FIFTH EDITION

Borkowski's Organizational Behavior and Leadership in Health Care

Katherine A. Meese, PhD
Faculty
University of Alabama at Birmingham, School of Health Professions,
Department of Health Services Administration

Nancy Borkowski, DBA, FACHE
Distinguished Professor
University of Alabama at Birmingham, School of Health Professions,
Department of Health Services Administration

World Headquarters
Jones & Bartlett Learning
25 Mall Road
Burlington, MA 01803
978-443-5000
info@jblearning.com
www.jblearning.com

Jones & Bartlett Learning books and products are available through most bookstores and online booksellers. To contact Jones & Bartlett Learning directly, call 800-832-0034, fax 978-443-8000, or visit our website, www.jblearning.com.

Substantial discounts on bulk quantities of Jones & Bartlett Learning publications are available to corporations, professional associations, and other qualified organizations. For details and specific discount information, contact the special sales department at Jones & Bartlett Learning via the above contact information or send an email to specialsales@jblearning.com.

31034-4

Production Credits
Vice President, Innovative Learning and Assessment Solutions: Ada Woo
Senior Director, Content Production and Delivery: Christine Emerton
Director, Product: Melissa Kleeman-Moy
Manager, Content Development: Bill Lawrensen
Product Manager: Sophie Fleck Teague
Content Manager: Christina Freitas
Content Coordinator: Rachelle Soden
Manager, Intellectual Properties and Content Production: Kristen Rogers
Content Production Manager: Michael Lepera
Senior Intellectual Property Specialist: Colleen Lamy
Senior Product Marketing Manager: Susanne Walker
Director, Product Fulfillment: Aaron McKinzie
Purchasing Manager: Wendy Kilborn
Composition: XBP Global
Project Management: XBP Global
Cover/Text Design: MPS Limited
Media Developer: Faith Brosnan
Intellectual Property Specialist: Lisa Passmore
Cover Image (Title Page, Part Opener, Chapter Opener): © greenyo/Shutterstock
Printing and Binding: Lakeside Book Company

Library of Congress Cataloging-in-Publication Data
Names: Meese, Katherine A. author | Borkowski, Nancy author
Title: Borkowski's organizational behavior and leadership in health care / Katherine A. Meese, PhD & Nancy Borkowski, DBA.
Other titles: Organizational behavior and leadership in health care
Description: Fifth edition. | Burlington, MA : Jones & Bartlett Learning, [2027] | Includes bibliographical references and index.
Identifiers: LCCN 2025034553 | ISBN 9781284307603 paperback
Subjects: LCSH: Health services administration | Health facilities–Personnel management | Organizational behavior | BISAC: BUSINESS & ECONOMICS / Industries / Healthcare | EDUCATION / General
Classification: LCC RA971 .M4435 2027
LC record available at https://lccn.loc.gov/2025034553

6048

Printed in the United States of America
30 29 28 27 26 10 9 8 7 6 5 4 3 2 1

Brief Contents

Contents

Preface

In the first edition of this book, Chapter 1 stated that "the U.S. healthcare industry has grown and changed dramatically over the past twenty-five years." That was an understatement! Since that time, the industry has experienced some of the most dynamic changes that healthcare managers have seen. In the coming years, more system-wide changes will occur as financing models evolve, the patient population and workforce ages, and artificial intelligence brings massive technological disruption. Healthcare managers are quickly learning that what worked in the past might not work in the future. This was the compelling reason to write an organizational behavior book specifically for healthcare managers who are on the front lines every day, motivating and leading others in a constantly changing, complex environment. This is not an easy task, as we know firsthand!

The purpose of this book is to provide healthcare managers and other professionals with an in-depth analysis of the theories and concepts of organizational behavior while embracing the uniqueness and complexity of the industry. Although healthcare is similar to other industries, it is also very different. As the nation's largest industry, health care employs more than 17 million people in numerous interrelated and interdependent segments.

Using an applied focus, this book provides a clear and concise overview of the essential topics in organizational behavior from the healthcare manager's perspective. It is our goal to give you a greater understanding of why and how people and groups behave as they do in the workplace. With this knowledge, you will be able to predict and effectively influence the behavior of the people you lead. Please let me know if we accomplish our goal! You can reach us at nborkows@uab.edu or kameese@uab.edu.

We have tried to ensure that we referenced all the individuals whose work contributed to the development of this book. However, if by chance we failed to give credit to someone along the way, please contact us so that we can make the necessary correction.

At this time, we wish to thank our families for their patience, understanding, and support over the years. Finally, we wish to thank the many wonderful and caring people employed throughout the healthcare industry with whom we have had and will continue to have the opportunity to work. Our lives continue to be blessed by these dedicated individuals!

Thank you for purchasing (and reading) our book. We welcome your comments and suggestions, and we wish you the best on your healthcare management and leadership journey.

With personal regards,
Katherine A. Meese, PhD
Nancy Borkowski, DBA, FACHE

About the Authors

Katherine A. Meese, PhD, is a faculty member in the Department of Health Services Administration at the University of Alabama at Birmingham. She earned her PhD in Health Services Administration with a specialization in strategic management from the University of Alabama at Birmingham in 2019. With 15 years of experience in healthcare management, leadership and research, Dr. Meese is an award-winning scholar and author in the field of organizational behavior. Her research interests are in wellness, burnout, engagement, quality and safety, and delivery models that enhance organizational learning. Dr. Meese has published numerous peer-reviewed journal articles and has served as a co-investigator and evaluator on multi-million-dollar federal grants. Her work has been published in *Anesthesia & Analgesia*, *Health Services Management Research*, *Journal of Healthcare Management*, *Journal of Health Administration Education*, and various other journals. She has co-authored five books, including *The Human Margin: Building the Foundations of Trust* and *Genfluence: Leading a Multigenerational Workforce*. Dr. Meese serves as an advisory board member for Belmont University Frist College of Medicine Collaborative for Health Systems Innovation.

Nancy Borkowski, DBA, FACHE, is a Distinguished Professor in the Department of Health Services Administration at the University of Alabama at Birmingham. She received her DBA with specializations in health services administration and accounting from Nova Southeastern University. Dr. Borkowski has over 20 years of experience in the healthcare industry and is a three-time past recipient of the American College of Healthcare Executives (ACHE) Regent's Senior Career Healthcare Executive Award (South Florida and Alabama), which recognizes individuals who have made significant contributions to the advancement of health management excellence. Dr. Borkowski is a nationally recognized author, with the first edition of her book *Organizational Behavior in Health Care* being referred to as "one of the most significant advances in the field of health services administration." It was awarded the AJN 2005 Book of the Year Award for nursing leadership and management. She is the author of three textbooks widely used in graduate and undergraduate health administration and nursing programs nationally and internationally.

Dr. Borkowski's work has been published in the *Journal of Ambulatory Care Management*, *Leadership in Health Services*, *Group & Organization Management*, *Organizational Behavior and Human Decision Processes*, *Health Care Management Review*, *Journal of Health Administration Education*, and various other journals. She currently serves as the editor for the *Journal of Health Administration Education*.

Dr. Borkowski's teaching interests are leadership, organizational behavior, and strategic management. She is a past recipient of the ACHE's Excellence in Teaching Award (District 2), given to faculty who engage in furthering academic excellence and the professional development of health management students, and the 2022 UAB Presidential Award for Excellence in Teaching in the School of Health Professions. In 2025, Dr. Borkowski was honored with the Association of University Programs in Health Administration's Gary L. Filerman Prize for Educational Leadership. In addition, Dr. Borkowski held a visiting professor appointment at the School of Health Services and Management at Southern Medical University in Guangzhou, China, from 2012 to 2020.

Over the past decade, Dr. Borkowski has served in various leadership roles for the Academy of Management's Health Care Management Division, the American College of Healthcare Executives' Southern Florida Regent's Advisory Council, the South Florida Healthcare Executive Forum, the Alabama Healthcare Executive Forum, and various other health-related organizations. In 2013, Dr. Borkowski received the Jessie Trice Hero Award for her leadership and commitment to improving the lives of underserved and minority populations. She has also been honored with the Exemplary Service Award from the American College of Healthcare Executives (2012) and the Frederick T. Muncie Gold Award from the Healthcare Financial Management Association (2017).

SECTION ONE

Micro Level—“The Individual”

PART I

Introduction

Part I includes four different but related topics. Chapter 1 discusses the history of organizational behavior and its importance to today's healthcare managers. Chapter 2 describes the changing environment in which healthcare managers find themselves. The chapter examines the numerous issues that have emerged within the healthcare industry because of the nation's changing demographics. Chapter 3 focuses on cultural intelligence and the skills managers need to adapt to the changing environment explored in Chapter 2. Chapter 4 deals with attitudes and perceptions, the foundation for understanding organizational behavior. Finally, Chapter 5 discusses the importance of communication. Research has revealed that 70% of small- to medium-sized businesses claim ineffective communication is their primary problem. Sentinel event data from The Joint Commission estimated that communication failure was the root cause of patient harm 70% of the time in 2,400 reported negative outcomes studied. No wonder communicating effectively is an essential job skill for today's healthcare managers and leaders.

CHAPTER 1

Overview and History of Organizational Behavior

LEARNING OUTCOMES

After completing this chapter, the student should be able to explain:

- The definition of organizational behavior.
- The significant challenges facing today's and tomorrow's healthcare organizations and managers.
- The importance of the Hawthorne Studies to the study of organizational behavior.
- The importance of McGregor's Theory X and Theory Y to studying organizational behavior.
- The differences between organizational behavior, organization theory, organizational development, and human resources management.

Overview

Organizational behavior (OB) is an applied behavioral science that emerged from psychology, sociology, anthropology, political science, and economics. OB is the study of individual and group dynamics in an organizational setting. Whenever people work together, numerous and complex factors interact. The discipline of OB attempts to understand these interactions so that managers can predict behavioral responses and, as a result, manage the resulting outcomes.

According to Ott (1996), OB asks the following questions:

1. Why do people behave the way they do when they are in organizations?
2. Under what circumstances will people's behavior in organizations change?
3. What impacts do organizations have on the behavior of individuals, formal groups (such as departments), and informal groups (such as people from several departments who have lunch together regularly)?
4. Why do different groups in the same organization develop different behavioral norms?

OB has three goals. First, OB attempts to explain why individuals and groups behave the way they do in organizational settings. Second, OB tries to predict how individuals and groups will behave based on internal and external factors. Third, OB provides managers with tools to assist in managing individuals' and groups' behaviors so that they willingly put forth their best effort to accomplish organizational goals. OB has become more important in the healthcare industry because people with different backgrounds, skills, experiences, and cultural values must work together effectively and efficiently.

Why Study Organizational Behavior in Health Care?

The largest U.S. industry is health care, which employs over 21 million individuals. The industry will account for almost a third of the nation's projected job growth from 2023 to 2033, adding approximately 2.2 million jobs. The projected 1% per year growth rate is the fastest among all industry sectors (Bureau of Labor Statistics, 2024).

Each segment of the healthcare industry (e.g., hospitals, home health, rehabilitation facilities) comprises different health-related occupations, ranging from highly educated licensed professionals, such as physicians and nurses, to those with on-the-job training. Furthermore, each industry segment has various economic structures (e.g., investor-owned, not-for-profit, governmental). Therefore, today's healthcare managers need the skills to communicate effectively, motivate, and lead diverse groups of people within a large, dynamic, and complex industry. Communication, motivation, and leadership are all concepts in the discipline of OB. Furthermore, managers need to understand the causes of workplace problems, such as low performance, turnover, conflict, and stress, so that they may be proactive and minimize these unnecessary negative outcomes. With a greater understanding of OB, managers can better predict and influence employees' behavior to achieve organizational goals.

Given the service-related nature of the healthcare industry, understanding individuals' behavior and group dynamics within health service organizations is critical to a manager's success. The primary reasons why managers fail stem from difficulty handling change, poor communication, being unable to work well in teams, and having poor interpersonal relations. There is a saying that employees do not leave organizations; they leave managers. While the reality is more nuanced, the manager plays a huge role in individual employees' daily experiences and performance.

The Healthcare Industry

Changes within the healthcare industry over the past 30 years have been powerful, far-reaching, and continuous. Because readers are probably familiar with most of these changes, either from their own experiences or from a previous healthcare delivery system course, the discussion will address some of the trends or future concerns that will affect tomorrow's healthcare industry.

Past changes and future trends are interrelated forces shaping tomorrow's healthcare organizations at the industry and organizational levels. Declining reimbursement, national staffing shortages, and an aging population deeply impact the industry. Technology has also caused significant changes in health care. Advances in biomedical and genetic research, big data, machine learning, expansion of telemedicine, and artificial intelligence are producing rapid changes in scientific understanding, clinical treatments, and care delivery. In addition, the industry has experienced changing government mandates and political pressures, leading to changes in how research and clinical care are prioritized, funded, and regulated. With an increased focus on chronic disease management, patients are living longer and requiring more long-term and home healthcare services now and in the future. Patients' and healthcare workers' characteristics are also changing. Both populations are becoming older and more diverse. Patients are better informed and have increasingly high expectations of healthcare professionals. This trend has changed how healthcare services are delivered, with a focus on patient satisfaction and safety as well as on the quality and value of services provided. Physician-patient relationships have changed because patients have easy access to health-related information. A growth in high-deductible insurance plans places a more significant financial responsibility on patients to manage their own health and reduce unnecessary health spending. The economics of health care are in a state of flux. For example, reimbursements are moving toward value-based payments; therefore, we see an increase in the use of evidence-based medicine. There are continuing staff shortages, especially in primary care physicians, nurses, imaging technicians, and pharmacists, leading to competition for well-qualified people. Changes are also taking place in the disease environment. Many factors of modern life contribute to the emergence of new diseases, the reemergence of old ones, and the evolution of pathogens immune to many of today's medications. In addition, because of the ease of global travel, healthcare providers are concerned with global pandemics, diseases, and bioterrorism preparedness.

Several healthcare organizations have adapted their organizational forms to deal with these changes by restructuring themselves into integrated delivery networks, which may be part of a local, regional, or national system. We have seen increased vertical, horizontal, and virtual integration. Vertical integration focuses on developing a continuum of care services to meet the patient's full range of healthcare needs. This integration model, in which a single entity owns and operates all the segments providing care, may include preventive services, specialized and primary ambulatory care, acute care, subacute care, long-term care, home health care, and a health plan. Horizontal integration through mergers and acquisitions is also on the rise. Consolidation in health care has risen sharply over the past 30 years (Kaiser Family Foundation, 2025). In recent years, 428 hospital and health system mergers occurred from 2018 through 2023 (Levinson et al., 2024). In addition, not-for-profit hospitals have merged with for-profit health systems due to competition and the need to reduce costs through economies of scale. Virtual integration, which emphasizes coordination of healthcare services through patient-management agreements, provider incentives, and/or information systems, has increased. This virtual integration has evolved to meet the need for better technology and information infrastructures for information sharing, patient care management, and cost control. The COVID-19 pandemic rapidly upended almost every element of healthcare work, expanding telemedicine, virtual and hybrid positions, changing the scope of practice for various positions, and changing national attitudes about public health measures like vaccinations.

Because of the dramatic changes and the future trends in the healthcare industry, most managers have had to change how they and other employees carry out their job responsibilities. These changes have been forced on the industry by the need to increase productivity, due to decreasing reimbursement and increasing competition. At the same time, healthcare providers must deliver patient-centered, value-based care. These are not easy tasks to balance. As a result, many healthcare providers are breaking down their traditional hierarchical structures and moving toward multidisciplinary team-managed environments. Employees are finding themselves in new roles with new responsibilities. All of these changes cause disruptions in the workplace. The study of

OB will assist healthcare managers in minimizing the adverse effects (such as stress and conflict) related to this "new" environment and in maximizing their ability to motivate staff and lead their organizations effectively.

History of Organizational Behavior

The beginnings of OB can be found in the human relations/behavioral management movement, which emerged during the 1920s as a response to the traditional or classic management approach. Beginning in the late 1700s, the Industrial Revolution was the driving force for the development of large factories employing many workers. Managers at that time were concerned "about how to design and manage work in order to increase productivity and help organizations attain maximum efficiency" (Daft, 2004). This traditional approach included Frederick Taylor's (1911) well-known framework of scientific management, or "Taylorism," as it is now labeled. Taylor believed efficiency was achieved by creating jobs that economized time, human energy, and other productive resources. Taylor scientifically divided manufacturing processes into small, efficient work units through his time-and-motion studies. Through Taylor's work, productivity significantly increased. For example, Henry Ford developed his assembly line according to the principles of Taylorism and could churn out Model Ts at a remarkable and economical pace (Benjamin, 2003).

Although the classic approach to management focused on efficiency within organizations, Taylor attempted to address the human relations aspect of the workplace. In his book *The Principles of Scientific Management*, Taylor stated that:

> In order to have any hope of obtaining the initiative (i.e., best endeavors, hard work, skills and knowledge, ingenuity, and goodwill) of his workmen, the manager must give some special incentive to his men beyond that which is given to the average of the trade. This incentive can be given in several different ways, as, for example, the hope of rapid promotion or advancement; higher wages, either in the form of generous piecework prices or of a premium or bonus of some kind for good and rapid work; shorter hours of labor; better surroundings and working conditions than are ordinarily given, etc., and, above all, this special incentive should be accompanied by that personal consideration for, and friendly contact with, his workers which comes only from a genuine and kindly interest in the welfare of those under him. Only by giving a special inducement or incentive of this kind can the employer hope even approximately to get the initiative of his workers.

Although Taylor included a concern for workers in the scientific management approach, the human relations or behavioral management movement did not begin until after the landmark Hawthorne Studies.

The Hawthorne Studies

Between 1924 and 1933, Elton Mayo, Frederick Roethlisberger, and colleagues from Harvard Business School conducted a series of experiments at the Hawthorne Plant of the Western Electric Company in Cicero, Illinois. These studies were pivotal in developing OB, demonstrating the significant influence of social and psychological factors on worker productivity. This research identified the concept known as the Hawthorne Effect—the phenomenon in which individuals modify their behavior because they know they are being observed (Roethlisberger & Dickson, 1939).

The Hawthorne Studies consisted of four major phases: (1) illumination experiments, (2) relay-assembly group experiments, (3) bank-wiring observation-room studies, and (4) the interviewing program. The initial purpose was to determine how physical working conditions influenced worker output.

Researchers assessed whether varying lighting levels would affect productivity in the illumination experiments. Unexpectedly, productivity improved in the experimental group (with altered lighting) and the control group (with no changes). This led researchers to conclude that the increase in output was due not to lighting but to the attention and interest shown by researchers—a finding that gave rise to the Hawthorne Effect.

The relay-assembly group experiments examined the impact of improved working conditions on six female workers over a 5-year period. Modifications included shorter workdays, more frequent rest breaks, free lunches, and enhanced consultation with workers. The group was also allowed to socialize freely during work and was supervised by a researcher who took an active interest in their well-being. These conditions led to a significant increase in productivity. In a subsequent phase, productivity remained high when original working conditions were reinstated. This indicated that the workers' sense of social cohesion and shared purpose, rather than the physical changes, was the primary driver of performance.

The bank-wiring observation-room study similarly placed workers in a controlled setting to examine the effects of group dynamics on productivity. Workers were paid based on a piece-work system that accounted for individual and group output. However, the team established its own informal productivity standard, deciding what constituted a "fair day's work." Workers who exceeded this standard, labeled "rate busters," were pressured by their peers to reduce output. Conversely, if someone produced less than the agreed-upon level, the group would redistribute tasks to maintain consistent overall performance. These behaviors reflected a shared understanding among workers and emphasized the role of informal group norms over formal incentives.

The insights from these studies led researchers to examine informal group structures and their powerful influence on individual behavior in organizations. The final phase of the Hawthorne Studies was the interviewing program, in which more than 21,000 interviews were conducted to understand workers' attitudes toward their jobs and the company. This effort revealed that employees are not isolated individuals but social beings whose attitudes toward work are shaped by their backgrounds and satisfaction from social interactions at work (Homans, 1950).

A key insight was that employee dissatisfaction often signals deeper underlying issues, whether in the workplace, at home, or from prior life experiences. As Roethlisberger and Dickson (1939) concluded, workers bring a set of values, expectations, and emotional experiences that shape how they respond to organizational change. The studies emphasized the importance of addressing work's human and social dimensions, marking a significant shift in management theory from mechanistic models to a more human-centered understanding of OB.

Theories X and Y

Another significant impact on the development of OB came from Douglas McGregor (1957, 1960) when he proposed two theories by which managers view their employees: Theory X (negative/pessimistic) and Theory Y (positive/optimistic). Theories X and Y reflect polar opposite positions and are ways of seeing and thinking about people, affecting their behavior.

Theory X states that employees are unintelligent and lazy. They dislike work, avoiding it whenever possible. Employees should be closely controlled because they have little desire for responsibility, have little aptitude for creativity in solving organizational problems, and will resist change. In contrast, Theory Y states that employees are creative and competent; they want meaningful work, contribute, and participate in decision-making and leadership functions.

Borrowing from Maslow's Hierarchy of Needs, McGregor stated that the autocratic (Theory X) managers were no longer effective in the workplace because they relied on an employee's lower needs for motivation (physiological concerns and safety), which, in modern society, mainly were satisfied and therefore no longer acted as motivators for the employee. For example, managers would ask, "Why aren't people more productive? We pay good wages, provide good working conditions, have excellent fringe benefits, and provide steady employment. However, people are unwilling to put forth more than minimum efforts." The answers to these questions were embedded in Theory X's managerial assumptions about people. If managers believed their employees had an inherent dislike for work and must be coerced, controlled, and directed to achieve organizational goals, the resulting employee behavior was nothing more than a self-fulfilling prophecy. The manager's assumptions caused the staff's "unmotivated" behavior.

At the opposite end of the spectrum from Theory X, McGregor proposed Theory Y, which suggested productivity increased when managers created opportunities, removed obstacles, and encouraged employee growth and learning. McGregor stated that participative (Theory Y) managers supported decentralization and delegation of decision making, job enlargement, and participative management because these allowed employees to direct their own activities and assume responsibility, thereby satisfying their higher-level needs (see **Figure 1-1**).

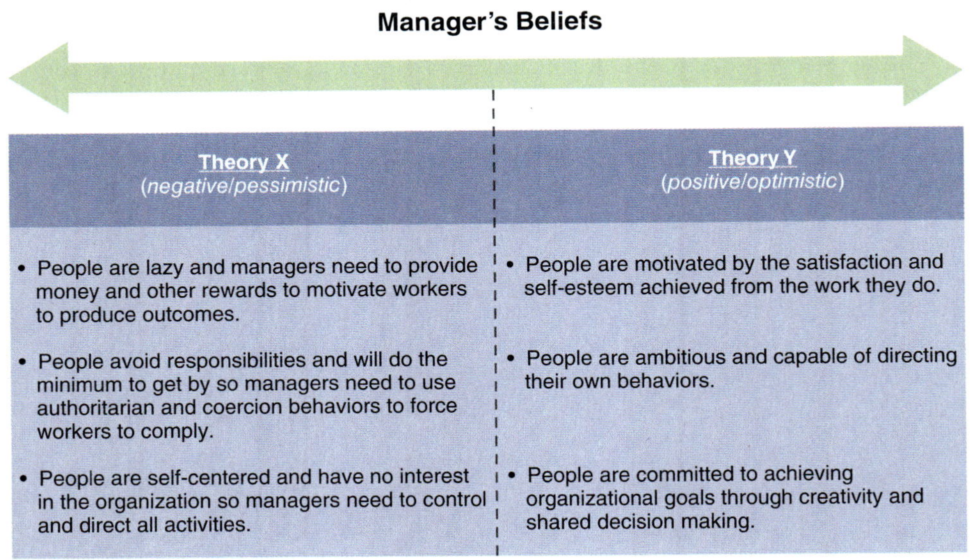

Figure 1-1 McGregor X–Y Theory Diagram

Related Disciplines

Before we conclude this chapter, we would like to explain the differences between OB and three other related fields: organization theory (OT), organizational development (OD), and human resources management (HRM). As was noted at the beginning of the chapter, OB is the study of individual and group dynamics within an organizational setting and, therefore, is a micro approach. OT analyzes the entire organization and is a macro perspective, since the organization is the unit examined. The field of OD describes a planned process of change that is used throughout the organization to improve the organization's effectiveness. Since, like OT, OD involves the entire organization, it is a macro examination. Finally, HRM can be viewed as a micro approach to managing people. The difference between HRM and OB is that the latter studies human behavior in various settings, emphasizing explaining, predicting, and understanding behavior in organizations. In contrast, HRM emphasizes systems, processes, procedures, and the like for personnel management and is usually housed in a functional unit within an organization.

Since 1960, a wealth of information has emerged within the study of OB, which will be addressed in this textbook. Part I discusses the issues of diversity, perceptions, attitudes, and communication. Part II addresses motivation and individual behaviors. Part III examines leadership from four approaches—power and influence, behavioral, contingency, and transformational. Part IV emphasizes the importance of intrapersonal and interpersonal issues within the context of stress and conflict management. Part V examines group dynamics, working in groups, teams, and team building. Part VI provides an overview of managing organizational change within the context of OD.

Discussion Questions

1. Define organizational behavior.
2. What are some significant challenges facing today's and tomorrow's healthcare organizations and managers? Why?
3. Why did the Hawthorne Studies impact the study of organizational behavior?
4. Why did McGregor's Theory X and Theory Y impact the study of organizational behavior?
5. Discuss the difference between organizational behavior, organization theory, organizational development, and human resources management.

What Do You Know About Organizational Behavior?

	Questions	True/False
1	OB is the study of individuals, groups, and organizations.	______
2	Under Theory Y, managers create opportunities, remove obstacles, and encourage employee growth and learning.	______

	Questions	True/False
3	Attitudes are very individual and subjective; therefore, we do not currently have ways to measure employees' attitudes about their jobs.	______
4	Extroverts do best in quiet, nonsocial jobs, such as computer work, while introverts perform best when they must work and present in front of large groups of people.	______
5	Motivation is the conscious or unconscious stimulus, incentive, or motive for action toward a goal resulting from psychological or social factors, which give purpose or direction to behavior.	______
6	Employee motivation has a direct impact on a health services organization's performance.	______
7	Process theories of motivation assist managers in predicting employees' behavior so that the behavior may be influenced if necessary.	______
8	An employee's degree of job satisfaction is proportional to the rewards the employee receives.	______
9	Power may be defined as the influence over people's beliefs, emotions, and behaviors.	______
10	A leader is a person who directs the work of employees and is responsible for results.	______
11	Management and leadership are both necessary for an organization to achieve its goals.	______
12	The leader who is able to respond to ever-increasing levels of environmental uncertainty by utilizing more than one style of leadership will most likely increase employees' motivation, satisfaction, and productivity.	______
13	Transactional leadership is about change, innovation, improvement, and entrepreneurship through vision and inspiration.	______
14	Transactional and transformational leadership approaches are clearly in opposition.	______
15	Because stress is a complex and highly personalized process, some individuals see a specific situation as a threat, whereas others see the same situation as a challenge or opportunity.	______
16	Managers are limited by time and resources, personal bias, and other factors, which make rational decision-making unrealistic.	______
17	Conflict is inevitable and unavoidable.	______
18	Individuals join groups to satisfy their need for safety and social interaction.	______
19	Barriers to effective teamwork fall within four categories: (1) lack of management support, (2) lack of resources, (3) lack of leadership, and (4) lack of training.	______
20	The two primary forces influencing an individual's perception, attitude, and response toward change are cumulative life experiences and social (informal group) forces.	______

Scoring

The correct answers to the above 20 questions are:

1. False
2. True
3. False
4. False
5. True
6. True
7. True
8. False
9. True
10. False
11. True
12. True
13. False
14. True
15. True
16. True
17. True
18. True
19. True
20. True

Interpretation

How much do you know about organizational behavior? If you scored well, that would be good for you! However, the previous questions represent only a tiny part of organizational behavior. If you didn't score high, don't be concerned. You will learn the many theories and concepts of organizational behavior that will provide you with the necessary skill set to manage and lead others successfully.

References

Benjamin, M. (2003, February 24). Fads for any and all eras. *U.S. News & World Report, 134*(6), 74–76.

Bureau of Labor Statistics, U.S. Department of Labor. (2024, August 29). *Employment projections: 2023–2033 summary*. https://www.bls.gov/news.release/ecopro.nr0.htm

Daft, R. L. (2004). *Organization theory and design* (8th ed.). Thomson South-Western.

Kaiser Family Foundation. (2025, August 9). *Ten things to know about consolidation in health care provider markets*. KFF. https://www.kff.org/health-costs/ten-things-to-know-about-consolidation-in-health-care-provider-markets/

Hawthorne Experiments. (n.d.). Hawthorne Experiments [PDF]. http://ncbgudi.com/wp-content/uploads/2018/01/Hawthorne-Experiments.pdf

Homans, G. C. (1950). *The human group*. Harcourt, Brace and Company.

Levinson, Z., Godwin, J., Hulver, S., & Neuman, T. (2024, April 19). *Ten things to know about consolidation in health care provider markets*. Kaiser Family Foundation. https://www.kff.org/health-costs/press-release/ten-things-to-know-about-consolidation-in-health-care-provider-markets/

McGregor, D. M. (1957). The human side of enterprise. *Management Review, 46*, 22–28.

McGregor, D. M. (1960). *The human side of enterprise*. McGraw-Hill Book Company.

Ott, J. S. (Ed.). (1996). *Classic readings in organizational behavior* (2nd ed.). South-Western.

Roethlisberger, F. J., & Dickson, W. J. (1939). *Management and the worker*. Harvard University Press.

Taylor, F. W. (1911). *The principles of scientific management*. Harper and Brothers.

CHAPTER 2

Diversity, Equity, and Inclusion in Health Care[1]

LEARNING OUTCOMES

After completing this chapter, the student should be able to:

- Define diversity, equity, and inclusion.
- Understand major trends in U.S. demographics.
- Understand why changes in U.S. demographics affect the healthcare industry.
- Understand the unique challenges facing different groups of people.

Overview

Demographics of the U.S. population have changed dramatically in the past three decades. These changes directly affect the healthcare industry regarding the patients we serve and our workforce. Over the next 40 years, there is expected to be a fundamental shift in which demographic groups represent the majority and minority percentages of the U.S. population. According to the U.S. Census Bureau, the White, non-Hispanic population will make up less than 50% of the nation's population by midcentury. The healthcare industry needs to change and adopt new ways to meet the diverse needs of our current and future patients and employees.

This chapter is presented in three parts. First, we define the terms "diversity," "equity," and "inclusion." Second, we discuss the changing demographics of the nation's population. Last, we examine how these changes affect health service delivery from the perspectives of patients and employees. Because diversity challenges faced by the healthcare industry are not limited to quality-of-care and access-to-care issues, in part three of our discussions, we explore how these changes will affect the health services workforce and, more specifically, the current and future leadership within the industry.

[1]We acknowledge the importance of using respectful and inclusive language when referring to various subgroups, yet also understand that terminology continues to evolve. In many instances, we have cited specific research for which we cannot change the terminology used in the original studies.

Diversity, Equity, and Inclusion Defined

The *American Heritage Dictionary of the English Language* (4th ed.) defines diversity as "having two main meanings: first, it refers to the state or characteristic of being varied or different, and second, it describes a specific aspect or area where things are not uniform." Dreachslin (1998) provides a more specific definition of diversity as "the full range of human similarities and differences in group affiliation, including gender, race/ethnicity, social class, role within an organization, age, religion, sexual orientation, physical ability, and other group identities." Therefore, diversity can mean many things, from differences in education, language, and background to race and gender identity. For our discussions, we will focus on the following characteristics: (1) race/ethnicity; (2) age; (3) biological sex at birth; and (4) sexual orientation, gender identity, and gender expression.

Equity is providing fair treatment, access, opportunity, and advancement for all people while striving to identify and eliminate barriers that have prevented the full participation of some groups. Improving equity involves increasing the fairness of the procedures and processes within the organization and their distribution of resources. Tackling equity issues requires understanding the root causes of outcome disparities within our society and organizations (Kapila et al., 2016).

Inclusion refers to the act of creating environments in which any individual or group can feel welcomed, respected, supported, and able to participate fully. An inclusive and welcoming climate embraces differences and offers respect in words and deeds to all people (Kapila et al., 2016). Inclusion allows people to have a sense of belonging.

Diversity, equity, and inclusion are not always present together. A diverse environment with people of different races, ethnicities, genders, or religions might not be equitable or inclusive. Therefore, simply increasing diversity is not enough. For example, suppose a manager does not offer the same mentorship and coaching to employees from underrepresented populations. Therefore, these employees do not get the same promotion opportunities as other employees. In that case, that is not an equitable environment. An environment can be diverse and equitable, but not inclusive. For example, maybe all employees can access the same coaching and career development opportunities, but the manager plans a celebratory lunch during an important Jewish religious holiday. This lunch would not be inclusive because Jewish employees could not attend due to their religious customs. One way to remember the differences between diversity, equity, and inclusion is by thinking about a theater production:

- Diversity is everyone getting a ticket to the show.
- Equity is everyone getting a seat where they can actually see the stage.
- Inclusion is everyone being invited to take part in the performance, not just watch it. (see **Case Study 2-1**).

Unfortunately, we all have implicit or unconscious biases that can affect how we treat people of certain genders, gender identities, sexual orientations, races, ethnicities, and ages. These are automatic assumptions we make about a person based on what we see or perceive about that person. Despite our best intentions, these implicit biases are often unknown even to ourselves, and they can lead us to create or accept environments in which certain people are treated poorly or are discriminated against. "Think of implicit bias as the thumbprint of the culture on our brain," says Harvard University social psychologist Mahzarin Banaji (Joplin & Kunitz, 2018). It is only by recognizing our unconscious and implicit biases that we can hope to change them. Instead of denying their existence—we *all* have them—we must actively work to understand and eliminate our blind spots that might lead us to treat certain people differently (see **Case Study 2-2**). Additionally, we must advocate for and implement systems that reduce opportunities for biased

CASE STUDY 2-1 Diverse but Not Inclusive

Jill, a young, White female, was hired to work at a healthcare consulting firm. The team was very diverse, with people from all over the world who had a variety of educations and backgrounds. Jill's coworkers had different religious and cultural beliefs, races, languages, and countries of origin. Jill felt she connected well with all her colleagues and appreciated the unique perspectives they all brought to the team. However, she noticed the senior vice president, Mark, had a small group of favorites. The younger White employees were the only people he would invite to lunch or have coaching sessions with. As individuals started to get promoted, White employees were promoted much more quickly than anyone else. Although these employees' promotions were usually deserved, other employees seemed to have a harder time gaining promotion, even if they had performed equally well. When Jill had been at the company for almost a year, Mark scheduled a team lunch at an expensive restaurant to thank the team for surpassing productivity targets. The lunch was scheduled during Ramadan, an important religious time for Muslims, which involves fasting during the day. Jill overheard one of her Muslim coworkers whispering to another coworker, "I mean, if he had just waited one more week to schedule the lunch, we could all enjoy it." Jill thought Mark might have been unaware of the poor timing, so she brought it to his attention at their next one-on-one meeting. When Jill raised the issue, Mark replied, "Well, I have got to keep the numbers down if I want us to go somewhere expensive. They are invited. It is not my problem if they choose not to eat."

Was this environment diverse, equitable, and inclusive? Why or why not?

CASE STUDY 2-2 You Do Not Look Like a Doctor

Tamika Cross, a young, Black physician who worked in Houston, was flying home from a wedding in Detroit. When the flight attendants asked if any physicians were on board to help a passenger who had become unresponsive, Dr. Cross raised her hand and offered to help. The flight attendant responded, "Sweetie, put your hand down. We are looking for actual physicians, nurses, or some type of medical personnel; we don't have time to talk to you."

When Dr. Cross tried to inform the flight attendant that she was a physician, she was repeatedly dismissed and asked to show her credentials. When she insisted she was a doctor, the flight attendants responded with surprise and disbelief. The crew continued to ask any physicians on board to press their call buttons. A few moments later, an older White male physician told the flight attendant that he was a physician, and Dr. Cross was returned to her seat.

Dr. Cross posted the account to her Facebook page, which then went viral on several social media sites and news outlets, sparking the #WhataDoctorLooksLike movement.

What implicit biases do you think the flight attendant held about what a physician should look like?

Modified from #TamikaCross. (n.d.). Twitter. https://twitter.com/hashtag/TamikaCross; #WhatADoctorLooksLike. (n.d.). Twitter. https://twitter.com/hashtag/whatadoctorlookslike

decision-making. For example, having a defined rubric for promotion instead of promoting based on the subjective feeling that somebody is "management material" can help guard against unconscious biases in the promotion process.

Changing U.S. Population

It is important to understand how our population is changing to better appreciate the need for more diverse, equitable, and inclusive environments. The demographic profile of the U.S. population is projected to undergo significant alterations in age, gender, and ethnicity over the next 40 years (see **Table 2-1**).

In 2020, 331.5 million people resided in the United States, an increase of 22.8 million people, or 7.4%, between 2010 and 2020. The 2016 census data showed a decline in the White, non-Hispanic population for the first time since the first census in 1790. This decline was almost a decade ahead of earlier projections. Additionally, there are currently more non-White children

Table 2-1 Projected Population of the United States by Age, Gender, and Race/Ethnicity (in Millions)

	2020		2060		2020–2060 Change	
	Number	Percent	Number	Percent	Number	Percent
Total population	331.5	100	364.3	100	32.8	9.9
Under age 18	73.1	22.1	64.3	17.7	−8.8	−12.0
Ages 18–64	202.6	61.1	211.2	58.0	8.6	4.2
Ages 65 and over	55.8	16.8	88.8	24.4	33.0	59.1
Males	162.7	49.1	180.1	49.4	17.4	10.7
Females	168.8	50.9	184.2	50.6	15.4	9.1
White	204.3	61.6	247.5	67.9	−43.2	−21.1
Non-Hispanic White	191.7	57.8	163.6	44.9	−28.1	−14.7
Black or African American	41.1	12.4	54.0	14.8	12.9	31.4
American Indian and Alaska Native	3.74	1.1	5.0	1.4	1.3	35.1
Asian	19.9	6.0	34.4	9.4	14.5	72.9
Native Hawaiian and Other Pacific Islander	0.7	0.2	1.3	0.34	0.6	85.7
Hispanic or Latino	54.6	16.5	98.0	26.9	43.4	79.5

Percentages do not add up to 100% due to rounding and because Hispanics may be of any race and are therefore counted under more than one category.

Data from U.S. Census Bureau. (2020). DP-1 United States: Profile of general population and housing characteristics: 2020 demographic profile data. https://www.census.gov; U.S. Census Bureau. (2023). National population projections tables: Main series. https://www.census.gov/data/tables/2023/demo/popproj/2023-popproj.html

than White children under 10 years old for those born after 2007 (Frey, 2018). As the youngest generation ages, we are on the verge of a fundamental shift in the diversity of patients and workers in the United States. In addition to the changing ethnic and racial composition of America, another trend is the aging population. The percentage of the population over age 65 is projected to increase from 17% to 24% by the year 2060, an increase of 31 million people (see Table 2-1).

Males and females are almost evenly divided in the total population, representing 49.1% and 50.9%, respectively (see Table 2-1); however, males outnumber females in the population under age 25 years. The male–female ratio reverses among older adults, with women outnumbering men, typically due to longer life spans (Vespa et al., 2018). This imbalance is expected to persist through 2060 and beyond. However, the gap between males and females over age 65 is narrowing as men live longer than women in previous generations.

Race/Ethnicity

The U.S. population continues to diversify racially as underrepresented populations continue to increase in size at a faster rate than the White population. Although the non-Hispanic White population still represents the largest group (57.8%) of the U.S. population, this number is expected to decrease by almost 15% by 2060.

In 2020, the Hispanic or Latinx population represented the largest minority population group in the United States, at almost 17% of the population. By 2060, Latinx individuals are expected to comprise approximately one-third of the U.S. population (26.9%). The remaining population is composed of 12.44% Black or African American, 6% Asian and Pacific Islanders, 1.1% American Indians and Alaska Natives, and 10.2% people who identify themselves as belonging to more than one race.

The Asian population in the United States is increasing rapidly as a percentage of the total population. From 2010 to 2020, the population of people identified as Asian (alone or in combination with another race) grew by over 50%, while the total population grew by only 7.4% (U.S. Census Bureau, 2023). In the next 40 years, the Asian population is expected to grow by almost 73% (see Table 2-1).

In addition to the resident population in the United States, healthcare organizations may encounter an even more diverse patient population due to the strong reputation of U.S. health care and its popularity as a destination for medical travel and medical tourism. The United States is a highly desirable destination for health care for people worldwide who cannot access various procedures or treatments in their home countries. Hundreds of thousands of visits from international patients from almost every country occur yearly at U.S. hospitals (Johnson & Garman, 2010). As the middle class expands in countries, such as China and India, this trend will continue as more patients worldwide can afford to travel for treatment. This means that healthcare workers will need additional skills and tools to deal with a vastly more diverse population of patients from other countries and the growing diversity in the domestic population.

Unfortunately, there are health and access disparities among people from underrepresented racial and ethnic groups; see **Figures 2-1**, **2-2**, and **Exhibit 2-1**. Disease burdens vary among groups, as do death rates and measures of access to care (Artiga & Orgera, 2019). These groups may also face additional challenges when interacting with the U.S. healthcare system. A survey by the Commonwealth Fund (2002) found that Black non-Hispanics, Asian Americans, and Hispanics are more likely than White non-Hispanics to experience difficulty communicating with their physician, to feel that they are treated with disrespect when receiving health care, to experience barriers to access to care, such as lack of insurance or not having a regular physician, and to feel

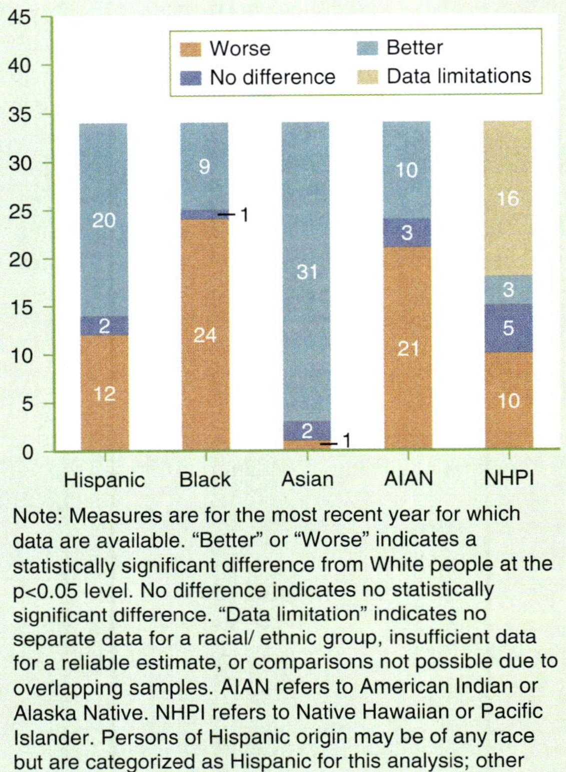

Figure 2-1 Health Status and Outcomes Among People of Color Compared to White People

Reproduced from Artiga, S., & Orgera, K. (2019, November 12). Key facts on health and health care by race and ethnicity. KFF. https://www.kff.org/report-section/key-facts-on-health-and-health-care-by-race-and-ethnicity-introduction/

that they would receive better care if they were of a different race or ethnicity. In addition, the survey found that Hispanics were more than twice as likely as White non-Hispanics (33% versus 16%) to cite one or more communication problems, such as not understanding the physician, not being listened to by the physician, or not asking questions they needed to ask. Twenty-seven percent of Asian Americans and 23% of Black non-Hispanics experience similar communication difficulties. According to AHRQ (2023), Alaska Natives/American Indians and Black Americans receive worse care on 44–52% of quality measures compared to White Americans.

Age

The world's population is aging at unprecedented rates. Slow population growth brought about by reductions in fertility leads to population aging; that is, it produces populations in which the proportion of older persons increases while that of younger persons decreases. For the first time in history, in 2018, the number of people over age 65 outnumbered the number of children under age 5. By 2050, the number of people over age 65 is projected to double that of people under age 5 (United Nations, 2019).

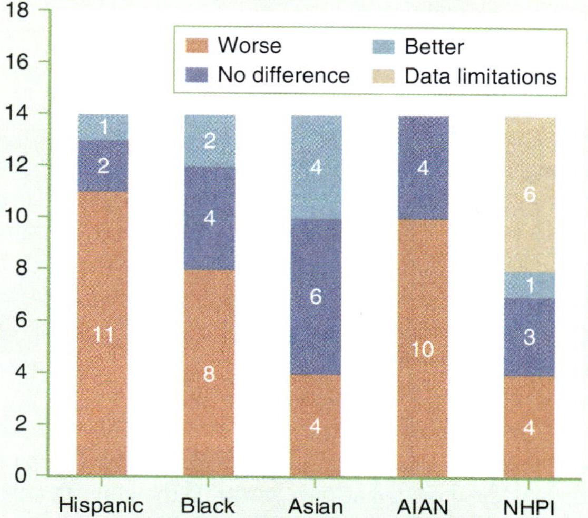

Note: Measures are for the most recent year for which data are available. "Better" or "Worse" indicates a statistically significant difference from White people at the p<0.05 level. No difference indicates no statistically significant difference. "Data limitation" indicates no separate data for a racial/ethnic group, insufficient data for a reliable estimate, or comparisons not possible due to overlapping samples. AIAN refers to American Indian or Alaska Native. NHPI refers to Native Hawaiian or Pacific Islander. Persons of Hispanic origin may be of any race but are categorized as Hispanic for this analysis; other groups are non-Hispanic.

Figure 2-2 Coverage, Access, and Use of Care Among People of Color Compared to White People

Reproduced from Artiga, S., & Orgera, K. (2019, November 12). Key facts on health and health care by race and ethnicity. KFF. https://www.kff.org/report-section/key-facts-on-health-and-health-care-by-race-and-ethnicity-introduction/

Exhibit 2-1 Unequal Treatment

A 2002 study by the Institute of Medicine titled *Unequal Treatment: Confronting Racial and Ethnic Disparities in Health Care* found that a consistent body of research demonstrates significant variation in the rates of medical procedures by race, even when insurance status, income, age, and severity of conditions are comparable. This research indicated that in the United States, members of underrepresented racial and ethnic groups receive fewer routine medical procedures and experience a lower quality of health services than the majority of the population. For example, members of underrepresented populations are less likely to be given appropriate cardiac medications or to undergo bypass surgery and are less likely to receive kidney dialysis or transplants. By contrast, they are more likely to be subjected to certain less desirable procedures, such as lower-limb amputations for diabetes. The study's recommendations for reducing racial and ethnic disparities in health care included increasing awareness among the general public, healthcare providers, insurance companies, and policy makers.

Data from Smedley, B. D., Stith, A. Y., & Nelson, A. R. (Eds.). (2002). Unequal treatment: Confronting racial and ethnic disparities in health care. National Academy Press.

The United States is experiencing the same trend. Between 2020 and 2060, the U.S. population under 18 is expected to shrink by 12%, and the population aged 45–64 is expected to grow by 4.2%. In stark contrast, the country is experiencing substantially faster growth rates for older ages. For example, the population over 65 is expected to grow by nearly 60% (U.S. Census Bureau, 2018; see Table 2-1). The significant growth in this age group is primarily attributable to the aging of the Baby Boomer population and longer life spans due to disease control and advances in medical technology.

One of the most striking characteristics of the older population is the change in the ratio of men to women as people age. As Howden and Meyer (2011) point out, this results from differences in mortality rates for men and women, in that women tend to live longer than men. For example, life expectancy for men in the United States is 73.2 years, whereas women's is 79.1 years (Arias et al., 2022).

While the older population is not as racially and ethnically diverse as younger generations, its racial and ethnic makeup is projected to diversify over the next four decades. As in the past, the most significant proportion of the U.S. population age 65 and over is White. However, the racial composition of the older population is changing; the percentage of Whites is projected to decrease by 2060, and the percentages of all other race groups will increase (Vespa et al., 2018).

Technology and other medical advances have given us the ability to increase longevity. As our citizens grow older, more services are required for the treatment and management of both acute and chronic health conditions. Healthcare professionals must devise strategies for the growing elderly patient population. America's older citizens often live on fixed incomes and have small or nonexistent support groups. Although this may be considered an infrastructure dilemma, the reality is that medical professionals must be able to understand and empathize with poor, sick, older adults of all races and genders.

The term "ageism" was coined in 1968 by Robert N. Butler, MD, a pioneer in geriatric medicine and a founding director of the National Institute on Aging (NIA). Butler (1969) was among the first to identify the phenomenon of age prejudice, initially describing it as "a systematic stereotyping of and discrimination against people because they are old."

Ageism is "any attitude, action, or institutional structure, which subordinates a person or group because of age or any assignment of roles in society purely based on age" (Traxler, 1980). Healthcare professionals often make assumptions about their older patients based on age rather than functional status (Bowling, 2007). This may be due to the limited training physicians receive in the care and management of geriatric patients. For example, Warshaw and colleagues (2002, 2006) related that medical residents have limited training in geriatric medicine. Warshaw et al.'s 2006 study compared findings with those from a similar 2002 survey to determine whether any changes had occurred. Of the participating 3-year residency training programs, only 9% required 6 weeks or more of training. As of 2002, the residency programs depended on nursing home facilities, geriatric preceptors in nongeriatric clinical ambulatory settings, and outpatient geriatric assessment centers for medical residents' geriatrics training. A report from the Alliance for Aging Research (2003) related that there continues to be shortcomings in medical training, prevention, screening, and treatment patterns that disadvantage older patients. The report outlined five domains of ageism in health care:

1. Healthcare professionals do not receive enough training in geriatrics to care for many older patients.
2. Older patients are less likely than younger people to receive preventive care.
3. Older patients are less likely to be tested or screened for diseases and other health problems.
4. Proven medical interventions for older patients are often ignored, leading to inappropriate or incomplete treatment.
5. Older people are consistently excluded from clinical trials, even though they are the largest users of approved drugs.

On a positive note, Perry (2012) relates that progress against systematic ageism in health care has partly begun due to the passing of the 2010 Affordable Care Act (ACA). He notes that the law's various provisions, such as Medicare's increased focus on chronic disease prevention, new models of care for reducing rehospitalizations, improved care coordination, and annual screening for cognitive impairment, will assist in changing attitudes toward elderly patients.

Gender

As was previously noted, according to the U.S. Census Bureau, in 2020, 50.9% of the U.S. population was female and 49.1% was male—almost identical to percentages in the 2000 Census. That translates to 97 men for every 100 women. That being said, the ratio of men to women varies significantly by age group. However, the male–female ratio declines as people age. The male–female ratio falls among older adults as women increasingly outnumber and outlive men.

Sexual Orientation, Gender Identity, and Gender Expression

Another important aspect of diversity in health care is sexual orientation, gender identity, and gender expression. The last decade has led to an increased focus on disparities that exist in the lesbian, gay, bisexual, transgender, and questioning plus community (LGBTQ+). Various surveys estimate that people over age 18 who identify as LGBTQ+ make up 2.8% to 7.2% of the total population (Kates et al., 2018; Dawson et al., 2023). The term "LGBTQ+" may encompass elements of sexual orientation, gender identity, and gender expression. Sexual orientation is defined by the Institute of Medicine report as "an enduring pattern of or disposition to experience sexual or romantic desires for, and relationships with, people of one's same sex, the other sex, or both sexes" (Graham et al., 2011). For many people, sexual orientation does not fall neatly into any specific category and may be better described as belonging somewhere along a spectrum. Gender identity refers to one's internal sense of being male, female, or something else (Kates et al., 2018). Because gender identity is internal, it is not necessarily visible to others. Gender expression refers to the outward and external portrayal of gender. Gender expression may include clothing, hairstyles, mannerisms, and taking on gender roles that are defined by one's culture. Both gender identity and gender expression may be different from one's biological sex at birth.

These aspects of identity and orientation can span all ages, races, and biological sexes. According to the Kaiser Family Foundation report, "while sexual orientation and gender identity are important aspects of an individual's identity, they interact with many other factors, including sex, race/ethnicity, and class. These characteristics' intersection helps shape an individual's health, access to care, and experience with the healthcare system" (Kates et al., 2018).

Individuals who identify as LGBTQ+ may experience unique health challenges that differences in race/ethnicity, age, or gender alone cannot explain. Because of discrimination and a variety of other factors, research has shown that self-identified lesbian, gay, and bisexual individuals are more likely to rate their health as poor and have higher prevalence of many chronic diseases, such as cancer and cardiovascular disease, as well as asthma, allergies, headaches, and disabilities. In addition to concerns about physical health, studies have found that people who identify as LGBTQ+ are at a higher risk for mental health conditions, often as a result of prejudice, discrimination, and stigma. Various studies show that LGBTQ+ individuals are 2.5 times more likely to suffer anxiety, depression, and substance misuse; are more likely to have experienced both sexual and physical violence; and have a substantially higher rate of suicidal ideation or attempts. In

Table 2-2 Healthcare Equality Index's Core Four Criteria Areas

Criteria	
Non-discrimination and staff training	Patient non-discrimination Equal visitation Employment non-discrimination LGBTQ+ patient services and support Staff training Gender affirming services and support
Patient services and support	Medical decision making Patient identification and data collection
Employee benefits and policies	Equal employee benefits, policies & practices Transgender-inclusive health insurance
Patient and community engagement	LGBTQ+ patients and the larger LGBTQ+ community engagement

addition to stigma and discrimination, LGBTQ+ individuals may face additional health disparities resulting from practices that pose barriers to accessing health services. For example, some insurance companies will not pay for mental health services for transgender individuals. Additionally, between 6% and 15% of employers reported not offering same-sex spousal benefits to workers. Although these numbers are improving, there is still a substantial disparity in this area (Kates et al., 2018).

However, there has been some progress toward better support for those identifying as LGBTQ+. Since 2007, the Healthcare Equality Index (HEI) of the Human Rights Campaign (HRC) Foundation has been available for hospitals and other organizations. This survey is a resource for healthcare organizations that are seeking to provide equitable, inclusive care to LGBTQ+ Americans and for LGBTQ+ Americans who are seeking healthcare organizations that have a demonstrated commitment to their care. In 2024, 1,065 facilities across the country participated in the HEI survey, with 36.1% designated as leaders and 43.4% as top performers, demonstrating that they have varying inclusive LGBTQ+ patient and employment policies (HRC, 2024). These non-discrimination policies are also required for Joint Commission accreditation. (See Chapter 3.) In addition, the Joint Commission requires that facilities allow visitation without regard to sexual orientation or gender identity. The HEI has four scoring criteria areas: (1) Non-Discrimination and Staff Training, (2) Patient Services and Support, (3) Employee Benefits and Policies, and (4) Patient and Community Engagement. The four criteria areas are reflected in **Table 2-2**.

Implications for the Healthcare Industry

The changing demographics of the U.S. population significantly affect the healthcare industry. Healthcare organizations need to work to reduce disparities in care and treatment provided to underrepresented populations and ensure that our healthcare systems are diverse, equitable, and inclusive places for both patients and employees.

Consider the following:

> *Scenario One:* An insulin-dependent, indigent English-speaking male was treated at a predominantly Spanish-speaking clinic near the Mexican border. Later, he was brought back to the clinic in a diabetic coma. When he awoke, the nurse who had counseled him asked whether he had followed her instructions. "Exactly!" he replied. When the nurse asked him to show her, the monolingual Spanish-speaking nurse was startled when the patient injected an orange and ate it.
>
> *Scenario Two:* An elderly, monolingual Latinx female was being prepared for surgery, which was not the primary reason for her visit. An English-speaking nurse told her designated interpreter (a young female relative) to tell Maria that the surgeon was the best in his field and Maria would get through this fine. The young interpreter told Maria, "The nurse says the doctor does best when he is in the field, and when it is over, you will have to pay a fine!"

Real-life experiences like these happen daily in the United States (Howard et al., 2001). Cultural differences between providers and patients affect the provider–patient relationship. For example, Fadiman (1998) related a true and poignant story of cultural misunderstanding within the healthcare profession. Fadiman described the story of a young female epileptic Hmong immigrant whose parents believed that their daughter's condition was caused by spirits called "dabs," which had caught their daughter and made her fall down, hence the name of Fadiman's book, *The Spirit Catches You and You Fall Down*. The patient's parents struggled to understand the prescribed medical care, which recognized only the scientific necessities but ignored the family's personal beliefs about the spirituality of one's soul in relation to the universe. From a unique perspective, Fadiman examined the roles of the caregivers (physicians, nurses, and social workers) in treating ill children. She studied how the medical care system responded to its perceptions that the family was refusing to comply with medical orders without understanding the meaning of those orders in the context of the Hmong culture, language, and beliefs.

Health and healthcare disparities in the United States have been documented for decades. The Kaiser Family Foundation (now known simply as KFF) and the Institute of Medicine both note that although many improvements in population health have occurred, numerous disparities have persisted and, in some cases, widened across many dimensions, including race/ethnicity, socioeconomic status, age, location, gender, disability status, and sexual orientation (Orgera & Artiga, 2018; Weinstein et al., 2017). As noted by Orgera and Artiga (2018), there is a complex and interrelated set of not only individual and provider factors but also a broad array of social and environmental factors both inside and outside of the healthcare system that affect individuals' health and ability to engage in healthy behaviors, such as economic status, neighborhood/physical environment, educational levels, and access to healthy food.

Summary

Healthcare organizations need to build diverse, equitable, and inclusive environments for the well-being of their patients and employees. The slower growth of the younger population of the United States will directly affect the healthcare industry's ability to recruit professionals to provide sufficient services in the future for a large elderly population. Young people representing all forms of diversity must be attracted to the healthcare industry as a career choice to meet the healthcare needs of the country's growing, aging, and increasingly diverse population. Additionally, structural barriers that prevent various groups from accessing and obtaining high-quality health care must be addressed.

Discussion Questions

1. Discuss what the terms "diversity," "equity," and "inclusion" mean.
2. Explain why and how U.S. demographics changes affect the healthcare industry.
3. What are the differences between diversity, equity, and inclusion?
4. Describe a situation that is diverse but not equitable or inclusive.
5. Describe a situation that is diverse and equitable but not inclusive.

Exercise 2-1

In 2012, the Alliance for Aging Research established the Healthspan Campaign, a coalition of organizations committed to solving the challenges brought about by the aging of the American population. With each passing year, the percentage of people in the United States—and much of the world—over age 65 increases. This "Silver Tsunami" is expected to bring a flood of chronic disease and disabilities due to aging that could overwhelm the healthcare systems of many nations. Watch the film *The Healthspan Imperative* at www.healthspancampaign.org. Discuss the effect of the aging population on our health system, and present recommendations for how these challenges could be addressed.

Exercise 2-2

Health equity should be a consideration in the selection of vendors and implementation of new technologies within the healthcare setting. Artificial intelligence algorithms can be skewed depending on how the models were trained. AI algorithms have been identified that can lead to patient harm for certain populations, such as worse diagnostic accuracy for heart attacks in women, or biases based on the specific words patients describe their ailments. As organizations pursue new technologies, leaders should consider the implications for health equity. Look up an article on how an AI tool has led to bias or harm in either health care or the workforce. What could management do to avoid negative consequences from the technological issues in the article you found?

Exercise 2-3

There are many different elements of diversity in addition to race/ethnicity, age, sex or gender that can have an impact on health equity. Some of these include urban versus rural, disabilities, education-levels, zip code, access to broadband internet, and income level. Choose an area that is interesting for you and search for information related to health disparities or health outcomes related to that group. Discuss your findings.

References

Agency for Healthcare Research and Quality (AHRQ). (2023, November). *2023 national healthcare quality and disparities report*. https://www.ahrq.gov/research/findings/nhqrdr/nhqdr23/index.html

Alliance for Aging Research. (2003, May 19). *Alliance exposes widespread ageism in U.S. healthcare*. https://www.agingresearch.org/press-release/alliance-exposes-widespread-ageism-in-u-s-healthcare/

Arias, E., Tejada-Vera, B., Kochanek, K. D., & Ahmad, F. B. (2022, August). Provisional life expectancy estimates for 2021. *Vital Statistics Rapid Release*, no 23. National Center for Health Statistics. https://www.cdc.gov/nchs/data/vsrr/vsrr023.pdf

Artiga, S., & Orgera, K. (2019, November 12). *Key facts on health and health care by race and ethnicity*. KFF. https://www.kff.org/report-section/key-facts-on-health-and-health-care-by-race-and-ethnicity-introduction/

Bowling, A. (2007). Honour your father and mother: Ageism in medicine. *British Journal of General Practice, 57*(538), 347–348.

Butler, R. (1969). Ageism: Another form of bigotry. *The Gerontologist, 9*(4), 243–246.

Commonwealth Fund. (2003, May 1). *2002 international health policy survey of adults with health problems*. https://www.commonwealthfund.org/publications/surveys/2003/may/2002-international-health-policy-survey-adults-health-problems

Dawson, L., Long, M., & Frederiksen, B. (2023, June 30). *LGBT+ people's health status and access to care*. KFF. https://www.kff.org/report-section/lgbt-peoples-health-status-and-access-to-care-issue-brief/

Dreachslin, J. L. (1998). Conducting effective focus groups in the context of diversity: Theoretical underpinnings and practical implications. *Qualitative Health Research, 8*(6), 813–820.

Fadiman, A. (1998). *The spirit catches you and you fall down*. Farrar, Straus and Giroux.

Frey, W. (2018, June 22). *US white population declines and Generation 'Z-Plus' is minority white, census shows*. The Brookings Institution. https://www.brookings.edu/blog/the-avenue/2018/06/21/us-white-population-declines-and-generation-z-plus-is-minority-white-census-shows/

Graham, R., Berkowitz, B., Blum, R., Bockting, W., Bradford, J., de Vries, B., et al. Institute of Medicine Committee on Lesbian, Gay, Bisexual, and Transgender Health Issues and Research Gaps and Opportunities. (2011). *The health of lesbian, gay, bisexual, and transgender people: Building a foundation for better understanding*. National Academies Press.

Hill, L., Artiga, S., & Damico, A. (2024). *Health coverage by race and ethnicity, 2010–2022*. https://www.kff.org/racial-equity-and-health-policy/issue-brief/health-coverage-by-race-and-ethnicity/

Houghton Mifflin. (2006). *The American Heritage dictionary of the English language* (4th ed.).

Howard, C., Andrade, S. J., & Byrd, T. (2001). The ethical dimensions of cultural competence in border healthcare settings. *Family and Community Health, 23*(4), 36–49.

Howden, L. M., & Meyer, J. A. (2011, May). Age and sex composition: 2010. *2010 Census Briefs*. U.S. Department of Commerce, Economics and Statistics Administration, U.S. Census Bureau. https://www.census.gov/content/dam/Census/library/publications/2011/dec/c2010br-03.pdf

Human Rights Campaign. (2024). *Healthcare equality index 2024*. https://reports.hrc.org/hei-2024

Johnson, T. J., & Garman, A. N. (2010). Impact of medical travel on imports and exports of medical services. *Health Policy, 98*(2–3), 171–177.

Joplin, A., & Kunitz, D. (2018, May 25). Can you change implicit bias? *Washington Post*. https://www.washingtonpost.com/video/national/can-you-change-implicit-bias/2018/05/29/e1d28542-604d-11e8-b656-236c6214ef01_video.html

Kapila, M., Hines, E., & Searby, M. (2016, October 6). *Why diversity, equity, and inclusion matter*. Independent Sector. https://independentsector.org/resource/why-diversity-equity-and-inclusion-matter/

Kates, J., Ranji, U., Beamesderfer, A., Salganicoff, A., & Dawson, L. (2018, May 3). *Health and access to care and coverage for lesbian, gay, bisexual, and transgender (LGBT) individuals in the U.S.* KFF. https://www.kff.org/disparities-policy/issue-brief/health-and-access-to-care-and-coverage-for-lesbian-gay-bisexual-and-transgender-individuals-in-the-u-s/

Ndugga, N., Hill, L., & Artiga, S. (2024). *Key data on health and health care by race and ethnicity*. KFF. https://www.kff.org/key-data-on-health-and-health-care-by-race-and-ethnicity/

Orgera, K., & Artiga, S. (2018, August 8). *Disparities in health and health care: Five key questions and answers*. KFF. https://www.kff.org/disparities-policy/issue-brief/disparities-in-health-and-health-care-five-key-questions-and-answers/

Perry, D. (2012). Entrenched ageism in healthcare isolates, ignores and imperils elders. *Aging Today, 33*(2), 1.

Traxler, A. J. (1980). *Let's get gerontologized: Developing a sensitivity to aging. The multi-purpose senior center concept: A training manual for practitioners working with the aging*. Illinois Department of Aging.

United Nations, Department of Economic and Social Affairs, Population Division. (2019). *World population prospects 2019: Highlights (ST/ESA/SER.A/423)*. https://population.un.org/wpp/Publications/Files/WPP2019_Highlights.pdf

U.S. Census Bureau (2025, February 12). *2023 national population projections tables: main series*. https://www.census.gov/data/tables/2023/demo/popproj/2023-summary-tables.html

U.S. Census Bureau. (2023). Profile of general population and housing characteristics: 2020 (DP-1). 2020 Census Demographic Profile Data. https://data.census.gov/table?tid=DECENNIALDP2020.DP1

U.S. Census Bureau. (2017). *Educational attainment in the United States: 2017*. https://www.census.gov/data/tables/2017/demo/education-attainment/cps-detailed-tables.html

U.S. Census Bureau. (2023). *Chinese, except Taiwanese, was the largest Asian alone or in any combination group; Nepalese population grew fastest*. https://www.census.gov/library/stories/2023/09/2020-census-dhc-a-asian-population.html

Vespa, J., Armstrong, D. M., & Medina, L. (2018). *Demographic turning points for the United States: Population projections for 2020 to 2060 (Current Population Reports, P25–1144)*. U.S. Census Bureau.

Warshaw, G. A., Bragg, E. J., Shaull, R. W., & Lindsell, C. J. (2002). Academic geriatrics programs in US allopathic and osteopathic medical schools. *JAMA, 288*(18), 2313–2319.

Warshaw, G. A., Bragg, E. J., Thomas, D. C., Ho, M. L., & Brewer, D. E. (2006). Are internal medicine residency programs adequately preparing physicians to care for the Baby Boomers? A national survey from the Association of Directors of Geriatric Academic Programs Status of Geriatrics Workforce Study. *Journal of the American Geriatrics Society, 54*(10), 1603–1609.

Weinstein, J. N., Geller, A., Negussie, Y., & Baciu, A. (Eds.). (2017). *Communities in action: Pathways to health equity*. National Academies Press.

Other Suggested Readings

Institute of Medicine. (2004). *In the nation's compelling interest: Ensuring diversity in the healthcare workforce*. National Academies Press. http://www.nap.edu/catalog/10885.html

Lantz, P. (2008). Gender and leadership in healthcare administration: 21st century progress and challenges. *Journal of Healthcare Management, 53*(5), 291–304.

Information relating to Anne Fadiman's book *The Spirit Catches You and You Fall Down* may be viewed at www.spiritcatchesyou.com

CHAPTER 3

Diversity Management and Cultural Humility in Health Care

LEARNING OUTCOMES

After completing this chapter, the student should be able to:

- Define diversity management.
- Define cultural intelligence and cultural humility.
- Understand the importance of cultural intelligence and cultural humility of the workforce in meeting the needs of patients.

Overview[1]

The population of the United States is changing rapidly and is becoming increasingly diverse. In response to the growing general population's diversity, healthcare organizations must be prepared to handle the unique needs of a changing population in two key ways. First, they must ensure that people of all backgrounds and experiences can succeed within the organization and feel a sense of belonging. Second, healthcare organizations must ensure that their workforce is equipped to handle the needs of an increasingly diverse patient population by developing cultural intelligence and cultural humility. Diversity management strategies and cultural intelligence are the focus of this chapter. Healthcare organizations need to be flexible to meet the needs of a diverse workforce and patient population.

> Diversity is now a given in both labor and customer markets. To benefit from it, organizations must adopt a long-term, systemic approach. When diversity is framed as an

[1]It is critically important to consider all standards of diversity in a healthcare setting within the context of current and evolving laws, including, without limitation, laws related to workforce diversity and employment practices. Healthcare organizations and leaders should consult with their human resources and legal counsel for guidance and direction on employment practices.

opportunity to learn and improve work together—supported by cooperative culture, leadership, and group process skills—it strengthens performance. Those who commit resources to harnessing diversity's potential will likely surpass organizations that neglect such investment.

Diversity Management

Creating diverse and inclusive work environments has important implications for organizational performance. Studies show that companies with women in the C-suite, CEO position, or Chair of the Board of Directors were associated with better financial performance (Noland et al., 2016; Nordea Bank, 2017). Companies in the top quartile for ethnic and cultural diversity on their executive teams were 33% more likely to have industry-leading profitability (Hunt et al., 2018). Additionally, a more diverse employee population within a healthcare system is better equipped to serve the diverse communities in which they operate.

Despite its importance, diversity management is a challenge for many organizations. Diversity management is "a strategically driven process whose emphasis is on building skills and creating policies that will address the changing demographics of the workforce and patient population" (Svehla, 1994; Weech-Maldonado et al., 2002). While some gains have been made in increasing diversity in healthcare management to better reflect the patient population, recent studies suggest that there is still ample room for improvement. The American Hospital Association Institute for Diversity in Health Equity published a 1992 study that minorities held fewer than 1% of top management positions in the industry. In 2020, the American College of Healthcare Executives reported that 11% of hospital CEOs were non-White, though this reflects nearly 40% of the population (ACHE, 2020). While some progress has been made, the healthcare workforce still does not reflect the population it serves.

The Future Workforce

For the first time in modern history, the U.S. workforce consists of four (soon-to-be) five separate generations working side by side, and the differences among generations is a challenge facing managers today. Each generation has stereotypical views and attitudes toward work, which may affect their behavior at work. While these stereotypes are broad generalizations and do not necessarily apply to individual employees, it is helpful to understand them in navigating the dynamics of an intergenerational workforce. In addition to managing differences among these generations in the workforce, there are also seven generations currently in the patient population.

Generational differences may (see **Table 3-1**) best be explained by "age, life stage, or career stage effects" (Becton et al., 2014, p. 176). The Silent Generation makes up a small percentage of the healthcare workforce, with Baby Boomers, Generation X, Millennials, Gen Z and Gen Alpha making up the majority of the workforce in the coming years:

- **Baby Boomers** generally place a high value on loyalty and stability, reflecting the era in which they entered the workforce, when long tenure was rewarded and organizational hierarchies were rarely questioned. They tend to be comfortable with structure and authority.

Table 3-1 Generations in the Patient Population

Generation Name	Birth Years	Stereotypes/Trends
Silent Generation	1928–1945	Loyalty, conformist, risk-averse, traditional values; value stability
Baby Boomers	1946–1964	Work-centric, competitive, goal-oriented, value job security; shaped by postwar prosperity and social change. Loyal to their organizations and employers.
Generation X	1965–1980	Independent, adaptable, and skeptical. Have experienced technological and social change.
Millennials	1981–1996	Tech-savvy, collaborative, value purpose and flexibility, seen as entitled. More likely to switch jobs and employers.
Generation Z	1997–2009	Digital natives, pragmatic, diverse, socially aware, value individuality. Increased rates of anxiety and depression. Shaped by social media and digital connectivity.
Generation Alpha	2010–2024	Still emerging, but likely highly digitally connected, most diverse; shaped by AI and virtual learning.
Generation Beta	2025–2039	Experts project them to be AI-natives, highly adaptive, raised in a world of automation and rapid change.

Note: Not all experts agree on the cutoff years for different generations, though this table represents common delineations.

Data from Pew Research Center. (2019, January 17). Where Millennials end and Generation Z begins. https://www.pewresearch.org/short-reads/2019/01/17/where-millennials-end-and-generation-z-begins/; Library of Congress. (2020). Generations - Doing Consumer Research: A Resource Guide. https://guides.loc.gov/consumer-research/market-segments/generations; ABC13. (2025, January 1). With the start of Gen Beta in 2025, get to know all the generations. Gen Beta kicks off in 2025: Your guide to all the generation names and years - ABC13 Houston; Haidt, J. (2024). The anxious generation: How the great rewiring of childhood is causing an epidemic of mental illness. Penguin Press; Twenge, J. M. (2023). Generations: The real differences between Gen Z, Millennials, Gen X, Boomers, and Silents—and what they mean for America's future. Atria Books.

- **Generation X** is often characterized by self-reliance and a degree of skepticism toward authority and bureaucracy. Many members of this cohort experienced childhood in households with two working parents or as children of divorce, circumstances that frequently required independence at an early age.
- **Millennials** typically seek purpose and meaning in their work, often prioritizing these factors over traditional markers of success. This orientation is shaped by formative experiences such as the September 11 terrorist attacks, the Great Recession, and escalating student debt. They also tend to value regular feedback and professional development, influenced by an upbringing that emphasized structured activities, achievement, and positive reinforcement. Millennials make up the largest portion of today's workforce, comprising 35% of the U.S. labor force (Fry, 2018).
- **Generation Z** grew up during a time with smartphones and the internet, and demonstrates a high level of digital fluency. Their formative years were further shaped by the COVID-19 pandemic and related social isolation, contributing to their reputation as the "loneliest generation." Consequently, a strong emphasis on emotional well-being is common among this group. Gen Z is making up a growing percentage of the healthcare workforce.

- **Generation Alpha**, still emerging, is expected to be the most digitally connected generation to date. Growing up with artificial intelligence, virtual learning, and rapid technological change, they are likely to expect inclusivity, flexibility, and highly personalized approaches to work and development.
- **Generation Beta** is newly formed, and little is known about their preferences, behaviors, or the global dynamics that will shape their lives in the future.

Generational diversity poses challenges for healthcare leaders. Workers of different ages and stages of life may have different requirements for flexibility, feedback, work-life balance, growth and training opportunities, professionalism, and part-time roles. Adapting to meet the needs of different generations at work allows organizations to maintain a workforce that brings together many different perspectives and skill sets, and remains sufficient to meet the care needs of an aging patient population.

Diversity in Healthcare Leadership

The American College of Healthcare Executives (ACHE), the National Association of Health Services Executives (NAHSE), the Institute for Diversity in Healthcare Management (IFD), the National Forum for Latino Healthcare Executives, and the Asian Healthcare Leaders Association released a study in 2015 that measured the representation of Black non-Hispanics, Hispanics, women, and other minorities in healthcare executive leadership roles. This study was a follow-up to similar studies that were completed in 1992, 1997, 2002, and 2008. The study, completed in 2014, was based on a random-sample survey of 1,409 healthcare executives. Respondents worked in a variety of settings: hospitals, healthcare provider organizations, government health agencies, and consulting and educational institutes. (see **Table 3-2**.)

Although there have been improvements since the initial 1992 survey, the composition of the (CEO) and chief operating officer (COO)/senior vice president positions still does not reflect the patient population. In the 2014 ACHE study, reflected in Table 3-2, 32% of White men are CEOs, compared to 25% of Hispanic men, 20% of Black men, and 9% of Asian men. These disparities are not as apparent among women; roughly 8–15% of women in each race hold CEO positions. Additionally, in 2014, members of minorities still reported the effects of discrimination in the workplace. Between 15% and 29% of minority respondents believed that they had not been hired for a position because of their race or ethnicity, compared to 2% of White respondents.

The 2015 Benchmarking Survey by the AHA Institute for Diversity and Health Equity highlighted that although there was some limited increase in the diversity of hospitals' leadership and governance, more positive movement is needed to reflect the growing diversity of the patient population. The study reported that minorities comprised:

- 14% of hospital board members (unchanged from 2013).
- 11% of executive leadership positions (a decrease from 12% in 2013).
- 19% of first- and middle-level management positions (an increase from 15% in 2011).

Dreachslin and Curtis (2004) noted that career advancement of women and racially and ethnically diverse individuals in healthcare management was characterized by (1) underrepresentation, especially in senior-level management positions; (2) lower compensation, even controlling for education and experience; and (3) more negative perceptions of equity and opportunity in the workplace. The researchers identified three areas that are key organization-specific factors for shaping career outcomes for women and racially and ethnically diverse individuals: (1) leadership and strategic orientation (i.e., senior management's commitment to successful implementation

Table 3-2 American College of Healthcare Executives 2014 Diversity Study

Position by race/ethnicity and gender[a]
For each ethnicity, the percentage holding a specific position type

	Males				Females			
	Black	White	Hispanic	Asian	Black	White	Hispanic	Asian
CEO (%)	20	32	25	9	8	14	11	0
COO/senior vice president	16	19	19	17	11	18	19	13
Vice president	23	20	13	18	20	22	19	8
Department head	30	16	31	36	36	31	31	38
Manager/supervisor/program director	2	3	1	5	7	4	6	7
Department staff/consultant/ other	9	10	10	16	18	11	14	24
Total %	100%	100%	99%	101%	100%	100%	100%	101%
N	219	182	158	153	224	218	108	132

[a]Responses may not total to 100 because of rounding.

of diversity initiatives), (2) organizational culture and climate (i.e., the depth and breadth of the organization's strategic commitment to diversity leadership and cultural competency), and (3) human resources practices (i.e., establishing best practices in advancing the management careers of women and racially and ethnically diverse individuals, such as formal mentoring programs, professional development, work-life balances, and flexible benefits).

To best serve their patient base, healthcare organizations and providers must be willing to invest the time, money, and effort needed to educate all their employees, from senior staff to front-line workers. Wilson-Stronks and Mutha (2010), Cejka Search and Solucient (2005), and Kochan et al. (2003) have linked the effects of diversity to business performance. Kochan and colleagues (2003) concluded that the impact of diversity depends on organizational culture, human resource practices, and strategy. In other words, the positive impact of diversity is directly related to the organization's ability to successfully manage a diverse environment. A recent review by Gomez and Bernet (2024) explores how diversity in healthcare organizations supports improved patient care. This review synthesized findings from 16 meta-analyses and studies focusing specifically on health care. Its main conclusions were:

- Increased workforce diversity is associated with improved patient satisfaction, more accurate diagnoses, greater patient compliance, and sometimes lower long-term costs.
- Diverse healthcare teams are linked to higher-quality patient outcomes, especially when care is culturally concordant or teams reflect the diversity of the patient population.
- The review further noted that a diversity-friendly environment boosts innovation, team communication, and reduces clinical uncertainty, all of which contribute to higher quality care.

Dreachslin (2007) reinforces the need for mass customization of diversity practices to be inclusive of disparities that are represented in the communities that healthcare organizations serve. In order to actively support business strategy, organizations will need to provide employees with skills that are inclusive of conflict-management skills, self-awareness, understanding of cultural differences, validation of alternative points of view, and methods to manage bias through effective training and development.

For healthcare managers to transform their organizations to provide an inclusive culture where all employees feel the opportunity to reach their full potential, Guillory (2004, pp. 25–30) recommended a 10-step process:

1. Development of a customized business case for diversity for your organization. In other words, how does diversity relate to the organization's overall success?
2. Education and training for your staff to develop an understanding of diversity, its importance to your organization's success, and diversity skills to apply on a daily basis.
3. Establishment of a baseline by conducting a comprehensive cultural survey that integrates performance, inclusion, climate, and work-life balance.
4. Selection and prioritization of the issues that lead to the greatest breakthrough in transforming the culture.
5. Creation of a 3- to 5-year diversity strategic plan that is tied to organizational strategic business objectives.
6. Leadership's endorsement of and financial commitment to the plan.
7. Establishment of measurable leadership and management objectives to hold managers accountable to top leadership for achieving these objectives.
8. Implementation of the plan, recognizing that surprises and setbacks will occur along the way.
9. Continued training in concert with the skills and competencies necessary to successfully achieve the diversity action plan.
10. Survey 1 to 1.5 years after initiation of the plan to determine how inclusion has changed.

Dreachslin (2007) stresses the need for organizations to manage diversity and invest in professional development so that team members have the tools needed to navigate their differences and effectively manage their biases.

Cultural Intelligence and Cultural Humility

In addition to supporting a diverse workforce, healthcare organizations must ensure that their employees can handle the diverse needs of their patient population. First, healthcare professionals and organizations must have cultural and linguistic understanding and skills to provide effective and efficient health services to diverse patient populations. This skill set has been referred to as cultural intelligence. Cultural intelligence has been defined as "the ability to engage in a set of behaviors that uses skills (i.e., language, or interpersonal skills) and qualities (e.g., tolerance for ambiguity, flexibility) that are tuned appropriately to the culture-based values and attitudes of the people with whom one interacts" (Peterson, 2004, p. 89). Supportive organizational practices include an ongoing commitment to appropriate practice and policies for diverse populations (Brach & Fraser, 2000; Weech-Maldonado et al., 2002; see Hofstede's Cultural Dimensions, **Exhibit 3-1**). The term "linguistic competency" has been defined as "the capacity of an organization and its personnel to communicate effectively, and convey information in a manner that is easily understood by diverse audiences, including persons of limited English proficiency, those

Exhibit 3-1 Hofstede's Cultural Dimensions

One of the most extensive cross-cultural surveys ever conducted is Hofstede's (1983) study of the influence of national culture on organizational and managerial behaviors. National culture is important to organizational studies because it incorporates political, sociological, and psychological components.

Hofstede's research was conducted over 11 years, with more than 116,000 respondents in more than 40 countries, and continued to be validated over the next 40 years. The researcher collected data about "values" from the employees of a multinational corporation located in more than 50 countries. Based on his findings, Hofstede proposed four dimensions of national culture within which countries could be positioned independently. Hofstede's (1983) original four dimensions of national culture, which have now been expanded to six dimensions, are labeled and described as follows (**Figure 3-1**):

- *Individualism–Collectivism*: Individualism measures culture along a self-interest versus group-interest continuum. Individualism is a preference for a loosely knit social framework wherein individuals are supposed to take care of themselves and their immediate families only. Its opposite, collectivism, is a preference for a tightly knit social framework in which individuals can expect their relatives, clan, or other in-group to look after them in exchange for unquestioning loyalty. Hofstede (1983) suggested that self-interested cultures (e.g., individualism) are positively related to the wealth of a nation.

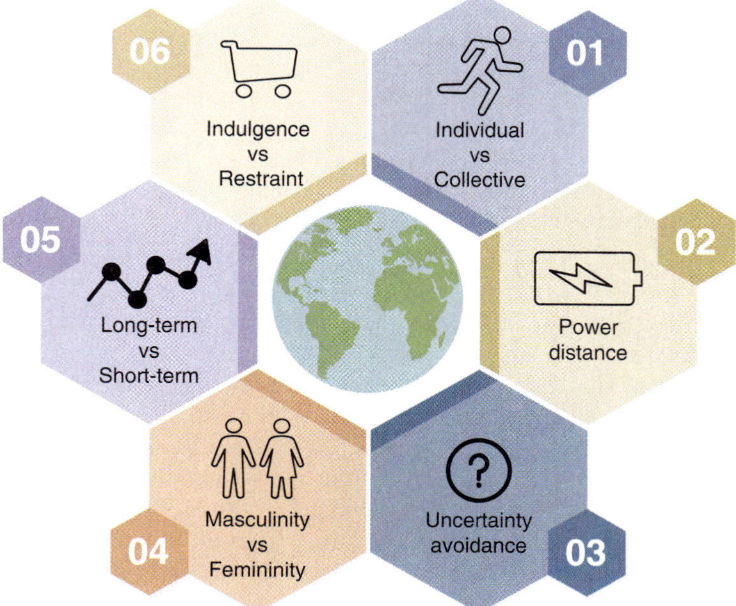

Figure 3-1 Hofstede's Cultural Dimensions

Data from Hofstede, G., Hofstede, G. J., & Minkov, M. (2010). *Cultures and organizations: Software of the mind* (3rd ed.). McGraw-Hill. https://geerthofstede.com/culture-geert-hofstede-gert-jan-hofstede/6d-model-of-national-culture/

(continues)

Exhibit 3-1 Hofstede's Cultural Dimensions *(continued)*

- *Power Distance*: Power distance measures how a society deals with physical and intellectual inequalities and how the culture applies power and wealth relative to its inequalities. People in societies with a large power distance accept a hierarchical order in which everybody has a place, which needs no further justification. People in societies with a small power distance strive for power equalization and demand justification for power inequalities. Hofstede (1983) indicated that group-interest cultures (e.g., collectivism) have large power distance.
- *Uncertainty Avoidance*: Uncertainty avoidance reflects the degree to which members of a society feel uncomfortable with uncertainty and ambiguity. The scale runs from tolerance of different behaviors (i.e., a society with a natural tendency to feel secure) to a society where institutions create security and minimize risk. Societies with substantial uncertainty avoidance maintain rigid codes of belief and behavior and are intolerant of deviant personalities and ideas. Societies with weak uncertainty avoidance maintain a more relaxed atmosphere where practice counts more than principles and deviance is more easily tolerated.
- *Masculinity versus Femininity*: Masculinity versus femininity measures the division of roles between the genders. The masculine side of the scale is a society in which the gender differences are maximized (e.g., need for achievement, heroism, assertiveness, and material success). Feminine societies are those in which there are preferences for relationships, modesty, caring for the weak, and the quality of life.
- *Long-Term Orientation versus Short-Term Normative Orientation*: Societies with a long-term orientation tend to value time-honored traditions and norms. In contrast, societies with a short-term orientation tend to value ingenuity and modernization (Hofstede, 1991).
- *Indulgence versus Restraint*: Societies valuing indulgence allow relatively free gratification of natural human drives, and prioritize enjoying life and having fun. Those valuing restraint adhere to strict social norms and value duty, discipline, and order (Hofstede & Minkov, 2010).

Hofstede proposed that the most important dimensions for organizational leadership are individualism–collectivism and power distance, and the most important for decision making are power distance and uncertainty avoidance.

who have low literacy skills or are not literate, and individuals with disabilities" (National Center for Cultural Competence, 2000, August).

Moving beyond cultural intelligence, healthcare providers must adopt the practice of cultural humility, which acknowledges that understanding another person's cultural preferences is not something that can be fully mastered—it is not a finite body of information to be memorized. Instead, one should adopt an attitude of humility in recognizing that they may not fully understand the culture or preferences of others, and must commit to openness, curiosity, self-reflection, and lifelong learning. Cultural humility "incorporates a lifelong commitment to self-evaluation and self-critique, to redressing the power imbalances in the patient-physician dynamic, and to developing mutually beneficial and non-paternalistic clinical and advocacy partnerships with communities on behalf of individuals and defined populations" (Tervalon, M., & Murray-Garcia, J., 1998, p. 117).

Because of our increasingly diverse population, healthcare professionals must be concerned about their cultural intelligence, which is more than cultural awareness or sensitivity. Regulatory and accreditation entities have set standards to assist healthcare practitioners in developing their cultural awareness and skills as they encounter more diverse patients. For example, the Liaison

Committee on Medical Education (LCME), the accrediting body of medical schools, introduced the following accreditation standard:

> The faculty and students must demonstrate an understanding of how people of diverse cultures and belief systems perceive health and illness and respond to various symptoms, diseases, and treatments. Medical students should learn to recognize and appropriately address gender and cultural biases in healthcare delivery while considering the health of the patient first.

This standard has given medical schools added impetus and emphasis on introducing cultural competency education into the undergraduate medical curriculum (Association of American Medical Colleges, 2005, p. 1). In addition, The Joint Commission has implemented patient-centered communication accreditation standards, which require hospitals to meet certain mandates related to qualifications for language interpreters and translators, identifying and addressing patient communication needs, collecting patient race and ethnicity data, patient access to a support individual, and nondiscrimination in care (The Joint Commission, 2014, July).

The Commonwealth Fund has led the effort "to eliminate the cultural and linguistic barriers between healthcare providers and patients, which can interfere with the effective delivery of health services" (Beach et al., 2006, p. vi). The Commonwealth Fund (2004), in addition to funding initiatives regarding quality of care for underserved populations, has initiated an educational program that assists healthcare practitioners in understanding the importance of communication between culturally diverse patients and their physicians, the tensions between modern medicine and cultural beliefs, and the ongoing problems of racial and ethnic discrimination. The goals of this program are for clinicians to:

1. Understand that patients and healthcare professionals often have different perspectives, values, and beliefs about health and illness that can lead to conflict, especially when communication is limited by language and cultural barriers.
2. Become familiar with the issues and challenges critical in caring for patients of different cultural backgrounds.
3. Consider each patient as an individual with many different social, cultural, and personal influences rather than using general stereotypes about cultural groups.
4. Understand how discrimination and mistrust affect the interaction of patients with physicians and the healthcare system.
5. Develop a greater sense of curiosity, empathy, and respect toward culturally diverse patients, and thus be encouraged to develop better communication and negotiation skills through ongoing instruction.

Modified from *Worlds Apart, Facilitator's Guide* by Alexander Green, MD, Joseph Betancourt, MD, MPH, and J. Emilio Carrillo, MD, MPH, The Commonwealth Fund, p. 4.

In addition to the Commonwealth Fund, the W. K. Kellogg Foundation has led efforts to lessen the recognized disparity of racial and ethnic minority groups' representation among the nation's health professionals. The Kellogg Foundation requested the Institute of Medicine's (2004) study entitled *In the Nation's Compelling Interest: Ensuring Diversity in the Health-Care Workforce*. The Institute of Medicine found that racial and ethnic diversity is important in the health professions for the following reasons:

1. Healthcare professionals who are members of racial and ethnic minorities are significantly more likely than their peers to serve minority and medically underserved communities, thereby helping to improve problems of limited minority access to care.

2. Minority patients who have a choice are more likely to select healthcare professionals of their own racial or ethnic background. Moreover, patients who are members of racial and ethnic minorities are generally more satisfied with the care that they receive from minority professionals, and minority patients' ratings of the quality of their health care are generally higher in racially concordant settings than in racially discordant settings.
3. Diversity in healthcare training settings may assist in efforts to improve the cross-cultural training and competencies of all trainees.

Other organizations are active in bridging cultural differences in an attempt to lessen health disparities. For example, the Office of Minority Health within the Department of Health and Human Services has developed a list of standards for Culturally and Linguistically Appropriate Services (CLAS), which healthcare organizations and practitioners should use to ensure equal access to high-quality health care by diverse populations (HHS OMH, 2025). The list of standards is included below:

Principal Standard:

1. Provide effective, understandable, and respectful quality care and services that respond to cultural health beliefs and practices, languages, health literacy, and other communication needs. Governance, Leadership, and Workforce:
2. Advance and sustain organizational governance and leadership that promotes CLAS through policy, practices, and allocated resources.
3. Recruit, promote, equip, and support a governance, leadership, and workforce that respond to the digital, cultural, and language needs of the population.
4. Educate and train governance, leadership, and workforce regularly on CLAS practices and resources.

Communication and Language Assistance:

5. Offer language assistance to individuals who have limited English proficiency and/or other communication needs, at no cost to them, to facilitate timely access to all health care and services.
6. Inform all individuals, in writing and orally, of the availability of language assistance services in English and other languages that serve their linguistic needs.
7. Ensure the competence of individuals providing language assistance through training and certification, when available, recognizing that the use of untrained individuals and/or minors as interpreters should be avoided and discouraged.
8. Provide easy-to-understand digital and print materials and signage in the languages commonly used by the populations in the service area.

Engagement, Continuous Improvement, and Accountability:

9. Establish culturally and linguistically appropriate goals, policies, and management accountability, and infuse them throughout the organization's planning and operations.
10. Conduct ongoing assessments of the organization's integration of CLAS-related activities and measures into quality improvement activities.
11. Collect and maintain accurate and reliable demographic data to monitor and evaluate the impact of CLAS on health outcomes and to inform service delivery.
12. Conduct regular assessments of community health assets and needs and use the results to plan and implement services that respond to the cultural and linguistic needs of populations in the service area.

13. Partner with the community to design, implement, and evaluate cultural and linguistically appropriate practices and impact.
14. Create culturally and linguistically appropriate processes to identify, prevent, and resolve conflicts, complaints, or grievances.
15. Communicate the organization's progress in implementing and sustaining CLAS to all stakeholders, constituents, and the general public.

Reproduced from the National CLAS Standards, Office of Minority Health, U.S. Department of Health and Human Services, 2025.

Summary

As the U.S. population changes and continues to become more diverse, healthcare organizations must ensure that they support the cultural intelligence and humility of their employees. When cultural intelligence and humility are organizational expectations, the results will be reduced health disparities, increased patient satisfaction, and a more engaged workforce.

Discussion Questions

1. Explain the meaning of cultural intelligence and cultural humility.
2. What is diversity management?
3. How does a diverse workforce help organizations address the needs of a diverse patient population?

Exercise 3-1

Visit the Hofstede Centre (https://geerthofstede.com/culture-geert-hofstede-gert-jan-hofstede/6d-model-of-national-culture/) and review the scores by country for the various cultural dimensions that Hofstede identified. In light of these scores, think about some interactions you have had with people (colleagues, patients, friends, etc.) who were born and raised in other countries. Do your interactions make more sense given this new insight?

Exercise 3-2

With diverse patient populations come language translation issues. Medical interpretation is a challenge facing most health organizations. Medical interpretation and translation services are costly. You are a member of your hospital's task force and are challenged to establish customer-focused, cost-efficient communication programs. Search the Joint Commission website for ideas (https://www.jointcommission.org/en-us). What recommendations would you make as a member of the task force?

References

ABC13 Houston. (2025, January 1). *Gen Beta kicks off in 2025: Your guide to all the generation names and years*. https://abc13.com/post/gen-beta-kicks-off-2025-guide-generation-names-years/15733724/

American College of Healthcare Executives. (2020, November 16). Increasing and sustaining racial diversity in healthcare leadership. https://www.ache.org/about-ache/our-story/our-commitments/policy-statements/increasing-and-sustaining-racial-diversity-in-healthcare-management

American College of Healthcare Executives. (2008). *A race/ethnic comparison of career attainments in healthcare management, summary report*. https://www.ache.org/-/media/ache/learning-center/research/report_tables.pdf

Association of American Medical Colleges. (2005). *Cultural competence education*. https://www.aamc.org/media/20856/download

Beach, M. C., Saha, S., & Cooper, L. A. (2006, October 1). *The role and relationship of cultural competence and patient-centeredness in health care quality*. The Commonwealth Fund. http://www.commonwealthfund.org/publications/fund-reports/2006/oct/the-role-and-relationship-of-cultural-competence-and-patient-centeredness-in-health-care-quality

Becton, J. B., Walker, H. J., & Jones-Farmer, A. (2014). Generational differences in workplace behavior. *Journal of Applied Social Psychology, 44*(3), 175–189.

Betancourt, J., Green, A. R., & Carrillo, J. E. (2002, October 1). *Cultural competence in health care: Emerging frameworks and practical approaches*. The Commonwealth Fund. https://www.commonwealthfund.org/publications/fund-reports/2002/oct/cultural-competence-health-care-emerging-frameworks-and

Brach, C., & Fraser, I. (2000). Can cultural competency reduce racial and ethnic health disparities? A review and conceptual model. *Medical Care Research and Review, 57*(Suppl. 1), 181–217.

Cejka Search and Solucient, LLC. (2005). *Hospital CEO leadership survey*.

Commonwealth Fund. (2004, February 1). *Worlds apart: A four-part series on cross-cultural health care*. https://www.commonwealthfund.org/publications/publication/2004/feb/worlds-apart-four-part-series-cross-cultural-health-care

Dotson, E., & Nuru-Jeter, A. (2012). Setting the stage for a business case for leadership diversity in healthcare: History, research, and leverage. *Journal of Healthcare Management, 57*(1), 35–46.

Dreachslin, J. L. (2007). Diversity management and cultural competence: Research, practice and the business case. *Journal of Healthcare Management, 52*(2), 79–86.

Dreachslin, J. L., & Curtis, E. F. (2004). Study of factors affecting the career advancement of women and racially/ethnically diverse individuals in healthcare management. *Journal of Health Administration Education, 21*(4), 441–484.

Fry, R. (2018, April 11). *Millennials are the largest generation in the U.S. labor force*. Pew Research Center. https://www.pewresearch.org/fact-tank/2018/04/11/millennials-largest-generation-us-labor-force/

Gómez, L. E., & Bernet, P. (2019). Diversity improves performance and outcomes. *Journal of the National Medical Association, 111*(4), 383–392. https://pubmed.ncbi.nlm.nih.gov/30765101

Guillory, W. A. (2004). The roadmap to diversity, inclusion, and high performance. *Healthcare Executive, 19*(4), 24–30.

Haidt, J. (2024, March 26). *The anxious generation: How the great rewiring of childhood is causing an epidemic of mental illness*. Penguin Press.

Hofstede, G. (1983). The cultural relativity of organizational practices and theories. *Journal of International Business Studies, 14*(2), 75–89.

Hofstede, G. (1991). *Cultures and organizations: Software of the mind*. McGraw-Hill.

Hofstede, G., Van Deusen, C. A., Mueller, C. B., Charles, T. A., & The Business Goals Network. (2002). What goals do business leaders pursue? A study in fifteen countries. *Journal of International Business Studies, 33*(4), 785–803.

Hofstede, G., Hofstede, G. J., & Minkov, M. (2010). *Cultures and organizations: Software of the mind: Intercultural cooperation and its importance for survival*. McGraw-Hill.

Hunt, D. V., Prince, S., Dixon-Fyle, S., & Yee, L. (2018, January 18). *Delivering through diversity*. McKinsey & Company. https://www.mckinsey.com/capabilities/people-and-organizational-performance/our-insights/delivering-through-diversity

Institute for Diversity in Health Equity. (2019). *About the institute*. https://web.archive.org/web/20190402030256/https://www.aha.org/about

Institute of Medicine. (2004). *In the nation's compelling interest: Ensuring diversity in the health-care workforce*. National Academy Press.

The Joint Commission. (2014, July). *A crosswalk of the national standards for Culturally and Linguistically Appropriate Services (CLAS) in health and health care to The Joint Commission Hospital Accreditation Standards*. https://web.archive.org/web/20150413054511/https://www.jointcommission.org/assets/1/6/Crosswalk-_CLAS_-20140718.pdf

Kochan, T., Bezrukova, R., Ely, R., Jackson, S., Jehn, K., Joshi, A., Leonard, J., Levine, D., & Thomas, D. (2003). The effects of diversity on business performance: Report of the diversity research network. *Human Resource Management, 42*(1), 3–21.

Library of Congress. (2020). *Generations - Doing consumer research: A resource guide*. https://guides.loc.gov/consumer-research/market-segments/generations

Nahavandi, A., & Malekzadeh, A. R. (1999). *Organizational behavior: The person-organization fit*. Prentice Hall.

National Center for Cultural Competence. (2000, August). Linguistic competence. Georgetown University Center for Child and Human Development. https://nccc.georgetown.edu/curricula/linguisticcompetence.html

Noland, M., Moran, T., & Kotschwar, B. (2016, February). *Is gender diversity profitable? Evidence from a global survey*. Peterson Institute for International Economics. https://www.piie.com/sites/default/files/documents/wp16-3.pdf

Nordea B. (2017, September 8). *Investing in female CEOs pays off.* https://www.nordea.com/en/press-and-news/news-and-press-releases/news-en/2017/investing-in-female-ceos-pays-off.html

Peterson, B. (2004). *Cultural intelligence: A guide to working with people from other cultures*. Nicholas Brealey.

Pew Research Center. (2019, January 17). *Where Millennials end and Generation Z begins*. https://www.pewresearch.org/short-reads/2019/01/17/where-millennials-end-and-generation-z-begins/

Svehla, T. (1994). Diversity management: Key to future success. *Frontiers of Health Services Management, 11*(2), 3–33.

Tervalon, M., & Murray-Garcia, J. (1998). Cultural humility versus cultural competence: A critical distinction in defining physician training outcomes in multicultural education. *Journal of Health Care for the Poor and Underserved, 9*(2), 117–125.

Twenge, J. M. (2023. April 25). *Generations: The real differences between Gen Z, Millennials, Gen X, Boomers, and Silents—and what they mean for America's future*. Atria Books.

U.S. Department of Health and Human Services, Office of Minority Health [HHS OMH]. (2025). *National standards for culturally and linguistically appropriate services in health and health care*. https://thinkculturalhealth.hhs.gov/assets/pdfs/EnhancedNationalCLASStandards_Revised_June2025.pdf

Weech-Maldonado, R., Dreachslin, J. L., Dansky, K. H., DeSouza, G., & Gatto, M. (2002). Racial/ethnic diversity management and cultural competency: The case of Pennsylvania hospitals. *Journal of Healthcare Management, 47*(2), 111–124.

Wilson-Stronks, A., & Mutha, S. (2010). From the perspective of CEOs: What motivates hospitals to embrace cultural competence? *Journal of Healthcare Management, 55*(5), 339–351.

CHAPTER 4

Attitudes and Perceptions

LEARNING OUTCOMES

After completing this chapter, the student should be able to:

- Appreciate the importance of attitudes to understanding behavior.
- Understand the three components of attitude.
- Understand how attitudes can be changed.
- Understand how perceptions allow individuals to simplify their worlds.
- Understand the four stages of the perception process.
- Understand social perception and the various subgroups.
- Understand the importance of using objective methods for employee selection.

Overview

This chapter explains how understanding the psychology of attitudes and perceptions helps us better manage the employees of the organizations in which we work. When applied to organizational behavior issues, psychological principles can help healthcare managers deal with staff fairly, make jobs enjoyable and satisfying, and motivate employees to higher productivity levels. By the end of this chapter, you will gain insights into attitudes and perceptions and how they relate to human behavior.

Attitudes

What is an attitude? Gordon Allport (1935) defined an attitude as a mental or neural state of readiness organized through experience, exerting a directive or dynamic influence on the individual's response to all related objects and situations. A simpler definition of attitude is a mindset or a tendency to act in a particular way toward an object or entity (i.e., a person, place, or thing) due to one's experience and temperament.

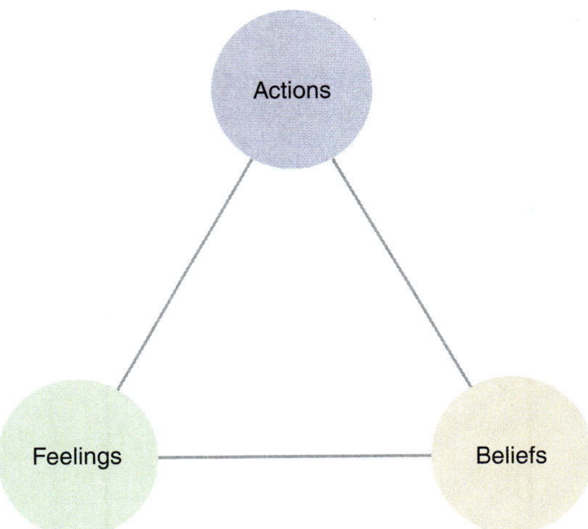

Figure 4-1 Tricomponent Model of Attitudes

When we refer to a person's attitudes, we attempt to explain their behavior. Attitudes are a complex combination of an individual's personality, beliefs, values, behaviors, and motivations. We understand when someone says, "She has a positive attitude toward work" versus "She has a poor work attitude." When we speak of someone's attitude, we are referring to the person's emotions and behaviors. A person's attitude toward preventive medicine encompasses their point of view about the topic (e.g., thought) and how the person feels about this topic (e.g., emotion), as well as the actions (e.g., behaviors) in which they engage as a result of their attitude toward preventing health problems. This is the tricomponent model of attitudes; see **Figure 4-1**. An attitude includes three components: an affect (a feeling), cognition (a thought or belief), and behavior (an action).

Attitudes help us define how we see situations and behave toward them. As the tricomponent model illustrates, attitudes include feelings, thoughts, and actions. Attitudes may be an enduring evaluation of a person or object (e.g., "I like John best of my coworkers") or other emotional reactions to objects and to people (e.g., "I dislike working on the department's annual budget" or "Jane makes me angry"). Attitudes also provide us with internal cognitions or beliefs and thoughts about people and objects (e.g., "Jane needs to work harder" or "Sam does not enjoy working in this department"). Attitudes cause us to behave in a particular way toward an object or person (e.g., "I return email messages within 24 hours because it upsets me when others do not follow up with me in a timely fashion"). Although the feeling and belief components of attitudes are internal to a person, we can often determine their attitude from their behavior.

Cognitive Dissonance

Alfred Adler (1870–1937), a Viennese physician who developed the theory of individual psychology, emphasized that a person's attitude toward the environment significantly influences their behavior. Adler suggested that a person's thoughts, feelings, and behaviors were transactions with the person's physical and social surroundings. The direction of influence flowed both ways: Our attitudes are influenced by our social world, and our attitudes influence our social world.

However, these interactions may cause conflict between our attitude and our behavior. This conflict is referred to as cognitive dissonance. Cognitive dissonance refers to any inconsistency that a person perceives between two or more of their attitudes or between the person's behavior and attitudes. Festinger (1957) stated that any form of uncomfortable inconsistency will prompt the person to reduce the dissonance (conflict). For example, suppose that Harry likes two coworkers, John and Mary, but John does not like Mary (i.e., inconsistency). Suppose Harry becomes too uncomfortable with the inconsistency. In that case, he may (1) try to change John's feelings about Mary, (2) change his feelings about either John or Mary, or (3) sever his relationship with either John or Mary (see **Case Study 4-1**).

Other approaches that a person may use to reduce the inconsistency are as follows:

- Eliminating their responsibility or control over an act or decision.
- Denying, distorting, or selectively forgetting the information.
- Minimizing the importance of the issue, decision, or act.
- Selecting new information that is consonant with an attitude or behavior.

CASE STUDY 4-1 Scott's Dilemma

Scott, a licensed physical therapist, has worked for a national rehabilitation company in an urban Southwest city for 4 years. Until recently, he was satisfied with his work environment, enjoying patient care and colleague interactions. However, after a health system reorganization, Scott's new supervisor, George, was transferred from a Midwest facility. From the outset, George criticized Scott's care plans and patient interactions, making Scott feel incapable despite his history of above-average performance evaluations.

Determined to meet George's expectations, Scott increased his workload and addressed every critique. Nevertheless, George continued to find fault. Staff meetings became a source of stress, as George repeatedly belittled Scott in front of colleagues. Over time, Scott felt alienated, his health and well-being deteriorated, and the career he once loved became a source of anxiety. He began calling in sick and experiencing disturbing thoughts of confrontation, leading to further guilt and distress.

George also influenced Scott's coworkers, encouraging them to isolate Scott. Over time, they began to perceive Scott as the problem, assuming George's authority validated his critiques. To maintain their standing, they distanced themselves, leaving Scott increasingly isolated.

Seeking resolution, Scott directly addressed his concerns with George, wanting to improve their working relationship. However, George interpreted this as insubordination, escalating his hostility toward Scott. Desperate for support, Scott turned to Human Resources (HR), where a manager advised him to document instances of mistreatment. When HR approached George to discuss the issue, George's resentment and retaliatory actions against Scott intensified.

Scott escalated his concerns to George's superior, Rebecca, as a last resort. After speaking with both parties, Rebecca sided with George, who framed Scott as an unproductive employee lacking respect for authority. Instead of relief, Scott received a formal reprimand for insubordination.

Discuss the cognitive dissonance reflected in Scott's Dilemma.

Data from Pinto, J., Vecchione, M., & Howard, L. (2004, October). Workplace bully [Conference presentation]. 12th Annual International Conference of the Association on Employment Practices and Principles, Ft. Lauderdale, FL.

For example, why do people continue to smoke cigarettes when the hazards of smoking are so well known? Using the cognitive dissonance theory, Kassarjian and Cohen (1965) attempted to analyze how smokers rationalize their behavior. They found that smokers justify their continued smoking by (1) eliminating their responsibility for their behavior ("I am unable to stop" or "It takes too much effort to stop"); (2) denying, distorting, misperceiving, or minimizing the degree of health hazard involved ("Many smokers live a long time" or "Lots of things are hazardous"); and/or (3) selectively relying on information that reduces the inconsistency of the smoker's behavior ("Smoking is better than excessive eating or drinking" or "Smoking is better than being a nervous wreck").

Although the theory of cognitive dissonance helps us understand how individuals try to make sense of the world, it does not predict what an individual will do to reduce or eliminate the dissonance. It only relates that the individual will be motivated to "do something" to bring attitudes and behaviors into balance. Cognitive dissonance theory has many practical managerial applications for motivating employees and is the theoretical basis for what are known as the equity theories of motivation (Ott, 1995). Equity theory predicts that employees will pursue a balance between their investments in work and the rewards gained from their work, such that their own investment/reward ratio will be the same as or similar to that of others. Disturbance of this balance results in behaviors that will attempt to relieve the dissonance. For example, suppose an employee perceives that a colleague is paid more for the same level of productivity. In that case, they will be motivated to ask for a raise, lower their level of productivity, or seek another job.

Formation of Attitudes

How are attitudes formed? Attitude formation results from learning, modeling other individuals' actions and attitudes, and direct experiences with people and situations. Attitudes influence our decisions, guide our behavior, and affect what we remember (which is not always the same as what we hear). Attitudes come in different strengths, and like most things learned or influenced through experience, they can be measured and *changed*.

Measurement of Attitudes

Since 1929 (Thurstone & Chave, 1929), organizations have widely used employee surveys to learn about workers' attitudes toward their environments. As Fottler and colleagues (1995) point out, "from responses to these surveys, management can learn how employees view their jobs, their supervisors, their wages and benefits, their working conditions, and other aspects of their employment." Thus, employee attitude survey responses help managers determine whether management is doing the right things to retain and motivate employees. For example, Lowe, Schellenberg, and Shannon (2003) found that workers who rated their work environments as "healthy" (in terms of task content, pay, work hours, career prospects, interpersonal relationships, security, etc.) reported higher job satisfaction, morale, and organizational commitment and lower absenteeism and intent to quit. Some typical questions are illustrated in **Figure 4-2**. Morrel-Samuels (2002) provided 16 guidelines for organizations to consider when designing an employee attitude survey (see **Exhibit 4-1**).

Effective managers use survey results to detect problem areas and implement the necessary changes.

Legend (check ☑ the correct number that applies to each question): 1 = Strongly disagree 2 = Disagree 3 = Neutral 4 = Agree 5 = Strongly agree	1	2	3	4	5
1. Do you feel that your salary reflects your worth to the organization?					
2. Do you feel appreciated for your work performance?					
3. Do you feel a sense of achievement for your work efforts?					
4. Are you provided the opportunity for growth/advancement to higher level tasks?					
5. Do you feel that you contribute to the overall success of the organization?					
6. Would you recommend the organization to family and friends?					
7. Are you given the opportunity to learn new skills through formal training?					
8. Do you feel the organization provides adequate resources to complete your work?					
9. Do you feel overwhelmed by your workload?					
10. Do you experience ongoing interests in your job/tasks?					

Figure 4-2 Employee Attitude Survey

Exhibit 4-1 Guidelines to Help Companies Improve Their Workplace Surveys

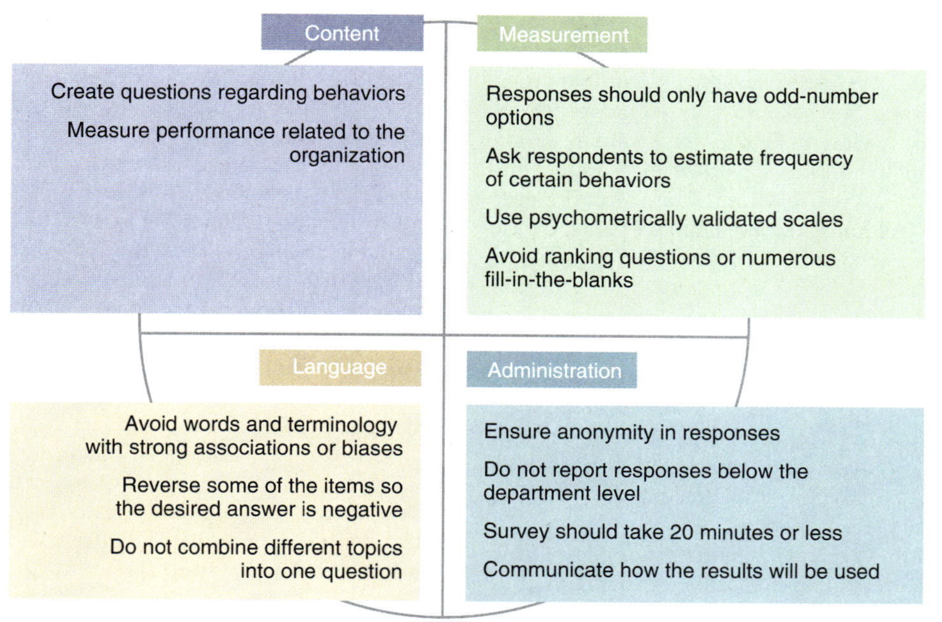

Data from Getting the truth into workplace surveys, by P. Morrel-Samuels, 2002, Harvard Business Review, 80(2), pp. 111–118.

Changing Attitudes

How do you change someone's attitude? You need to address the cognitive and emotional components to change a person's attitude. How would you convince another person to start an exercise program when the individual may say, "I do not have enough time" or "I am just too busy"? One approach would be to challenge the person's behavior by providing new information. For example, explain to the other person how you made time in your day and how, as a result, both your cholesterol level and your blood pressure decreased. This is a cognitive approach when a person is presented with new information. Providing new information is one method for changing a person's attitude and, therefore, their behavior. Attitude transformation takes time, effort, and determination, but it can be done. It is important not to expect to change a person's attitudes quickly.

Managers must understand that attitude change takes time and rapid change is unlikely. Attitudes are formed over a lifetime through an individual's socialization process. This process includes the formation of values and beliefs during childhood, influenced not only by family, religion, and culture but also by socioeconomic factors. This socialization process affects a person's attitude toward work and related behavior (see **Case Study 4-2**).

CASE STUDY 4-2 What Changed in the Housekeeping Department?

Betty, the newly assigned manager of the hospital's housekeeping department, was puzzled. Her employees never suggested ways to improve their work. She believed they should be telling her how to clean more effectively, not vice versa.

Finally, during a performance evaluation, Sally, a 24-year-old immigrant from Sierra Leone and housekeeping employee for the past 5 years, confided, "I do not offer suggestions because I am only a housekeeper with no formal education. I don't want to look stupid."

Determined to change this mindset, Betty implemented a 3-month training program to build confidence, help employees recognize problems, and contribute solutions. The program clarified performance expectations and demonstrated how housekeeping fit into the hospital's larger operations.

Midway through the training, Betty introduced Friday afternoon staff meetings to discuss weekly challenges. Though she always invited input, the room remained silent—until one Friday, when Sally hesitantly raised her hand.

"I overheard a doctor talking to the ED manager about delays in moving patients from the ED to the floors. I think part of the problem is that rooms aren't cleaned fast enough after discharge. We don't get told a patient is leaving until after they're gone, and by the time we can get to the room, it's been an hour or more. Why can't the nursing station secretaries tell us before a patient is discharged so we can plan ahead?"

Betty agreed and promised to investigate. She contacted Mary, the vice president of nursing, who acknowledged the problem. "Administration has noticed that sometimes it takes up to 3 hours from when a bed is empty to when it's reported clean."

A task force was formed, including nurse managers, supervisors, floor nurses, unit secretaries, and housekeeping staff—including Sally—to find a solution. They devised a simple, low-cost, and low-tech system:

1. Nursing supervisors would email housekeeping a list of anticipated discharges by midnight.

2. Evening housekeepers would retrieve and post the list for the morning shift to plan their day.
3. Two jars were placed at each nursing station—one for dirty rooms, one for clean rooms.
4. A nurse would drop a red slip with the room number into the dirty-room jar when a patient was discharged.
5. After housekeeping cleaned the room, they would remove the red slip and place a green slip in the clean-room jar.
6. The green slip signaled to the unit secretary that the bed was ready when the ED called for an open room.

One month later, Mary called Sally. "I wanted to thank you for your proactive observation. The new system reduced bed turnaround time from 3 hours to 30 minutes!"

At the next Friday meeting, Betty shared the news. "Your input makes patient transfers smoother, and physician satisfaction has improved. This was a team effort—thank you!"

Then she asked, as always, "Does anyone have anything else to discuss?"

This time, hands went up. Sally spoke first. "Barry and I noticed that we're using too many paper towels. We have some ideas that could save the hospital money."

Joe added, "I've been thinking about how we can start recycling paper waste. It could cut costs and reduce our workload."

Tina chimed in. "I have a few suggestions about ..."

Betty smiled, listening as her once-silent team eagerly shared ideas.

Discuss why Sally and the other housekeeping staff's attitudes changed.

* The University Hospital of the University Health System reported portions of the solution as being implemented. See Blueprint at the Seams: Improving Patient Flow to Help America's Emergency Department. Available from the Robert Wood Johnson Foundation Urgent Matters Program. Adapted with permission.

Data from Robert Wood Johnson Foundation Urgent Matters Program. (n.d.-a). *Bursting at the seams: Improving patient flow to help America's emergency department.*

Healthcare managers may use techniques from counseling and conflict-resolution fields to develop a step-by-step process for changing employees' attitudes when necessary (see **Exhibit 4-2**). The importance of attitude assessment and change cannot be underestimated. One person with a consistently and vocally bad attitude can lower the morale of an entire workgroup in an otherwise "healthy" organization. Employees who demonstrate counterproductive work behaviors, also referred to as "toxic behavior," can seriously debilitate individuals, teams, and the organization over the long term (Kusy & Holloway, 2009). For example, Rosenstein (2011) reported, based on a survey of more than 4,500 respondents in over 100 hospitals, that there was a strong perceived correlation between disruptive behaviors and the occurrence of medical error, compromised quality, adverse events, compromises in patient safety, and increased patient mortality.

The first step in the change process is identifying the problem, followed by efforts to adjust attitudes, reduce conflict, and seek solutions (see **Exhibit 4-3**). Open communication creates environments where workers feel safe to dissent and their opinions are respected. Everyone has attitudes, both positive and negative. Helping workers realize their full potential requires ongoing efforts.

Perception

Perception is closely related to attitudes. Perception is the process by which organisms interpret and organize sensations to produce a meaningful experience of the world (Lindsay & Norman, 1977). In other words, when confronted with a situation or stimulus, the person interprets the

Exhibit 4-2 Step-by-Step Process for Changing Attitudes in the Workplace

1. Assessment of Attitudes
   a. Identification—Recognize common workplace attitude problems.
   b. Environment—Identify challenges in the workplace environment.

   Participants are introduced to typical examples of "attitude-challenged" workers. Group activities help participants identify and role-play different types of attitude challenges. The goals are to assess the impact of negative attitudes on workers, management, and patients/customers and to identify the causes of problems.
2. Adjusting Attitudes
   a. How listening, coaching, and providing feedback are the tools for attitude change.
   b. Role-play to practice how to use coaching and provide feedback with staff.
   c. Identify payoffs and rewards.

   Participants learn how to use open-ended questions, active listening, and tactful confrontation to address attitude problems in the workplace.
3. Common Management Mistakes
   a. How can we be realistic and patient when dealing with attitude change?
   b. Why scolding employees does little to stop the problem.
   c. How to stop the culture of complaining and work to effect attitude change positively.
   d. Group activities include examples of common management mistakes and exercises to practice more realistic and positive ways to provide employee feedback, facilitate group discussion, and role-play the best methods for confronting negative attitudes.
4. Resolving Conflict
   a. There is a need to confront negative behaviors so they will not continue.
   b. Clarifying expectations and management directives.
   c. Recognizing personal conflict styles of workers and how to deal with them.

   Exercises include ways to analyze communications to identify employee styles, planning the conflict resolution meeting, and working collaboratively to discover win/win solutions.
5. How to Work with Problem Behaviors and Attitudes
   a. Analyze the cause of the problem.
   b. Privately confront with a calm, non-defensive professional demeanor.

   In this session, participants role-play using their preferred style for handling difficult employees. Managers and employees exchange roles and must reprimand or confront problem behaviors.
6. The Last Resort: Employee Termination and Legal Issues
   a. Legal issues of employee terminations.
   b. Requirements, documentation, and procedure.

   Exercises use case studies to develop remedial and probationary systems and fully document intervention efforts before termination or reassignment is necessary.
7. Creating a Positive Work Environment
   a. Evoke a collaborative team environment.
   b. Top motivators include non-monetary rewards.
   c. Characteristics of managing motivation in the workplace.

   Exercises include engaging workers in teams, providing employee recognition awards, and changing the climate by launching career development and advancement initiatives, leadership training, multicultural skills, and other positive incentive programs.

Exhibit 4-3 **Facilitating an Attitude Workshop for Employees**

Discussion groups are a great way to diagnose and treat attitude problems. To alleviate any anxiety and set a positive tone, begin by stating the session guidelines. Create a supportive atmosphere so that participants feel safe examining their attitudes and beliefs.

The manager's role should be as a facilitator rather than guiding a question-and-answer session. One task of the effective facilitator is activating the group's resources to bring out the best in the group. For example, plan activities where people interact with one another at the start (e.g., an icebreaker type of exercise). Work with the group's energy; use humor, laughter, and healthy competition. These interactions build trust and help people to feel comfortable sharing ideas and considering new options.

The second task of the facilitator is to activate participants' internal wisdom. Ask questions and let people discover their answers. You can assist participants by keeping the dialogue going to enable them to sort out their values and priorities, explore beliefs and assumptions, and feel encouraged to alter their work lives in their chosen ways.

The third task is facilitating personal reflection by asking questions to help participants test the ideas being developed against their own experiences—list issues, goals, problems, and solutions that come up in the group dialogue. Write the main ideas on a board, perhaps focusing on negative attitudes and aspects of the workplace that may cause them. Ask participants to expand on these. Give personal examples, and ask how poor attitudes in others can make them feel.

Throughout the process, the facilitator's goal is to foster interpersonal support. Having participants share ideas and experiences initiates the process of people supporting one another. Encourage team building and interpersonal support as part of creating a work atmosphere where negative attitudes are exposed and positive attitudes flourish.

At the end of each session, it is important to provide a summary. This communicates to the participants that you have been actively listening and are prepared to offer a synthesis of the group's observations and insights. Begin by saying, "What I heard today is . . ." Offer participants a chance to compare notes with one another for feedback. You might also ask participants to jot down ideas and feelings about the attitude dialogue to bring to the next meeting. Always provide a "take-home message" of commitment to change. Everyone should leave with at least one clear idea about what they will do next.

Discussions to identify negative workplace attitudes can be very effective. These discussions lead to solutions and group commitment to improved morale.

Data from Kreitlow, B., & Kreitlow, D. (1997). Creative planning for the second half of life. Whole Person Associates.

stimulus as something meaningful based on prior experiences. However, what an individual interprets or perceives may differ from reality.

The perception process follows four stages: stimulation, registration, organization, and interpretation (see **Figure 4-3**).

Awareness and acceptance of stimuli play an important role in the perception process. Receptiveness to stimuli is highly selective and may be limited by a person's existing beliefs, attitudes, motivation, and personality (Assael, 1995). Individuals will select stimuli that satisfy their immediate needs (perceptual vigilance) and may disregard stimuli that may cause psychological anxiety (perceptual defense).

Broadbent (1958) addressed the concept of perceptual vigilance with his filter model. Broadbent argued that, on the one hand, because of limited capacity, a person must process information

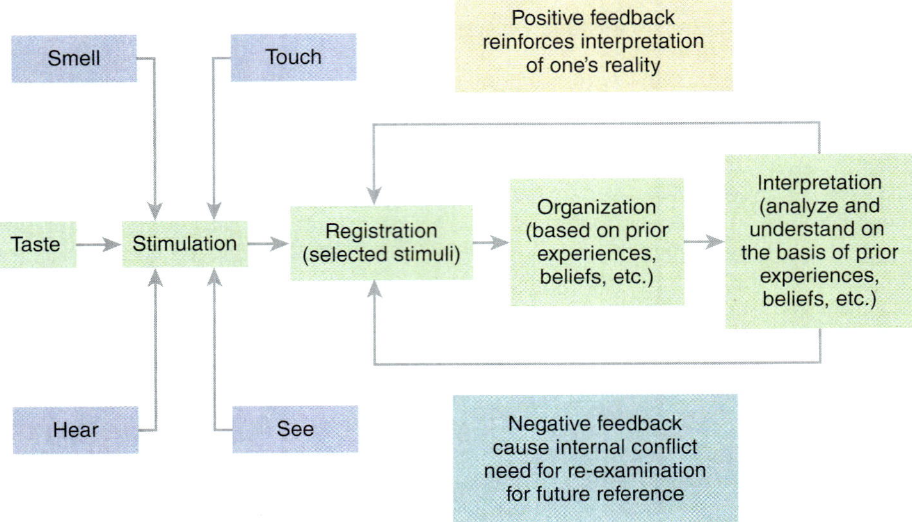

Figure 4-3 Perception Processing System

selectively; therefore, when presented with information from two different channels (such as visual *and* auditory), an individual's perceptual system processes only that which they believe to be most relevant. However, perceptual defense creates an internal barrier that limits the external stimuli from passing through the perception process when the stimuli are not congruent with the person's current beliefs, attitudes, motivations, and personality. This is referred to as selective perception. Selective perception occurs when an individual limits the processing of external stimuli by selectively interpreting what they see based on beliefs, experience, or attitudes (Sherif & Cantril, 1945).

Others suggest that filtering is not just a consequence of capacity limitations but is also driven by goal-directed actions (Allport, 1987, 1993; Neumann, 1987; Van der Heijden, 1992). The concept is that any action requires the selection of relevant aspects of the environment and other aspects that are irrelevant to the action are filtered out. When working toward a goal, one will skip over information that does not support one's plan. Studies of the brain have also led to models suggesting that there are multiple processing channels (Pashler, 1989) and that selective perception occurs due to activation of cortical maps and neural networks (Rizzolatti & Craighero, 1998). People are selective in what they perceive and tend to filter information based on their capacity to absorb new data, combined with preconceived thoughts. In short, people hear what they want to hear.

Social Perception

Social perception is how an individual "sees" others and how others perceive an individual. This is accomplished through various means, such as classifying an individual based on a single characteristic (halo effect), evaluating a person's characteristics by comparison to others (contrast effect), perceiving others in ways that reflect a perceiver's attitudes and beliefs (projection), judging someone based on one's perception of the group to which that person belongs (stereotyping), causing a person to act erroneously based on another person's perception (Pygmalion effect), or controlling another person's perception of oneself (impression management).

Halo Effect

The halo effect occurs when an individual forms a general impression about another person based on a single characteristic, such as intelligence, sociability, or appearance. The perceiver may evaluate the other individual as high on many traits because they believe that the individual is high in one trait. For example, suppose an employee performs a difficult accounting task well and the manager believes that the employee is highly intelligent. In that case, the manager may also erroneously perceive the employee as having competencies in other areas, such as management or technology.

The halo effect applies to individuals' perceptions of others and organizations. For example, a hospital that is well known for its open-heart and cardiac programs may be perceived in the community as excellent in other clinical areas, such as obstetrics or orthopedics, whether that is true or not.

Opposite to the halo effect is the horn effect, whereby one person evaluates another as low on many traits because of a belief that the individual is low on a trait that is assumed to be critical (Thorndike, 1920). A study on obesity conducted with healthcare professionals and researchers reflects the horn effect. Study participants were asked to complete the Implicit Association Test to assess overall implicit weight bias (associating "obese people" and "thin people" with "good" versus "bad") and three ranges of stereotypes: lazy–motivated, smart–stupid, and valuable–worthless. The study respondents were much quicker to pair "fat" with "lazy" and other negative traits and/or stereotypes (Schwartz et al., 2003).

Halo/horn-effect cognitive bias is a challenge that healthcare managers face when they perform workers' evaluations. Managers need to avoid the tendency for an employee's positive or negative trait to spill over into other areas of the evaluation. For example, if an employee has been late to work for 3 days, the manager might conclude that this person has a poor attitude and does not care about their job. However, there may be external reasons for the employee's lateness, such as a car breaking down, a delay in public transportation, the babysitter being late, or bad weather. Because of the lateness, the manager who assumes that the employee is a poor worker will unfairly give the employee a negative overall evaluation. Managers must critically evaluate employees' strengths and weaknesses using as much objective information as possible so that specific traits do not bias their perceptions.

Contrast Effects

Perceptions are also subject to contrast effects. Contrast effects relate to an individual's evaluation of another person's characteristics based on (or affected by) comparisons with people who rank higher or lower on the same characteristics. For example, Wedell, Parducci, and Geiselman (1987) found that, if compared to a highly attractive person, a target person of average attractiveness is judged less attractive than they would have been judged if rated on their own. When asked to contrast a target person with highly attractive people, ratings of the target's attractiveness went down. When the target person was compared with less attractive people, the target seemed more attractive by comparison (Thornton & Moore, 1993). In other words, the contrast effect relates to how others around them perceive an individual. Like perceived attractiveness, contrast effects influence self-esteem, public self-consciousness, and social anxiety (Thornton & Moore, 1993). A worker's performance may be judged in contrast to those around them. However, managers must be aware of this contrast-effect bias when interviewing job candidates or evaluating a worker's performance. Just because others do a great job does not mean the employee performs poorly.

Contrast is an important principle by which we make decisions. When we make judgments, they are not absolute judgments. We judge an individual or object compared to someone else or something else. By using the perceptual contrast-effects principle, one can persuade other people in their judgments by leveraging the following comparisons (changingminds.org):

- *Shortlists*: People have a hard time choosing from a large group because there are too many options. When dealing with many candidates for a job, we quickly simplify the decision by narrowing it down to a very short list.
- *Simplified Selection Process*: People find it hard to choose from many options due to overwhelming differences. During the hiring process, decision-makers quickly narrow down a large pool of applicants to a few manageable candidates, making the choice easier.
- *Binary Choice Preference*: Humans perform better at decision-making when only two options are available. Limiting choices to a small list helps by decreasing the number of comparisons needed. Even with a shortlist, people often further restrict their options to compare just the top two or three candidates individually.
- *Extreme Categorization*: To differentiate options, people emphasize perceived differences by pushing their judgments to opposite ends of a spectrum. This black-and-white thinking, although less accurate, offers mental comfort in uncertain situations. Many prefer taking firm stances rather than accepting doubt. This process focuses on supporting evidence while ignoring contradictory facts, leading to biased views. This tendency is especially strong when distinguishing social groups, particularly about values, where people see their group as virtuous and view others negatively.
- *Idealized Standards*: People form mental images of perfect combinations of qualities they desire, based on positive experiences. When assessing job applicants, recruiters often compare candidates to these imaginary perfect standards that blend the best traits from different sources.
- *Convenience-Based Comparisons*: People depend on easily accessible reference points when making evaluations instead of seeking the best comparisons. The desire for mental efficiency causes choosing immediately available options over more suitable but harder-to-remember ones. For example, when viewing an unattractive person next to someone average-looking, the average person seems more attractive than they would alone.
- *Social Benchmarking*: Self-evaluation mainly happens through comparing oneself to others, as people assess their own happiness, attractiveness, or success relative to peers. Usually, individuals compare themselves to similar people within their social groups. As a result, wealthy individuals often compare themselves to others who are also wealthy and may feel financially inadequate, while intelligent people tend to compare themselves to other smart individuals. This pattern explains why material success, influence, creativity, and achievements don't always lead to happiness—there's always someone doing better.

Projection

Projection is the attribution of one's attitudes and beliefs onto others. All of us are guilty of unconsciously projecting our own beliefs onto others. Sigmund Freud (1894–1966) and his daughter Anna Freud (1936–1967) suggested that projection is a defensive mechanism where we attribute our attitudes onto someone else as a defense against our feelings of anxiety or guilt. Projection occurs when individuals attribute their feelings, traits, or impulses to others, avoiding self-awareness and reducing anxiety. For example, if you dislike someone but do not want to admit it, you might believe that they dislike you instead. This defense mechanism protects self-esteem by externalizing negative qualities. A rude person, for instance, may frequently accuse others of being rude, thereby avoiding the discomfort of acknowledging their behavior. By shifting blame, projection allows individuals to maintain a positive self-image. It is a common tendency—who has not blamed others for making them late, causing them to break a diet, or ruining their mood? Projection helps individuals cope with uncomfortable emotions by perceiving in others what exists within themselves. This unconscious process provides psychological comfort, even if it distorts reality.

Stereotyping

In 1798, printers invented a new way to fix and reproduce visual images permanently. This precursor to modern photographic printing processes was called stereotyping. Over time, the word "stereotype" came to apply not just to visual printed images, but also to how we fit attributes of ability, character, or behavior to groups and/or populations to generalize. The term is now most often defined to mean a conventional image applied to whole groups of people and the treatment of groups according to a fixed set of generalized traits or characteristics.

Although stereotyping can help us to organize a complex world, it may be considered negative if it leads to overly generalized views about groups of individuals. Researchers suggest that stereotypes wield a strong, covert influence on human behavior (even among those who disagree with stereotypes). Social researchers have revealed that it is relatively easy for stereotypes to be activated across a wide range of contexts and situations because of many factors, including race, gender, religion, physical appearance, disability, and occupation (Bargh et al., 1996).

Stereotyping regarding race and ethnicity is problematic for healthcare professionals and health service organizations. The Institute of Medicine (2003) found that "racial and ethnic minorities tend to receive a lower quality of health care than non-minorities, even when access-related factors, such as patients' insurance status and income are controlled . . . and found evidence that stereotyping, biases, and uncertainty on the part of health care providers can contribute to unequal treatment" (p. 1).

In addition to stereotyping racial and ethnic minorities, healthcare professionals tend to stereotype other groups, such as older adults, homeless people, people with disabilities, and those dealing with obesity. People tend to stereotype unhoused individuals as people they may have seen on the street asking for money. However, homelessness also affects families, children, and young people—groups that do not fit the stereotypes. When it comes to obesity, Puhl and colleagues (2010) have published numerous studies documenting "harmful weight-based stereotypes that overweight and obese individuals are lazy, weak-willed, unsuccessful, unintelligent, lack self-discipline, have poor willpower, and are noncompliant with weight-loss treatment."

One of the most common forms of stereotyping involves gender and leadership. Women hold positions at all levels in healthcare organizations, but only between 10% and 18% of chief executive officer positions are held by women (Russell et al., 2019). The influence of gender stereotypes is one possible reason why it is sometimes difficult for people to accept women as leaders in the workplace. Traits that are often attached to leadership are stereotypically "masculine" qualities, such as courage, persuasiveness, and assertiveness. An aggressive male leader may be viewed as "ambitious," compared with an assertive female leader, who may be viewed as "pushy." This is partly because the assertive female leader's behavior violates the gender stereotype that women should be less authoritarian and more sensitive, gentle, and nurturing (see **Exhibit 4-4**).

Whether we know it or not, we all use stereotypes because they help simplify our world. However, we often do not take the time to understand why we perceive groups in a certain way.

Exhibit 4-4 Gender stereotyping

Gender roles and stereotypes provide specific expectations of male and female behavior in each culture. When those expectations are violated (as in the case of a woman acting assertively), a negative label is often used to describe the person who is violating the expectation. This was at issue in *Price Waterhouse v. Hopkins*, 490 U.S. 228 (1989), as cited by Lord and Maher (1991).

Ann Hopkins was a high-performing but masculine-acting prospective partner at Price Waterhouse. When denied a partnership at Price Waterhouse, she charged that gender stereotyping had played a role in the decision (Fiske et al., 1991). At the time of her eligibility and consideration for promotion to partner, Hopkins was the only woman among 88 candidates nominated for partnership. Her close colleagues submitted an evaluation noting her "outstanding performance" and strongly urged her admission to the partnership. She sued when she was not accepted as a partner by the promotion board.

In response to the suit, Price Waterhouse countered that Hopkins had interpersonal problems and was considered too "macho" for the position. The person explaining the board's decision to Hopkins advised her that to improve her chances for partnership, she "should walk more femininely, talk more femininely, dress more femininely, wear make-up, have her hair styled, and wear jewelry." Another board member repeatedly commented that "he could not consider any woman seriously as a partnership candidate and believed that women were not even capable of functioning as partners." Hopkins brought her gender discrimination lawsuit to the U.S. Supreme Court and won.

Data from Lord, R. G., & Maher, K. J. (1991). *Leadership and information processing: Linking perceptions and performance.* Unwin Hyman.

We revert to our cognitive prototypes and ignore relevant information. These habits and biases are learned and, thus, can be unlearned. Training exercises can help to sensitize individuals to issues of bias, such as racism, sexism, and ageism. One goal of management is to assist staff in recognizing that stereotypes are illogical by challenging these faulty cognitions. Considering how our perception of groups can influence our behavior, including hiring and management practices and interactions with workers, is important. Stereotypes may lead to discrimination. Negative stereotypes can be problematic for any organization, and proper training can effectively minimize widely held false beliefs (see **Exhibit 4-5**).

Exhibit 4-5 Exercise to Identify Stereotypes Within Our Organizations and Profession

Discussion: Have you seen any evidence of stereotypes in your workplace?

Which of the following positions are filled more by MEN or by WOMEN:

Physician ____________ Pharmacist ____________ Nurse ____________

Computer Programmer ____________ Nurses Aide ____________ Chief of Staff ____________

Medical Receptionist ____________ Radiology Technician ____________

Statements:

Health services administrators need to be ____________ to be effective.

The hospital cafeteria is staffed by people who are ____________.

Older people that I have worked with are ____________.

Young people these days are ____________.

Pygmalion Effect

The Pygmalion effect, or self-fulfilling prophecy, describes how a person modifies their behavior based on another individual's perception, whether or not it is accurate. Once another person makes an expectation known, an individual tends to behave in ways that are consistent with the expectation. This can have negative or positive results. If a manager sets high standards for an employee's performance, the employee is likely to respond accordingly with high performance. Similarly, the resulting work performance will likely be low if a manager sets low expectations because of perceived lack of ability or motivation. Managers' expectations directly influence employees' performance. In other words, what a manager communicates as the expectation is what will result. Livingston (1969) stated that what was critical in communicating expectations was not what the manager said but how the manager behaved. Indifferent and noncommittal treatment communicated low expectations and led to poor performance. Livingston related that managers were more effective at communicating low expectations than high expectations.

Closely related to the self-fulfilling prophecy is the "Galatea effect." This effect relates to the expectations we have for ourselves rather than the expectations others have for us. To illustrate this concept, Livingston (1969) referred to "Sweeney's Miracle." James Sweeney, an industrial management professor at Tulane University, wished to disprove the theory that a certain IQ level was needed to learn how to program computers. Sweeney trained a poorly educated janitor whose IQ indicated he could not learn to type, much less program. The janitor learned to program and eventually took charge of the computer room and the responsibility of training new employees to program and operate the computers. As Livingston pointed out, Sweeney's expectations were based on what he believed about his teaching ability (internal expectations), not on the janitor's learning capabilities. Livingston's work highlights how the expectations of superior managers are primarily influenced by their self-perception, particularly their confidence in selecting, training, and motivating team members. This self-assessment subtly shapes their beliefs about their team members, their expectations of them, and, ultimately, how they interact with them (Livingston, 1969).

Managers need to understand the effects of their self-expectations and how these expectations interact with the expectations they hold and communicate about their subordinates' performance. Managers set the tone and culture of the workplace. Managers can set high but realistic performance expectations for their subordinates by understanding the Pygmalion and Galatea effects. Managers who rate subordinates as "excellent" will continue their previous work behaviors. Managers can also have workers rate their performance. Expectations about ourselves tend to be self-sustaining.

Impression Management

"You never get a second chance to make a first impression." This classic statement is all about impression management, whereby people try to shape others' impression of them. Impression management incorporates what we do, how we do it, what we say, and how we say it as we try to influence the perceptions others have of us. Individuals will try to present themselves in ways that lead to positive evaluations by others by highlighting their achievements and hiding failures. This behavior is common on social media, where people share only their best moments and pictures. Giacalone and Rosenfeld (1989) point out that impression management is inherently neither good nor bad; rather, it is a fundamental part of our social and work lives, and we need to view it in the situations in which it is used. For example, consider the concept of self-sabotage. Self-sabotage occurs when people place obstacles in their way so that if they fail, they can blame the obstacles, or if they are successful, they can brag about performing successfully despite these barriers.

Schlenker and Weigold (1992) view impression management as a broad phenomenon in which we try to influence the perceptions and behaviors of other people by controlling the information they receive. People actively carry out impression management to achieve their objectives and goals, individually and as part of groups and organizations. This can be done consciously and deliberately (e.g., by perfecting job-interview skills), or it may be unconscious. At times, the managed impression serves to bolster or protect our self-image (e.g., dressing for success); at other times, we manage impressions in hopes of pleasing significant audiences. Sometimes, impression management is truthful and accurate. Sometimes, it involves "false advertising" through exaggeration, fabrication, deception, and lies (Schlenker & Weigold, 1992). Sadly, according to HireRight's 2017 employment screening benchmark report, 85% of surveyed employers uncovered a misrepresentation or falsehood on a candidate's resume or job application. Over the years, cases of falsifying one's professional credentials have been reported in the popular press with negative consequences for the dishonest individual. For example, an Australian woman recently falsified her resume and faked references to obtain a high-paying governmental job. She was imprisoned for "deception, dishonesty, and abuse of public office" (Cheung, 2019).

Employee Selection

Because perceptions determine our behavior toward others and can cloud our judgments of them, one area that benefits from using psychological principles is employee selection. The goals of selection are (1) to identify the knowledge, skills, abilities, and qualities necessary to perform a job well; (2) to design tests to measure applicants' levels on those key job requirements; (3) to administer and score the tests; and (4) to determine which applicants are most suitable for a given position, ensuring that the process is accurate and fair and does not discriminate against members of protected groups. The basis for this employee selection process is the ability to identify key invariant qualities of individuals (e.g., skills, character, motivation, attitude, leadership potential, and personality) that match up well with the job.

Psychometrics involves the measurement of human ability, potential, and attitude. This is most visible when employers use tests and special interview techniques in employee selection. Job analysis is designed to identify the skills, abilities, and attributes needed to perform well. Context-specific tests can measure applicants' skill levels regarding key job requirements. As with any tool, instruments used to measure human ability can be misused or misleading. Instruments that rely on self-reporting personal information are subject to bias (such as impression management), and the interpretation of aptitude scores is also subject to bias (such as stereotypes and halo effects). Therefore, managers should look for many data sources to determine the qualities essential to the job, such as personality (see **Exhibit 4-6**).

One goal in this discussion is to help managers make accurate and fair assessments of staff members or potential staff members for various positions in their organizations. Who

Exhibit 4-6 Five-Factor Model of Personality

Personality traits are the regularities that we observe in someone's behavior, attitudes, and expressions. Prior research suggests that virtually all personality measures can be reduced or categorized under the Five-Factor Model of Personality, also known as the "Big 5." The Big 5's dimensionality has been found to be applicable across all cultures.

The Big 5 model is based on the concept that personality can be described and measured on five broad dimensions or traits: openness, conscientiousness, extraversion, agreeableness, and neuroticism.

Dimension/Trait	Description
Openness	Imaginative, innovative, open-minded
Conscientiousness	Competent, responsible, dependable, hardworking, goal-oriented, self-disciplined
Extraversion	Assertive, social, positive emotions
Agreeableness	Trusting, straightforward, compliant, warmhearted, generous, modest
Neuroticism	Emotional, insecure, self-conscious, impulsive, vulnerable

Data from McCrae, R. R., & John, O. P. (1992). An introduction to the five-factor model and its application. Journal of Personality, 60, 175–215.

should function in positions of high contact with patients? Who is better at working with new technologies? Who can most effectively direct a unit to promote the best clinical care? Who is best suited to manage the business office? How can we help employees not ready to assume a leadership role develop the skills for leadership while still working in their current positions? These are the questions a manager or administrator must answer when making personnel decisions. To do so requires the manager to perceive the unchanging qualities of a person across situations, or the key "traits" that underlie success in a job.

Many instruments used to assess personnel and management/leadership potential, such as the DISC profile, CliftonStrengths, Hogan Assessments or the Enneagram of Personality, are trying to identify "constants" of personality and work style. Another commonly used scale is the Myers-Briggs Type Indicator (MBTI), an instrument for measuring a person's preferences using four opposing-pole dimensions (extraversion/introversion, sensing/intuiting, thinking/feeling, and judging/perceiving). This instrument assigns a personality type based on how someone answers a series of questions. Each personality type may be better suited for specific occupations. Using any instrument as the sole selector of occupational areas based on type has many pros and cons. On the positive side, these instruments pick up patterns (invariants) in self-reported behavioral characteristics and categorize types that may be useful in assessing certain qualities relevant to leadership and workplace issues. They may also help managers identify areas where specific coaching or development might benefit the individual. On the negative side, these tests generalize a person's likely traits, which may not accurately reflect that individual or how they express those traits, and can lead to incorrect stereotyping.

Summary

In this chapter, we reviewed several important concepts of social psychology that managers need to understand. These can influence and bias our perceptions; therefore, we need to understand them to temper and inform our perceptions. In discussing attitudes and how to change them, we become more aware of those distinctly unique human qualities that complicate the workplace and make it so enjoyable. If we understand how workers see the world, we are in a better position to facilitate a productive workplace. Today's healthcare managers have many resources, including a wide-ranging scientific literature on organizational behavior, psychology, and human resource issues in the workplace. Ideally, this chapter will encourage you to develop and use your skills as a social perceiver and give you some confidence that you can foster positive attitudes. We are always learning, improving, and building skills in social perception. In this way, we will continue to use our understanding of human behavior to create a positive and healthy workplace.

Discussion Questions

1. Define attitudes and provide examples.
2. What is meant by cognitive dissonance?
3. What are standard methods to measure a person's attitude?
4. List and describe ways in which attitudes can be changed.
5. What is the difference between the halo and horn effects?
6. Define the four stages of the perception process.
7. Define social perception.
8. What is the difference between contrast effect and projection?
9. Is stereotyping negative or positive? Why?
10. Why is stereotyping so problematic for the healthcare industry?
11. What is the difference between the Pygmalion effect and the Galatea effect?
12. Is impression management negative or positive? Why?
13. Is employee selection an unbiased process? Why?

CASE STUDY AND EXERCISES

Exercise 4-1 Gender Stereotyping in Organizations

Role-Play

Choose a male and a female volunteer. Each member of the pair will argue over a situation in the workplace, such as departments negotiating over which gets to purchase a piece of new medical equipment (limited financial resources), deciding whether laptops or PCs are appropriate for the nursing stations, or choosing which color to paint the hospital's hallways.

Designate one of the participants as the "influencer," who should try to "win" the argument. Designate the other as the "influencee," who should resist.

The influencer has a fixed amount of time, perhaps one minute, to persuade the influencee.

After you have observed the interaction, break into groups for discussion of the influencer (i.e., leader), and make a list of adjectives used to describe the influencer. For example, was the leader "bossy" or "dominating" or "assertive"?

Have the male and female reverse roles with a new situation and repeat the discussion. Now discuss the two leadership influencers in both of the role-play episodes. Which one had more skill and fit your image of a leader? Record your responses.

Break into groups again and describe the second influencer with an adjective list. Continue until several male–female dyads have role-played as influencers and influencees. Record the descriptive adjectives. Rate the overall leadership of each influencer. Record the responses.

Discussion Questions

1. Were differences in leader perceptions due to gender stereotypes or behavioral differences?
2. What social invariants (constants or traits) can you identify as being important for leadership positions?
3. Why are leadership perceptions important? Can attributions about leadership ability affect the behaviors of followers? If so, how?

Debriefing

Research by Butler and Geis (1990) suggests that in role-play exercises, such as those in the preceding activity, the female leader was described differently in terms of her personality traits and was more likely to be the recipient of covert gender stereotyping compared with males. How do their findings match your results?

Exercise 4-2 Implicit Association Test

An interesting approach to uncovering personal hidden biases is the Implicit Association Test (IAT). IAT is a component of Project Implicit, a collaborative research effort between researchers at Harvard University, the University of Virginia, and the University of Washington. IAT may be accessed at https://implicit.harvard.edu/implicit/.

This web-based self-assessment prompts the user to link words with images that appear on the computer screen. The links reveal the user's mental associations or automatic preferences, which are indicative of the user's tendency to view one identity group more positively over another. Millions of individuals have taken the IAT. An array of implicit bias assessments and answers to frequently asked questions about the IAT can be found at https://implicit.harvard.edu/implicit/. As the website cautions, the test sometimes provides some challenging personal feedback!

Exercise 4-3 Jung Typology Test: Personality Assessment

A 72-item web-based assessment is available at www.humanmetrics.com. After completing the questionnaire, you will be given a description of personality types and your type formula according to the Carl Jung and Isabel Myers-Briggs typology. There are no right or wrong answers; the test is only for your own self-assessment.

Did the results accurately describe your personality traits? Share your results with a significant other. Does your significant other agree with your results? (Note: Short questionnaires, tests, and assessments can be unreliable in certain situations.) This web-based assessment is designed primarily to stimulate your thinking about yourself.

CASE STUDY 4-3 Only 15 weeks to Thanksgiving!

Scene I

"I just hate the thought of going back to work," Mary told her brother Tom. It was the last night of her vacation, and she dreaded returning. "It's 15 weeks until Thanksgiving."

"I know you're miserable," Tom replied. "You've been unhappy there for years. You're a different person on vacation. Haven't we talked about this enough? Isn't there something else you can do?"

"Don't you think I would if I could?" Mary snapped. "I'm sorry, I know you're trying to help. But I feel trapped. With my diabetes and high blood pressure, I can't afford to retire early—I need the health insurance. Social Security starts at 62, but healthcare coverage doesn't kick in until 65. A supplemental plan would be too expensive, if I could even get one. The moment I'm back at work, my stress will spike my blood pressure and sugar."

"Yes," Tom sighed. "And you'll start counting the days to the weekend. You've already marked Thanksgiving! There has to be a way out."

"Sure, winning the lottery!" Mary said bitterly. "That's all I've got."

Scene II

Dan, the health information department manager at a large South Florida healthcare system, finished his coffee with a sigh. "Mary's back tomorrow. I keep hoping she'll come back less stressed, but it's always the same. She has so much experience, she could be a great mentor, but I can't turn her attitude around. I've tried everything—special projects, adjusted hours, more responsibility, advanced training—but nothing works."

"She's just jealous of you," his wife Sonia replied. "You've tried hard enough. Why doesn't she just retire?"

Dan laughed. "Good thing HR didn't hear that! You're wrong about Mary. She knows everything about the department. I couldn't have managed when I started without her help. I just wish she weren't so unhappy."

"I think she enjoys being miserable," Sonia scoffed.

"Jean and Mary started here together 20 years ago," Dan mused. "Jean says Mary's always been independent—stubborn, even. She speaks her mind, and she's usually right, but her delivery rubs people the wrong way. Apparently, she even got thrown out of college once for protesting a policy—and fought her way back in when the school didn't follow due process."

Sonia said, "Dan, let it go. You can figure her out tomorrow. Right now, let's watch the Dolphins beat the Bucs. Can you believe they're favoring the Bucs?"

In Scene I, what is Mary's attitude? Are you able to identify the three elements of an attitude in what she says?

In Scene II, Dan and Sonia have very different perceptions about Mary. Why?

References

Allport, A. (1987). Selection for action: Some behavioral and neurophysiological considerations of attention and action. In H. Heuer & F. Sanders (Eds.), *Perspectives on perception and action* (pp. 395–419). Lawrence Erlbaum Associates.

Allport, A. (1993). Attention and control: Have we been asking the wrong questions? A critical review of twenty-five years. In S. Kornblum & D. E. Meyer (Eds.), *Attention and performance XIV* (pp. 183–218). MIT Press.

Allport, G. W. (1935). Attitudes. In C. Murchison (Ed.), A *handbook of social psychology* (pp. 798–844). Clark University Press.

Assael, H. (1995). *Consumer behavior and marketing action* (5th ed.). *South-Western College Publishing.*

Bargh, J. A., Chen, M., & Burrows, L. (1996). Automaticity of social behavior: Direct effects of trait construct and stereotype-activation on action. *Journal of Personality and Social Psychology, 71*(2), 230–244.

Broadbent, D. E. (1958). *Perception and communication*. Pergamon Press.

Butler, D., & Geis, F. L. (1990). Nonverbal affect responses to male and female leaders: Implications for leadership evaluations. *Journal of Personality and Social Psychology, 58*(1), 48–59.

Changingminds.org. (n.d.). How we change what others think, feel, believe and do. https://changingminds.org

Cheung, E. (2019, December 4). *A woman lied on her resume to land a $185,000-a-year job. Now she's going to jail*. CNN. https://www.cnn.com/2019/12/04/australia/australia-woman-jailed-fake-resume-intl-hnk-scli/index.html

Daley, D. (1996, January). Attribution theory and the glass ceiling: Career development among federal employees. *Public Administration and Management: An Interactive Journal, 1*(1). https://www.researchgate.net/publication/285991553_Attribution_Theory_and_the_Glass_Ceiling_Career_Development_Among_Federal_Employee

Dobbin, F., Kalev, A., & Kelly, E. (2007). Diversity management in corporate America. *Contexts, 6*(4), 21–27.

Festinger, L. (1957). *A theory of cognitive dissonance*. Stanford University Press.

Fiske, S. T., Bersoff, D. N., Borgida, E., Deaux, K., & Heilman, M. E. (1991). Social science research on trial: Use of sex stereotyping research in Price Waterhouse v. Hopkins. *American Psychologist, 46*(10), 1049–1060.

Fottler, M. D., Crawford, M., Quintana, J. B., & White, J. B. (1995). Evaluating nurse turnover: Comparing attitude surveys and exit interviews. *Hospital & Health Services Administration, 40*(2), 278–295.

Freud, A. (1966). The *ego and the mechanisms of defence: Vol. 2. The writings of Anna Freud*. International Universities Press. (Original work published 1936).

Freud, S. (1966). The neuro-psychoses of defense. In J. Strachey (Trans.), *The standard edition of the complete psychological works of Sigmund Freud* (3rd ed., pp. 45–61). Hogarth Press. (Original work published 1894).

Giacalone, R. A., & Rosenfeld, P. (Eds.). (1989). *Impression management in the organization*. Lawrence Erlbaum Associates.

Halvorson, H. G., & Rock, D. (2015). Beyond bias. *Strategy+Business, 80*, 1–10.

Heider, F. (1958). *The psychology of interpersonal relations*. John Wiley & Sons.

HireRight. (2017). *2017 employment screening benchmark report*. https://www.hireright.com/benchmarking

Institute of Medicine. (2003). *Unequal treatment: Confronting racial and ethnic disparities in health care*. The National Academies Press. books.nap.edu/catalog/10260.html

Kassarjian, H. H., & Cohen, J. B. (1965). Cognitive dissonance and consumer behavior: Reactions to the Surgeon General's report on smoking and health. *California Management Review, 8*(1), 55–64.

Kelley, H. H. (1967). Attribution theory in social psychology. In D. Levine (Ed.), *Nebraska Symposium on Motivation* (Vol. 15, pp. 129–238). University of Nebraska Press.

Kelley, H. H. (1973). The process of causal attribution. *American Psychologist, 28*(2), 107–128.

Kusy, M., & Holloway, E. (2009). *Toxic workplace!: Managing toxic personalities and their systems of power*. Jossey-Bass.

Lindsay, P., & Norman, D. A. (1977). *Human information processing: An introduction to psychology*. Academic Press. Harcourt Brace Jovanovich.

Livingston, J. S. (1969). Pygmalion in management. *Harvard Business Review, 81*(1), 97–106.

Lord, R. G., & Maher, K. J. (1991). *Leadership and information processing: Linking perceptions and performance*. Unwin Hyman.

Lowe, G., Schellenberg, G., & Shannon, H. (2003). Correlates of employees' perceptions of a healthy work environment. *American Journal of Health Promotion, 17*(6), 390–399.

Mitchell, T. R., Green, S. G., & Wood, R. E. (1981). An attributional model of leadership and the poor performing subordinate. *Research in Organizational Behavior, 3*(1), 197–235.

Morrel-Samuels, P. (2002). Getting the truth into workplace surveys. *Harvard Business Review, 80*(2), 111–118.

Neumann, O. (1987). Beyond capacity: A functional view of attention. In H. Heuer & A. F. Sanders (Eds.), *Perspectives on perception and action* (pp. 361–394). Lawrence Erlbaum Associates.

Ott, J. S. (1995). *Classic readings in organizational behavior* (2nd ed.). Wadsworth Publishing Company.

Pashler, H. (1989). Dissociations and dependencies between speed and accuracy: Evidence for a two-component theory of divided attention in simple tasks. *Cognitive Psychology, 21*(4), 469–514.

Price Waterhouse v. Hopkins, 490 U.S. 228 (1989).

Puhl, R. M., & Heuer, C. A. (2010). Obesity stigma: Important considerations for public health. *American Journal of Public Health, 100*(6), 1019–1028.

Rizzolatti, G., & Craighero, L. (1998). Spatial attention: Mechanisms and theories. In M. Sabourin, F. Craik, & M. Robert (Eds.), *Advances in psychological science: Vol. 2. Biological and cognitive aspects* (pp. 171–198). Psychology Press.

Rosenstein, A. H. (2011). The quality and economic impact of disruptive behaviors on clinical outcomes of patient care. *American Journal of Medical Quality, 26*(5), 372–379.

Russell, M. S., Krentz, M., Abouzahr, K., & Doyle, M. (2019, January 7). *Women dominate health care—Just not in the executive suite*. Boston Consulting Group. https://www.bcg.com/en-us/publications/2019/women-dominate-health-care-not-in-executive-suite.aspx

Schlenker, B. R., & Weigold, M. F. (1992). Interpersonal processes involving impression regulation and management. *Annual Review of Psychology, 43*, 133–168.

Schwartz, M. B., Chambliss, H. O., Brownell, K. D., Blair, S. N., & Billington, C. (2003). Weight bias among health professionals specializing in obesity. *Obesity Research, 11*(9), 1033–1039.

Sherif, M., & Cantril, H. (1945). The psychology of attitudes: Part I. *Psychological Review, 52*(6), 295–319.

Thorndike, E. L. (1920). A constant error in psychological rating. *Journal of Applied Psychology, 4*(1), 25–29.

Thornton, B., & Moore, S. (1993). Physical attractiveness contrast effect: Implications for self-esteem and evaluations of the social self. *Personality and Social Psychology Bulletin, 19*(4), 474–480.

Thurstone, L. L., & Chave, E. J. (1929). *The measurement of attitude*. University of Chicago Press.

Van der Heijden, A. H. C. (1992). *Selective attention in vision*. Routledge.

Wedell, D. H., Parducci, A., & Geiselman, R. E. (1987). A formal analysis of ratings of physical attractiveness: Successive contrast and simultaneous assimilation. *Journal of Experimental Social Psychology, 23*(3), 230–249.

Weiner, B. (1979). A theory of motivation for some classroom experiences. *Journal of Educational Psychology, 71*(1), 3–25.

CHAPTER 5

Workplace Communication

LEARNING OUTCOMES

After completing this chapter, the student should be able to:

- Describe the communication process.
- Understand the importance of feedback in the communication process.
- Identify various verbal and nonverbal methods of communication.
- Explain the common barriers to communication and apply strategies to overcome these barriers.
- Discuss the elements of effective communication for knowledge management.
- Describe the various components of effective strategic communication.
- Understand the flow of intraorganizational communication.
- Comprehend the challenges of cross-cultural communication.
- Understand the flow of communication with external stakeholders and the public sector.

Overview

Effective communication leads to higher employee engagement and a lower likelihood of employee turnover. Despite its importance, only 7% of U.S. employees strongly agree they get timely, accurate, and transparent communication at work (Robison, 2021). Fundamental and vital to all healthcare managerial functions, communication is a means of transmitting information and making oneself understood by others. Communication is a major challenge for managers because they are responsible for providing information that should result in efficient and effective organizational performance. Every managerial function or activity involves some form of communication. A manager must communicate with and through others to plan, organize, direct, or lead. Managerial decisions are effective only if they are communicated and understood by the people responsible for enacting them. Furthermore, employee motivation and satisfaction depend on effective communication. Communication is essential to building and maintaining relationships in the workplace. Communication is the creation or exchange of thoughts, ideas, emotions, and understanding between the sender and the receiver. Managers who understand this exchange can better analyze their communication patterns, resulting in more effective communication in the workplace.

Although managers spend most of their time communicating (e.g., sending or receiving information), one cannot assume that meaningful communication occurs in all exchanges (Dunn, 2006). Once a message has been sent, many are inclined to believe that communication has taken place. However, communication does not occur until information and understanding have passed between the sender and the intended receiver. For example, a receiver may hear a sender, but might not have comprehended the sender's meaning. Effective communication occurs only when the message received is the same as the one intended. Communication enables people to establish and maintain positive interactions in the workplace. An effective communicator overcomes barriers to engage in more meaningful and successful communication.

Communication Process

Communication is a complex and dynamic process. **Figure 5-1** illustrates the S-M-C-R model of the communication process. Information originates from the sender (S) and is encoded into a message (M) that is forwarded through a selected channel (C) to the designated receiver (R). Messages are received and decoded or interpreted by the receiver. Decoding is affected by the receiver's prior experiences and frames of reference. Accurate decoding of the message by the receiver is critical to effective communication. The closer the decoded message gets to the intent of the sender, the more effective the communication. However, environmental and personal barriers can hamper the communication process. To ensure that messages are received as intended, feedback is a necessary component of the communication process. Feedback is the destination's

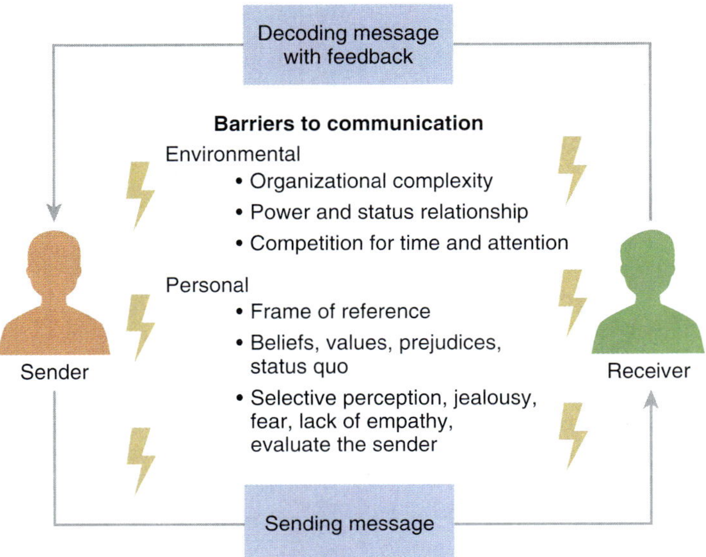

Figure 5-1 The Communication Process

reaction to a message (Certo, 1992). The receiver creates feedback to a message and encodes it before transmitting the feedback to the sender. The sender receives and decodes the feedback. It is an important element of communication because it allows for information to be shared between the receiver and sender in a two-way communication process.

Feedback

Effective communication takes place when the receiver fully understands the sender's message. In essence, feedback is a response (i.e., a signal) from the receiver that enables the sender to determine whether a message has been received in its intended form. The response or signal may take the form of an oral comment, a written message, a smile, a sigh, raised eyebrows, or some other action. Even a lack of response by the receiver may be interpreted as a form of feedback. Without feedback, the sender cannot confirm that the receiver has interpreted the message correctly. Feedback is a key component in the communication process because it allows the sender to evaluate whether the message was decoded as intended or if a corrective action is needed to clarify the intended message. For instance, a manager needs feedback to determine the level of staff acceptance of a new policy requiring employees to call and verbally confirm all patients' appointments 48 hours in advance.

The feedback process suggests that both the sender and receiver need to adjust their outputs in relation to the information transmitted. In the absence of feedback, when the communication process does not allow for sufficient feedback to develop, or when feedback is ignored, a certain amount of feedback will occur spontaneously and will tend to take a negative form. For example, suppose an employee emails their manager on a sensitive issue, and the manager never replies. This lack of feedback may be interpreted as negative feedback (e.g., the manager did not think the issue was important).

In one-way communication, a person sends a unidirectional message without interaction. For example, after reviewing a patient's lab results, a physician orders a medical test for the patient. The physician instructs the medical assistant to arrange the appointment within the week and notify the patient. The physician's order is an example of one-way communication that does not provide the opportunity for the patient to pose questions directly to the physician. Negative feedback may occur if the patient expresses frustration at the physician for not directly explaining the necessity of the medical test. However, the same patient could express appreciation toward the medical assistant who explains the purpose of the medical test based on the patient's lab results. The opportunity for feedback results in two-way communication between the patient and the medical assistant. Two-way communication is more accurate and information-rich when the message is complex, although one-way communication is more efficient, as in the case of the physician's written order.

Effective communication must allow opportunities for feedback. Feedback can take several forms, each with a different intent. Keyton (2002) describes three different forms of feedback: descriptive, evaluative, and prescriptive.

- *Descriptive Feedback*: Feedback that identifies or describes how a person communicates. For instance, a director attends a manager's staff meeting. After the meeting, the director tells the manager that she was very clear and detailed as she explained the new software for managing patient accounts. In this example, the director provides descriptive feedback on the manager's communication with staff.

- *Evaluative Feedback*: Feedback that provides an assessment of the person who communicates. If a director attends a manager's staff meeting and points out that the manager seemed like a warm and caring leader because of how she communicated with empathy, then the director has provided positive evaluative feedback of the manager's interaction with her staff.
- *Prescriptive Feedback*: Feedback that provides advice about behavior or communication. For example, the manager asks the director what changes she could have made to better communicate her message to her staff. The director suggests that she be friendlier and more cooperative by giving the staff specific times when she is available for help with the new computer database. This type of advice is prescriptive feedback.

In addition to forms and intent, there are also four levels of feedback. Feedback can focus on a group or an individual working with specific tasks or procedures. It can also provide information about relationships within the group or individual behavior within a group (Keyton, 2002).

- *Task or Procedural Feedback*: Feedback at this level involves issues of effectiveness and appropriateness. Specific issues related to task feedback include the quantity or quality of a group's output. For instance, are patients satisfied with the new outpatient clinic? Did the group complete the project on time? Procedural feedback refers to whether a correct procedure was used appropriately by the group at the time.
- *Relational Feedback*: This type of feedback provides information about interpersonal dynamics within a group. It emphasizes how a group gets along while working together and is effective when combined with descriptive and prescriptive forms of feedback.
- *Individual Feedback*: Feedback that focuses on a particular individual in a group. For example, is an individual in the group knowledgeable? Does the individual have skills that are helpful to this group? What attitudes does the individual have toward the group as the members work together to accomplish their tasks? Can the individual plan and organize within a schedule that contributes to the group's goal attainment?
- *Group feedback*: This type of feedback focuses on how well the group is performing. Questions like those raised at the individual feedback level are asked of the group. Do team members in the group have adequate knowledge to complete a task? Have they developed a communication network to facilitate their objectives?

Feedback can take the form of email or text responses, questionnaires, surveys, or audio or video recordings of group interaction. It can also occur in activities, such as market research, client surveys, accreditation, and employee evaluations (Liebler & McConnell, 2008). Feedback should be used to help a group communicate more effectively by encouraging group members to identify with the group and increase its efficacy. Feedback should not be viewed as a negative process. O'Hair, Stewart, and Rubenstein (2007) point out that negative feedback does not imply "bad" and positive feedback does not imply "good." Negative feedback indicates that you should do less of what you are doing or change to something else. Positive feedback encourages you to increase what you are doing. Thus, managers should use feedback as a strategy to enhance goals, awareness, and learning.

Feedback is a managerial tool that enables managers to anticipate and respond to changes. Structured feedback enhances managerial planning and controlling functions. Because of its value, managers should encourage and evaluate feedback systematically.

Gallup has found that of employees who strongly agree they receive valuable feedback from their coworkers, 80% are highly engaged. Feedback is more effective when it is meaningful to employees. The top five characteristics of meaningful feedback are (McLain & Nelson, 2024):

1. Recognition or appreciation for recent work
2. Connection, collaboration, and relationships
3. Clarifying role, goals, and priorities
4. Frequent and short (15–30 minutes, ideally weekly)
5. Focus on employee strengths

The Johari Window

The process of feedback can also be illustrated by the Johari Window, a useful communication model to improve understanding between individuals. Joe Luft and Harry Ingham created it in 1955 (hence the name "Johari") (Luft, 1984). The Johari Window model has two key concepts: (1) You can build trust with others by disclosing information about yourself, and (2) with the help of feedback from others, you can learn about yourself and come to terms with personal issues.

As shown in **Exhibit 5-1**, windowpane 1 is considered the open area, in which information about you is known both to you and to others. This includes your behavior, knowledge, skills, attitudes, and "public" history. Tubbs (2001) described this area as the general cocktail party conversation, in which an individual willingly shares personal information with others. For instance, at an office picnic, you might reveal to your coworkers that you are a vegetarian to support your desire for a healthier lifestyle. What is posted on social media may also be considered public. Windowpane 2 refers to a blind area in which others know information about you that you are unaware of, or things that you do unthinkingly. For example, your colleagues know that although you are a nice and caring person, you chronically interrupt and talk over others in conversation.

The third windowpane is the hidden area, in which you have likes and dislikes that you are unwilling to share with others. This area includes your values, beliefs, fears, and past experiences that you would not wish to reveal. The fourth and last windowpane is the unknown—things that are unknown to you and are also unknown to others. This is an area of potential growth or self-actualization. It represents all the things that you have never tried, participated in, or experienced.

Increasing mutual understanding through feedback and disclosure allows one to increase the open area and reduce the blind, hidden, and unknown areas of oneself (McShane & Von Glinow, 2003). Luft (1984) argues for increasing the open area in the Johari Window so that you and your coworkers are aware of your limitations. This is done by receiving more feedback from others and decreasing one's blind area (windowpane 2) and by reducing the hidden area (windowpane 3) through disclosing more about oneself. The combination of feedback and disclosure may also help produce more information in the unknown area (windowpane 4).

The Johari Window can be used to open channels of communication. Open communication is important for improving employee morale and increasing worker productivity. Open communication allows supervisors and subordinates to freely discuss organization-related issues, such as goals and conflicts. Nevertheless, Luft (1984) is cautious about the use of the Johari Window for all situations. He offers several guidelines for the appropriateness of self-disclosure. He recommends that self-disclosure is a function of an ongoing relationship. The timing and extent of disclosure are also critical. A competent communicator knows when, with whom, and how much to disclose.

Exhibit 5-1 The Johari Window

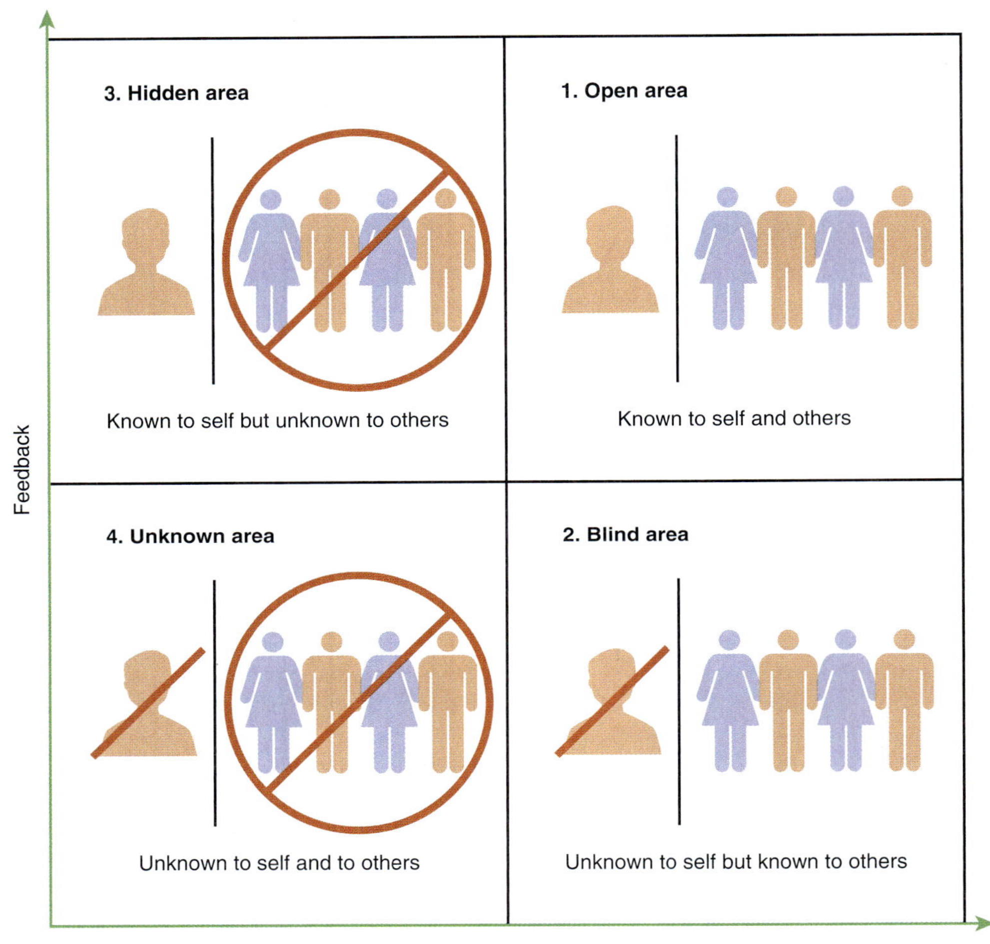

Communication Channels

Another important component of the communication process is selecting an appropriate communication channel. This is the means by which messages are transmitted. As Mazurenko and Hearld (2015) note, "Individuals may have different attitudes toward [these] different communication channels, often varying as a function of different personal and contextual factors, which can result in recipients responding differently to the same message received via different channels."

There are two types of channels: verbal and nonverbal. Various channels of communication and the amount of information transmitted through each type are illustrated in **Figure 5-2**.

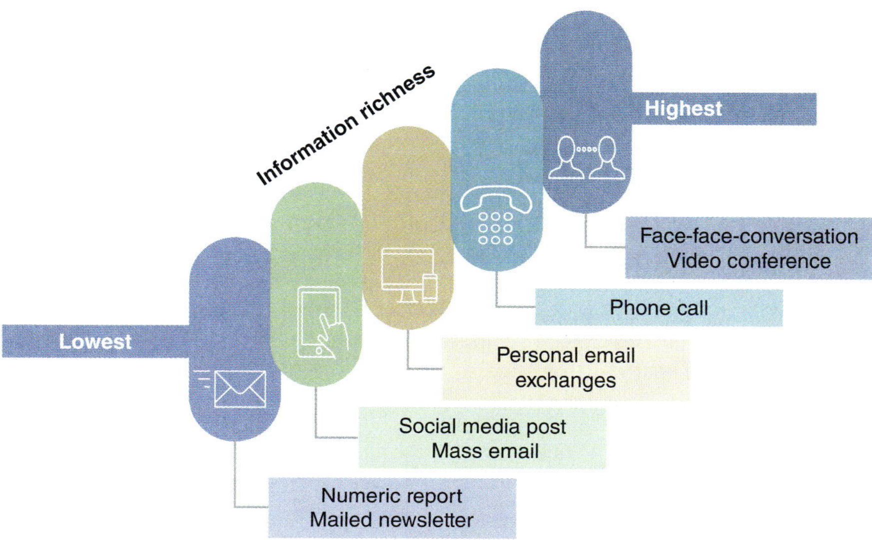

Figure 5-2 Communication Channels

Modified from Daft, R. L., & Lengel, R. H. (1984). Information richness: A new approach to managerial behavior and organizational design. In B. Staw & L. Cummings (Eds.), *Research in organizational behavior* (pp. 191–233). JAI Press.

Verbal Communication

Verbal communication relies on spoken or written words to share information with others. Dialogue, a form of verbal communication, is a discussion or conversation between people in which participants may be exposed to new information. In an organization, the process may involve a series of meetings of organizational members representing different views on issues of mutual interest. According to Edgley and Robinson (1991), for dialogue to be successful, there are several fundamental principles: Engage motivated people, use a facilitator and a recorder to manage the process, have the group develop procedures and live by them, ensure confidentiality, and let the process move at its own pace. Adhering to these principles will improve dialogue and result in more effective communication.

Different forms of verbal communication should be used for different situations. Face-to-face meetings are information-rich, allowing for emotions to be transmitted and immediate feedback to take place. Written communication is more appropriate for describing details, especially technical ones, as in the example of monitoring a patient's complex medical condition. Although traditional written communication was comparatively slow, the development of email and other forms of electronic communication, such as texting, has enabled written communication through these channels to dramatically improve efficiency (see **Case Study 5-1**).

Electronic Communication

The use of information technology is dramatically affecting how we communicate. Consider the following:

> When Martin Luther King Jr. wanted to expose racial injustices in the American South during the 1950s and 1960s, he relied on the written and spoken word—his letters and speeches, newspaper articles by sympathetic journalists, and published

CASE STUDY 5-1 Are We Getting the Message Across?

James Warick, director of physical plant at Southern Hospital, emailed Diane Curtis, director of nursing, informing her of a water leak in Operating Room 1, which would need to be shut down for repairs early the next morning. Curtis forwarded the message to Joanne Messing, the night shift's operating room nurse supervisor on duty. Messing, tired from a long night's work, handwrote a message to the nurse supervisor on the day shift to switch the 8:00 a.m. operation from Room 1 to Room 8 and taped the message onto the bulletin board. David Swanson, the day-shift nurse supervisor, arrived at 7:30 a.m. and found Dr. Roberts shouting that his patient was ready for surgery, but no rooms were available because Dr. Jones had already taken Room 8.

Discussion Questions

1. What were the channels of communication used by each person?
2. Should a different channel of communication have been used instead?
3. What can be done to resolve the problem?
4. What policies should be implemented to prevent this from occurring again?

accounts from civil rights workers provided evidence of discrimination and violence. Looking through the lens of the 21st century, King's message traveled slowly and only to limited parts of the world. Fast-forward half a century, and activists organizing the global climate strikes led by youth movements coordinated their efforts using social media platforms, instant messaging, livestreams, and viral hashtags. Videos and images of millions of protesters across continents were instantly available to the world in real time. In response to this widespread visibility, numerous governments and corporations announced new climate commitments and policies, acknowledging the activists' demands for urgent environmental action.

Today, most information sharing is done electronically through various channels, including emails, texts, and messaging through various apps. With the growth of AI, many communication processes are also being automated.

These digital forms of communication have revolutionized the communication process, allowing for rapid information exchange across any distance. These messages allow information to be quickly created, changed, saved, and sent to many people simultaneously. Although these are convenient forms of communication, they have several problems and limitations. The most obvious is information overload. Users can become overwhelmed by the number of messages and notifications they receive daily, many of which are unnecessary to the receiver. Another problem is their ineffectiveness in communicating emotion. The tone of a message can easily be misinterpreted, causing misunderstandings between sender and receiver. Icons known as emoticons or emojis have been developed to represent emotions in email and text messages, though they may be perceived to be unprofessional. Electronic messaging can also reduce politeness and respect for others when nonverbal cues are absent. Flaming is the act of sending an emotionally charged message to others, especially before emotions subside. This common problem occurs frequently in electronic communication because the sender does not have to bear the discomfort of having a heated discussion face-to-face. In a face-to-face discussion, scheduling and coordinating an in-person meeting allows one to cool down and develop second thoughts. A face-to-face meeting may allow the receiver of the heated message to respond quickly with feedback that may be uncomfortable for the sender. When you are tempted to respond with an emotionally charged message, it is best to acknowledge that you have received the message but to wait at least 24 hours before crafting your response, to allow emotions to subside. There are many recommended practices to reduce these communication problems; see **Table 5-1**.

Table 5-1 Written Communication Etiquette

Before pressing send on an email, text, or message, consider how your message would be perceived if it were forwarded to your entire organization. Keep your audience in mind before discussing private matters, expressing anger, or criticizing others. Emails last forever, and there is no guarantee that your messages will stay private.

General Best Practices

- Managers should communicate expectations regarding communication etiquette. Do not assume your team already knows the best practices. Set the standard and communicate it.
- Use calls or video meetings for longer, more complex discussions or when tone and context are essential. If a discussion takes over three email exchanges, it may be time to call or meet. However, do not waste another's time with a meeting that could be easily handled via email.
- Follow organizational policies on communication tools and etiquette, and use status indicators to reflect availability.
- Send follow-up emails summarizing key points from calls or in-person meetings to ensure clarity and documentation.

Composing Messages

- Write concise, clear messages tailored to your audience, using proper spelling, grammar, and punctuation.
- Avoid text shorthand (e.g., "u" for "you") or excessive emojis/emoticons/GIFs to maintain professionalism.
- Introduce yourself briefly when contacting someone for the first time. Please do not assume they already know who you are or remember you from one interaction.
- Use clear, direct subject lines for emails or state your purpose at the beginning of a text or instant message.
- Proofread messages before sending them to prevent errors and misunderstandings.
- Make sure your subject line is clear and direct. It should concisely describe the crux of your message. Do not be vague. Make it easy for someone with a clogged inbox to see and understand your message immediately.
- If your message is on a new topic, start a new thread. Do not reply to an old email with a message unrelated to the previous conversation. If the topic changes, change the subject line in your reply.
- Do not "reply all" unless all the recipients need to know your response. Avoid clogging people's inboxes with conversations that are irrelevant to them.

Content and Tone

- Maintain a respectful, courteous, and professional tone; avoid sarcasm or humor that could be misinterpreted.
- Match the tone of the message receiver. If formal, keep it formal; if more casual, you may respond with a more casual (yet still professional) tone.

(continues)

Table 5-1 Written Communication Etiquette *(continued)*

- Avoid discussing sensitive, complex, or confidential topics in email, text, or instant messages unless appropriate and secure.
- Keep messages concise, avoiding long blocks of text or unnecessary information. When asking multiple questions, use lists or numbering for clarity.

Timing and Frequency

- Send messages during regular working hours, considering recipients' time zones and routines.
- Respond promptly to emails, ideally within one or two business days; acknowledge messages needing a delayed response.
- Limit the number of messages to avoid overwhelming recipients. Instead of several short messages, use a single, comprehensive message.
- Reserve communication outside business hours for urgent matters and respect work-life boundaries.

Data from Silberman, L. (n.d.). 25 tips for perfecting your email etiquette. Inc. https://www.inc.com/guides/2010/06/email-etiquette.html

Nonverbal Communication

Nonverbal communication is sharing information without using words to encode messages. Mehrabian (1980) demonstrated that only 7% of any message is conveyed through words, 38% by the way the words are said, and 55% through nonverbal elements, such as facial expressions, gestures, and posture.

First impressions are made within 7 seconds, so being mindful of our nonverbal communication is important from the very first interaction (Goman, 2018). There are many forms of nonverbal communication (Cooks-Campbell, 2023; Nelson & Quick, 2003; Wilson, 2021), including:

- **Proxemics:** The study of an individual's perception of and use of space. Territorial space and seating arrangement are two examples. Taking up a large amount of space can convey confidence. Sitting on the same side of the table to work on a project can convey cooperation.
- **Kinesics:** Body language and gesture can convey meaning and messages. Pacing and drumming fingers are signs of nervousness. Wringing the hands and rubbing the temples signal stress. Raised eyebrows can express concern, and animated hand gestures communicate passion or excitement.
- **Gaze:** The frequency and duration of eye contact can convey meaning (Perry, 2021). Maintaining eye contact generally means that someone is comfortable and telling the truth. In contrast, avoiding eye contact might suggest they are nervous or hiding something. For example, when a healthcare manager interviews a candidate for a position as a clinical care coordinator, the manager attaches meaning to frowns and eye contact. Avoiding eye contact tends to close communication. However, cultural and individual differences influence appropriate eye contact. Moderate direct eye contact communicates openness, while too much direct eye contact can be intimidating.
- **Haptics:** The use of touch. While touch is rarely used within the workplace, there are many personal preferences regarding touch. While handshakes are a common form of greeting, they became less common for healthcare workers during the COVID-19 pandemic.
- **Paralanguage and Vocalics:** These are the features of our voice and how we speak, rather than our words. This includes pitch, volume, speech rate, tone, quality, tempo, rhythm, and

articulation. Rapid and loud speech may be taken as signs of anger or nervousness, while slow speech may be interpreted as confusion or uncertainty.

- **Chronemics:** The study of time and how it is used. Delaying an answer can be interpreted as anger or disappointment. Arriving late can convey power, a lack of care, or a lack of concern.
- **Appearance:** One's appearance, including hygiene, grooming, and clothing choices, can convey a message. Wearing more formal attire can convey seriousness, whereas a sloppy appearance can convey a lack of care for the conversation's subject.
- **Physiological Responses:** Sometimes, despite our best efforts, our physiology betrays us. Blushing, sweating, or crying can all betray our true feelings or responses, regardless of the words we use.

Negative nonverbal cues can impede communication. For example, arriving late for an interview with the vice president of finance, talking very fast, avoiding eye contact, and getting too close during a conversation or in a seating arrangement for a committee meeting can all have negative effects on communication.

To determine the most appropriate channel of communication for sending messages, one needs to identify whether verbal or nonverbal communication should be used. At the same time, ideal communication channels can be selected by examining the richness of information and the symbolic meaning of messages (Daft & Lengel, 1984). Information richness refers to the volume and variety of information that can be transmitted. Figure 5-2 shows that face-to-face meetings have the highest information-carrying capability because the sender can use verbal and nonverbal communication channels, and the receiver can provide instant feedback. When the wrong communication channel is used, this wastes time and leads to more misunderstandings. Information-rich channels are required for more effective communication when communication is nonroutine or unclear. For example, suppose a gunshot victim is brought into a trauma center. Organizing the care of this patient requires face-to-face instructions to quickly coordinate workflow and minimize the risk of confusion among various care providers. However, for routine communications, less information-rich channels can be used.

Choosing one communication channel over another lends meaning to the message; that is, there is symbolic meaning to selecting a particular communication channel beyond the message content. For example, when a manager tells an employee they must meet in person, this symbolizes that the issue is important, compared with a brief email message with instructions.

Barriers to Communication

As the middle of Figure 5-1 shows, several types of barriers can impede the communication process. Longest, Rakich, and Darr (2000) classify these barriers into two categories: environmental and personal. Both barriers can block, filter, or distort messages when they are sent and received.

Environmental Barriers

Common Environmental Barriers

Environmental barriers are characteristic of the organization and its environmental setting:

- Competition for Attention
- Time Pressure
- Hierarchy

- Organizational Philosophy
- Power Dynamics
- Complex Systems
- Technical Language

Environmental barriers include competition for attention and time between senders and receivers. Multiple and simultaneous demands cause messages to be incorrectly decoded. Sometimes the receiver hears the message but does not understand it. A receiver not paying adequate attention to the message is not listening. With abundant notifications from texts, apps, watches, and calendars, listening intently is becoming increasingly difficult. Listening is a process that integrates physical, emotional, and intellectual inputs into the quest for meaning and understanding. Listening is effective only when the receiver understands the sender's messages as intended. Thus, the receiver fails to comprehend the message without active or mindful listening. Mindful listening is a skill that managers need to develop to be effective in the busy 24/7 world of health care. According to communication expert Rebecca Shafir (2003), the goal of mindful listening is to silence the noise and distractions of our external environment and our thoughts so that the sender's entire message can be heard and understood.

Time is another barrier. Lack of time prevents the sender from carefully considering messages and structuring them accordingly. It also limits the receiver's ability to decipher messages and determine their meaning.

Other environmental barriers include the organization's managerial philosophy, multiple levels of hierarchy, and power or status relationships between senders and receivers. Managerial philosophy can promote or inhibit effective communication. Managers who fail to promote intraorganizational communication upward or disseminate information downward will create procedural and organizational blockages. A managerial philosophy requiring that all communication follow the chain of command shows a lack of attention and concern toward employees and restricts communication flow. Furthermore, when subordinates encounter managers who fail to act, the subordinate might be unwilling to communicate upward in the future because of a perception that communications are not taken seriously.

Managerial philosophy affects communication within the organization and the organization's communications with external stakeholders. For instance, when one hospital's chief executive officer (CEO) became aware that patients might have been exposed to a dangerous infection while hospitalized, he immediately decided to cover up the incident. He communicated that message down to his managers. However, another hospital CEO dealt with this situation very differently. She used public media as a communication channel to encourage patients to come forward and be tested. These reactions to similar events reflect different managerial philosophies about communication.

Multiple hierarchy levels and complexities, such as the size and degree of activity conducted in an organization, cause message distortion. When multiple links exist in the communication chain, information could be misinterpreted. As a result, a message sent through many levels is likely to be distorted or blocked. For example, the CEO of a healthcare organization asked department administrators to relay his message of sincere congratulations and appreciation to the staff for their hard work toward reaccreditation from The Joint Commission. This message was transmitted downward through several layers in the organization and was received more nonchalantly than was initially intended. In another scenario, a report generated by the management information system analyst was given to his supervisor, who went on vacation and left it on his desk without giving it to the vice president, who had requested it a week earlier. In this case, the message did not reach its destination.

Power or status relationships can also affect the transmission of a message. An inharmonious supervisor–subordinate relationship can interfere with the flow and content of information. Moreover, a staff member's previous experiences in the workplace may prevent open communication because of fear of adverse reactions. For instance, a poor supervisor–subordinate relationship inhibits the subordinate from reporting that the project is not going as planned. A subordinate who is fearful of the manager's power and status might prevent effective communication from taking place. Gardezi and colleagues (2009) observed silence as a form of communication in the operating room. They found that nurses often used silence because of a lack of understanding, fear of asking questions, and intimidation. They also found that silence was used in the operating room to communicate disrespect or power.

> During a 45-minute operation, the surgeon repeatedly requests "burning forceps." Instead of returning them to the scrub nurse, he leaves them on a mat across the patient's chest. Each time, the nurse must step down, maneuver around the resident, climb back up, and pass the instrument across the abdomen. Observing this, the surgeon remarks, "Just tell me it is up… We will try to remember to pass it back." He repeats, "Just tell me it is up!" while the nurse, looking confused, sometimes retrieves it anyway and once quietly responds, "Up." His tone remains calm throughout.

Another environmental barrier that may lead to miscommunication is using specific terminology unfamiliar to the receiver, especially in complex messages. Managers and clinical staff members in healthcare organizations use medical terminology, which may be unfamiliar to external stakeholders. Communication between individuals who use different terminology can be unproductive simply because people attach different meanings to the same words. Thus, misunderstandings can occur as a result of unfamiliar terminology.

Personal Barriers

Common Personal Barriers

Personal barriers arise from an individual's nature and their interactions with others.

- Personal Point-of-View
- Beliefs and Values
- Lack of Empathy
- Information Overload
- Selective Perception / Filtering
- Skepticism about the Source of Information
- Fear / Jealousy / Bias

Personal barriers arise because of an individual's frame of reference or beliefs and values. These barriers are based on one's socioeconomic background and prior experiences, shaping how messages are encoded and decoded. One may also consciously or unconsciously engage in selective perception or be influenced by fear or jealousy. For example, some cultures believe in the sayings "do not speak unless spoken to" or "never question elders" (Longest et al., 2000). These beliefs inhibit communication. Others accept all communication at face value without filtering out erroneous information. Still others provide self-promotion information, intentionally transmitting and distorting messages for personal gain. Unless one has had the same experiences as another individual, it can be challenging to understand the other individual's message thoroughly. In addition to the frame of reference, one's beliefs, values, and prejudices can alter and block messages. Preconceived opinions and prejudices are formed based on varying personalities and backgrounds. Selective perception tends to retain positive parts of the message and filter out negative parts. When a person is overloaded with information, they will do more filtering.

Two additional personal barriers are the status quo and evaluating the source (or the sender) to determine whether the receiver should retain or filter out messages. For instance, a manager always ignores complaints from Melissa, the medical receptionist, because Melissa tends to exaggerate issues and events. However, one must carefully evaluate and distinguish exaggerations from legitimate messages. Status quo is when individuals prefer the present situation. They intentionally filter out unpleasant information. For example, a manager does not tell staff and patients that their favorite physician, Dr. Ames, has decided to leave the clinic. To prevent staff and patients from leaving to follow Dr. Ames to the new clinic, the manager postpones the communication to retain the status quo.

A final personal barrier is a lack of empathy—in other words, insensitivity to the emotional states of senders and receivers. When a physician shouts for his assistants to hurry with preparing clean rooms because 50 patients are in the waiting room, his assistants should empathize with the physician and understand that he is under stress and pressure to see his patients, who are complaining that they have been waiting for up to 3 hours. At the same time, the physician should empathize with his assistants because the office is understaffed due to one of the three assistants calling in sick.

Overcoming Barriers to Improve Communication

Recognizing environmental and personal barriers is the first step to effective communication, but they can be difficult to overcome. By becoming cognizant of their existence, one can consciously minimize their impact. However, positive actions are needed to overcome these barriers. Below are some recommended ways in which managers can overcome some of these barriers:

- **Foster Open Communication Culture**
  Encourage a management philosophy that promotes transparency and the free flow of information across all organizational levels and departments. Diagonal communication through cross-functional teams or task forces can enhance inclusivity and engagement.
- **Streamline Communication Channels**
  Minimize the number of hierarchical layers or intermediaries between the sender and receiver to reduce distortion. Utilize cross-organizational processes rather than limiting communication to departmental silos.
- **Adapt Language and Symbols for Clarity**
  Tailor messages using clear, accessible language. Reinforce verbal communication with consistent actions and ensure that technical terminology is defined for diverse audiences.
- **Use Multiple, Appropriate Channels**
  Communicate complex or critical messages through several channels (e.g., verbal, written, visual) to reinforce understanding and reduce misinterpretation.

- **Leverage Management and HR Systems**
  Implement human resources strategies, such as job training and rotation to improve cooperation and mutual understanding among staff. Use conflict resolution mechanisms to address issues equitably and maintain open lines of communication.
- **Prioritize Active Listening and Empathy**
  Dedicate sufficient time and attention to listening. Encourage all parties to be aware of their own and others' beliefs, perceptions, and emotional states to reduce misunderstandings and foster empathy.

Effective Communication for Knowledge Management

Communication plays an important role in knowledge management. Employees are the organization's brain cells, and communication represents the nervous system that carries information and shared meaning to vital parts of the organizational body. Effective communication brings knowledge into the organization and disseminates it to employees who require it. Agarwal, Sands, and Schneider (2010) attempted to quantify the economic waste associated with communication inefficiencies in hospital settings at a national level. They found that U.S. hospitals waste more than $12 billion annually due to communication inefficiency among care providers.

Effective communication minimizes the "silos of knowledge" problem that undermines an organization's potential and also allows employees to make more informed decisions about corporate actions. Effective communication is one of the most critical goals of organizations (Spillan, Mino, & Rowles, 2002). Research suggests that an effective manager spends considerable time on staffing, motivating, and reinforcing activities (Luthans, Welsh, & Taylor, 1988).

Shortell (1990) identified multiple key elements to effective communication in a model developed for physicians and hospital administrators to improve communication abilities to disseminate knowledge within the organization. The following list summarizes these key elements:

- An effective communicator must have a desire to communicate, which is influenced by one's personal values and the expectation that the communication will be received meaningfully.
- An effective communicator must understand how others learn, which includes considering differences in how others perceive and process information (e.g., analytic versus intuitive, abstract versus concrete, verbal versus written).
- The receiver of the message should be cued as to the message's purpose—whether the message is intended to provide information, elicit a response or reaction, or arrive at a decision.
- The message's content, importance, and complexity should be considered in determining how the message is communicated.
- The credibility of the sender affects how the message will be received.
- The time frame associated with the content of the message (long versus short) must be considered when choosing how the message is communicated. More precise cues with shorter time frames are needed; see **Figure 5-3**.

Research suggests that to improve healthcare organizational communication and cohesion, exchanges between employees and leaders should involve leaders' direct support and encouragement of employees' constructive expressions of dissatisfaction and innovative ideas (Sobo & Sadler, 2002) (see **Case Study 5-2**).

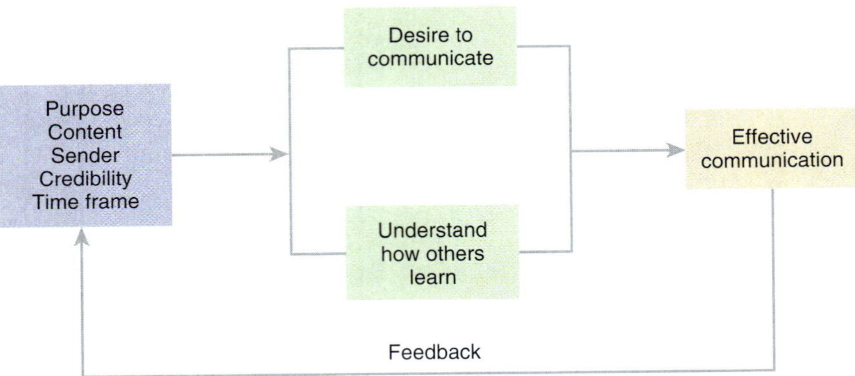

Figure 5-3 Interrelationships of Effective Knowledge-Management Communication

Reproduced from Shortell, S. M. (1990). *Effective hospital-physician relationships*. Health Administration Press.

Strategic Communication

Strategic communication is an intentional process of presenting ideas clearly, concisely, and persuasively. A manager must intentionally master communication skills and use them strategically—that is, consistently according to the organization's values, mission, and strategy. To plan strategic communication, managers must develop a methodology for thinking through and effectively communicating with superiors, staff, and peers. Sperry and Whiteman (2003) provide us with a strategic communication plan that consists of five components:

1. *Outcome*: The specific result that an individual wants to achieve.
2. *Context*: The organizational importance of communication.

CASE STUDY 5-2 What Should We Do Now?

Jenny Taylor, receptionist at Caring Physicians Clinic, called patients to remind them of their appointments. Dr. Ann Ryan, medical director of the clinic, found Jenny hardworking and pleasant to the patients. One morning, Dr. Ryan arrived and found Jenny crying in the supply room. When she questioned Jenny, Jenny sobbed that for the past 3 months she had kept forgetting to order supplies. Jenny had been borrowing supplies from the pediatrics office next door. Now they were unwilling to lend her more. Jenny said that she had called the supply center once and faxed a list of supplies, but had not followed through. This morning, Jenny called the supply center again and found they were out of business. Jenny told her immediate supervisor, Barbara Lakes, patient care coordinator for the clinic. Lakes fired Jenny for incompetence. In the meantime, patients were waiting, and there were no clean sheets, gloves, or gowns.

Discussion Questions

1. What was the beginning of the problem?
2. What should Jenny have done?
3. Using the elements of effective communication, discuss what Dr. Ryan and Barbara Lakes should do now.

3. *Messages*: The key information that staff members need to know.
4. *Tactical reinforcement*: Tactics or methods used to reinforce the message.
5. *Feedback*: How the message is received and its impact on the individual, team, unit, or organization.

Strategic communication requires forethought about the message's purpose and outcome. Managers must be able to link the staff's needs to the organization's mission and deadlines.

Flows of Intraorganizational Communication

Communication can flow upward, downward, horizontally, and diagonally within organizations. Upward communication occurs between supervisors and subordinates. Downward communication primarily involves passing on information from supervisors to subordinates. Horizontal flow is from manager to manager or from coworker to coworker. Diagonal flow occurs between different levels of different departments. Longest et al. (2000) provide several forms of intraorganizational communication for healthcare organizations, as described in the following paragraphs.

Upward Flow

The purpose of upward communication flow is to provide managers with information to make decisions, identify problem areas, collect data for performance assessments, determine staff morale, and reveal employees' thoughts and feelings about the organization. Upward flow becomes especially important with increased organizational complexity. For example, as Adelman (2012) noted, the Institute of Medicine's 2004 report, titled *Keeping Patients Safe: Transforming the Work Environment of Nurses,* related that "a lack of critical upward feedback in the hospital setting has adverse effects on direct patient care and health outcomes." Therefore, managers must rely on effective upward communication and encourage it as an integral part of the organizational culture. Upward communication flow helps employees meet their personal needs by allowing those in positions of lesser authority to express opinions and perceptions to those in positions of higher authority. As a result, the employees contribute to the organization and participate in the decision-making process. Adelman (2012) found that award-winning, high-performance hospitals' leaders have four key areas that promote effective upward communication:

1. Establishing a culture of excellence, in which employees feel comfortable voicing their concerns for improvement.
2. Using formal and informal communication channels, creating employee voice opportunities through leaders' visibility and approachability.
3. Reinforcing employee voice instrumentality—whereby leaders interact with employees often to actively solicit comments and provide feedback on decisions.
4. Removing risks and costs—a climate of safety (i.e., trust) that allows employees to take interpersonal risks regarding communicating improvement ideas to the organization's leaders.

The hierarchical structure (chain of command) is the primary channel for upward communications in healthcare organizations. To increase the effectiveness of upward communication, Luthans (1989) recommends using grievance procedures, open-door policies, counseling, employee questionnaires, exit interviews, participative decision-making techniques, and an ombudsperson.

- *Grievance Procedure*: The grievance procedure allows employees to appeal upward beyond their immediate supervisor. It protects individuals from arbitrary action by their direct supervisor and encourages communication about complaints.
- *Open-Door Policy*: The supervisor's door is always open to subordinates. It is an invitation for subordinates to talk to the supervisor about problems that trouble them, seek advice, or share information.
- *Counseling, Questionnaires, and Exit Interviews*: The department of human resources in a healthcare organization can facilitate subordinate-initiated communication by conducting confidential counseling, administering attitude questionnaires, and holding exit interviews for those leaving the organization. Information gained from these forms of communication can be used to make improvements.
- *Participative Decision-Making Techniques*: Participative techniques can improve employee performance and satisfaction by involving subordinates in informal or formal programs, such as quality-improvement teams, union–management committees, and suggestion boxes. Because employees can participate in decision-making, they feel they can contribute valuable information to the organization.
- *Ombudsperson*: An ombudsperson provides an outlet for people who feel they have been treated unfairly. An ombudsperson is a neutral party designated to help resolve conflicts and mediate between employees, including between lower-level employees and management.

In upward communication, subordinates can provide two types of information to supervisors: (1) personal information about ideas, attitudes, and performance, and (2) technical information to provide feedback. Managers who encourage feedback enhance the upward flow of communication.

Downward Flow

Downward communication involves passing information from supervisors to subordinates. This includes verbal and nonverbal communication, such as instructions for completing tasks and one-to-one communication. Downward communications include meetings with employees, written memos, emails, newsletters, procedural manuals, and clinical and administrative information systems.

Horizontal Flow

Relying only on upward and downward communication is inadequate for effective organizational performance. In complex healthcare organizations, horizontal flow, or lateral communication, must also occur. The purpose of lateral communication is to share information among peers at similar levels to keep organizational staff informed of all current practices, policies, and procedures (Spillan et al., 2002). For example, coordinating the patient care continuum requires communication among multiple units. Committees, task forces, and cross-functional project teams are all valuable forms of horizontal communication.

Diagonal Flow

The least-used communication channel in healthcare organizations is diagonal flow, although it is growing in importance. Although diagonal flow does not follow the typical hierarchical chain of command, it is especially useful for efficient communication and coordination of patient care. For example, diagonal communication occurs when the director of nursing asks the data analyst in the medical records department to generate a monthly report for all patients in the intensive care unit (see **Case Study 5-3**).

CASE STUDY 5-3 Communication Flows

At Sunny Nursing Home, a charge nurse approved a schedule change for a nurse who requested a more flexible shift to accommodate personal issues. She intended to inform the facility's president during an informal meeting after work. Another nurse overheard the conversation and, perceiving favoritism, sought a similar schedule change from the director of nursing. Wanting to maintain staff morale, he approved the request without consulting others.

This nurse then shared her new schedule with a colleague, who requested the same adjustment from the chief of staff. The chief of staff, believing it to be a valid request, forwarded it to his assistant for implementation.

On Monday, the schedule was updated without coordination among stakeholders. Three nurses were off for five consecutive days, leaving only one nurse on duty.

Discussion Questions

1. What are the different communication flow forms in this scenario?
2. What changes should have been implemented?
3. What should be done now?

Communication Networks

Flows of communication can be combined into patterns called communication networks, which are interconnected by communication channels. A communication network is the interaction pattern between and among group members. A network creates a structure for the group because it controls who can and should talk to whom (Keyton, 2002). Groups generally develop two types of communication networks: centralized and decentralized (**Figure 5-4**).

Decentralized networks allow each group member to talk to every other group member without restrictions. An open, all-channel, or decentralized network is best used for group discussions, decision-making, and problem-solving. The all-channel network tends to be faster and more accurate than the centralized network, such as the chain or Y-pattern network (Longest et al., 2000). Nevertheless, a decentralized network can create communication overload, in which too much information or excessively complex communication may occur (Keyton, 2002). When communication overload is produced, messages may conflict, resulting in confusion or disagreement. To reduce communication overload, a facilitator should be used to monitor group discussions.

A centralized network restricts the number of individuals in the communication chain. In a group setting where a dominant leader takes over group discussions by controlling the number of messages and information being passed, group members do not interact except through the leader. Such a network can create communication underload, in which too few or simple messages are transmitted. In this type of network, group members feel isolated from group discussions and generally feel dissatisfied. In the chain network, communication occurs upward and downward, following line authority relationships. An example is a staff nurse who reports to the charge nurse, who reports to the director of nursing, who reports to the vice president for clinical services, and who finally reports to the CEO of a large hospital. This network delineates the chain of command and shows clear lines of authority.

Other types of centralized networks include the Y-pattern, the wheel pattern, and the circle network. The Y-pattern is similar to the chain network, with its hierarchical structure, except that

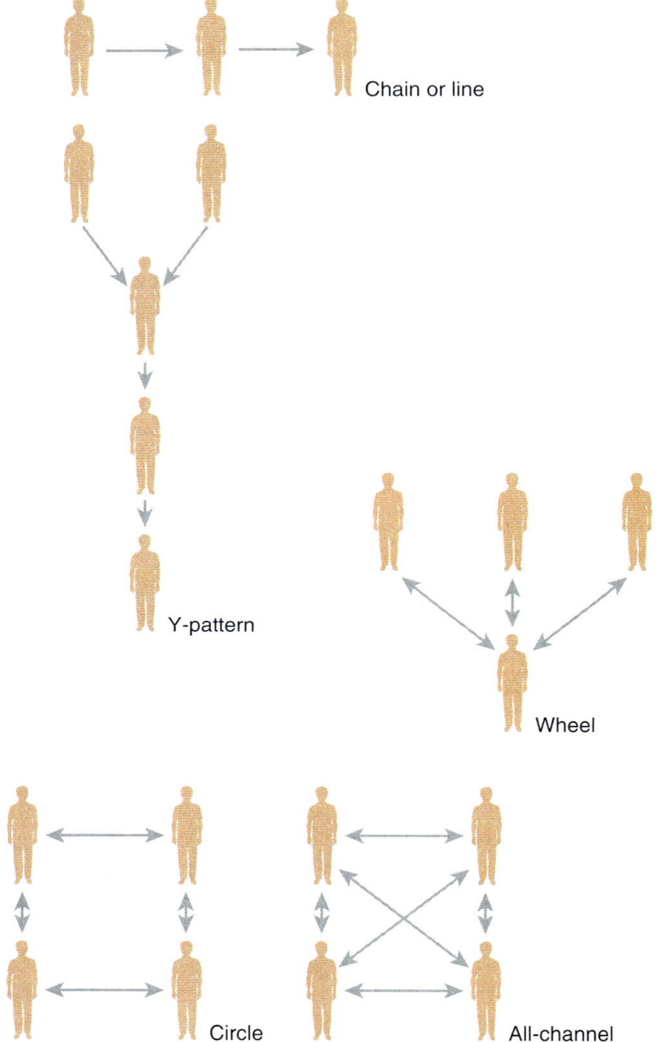

Figure 5-4 Two Types of Communication Networks: Centralized and Decentralized

it shows two employees at the same level who then follow the chain. An example is two medical assistants in the organ transplant division who report to the clinical administrator for the division, who reports to the clinical administrator for the department of surgery, who reports to the vice president of clinical services, who finally reports to the hospital's CEO.

The wheel pattern shows four subordinates reporting to one supervisor. Subordinates do not interact, and all communications are channeled through the manager at the center of the wheel. This pattern is rare in healthcare organizations and systems. However, elements of it can be found in the example in which four vice presidents report to a president if the vice presidents have little interaction with one another. Even though this network pattern is not routinely used, it may be used when urgency or secrecy is required. For example, the president with an organizational emergency might communicate with the vice presidents in a wheel pattern because time does not permit using other modes. Similarly, if secrecy is important, such as when investigating possible embezzlement, the president might require that all relevant communication with the vice presidents be kept confidential. The wheel pattern works well with time pressure, secrecy, and accuracy.

The circle pattern allows communicators in the network to communicate directly only with two others. Because each person communicates with another in the network, there is no central authority or leader. The circle network works well with open communication channels among all parties. However, it can slow down the communication process to enable everyone access to information.

No one type of communication network is right for all situations. Different forms can be applied under varying circumstances. To be effective, healthcare managers must be able to select the appropriate flows of communication for specific situations. Identifying the best communication network for the situation is critical to successful communication. Health problems range from simple to complex, and simple problems can be easily resolved using simple networks. For example, scheduling patient appointments for Dr. Davis can be easily accomplished through the superior–subordinate chain network. However, complex problems require many levels of decision-making. For instance, whether Horizons Hospital should merge with its major competitor to gain more market share at the risk of making a significant capital investment can be accomplished through the all-channel network, which is more valuable and practical for tackling complex problems. Hellriegel and Slocum (2004) compared the five communication networks using four assessment criteria:

1. *Degree of Centralization*: The degree of centralization is the extent to which team members have access to more communication than others. The wheel network is the most centralized network because communication flows from and to only one member. By contrast, the all-channel network provides everyone with the same opportunity for communication; thus, it is the least centralized network.
2. *Leadership Predictability*: Leadership predictability is the ability to anticipate which member of the communication network is likely to emerge as the leader. In the Y-pattern and the wheel pattern, the most centrally positioned individual is the most likely person.
3. *Average Group Satisfaction*: Average group satisfaction reflects members' satisfaction level in the communication network. In the wheel network, average member satisfaction is the lowest compared to other networks because the most centrally positioned person plays the most crucial roles, leaving less important decision-making responsibilities for the people around the wheel.
4. *Range of Individual Member Satisfaction*: The range of an individual's satisfaction within the communication network has an inverse relationship with the average group satisfaction. Again, in the wheel, although average member satisfaction is low, the range of individual member satisfaction is high because they are highly dependent on the individual in the middle. In the case of the all-channel network, average group satisfaction is high because there is greater participation by all members of the communication network, but individual satisfaction tends to be low.

Informal Communication

In addition to formal communication flows and networks within healthcare organizations, informal communication flows have their own networks. Employees have always relied on the oldest communication channel: the grapevine. The grapevine is an unstructured and informal network founded on social relationships rather than organizational charts or job descriptions. According to some estimates, 75% of employees typically receive news from the grapevine before they hear about it through formal channels (McShane & Von Glinow, 2003).

Early research identified several unique features of the grapevine. One feature of note is that it transmits information rapidly in all directions (Newstrom & Davis, 1992). **Figure 5-5** illustrates four common patterns that the grapevine can take.

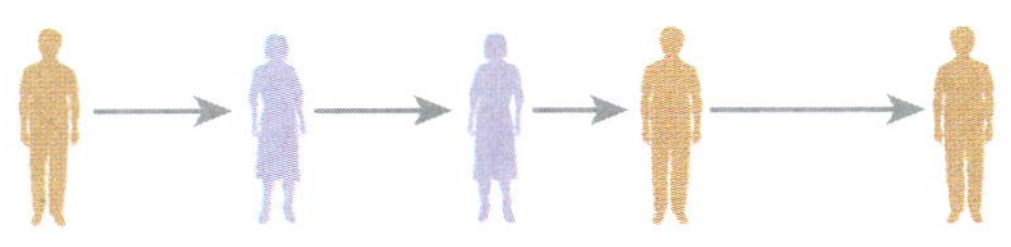

Single strand – information travels from one person to the next person

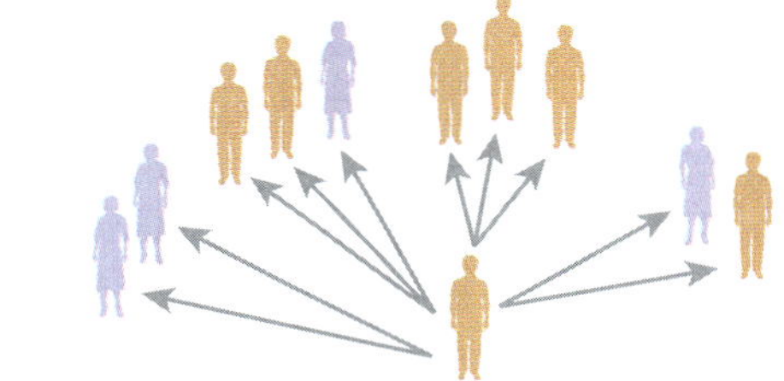

Gossip – one individual transmits the message to others

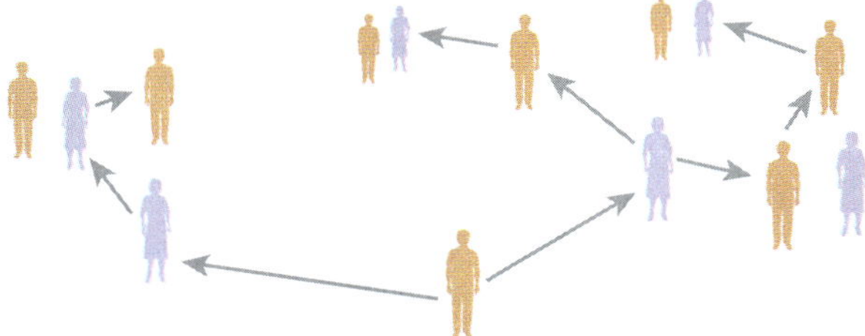

Probability – one individual randomly selects others to communicate the message and these secondary people randomly pick others

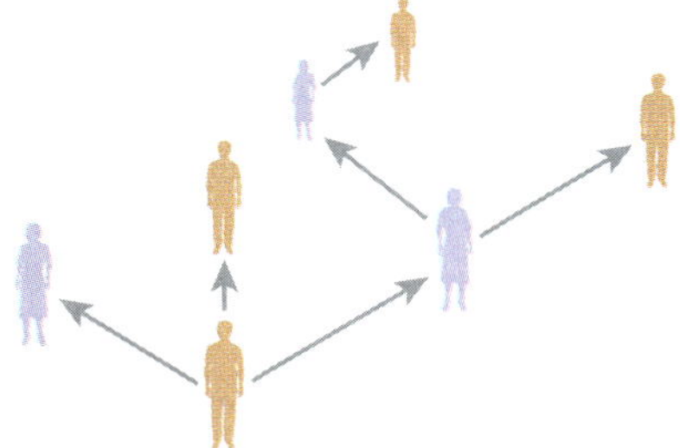

Cluster – one individual randomly selects others to communicate the message

Figure 5-5 Grapevine Networks

CASE STUDY 5-4 Did You Hear the Latest?

Sally Reeds, a medical secretary for the Department of Neurology at Western Heights Hospital in Colorado, checked her phone last night and found a post on social media from her friend and coworker, Justin Zeels, a social worker in the same hospital. Justin wrote that Dr. Sites, medical director of neurology, had been found under a bench outside the emergency department. The hospital security officers had allegedly reported that Dr. Sites was completely intoxicated, and he had been rushed home. Sally spiced up the tale and immediately reposted it. This morning, Sally looked up and noticed Dr. Sites seeing his patients as if nothing had happened. She confronted him and asked how he could face everyone after what happened last night. Dr. Sites looked confused until another staff member showed a screenshot of Zeels's post to Dr. Sites. After reading it, Dr. Sites became livid and fired Justin for spreading such a malicious rumor. Meanwhile, another medical secretary who saw the incident unfold took a video and texted it to her friends.

Discussion Questions

1. What did Sally do wrong?
2. What should Justin have done?
3. What should the organization do to prevent the spread of gossip through the grapevine?

The typical grapevine pattern is a cluster chain, whereby a few people actively transmit rumors to many others. The grapevine works through informal social networks, so it is more active for employees who have similar backgrounds and can communicate easily. Many rumors seem to have a small quantity of truth, possibly because rumors are transmitted through information-rich communication channels and employees are motivated to communicate effectively. Nevertheless, the grapevine distorts information by deleting fine details and exaggerating parts of the message.

In this era of information technology, messaging and social media have replaced the traditional watercooler site of grapevine gossip. Instead, networks have expanded as employees can communicate with one another instantly. Social media and public review sites have become virtual water coolers for posting comments about specific companies. This technology extends gossip to anyone, not just employees. A manager must selectively utilize the informal network to benefit the organization's goals (see **Case Study 5-4**).

Cross-Cultural Communication

Increasing information technology, globalization, and cultural differences can present organizational communication opportunities and challenges. Organizational personnel must be sensitive and competent in cross-cultural communication. While different cultures and perspectives enrich the environment, they can also cause communication barriers that impede efficient and effective service delivery. Communication difficulties arise from differences in cultural values, languages, and points of view. For instance, one significant barrier in the healthcare industry is language, because numerous languages may be encountered among staff and patients. More than 65 million people in the United States speak a language other than English at home. That is almost 22% of the total population! In the country's five largest cities, this percentage rises to nearly half the city's population (Zeigler & Camarota, 2018). Because language is the most obvious cross-cultural barrier, words can be easily misunderstood in verbal communication (Dutton, 1998). To be effective in cross-cultural communication, several guidelines are important:

- Understand your own identity. To develop sensitivity to other cultures, you must first understand your own culture and identity, which encompasses who you are and who you want to be. Your communication style, assumptions, and understanding may be influenced by various factors that have shaped your perspectives, including education, demographics, and upbringing.
- Enhance personal and social interactions. Globalization has increased our opportunities to associate and develop close interactions with individuals different from us. The conscious decisions that we make to become more accommodating, flexible, and understanding of others will broaden our views of the world and enrich our perspectives. Our relationships with people of different cultures help us learn more about the world and break stereotypes. These interactions also enable us to develop new communication skills and learn from others.
- Resolve misunderstandings, miscommunications, and mistrust. Make the effort to study, understand, and appreciate individuals of different cultures. Open, honest, and positive communication can help resolve misunderstandings, miscommunications, and mistrust.
- Enhance and enrich the quality of the work environment. Recognizing and respecting cultural differences through more open communication are the first steps toward valuing various perspectives and enriching the quality of the work environment (Hybels & Weaver, 2007).

Communicating with External Stakeholders

In healthcare organizations, managers must be competent communicators because they spend most of their time and energy communicating with external stakeholders: individuals, groups, and other organizations. A competent communicator is an individual who can identify appropriate communication patterns in a given situation and achieve goals by applying that knowledge. Competent communicators quickly understand how listeners interpret certain words and symbols, and they know which communication channel is most appropriate in a particular situation. Moreover, competent communicators use this knowledge to communicate in ways that achieve personal, team, and organizational objectives. A manager with high communication competence would be better than others at determining whether an email, call, or personal visit would be the best way to convey a message to an employee.

To competently communicate with external stakeholders, organizations and their managers are responsible for assessing the environment to gain information to make strategic decisions. Managers must utilize their roles as liaisons and monitors to scan the environment for opportunities and minimize threats. Furthermore, managers must use their strategic role to formulate and implement policies consistent with their organization's strategic goals and plans (Guo, 2003). **Exhibit 5-2** shows steps for analyzing stakeholders to increase the acquisition of useful information.

First, scanning the macroenvironment and the microenvironment yields information about stakeholders. **Figure 5-6** illustrates the variety of stakeholders for a community hospital.

Relationships between the organization and its external stakeholders are complex and affect communication because the organization is a dynamic, open system operating in a turbulent external environment. The size and variety of external stakeholders make communication

Exhibit 5-2 Stakeholder Analysis

1. Conduct a comprehensive environmental analysis (broad external factors: economy, regulations, social/cultural dynamics, politics, population trends, competition, technological advances; specific context: healthcare sector)
2. Pinpoint critical strategic concerns (e.g., determine key stakeholder groups)
3. Track ongoing developments (observe and record stakeholder perspectives and stances)
4. Project future directions (anticipate shifts in stakeholder opinions and positions)
5. Evaluate strategic significance (analyze how stakeholder perspectives and positions will impact the organization)
6. Distribute insights (share stakeholder intelligence with relevant decision-makers)

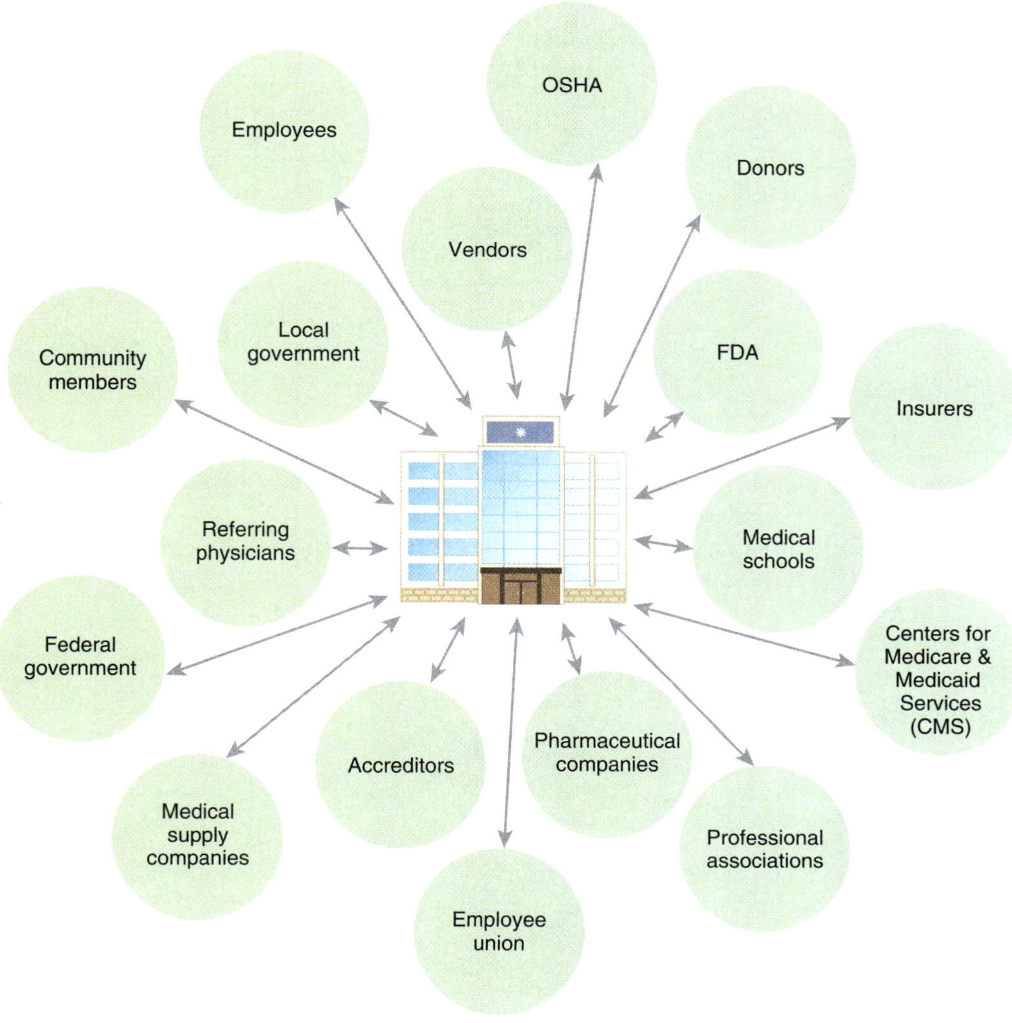

Figure 5-6 External Stakeholders

complex, especially because stakeholders attempt to influence organizational decisions. Fottler, Blair, Whitehead, Laus, and Savage (1989) examined communication between a large hospital and its stakeholders and found different relationships—positive and negative. Positive relationships with external stakeholders are easier to manage, and communication tends to be more effective than is the case in negative relationships.

The environmental scan identifies important issues and stakeholders in the stakeholder analysis. Next, monitoring stakeholders' activities is crucial. Managers must be able to take stakeholders' views and incorporate trends into their decisions. Finally, managers must evaluate the value of the information gathered and transmit it to those who need it.

Another way to describe communication with external stakeholders is known as boundary spanning. Boundary spanning, or external communication links, provides opportunities for organizational learning in areas, such as strategic planning or marketing (Johnson & Chang, 2000). Communicating with all external stakeholders is essential; however, each stakeholder may be viewed for its unique position and benefits to the organization. For instance, in interactions with the public sector, healthcare organizations are affected by public policies. The government is a major stakeholder because of its legislative and regulatory powers and because it is one of the largest purchasers of health services. For example, issues, such as access to care, cost containment, and quality concerns have driven federal government debate, reforms, and involvement in health care. Therefore, healthcare organizations cannot be insulated from public policies and must make strategic responses to reflect the needs of the public sector. A healthcare organization has a special relationship with the geographical community where the organization is located. Meeting the community's particular needs is a primary goal of healthcare organizations.

For effective communication to take place, both parties must form realistic expectations. Healthcare organizations have six areas of responsibility toward their communities (Longest et al., 2000):

1. Engaging in the core, health-enhancing activities in the community
2. Providing economic benefits to the community
3. Offering unique benefits or a niche to the community
4. Pursuing philanthropic activities in a broad and generous manner
5. Being in full compliance with legal requirements
6. Meeting ethical and fiduciary obligations

Summary

Communication in the workplace is critical for establishing and maintaining high-quality working relationships in organizations. Communication is the creation or exchange of thoughts, ideas, emotions, and understanding between sender(s) and receiver(s). Feedback is information that individuals receive about their behavior. Feedback can be used to promote more effective communication. The Johari Window is a model to improve an individual's communication skills through identifying one's capabilities and limitations. The channels of communication are how messages are transmitted. Verbal communication relies on spoken or written words to share information with others. Electronic communication, such as email and texts, has dramatically enhanced communication. Especially in health care, other forms of technology (such as high-speed, high-definition images; telemedicine; and wireless handheld, digital, electronic medical records) can bridge communication gaps between clinicians and administrators. Nonverbal communication is the sharing of information without using words to encode messages. This includes proxemics, kinesics, gaze, haptics, paralanguage and vocalics, chronemics, appearance, and physiological responses.

There are two types of barriers to communication: environmental and personal. Barriers can be overcome by conscious efforts to devote time and attention to communication, reduce hierarchical levels, tailor words and symbols, reinforce words with action, use multiple communication channels, and understand one another's frame of reference and beliefs.

Key elements of effective communication include the desire to communicate, understanding how others learn, the intent, the content, the sender's credibility, and the time frame. Strategic communication is an intentional process of presenting ideas clearly, concisely, and persuasively. Five components of strategic communication are outcome, context, messages, tactical reinforcement, and feedback.

Intraorganizational communication flows upward, downward, horizontally, and diagonally. Various communication flows can be combined to form communication networks, such as the chain, Y-pattern, wheel, circle, and all-channel. Specific networks may work better than others, depending on the situation. A manager must determine the best network for complex or straightforward communications. Informal communication results from interpersonal relationships developed in the workplace. Although informal networks can be helpful, they can also be misused.

Cross-cultural communication can be challenging. Communication difficulties arise from differences in cultural values, languages, and points of view. Organizational personnel must be sensitive and competent in cross-cultural communication. Several techniques and guidelines for improving cross-cultural communication are provided.

Healthcare organizations must manage relationships with a large number of external stakeholders: individuals, groups, and organizations interested in the organization's actions and decisions. Effective communication with external stakeholders involves environmental assessments to enable managers to identify and make strategic decisions for their organizations.

Discussion Questions

1. What are the various components of the communication process?
2. What are the three forms and four levels of feedback?
3. What is the Johari Window? How is it used in communication?
4. What is verbal communication? Give an example.
5. What are the different types of nonverbal communication?
6. What are the appropriate uses of verbal and nonverbal communication channels?
7. What are the two types of barriers to effective communication?
8. What methods are available to overcome these barriers?
9. What are the elements of effective communication?
10. What are the five components of a strategic communication plan?

11. What are the different forms of intraorganizational flows of communication?
12. What are the various networks available for formal and informal communication?
13. Why is cross-cultural communication important to today's health services organizations?
14. What competencies are needed by managers for communicating with external stakeholders?

CASE STUDY 5-5 "Now We Can Finally Talk"

Comfort Zone is a 60-bed, for-profit intermediate-care facility in Northern California. The rehabilitative department manager, Jamie Richards, has been working there for only six months. She holds monthly staff meetings and additional individual meetings with staff members to address specific patient-related issues. On most days, she eats lunch in a quiet corner of the cafeteria so that she can catch up on her paperwork at the same time.

Catherine Williams, one of her staff members, who has been working at the facility for more than 25 years, spotted her in the cafeteria one day and sat down uninvited. Catherine has never attended any of the monthly meetings and always has an excuse for not attending. Catherine said, "I have been waiting to tell you this since you began working here, but I wanted you to get adjusted first. Now we can finally talk. I have been here for a long time and have seen all kinds of comings and goings."

Catherine proceeded to tell Jamie about members of her staff who were constantly tardy or absent. She also told Jamie about what the staff members had been doing behind her back, such as using work time and technology to do side business, going shopping during lunch hour, coming back late, and going home early without permission. Catherine concluded, "At your monthly meetings, the staff shows up to tell you that everything is just fine when I know differently. I am too busy working to attend these meetings. I would fire them all if you want my opinion, since they are incompetent."

Discussion Questions

1. How should Jamie deal with the information that Catherine provided?
2. What do you think of Jamie's communication methods with her staff?
3. Do you think Jamie should use a different form of communication with Catherine?

CASE STUDY 5-6 It's Not My Job

In the Northeastern Medical Center's medical unit, Leah Hernandez is an insurance claims specialist who works with one nurse, one certified nursing assistant, and one medical assistant/receptionist. The physician and the administrator are located in a separate building. The administrator, Dan Jules, spends 3 hours a day in the clinic, from 9:00 to 10:30 every morning and from 2:00 to 3:30 every afternoon. He never varies the times that he is in the clinic.

One morning at 9:00 a.m., Dan was in the clinic with nurse Kate Williams, addressing the concerns of the patient in room 2, when the phone rang. A second phone line rang a few seconds later, and then a third. The nursing assistant was in room 1 with the physician, and the medical assistant/receptionist was in room 3 with another patient. The only staff member available to answer the phone was Leah, who was on the line with an insurance company. She yelled, "Anybody? Somebody, pick up the phone already! It is driving me crazy!" Everyone in the clinic, including the patients, heard her shouting. Kate rolled her eyes and told Dan it was like this every day. Dan excused himself and rushed into the reception area to pick up the phone. Later, Dan asked Leah why she could not pick up the phone. Leah answered, "It is not my job. I was busy with the insurance company."

Discussion Questions

1. What should Dan do to address the problem?
2. Should Dan meet with Leah or communicate with all staff members?
3. Because Dan works in a different building, who should have communicated this ongoing problem to Dan?

References

Adelman, K. (2012). Promoting employee voice and upward communication in healthcare: The CEO's influence. *Journal of Healthcare Management, 57*(2), 133–148.

Agarwal, R., Sands, D. Z., & Schneider, J. D. (2010). Quantifying the economic impact of communication inefficiencies in U.S. hospitals. *Journal of Healthcare Management, 55*(4), 265–282.

Certo, S. C. (1992). *Modern management: Quality, ethics, and the global environment* (5th ed.). Allyn & Bacon.

Coile, R. C., Jr. (2002). Physician executives explore "new science" frontier: Bridging the communications gap between medical staff and administration. *Physician Executive, 28*(1), 81–83.

Cooks-Campbell, A. (2023, February 8). *What is nonverbal communication? 10 different types (with examples)*. BetterUp. https://www.betterup.com/blog/types-of-nonverbal-communication

Daft, R. L., & Lengel, R. H. (1984). Information richness: A new approach to managerial behavior and organizational design. In B. Staw & L. Cummings (Eds.), *Research in organizational behavior* (pp. 191–233). JAI Press.

Dunn, R. (2006). *Haimann's healthcare management* (8th ed.). Health Administration Press.

Dutton, G. (1998). One workforce, many languages. *Management Review, 87*(11), 42–47.

Edgley, G., & Robinson, J. (1991). The dialogue process. *Association Management, 43*(10), 37–41.

Extejt, M. M. (1998). Teaching students to correspond effectively electronically: Tips for using electronic mail properly. *Business Communication Quarterly, 61*(2), 57–67.

Fottler, M. D., Blair, J. D., Whitehead, C. J., Laus, M. D., & Savage, G. T. (1989). Assessing key stakeholders: Who matters to hospitals and why? *Hospital & Health Services Administration, 34*(4), 525–546.

Gardezi, F., Lingard, L., Espin, S., Whyte, S., Orser, B., & Baker, G. R. (2009). Silence, power, and communication in the operating room. *Journal of Advanced Nursing, 65*(7), 1390–1399.

Goman, C. K. (2018, August 26). *5 ways body language impacts leadership results*. Forbes. https://www.forbes.com/sites/carolkinseygoman/2018/08/26/5-ways-body-language-impacts-leadership-results/?sh=5c1b235c536a

Guo, K. L. (2003). A study of the skills and roles of senior-level health care managers. *Healthcare Manager, 22*(2), 152–158.

Hellriegel, D., & Slocum, J. W., Jr. (2004). *Organizational behavior* (10th ed.). South-Western.

Hicks, J. M. (2011). Leader communication styles and organizational health. *Health Care Manager, 30*(1), 86–91.

Hybels, S., & Weaver II, R. L. (2007). *Communicating effectively* (8th ed.). McGraw-Hill.

Institute of Medicine. (2004). *Keeping patients safe: Transforming the work environment of nurses*. National Academies Press. https://doi.org/10.17226/10851

Johnson, J. D., & Chang, H. J. (2000). Internal and external communication, boundary spanning and innovation adoption: An over-time comparison of three explanations of internal and external innovation communication in a new organizational form. *Journal of Business Communication, 37*(3), 238–263.

Keyton, J. (2002). *Communicating in groups: Building relationships for effective decision making* (2nd ed.). McGraw-Hill.

Liebler, J. G., & McConnell, C. R. (2008). *Management principles for health professionals* (5th ed.). Jones & Bartlett Publishers.

Longest, B. B., Rakich, J. S., & Darr, K. (2000). *Managing health services organizations* (4th ed.). Health Professions Press.

Luft, J. (1984). *Group processes: An introduction to group dynamics* (3rd ed.). Mayfield.

Luthans, F. (1989). *Organizational behavior* (5th ed.). McGraw-Hill.

Luthans, F., Welsh, D. H. B., & Taylor III, L. A. (1988). A descriptive model of managerial effectiveness. *Group & Organization Studies, 13*(2), 148–162.

Mazurenko, O., & Hearld, L. R. (2015). Environmental factors associated with physicians' engagement in communication activities. *Health Care Management Review, 40*(1), 79–89. https://doi.org/10.1097/HMR.0000000000000003

McLain, D., & Nelson, B. (2024, January 19). *How effective feedback fuels performance*. Gallup. https://www.gallup.com/workplace/357764/fast-feedback-fuels-performance.aspx

McShane, S. L., & Von Glinow, M. A. (2003). *Organizational behavior: Emerging realities for the workplace revolution* (2nd ed.). McGraw-Hill.

Mead, R. (1993). Cross-cultural management communication. In J. V. Thill & C. L. Bovee (Eds.), *Excellence in business communication* (2nd ed., pp. 161–162). McGraw-Hill.

Mehrabian, A. (1980). *Silent messages*. Wadsworth Publishing.

Nelson, D. L., & Quick, J. C. (2003). *Organizational behavior: Foundations, realities and challenges* (4th ed.). South-Western.

Newstrom, J. W., & Davis, K. (1992). *Organizational behavior: Human behavior at work* (9th ed.). McGraw-Hill.

O'Hair, D., Stewart, R., & Rubenstein, H. (2007). *A speaker's guidebook: Text and reference* (3rd ed.). Bedford/St. Martin's.

Peck, R. (1997, June 5). Learning to speak computer lingo. *Times-Picayune*, E1.

Perry, E. (2021, September 9). Eye contact is important (crucial really) in communication. BetterUp. https://www.betterup.com/blog/why-is-eye-contact-important

Robison, J. (2021, June 28). *Communicate better with employees, regardless of where they work.* Gallup Workplace. http://gallup.com/workplace/351644/communicate-better-employees-regardless-work.aspx

Shafir, R. Z. (2003). *The zen of listening: Mindful communication in the age of distraction*. Quest Books.

Shortell, S. M. (1990). *Effective hospital-physician relationships*. Health Administration Press.

Silberman, L. (2020, February 6). *25 tips for perfecting your email etiquette*. Inc. https://www.inc.com/guides/2010/06/email-etiquette.html

Sobo, E. J., & Sadler, B. L. (2002). Improving organizational communication and cohesion in a healthcare setting through employee-leadership exchange. *Human Organization, 61*(3), 277–287.

Sperry, L., & Whiteman, A. (2003). Communicating effectively and strategically. In L. Sperry (Ed.), *Becoming an effective healthcare manager: The essential skills of leadership* (pp. 75–98). Health Professions Press.

Spillan, J. E., Mino, M., & Rowles, M. S. (2002). Sharing organizational messages through effective lateral communication. *Communication Quarterly, 50*(2): Research Library Core, Q96.

Thiederman, S. (1996). Improving communication in a diverse healthcare environment. *Healthcare Financial Management, 50*(11), 72–75.

Tubbs, S. L. (2001). *A systems approach to small group interaction* (7th ed.). McGraw-Hill.

Wilson, C. R. (2021, June 8). *Nonverbal communication skills: 19 theories & findings*. PositivePsychology.com. https://positivepsychology.com/nonverbal-communication/

Zeigler, K., & Camarota, S. (2018, September 19). *Almost half speak a foreign language in America's largest cities.* Center for Immigration Studies. https://cis.org/Report/Almost-Half-Speak-Foreign-Language-Americas-Largest-Cities

PART II

Understanding Individual Behaviors

In *Motivation and Personality* (1954), Abraham Maslow asked, "What conditions of work, what kinds of work, what kinds of management, and what kinds of reward or pay will help motivate humans?" In Part II, we answer Maslow's questions in three chapters that are dedicated to the discussion of motivation.

In Chapter 6, we describe and explain five content theories of motivation: (1) Maslow's Hierarchy of Needs, (2) Alderfer's Existence, Relatedness, and Growth (ERG) Theory, (3) Herzberg's Two-Factor Theory, (4) McClelland's Three-Needs Theory, (5) Self-Determination Theory. These theories attempt to explain what motivates employees, and each theory contains some parts of the others.

In Chapter 7, we examine five process theories of motivation: (1) Expectancy Theory, (2) Equity Theory, (3) Satisfaction–Performance Theory, (4) Goal-Setting Theory, and (5) Reinforcement Theory. Although Reinforcement Theory is not usually included with process theories of motivation, it does assist managers with understanding what reinforcements control an individual's behavior. Process theories contain some components of the content theories and vice versa.

In Chapter 8, we examine attribution theory. Discussing attribution theory and its relevance in the workplace gives managers a better understanding of the highly cognitive and psychological mechanisms that influence individuals' motivation levels.

CHAPTER 6

Content Theories of Motivation

LEARNING OUTCOMES

After completing this chapter, the student should be able to understand:

- The definition of motivation.
- The difference between content theories and process theories of motivation.
- Maslow's Hierarchy of Needs Theory and its criticisms.
- Alderfer's ERG Theory.
- Herzberg's Two-Factor Theory and how it relates to job design.
- Hackman and Oldham's Job Characteristics Model.
- McClelland's Three-Needs Theory.
- Self-Determination Theory.

Overview

We will begin by defining motivation before exploring two groups of motivation theories: content and process. Motivation is the conscious or unconscious reason for acting in a particular way, and one's general desire or willingness to do something; see **Figure 6-1**. Motivation is the psychological process through which unsatisfied needs or wants lead to desires that are the basis for goals or incentives. The purpose of an individual's behavior is to satisfy needs or wants. In this context, a need is anything a person requires or desires. A want is the conscious recognition of a need. An unsatisfied need or want creates an internal tension, from which an individual seeks relief.

The concept of motivation has been researched extensively in organizational behavior over many years. Through this research, we have identified and categorized motivation theories into two groups: content and process.

Content theories of motivation explain the specific factors or needs that motivate people. The content approach assumes that individuals are motivated by the desire to satisfy their inner needs.

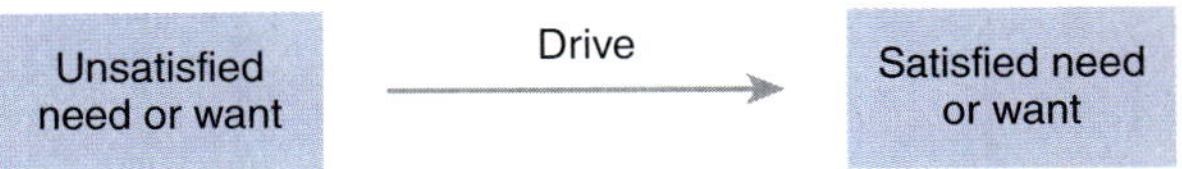

Figure 6-1 Process of Motivation

Content theories answer the question, "What drives behavior?" Content theories help managers understand what arouses, energizes, or initiates employee behavior.

Process theories of motivation focus on the cognitive processes underlying an individual's level of motivation. This approach describes and analyzes how behavior is energized, directed, sustained, and stopped. Process theories help explain how an employee's behavior is initiated, redirected, and halted.

Employee motivation directly impacts organizational performance; therefore, managers need to understand what motivates employees. By understanding what motivates them, managers can assist employees in reaching their fullest potential. There are some factors the manager can control, such as extrinsic factors (e.g., salary, working conditions, interpersonal relationships). For the motivating factors that are intrinsic to the employee (e.g., need for recognition, achievement), managers can be influential by providing a work environment that allows employees the opportunity to satisfy their personal needs and, simultaneously, the organization's goals.

Motivating staff is not about hanging posters with cute sayings in the office. Managers motivate by establishing an organizational structure and environment that allows employees to satisfy both their intrinsic and extrinsic needs. Remember, motivation is an individual's voluntary drive to satisfy a need or want!

Maslow's Hierarchy of Needs Theory

The most popular and widely cited human motivation theorist is Abraham Maslow. Maslow (1954) is considered the father of humanistic psychology. Briefly, humanistic psychology incorporates aspects of both behavioral psychology and psychoanalytic psychology. Behaviorists believe that external environmental factors control human behavior, whereas psychoanalytic psychology is based on the idea that internal unconscious forces control human behavior. Early in his career, Maslow concluded that human behavior is controlled by internal and external factors (e.g., needs). He also proposed that some factors have precedence over others. Maslow created his five-tier Hierarchy of Needs from this concept (see **Figure 6-2**).

According to Maslow, humans have five levels of needs and are driven to fulfill these needs. The most basic physiological needs include air, water, and food. After the basic physiological needs are met, an individual moves toward satisfying safety and security needs. At this lower level of the hierarchy, individuals are interested in having a home in a safe neighborhood, job security, a retirement plan, and health insurance. Because employees are concerned about satisfying these external (extrinsic) needs, these motivators need to be addressed by employers, such as by providing employees with an adequate benefits package. The next three levels in Maslow's Hierarchy of Needs Theory are somewhat less tangible and more psychological. The third level in the hierarchy is a desire for love, belonging, and approval. Humans have a drive to feel needed and loved. In the workplace, employees seek a sense of community and belonging. To achieve this, they seek their peers' and supervisors' approval and acceptance. Helping staff feel connected to the organization and its mission can support

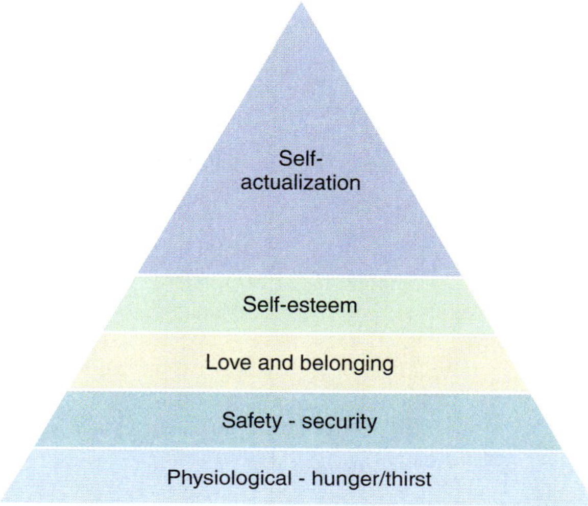

Figure 6-2 Maslow's Hierarchy of Needs

Reproduced from Maslow, A. H. (1954). *Motivation and personality.* Harper & Row.

this sense of belonging and community. After an individual's physiological, safety, and belonging needs are satisfied, self-esteem is the next tier in the hierarchy. Maslow noted two types of esteem needs: lower (external) and higher (internal). External esteem is satisfied by achieving the respect of other people, social and professional status, recognition, and appreciation. The higher form of esteem, internal esteem, involves the need for self-respect, a feeling of confidence, achievement, and autonomy. Individuals want to be competent in what they do, and self-esteem increases when they receive attention and recognition from others for their accomplishments. Therefore, careful use of praise and positive feedback to staff members is essential to motivating them. A word of praise or encouragement for a job well done or other forms of positive feedback go a long way toward motivating staff to perform. Managers should also provide employees with opportunities to demonstrate their competence. Encouraging staff participation in continuing education and other professional development activities and providing opportunities for challenging and meaningful work are effective motivators. These opportunities allow employees to achieve feelings of self-esteem and accomplishment.

Maslow described the preceding four levels (physiological, safety, belonging, and self-esteem) as deficiency needs (D-needs) because if any of these motivators are not satisfied, an inner tension is created within the individual that must be relieved (see **Case Study 6-1**). However, if these needs have been satisfied, they cease to motivate the individual, who moves to the next level in the hierarchy. Maslow believed that individuals must satisfy their lower-level needs, *at least to an acceptable state*, before they can be motivated to achieve the higher levels in the hierarchy.

The highest level of need is an individual's desire to become all that they can be. Although Maslow used a variety of terms to refer to this level, it is most commonly referred to as self-actualization. Self-actualization is the desire to become more of what one is and everything one can become. It is referred to as a "being need" (B-need) because it motivates without a deficiency, as with the D-needs. In Maslow's view, self-actualization is not an endpoint; rather, it is an ongoing process that involves many growth choices that entail risk and require courage (O'Connor &

CASE STUDY 6-1 Poor Cindy, What Should She Do?

Cindy has worked at Memorial Health System for 25 years, progressing through the ranks. After earning her bachelor's degree, she started as a medical coder. After 10 years, she pursued a master's in health services administration to qualify for management roles. Through years of dedication, she became the director of compliance. Recently, she has heard rumors of impending layoffs due to national health reform, which has caused her significant stress. Memorial is the only organization she has ever worked for.

Her anxiety worsened after she spoke with Harry, a former classmate who relocated for a job with a larger healthcare system. Harry was laid off 3 months ago and has struggled to secure interviews due to industry uncertainty. His experience has made Cindy increasingly fearful of job loss. Seeking reassurance, she approached her boss but received vague responses.

Cindy's preoccupation with job security has impacted her performance. She struggles to focus, misses project deadlines, and has become forgetful. Her stress manifests physically—she has experienced stomach cramps and headaches and has called in sick multiple times over the past month.

Discuss Cindy's situation using Maslow's Hierarchy of Needs.

Yballe, 2007). In addition to describing what is meant by self-actualization in his theory, Maslow (1970) identified key characteristics of a self-actualized person:

- *Acceptance and Realism*: Self-actualized people have realistic perceptions of themselves, others, and the world around them. They easily accept themselves and others as they are.
- *Problem-Centering*: Self-actualized individuals are concerned with solving problems outside of themselves. They often dedicate themselves to a larger purpose in life based on ethics or a sense of personal responsibility.
- *Spontaneity*: Self-actualized people are spontaneous, natural, and open in their behavior and thoughts. However, they can easily conform to conventional rules and expectations when situations demand such behavior.
- *Autonomy and Solitude*: Although they accept and enjoy other people, self-actualized individuals strongly need privacy and independence. They focus on their own potential and development rather than on the opinions of others.
- *Continued Freshness of Appreciation*: Self-actualized people continue to appreciate life's simple pleasures with awe and wonder.
- *Peak Experiences*: Self-actualized people commonly have peak experiences, or moments of intense ecstasy, wonder, and awe during which their sense of self is lost or transcended. These peak experiences may transform and strengthen the self-actualized person.

Although progress to self-actualization is often interrupted by failure to meet lower-level needs as a result of situations, such as illness (lack of physiological well-being), loss of a job (lack of security), or divorce (lack of sense of being loved), individuals can learn that satisfying basic needs becomes an integrated, consciously managed aspect of a whole life and is not compulsive or dominating of all other concerns. As O'Connor and Yballe (2007) point out, "a paradigm shift takes place. An individual becomes a person who has needs, not a needy person."

Managers need to ask themselves, "How can I motivate my employees?" When answering this question, managers need to be conscious of the fact that not all employees are driven by the same needs, nor is any employee driven by only one need at a time. For example, as you read this

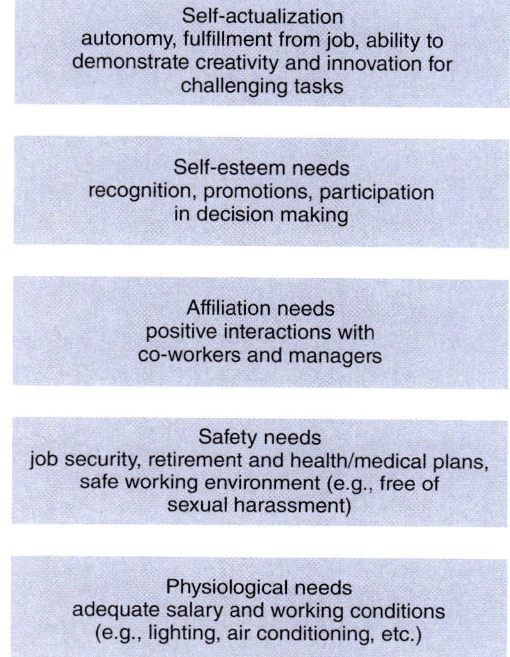

Figure 6-3 How Managers Can Satisfy Employees' Needs at Different Levels of Maslow's Hierarchy of Needs

book, you may have several needs operating simultaneously—curiosity, new knowledge, or thirst. Managers need to recognize the needs of each employee individually. Managers who simultaneously address each employee's lower level of needs will benefit from workers who are motivated to achieve the higher levels of Maslow's Hierarchy of Needs; see **Figure 6-3**.

Although Maslow introduced his Hierarchy of Needs Theory more than 60 years ago, only a limited number of studies support his theory, and those published have reported mixed findings (Alderfer, 1972). Some research contradicts Maslow's specific ordering of needs. For example, Huizinga (as cited in Griffin, 1991) attempted to validate the theory in the workplace. Huizinga's study is a broad effort to verify hierarchy principles, surveying 600+ managers across five Dutch industries. Participants spanned production, personnel, R&D, finance, and top management, aged 20–65, with education levels ranging from grade school to university. Huizinga found that no matter how many ways he analyzed the data, there was no evidence that workers had a single dominant need, much less that the need diminished in strength when gratified (Griffin, 1991).

Maslow's needs theory also had difficulty explaining individuals, such as Mother Teresa, who neglected her lower-level needs in pursuit of her spiritual calling to serve people experiencing poverty in India. Even though Maslow himself used the example of a starving artist pursuing his creativity needs (i.e., self-actualization) while ignoring physiological needs, he saw these as exceptions to the rule. Despite the gap in empirical research to support Maslow's Hierarchy of Needs Theory, it remains a popular theory because it is simple, relatable, and easy to translate to the organizational context.

Alderfer's ERG Theory

To address the criticisms of Maslow's Hierarchy of Needs, in the late 1960s, Clayton Alderfer (1972) introduced an alternative needs hierarchy, referred to as the ERG Theory. Alderfer's hierarchy relates to three identified categories of needs: existence, relatedness, and growth; see **Table 6-1**.

- *Existence* refers to an individual's concern with basic material and physiological requirements, such as food, water, pay, fringe benefits, and working conditions.
- *Relatedness* refers to the need to develop and sustain interpersonal relationships, such as those with family, friends, supervisors, coworkers, subordinates, and other significant groups.
- *Growth* refers to an individual's intrinsic need to be creative and to make useful and productive contributions, including personal development with opportunities for personal growth.

When compared with Maslow's Hierarchy of Needs, Alderfer's ERG Theory differs on three points. First, the ERG Theory allows for an individual to seek satisfaction of higher-level needs before lower-level needs have been satisfied. In other words, the ERG Theory does not require a person to satisfy a lower-level need for a higher-level need to become the driver of the person's behavior. Although the ERG Theory retains the concept of a needs hierarchy, it does not require a strict ordering, as in Maslow's theory.

Second, the ERG Theory accounts for differences in need preferences between cultures; therefore, the order of needs can be different for different people. This flexibility allows the ERG Theory to account for a wider range of observed behaviors. For example, it can explain Mother Teresa's behavior of placing spiritual needs above existence needs.

Third, and perhaps the most important aspect of the ERG Theory, is the frustration–regression principle. The frustration–regression principle explains that when a barrier prevents an individual from satisfying a higher-level need, the person may "regress" to a lower-level need to achieve feelings of satisfaction. For example, a person wants existence-related objects when their relatedness needs are not satisfied; a person wants relationships with significant others when growth needs are not being met.

Managers must recognize that an employee may have multiple needs to satisfy simultaneously, and focusing exclusively on one need will not effectively motivate an employee. In addition,

Table 6-1 Alderfer's ERG Theory

Level of Need	Definition	Properties
Existence	Includes all of the various forms of physiological and material desires.	When resources are limited and must be divided among people, one person's gain is another's loss.
Relatedness	Involves relationships with significant other people.	Satisfied by mutually sharing thoughts and feelings, acceptance, confirmation, understanding, and influence.
Growth	Drives a person to make creative or productive effects on themselves and the environment.	Satisfied through a person using their capabilities entirely (and developing additional ones) in problem solving; creates a greater sense of wholeness and fullness as a human being.

CASE STUDY 6-2 I Get By with a Little Help from My Friends

Jennifer Smith, RN, has worked at St. Joe's Medical Center for 5 years as an operating room nurse. She enjoys her job and has built strong friendships with her coworkers, often spending time together outside work. Helen Jones, director of surgical services, has praised their teamwork and cohesiveness.

Over the past year, Jennifer has expressed frustration about her career stagnation. She feels unchallenged and regrets earning her MSN since she hasn't applied her new skills. Considering a job change, she was encouraged by coworkers to apply for an assistant clinical manager position. Confident in her experience and education, she submitted her application, expecting Helen to offer her the role.

However, Helen selected another candidate with more management experience. Disappointed, Jennifer questioned whether to leave St. Joe's but hesitated due to her strong friendships. Her coworkers supported her, reminding her that more opportunities would come. Their encouragement helped her regain enjoyment in her work.

A few weeks later, Helen introduced Jennifer to a hospital mentorship program designed to provide hands-on management experience. Seeing this as a chance to grow, Jennifer quickly enrolled. Now, she feels prepared for future leadership opportunities.

Discuss how Jennifer displayed the frustration–regression principle of Alderfer's ERG Theory.

the frustration–regression principle affects workplace motivation. For example, if growth opportunities are not provided, employees might regress to relatedness needs and socialize more with coworkers, or they might look to other types of organizations for satisfaction of this need—for example, a union. If the work environment does not satisfy an employee's need for social interaction, the employee might feel an increased desire for more money or better working conditions. If a manager is able to recognize these conditions, steps can be taken to satisfy the employee's frustrated needs until the employee is able to pursue growth again (see **Case Study 6-2**).

Herzberg's Two-Factor Theory

Frederick Herzberg developed his Two-Factor Theory, also known as the Motivation–Hygiene Theory, from a study designed to test the concept that people have two sets of needs: (1) avoidance of unpleasantness and (2) personal growth. In Herzberg's original study (1959), 200 engineers and accountants were asked about events they had experienced at work that had resulted in either a marked improvement in job satisfaction or a marked reduction in job dissatisfaction. From Herzberg's research (1966), five factors stood out as strong determiners of job satisfaction (i.e., motivator factors) and are related to job content: (1) achievement, (2) recognition, (3) work itself, (4) responsibility, and (5) advancement. The determinants of job dissatisfaction (i.e., hygiene factors) that are related to job context were found to be (1) company policies, (2) administrative policies, (3) supervision, (4) salary, (5) interpersonal relations, and (6) working conditions. It is important to note that Herzberg used the term "hygiene" to describe factors that are necessary to avoid dissatisfaction but that by themselves do not provide satisfaction or motivation (see **Exhibit 6-1**).

Herzberg's research findings are significant to managers because the factors involved in producing job satisfaction are separate and distinct from those that lead to job dissatisfaction. As Exhibit 6-1 illustrates, these two factors are not opposites. As Herzberg pointed out, the opposite

Exhibit 6-1 Job Satisfaction

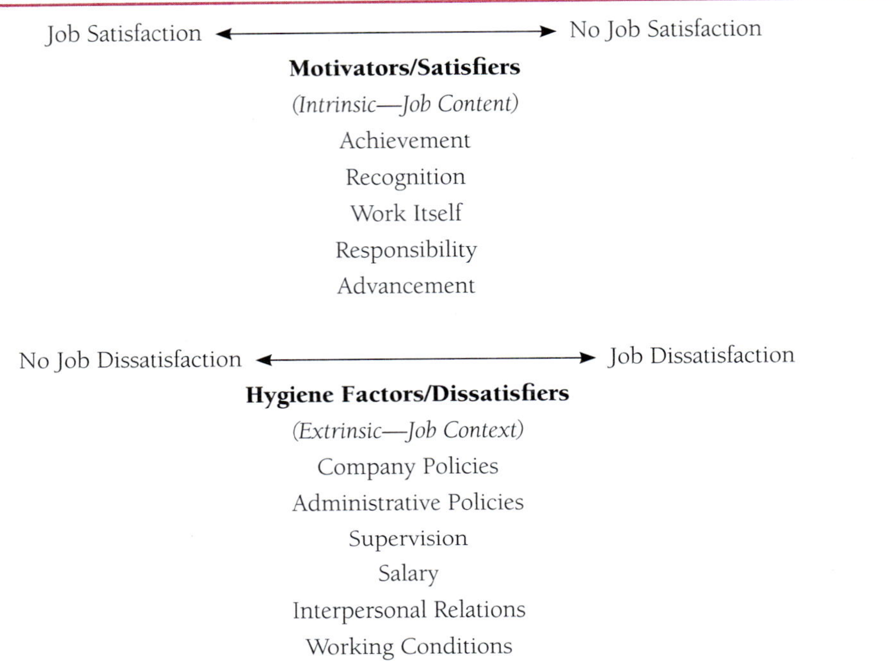

of job satisfaction is not job dissatisfaction but no job satisfaction. Similarly, the opposite of job dissatisfaction is no job dissatisfaction, not satisfaction with one's job.

In a practical sense, this means that dissatisfiers, referred to as hygiene factors, support and maintain the structure of the job (job context), while satisfiers, referred to as motivators, assist employees in increasing their motivation to do their work (job content). Unfortunately, Timmreck's (2001) study of health services middle managers found that only a small percentage believed in and used motivators to stimulate subordinates' behavior.

One of the criticisms of Herzberg's Two-Factor Theory is that a factor may be a motivator for one person but cause job dissatisfaction for another. For example, increased responsibility may be welcomed by one employee but avoided by another. Another criticism has been Herzberg's placement of salary or pay in the dissatisfier category, which has caused some people to believe that Herzberg did not value money as a motivator. However, what Herzberg meant was that if pay did not meet expectations, employees were dissatisfied, but if pay met employees' expectations, salary was not a need to achieve satisfaction.

This view is reiterated in Daniel Pink's (2011) book, *Drive: The Surprising Truth About What Motivates Us*. Pink refers to an employee's salary as a "baseline reward." If this baseline reward is not adequate, then employees will focus on the inadequacy of their remuneration, which will lead to anxiety about their financial circumstances, resulting in very little motivation. Herzberg believed that the absence of good hygiene factors, including money, would lead to dissatisfaction and thus potentially block any attempt to motivate the worker (see **Exhibit 6-2**).

Exhibit 6-2 Stop Demotivating Before You Start Motivating

Gallup research shows that 42% of employee turnover is preventable but often ignored (Tatel & Wigert, 2024). Many organizations focus on rewards—raises, promotions, flexible shifts, or recognition—to motivate employees. However, motivation alone is insufficient if underlying frustrations push employees away. Before encouraging employees to stay, organizations must remove the demotivating factors that make them want to leave.

Employees face two types of workplace influences: Pushes and Pulls. Pushes are workplace frustrations that cause disengagement and prompt employees to consider quitting, such as poor management, scheduling issues, or inadequate compensation. Pulls inspire employees to stay, such as career growth, meaningful work, or a strong organizational culture.

For example, a nurse at a teaching hospital, Pat, loves her job because it allows her to participate in research, which is a significant pull. However, a recent schedule change disrupted her childcare arrangements, creating a significant Push. Until her scheduling issue is resolved, no amount of research opportunities will restore her enthusiasm. Many leaders fail to distinguish between Pushes and Pulls, mistakenly trying to compensate for Pushes by offering more Pulls.

Many workplaces unknowingly push employees away by ignoring these frustrations. Employees experiencing excessive Pushes become retention risks, while those with neither Pushes nor Pulls remain disengaged and vulnerable to external job offers. To build long-term commitment, leaders must eliminate Pushes and reinforce Pulls. Meeting employees' basic needs while providing meaningful growth opportunities is key to reducing preventable turnover.

Dent (2002) relates that when Herzberg first presented his work, it was very controversial in the academic community but very popular in industry because it helped answer employers' questions as to why the level of an employee's productivity does not equate to the compensation received.

In the late 1950s, the U.S. economy was experiencing a tremendous upswing. The issue of motivation was critical for retaining good people, who often had several other opportunities. The primary advice coming from industrial psychologists was to motivate through compensation packages. As a result, employers were paying higher and higher salaries but felt that they were not getting higher levels of performance in return. Herzberg's work validated what the employers were feeling. Herzberg suggested that higher performance levels would come not from higher salaries but from giving employees the opportunity to create and affect their own environments (Dent, 2002).

Although managers need to provide employees with a reasonable salary, a degree of job security, and safe and comfortable working conditions (hygiene factors), focusing on these matters will not contribute to an employee's motivation or performance improvement (Sashkin, 1996). Herzberg promoted the concept that if the work one does is significant, it will ultimately lead to satisfaction with the work itself. In other words, employees will be motivated to do work that they perceive to be significant (see **Case Study 6-3**).

To build on this concept, jobs should be designed with special attention for opportunities relating to achievement, responsibility, meaningfulness, and recognition. Pink (2011) relates that organizations need to focus on individuals' intrinsic needs for autonomy (providing employees with the control over some or all of their work), mastery (allowing employees to become better at

CASE STUDY 6-3 Why Don't I Just Quit?

Robin sat at her desk, sorting her mail, and asked herself again, "Why don't I just quit?" She had enough savings to last a year, and with her MSW from a top school, she could find work anywhere.

For 4 years, Robin had been a social worker at Alpine Medical Center. She loved helping clients navigate the system to meet their social and medical needs. But the 60-hour workweeks and low salary frustrated her—especially when her friends with AS/Nursing degrees earned more.

Her boss, whom she had called incompetent, seemed to be setting her up for failure. He couldn't even secure funding for a computer she desperately needed. Her coworkers were no better, never inviting her to lunch or acknowledging her birthday. She felt unappreciated and isolated.

As she mulled over her frustrations, she opened a letter from a former client. He thanked her for her help during his illness, saying she had made it possible for him to remain at home instead of entering a nursing home.

Robin smiled and set the card aside. She still didn't know why she hadn't quit—but for now, something was keeping her there.

Using Herzberg's Two-Factor Theory, discuss why Robin has not resigned from her position.

something that matters to them), and purpose (fulfilling employees' natural desire to contribute to a cause greater and more enduring than themselves).

According to Herzberg, motivation comes from job content. Therefore, it is important for managers to consider the nature of the jobs that they ask their employees to do. Herzberg's approach can be summarized as follows: "If you want people to do a good job for you, then you must give them a good job to do." As Sethi and Stubbing (2019, p. 1) explain, "People want to do good work, in two ways: (1) they want intrinsically rewarding experiences, and (2) they want to make a contribution that fits their values." Managers need to be concerned with job-design characteristics, including job enrichment. Job enrichment is the vertical expansion or loading of the job, as opposed to a horizontal expansion (job enlargement). In other words, vertical loading is providing employees more responsibility in order to develop their skills. This could be accomplished by removing some of the controls over their work, assigning more difficult tasks, or allowing them to develop specific expertise over certain tasks (Herzberg, 2003).

Job Design

Job-design research in the past 4 decades has generated many insights into the relationship between job characteristics and job satisfaction. The well-known and widely researched Job Characteristics Model was developed by Hackman and Oldham (1976, 1980); see **Figure 6-4**.

Hackman and Oldham (1980) outlined five essential job characteristics that influence employee motivation.

Skill variety indicates the extent to which a job involves a range of different activities that demand diverse skills and talents from the employee.

Task identity describes how much a job allows an individual to complete an entire task, resulting in a clear and measurable outcome.

Task significance assesses the impact of a job on the lives of others, including colleagues in the organization and individuals in the wider community.

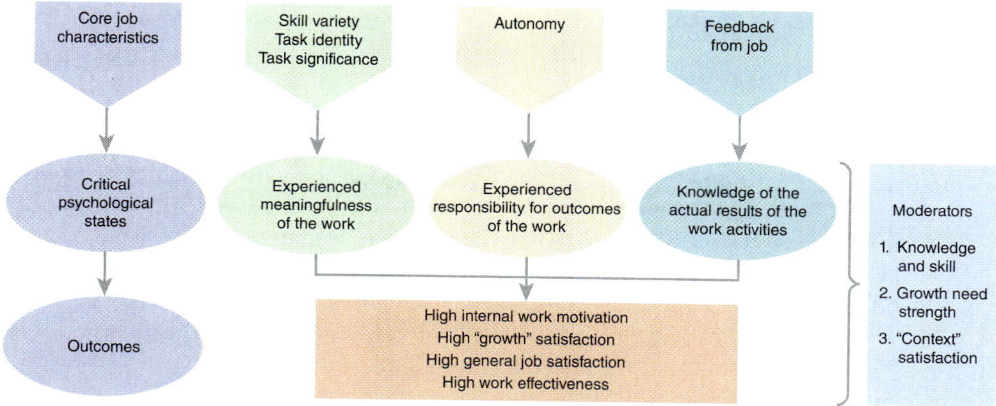

Figure 6-4 The Job Characteristics Model of Work Motivation

Data from Hackman, J. R., & Oldham, G. R. (1980). Work redesign. Addison-Wesley.

Autonomy reflects the level of freedom, independence, and discretion employees possess in organizing their work and deciding how to accomplish their tasks.

Feedback reveals how performing job tasks provides employees with clear information about their performance.

As reflected in Figure 6-4, each core job characteristic or combination of factors leads to critical psychological states for an employee. Hackman and Oldham (1980) relate that the combination of skill variety, task identity, and task significance leads to the psychological state of experienced meaningfulness, in which the worker perceives that the job is significant. Autonomy leads to the psychological state of experienced responsibility for outcomes (i.e., the employee feels individual responsibility for the work), and feedback leads to the psychological state of knowledge of the actual results of work activities. These critical psychological states lead to an employee's high levels of internal motivation, growth, job satisfaction, and work effectiveness (quality and quantity).

Using the moderators in the Job Characteristics Model, Hackman and Oldham (1980) attempted to explain why some employees "take off" on jobs that are high in motivating potential and others are "turned off." The first moderator is knowledge and skills. If people have sufficient knowledge and skills to perform their jobs well, they will experience positive feelings as a result of their work activities. However, people who are not competent to perform their tasks well will experience unhappiness and frustration at work.

The second moderator is growth-need strength. Some people have strong needs for personal accomplishment, for learning, and for developing themselves beyond where they currently are. These people are said to have strong "growth needs." Other people have less strong needs for growth or personal accomplishment. Therefore, individuals with high growth needs respond positively to the opportunities provided by enriched work. However, individuals with low growth needs might not recognize the existence of enriching opportunities, might not value them, or might find them threatening or complain about being stretched too far at work.

The third moderator is satisfaction with the work context. Employees who are relatively satisfied with their job context (pay, job security, coworkers, etc.) will respond more positively to enriched and challenging jobs than will employees who are dissatisfied with their job context.

Managers need to pay close attention to the moderators. If an employee is fully competent to carry out the work required by a complex and challenging task, has strong needs for personal growth, and is well satisfied with the work context, then the manager should expect the employee to exhibit high personal satisfaction and work motivation and performance. If an employee lacks any of these moderators, the opposite results are likely to occur.

To assist managers in designing jobs that will increase motivation for employees, Hackman and Oldham (1975) developed the Job Diagnostic Survey (JDS). The JDS measures the degree to which the various job characteristics are included in the job. The job characteristics can then be altered to enrich the job and increase its motivational potential (Lunenburg, 2011). The JDS generates a summary score reflecting the overall motivating potential of a job in terms of the core job dimensions (Hackman & Oldham, 1975). The motivating potential score (MPS) is calculated as follows:

$$\text{MPS} = \frac{(\textit{Skill Variety} + \textit{Task Identity} + \textit{Task Significance})}{3} \times \textit{Autonomy} \times \textit{Feedback}$$

The core job characteristics of skill variety, task identity, and task significance are combined, whereas the job characteristics of autonomy and feedback stand alone. Because of the additive and multiplicative relationships of the job characteristics in the MPS formula, one or more of skill variety, task identity, and task significance could be missing or measured as zero, and the employee could still experience the work as meaningful. However, if either autonomy or feedback were missing, the job would offer no motivating potential (MPS = 0) because of the multiplier effect (Lunenburg, 2011).

In 2011, Grant, Fried, and Juillerat found that job redesign for bank tellers increased both job performance and job satisfaction, with positive effects lasting up to four years. Grant's and his colleagues' work supports the idea that careful job redesign that increases performance and satisfaction is an important factor not only for employees but also for organizations. Grant's research was conducted at a large bank where managers, using a research survey, found that bank tellers were very dissatisfied with their jobs, stating that they were "just glorified clerks"—micromanaged with boring jobs and no decision-making responsibilities. The bank managers decided to redesign the teller jobs. New tasks were added to provide variety and require a broad range of skills. The tellers were also given more autonomy in their roles as well as decision-making responsibilities. Job satisfaction increased, and when a survey was administered six months later, it showed that the tellers not only were more satisfied with their roles but also were more committed to the organization (Grant et al., 2011).

McClelland's Three-Needs Theory

David McClelland (1985) experimented with individuals' responses to pictures of various groups of people gathered together. On the basis of the participants' responses, McClelland identified three types of motivational needs: achievement, power, and affiliation.

- Achievement (*n*-Ach) is described as the need to excel or succeed. In general, high achievers tend to seek moderately challenging tasks, take personal responsibility for their performance, and require feedback to confirm their successes.

- Power (*n*-Pow) is described as an individual's need to influence others. This can be positive or negative, as we will discuss later.
- Affiliation (*n*-Aff) is described as an individual's need to be liked and approved of by others. As such, *n*-Aff people have a strong need for interpersonal relationships.

McClelland (1985) believed that most people have a combination of these motivational needs, with some exhibiting a stronger tendency to one particular motivational need (e.g., a high power need versus a high achievement need). This tendency affects a person's behavior and management style. For example, McClelland suggested that a high affiliation need weakens a manager's objectivity and decision-making capability because of the manager's need to be liked by subordinates, colleagues, and supervisors. Although individuals with high power needs are attracted to leadership roles, they might not have the required flexibility and human relations skills necessary to be effective. McClelland argues that individuals with strong achievement needs make the best leaders, although they can have a tendency to demand too much of their staff in the belief that they are all similarly and highly focused on achievement (i.e., results-driven). One interesting aspect of McClelland's theory is that individuals can learn or acquire a need for achievement by being associated with success and failure in the past (and the effect that accompanies success and failure).

Achievement

A significant part of McClelland's research focused on the achievement motivational need (*n*-Ach). Through his research, McClelland concluded that while most people do not possess a strong *n*-Ach motivation, those who do have it display a consistent behavior of moderate risk-taking. To support his theory, McClelland (1985) performed the now famous ring-toss experiment.

Participants played a ring-toss game in which the subjects determined how close or far away they would stand from the peg. One group of participants stood very close to the peg to ensure that they would never miss. Another group stood so far away that if they actually did place the ring on the peg, it was because of chance, not ability. The third group calculated their distance from the peg. They did not stand so far away as to make the task impossible, nor did they stand so close as to make it too easy. If they missed the first toss, they would move closer; if they made the toss, they would take a step back for the next toss. McClelland referred to the third group as moderate risk-takers—individuals who desired a challenge but whose success was based on their abilities, not chance, as with the second group.

McClelland (1961) relates that *n*-Ach people have various attributes. First, *n*-Ach individuals are not high risk-takers as compared to a gambler who has no control over the outcomes. High achievers are moderate risk-takers. Achievement-motivated individuals set difficult goals, but these are goals that they believe to be achievable through their efforts and abilities. High achievers work harder and more efficiently when the task is challenging and requires creativity, such as designing new systems or a better way of doing things. Second, *n*-Ach individuals view goal achievement as their reward and require quantifiable and factual feedback. They view more money and/or higher profits as the measurement or feedback of their success. Job security is not an important issue for *n*-Ach people. They prefer occupations that allow them the flexibility and the opportunity to set their goals, such as in sales, business, or entrepreneurial roles. Although high achievers can work in groups, they are satisfied knowing they initiated an action that contributed to the group's success.

McClelland (1961) believed that *n*-Ach individuals are the ones who make things happen and get results in an organization. They successfully obtain the resources, including employee buy-in, to achieve organizational goals. However, because of their results-driven attitude, high achievers may be viewed as demanding of staff and insensitive to the needs of others.

Power

McClelland (1985) relates that a high need for power may be expressed as personalized power or socialized power. Individuals with a high need for personalized power tend to display impulsive or aggressive actions, abuse alcohol, and collect prestige "toys," such as fancy cars. They seek to control others for their benefit. Their attitude is "I win, you lose." Individuals with a high need for personalized power demand personal loyalty from staff, not loyalty to the organization. Yukl (2001) points out that when a highly personalized power leader leaves an organization, the result is usually chaos, loss of direction, and low morale.

Socialized power is needed for effective leadership. These leaders direct their power in ways that benefit others and the organization rather than for their gain. As McClelland (1985) and Yukl (2001) relate, these leaders are interested in seeking power because it is through power that they can influence other people to accomplish tasks. They empower others who use that power to enact and further the leader's vision for the organization.

Affiliation

Individuals with a high need for affiliation seek to be with and interact with others. McClelland (1985) relates that they are concerned with establishing, maintaining, or restoring positive relationships with others. High-affiliation individuals want to please and engage in more dialogue with others. Individuals are very important to *n*-Aff people. They prefer friends over experts when working in groups (*n*-Ach individuals prefer experts over friends as working partners) and prefer feedback on how well the group gets along rather than how well they perform on the task. They avoid conflict and criticism and have a fear of rejection by others. Therefore, individuals with a high need for affiliation do not always make good managers (see **Case Study 6-4**).

Self-Determination Theory

Self-Determination Theory (SDT) provides a framework for understanding human motivation and behavior. Developed by Deci and Ryan (1985, 2000), SDT identifies three fundamental psychological needs: autonomy, competence, and relatedness. Autonomy involves having control over one's actions, competence refers to mastering challenges and feeling effective, and relatedness pertains to establishing meaningful connections with others.

SDT categorizes motivation into autonomous and controlled types. Intrinsic motivation, where individuals engage in activities for inherent satisfaction, is considered the prototype of autonomous motivation. In contrast, extrinsic motivation varies in its degree of autonomy, ranging from external regulation (controlled) to integrated regulation (autonomous).

SDT posits that fulfilling these three basic psychological needs is crucial for optimal functioning in the workplace (McAnally & Hagger, 2024).

CASE STUDY 6-4 The Office Manager's Dilemma

When Mayra was promoted to office manager at Dr. Green's orthopedic practice, she was thrilled. After 6 years with the practice, she saw her coworkers as family. She organized social events, celebrated staff milestones, and ensured a positive work environment.

Mayra was also highly skilled in office operations. Hired as an X-ray technician, she had filled in for reception, medical records, and billing whenever needed. She also managed supplies and surgery scheduling. Confident in her abilities, she expected an easy transition into management.

For the first few months, things went smoothly. However, in her fourth month, staff began complaining about Kiara, the new appointment-scheduling clerk. Kiara was making critical scheduling errors—booking patients when Dr. Green was at the hospital, during staff lunch breaks, and overscheduling, leading to long wait times.

Mayra intended to address the issue but found herself paralyzed by anxiety. Each time she approached Kiara, she avoided confrontation, asking vague questions like, "How is everything going?" Unaware of the problems, Kiara remained cheerful, saying she loved the office.

As scheduling errors worsened, staff grew frustrated and warned Mayra that the added workload was unsustainable. They pressed her for updates, and Mayra lied, saying she was too busy but would address it soon. She feared upsetting Kiara but also dreaded disappointing Dr. Green, who might doubt her leadership abilities.

Tensions escalated as staff threatened to quit if the issue remained unresolved. Determined, Mayra scheduled a meeting with Kiara for the next morning. However, stress took a toll—she woke up with a rash and called in sick. Unable to face the confrontation, she postponed the conversation once again.

Using McClelland's Three-Needs Theory, discuss whether Dr. Green made the right decision in promoting Mayra to office manager. Why or why not?

- **Autonomy:** Employees who experience a sense of choice and control over their work report higher levels of job satisfaction and engagement.
- **Competence:** Feeling capable and effective in one's role is associated with increased work engagement and job performance.
- **Relatedness:** Strong workplace relationships and a sense of belonging contribute to higher job satisfaction and lower turnover intentions.

Summary

When the content theories of motivation are compared, there are notable similarities; see **Table 6-2**. The theories describe an individual's various needs in similar terms. Herzberg's hygiene factors parallel Maslow's physiological, security, and belongingness needs and Alderfer's existence and relatedness needs. Maslow's self-esteem and self-actualization needs are similar to Herzberg's motivators and Alderfer's growth requirement. McClelland's achievement is closely related to Herzberg's motivators, and his power and affiliation can be related

Table 6-2 Comparisons of Content Theories of Motivation

Herzberg's Two-Factor Theory	Maslow's Hierarchy of Needs	Alderfer's ERG Theory	McClelland's Three-Needs Theory	Self-Determination Theory
Motivators	Self-actualization	Growth	Achievement	Autonomy
	Self-esteem			
Hygiene factors	Love	Relatedness	Power (influencing others)	Competence
			Affiliation (exchange of warm feelings)	Relatedness
	Safety	Existence		
	Physiological			

to Alderfer's relatedness needs because of an individual's need to influence (power) or satisfy a need for warm feelings (affiliation) (Alderfer, 1972). It is clear that Maslow's Hierarchy of Needs Theory has greatly influenced the study of organizational behavior and continues to do so even after 70 years (Latham & Pinder, 2005).

Discussion Questions

1. Define motivation.
2. Connect the five tiers of Maslow's Hierarchy of Needs to the workplace.
3. Discuss how Alderfer's ERG Theory satisfied the criticisms of Maslow's Hierarchy of Needs.
4. Explain Herzberg's Two-Factor Theory as it relates to job design.
5. Explain the various components of Hackman and Oldham's Job Characteristics Model.
6. Discuss McClelland's Three-Needs Theory as it relates to a manager's success in the workplace.
7. Discuss the relationship between the various content theories of motivation.

CASE STUDY 6-5 Motivated but Exhausted

Monica Reynolds, a nurse manager at Northside Regional Medical Center, sat in her car an extra five minutes before heading into work. She hadn't slept more than 4 hours the night before—again. Between coordinating coverage for short-staffed shifts and checking in on her aging mother after dinner, there hadn't been a moment to rest.

Inside, tensions were high. Several nurses had asked to meet with her after hearing that their requests for pay adjustments had been denied. With an ongoing national nursing shortage and a system-wide hiring freeze, schedules had become unpredictable. "We're working harder than ever, and it feels like no one's listening," one nurse said. Monica understood their frustration—she felt it too. But without budget flexibility, she had few solutions to offer.

Later that day, Monica met with the director of clinical operations about a potential promotion. She had been working toward this next step for over a year, completing leadership coursework on weekends and picking up extra responsibilities. It was the opportunity she had been hoping for—but it would mean even longer hours.

As she pulled into her driveway that evening, her 8-year-old daughter, Ava, ran out holding a crumpled paper. "You forgot picture day again," Ava said quietly. Monica's heart sank. She had set a reminder but missed it in the flurry of shift changes and emails.

Her phone buzzed again—her brother texting about who would take their mom to her next doctor's appointment. She hadn't seen her close friends in months, and even simple messages in their group chat now felt like a luxury she couldn't afford.

Monica stood in the doorway, unsure whether to open her laptop again or sit down at the table with Ava. She wasn't sure how much longer she could keep all of it going. She was highly motivated, but somehow wanting to be the best manager, mother, and friend felt out of reach. "With just a little more sleep ..." she thought.

Discuss the various motivation theories reflected in this case study.

CASE STUDY 6-6 Develop a Motivation Plan

Aliyah, director of nursing at a 400-bed nonprofit hospital, faces rising tensions due to high patient census, staff shortages, and an upcoming accreditation visit. With limited time, she skipped performance evaluations but approved a 5% pay increase, making the hospital's nurses the highest paid in the region. She believes this offsets their increased workload and stress.

After relocating from the Northeast, Susan Smith, 30, joined the hospital 3 years ago. A staff nurse for 10 years, she balances work with raising two young children and a lawyer husband.

Initially, Susan was hardworking and error-free, but her productivity has dropped in the past 3 months. She argues with physicians and nurses over patient care and frequently complains that no one listens to or values her input. Aliyah often hears Susan complaining that "no one listens to me," "no one wants to hear my opinion," and "they do not pay me enough to do this job."

Susan was once a highly motivated, productive member of the nursing staff. Aliyah understands that everyone is experiencing more stress than usual because of the increased workload, but what can be done to motivate Susan to return to her prior performance?

Using the principles of Maslow, Herzberg, and Alderfer's content theories, explain to Aliyah why Susan has behaved the way she has over the past 3 months.

CASE STUDY 6-7 Employees' Motivation Needs

Although cash bonuses can improve physician executive job performance, a recent survey found that money isn't very helpful in improving job satisfaction.

According to a survey of physician executives, personal growth, personal development, life/work balance, effective communications, and personal relationships are the keys to improving satisfaction. The informal survey questioned 104 physician leaders, including CEOs, medical affairs vice presidents, medical directors, department chairs, and consultants. It examined both individual and organizational views of job satisfaction. When asked to describe successful methods of improving job satisfaction for their staff, the responses were as follows:

- 46% of respondents described improving communications and personal relationships.
- 9% mentioned improving leadership quality.

- Only 3% of respondents stated that bonuses could be successfully used to improve satisfaction at the staff level.

When dealing with staff, "listen to them and treat them with respect," one survey respondent said. "Give them credit for their help and ideas whenever there is an opportunity, especially in front of bosses or a large group. Ask them what they need to do their job better, and then try to give it to them. If we cannot give it to them, be honest and ask for other suggestions." Another participant said more money is certainly not the answer. "Added pay for added responsibility does not work if they did not want the responsibility in the first place."

Using Herzberg's Two-Factor Theory, explain the informal survey results regarding employees' motivation needs.

Reproduced from Matheny, G. L. (2008). Money is not key to happiness, survey finds. *Physician Executive, 34*(6), 14–15.

CASE STUDY 6-8 We Only Wanted to Scare Management into Making Changes!

A small group of nurses at a large community hospital met daily to discuss their growing dissatisfaction with their work environment. A management change created uncertainty, while a hiring freeze left nurses overworked, skipping breaks, working overtime, and taking extra on-call shifts. Their workload was increasing with a high patient occupancy rate and sicker patients.

Compounding their frustration, wages had been stagnant for 2 years, despite a 10% rise in the cost of living. Some nurses were barely able to afford the higher costs of rent and childcare. They felt they were doing more with fewer resources and receiving no appreciation for their efforts.

The lack of support staff meant nurses spent valuable time searching for medications and supplies, reducing patient care time and jeopardizing safety. Additionally, physicians' verbal abuse and management's inaction on complaints added to their dissatisfaction.

Feeling unheard, the nurses contacted a labor union, which launched a six-week campaign. Peer pressure grew, and even well-respected nurses—who were not part of the original group—became vocal supporters of unionization.

When the vote was held, two-thirds of the nursing staff approved union representation. The original group of nurses was surprised, realizing they had only intended to pressure management into improving conditions, not necessarily unionize.

1. Using Maslow's Hierarchy of Needs, diagram the nurses' issues within each level.
2. Explain why the nurses were motivated to contact the labor union using Herzberg's Two-Factor Theory.

Exercise 6-1 Job Survey

Introduction

Objective: To learn how job design affects performance.

Time: About 25 minutes.

Instructions: Take the survey below. Once you have completed it, total your scores. Compare your final score with others in the class and discuss the following questions:

- Normally, leaders will have scores that are higher than their workers'. Why is this?
- If your employees were to take this survey today, what do you think their average scores would be?

- Discuss Hackman and Oldham's five dimensions and how they help motivate a job holder. Ask for a few examples of how a job could be redesigned under each of the five dimensions.

Job Design Questionnaire

Directions: Listed below are some statements about your job. For each statement, write in your response based on how much you agree or disagree with it.

Strongly Disagree	Slightly Disagree	Disagree	Undecided	Slightly Agree	Agree	Strongly Agree
(1)	(2)	(3)	(4)	(5)	(6)	(7)

My job:

- Provides much variety. __________
- Allows me the opportunity to complete the work I start. __________
- Is one that may affect a lot of other people by how well the work is performed. __________
- Lets me be left on my own to do my own work. __________
- Provides feedback on how well I am performing as I am working. __________
- Provides me with a variety of work. __________
- Is arranged so that I have a chance to do the job from beginning to end. __________
- Is relatively significant in the organization. __________
- Provides the opportunity for independent thought and action. __________
- Provides me with the opportunity to find out how well I am doing. __________
- Gives me the opportunity to do a number of different things. __________
- Is arranged so that I may see projects through to their completion. __________
- Is very significant in the broader scheme of things. __________
- Gives me considerable opportunity for independence and freedom in how I do my work. __________
- Provides me with the feeling that I know whether I am performing well or poorly. __________

Summary

Scoring for Job Design Questionnaire

The survey is designed to analyze five dimensions of the job:

- Skill Variety: Total the scores for questions 1, 6, 11 __________
- Task Identity: Total the scores for questions 2, 7, 12 __________
- Task Significance: Total the scores for questions 3, 8, 13 __________
- Autonomy: Total the scores for questions 4, 9, 14 __________
- Feedback About Results: Total the scores for questions 5, 10, 15 __________

The lower-scoring dimensions (normally, anything below 15) should be investigated to see whether the job environment can be improved.

About the Survey

Hackman and Oldham's Five Dimensions of Motivating Potential

- *Skill Variety*: The degree to which a job requires a variety of challenging skills and abilities.
- *Task Identity*: The degree to which a job requires completion of a whole and identifiable piece of work.

- *Task Significance*: The degree to which the job has a perceivable impact on the lives of others, either within the organization or in the world at large.
- *Autonomy*: The degree to which the job gives the worker freedom and independence in scheduling work and determining how the work will be carried out.
- *Feedback*: The degree to which the worker gets information about the effectiveness of their efforts, either directly from the work itself or from others.

Exercise 6-2

Social determinants of health are important nonclinical elements affecting the health of individuals. Often, these factors can influence whether or not patients will become ill, engage in healthy lifestyles, have access to preventive care, or address more pressing health concerns before they progress. Navigating the complex system of hospitals and insurance can take significant motivation and initiative on the part of the patient. As healthcare institutions focus on caring for the health of their populations instead of just handling acute cases that come into the hospital, administrators need to understand what motivates members of the community to take care of their health. Discuss how each of the elements below relates to Maslow's Hierarchy of Needs and how barriers in these areas might affect one's motivation to engage in a healthy lifestyle.

- Economic Stability
  - Employment
  - Food Insecurity
  - Housing Instability
  - Poverty
- Education
  - Early Childhood Education and Development
  - Enrollment in Higher Education
  - High School Graduation
  - Language and Literacy
- Social and Community Context
  - Civic Participation
  - Discrimination
  - Incarceration
  - Social Cohesion
- Health and Health Care
  - Access to Health Care
  - Access to Primary Care
  - Health Literacy
- Neighborhood and Built Environment
  - Access to Foods That Support Healthy Eating Patterns
  - Crime and Violence
  - Environmental Conditions
  - Quality of Housing

Modified from U.S. Department of Health and Human Services Social Determinants of Health. https://www.healthypeople.gov/2020/topics-objectives/topic/social-determinants-of-health

References

Alderfer, C. (1972). *Existence, relatedness, and growth*. Free Press.

Deci, E. L., & Ryan, R. M. (1985). *Intrinsic motivation and self-determination in human behavior*. Plenum.

Dent, E. B. (2002). The messy history of OB&D: How three strands came to be seen as one rope. *Management Decision, 40*(3), 266–280.

Grant, A. M., Fried, Y., & Juillerat, T. (2011). Work matters: Job design in classic and contemporary perspectives. In S. Zedeck (Ed.), *APA handbook of industrial and organizational psychology* (Vol. 1, pp. 417–453). American Psychological Association.

Griffin, E. (1991). *A first look at communication theory*. McGraw-Hill.

Hackman, J. R., & Oldham, G. R. (1975). Development of the job diagnostic survey. *Journal of Applied Psychology, 60*(2), 159–170.

Hackman, J. R., & Oldham, G. R. (1976). Motivation through the design of work: Test of a theory. *Organizational Behavior and Human Performance, 16*(2), 250–279.

Hackman, J. R., & Oldham, G. R. (1980). *Work redesign*. Addison-Wesley.

Herzberg, F. (1966). *Work and the nature of man*. World Publishing Company.

Herzberg, F. (2003). One more time: How do you motivate employees? *Harvard Business Review, 81*(1), 93–173.

Herzberg, F., Mausner, B., & Snyderman, B. (1959). *The motivation to work*. John Wiley & Sons.

Latham, G. P., & Pinder, C. C. (2005). Work motivation theory and research at the dawn of the twenty-first century. *Annual Review of Psychology, 56*, 485–516.

Lunenburg, F. C. (2011). Motivating by enriching jobs to make them more interesting and challenging. *International Journal of Management, Business, and Administration, 15*(1), 1–11.

Maslow, A. H. (1954). *Motivation and personality*. Harper & Row.

Maslow, A. H. (1970). *Motivation and personality* (2nd ed.). Harper & Row.

McAnally, K., & Hagger, M. S. (2024). Self-determination theory and workplace outcomes: A conceptual review and future research directions. *Behavioral Sciences, 14*(6), 428. https://doi.org/10.3390/bs14060428

McClelland, D. C. (1961). *The achieving society*. Free Press.

McClelland, D. C. (1985). *Human motivation*. Scott, Foresman.

O'Connor, D., & Yballe, L. (2007). Maslow revisited: Constructing a road map of human nature. *Journal of Management Education, 31*(6), 738–756. https://doi.org/10.1177/1052562907307639

Pink, D. H. (2011). *Drive: The surprising truth about what motivates us*. Riverhead Books.

Ryan, R. M., & Deci, E. L. (2000). Self-determination theory and the facilitation of intrinsic motivation, social development, and well-being. *American Psychologist, 55*(1), 68–78.

Sashkin, M. (1996). *The MbM questionnaire: Managing by motivation* (3rd ed.). Human Resource Development Press.

Sethi, B., & Stubbings, C. (2019, February 18). Good work. *Strategy+Business, 94*, 1–13. https://www.strategy-business.com/feature/Good-Work?gko=89684

Tatel, C., & Wigert, B. (2024, July 10). *42% of employee turnover is preventable but often ignored: With more employees now eyeing the job market, organizations must intervene*. Gallup. https://www.gallup.com/workplace/646538/employee-turnover-preventable-often-ignored.aspx

Timmreck, T. C. (2001). Managing motivation and developing job satisfaction in the health care work environment. *Health Care Manager, 20*(1), 42–58.

Yukl, G. A. (2001). *Leadership in organizations* (5th ed.). Pearson Education.

Other Suggested Readings

Campbell, J. P., Dunnette, M. D., Lawler, E. E., & Weick, K. E. (1970). *Managerial behavior, performance and effectiveness*. McGraw-Hill.

Maslow, A. H. (1943). A theory of human motivation. *Psychological Review, 50*(4), 370–396.

CHAPTER 7

Process Theories of Motivation

LEARNING OUTCOMES

After completing this chapter, the student should be able to understand:

- The various components of Expectancy Theory and how they affect an individual's level of motivation.
- Equity Theory and the methods to resolve inequity tension.
- The significance of the Satisfaction–Performance Theory.
- Goal-Setting Theory and the steps necessary for successful implementation.
- Reinforcement Theory and the four types of reinforcement.

Overview

Understanding individuals and what motivates them is a conundrum for healthcare managers, especially since we need to manage such different groups of employees. These employees vary not only in culture, age, race, and gender but also in their varying levels of education and experience. Daily, we manage a range of individuals, from staff with minimal education to highly skilled licensed healthcare professionals. Process theories can assist us in predicting employees' behavior so that we may influence their behavior, if necessary.

In this chapter, we examine five theories of motivation: (1) Expectancy Theory, (2) Equity Theory, (3) Satisfaction–Performance Theory, (4) Goal-Setting Theory, and (5) Reinforcement Theory.

Expectancy Theory

One widely cited theory of motivation is Victor Vroom's (1964) Expectancy Theory (also referred to as the VIE Theory). Expectancy Theory suggests that for any given situation, the level of a person's motivation ("force" in Vroom's conceptualization) concerning performance

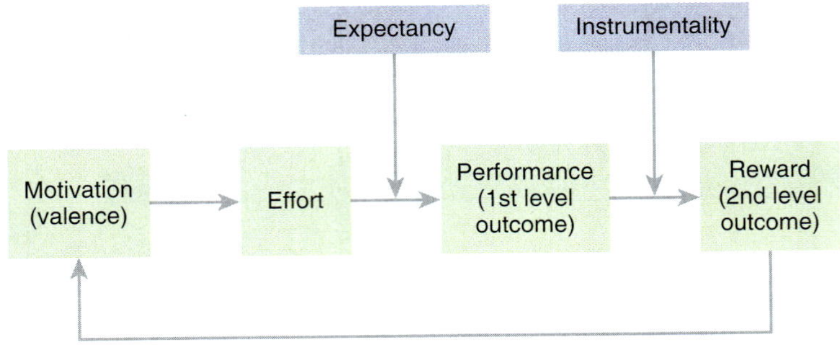

Figure 7-1 Vroom's Expectancy Theory (VIE)

depends on (1) the desire for a particular outcome, (2) the perception that individual job performance is related to obtaining the desired outcome, and (3) the perceived probability that individual effort will lead to the required performance. The theory may be expressed as $M = V \times I \times E$; see **Figure 7-1**.

Vroom (1964) explains that the force that drives a person to perform depends on valence, instrumentality, and expectancy.

Valence is the strength of an individual's want, need, or dislike of a particular outcome. An outcome has a positive valence when the person wants to attain the outcome, a valence of zero when the person is indifferent to achieving the outcome, and a negative valence when the person does not wish to obtain the outcome. Thus, valence can have a wide range of positive and negative values. The strength of a person's desire for, or aversion to, an outcome is based on the intrinsic properties of an outcome that are valued or not (a second-level outcome in Vroom's conceptualization) and/or on the anticipated satisfaction or dissatisfaction associated with other outcomes that are related to any given outcome (a first-level outcome in Vroom's conceptualization). For example, some workers may value an opportunity for a promotion because of their need for achievement. For these individuals, the promotion is positively related to or instrumental to obtaining another outcome, achievement. Others might not want the promotion because it would require an additional commitment of time and, therefore, would reduce time with family or friends. For these individuals, the promotion is negatively related to or instrumental to another outcome: the need for affiliation.

Instrumentality is an individual's perception that their performance is positively or negatively related to other outcomes. It is an outcome–outcome association. In other words, an individual will perform in a specific manner because they believe that behavior will be rewarded with something of value to the person. For example, one might assume that producing both high-quality and high-quantity work will result in a promotion.

Expectancy is the perception that effort will positively influence performance. It is an action–outcome association. It is a momentary belief concerning the likelihood that a particular act (effort) will be followed by a specific outcome (performance). Expectancies can be described in terms of their strength. Maximal strength is indicated by the certainty that the act *will* be followed by the outcome, while minimal (or zero) strength is indicated by the certainty that the act will *not* be followed by the outcome. For example, one might perceive that if they work overtime, the management report will be completed by the deadline (maximal strength).

However, the expectancy strength is minimal if the employee perceives the deadline as unrealistic because of the time required to complete the report.

Newsom (1990) summarized Expectancy Theory with what he termed the "Nine C's":

1. *Challenge*: Does the individual have to work hard to perform the job well? Managers need to review an employee's job design. Is the job routine and unchallenging? Does it incorporate Herzberg's Two-Factor Theory motivators?
2. *Criteria*: Does the individual know the difference between good and poor performance? Managers need to effectively communicate to employees the task's responsibilities, requirements, and how the employee will be measured for their successful completion. A manager should not assume that an employee knows the criteria for performing satisfactorily. In addition, managers need to provide feedback so that employees are aware of what they are doing right and what needs to be improved.
3. *Compensation*: Do the outcomes associated with good performance reward the individual? Nadler and Lawler (1983) discussed the mixed message an organization sends to employees when employees are rewarded for seniority rather than performance. The organization gets behavior-oriented toward safe, secure employment rather than efforts directed at performing well.
4. *Capability*: Does the individual have the ability to perform the job well? Employees lacking the necessary skills, knowledge, and experience to perform a task well will become frustrated and will likely avoid future growth opportunities.
5. *Confidence*: Does the individual believe they can perform well? Employees need to believe that they can perform a task well. An employee might have knowledge and skills, but might not see themselves as having the ability to perform the task well. This may be based on past experiences of failure.
6. *Credibility*: Does the individual believe that management will deliver on promises? Managers must deliver what they promised.
7. *Consistency*: Does the individual believe that all workers receive similar preferred outcomes for good performance and similar less-preferred outcomes for poor performance? Managers need to treat all employees equally based on objective criteria.
8. *Cost*: What does it cost an individual in time and effort to perform well?
9. *Communication*: Does management communicate well and consistently with the individual to affect the other eight Cs? Managers need to set clear goals and provide the right rewards for different people, as shown in **Figure 7-2**.

Expectancy Theory benefits managers because it helps them understand a worker's behavior. An employee's lack of motivation may be caused by indifference toward, or desire to avoid, the existing outcomes. Expectancy theory assumes that individuals calculate the costs and benefits when choosing among alternative behavioral actions. For example, if an employee wants to move up the corporate ladder, then a promotion has a high *valence* for that employee. If the employee believes that high performance will result in excellent evaluation ratings, then the employee has a high *expectancy*. However, suppose the employee thinks the organization will not promote from within. In that case, the employee has low *instrumentality* and will not be motivated to perform their job at a high level. So the important question for managers to ask is, "What rewards (outcomes) do my employees value?" (see **Case Study 7-1**).

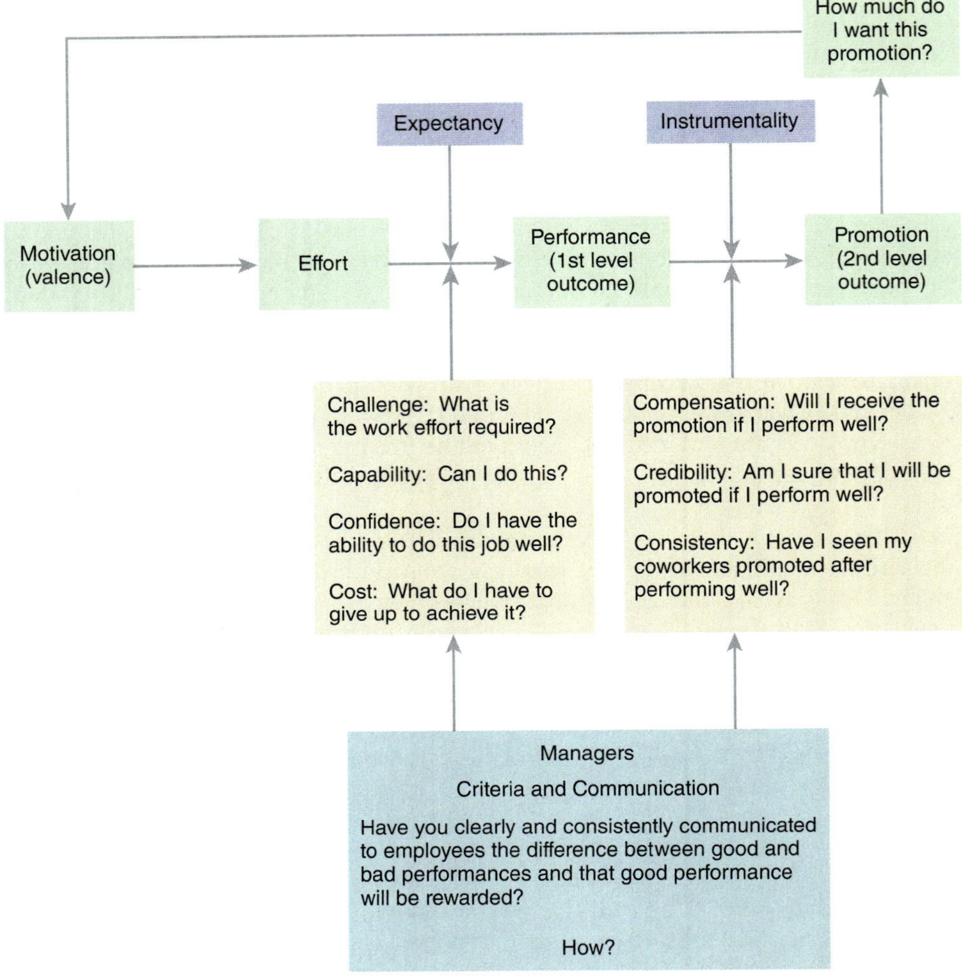

Figure 7-2 Application of Expectancy Theory Using Newsom's Nine C's

CASE STUDY 7-1 A Step Forward

Ashley Brooks, a 27-year-old registered nurse, lives with her two young children in a modest townhouse near the hospital where she has worked for the past 5 years. She enjoys the familiarity of her current unit, supportive colleagues, and a stable schedule of three 12-hour shifts each week. Her mother helps with childcare during the week, making the arrangement sustainable.

Recently, Ashley learned that a neighboring health system is offering tuition support for nurses who enroll in a full-time master's program in nursing leadership. The program begins in August and requires a commitment to work part-time evening or weekend shifts at the sponsoring hospital while attending on-campus classes during the day. In return, tuition is covered, and graduates are given preference for internal leadership roles upon completion.

To participate, Ashley would need to resign from her current role and start over as a new employee at the other facility. This would mean adjusting to a different culture, navigating a new team, and temporarily giving up her seniority. The timing is difficult—her children will be starting school soon, and she relies on a consistent routine to manage their care. She also worries about missing key moments in their lives, as well as losing touch with friends and extended family during such a demanding period.

Still, the opportunity to advance her career and secure a more stable future is compelling.

Using Vroom's Expectancy Model, explain Ashley's motivation to pursue her education.

Data from Gyurko, C. G. (2011). A synthesis of Vroom's model with other social theories: An application to nursing education. *Nursing Education Today*, 31(5), 507. https://doi.org/10.1016/j.nedt.2010.09.004

Equity Theory

In his Equity Theory, J. Stacy Adams (1963, 1965) proposed that a person evaluates their outcomes and inputs by comparing them with those of others. Adams's Equity Theory is grounded in social-exchange theories and rests on two key assumptions. The first is that individuals evaluate their social relationships similarly to how they assess economic transactions. Social relationships function as exchange processes, where individuals contribute (invest) with the expectation of receiving certain outcomes (Mowday, 1983).

The second assumption focuses on how individuals determine whether an exchange is satisfactory. Satisfaction is likely when the balance between contributions and outcomes is perceived as equal among all parties (Mowday, 1983). However, dissatisfaction arises if an individual perceives an imbalance, creating internal tension. For instance, an employee who believes their salary fairly reflects their experience and education may feel demotivated upon discovering that colleagues with similar credentials earn more, potentially leading to reduced productivity.

Equity Theory identifies two main components: inputs and outcomes. Inputs include an employee's experience, education, effort, skills, and abilities. Outcomes consist of rewards from the exchange, such as salary, bonuses, promotions, and recognition. Equity exists when an individual's input-to-outcome ratio is proportionate to that of others; see **Figure 7-3**.

Adams's theory has several important aspects. First, the determination of whether inequity exists is based on the individual's perceptions of input and outcomes, which may or may not be reality. Second, inequity will not exist if the person has high inputs and low outputs, as long as the other person has a similar ratio. Third, inequity exists when a person is either underpaid or overpaid. For example, if employees perceive that they are overcompensated, they may increase their level of productivity. If employees perceive that they are undercompensated, they may either decrease their level of productivity or attempt to obtain additional compensation.

Adams (1965) proposed that when an individual perceives an inequity, (1) it creates tension within the person, (2) the tension is proportional to the degree of inequity, (3) the tension created within the individual motivates them to relieve it, and (4) the strength of the motivation to reduce the tension is proportional to the perceived inequity. Adams states

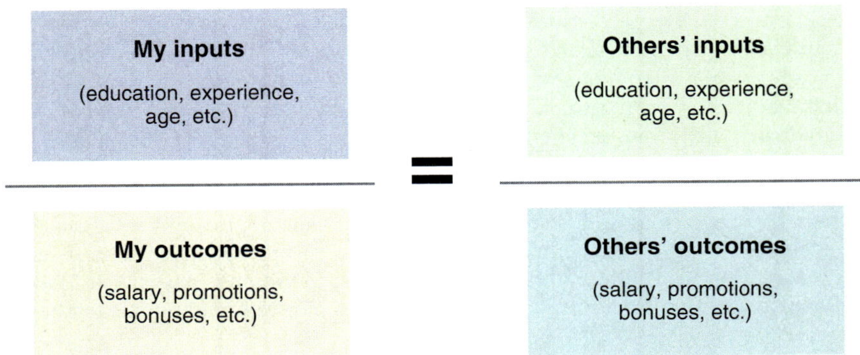

Figure 7-3 Adams's Equity Theory

that several cognitive and behavioral mechanisms are available to individuals to reduce the psychological discomfort (i.e., inequity tension) associated with the perceived inequity. He refers to these cognitive and behavioral mechanisms as methods of inequity resolution. The six methods described by Adams are as follows:

1. *Altering Inputs*: Reduce productivity, take longer breaks, and use sick days for personal activities, disengagement, and doing as little as possible.
2. *Altering Outcomes*: Try to obtain an increase in pay, a bonus, or a new job title, or resort to taking supplies from the company for personal use (i.e., stealing).
3. *Cognitively Distorting Inputs or Outcomes (Self)*: Describe how much harder they are working compared to others.
4. *Leaving the Field*: Transfer to another department or quit the organization.
5. *Distorting the Inputs or Outcomes of the Comparison Other*: Describe the other person's job as routine and unchallenging.
6. *Changing the Comparison Other*: Find someone in the organization more like themselves—another high-performing worker.

Equity Theory does not predict which method the individual will select. The behavior chosen by the individual depends on the situation with the goal of maximum utility (see **Case Study 7-2**). According to Mowday (1983), distorting the other's inputs and outcomes is the easiest method. Leaving the organization will be considered only in extreme cases. Managers need to be aware of how employees perceive inequities in the work environment because individuals will respond to feelings of inequity in various ways. For instance, in general, the level of demotivation displayed by the person will be proportional to the perceived inequity with others. However, for some employees, the slightest indication of negative inequity between themselves and others may cause deep disappointment and a feeling of injustice, resulting in demotivation or hostile behavior toward others. Other employees may lower their level of productivity and become disruptive in the workplace, expressing negative attitudes toward management, their peers, or both. Others may request additional compensation to increase outputs or seek a new position that provides for higher levels of outputs. In conclusion, if subordinates perceive that they are not being dealt with fairly, it is difficult, if not impossible, to motivate them.

CASE STUDY 7-2 I Don't Know What to Do

Katie was frustrated with her work situation and considered applying for an open RN position in the hospital's ambulatory surgery center to escape the ICU. At 39, she had worked at Good Point Hospital for 10 years, starting in housekeeping before earning her nursing degree through the hospital's tuition reimbursement program. Balancing full-time work, school, and raising three children was challenging, but she was proud to be the first in her family to earn a college degree. For 4 years, she enjoyed working as an RN in the ICU—until Beth joined the staff a year ago.

Talking to her husband, Mike, Katie vented her frustrations. "Beth has no work ethic. She spends half her shift on her phone, calls in sick before weekends, and constantly complains about being too busy." She explained that Beth's unfinished tasks, such as incomplete patient charts, created extra work. "I do not mind helping, but it takes 30 minutes, and with overtime frozen, I do not get paid to cover for her laziness."

Beth's attitude toward seniority also annoyed Katie. "She whines that I get first pick for vacations, but I reminded her I worked my way up. Everyone has to." Katie had spoken to their manager, Terry, several times, but nothing changed. "He says he'll talk to her, but he never does. He is too overwhelmed managing three departments."

Feeling unsupported and overburdened, Katie was unsure what to do. "I'm not Beth's supervisor, but I'm stuck covering for her. I'm so frustrated, I'm ready to leave the ICU."

Using Adams's Equity Theory, discuss Katie's motivation to quit the ICU.

Satisfaction–Performance Theory

One of the major criticisms of Expectancy Theory is that it does not take into account the relationship between employee performance and job satisfaction. Therefore, Lyman Porter and Edward Lawler (1968a) extended the expectancy theory and incorporated equity theory into a model to reflect the relationship between an employee's performance and job satisfaction. Job satisfaction is related to absenteeism, turnover, and well-being. This is of great concern to organizations because turnover and absenteeism directly influence an entity's effectiveness (Lawler, 1983). As Lawler points out,

> Absenteeism is very costly because it interrupts scheduling, creates a need for overstaffing, increases costs; turnover is expensive because of the many costs incurred in recruiting and training replacement employees. Because satisfaction is manageable and influences absenteeism and turnover, organizations can control them. By keeping satisfaction high and specifically by seeing that the best employees are the most satisfied, organizations can retain those employees they need the most. (p. 87)

Interestingly, prior to Porter and Lawler (1968a), no motivational model had directly dealt with the relationship between satisfaction and performance (Luthans, 2002). The Porter and Lawler model does not predict who is satisfied; it simply gives the conditions that lead to employees experiencing feelings of satisfaction or dissatisfaction (Lawler, 1983). The researchers believe that performance leads to satisfaction rather than satisfaction leading to improved performance.

The Porter and Lawler model reflects the idea that satisfaction results from performance itself, the rewards for performance, and the perceived equitability of those rewards (see **Figure 7-4**).

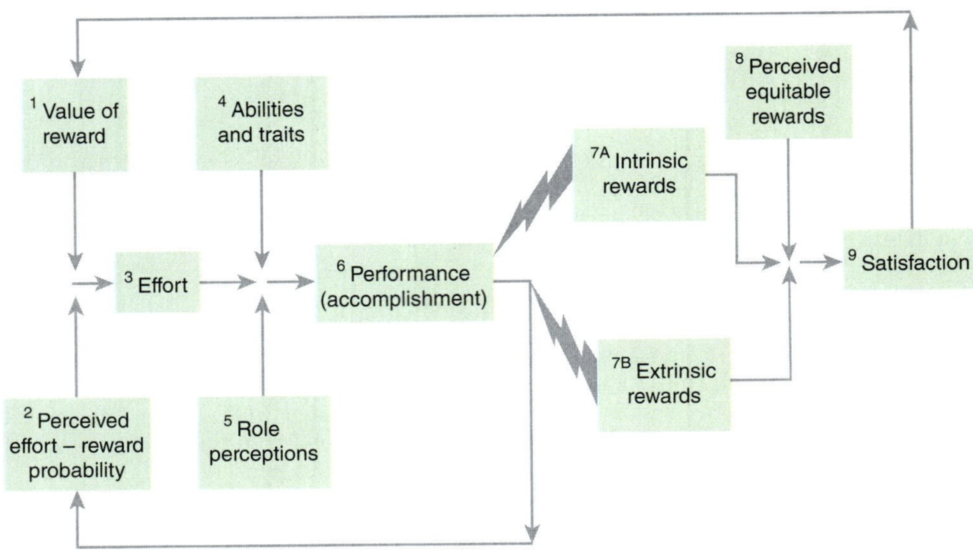

Figure 7-4 Porter–Lawler Satisfaction–Performance Model

Porter and Lawler (1968a) stated that job satisfaction is generated when an employee receives rewards for their performance. These rewards can be intrinsic (e.g., sense of accomplishment) or extrinsic (e.g., bonus). An employee's degree of satisfaction will be proportionate to the rewards they believe they are receiving.

An important aspect of Porter's and Lawler's theory is that the amount of the reward an employee receives may be unrelated to how well they have performed (e.g., pay increases based on seniority or labor union agreements). There will be minimal correlation between satisfaction and job performance for employees whose rewards are tied to external factors versus receiving rewards based on performance. However, if an employee holds a position (e.g., manager) in which rewards are received based on the quality and quantity of the employee's performance, there would be a correlation between satisfaction and performance. Porter's and Lawler's (1968a, b) research found that managers who are ranked high by their supervisors report significantly greater satisfaction than the low-ranked managers. More important is that, although the best-performing managers did not report receiving any greater extrinsic rewards (e.g., pay and security) compared to their counterparts, they did report receiving greater intrinsic rewards (e.g., expressed autonomy and the ability to obtain self-realization in the job). Therefore, the question is, "Does the organization actively and visibly give rewards directly in proportion to the quality of job performance for all of its employees?" If the answer is yes, then high satisfaction should be more closely related to higher performance if the employees value the rewards distributed.

The Satisfaction–Performance Model tells us two things. First, an employee will demonstrate higher performance if they value the reward, believe that increased effort will lead to that reward, and possess the necessary skills and clear role expectations. Second, an employee will experience satisfaction if the intrinsic and extrinsic rewards for their performance are perceived as fair—where satisfaction is determined by the alignment between perceived fairness and actual rewards. Job satisfaction is a complex and multifaceted concept. It is circumstantial and subjective for each employee and situation being assessed.

Goal-Setting Theory

In the 1960s and 1970s, Gary Latham and Edwin Locke (1983) performed laboratory and field research studies that determined that participants who were given specific, challenging goals outperformed those who were given vague goals, such as "Do your best." For example, in a 1974–1975 study, Latham found that unionized truck drivers increased the number of logs loaded onto their trucks from 60% to 90% of the legal allowable weight as a result of setting goals. They saved the company $250,000 in 9 months. In 1982, another group of unionized drivers saved $2.7 million in 18 weeks by adhering to assigned goals of increasing their daily trips to the mill (Locke & Latham, 2002). Based on their studies, Latham and Locke developed a goal-setting model. Although goal setting is a simple concept, it requires careful planning and forethought on the part of the manager; see **Figure 7-5**. A goal is the aim of an action or task that a person consciously desires to achieve or obtain (Locke & Latham, 2002, 2006). Goal setting involves the conscious process of establishing levels of performance in order to obtain desirable outcomes.

Latham and Locke suggest that there are three steps to be followed in successful goal setting: (1) setting the goal, (2) obtaining commitment to the goal, and (3) providing support elements.

1. *Setting the Goal*: The goal that is set should have two main characteristics. First, it should be specific, rather than vague, and measurable. For example, a goal statement, such as "Increase elective outpatient surgeries by 5% within the next 6 months" is specific, with a time limit for goal accomplishment. Second, the goal should be challenging yet reachable. Difficult

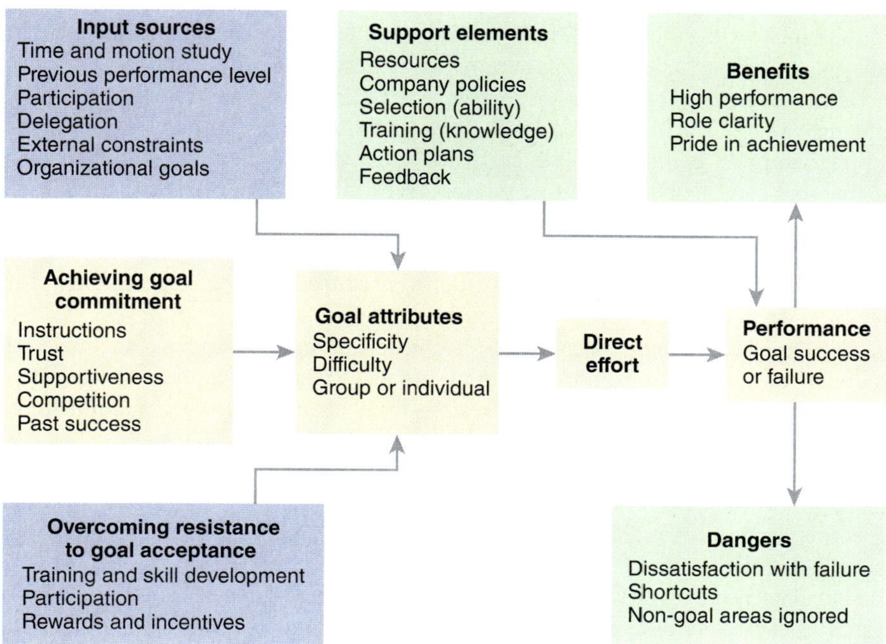

Figure 7-5 Latham and Locke's Goal-Setting Model

Reproduced from Latham, G. P., & Locke, E. A. (1979). Goal setting—A motivational technique that works. *Organizational Dynamics, 8*(2), 68.

goals lead to better performance. However, for employees with low self-confidence or ability, goals should initially be set at a level that is easy and attainable. For employees with high self-confidence and ability, goals should be made difficult but attainable. If employees perceive the goals as unattainable, they will not accept them and performance will not improve. In fact, the employees may experience dissatisfaction and frustration. Managers need to be conscious that setting unattainable goals may cause employees to view management with suspicion and distrust.

Latham and Locke stated that there are five possible methods, in addition to an employee's confidence and ability levels, that managers may use to determine goals for an employee. First, the manager could use time-and-motion studies to set an appropriate goal level. A second option, which would probably be more readily accepted, would be setting future goal levels on the basis of the average past performance of the employee. However, if the employee's past performance was unacceptably low, upward adjustments would need to be made. A third option would allow for the supervisor and subordinate to jointly set the goal. This participative approach has the advantages of being readily acceptable by both parties and promotes role clarity. The fourth method may be determined by external sources. This is very common in the healthcare industry; because third parties determine reimbursements, the goal is to deliver service at the lowest possible cost without reducing quality. The fifth method is determining individual goals that correspond to the long-term goals of the health services organization as determined by the organization's board of trustees.

2. *Obtaining Commitment to the Goal*: If goal setting is to be successful, the manager needs to ensure that subordinates will accept and remain committed to the goals. Appropriate pay (i.e., rewards) with the manager's supportiveness is usually sufficient for goal acceptance and commitment by the employee. Employees receive a feeling of satisfaction for reaching challenging, fair goals, which reinforces acceptance of future goals.

   Generally, employees resist goals for two reasons. First, they might perceive themselves as being incapable of reaching the goals. To overcome this resistance, managers need to provide training to improve employees' skills and knowledge, thereby increasing their self-confidence that the goal can be achieved. Second, employees might not see any relationship between their personal benefits (i.e., feeling of accomplishment or external rewards) and attaining the goals. Managers may use a participative approach so that employees have a feeling of control over the situation. Reward systems must be in place to directly compensate employees for reaching the agreed-upon goals.
3. *Providing Support Elements*: Managers must ensure that employees have adequate resources (e.g., financial, equipment, time, training, assistance) to reach their goals. Furthermore, company policies and procedures must not create barriers to employees' goal attainment. Employees need to trust that managers are supporting, not undermining, their efforts. For example, perhaps the goal is to train employees on new safety protocols. However, the manager's bonus depends upon the organization's financial performance, not the employee's implementation of the safety procedures. Therefore, the manager might not be motivated to allow employees to stop their daily tasks to complete the training (Fusion, 2019).

   Managers need to provide employees with an action plan of agreed-upon goals and rewards so clarity is in the process. In addition, feedback is essential. Employees must have access to information as to the status of their goal attainment. Finally, Latham and Locke point out that goal setting is not a solution to problems due to poor management or poor compensation of employees.

Reinforcement Theory

Reinforcement theory is based primarily on the work of B. F. Skinner (1953), who experimented with the theories of operant conditioning. Skinner's research found that an individual's behavior could be redirected through the use of reinforcement. Reinforcement theory suggests that an employee's behavior will be repeated if it is associated with positive rewards and will not be repeated if it is associated with negative consequences. Although reinforcement theory is not a motivation theory (at least not in the context we have been discussing), it does help managers to understand and influence, when necessary, behavioral change through the reinforcements they use. Reinforcement is a behavioristic approach, which argues that reinforcement conditions behavior (Robbins, 2003). Since reinforcement is an important means of understanding what controls an individual's behavior, it is included in motivation discussions; see **Figure 7-6** (Robbins, 2003; Tosi & Mero, 2003).

There are four types of reinforcement: positive, negative, punishment, and extinction.

Positive reinforcement occurs when a desirable outcome is associated with a behavior. Desirable outcomes can be simple and symbolic, such as words of praise, a certificate of accomplishment, or a month's use of the parking space directly outside the hospital's main entrance. To fully appreciate its effect, managers should use positive reinforcement only when an employee displays the desired behavior. For example, the director of nursing has attempted to reduce the turnover time (i.e., time required to set up an operating room [OR] after each surgical procedure) of the hospital's ORs to improve efficiency. The OR nurses formed a task group, and after many months and careful planning with full cooperation of the physicians and support staff, the daily turnover time decreased by 15% within a 6-month period. The decrease in OR turnover time allowed for one additional case to be scheduled per day. The director of nursing recognized the team's accomplishment by publishing it in the health system's newsletter and hosting a thank-you lunch for the department.

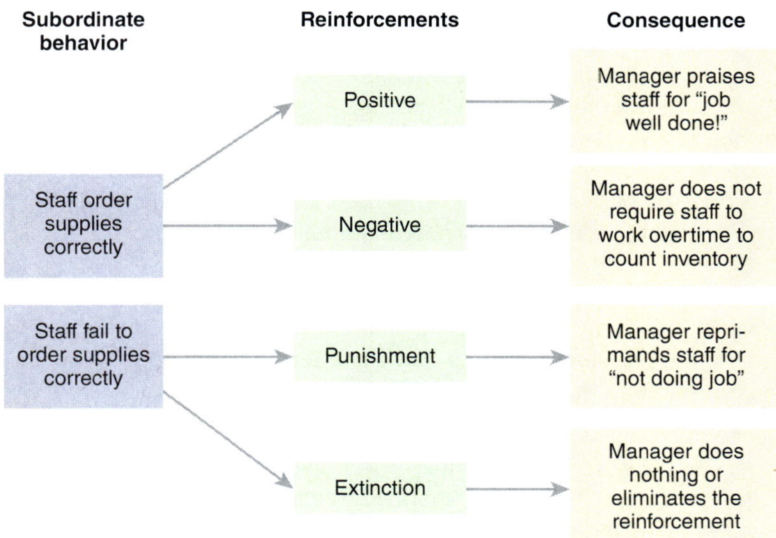

Figure 7-6 Reinforcement Theory and Types of Reinforcements

Negative reinforcement occurs when an unpleasant effect is eliminated or avoided, which, like positive reinforcement, encourages repeated positive behavior. In our OR example, the nurse responsible for ordering surgical supplies, by working with the hospital's technology department, designed an inventory system using bar codes that alert her when supplies are at a reordering level. With the use of technology, the system automatically transmits a message that an order must be placed to the purchasing department. By designing and implementing the new inventory ordering system, the nurse has eliminated her need to work overtime counting inventory and has eliminated the negative consequences (e.g., unhappy patients and physicians, lost revenues) that occur when a surgery case has to be canceled and rescheduled because the hospital did not have the necessary supplies on hand.

Punishment can come in two forms: negative consequences and positive consequences, both undesirable. A negative consequence is an undesirable response to an employee's behavior that is intended to stop the behavior from being repeated. For example, an OR nurse responsible for ordering supplies was reprimanded by the department's manager when she failed to order a required surgical instrument, causing an OR case to be canceled. (This reprimand motivated the OR nurse to design an inventory system so that the situation would not occur again.) A positive consequence occurs when something desirable is removed from the employee. For example, when the OR nurse failed to order the necessary surgical instrument, the department's manager required them to update the inventory supply list within 24 hours, meaning they had to work on their scheduled day off and cancel their trip to Disney World.

Extinction is the removal of an established reinforcement (positive or negative) previously used to reinforce an employee's behavior. This removal may weaken an employee's future behavior. For example, one hospital's OR department had a policy that if the room charge nurse's surgical cases started and ended on time (measured weekly), they would receive a gift certificate to a local restaurant. When there was a change in the hospital's senior management, this positive reinforcement was abruptly eliminated and the following message was issued: "It is your job to make sure the OR is run efficiently, which includes having the cases start and end on time. Therefore, we are eliminating the previously awarded gift certificate. If you have any questions regarding this new policy, please contact your manager."

Managers need to be careful about the administration of punishment reinforcements. Unless it is done carefully and appropriately, the effects can cause long-term consequences for the organization. Punishment can cause employee resentment, hostility, and turnover. Managers should punish only undesirable behavior and be very clear as to what constituted the undesirable behavior when discussing the situation with the employee; give reprimands or discipline actions as soon as possible after the behavior has occurred; administer punishment in private; and, when possible, combine negative and positive reinforcements.

Reinforcement schedules refer to the timing and frequency with which the consequences are associated with behavior. The scheduling of the reinforcement is important because the frequency will determine the time it takes to learn a new behavior (Tosi & Mero, 2003). Reinforcement schedules can be continuous, fixed interval, variable interval, fixed ratio, or variable ratio.

- A *continuous* reinforcement schedule requires the specific employee's behavior to be reinforced each time it occurs (e.g., the chief executive officer rewards all employees every time the hospital passes its Joint Commission accreditation). Research suggests that continuous reinforcement is the fastest way to establish new behaviors or to eliminate undesired behaviors.
- In a *fixed-interval* reinforcement schedule, the reinforcement is administered at predetermined periods (e.g., annual performance appraisals, weekly paycheck). A fixed-interval reinforcement

schedule does not appear to be a particularly strong way to elicit desired behavior, and behavior learned in this way may be subject to rapid extinction.

- A *variable-interval* reinforcement schedule allows reinforcements to be administered at irregular intervals (e.g., special recognition for successful performance, promotions to higher-level positions). This reinforcement schedule appears to elicit desired behavioral change that is resistant to extinction.
- A *fixed-ratio* reinforcement schedule requires the reinforcement to be administered after a predetermined number of behaviors have occurred (e.g., sales commission based on a number of units sold). Fixed-ratio reinforcement schedules can produce high rates of responses that continue as long as the reinforcement has value to the employee.
- A *variable-ratio* reinforcement schedule is evident when the number of behaviors necessary for reinforcement varies (e.g., bonuses or special awards that are applied after varying numbers of desired behaviors occur). Variable-ratio reinforcement schedules appear to produce desired behavioral change that is consistent and very resistant to extinction. (Tosi & Mero, 2003).

Consider the following scenario:

A hospital CEO is discussing her facility's experiences at trying to effectively manage the ordering and tracking of supplies in the hospital's OR department.

"We started looking at some product line assessments. As an example, a couple of years ago we met with two different groups of ophthalmologists to look at their costs on a case-by-case basis. We then compared what they used and might use, and determined the areas in which we might be able to standardize products and equipment... We had the ophthalmologists work with vendors and use a case supply cap, and we saved some money that way. Recently though, we've noticed that some of the ophthalmologists are drifting back to their old routines again, so I think this is something that you can't just do once and expect it to manage itself."

What reinforcement schedule would you advise the CEO to use in the future? Why?

Summary

In this chapter, we discussed various process theories of motivation. These motivation theories help healthcare managers to predict employee behavior. Managers can then effectively influence that behavior, achieving organizational success through increased job satisfaction.

Discussion Questions

1. Discuss the various components of Expectancy Theory.
2. Explain Newsom's Nine C's.
3. Discuss the two components of Equity Theory.
4. Explain the methods of inequity resolution.

5. Discuss the significance of the Satisfaction–Performance Theory.
6. Explain how the Satisfaction–Performance Theory relates to Expectancy Theory and Equity Theory.
7. Discuss the three components of the Goal-Setting Theory.
8. Explain how goals can be determined under the Goal-Setting Theory.
9. Explain management's responsibilities under the Goal-Setting Theory.
10. Explain why we include Reinforcement Theory in motivation discussions.
11. Discuss the types of reinforcements that are available to managers for changing an employee's behavior.
12. Discuss the various reinforcement schedules and why their timing and frequency are important.

CASE STUDIES

Case Study 7-3 What Can Joe Do About Betty?

Just before quitting time, Joe, the hospital's health information department manager, watched his three new trainees struggling with the complicated electronic medical records software they had to learn to use to do their jobs. Across the room, Betty, who was an expert with the software, was preparing to leave for the day, her tasks done ahead of time as usual. Also as usual, she gathered up her belongings and left without saying good-bye to any of her coworkers. "There goes the answer to my problem," thought Joe, "if only I knew how to reach her." With her expertise and experience in using the system, Betty would seem to be an ideal coach for the new employees. However, she had begged off from taking on training duties when Joe had asked her. Her reasons were that she wasn't comfortable telling anyone else what to do, didn't want the responsibility for someone else's work, and preferred to work by herself at her own job.

Joe was stunned by her refusal. He enjoyed helping his coworkers and thought that it was why he had advanced to department manager last year instead of Betty, who had more seniority and experience with the company than he did. Since her work was excellent, Joe hesitated to make it an "either you do what I want or you're in trouble" situation; he believed that employees worked best at what they wanted to work at. But his problem still remained: There was no money in the training budget, and there were no other employees as skilled with the system as Betty was. Was there an approach he hadn't thought of that he could use to convince her to help?

As Betty walked to the hospital's parking lot, she thought, "How could Joe think I would lift a finger to help him? I should have been the one promoted to department manager last year, not him. I'm the one with seniority and the necessary experience. In fact, I was the one who trained Joe when he first joined the hospital! Just because he has a master's in health information management and I don't should not have been the determining factor, but obviously senior management thought so when they selected him over me. I could care less what happens from this point forward. I only have 5 more years until I can retire with my full pension. As long as my work continues to be excellent, there is no way Joe can upset my plans. Not that he could, since he hardly understands the complexity of the software we use. It requires a person with a lot of technology knowledge and experience."

Using Vroom's Expectancy Theory (VIE), explain Betty's lack of motivation.

Case Study 7-4 How Much Longer Can Alice Continue Working for MGM Healthcare?

Alice has been a business/finance trainer for MGM Healthcare Consulting Group's clients for 3 years. She has enjoyed her job, coworkers, and the opportunity to combine her passion for teaching with healthcare finance. Though she wishes for a higher salary, she considers her pay fair given her responsibilities, experience, and education. Alice holds an MHSA degree, is certified as a healthcare finance professional through HFMA, and has a Lean Six Sigma Green Belt. Each year, her director has recognized her strong performance.

Alice's job requires extensive travel—8 months a year, working 12-hour days, 6 days a week. During the remaining 4 months, she works from the office, preparing training materials and conducting webinars. While this schedule is demanding, she has accepted it because it balances out over the year. She has never requested time off during her travel periods, and her director assured her that coverage would be available if needed.

Now, just as her latest travel period begins, Alice learns that her mother needs surgery and a week of complete bed rest. Her father can help, but Alice wants to be there for her. She informs her director, expecting flexibility, but is denied time off due to staffing shortages. Frustrated, Alice feels unappreciated—especially since this is her first request in 3 years.

Adding to her dissatisfaction, Alice has long struggled with her director's micromanagement. Every training manual revision and webinar must receive approval, causing delays, missed deadlines, and client complaints. These delays also impact her ability to earn bonuses for bringing in new clients. Additionally, the company is small, and after 3 years, Alice has hit the highest position and salary possible below the director level, leaving her with no clear path for advancement.

Although Alice enjoys her work and colleagues, she is growing increasingly disillusioned. She resents sacrificing her weekends for most of the year, losing income due to managerial inefficiencies, and facing a lack of career growth. Her motivation is fading, and she is unsure how much longer she can stay at MGM Healthcare Consulting Group.

Using Porter–Lawler's Satisfaction–Performance Theory, discuss Alice's job dissatisfaction and lack of motivation.

Case Study 7-5 Problems in the Purchasing Department

Employees in the purchasing department of a large hospital were suffering from lack of motivation. On the day shift, there had always been a few employees who were less productive than others. The other employees would have to pick up the slack to ensure that all supplies for the hospital were ordered on a timely basis. This would cause the departmental staff who were performing their jobs properly to become frustrated and angry because the other employees were not being held accountable for their low levels of productivity. There was clearly a disconnect between what was expected of all employees and what was actually being done.

Jack and Chris consistently worked hard and consistently exceeded the requirements of their jobs. They made sure that all daily requests for supplies were ordered so that there was no backlog to deal with at the beginning of each shift. However, they started to notice that Page and Betty were spending more time doing things other than their assigned jobs in the purchasing department.

Jack and Chris became less motivated to work as hard because they felt that they were picking up the slack for undeserving coworkers. The overperformance levels for the department began to fall. Backlogs started to increase, as did complaints from the other functional units of the hospital when requested supplies were not received in a timely fashion. Some surgical cases had to be canceled and rescheduled because the proper supplies were not available for the surgeons. Something had to be done!

Using the Goal-Setting Theory, create a plan that will motivate all the departmental staff to work to their full potential and perform more efficiently.

Case Study 7-6 How to Motivate Physicians to Improve Compliance

A hospital, located within a highly competitive market, is concerned over a decline in its performance on national quality indicators. Although many members of the medical staff are cooperative and compliant with the required documentation, a group of physicians don't seem to understand the importance of these measures. When either the hospital administration or members of the medical staff leadership confront these physicians, they often state they will try harder to be compliant, but ultimately don't change their behavior. Others simply choose to ignore letters sent to them or any attempts to discuss their noncompliance. Frustrated by the lack of cooperation by these physicians, the hospital and medical staff leadership decide to get tough on enforcement. They design a tiered response system. Physicians who do not meet the documentation requirements will be sent a warning letter. Failure to improve or respond will result in temporary loss of privileges. Continued lack of compliance will lead to loss of privileges.

Will this punitive system work to motivate physicians to improve compliance? If not, why not? Develop recommendations as to how to motivate these physicians to improve their compliance.

Reproduced from Tarantino, D. P. (2008). If you want to motivate physicians, you have to understand and fulfill what drives human behavior. *Physician Executive, 34*(5), 84–85.

Case Study 7-7 All in a Day's Work

Sarah Goodman, senior manager of network development for the Holy Managed Care Company, has just returned from a lunch meeting with the adviser for the Master of Health Services Administration program at State University, and now she is back on the job attending more meetings. At 1:30 p.m. she has a meeting to discuss pay issues. The Human Resources Department has evaluated the salary picture for the entire organization and is concerned that women are not being paid as well as men. They want input on a strategy to bring the pay issue into line so as to avoid a gender discrimination charge. Personally, Sarah wondered if she got paid as well as Dave, her counterpart in Tampa. Certainly, she has been there as long and worked about twice as hard as he seems to! He does seem to benefit from the "good old boy network," however.

At 3:00 there is a performance appraisal Sarah had scheduled with her assistant Maria. Sarah wasn't sure what to do about Maria. Her work was terrific from the standpoint of accuracy and amount. As long as she got a pat on the back pretty frequently, Maria was an ideal employee in a lot of ways. Sarah knew that Maria would be prepared for the interview, including her goals for the next 6 months. The problem was that Sarah really wanted to get Maria more involved with others in the department. If she wasn't able to get Maria ready to assume her position, how could Sarah ever hope to be promoted? Productive as she was, Maria just wasn't a "people person."

Then at 4:00, there is another performance appraisal scheduled. This one was going to be difficult. Janine was a fairly new employee and

Sarah loved the work she produced, but she didn't think she'd ever seen a more uptight person! She seemed to need to be told at each step what to do next and worried constantly about breaking the rules. Sarah had begun to think Janine had even invented some new rules! Last week, for example, Sarah had asked Janine to stay a little late to finish a project. She didn't discover until the next day that Janine had been late picking up her baby from the babysitter. Overtime wasn't required, and Sarah felt bad about causing the problem. She could have asked someone else to do the work but thought it might be a way of encouraging Janine to "get out of the box" a little.

By the time the meetings were over, Sarah figured she'd just have time to return her phone calls and scan the mail before it was time to go home. She'd promised Richard something special for dinner, mostly because she was planning to tell him about graduate school. The traffic would be awful, and she needed to stop by the store on the way. "Oh well! It's all in a day's work," she thought.

Discuss the various motivation theories reflected in this case study.

Case Study 7-8 Why Aren't My Employees Motivated?

Roger Harris, founder and managing partner of a health management consulting firm, oversees six partners and 20 professional staff members, all holding graduate degrees in health administration. The staff is evenly split between males and females, ranging from 25 to 35 years old. Among the 10 married employees, two have spouses working outside the home, and all married staff members have at least two children under 10 years old.

The firm emphasizes client service, enjoyment in work, and profitability. To attract top talent in a competitive labor market, salaries exceed market rates. Employees enjoy private offices, daily breakfast, weekly car washes, and office dry-cleaning delivery. Additionally, the firm provides home computers for weekend work during its peak season, from October to May.

During this period, employees work 55–60 hours per week. Benefits include two weeks of vacation, one week for continuing education, and one week of personal time, used by all employees. Despite increased billable hours for partners—up 12% in 2 years—staff billable hours declined by 14%. Employee turnover surged to 50%, a sharp rise from 10% 5 years earlier.

To address productivity and retention, Roger introduced a bonus program: employees billing 2000 hours annually received a 5% salary bonus, with double pay for hours beyond this threshold. While all employees met the minimum requirement, productivity did not increase beyond 2000 hours.

Seeking further improvement, Roger encouraged staff to publish in health management journals, agreeing to count writing time toward their billable hours. Employees welcomed this opportunity under that condition. To incentivize long-term commitment, Roger also promised partnership opportunities for those demonstrating technical competence and client retention skills. Historically, four of six partners had been promoted internally after 8–10 years of service. However, the most recent partner, hired externally, was promoted after just 3 years with the firm.

Roger views the firm as an excellent workplace, offering stimulating projects, strong compensation, and career growth. However, he remains perplexed by the persistent decline in staff productivity and rising turnover rate. Using Expectancy Theory, explain to Roger why nonpartner productivity level is low and why the firm is experiencing a high turnover rate among its professional staff.

References

Adams, J. S. (1963). Toward an understanding of inequity. *Journal of Abnormal and Social Psychology, 67*(5), 422–436.

Adams, J. S. (1965). Inequity in social exchange. In L. Berkowitz (Ed.), *Advances in experimental social psychology* (Vol. 2, pp. 267–300). Academic Press.

Fusion, J. (2019, February 12). *Motivation & goal setting theory*. Chron. http://www.smallbusiness.chron.com/motivation-goal-setting-theory-1187.html

Latham, G. P., & Locke, E. A. (1979). Goal setting—A motivational technique that works. *Organizational Dynamics, 8*(2), 68.

Latham, G. P., & Locke, E. A. (1983). Goal setting—A motivational technique that works. In J. R. Hackman, E. E. Lawler, & L. W. Porter (Eds.), *Perspectives on behavior in organizations* (pp. 296–304). McGraw-Hill.

Lawler, E. E. (1983). Satisfaction and behavior. In J. R. Hackman, E. E. Lawler, & L. W. Porter (Eds.), *Perspectives on behavior in organizations* (pp. 78–87). McGraw-Hill.

Locke, E. A., & Latham, G. P. (2002). Building a practically useful theory of goal setting and task motivation: A 35-year odyssey. *American Psychologist, 57*(9), 705–717.

Locke, E. A., & Latham, G. P. (2006). New directions in goal-setting theory. *Current Directions in Psychological Science, 15*(5), 265–268.

Luthans, F. (2002). *Organizational behavior* (9th ed.). McGraw-Hill.

Mowday, R. T. (1983). Equity theory predictions of behavior in organizations. In J. S. Ott (Ed.), *Classic readings in organizational behavior* (pp. 94–102). Wadsworth.

Nadler, D. A., & Lawler, E. E. (1983). Motivation: A diagnostic approach. In J. R. Hackman, E. E. Lawler, & L. W. Porter (Eds.), *Perspectives on behavior in organizations* (pp. 67–78). McGraw-Hill.

Newsom, W. B. (1990, February). Motivate, now! *Personnel Journal, 69*(2), 51–55.

Porter, L. W., & Lawler, E. E. (1968a). *Managerial attitudes and performance*. Irwin.

Porter, L. W., & Lawler, E. E. (1968b). What job attitudes tell about motivation. *Harvard Business Review, 46*(1), 118–126.

Robbins, S. P. (2003). *Organizational behavior* (10th ed.). Prentice Hall.

Skinner, B. F. (1953). *Science and human behavior*. Macmillan.

Tosi, H. L., & Mero, N. P. (2003). *The fundamentals of organizational behavior: What managers need to know*. Blackwell Publishing.

Vroom, V. H. (1964). *Work and motivation*. John Wiley & Sons.

CHAPTER 8

Attribution Theory and Motivation

Paul Harvey, PhD, and Mark J. Martinko, PhD

LEARNING OUTCOMES

After completing this chapter, the student should be able to understand:

- The basic premises of attribution theory.
- The differences between optimistic, pessimistic, and hostile attribution styles.
- The role of attributions, emotions, and expectations in motivating employees.
- Techniques that managers can use to promote accurate and motivational attributions.

Overview

This chapter discusses how attribution theory is used to understand the highly cognitive and psychological mechanisms that influence motivation levels. The chapter begins with an overview of attribution theory. We then discuss the different attribution styles that can bias the accuracy of causal perceptions, potentially undermining the effectiveness of motivational strategies. We then describe the impact of attribution-driven emotions and expectations on motivation. This is followed by an overview of techniques that healthcare managers can use to promote employee motivational attributions.

Attribution Theory

Before we describe the basic tenets of attribution theory, it is helpful to understand precisely what is meant by the term "attribution." An attribution is a causal explanation for an event or behavior. For example, a nurse who observes a colleague performing a procedure incorrectly will likely try to form an attributional explanation for this behavior. The nurse might conclude that the colleague is poorly trained, attributing the behavior to insufficient skills. People also form attributions for their behaviors and outcomes. For example, a physician might attribute their success in diagnosing a patient's rare disease to their intelligence, training, or good luck.

People typically engage in the attribution process countless times each day. For many of us, the process is so automatic and familiar that we do not notice it. However, research indicates that forming causal attributions is vital for adapting to changing environments and overcoming the challenges that we confront in our daily lives. When we experience desirable outcomes, attributions help us to understand what caused those events so that we can experience them again. When we experience unpleasant outcomes, attributions help us to identify and avoid the behaviors and other factors that caused them.

Fritz Heider (1958) argued that all people are "naïve psychologists" who desire to understand the causes of behaviors and outcomes. Attribution theory holds that attributions for these behaviors and outcomes ultimately help to shape emotional and behavioral responses (Weiner, 1985). A simplified depiction of this attribution–emotion–behavior process is shown in **Figure 8-1**. To understand these relationships, it is important to be familiar with the various dimensions along which attributions can be classified.

First, attributions can be classified along the dimension of *locus of causality*, which describes the internality or externality of an attribution. A physician who misdiagnoses a patient and attributes this medical error to their own carelessness (e.g., they overlooked one of the patient's symptoms) is making an internal attribution. If the misdiagnosis is attributed to faulty laboratory results, the physician is making an external attribution. The locus of causality dimension is particularly relevant to emotional reactions. Internal attributions for undesirable events or behaviors are frequently associated with self-focused negative emotions, such as guilt and shame. External attributions for the same behaviors and outcomes are generally associated with externally focused negative emotions, such as anger and resentment (Gundlach et al., 2003; Weiner, 1985).

Attributions can also be categorized along the *stability* dimension. Stable causes consistently influence outcomes and behaviors over time and across situations. Causes, such as intelligence and physical or governmental laws, are generally considered relatively stable because they are difficult to change. Unstable causal factors, such as the amount of effort exerted on doing a task, are comparatively easy to change. Unlike the locus of causality dimension, which primarily influences emotional reactions to events and behaviors, the stability dimension affects individuals' future expectations (Kovenklioglu & Greenhaus, 1978). When an outcome, such as poor performance, is attributed to a stable cause, such as low intelligence, it is logical to expect that the employee's performance will not change. Suppose the same poor performance is attributed to a less stable factor, such as temporary illness or insufficient effort. In that case, we can expect that the employee could improve their performance in the future.

We can consider attributions that are internal and stable (e.g., intelligence), external and stable (e.g., laws), internal and unstable (e.g., effort), or external and unstable (e.g., temporary organizational policies). Before examining the influence of these attributions on motivational states, it is useful to understand how attribution styles can bias and distort the attributions that individuals form.

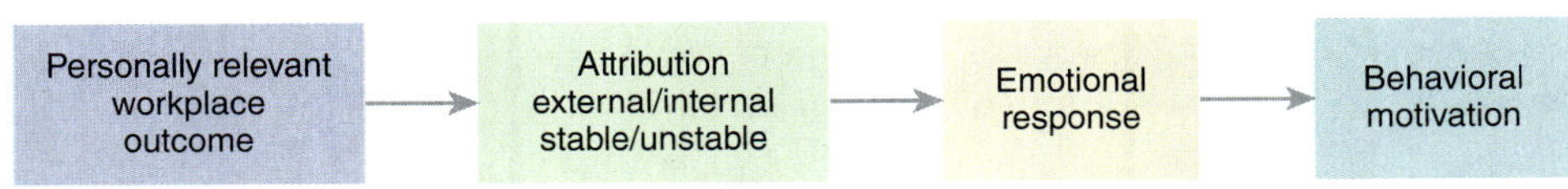

Figure 8-1 Attribution–Emotion–Behavior Process

Attribution Style

As with all perceptions, attributions do not always accurately reflect reality. We can probably all think of an instance in which someone failed at a task because of their actions but erroneously blamed the failure on others or circumstances. If we are honest with ourselves, we can each probably recall making such false attributions ourselves.

Astute observers may also notice that some people make these attributional errors more frequently than others. These individuals are said to have a biased *attribution style*. An attribution style is defined as a tendency to consistently attribute positive and negative outcomes to a specific type of cause (e.g., internal or external, stable or unstable). An **optimistic** attribution style is the tendency to attribute negative outcomes to external factors and to attribute positive outcomes to internal factors. This self-serving attribution style is called an optimistic one (Abramson et al., 1978; Douglas & Martinko, 2001). People with an optimistic attribution style often feel good about themselves and their capacity for success. However, this personal optimism may be unfounded and can set the individual up for disappointments in the future. Not surprisingly, employees with an unjustified sense of entitlement typically demonstrate high levels of this type of bias (Harvey & Martinko, 2009).

A **pessimistic** attribution style denotes the opposite tendency. This attributional tendency frequently attributes undesirable events to internal and stable factors, such as low intelligence, while attributing desirable outcomes to external and unstable factors, such as good luck. As the name of this style suggests, people who exhibit this tendency often lack confidence in themselves and are pessimistic about their chances for success (Abramson et al., 1978). This tendency can also promote depression and learned helplessness.

A **hostile** attribution style is similar to the optimistic style, with a tendency toward external attributions for negative outcomes. However, the two styles differ in that the external attributions for undesirable events associated with a hostile style are also stable. A study by Douglas and Martinko (2001) suggested that the stability of these attributions could promote anger toward the external entity (e.g., one's manager) and increase the likelihood of an aggressive response. Many highly publicized incidents of violence that have occurred in the United States were committed by individuals with a history of consistently external and stable causal explanations for the negative events in their lives. We can conclude that hostile attribution styles in the workplace are not only unproductive but can also be dangerous.

Before we discuss the implications of these attribution styles (see **Table 8-1**), and of attributions in general for employee motivation, one point should be clarified. In many situations, the causes of an event are clear. A driver who is rear-ended while stopped at a red traffic light is going to blame the other driver regardless of their attribution style. Attribution styles are unlikely to have an effect in situations where the causes of an outcome are obvious. However, when the causes are ambiguous, attribution styles are more likely to have an effect. A manager's goal should be to make (as well as to encourage) accurate and unbiased attributions so that employees' successes can be repeated and the causes of problems can be rectified (see **Exercise 8-1** at the end of the chapter).

Attributions and Motivational States

Our discussion of attributions and motivational states is divided into four sections, each of which describes a desirable or undesirable motivational state and the capacity of specific attributions and attribution styles to bring about these states. We first discuss two undesirable

Table 8-1 Summary of Attribution Styles

Attributional Style	Impact on Attributions	Examples
Optimistic	Biased toward internal (often stable) attributions for positive outcomes and external (often unstable) for negative outcomes.	Successful diagnoses are attributed to personal ability; misdiagnoses are attributed to inadequate information from others.
Pessimistic	Biased toward internal (often stable) attributions for negative outcomes and external (often unstable) for positive outcomes.	Successful outcomes are attributed to good luck; poor outcomes are attributed to a lack of personal ability.
Hostile	Biased toward external, stable attributions for negative outcomes.	Most workplace problems are attributed to a biased and vengeful manager.

states, learned helplessness and aggression (see **Case Study 8-2** at the end of the chapter). We then discuss two desirable motivational states: empowerment and resilience.

Learned Helplessness

After repeated punishments and failures, a person may become passive and unmotivated and stay that way even after the environment changes (Abramson et al., 1978; Martinko & Gardner, 1987). This phenomenon has been labeled "learned helplessness" because it describes a situation in which individuals believe that effort is futile because failure is inevitable. They have learned to be helpless because their efforts have not resulted in the desired outcome in the past.

Learned helplessness is a consequence of the reinforcement process. When people see that behaviors lead to desired rewards and outcomes, they are motivated to repeat those behaviors. When specific behaviors do not achieve desired outcomes, the motivation to perform those behaviors is lost. Learned helplessness was first observed by Overmier and Seligman (1967) in dogs that had been placed in a box with two sides in an experiment that would likely be considered cruel today. One side had an electric grid, and the other side was safe. Initially, the dogs were tethered to the electrified half of the chamber. Before the administration of an unpleasant but nonlethal shock, a light flashed. Because of classic conditioning, the dogs quickly learned to associate the flash of light with the impending electrical shock. After the conditioning was complete, the experimenters removed the tethers, which made escaping the chamber possible. Instead of leaping to safety when the light flashed, most of the dogs froze and braced themselves for the shock. The researchers concluded that the dogs had learned to be helpless, believing that the shock was inevitable regardless of their efforts.

This tendency toward learned helplessness is also common in people where organizational rules and norms can cause learned helplessness among employees (Martinko & Gardner, 1987). Specifically, organizational policies, norms, and leaders' behaviors that cause employees to feel that success or recognition is unobtainable are likely to inhibit motivation. For instance, a manager who routinely takes credit for their subordinates' successes while blaming them for their failures may find themselves with employees who see little reason to work any harder than is necessary to keep their jobs. Similarly, an organization that forces employees to follow outdated and ineffective procedures may find itself with employees who show little urgency or interest in their work, given that they expect the effort to fail. For example, a new nurse tries many times to bring up ideas for improving an inefficient process on their unit. They are repeatedly met with resistance and told they are too new to have an opinion. Eventually, they give up and stop trying to make a positive change. If you expect to fail, why bother trying?

The significance of organizationally induced learned helplessness is that, as Overmier and Seligman's experiments with dogs demonstrated, the helplessness often remains even when the barriers to success are removed. To continue the previous examples, if the unfair manager is replaced or restrictive policies are removed, we might expect employee motivation and performance to improve immediately. However, the reality is that employees who work under such conditions for an extended period often retain their learned helplessness and remain unmotivated even after the situation and conditions have changed.

The attribution process can explain this tendency. External barriers to success in the workplace can, ironically, promote internal and frequently stable attributions for failures while promoting external attributions for successes. Over time, these attributions can manifest themselves as a pessimistic attribution style, causing employees to accept blame for failures they did not contribute to while attributing successes to their manager or other external factors. To illustrate, a manager who consistently takes credit for departmental successes while blaming employees for failures can, over time, cause employees to believe and feel that they are incompetent at their jobs. This perception can remain even after removing the manager if proper steps to restore employees' confidence are not taken. This example also illustrates one of the downsides of the optimistic attribution style. Organizational leaders who demonstrate this tendency may feel good about themselves, but their tendency to take credit for successes and attribute blame for failures to others may cause their employees to lose confidence and experience learned helplessness.

Aggression

Aggression, another undesirable motivational state, differs from learned helplessness in several ways. Perhaps most significantly, unlike the diminished motivation associated with learned helplessness, aggression refers to a state of heightened motivation. The problem is that this motivation is focused on an undesirable behavior or goal.

Instrumental aggression describes behaviors targeted at obtaining a goal that the employing organization is not providing. For instance, an employee who feels that they are underpaid and steals from their employer is performing instrumental aggression. Hostile aggression refers to behaviors aimed primarily at harming another person or entity. For example, an employee who physically attacks a manager probably does not expect to get anything from the manager except the satisfaction of inflicting pain. Beyond the obvious surface-level differences in these forms of aggression, there are different underlying motivations (Martinko et al., 2005). Whereas instrumental aggression is motivated primarily by a desire to obtain something, hostile aggression is motivated by a desire to retaliate and harm others.

Both types of motivation may be sparked by the causal perceptions associated with hostile attribution styles. **Case Study 8-1**, at the end of the chapter, describes a study that indicated that individuals can more easily justify instrumental acts of deviance, such as forging paperwork or lying about their performance, in response to negative workplace events that were attributable to stable organizational factors (e.g., inadequate resources). Research has also shown that attribution of undesirable workplace outcomes to external and stable causes can increase the likelihood of a hostile response. Individuals with a hostile attribution style are more likely to engage in acts of hostile aggression than other people (Douglas & Martinko, 2001). In addition to empirical research evidence, anecdotal reports suggest that individuals with external attributional tendencies perpetrated a number of workplace shootings in the United States.

Several studies have suggested that an employee with a hostile attribution style can pose dual problems for managers. In addition to having a heightened tendency toward aggressive behaviors, employees with hostile attribution styles are more prone to perceive that they are also victims of such behavior. One study found that employees with hostile attribution styles were significantly more likely than other employees to view their supervisors as abusive in their behaviors toward them (Martinko et al., 2011). Building on this finding, a later study compared pairs of employees who shared the same supervisor and found that employees with a stronger hostile bias consistently rated the shared supervisor as being more abusive than more objective employees did. Although the perceptions of mistreatment in these employees may have been inaccurate, they were correlated with retaliatory behavior targeting the employees' supervisors (Harvey et al., 2014).

Employees who attribute negative events at work to external and stable causes are more likely than others to become motivated to engage in aggressive behaviors. A key element in determining the likelihood and type of aggression appears to be the perceived intent of the responsible party. Aggression becomes less likely when an undesirable workplace event is deemed to be caused by factors beyond the control of any specific party (e.g., an economic downturn) (Harvey et al., 2007). However, there is some evidence that some individuals will remain motivated to engage in acts of instrumental aggression in these situations (Martinko et al., 2005). When such individuals perceive that an external and stable factor caused a negative outcome and could have been prevented, hostile aggression toward the "guilty" party becomes more likely. This is probably due to the feelings of anger associated with such perceptions (Weiner, 1995). When causality and intent can be attributed to a specific person or entity, people often feel anger, which, in turn, frequently motivates acts of hostility.

Empowerment

Turning our attention to desirable motivational states, we first discuss the notion of empowerment. Empowerment refers to a heightened state of motivation caused by optimistic effort–reward expectations (Conger & Kanungo, 1994). Empowered individuals expect their efforts toward their goals to succeed and are, therefore, motivated to exert high levels of effort. Empowerment is also associated with high levels of innovation and managerial effectiveness (Spreitzer, 1995).

Empowerment among employees is generally good for overall organizational effectiveness. Research has shown that the causal attribution process explains how employees become empowered. Unlike learned helplessness, empowerment appears to result from attributing adverse workplace events to factors that are either internally controllable or external, unstable, and uncontrollable. Thus, a physician who misdiagnoses a patient's disease but believes that the error was due to a factor that is under their control (e.g., "I did not think to check for this disease, but I will know to do so in the future") is less likely to experience strongly negative emotions and learned helplessness than is a physician who attributes the error to their incompetence. Similarly, a physician who attributes a similar error to an external, unstable, and uncontrollable factor (e.g., the patient gave incomplete information and there was not enough time to run a whole battery of diagnostic tests) will likely feel optimistic about their future chances for successful diagnoses.

We can also expect individuals attributing positive events to internal factors, such as intelligence, skill, and effort, to experience empowerment (Martinko & Gardner, 1987). Individuals with an optimistic attribution style are likelier to demonstrate empowerment than those with pessimistic or hostile attribution styles. Recall that attribution styles can cause individuals to form inaccurate perceptions of causality. Therefore, sometimes people with an optimistic attribution style may feel empowered even when their skills and abilities are lacking. Promoting accurate attributions may be more important than encouraging optimistic attributions.

Resilience

Resilience is a "staunch acceptance of reality ... strongly held values, and an uncanny ability to improvise and adapt to significant change" (Coutu, 2002, p. 47). Research suggests that resilient people are relatively good at developing accurate attributions (Huey & Weisz, 1997). People with low levels of resilience tend to be overly external or internal in their attributions for adverse outcomes. Those with low resilience are likely to err in their attributions and are prone to blame others or themselves for their failures. Either of these attributional errors can promote adverse motivational outcomes. High levels of resilience have the opposite effect, helping people to keep their attributions in line with reality. If you can correctly identify the cause of something, your solution is more likely to work, which helps you bounce back faster.

Resilience, then, can be thought of as a factor that helps individuals avoid the attributional errors that can hurt motivation levels. By promoting accurate causal perceptions, resilience helps to keep people grounded in reality and prevent pessimistic and hostile attributional tendencies. It is also likely that resilience can help to prevent overly optimistic attributions, disillusionment, and unfounded optimism.

If we assume that resilience is good for promoting motivation through accurate attributions, the next logical question is, "Where does resilience come from?" We begin the next section by addressing this question, after which we discuss additional techniques for promoting empowerment while discouraging learned helplessness and aggression (**Table 8-2**).

Promoting Motivational Attribution Processes

In this section, we summarize five techniques that managers can use to promote and maintain employee motivation. These techniques are grounded in the formation of accurate and empowering attributions.

Table 8-2 Summary of Attributions Associated with Motivational States

Motivational State	Associated Attributional Tendency
Learned helplessness	Tendency to favor internal and stable attributions for failures, external attributions for successes
Aggression	Tendency to favor external and stable attributions for failures
Empowerment	Tendency to favor internal and stable attributions for successes, external and unstable attributions for failures
Resilience	Tendency to favor accurate attributions, not biased toward overly internal or external attributions for successes or failures

Screening for Resilience

In the previous section, we discussed the benefits of resilience for forming accurate and motivational attributions. Individuals' baseline levels of resilience appear to form very early in life (Masten, 2001). With proper emotional support, children have shown remarkably high levels of resilience in dealing with undesirable circumstances, such as poverty and violence. Conversely, we are probably all familiar with children and adults who break down in response to relatively minor problems. This suggests that resilience levels begin to form early in life. Drastic events, such as war and severe disease, often result in increased resilience levels in adults, but these do not fall under the umbrella of "regular life events."

Employers may determine that their organization requires a high level of resilience among employees. Hospitals, for example, can provide a very stressful and emotionally draining working environment. If employees form overly hostile or pessimistic attributions in response to the negative events that are bound to happen in such settings, motivational problems are likely to arise. This type of organization will probably benefit from a resilient workforce. A less stressful organization, by contrast, might not require such resilience among employees.

Organizations, such as hospitals, that require high levels of resilience should try to attract and hire individuals who demonstrate high levels of resilience. Although it is unlikely that they can drastically increase their employees' resilience levels in the short term, managers can try to form a workforce with high preexisting levels. Asking potential candidates to describe past hardships and how they responded to them is likely to shed light on both candidates' resilience levels and attributional tendencies (Campbell & Martinko, 1998).

Attributional Training

Although resilience is a relatively stable and unchanging personal characteristic, accurate and optimistic attributional tendencies can be fostered in other ways; one technique for accomplishing this is attributional training (Martinko & Gardner, 1987). This can take several forms, one of which is measuring employees' attribution styles with an existing assessment device (for examples of these instruments, Kent & Martinko, 1995; Lefcourt, 1991; Lefcourt et al., 1979; Peterson et al., 1985; Peterson et al., 1982; Russell, 1982) and discussing their attributional biases with them. Often, by simply realizing that they favor overly optimistic, pessimistic, or hostile attributions, individuals can begin to deliberately adjust their "perceptual lenses" to correct for their biases. Over time, this correction can become subconscious, allowing employees to form accurate attributions without additional cognitive effort.

A second form of attributional training is less formal and involves discussing the causes of employees' successes and failures on a case-by-case basis. This can help employees understand both the internal and external factors involved with workplace outcomes by helping them see the big picture in terms of the multiple personal and situational factors that are likely to contribute to positive and negative events. This promotes a more thorough causal search process and can help employees avoid the cognitive shortcuts that enable overly optimistic, pessimistic, or hostile attributions.

Immunization

Another technique Martinko and Gardner (1987) recommended is to immunize against demotivational attributions by enabling successes early in an employee's career or tenure with an organization. An employee who fails miserably at the first few tasks assigned in a new position may quickly decide that they cannot succeed (an internal and somewhat stable attribution). However, suppose they can tackle easier assignments before engaging in more difficult tasks. In that case, they will likely see that they have the basic ability to succeed at the job. This will probably promote optimistic attributions throughout the employee's tenure by initially providing a basic confidence level.

Increasing Psychological Closeness

In addition to individual attributional biases, employees can become the unwitting victims of their managers' inaccurate attributional tendencies (Martinko, 1995). Managers provide an important and often highly valued source of feedback for employees. Suppose this feedback consistently attributes blame for negative outcomes to employees' internal characteristics. In that case, employees might accept the feedback as accurate even if it is not and might then experience organizationally induced learned helplessness (Martinko & Gardner, 1987).

Research suggests that people in observational capacities (which is often the case for managers) frequently tend to be overly dispositional in their attributions for others' performance (Jones & Nisbett, 1971). They tend to focus on the influence of actors' effort and ability levels while overlooking situational factors that contribute to performance. In other words, managers can be overly burdensome on employees with low performance. Managers might also demonstrate an optimistic attribution style and take credit for the successes of their departments without giving credit to their subordinates, while also blaming employees when the department's performance suffers. Again, these tendencies can be demotivational, particularly if employees believe their managers' attributional explanations for their performance.

One technique for avoiding this tendency is to promote psychological closeness. Psychological closeness describes the extent to which two or more people form the same perceptions of their situation. Research has shown that managers with direct experience with their employees' work are less likely to form inaccurate attributions regarding employee performance. Managers who have little or no experience with their employees' tasks (or who have not performed them in a long time) appear to be less familiar with the situational challenges associated with the work and are more likely to blame employees' effort and ability levels when their performance is low (Fedor & Rowland, 1989).

To increase psychological closeness between managers and employees, organizations can work to ensure that managers have experience with the work their subordinates perform. This can be accomplished through internal promotions (i.e., selecting future managers from the pool of employees currently performing the job to be supervised) and by requiring existing managers to perform the jobs they manage from time to time. These techniques ensure that managers are familiar with the internal and external factors associated with performance, allowing more accurate and motivational attributional feedback to be formed and communicated to employees.

Multiple Raters of Performance

A final recommendation for improving the accuracy and motivational capacity of employees' attributions is to use multiple performance raters when possible (Martinko, 2002). As mentioned previously, managers can demonstrate attribution styles that bias them toward demotivational explanations for employee performance. The use of multiple performance raters can offset this tendency.

An illustrative example of this style of judging performance is using multiple judges to evaluate figure skaters in the Olympics. This system is used to help ensure that potential biases held by one or more raters can be offset by the accuracy or counteracting biases of other judges. Similarly, organizations can use more than one individual to rate the performance of employees. A common example is known as 360-degree evaluations, in which peers, managers, subordinates, customers, and employees rate performance. Although each of these parties may demonstrate some attributional inaccuracy, the hope is that through the use of multiple sources, an accurate picture of the causes of each employee's successes and failures will emerge. With this information, the proper steps can be taken to correct poor performance and encourage future successes, ultimately promoting employee empowerment (see Case Study 8-1 at the end of the chapter).

Conclusion

Our overarching goal in this chapter is to illustrate the importance of attributional perceptions in predicting employee motivation. One of the key findings from research on this topic is that internal and stable attributions for successes in the workplace and external and unstable attributions for adverse workplace events are associated with higher levels of empowerment. However, such attributions are desirable only when they are accurate. If an employee fails at a task because they are not cut out for the type of work being performed, it is generally better for them to realize that the task is too demanding. Similarly, suppose failures are caused by unstable internal factors, such as insufficient effort. In that case, employees must make that attribution even if it is not the most desirable short-term conclusion. These accurate attributions help steer employees toward empowerment, and managers can assist in the process by providing honest and accurate assessments of the causes of employees' performance.

Discussion Questions

1. What is an attribution?
2. Differentiate between optimistic, pessimistic, and hostile attribution styles.
3. Why might an optimistic attribution style be undesirable?
4. How can different types of attributions and attribution styles encourage high or low levels of learned helplessness, aggression, and empowerment?
5. How does resilience promote motivational attributions?
6. How can organizational leaders promote accurate and motivating attributions among their employees?

CASE STUDIES AND EXERCISE

Case Study 8-1 Managing Employees' Attributions

David, who was just promoted to manage a small medical transcription department, has inherited a problem. His predecessor recently completed the staff's annual performance evaluations, and it is now time to distribute annual raises based, in large part, on these evaluations. Of the seven employees whom David now manages, all received fairly strong evaluations, mostly in the "above average" range, although none received the highest rating of "excellent." The budget for David's department will not be growing much for the next few years, and there is very little room for salary increases. Had any of the employees achieved the highest performance level, David might have been able to apply for extra merit pay funding, but this does not appear to be an option.

Because all seven employees received relatively strong evaluations and there was not much difference between the highest and lowest performers, David has decided to allocate the raises equally among them. However, these raises will probably be disappointingly small. David is trying to decide how to break the disappointing news to his staff in the least demotivational way possible. He is weighing the following options:

1. Explain to the staff that they deserve larger raises but, given the long-term departmental budget, this was the best he could do for them.
2. Explain to the staff that he could have gotten them larger raises if their performance levels had been higher.
3. Explain to the staff that they deserve larger raises and that he, as their manager, failed them by not doing more for them.
4. Explain to the staff that these raises are fair, given their performance levels.

Discussion Questions

1. What attributions are being communicated in each of these explanations? Are they internal or external? Are they stable or unstable?
2. From a motivational standpoint, what potential pros and cons do you see for each of these explanations?
3. Which of these four options (or which combination of two or more) do you think would be the least demotivational for the staff? Why?

Case Study 8-2 "Unhealthy" Motivation: How Physicians Justify Deviant Behavior

We probably all know the feeling: something bad happens at work, and there are a few choices for dealing with it. You can go "by the book" and potentially suffer some unpleasant consequences, or you can bend the rules just a bit to make the whole thing go away. For example, suppose you miss a deadline by a few hours. You can choose to tell your manager or, because your manager happens to be in a long meeting, finish the job late and slip it under some paperwork on their desk, claiming that it has been there all day. You know what you *should* do, but you also know that the sneakier alternative is probably the path of least resistance. What would you do?

Your answer to this question would probably depend, at least in part, on why you missed the deadline in the first place. If you missed the deadline because you procrastinated all week and took an extended lunch break on the day the work was due, you might feel some guilt over lying to your manager. Attribution theory suggests that this is because you are attributing the missed deadline to an internal and unstable/controllable factor: insufficient effort. This guilt might, depending on other factors, such as your values and the consequences if your manager learns of the missed deadline, reduce your willingness to lie about finishing the work on time.

Your response might be different if you believe that you missed the deadline because the amount of time your manager gave you to complete the work was unreasonably short. If you worked late and skipped lunch all week but still needed a couple of extra hours to get the work done, you are much less likely to blame yourself. Instead, you will probably attribute the missed deadline to an external and relatively stable factor: your manager. Such attributions are associated with anger, which is a strong motivator of deviant behavior. This attribution-driven anger might help you feel justified in sneaking the work onto your manager's desk. After all, why should you get in trouble if the request was unreasonable?

To test the strength of attributions, such as these to motivate deviant behaviors, Harvey et al. (2007) examined the relationship between attributions, emotions, and the justification of workplace deviance using a sample of physicians. The researchers gave the physicians a hypothetical scenario similar to the one just described and asked them whether they would feel comfortable altering dates on paperwork to disguise the fact that a nonlethal procedural mistake had been made in diagnosing a patient. Each physician was given the same hypothetical scenario with one difference: The cause of the mistake (i.e., the attribution) was varied so that in some cases the mistake was due to internal and stable or unstable factors (the physician has poor attention to detail or was distracted) and in other cases it was due to external and stable or unstable factors (the physician's department is chronically understaffed, or an emergency meeting was called and the required test could not be ordered on time).

As you might expect, physicians were more likely to say that they would alter the paperwork when the cause of the mistake was beyond their control and was stable (i.e., likely to occur again). Before taking an overly dim view of these physicians, remember that the hypothetical mistake described in the scenarios was deliberately designed to be minor and inconsequential. Still, this study provides some insight into the power of attributions to motivate behaviors that we might not normally consider.

This justification process is an almost unavoidable part of life. There are always going to be times when it is tempting to break the rules because we feel that it is a justifiable response to a wrongdoing we have suffered. Indeed, many timeless stories are based on the notion of justifiable wrongdoing—Robin Hood returning the king's wealth to the peasants, for example.

There is a decidedly darker side to the justification process, however. Perpetrators of many serious crimes throughout history have, at least at the time of the crime, convinced themselves that they were justified in their behavior. In many cases, the justification can be traced to a desire for revenge resulting from the attribution of negative events to externally controllable, stable factors. Thus, we can see that there is more at stake than productivity when it comes to forming accurate attributions.

Exercise 8-1 Attribution Style Self-Assessment: Measure Your Attribution Style for Negative Events

To complete this assessment, begin by reading each of the hypothetical scenarios below and imagine them happening to you. Then, try to imagine what the most likely cause of each event would be if it *did* happen to you.

1. You recently received a below-average performance evaluation from your supervisor.
   What is the most likely cause of this outcome? ____________________
   a. To what extent was this outcome caused by something about you?
      Nothing to do with me 1 2 3 4 5 6 7 Totally due to me
   b. Will this cause be present in similar future situations?
      Never present 1 2 3 4 5 6 7 Always present
2. Today, you were informed that suggestions you made to your supervisor in a meeting would not be implemented.
   What is the most likely cause of this outcome? ____________________
   a. To what extent was this outcome caused by something about you?
      Nothing to do with me 1 2 3 4 5 6 7 Totally due to me
   b. Will this cause be present in similar future situations?
      Never present 1 2 3 4 5 6 7 Always present
3. You recently learned that you will not receive a promotion that you have wanted for a long time.
   What is the most likely cause of this outcome? ____________________
   a. To what extent was this outcome caused by something about you?
      Nothing to do with me 1 2 3 4 5 6 7 Totally due to me
   b. Will this cause be present in similar future situations?
      Never present 1 2 3 4 5 6 7 Always present

4. You recently discovered that you are being paid considerably less than another employee who holds a position similar to yours.
   What is the most likely cause of this outcome? ____________________
   a. To what extent was this outcome caused by something about you?
      Nothing to do with me 1 2 3 4 5 6 7 Totally due to me
   b. Will this cause be present in similar future situations?
      Never present 1 2 3 4 5 6 7 Always present
5. You recently received information that you failed to achieve all of your goals for the last performance reporting period.
   What is the most likely cause of this outcome? ____________________
   a. To what extent was this outcome caused by something about you?
      Nothing to do with me 1 2 3 4 5 6 7 Totally due to me
   b. Will this cause be present in similar future situations?
      Never present 1 2 3 4 5 6 7 Always present
6. You have a great deal of difficulty getting along with your coworkers.
   What is the most likely cause of this outcome? ____________________
   a. To what extent was this outcome caused by something about you?
      Nothing to do with me 1 2 3 4 5 6 7 Totally due to me
   b. Will this cause be present in similar future situations?
      Never present 1 2 3 4 5 6 7 Always present
7. You just discovered that a patient recently complained about the services you provided.
   What is the most likely cause of this outcome? ____________________
   a. To what extent was this outcome caused by something about you?
      Nothing to do with me 1 2 3 4 5 6 7 Totally due to me
   b. Will this cause be present in similar future situations?
      Never present 1 2 3 4 5 6 7 Always present
8. A large layoff has been announced at your organization, and you are told that you will be one of those laid off.
   What is the most likely cause of this outcome? ____________________
   a. To what extent was this outcome caused by something about you?
      Nothing to do with me 1 2 3 4 5 6 7 Totally due to me
   b. Will this cause be present in similar future situations?
      Never present 1 2 3 4 5 6 7 Always present

Enter the sum of your **A** scores here:
Enter the sum of your **B** scores here:

Scoring Key

Your **A** score represents the *locus of causality* dimension of your attribution style for negative outcomes. A score above 28 represents an internal attribution style, with scores closer to the maximum of 56 indicating a relatively more internal style (i.e., a tendency to attribute negative outcomes to internal causes). A score below 28 represents an external attribution style, with scores closer to zero indicating a relatively more external style (i.e., a tendency to attribute negative outcomes to external causes).

Your **B** score represents the *stability* dimension of your attribution style for negative outcomes. A score above 28 represents a stable attribution style, with scores closer to the maximum of 56 indicating a relatively more stable style (i.e., a tendency to attribute negative outcomes to stable causes). A score below 28 represents an unstable attribution style, with scores closer to zero indicating a relatively less stable style (i.e., a tendency to attribute negative outcomes to unstable causes).

Discussion Questions

1. According to this test, do you have an attribution style that favors internal or external attributions for negative outcomes?
2. According to this test, do you have an attribution style that favors stable or unstable attributions for negative outcomes?
3. Would you characterize your attribution style as optimistic? Pessimistic? Hostile?
4. If you were managing an employee with the attribution style that you identified, how would you help them to stay motivated when negative events occur?

Modified from Kent, R. L., & Martinko, M. J. (1995). The measurement of attributions in organizational research. In M. J. Martinko (Ed.), *Attribution theory: An organizational perspective* (pp. 53–75). St. Lucie Press.

References

Abramson, L. Y., Seligman, M. E. P., & Teasdale, J. D. (1978). Learned helplessness in humans: Critique and reformulation. *Journal of Abnormal Psychology, 87*(1), 49–74.

Campbell, C. R., & Martinko, M. J. (1998). An integrative attributional perspective of empowerment and learned helplessness: A multi-method field study. *Journal of Management, 24*(2), 173–200.

Conger, J. A., & Kanungo, R. N. (1994). Charismatic leadership in organizations: Perceived behavioral attributes and their measurement. *Journal of Organizational Behavior, 15*(5), 439–452.

Coutu, D. L. (2002). How resilience works. *Harvard Business Review, 80*(5), 46–55.

Douglas, S. C., & Martinko, M. J. (2001). Exploring the role of individual differences in the prediction of workplace aggression. *Journal of Applied Psychology, 86*(4), 547–559.

Fedor, D. B., & Rowland, K. M. (1989). Investigating supervisor attributions of subordinate performance. *Journal of Management, 15*(3), 405–416.

Gundlach, M. J., Douglas, S. C., & Martinko, M. J. (2003). The decision to blow the whistle: A social information processing framework. *Academy of Management Journal, 28*(1), 107–123.

Harvey, P., Harris, K. J., Gillis, W. E., & Martinko, M. J. (2014). Abusive supervision and the entitled employee. *The Leadership Quarterly, 25*(2), 204–217.

Harvey, P., & Martinko, M. J. (2009). An empirical examination of the role of attributions in psychological entitlement and its outcomes. *Journal of Organizational Behavior, 30*(4), 459–476.

Harvey, P., Martinko, M. J., & Borkowski, N. (2007, August 3–8). *Unethical behavior among physicians and students: Testing an attributional and emotional framework* [Conference presentation]. 2007 Academy of Management Conference, Philadelphia, PA.

Heider, F. (1958). *The psychology of interpersonal relations*. Wiley.

Huey, S. J., Jr., & Weisz, J. R. (1997). Ego control, ego resiliency, and the Five-Factor Model as predictors of behavioral and emotional problems in clinic-referred children and adolescents. *Journal of Abnormal Psychology, 106*(3), 404–415.

Jones, E. E., & Nisbett, R. E. (1971). The actor and the observer: Divergent perceptions of the causes of behavior. In E. E. Jones, D. E. Kanouse, H. H. Kelley, R. E. Nisbett, S. Valins, & B. Weiner (Eds.), *Attribution: Perceiving the causes of behavior* (pp. 79–94). General Learning Press.

Kent, R. L., & Martinko, M. J. (1995). The measurement of attributions in organizational research. In M. J. Martinko (Ed.), *Attribution theory: An organizational perspective* (pp. 53–75). St. Lucie Press.

Kovenklioglu, G., & Greenhaus, J. H. (1978). Causal attributions, expectations, and task performance. *Journal of Applied Psychology, 63*(6), 698–705.

Lefcourt, H. M. (1991). The multidimensional-multiattributional causality scale. In J. P. Robinson, P. R. Shaver & L. S. Wrightsman (Eds.), *Measures of personality and social psychological attitudes* (Vol. 1, pp. 454–457). Academic Press.

Lefcourt, H. M., von Baeyer, C. L., Ware, E. E., & Cox, D. J. (1979). The multidimensional-multiattributional causality scale: The development of a goal specific locus of control scale. *Canadian Journal of Behavioural Science, 11*(4), 286–304.

Martinko, M. J. (1995). The nature and function of attribution theory within the organizational sciences. In M. J. Martinko (Ed.), *Attribution theory: An organizational perspective* (pp. 7–16). St. Lucie Press.

Martinko, M. J. (2002). *Thinking like a winner: A guide to high performance leadership*. Gulf Coast.

Martinko, M. J., Douglas, S. C., Harvey, P., & Joseph, C. (2005). Managing organizational aggression. In R. Kidwell & C. Martin (Eds.), *Managing organizational deviance: Readings and cases* (pp. 237–260). Sage.

Martinko, M. J., & Gardner, W. L. (1987). The leader/member attribution process. *Academy of Management Journal, 12*(2), 235–249.

Martinko, M. J., Harvey, P., Sikora, D., & Douglas, S. C. (2011). Perceptions of abusive supervision: The role of subordinates' attribution style. *The Leadership Quarterly, 22*(4), 751–764.

Masten, A. S. (2001). Ordinary magic: Resilience processes in development. *American Psychologist, 56*(3), 227–238.

Overmier, J. B., & Seligman, M. E. P. (1967). Effects of inescapable shock upon subsequent escape and avoidance learning. *Journal of Comparative and Physiological Psychology, 63*(1), 28–33.

Peterson, C., Berres, B. A., & Seligman, M. E. P. (1985). Depressive symptoms and unprompted causal attributions: Content analysis. *Behaviour Research and Therapy, 23*(4), 379–382.

Peterson, C., Semmel, A., von Baeyer, C., Abramson, L., Metalsky, G., & Seligman, M. E. (1982). The attributional style questionnaire. *Cognitive Therapy and Research, 6*(3), 287–300.

Russell, D. (1982). The causal dimension scale: A measure of how individuals perceive causes. *Journal of Personality and Social Psychology, 42*(6), 1137–1145.

Spreitzer, G. M. (1995). Psychological empowerment in the workplace: Dimensions, measurement, and validation. *Academy of Management Journal, 38*(5), 1442–1465.

Weiner, B. (1985). An attributional theory of achievement motivation and emotion. *Psychological Review, 92*(4), 548–573.

Weiner, B. (1995). *Judgments of responsibility: A foundation for a theory of social conduct.* Guilford Press.

Other Suggested Readings

Schermerhorn, J. R., Jr. (1987). Improving health care productivity through high-performance managerial development. *Health Care Management Review, 12*(4), 49–55.

Sharma, M. K., Amudhan, S., Achar, M., & Vishwakarma, A. (2022). COVID-19 pandemic, risk, and blame attributions: A scoping review. *Indian Journal of Psychological Medicine, 44*(3), 227–233. https://doi.org/10.1177/02537176221091675

PART III

Leadership

Power is influencing other people's actions, thoughts, or emotions. When discussing power, the topic of leadership always enters into the conversation because the two terms are almost inseparable. In Part III, we attempt to answer the question, "What does it take to be an effective leader?" In Chapter 9, we provide an overview of the definition of power, the types, sources, and uses of power, and organizational politics. In Chapter 10, we discuss the early theories of leadership, such as the Great Man theory and trait theory. Chapter 11 focuses on the next generation of leadership theories: contingency theories and situational models. These theories state that leaders apply different styles in different situations, depending on the factors involved. Chapter 12 provides insight into some of the contemporary theories in leadership, such as transformational, servant, and collaborative leadership. These contemporary leadership theories look to the person and the organization's culture to determine what it takes to be an effective leader.

CHAPTER 9

Power, Politics, and Influence

LEARNING OUTCOMES

After completing this chapter, the student should be able to understand the:

- Definition of power.
- Difference between potential and kinetic power.
- Different sources of power.
- Ways in which managers develop a power base.
- Definition of organizational politics and the various political behaviors.
- Definition of upward influence and the various influence tactics categories.
- Effect of empowering leadership on individual and organizational performance.

Overview

Since 2002, *Modern Healthcare* has annually published a list of the 100 most powerful people in health care. *Modern Healthcare*'s readers develop the list. The readers are asked first to nominate and then to vote for individuals they believe have the greatest power to influence the U.S. healthcare delivery system. Burda (2003) related that the one theme that caught his attention was control. He stated, "Controlling something of value makes you powerful, and that's what the people on the list have in common" (p. 36). It should be no surprise to learn that many of the top 100 influential people each year are elected or appointed federal employees (with the President of the United States often taking the number-one position) who hold the purse strings on an annual budget over $6 trillion or have the power to impose, delay, or eliminate costly regulatory requirements on healthcare providers.

Power has been defined in various ways. Thibaut and Kelley (1959) defined power as having behavioral or fate control over another person's behavior. Mechanic (1962) defined power as any force that results in behavior that would not have occurred if the force had not been present. Siu (1979) defined power as the influence over people's beliefs, emotions, and behaviors, which is the definition adopted for our discussions.

Power exists only when there is an unequal relationship between two people and one is dependent upon the other (Emerson, 1962). Using the example of the annual 100 most powerful people ranking in health care reflects these two components of power: unequal relationship and dependency. Healthcare providers depend on the federal government for reimbursement, specifically from the Medicare and Medicaid programs. Any change in the levels of reimbursement can have significant positive or negative effects on the industry. For example, the Affordable Care Act of 2010 transformed Medicare from a passive payer to an active purchaser of higher-quality, more efficient health care through the value-based purchasing (VBP) initiative. The Centers for Medicare and Medicaid Services rule that denies payment for hospital-acquired conditions, referred to as "never events," strongly encourages patient safety efforts. There is an unequal relationship because of the federal government's ability to enact new regulations that require significant changes in how healthcare providers and suppliers conduct business (e.g., the Affordable Care Act of 2010 and the Medicare Access and CHIP Reauthorization Act of 2015).

Potential power exists when an individual has the ability to influence but does not use it (e.g., a supervisor sits at her desk completing paperwork but does not interact with staff). When the individual actually uses the power to influence, it is referred to as kinetic power (e.g., a supervisor awards a bonus to a subordinate for completing a challenging task on time and correctly) (Siu, 1979).

The concept of power is an integral part of organizational behavior. For example, power is central to attitudes, perception, and motivation, as well as leadership, group dynamics, and change management.

Sources of Power

French and Raven (1959) identified five bases or sources of social power: reward power, coercive power, legitimate power, referent power, and expert power. An individual is not limited to one source of power; individuals may hold and exercise multiple sources of power simultaneously.

1. *Reward power* is defined as the ability to give rewards, something that holds value to another individual. Reward power has two components. First, the individual (P) must perceive that the other person (O) has the ability to reward. Second, the reward must have some value to P. If O offers a reward to P and then fails to deliver, future attempts by O to change P's behavior by using reward power will have been diminished.
2. *Coercive power* is defined as the ability to punish by administering a punishment or withholding something an individual needs or wants. Coercive power stems from P's expectation that O will administer a punishment if P fails to conform to the influence attempt. As with reward power, for coercive power to be effective, P must perceive that O has the ability to punish or sanction, and this negative valence must have some value (e.g., avoidance of punishment) to P.
3. *Legitimate power* is authority given to an individual on the basis of a given role or position. There are three bases of legitimate power: culture, social structure, and delegation of power. In some cultures, certain groups are granted the right to prescribe behavior for others. For example, in some cultures, the elders or members of one sex are granted the power to demand conformity of behavior by others. Social structure is the second basis for legitimate power. In formal organizations, this power is granted by the position that someone holds in the company's hierarchy. The third base of legitimate power is the delegation of power by the legitimizing agent. For example, a department manager may accept the authority of a vice president in certain areas because the organization's president has specifically delegated the

authority to the vice president. It is important to remember that O holds legitimate power only if P accepts O as holding a legitimate power position.

4. *Referent power* stems from P's affective regard (i.e., attraction) for, or identification with, O. Interestingly, O has the ability to influence P even though O may be unaware of this referent power. Also, because P desires to be associated with or identified with O, P will assume attitudes, beliefs, or behavior displayed by O. Therefore, the greater the attraction, the greater the identification and the greater the referent power.
5. *Expert power* exists when P awards power to O on the basis of P's perception of O's knowledge in a given area. P evaluates O's expertness in relation to their own knowledge as well as against an absolute standard. The expert is seen as having superior knowledge or ability in very specific areas. Therefore, attempting to exert expert power outside of the specific area will reduce that expert power, and an undermining of confidence may occur.

Two other sources of power have been discussed: informational and connection (Hersey & Blanchard, 1982). A person who has access to valuable or important information possesses informational power. Connection power is related to who you know, vertically and horizontally, both within and outside the organization. These two sources of power are discussed further in the following sections.

Other Sources of Power in an Organization

David Mechanic (1962) found that employees without formally defined power positions exercise significant personal power within an organization by creating a sense of dependency. Employees create this dependency by controlling access to the following:

1. Instrumentalities, which include any aspect of the organization's physical plant or its resources (e.g., equipment, materials, and budgets).
2. People, including anyone within the organization or outside the organization, on whom the organization is in some way dependent.
3. Information, which includes knowledge of the norms, procedures, and techniques of doing business within the organization.

The most effective way for lower-level employees to achieve power is to have higher-ranking employees be dependent on them. Thomas Scheff's research (1961) provides us with an illustration of this dependency relationship and its power. Scheff's study involved a state mental hospital that failed to implement reforms because of the opposition of the hospital attendants. The failure was due largely to the ward physicians' dependency on the attendants. The dependency resulted from the physicians' short tenure, lack of interest in administration, and the many administrative responsibilities they assumed. An implicit trading agreement was developed between physicians and attendants whereby attendants would take on some of the responsibilities and obligations of the ward physicians in return for increased power in decision-making processes involving patients. Failure of the ward physician to honor their part of the agreement resulted in information being withheld, disobedience, lack of cooperation, and unwillingness of the attendants to serve as a barrier between the physician and a ward full of patients demanding attention and recognition. When the attendants withheld cooperation, the physicians had difficulty making graceful entrances and departures from the ward, handling necessary paperwork (officially their responsibility), and obtaining information needed to deal adequately with daily treatment and behavior problems. When the attendants opposed change, they could wield influence by refusing to assume responsibilities that were officially assigned to the physician.

Another example is the dependency of new physician residents on floor nurses in a large teaching hospital. These new physicians depend on the nurses to provide information to help them maneuver through the hospital maze to obtain the necessary patient care. How are tests ordered? What paperwork must be completed? Does the patient need authorization from their insurance company? The new residents depend on the nurses' goodwill. If the nurses withhold their cooperation, the physicians have little or no alternative but to attempt to decipher the hospital's policies and procedures by themselves, which would be a very time-consuming process.

Increasing complexity in organizations has made the expert or staff person more powerful as a result of the organization's dependency on their specialization, knowledge, and skills. Experts have tremendous potential for power by withholding information or providing incorrect information. For example, Mechanic (1962) discusses the situation of a lay hospital administrator (in contrast to a hospital administrator who is also a physician) who makes an administrative decision that physicians oppose on the basis of medical necessity. A lay administrator is not in a position to contest these claims independently. To evaluate these claims, the administrator would need to engage medical consultants to serve as a buffer between the medical staff and the lay administration.

Employees also form coalitions that demonstrate the power to get things done in a highly functionally structured organization, such as a hospital. Hospitals are complex entities organized into functional units, such as medical, nursing, administration, and physical plant, controlled at high authority levels. It is not unusual for coalitions to form at the intermediate and lower levels that overlap the functional units. For example, the hospital's orthopedic unit secretary knows the person in patient support services who schedules patient transport or the person in the centralized supply unit who coordinates deliveries to the various departments. The secretary can handle informally what would be very time-consuming if handled formally. Thus, managers become dependent on employees who know how to get around the system, which gives those employees power.

Employees also gain power because others have delegated responsibilities to them that the others do not want to do themselves, but that bring with them a certain amount of power. For example, a physician usually delegates the responsibility of scheduling their appointments to a secretary. The secretary schedules both patient and nonpatient appointments and therefore wields an enormous amount of power in terms of who will or will not see the physician during any given time period. Ask any pharmaceutical representative trying to schedule an appointment to discuss a new drug with a physician! An administrative assistant in a primary care physician's (PCP's) office who issues patient referrals has the power to select what specialists the physician's patients will be referred to within the managed care network. A specialist could experience a decrease in their patient referrals by not cooperating with the PCP's administrative staff's requests (e.g., seeing referred patients in a timely fashion).

Uses of Power

Recall that McClelland (1985) relates that a high need for power may be expressed as personalized power or socialized power. Individuals with a high need for personalized power tend to display impulsive, aggressive actions, abuse alcohol, and collect prestige "toys," such as fancy cars. They seek to control others for their own benefit. Their attitude is "I win, you lose." Individuals with a high need for personalized power demand personal loyalty from staff, not loyalty to the organization. Yukl (2001) points out that when a highly personalized power leader leaves an organization, the result tends to be chaos, loss of direction, and low morale.

Socialized power is needed for effective leadership. These leaders direct their power in ways that benefit others and the organization rather than for their own personal gain. As McClelland (1985) and Yukl (2001) relate, these leaders are interested in seeking power because it is through power that they can influence other people to accomplish tasks. They empower others who use that power to enact and further the leader's vision for the organization.

Magee and Langner (2008) provide the following example of individuals using personalized and socialized power. Three individuals decide to pursue a career in politics. One of them, who is highly motivated by socialized power but not personalized power, pursues this career to improve the welfare of a constituent group. Another, high in personalized power motivation but not socialized power motivation, seeks political office to achieve recognition and coerce others into benefiting that individual. The third, who is high in both types of power motivation, is motivated both by the promise of helping others and by the trappings of political office.

Developing a Power Base

Managers are dependent on others because of two organizational factors: division of labor and limited resources (Kotter, 1977). Managers are dependent on subordinates, peers, supervisors, other units within the organization, outside suppliers, and many others. Managers are sensitive to this issue and cope with their dependency by eliminating it, limiting it, or establishing power over others (Kotter, 1977). Kotter describes four ways in which managers have been successful in developing a power base:

- *Creating a Sense of Obligation*: Managers will go out of their way to do favors for people, and they expect those people to feel obligated to return those favors.
- *Building a Reputation as an Expert in a Certain Area*: Managers will establish themselves as experts in one or more areas so that others will defer to them on those matters. This can be accomplished through visible achievement (e.g., professional reputation and track record, executing a successful high-profile project).
- *Identification*: Managers will try to foster other people's unconscious identification with them or ideas for which they stand. Managers try to look and behave in ways that others respect. They go out of their way to be visible to their employees and give speeches about their organization's goals, values, and so on.
- *Perceived Dependence*: Managers will attempt to have other people believe that they are dependent on the manager for either help or not being hurt. The manager can accomplish this by securing resources that an employee requires to perform their job. At the same time, the manager makes it known that they can also have the same resources removed. Managers may also resort to influencing others' perception of the manager's available resources, which may be more than they possess in reality. In trying to influence people's judgments, managers pay attention to the trappings of power and to their own reputations and images. They associate with people and organizations that are known to be powerful.

Kotter (1977) notes that managers who build their power based on perceived expertise or identification can often use it to influence attitudes and someone's immediate behavior, which would result in a lasting impact.

Organizational Politics

Allen et al. (1979) describe organizational politics as the intentional acts of influence to enhance or protect the self-interest of individuals or groups. On the basis of their research, eight types of political behaviors were identified:

- *Attacking or Blaming Others*: Attacking or blaming others is often associated with scapegoating—blaming others for a problem or failure. It may also include trying to make a rival look bad by minimizing their accomplishments.
- *Using Information as a Political Tool*: Using information as a political tool may include withholding important information when doing so might further an employee's political interests. This type of behavior can also include information overload—for example, by burying or obscuring, among other things, some important (but potentially damaging) details that the employee hopes will go unnoticed.
- *Creating and Maintaining a Favorable Image*: Creating and maintaining a favorable image includes drawing attention to one's successes and the successes of others, creating the appearance of being a player in the organization, and developing a reputation of possessing qualities considered to be important to the organization (i.e., impression management). The behavior also includes taking credit for the ideas and accomplishments of others.
- *Developing a Base of Support*: Examples of developing a base of support include getting prior support for a decision before a meeting is called and getting others to contribute to an idea to secure their commitment.
- *Ingratiation and Praising Others*: Ingratiation and praising includes praising other people and establishing good rapport for self-serving purposes. Organizational jargon for this behavior includes buttering up the boss, apple polishing, and brown-nosing.
- *Developing Allies and Forming Power Coalitions*: Developing allies and forming power coalitions includes developing networks of coworkers, colleagues, and friends within and outside the organization to support or advocate a specific course of action.
- *Associating with Influential People*: Associating with influential people includes developing professional connections with organizations and people known to be powerful.
- *Creating Obligations and Reciprocity*: Creating obligations and reciprocity includes performing favors to create obligations from others, commonly known as "you scratch my back and I'll scratch yours."

From an organizational perspective, withholding and distorting information are the most dysfunctional and should be safeguarded against by the company. Note the similarities between Kotter's power bases and Allen et al.'s types of political behavior: creating a favorable image, developing allies and forming power coalitions, creating obligations, and associating with influential people. Although Kotter and Allen et al. developed their arguments 40 years ago, they are still valid today.

Upward Influence

There has been a growing recognition among organizational behavior researchers that a political influence perspective is a useful way to examine the effectiveness of managers (Falbe & Yukl, 1992; Farmer & Maslyn, 1999; Pfeffer, 1992). This perspective has focused on employees' influence tactics directed upward at those higher levels in the formal organizational structure. Kipnis et al. (1980), on the basis of their research, grouped influence tactics into various categories, of which six relate to upward influence:

- *Assertiveness* includes such influence tactics as demanding compliance, ordering, setting deadlines, nagging, and expressing anger.
- *Ingratiation* includes behaviors, such as praising, politely asking, acting humble, making the other person feel important, and acting friendly.
- The *rationality tactic* consists of using reason, logic, and compromise in attempting to influence others. This also includes attempts to convince others that certain actions are in their own best interests.
- The *exchange category* refers to such behavior as offering to help others in exchange for reciprocal favors.
- *Upward appeal* is indicated by behavioral attempts to gain support from superiors in an organization.
- *Coalition formation* refers to attempts to build alliances with others.

Kipnis and Schmidt (1988) assessed the use of upward influence with hospital supervisors, clerical workers, and chief executive officers. Using the tactics of the six categories of upward influence, Kipnis and Schmidt identified four clusters:

- *Shotguns*: Individuals who use all tactics, especially assertiveness and higher authority.
- *Tacticians*: Individuals with a high use of reason or rationality but average use of other tactics.
- *Bystanders*: Individuals with lower-than-average scores on all tactics.
- *Ingratiators*: Individuals with the highest use of friendliness or ingratiation tactics but average use of other tactics.

This research stream has been productive in the early stages. There is growing knowledge of how various tactics that employees use to influence behaviors of those in higher positions in the organization work or do not work under certain circumstances and in different cultures (Farmer & Maslyn, 1999; Ralston et al., 2005; Ralston et al., 2001).

A study by Carney et al. (2010) explored the use of body language to increase one's power position. The researchers found that when people posed in high-power displays (such as having a more open or expansive posture or stance), there was a physiological reaction in the body that released chemicals which increased feelings of power and risk tolerance, and lowered stress. This release of chemicals, in turn, influenced behaviors. In short, our body language and posture can influence our feelings of power, and thus our behaviors.

Empowering Leadership

More recent research has found that when a leader gives power away to others, it can benefit organizational and individual outcomes. Empowering leadership suggests that one of the main goals of the leader is not to have followers, but rather to create self-leaders. For leaders, this approach fosters trust and effectiveness by reducing reliance on direct supervision and encouraging self-management and psychological empowerment among team members (Amundsen & Martinsen, 2014). Such empowerment translates into positive work behaviors. Kim et al. (2018) performed a meta-analysis on empowering leadership, finding it had positive relationships with evaluations of the leader, trust, employee motivation, role clarity, attitudes, and performance. This indicates that empowering leadership can be an effective approach for improving various employee outcomes.

Organizations benefit from empowering leadership through enhanced innovation and adaptability. This leadership style encourages employees to pursue novel solutions and take calculated risks by fostering a climate of trust and autonomy, improving creativity and long-term resilience (Zhang & Bartol, 2010; Audenaert & Decramer, 2018). When it comes to leaders and power, sometimes giving is better than receiving.

Conclusion

In this chapter, we discussed power and how individuals can use it to influence others. The concept of power is an integral part of organizational behavior. Power is central to leadership, both building it and giving it away strategically.

Discussion Questions

1. Discuss what is meant by the term "power."
2. Explain the difference between potential and kinetic power.
3. Describe the different sources of power.
4. Explain a manager's power base and how managers develop it.
5. Describe organizational politics and the resulting political behaviors.
6. Discuss what upward influence means and the various influence tactics categories associated with it.
7. How does giving away power lead to better performance?

CASE STUDIES

Case Study 9-1 What Can Alex Do About Olivia?

Just before quitting time, Alex, the hospital's health information department manager, watched his three new trainees struggle with the complex electronic medical records software. Across the room, Olivia, an expert with the system, finished her tasks early, gathered her belongings, and left without acknowledging her coworkers.

"There goes the answer to my problem," Alex thought. Olivia would be the ideal trainer, but she had refused when asked, citing discomfort with instructing others, reluctance to take responsibility for their work, and a preference for working independently.

Alex was surprised by her refusal. He enjoyed helping others and believed his willingness to do so contributed to his promotion last year over Olivia, who had more seniority and experience. Since her performance was excellent, he hesitated to force the issue, believing employees worked best when doing what they preferred. However, with no training budget and no other employees as skilled as Olivia, he was stuck. Could he find another way to persuade her?

As Olivia walked to the parking lot, she fumed. "Why would Alex think I'd help him? I should have been promoted, not him. I have seniority and experience—he only has a master's in health information management. That shouldn't have been the deciding factor, but leadership thought otherwise."

Olivia had trained Alex when he first joined, and now he was her boss. She felt overlooked and undervalued. "I don't care what happens from here. I have five years until retirement, and as long as my work is excellent, Alex can't interfere with my plans. Not that he could, anyway—he barely understands how complex this system is. It takes real technical knowledge."

Olivia's resentment and Alex's challenge left a clear problem: Alex needed a skilled trainer, and Olivia had no interest in stepping up. How could Alex navigate this situation without damaging morale or forcing compliance? Could he appeal to Olivia in a way that acknowledged her expertise while addressing her concerns?

Alex needed a solution—one that aligned both their interests. Describe French and Raven's five sources of power. In this case, who has power(s) and why?

Case Study 9-2 Ethan's Dilemma

Ethan, a licensed physical therapist, worked for a national rehabilitation company in a busy Southwest city. For four years, he had enjoyed his job, valued his relationships with colleagues, and took pride in helping patients recover.

Last year, the health system underwent a reorganization, bringing in new leadership and reassigning staff. Ethan's new supervisor, Taylor, was transferred from a Midwest facility. Almost immediately, Taylor criticized Ethan's care plans, patient interactions, and overall performance. Despite consistently strong performance evaluations in previous years, Ethan's first review under Taylor was shockingly low.

Determined to prove himself, Ethan worked harder, staying late and making every effort to meet Taylor's expectations. Yet, no matter how much he adjusted, Taylor continued to find fault. Staff meetings became a source of stress, as Taylor often belittled Ethan in front of colleagues.

Ethan's stress began affecting his well-being. His sleep and eating habits deteriorated, and his once fulfilling career became a source of anxiety. Feeling isolated, he withdrew from family, friends, and coworkers. He started calling in sick more often and struggled with intrusive thoughts of confronting Taylor, which only compounded his guilt.

As time went on, Taylor subtly encouraged others to distance themselves from Ethan. Colleagues, wanting to stay on Taylor's good side, began questioning Ethan's competence. Rumors spread, and soon, he was treated as an outsider. Conversations would stop when he entered the room, and his once-supportive coworkers hesitated to be associated with him.

Hoping to resolve the situation, Ethan approached Taylor directly, expressing his concerns and asking how they could work together more effectively. Taylor, however, viewed this as insubordination. His hostility increased, and his criticism became even harsher.

Desperate, Ethan turned to the Human Resources Department (HRD). A manager listened to his concerns and advised him to document instances of mistreatment. In an attempt to mediate, HRD met with Taylor, but rather than improving, the situation worsened. Taylor, now aware that Ethan had gone to HR, retaliated with even more aggressive behavior.

With no improvement, Ethan escalated the issue to Taylor's supervisor, Isabella. She met with Taylor to discuss the complaints. However, Taylor painted Ethan as an underperforming employee with a lack of respect for authority. Without strong documentation to counter Taylor's claims, Ethan was issued a formal reprimand for insubordination.

Feeling trapped and unsupported, Ethan faced a difficult decision: endure a toxic work environment or leave the job he once loved. Describe French and Raven's five sources of power. What power(s) do the individuals in Ethan's dilemma hold?

Data from Pinto, J., Vecchione, M., & Howard, L. (2004, October). *Case discussion: Workplace bully.* Paper presented at the 12th Annual International Conference of the Association on Employment Practices and Principles, Ft. Lauderdale, FL.

References

Allen, R. W., Madison, D. L., Porter, L. W., Renwick, P. A., & Mayes, B. T. (1979). Organizational politics: Tactics and characteristics of its actors. *California Management Review, 22*(1), 77–83.

Amundsen, S., & Martinsen, Ø. L. (2014). Empowering leadership: Construct clarification, conceptualization, and validation of a new scale. *The Leadership Quarterly*, *25*(3), 487–511. https://doi.org/10.1016/j.leaqua.2013.11.009

Audenaert, M., & Decramer, A. (2018). When empowering leadership fosters creative performance: The role of problem-solving demands and creative personality. *Journal of Management & Organization*, *24*(1), 4–18. https://doi.org/10.1017/jmo.2016.20

Burda, D. (2003, August 25). Command and control: To make powerful list, you need to hold the purse strings or hire the workers. *Modern Healthcare*, p. 36.

Carney, D. R., Cuddy, A. J. C., & Yap, A. J. (2010). Power posing: Brief nonverbal displays affect neuroendocrine levels and risk tolerance. *Psychological Science, 21*(10), 1363–1368.

Emerson, R. M. (1962). Power-dependence relations. *American Sociological Review, 27*(1), 31–41.

Falbe, C. M., & Yukl, G. (1992). Consequences for managers of using single influence tactics and combinations of tactics. *Academy of Management Journal, 35*(3), 638–652.

Farmer, S. M., & Maslyn, J. M. (1999). Why are styles of upward influence neglected? Making the case for a configurational approach to influences. *Journal of Management, 25*(5), 653–682.

French, J. R. P., Jr., & Raven, B. (1959). The bases of social power. In D. Cartwright (Ed.), *Studies in social power* (pp. 150–167). University of Michigan Press.

Hersey, P., & Blanchard, K. H. (1982). *Management of organizational behavior: Utilizing human resources* (4th ed.). Prentice Hall.

Kim, M., Beehr, T. A., & Prewett, M. S. (2018). Employee responses to empowering leadership: A meta-analysis. *Journal of Leadership & Organizational Studies, 25*(3), 257–276. https://doi.org/10.1177/1548051817750538

Kipnis, D., & Schmidt, S. M. (1988). Upward influence styles: Relationship with performance evaluations, salary, and stress. *Administrative Science Quarterly, 33*(4), 528–542. https://doi.org/10.2307/2392642

Kipnis, D., Schmidt, S. M., & Wilkinson, I. (1980). Intraorganizational influence tactics: Explorations in getting one's way. *Journal of Applied Psychology, 65*(4), 440–452. https://doi.org/10.1037/0021-9010.65.4.440

Kotter, J. P. (1977). Power, dependence, and effective management. *Harvard Business Review, 55*(4), 125–136.

Magee, J. C., & Langner, C. A. (2008). How personalized and socialized power motivation facilitate antisocial and prosocial decision-making. *Journal of Research in Personality, 42*(6), 1547–1559.

McClelland, D. C. (1985). *Human motivation*. Scott, Foresman.

Mechanic, D. (1962). Sources of power of lower participants in complex organizations. *Administrative Science Quarterly, 7*(3), 349–365.

Pfeffer, J. (1992). *Managing with power: Politics and influence in organizations*. Harvard Business School Press.

Ralston, D. A., Hallinger, P., Egri, C. P., & Naothinsuhk, S. (2005). The effects of culture and life stage on workplace strategies of upward influence: A comparison of Thailand and the United States. *Journal of World Business, 40*(3), 321–337.

Ralston, D. A., Vollmer, G. R., Srinivasan, N., Nicholson, J. D., Tang, M., & Wan, P. (2001). Strategies of upward influence: A study of six cultures from Europe, Asia, and America. *Journal of Cross-Cultural Psychology, 32*(6), 728–755.

Scheff, T. J. (1961). Control over policy by attendants in a mental hospital. *Journal of Health and Human Behavior, 2*(2), 93–105.

Siu, R. G. H. (1979). *The craft of power*. Wiley.

Thibaut, J. W., & Kelley, H. H. (1959). *The social psychology of groups*. Wiley.

Yukl, G. A. (2001). *Leadership in organizations* (5th ed.). Pearson.

Zhang, X., & Bartol, K. M. (2010). Linking empowering leadership and employee creativity: The influence of psychological empowerment, intrinsic motivation, and creative process engagement. *Academy of Management Journal, 53*(1), 107–128. https://doi.org/10.5465/amj.2010.48037118

CHAPTER 10

Trait and Behavioral Theories of Leadership

LEARNING OUTCOMES

After completing this chapter, the student should be able to describe the:

- Difference between leaders and managers.
- Importance of early behavioral and trait studies.
- Role of behavioral and trait theories in the evolution of leadership research.
- Contributions of the early leadership studies at Ohio State University and the University of Michigan.
- Design and application of Blake and Mouton's Managerial (Leadership) Grid.

Overview

What is leadership? *Leadership* is a complex process by which a person sets direction and influences others to accomplish a mission, task, or objective. It also directs the organization to make it more cohesive and coherent (Winder, 2003). What makes an individual a leader? What makes a leader effective? The answers to these questions have been the focus of organizational researchers for nearly a century and philosophers for millennia. In this chapter, we discuss some of the earlier studies in leadership, referred to as the trait and behavioral theories, that laid the foundation for other leadership theories such as contingency theories and contemporary or transformational theories.

In exploring leadership in organizations, the first question is, "Are managers leaders?" or "Is there a difference between managers and leaders?" Kotter (1988) believes managers and leaders perform different but complementary activities. Winder (2003) and Hellriegel, Slocum, and Woodman (1995) point out that a manager is a person who directs the work of employees and is responsible for results. By contrast, a leader inspires employees with a vision and helps them to cope with change. Leaders make people want to achieve an organization's goals and objectives, while managers direct people to accomplish tasks or objectives. In the words of Peter Drucker and Warren Bennis, "Management is doing things right; leadership is doing the right things."

Table 10-1 Leaders Versus Managers

Leaders	Managers
Inspire employees with a vision.	Direct employees' work and devise systems to monitor employees' progress toward achieving preset goals.
Help employees to cope with change.	Determine how to achieve preset goals and be responsible for achieving them.
Make people want to achieve high goals and objectives.	Tell employees to accomplish a particular task or objective.
Articulate a direction or vision of what the future might look like.	Handle activities through planning and budgeting.
Develop strategies for producing changes needed to move in a new direction.	Achieve preset goals by organizing and staffing.
Recruit and keep employees who understand and share their vision.	Create an organizational structure and sets of jobs to accomplish the organization's strategies.

Khan (2010) emphasizes that organizations need strong leadership *and* management for optimum effectiveness. Robbins relates (as cited by Khan, 2010) that in today's dynamic world, organizations require leaders who can challenge the status quo, create the needed vision, and motivate followers toward achieving that vision. To achieve the vision, leaders need strong managers who can successfully develop the plans, create the structure and processes, and efficiently handle the daily operations.

Management and leadership are separate behaviors, but both are necessary for an organization (see **Table 10-1**). The distinctions in the table are based on *behaviors*, not particular characteristics, personality, or traits. Therein, we begin to discover the distinct contributions and applications of the theories presented in this chapter: trait and behavioral.

Trait Theory

The belief that innate traits could be found and be the basis for identifying leaders is illustrated by the following quote from Henry Ford: "The question 'who ought to be boss' is like asking 'who ought to be the tenor in the quartet?' The man who can sing tenor." One might conclude that not all of us are born to sing tenor, and not all of us are born to lead. In the early 20th century, many people accepted the belief that individuals possess different degrees of intelligence, energy, and moral force and that the masses of society, in whatever direction they may be influenced, are always led by the superior few (Bass, 1990). Leaders were believed to be born with personality, social, and physical characteristics that set them apart—traits that made them distinct from nonleaders.

The earliest trait studies of leadership reflect their times' social and psychological context. These studies generally assumed that leaders were born—the Great Man theory—and that these born leaders possessed specific characteristics or traits that set them apart. More than 100 studies summarized by Stogdill (1948) and Mann (1959) sought to distinguish leaders from nonleaders based on personality characteristics and individual traits, including intelligence, initiative, understanding of the task, and preference for a position of control and dominance. Early trait theorists suggest that traits such as intelligence, maturity, inner motivation, achievement drive, and employee-centeredness are more likely to be found in middle-level and top managers than in team leaders or first-line supervisors. Leaders tend to be emotionally mature, have a broad range of interests, and are high achievers. They can work effectively with employees in various situations, and they respect other people and realize that to accomplish tasks, they must be considerate of others' needs and values (Stogdill, 1974).

As research on leadership traits continued, a review by Geier (1967) of 20 different studies demonstrated the wide variance in the leadership traits chosen for investigation. Nearly 80 traits were identified across the 20 studies, and only five traits were common to four or more investigations. Thus, no clear set of traits by which we can distinguish great leaders emerged. Despite the difficulties in linking traits to successful leaders, evidence based on observed characteristics of successful and unsuccessful leaders reveals that many leaders share some basic traits (see **Exhibit 10-1**). Other studies established differences in drive (achievement, ambition, energy, tenacity, and initiative), cognitive ability, honesty and integrity, self-confidence, knowledge of business, and desire to lead (Kirkpatrick & Locke, 1991). However, as Robbins (2005) notes, the power of these traits to predict leadership was modest. No consistent patterns between specific traits and effective leadership materialized. Lussier and Achua (2012) note that no universal list of traits that all great leaders possess or that will guarantee leadership success in all situations has emerged. Leadership emerges from the combined influence of multiple traits (Zaccaro, Kemp, & Bader, 2004). This is consistent with research from the GLOBE study, which involved over 200 researchers across 62 cultures over the course of more than 20 years. This study found that although some elements of leadership were universally valuable, some elements of desirable leadership are culturally contingent and cannot necessarily be translated across cultures.

Exhibit 10-1 Trait Theory

One researcher studied a large number of North American organizations and leaders and concluded that leaders possess some common traits. Leaders who possess these traits are able to lead in a variety of situations:

- Physical vitality and stamina
- Intelligence and action-oriented judgment
- Eagerness to accept responsibility
- Task competence
- Understanding of followers and their needs
- Skill in dealing with people
- Need for achievement
- Capacity to motivate people
- Courage and resolution
- Trustworthiness
- Decisiveness
- Self-confidence
- Assertiveness
- Adaptability and flexibility

Data from Gardner, J. (1989). *On leadership*. Free Press.

Furthermore, this research found that leaders who acted according to the cultural values and expectations of leaders in their specific context tended to be more effective (Dorfman et al., 2012; Hernandez et al., 2018).

Winder (2003) points out another criticism of early trait theory related to its reference to leaders' physical characteristics, such as appearance, physique, energy, and health. This is not surprising when one considers that the early leadership studies were conducted in the 1930s. Leaders during that period would have typically been male, White, authoritarian, and educated. Aside from these traits, finding more than minor differences from one organizational leader to the next would have been difficult. However, as we recognize today, physical characteristics are not requirements for leadership.

The failure of early studies to determine a clear set of leadership traits led several researchers to question the value of trait leadership theory and explore another area of distinction: leader behavior. Rather than asking what traits distinguish leaders, behavioral theories ask, "How do leaders act or behave differently than nonleaders?" The underlying assumption or hypothesis shifts from being born with innate leadership abilities to being able to acquire leadership behaviors. Can we identify and teach particular behaviors that promote effective leadership? Many researchers support that leadership can be learned, cultivated through work experience, training, education, opportunity, motivation, and even a little luck (Kotter, 1988).

Lewin's Behavioral Study

One of the earliest studies to examine the effect of leadership behavior was performed in the 1930s under the direction of Kurt Lewin, who is recognized as the father of group dynamics. Lewin (1951) and his colleagues observed children's behavior under different leadership styles used by the adult participants. The study involved 10-year-old boys participating in an arts and crafts club. The boys were placed into groups matched on personal characteristics (e.g., IQ, popularity), and all groups worked on the same project (producing the same item). Each group was exposed to three types of leadership styles:

- *Authoritarian*: The authoritarian leader remained aloof and directed the group's activities by giving orders (without consultation).
- *Democratic*: The democratic leader guided and encouraged the children while they actively participated in the group's activities.
- *Laissez-faire*: The laissez-faire leader gave the children knowledge but did not direct the activities, nor did this leader become involved or participate in the group's activities.

The researchers measured and recorded both the amount of work produced and the levels of aggression displayed by the children. The results established that leadership style had clear impacts on group productivity, behaviors, and interpersonal relationships among group members. Under the democratic leadership style, group morale was high, and relationships between the group members and the leader were friendly. When the group leader was absent, the children continued with their work. The group's work reflected levels of originality and quality. However, members of the group did not produce as many items as did the group under the authoritarian leader. Under authoritarian leadership, the group displayed two types of behaviors: aggressive and apathetic. The aggressive children were defiant and continually wanted the leader's attention. They blamed one another when anything went wrong within the group. Although the apathetic children placed fewer demands on the leader, they displayed outbursts of aggression when the leader was absent. Under the laissez-faire leadership style, the children displayed low satisfaction and a low tendency to work independently. Group members displayed little cooperation. The group produced the least number of items, and the items were of low quality.

Overall, the democratic leadership style appeared to be the most successful. However, some of the children reported that they preferred the authoritarian style. This study provided us with our initial examination of leadership behavior and also alerted us to the possibility that followers may prefer specific leadership styles. Gladding (1995) suggested that different types of groups prefer specific styles. He contended that members' preferences would be based on the leadership style they perceived as right or natural according to their socialization process.

Comprehensive research projects conducted at Ohio State University and the University of Michigan during the 1940s focused further attention on identifying leader behaviors. These foundational studies impacted future conceptualizations and the research leadership theorists.

Ohio State Leadership Studies

In the late 1940s, researchers at Ohio State University focused on identifying independent dimensions of leadership behavior. They developed an assessment tool, the Leader Behavior Description Questionnaire, to discover how leaders carry out their activities. Leaders from the military, educational, manufacturing, and other sectors were included in the research project. The researchers found that two dimensions of leadership were consistent among the studied groups: consideration for people and initiating structure.

The dimension of consideration for people was focused on the human side of the business and was also called relationship behavior. This dimension recognizes that individuals have needs and require relationships. The initiating structure dimension places importance on tasks and goals. These findings were important to the study of organizational behavior and leadership by identifying these concepts and recognizing that the two dimensions were independent. In other words, consideration for workers and initiating structure existed simultaneously and to different degrees. A matrix was created that showed the various combinations and quantities of the elements; see **Figure 10-1**.

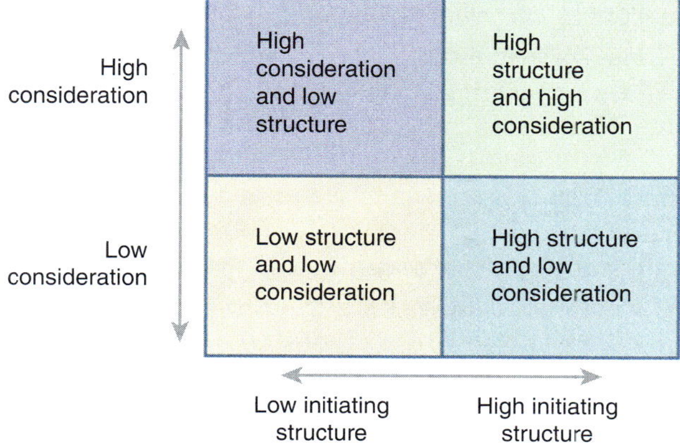

Figure 10-1 Ohio State Studies

Leaders who ranked high on both dimensions were more likely to influence the workforce to higher levels of satisfaction and performance. A weakness noted in the Ohio State studies was that situational factors were absent from the research. Although a combination of the dimensions was developed, the effectiveness of each combination in relation to workplace situations was not identified. Not all workplace situations require an emphasis on initiating structure. For example, healthcare professionals who are intrinsically motivated and highly skilled might not require initiating structure from their manager to the same degree.

University of Michigan Studies

During the same time as the Ohio State studies, researchers at the University of Michigan were researching the most effective leadership style based on two dimensions of leadership behavior: an employee-centered focus or a production-centered focus. Employee-centered leaders emphasized interpersonal relations, took a personal interest in the needs of their subordinates, and accepted individual differences among members. Production-centered leaders emphasized the technical aspects of the job, focused on accomplishing the tasks, and saw the members as a means to an end—getting tasks done. The researchers found that general supervision (i.e., providing support and direction without being authoritarian) created higher levels of productivity than production-centered supervision and that low-producing supervisors emphasized production, displaying little concern for their employees. Years of research have confirmed the University of Michigan studies (Luthans, 2002).

Likert (1961) expanded on the Michigan studies with extensive research into what differentiates effective managers from ineffective managers. Likert related that job-centered managers were found to be the least productive, while employee-centered managers were found to be the most effective. In addition, effective managers set specific goals but gave employees freedom in how they achieved those goals (i.e., empowerment).

Blake and Mouton's Leadership Grid

During the 1960s, Blake and Mouton reexamined the two dimensions of leaders identified in the Ohio State studies—consideration for people and initiating structure. Their work developed a two-factor framework (Razik & Swanson, 1995). The Leadership Grid is based upon the assertion that one best leadership style exists. The Leadership Grid provides the manager with a conceptual assessment of their current leadership style and an avenue for developing into an ideal manager.

Although there is a possibility of being categorized in one of 81 possible positions on the grid, we will examine five positions to assist our understanding of the Leadership Grid. The Leadership Grid, in **Figure 10-2**, identifies a vertical axis, on a scale from one to nine, describing a concern for people. A horizontal axis, also on a scale from one to nine, identifies a concern for production or results. The five notable positions are: impoverished management (1,1); authority-compliance (9,1); middle-of-the-road management (5,5); country club management (1,9); and team management (9,9).

Let us examine leadership characteristics in each of the five positions to understand how the grid functions. At the lower left position on the grid (1,1), the impoverished manager (also referred to as a laissez-faire-type leader) exercises minimal effort to accomplish the task, doing only the amount of work required to sustain their position within the organization. Additionally, the impoverished manager is much more focused on their own well-being than on the employees

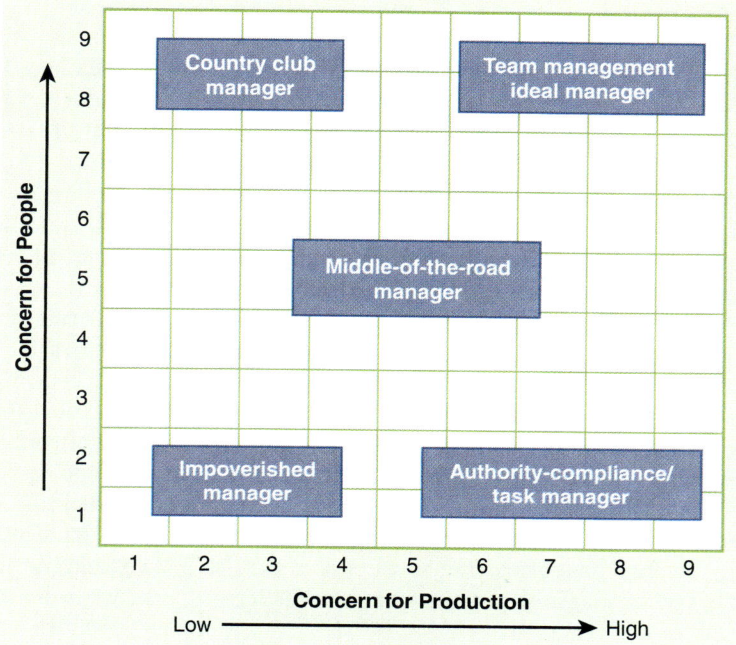

Figure 10-2 Blake and Mouton's Leadership Grid

they supervise. This manager has a low concern for people and a low concern for production. Such managers do just enough to get by, avoiding conflicts, having little social contact with employees, and so on.

The authority-compliance/task manager is positioned at the lower right on the grid (9,1). This manager exhibits an autocratic presence and is often called a dictator. The managerial focus in this position is efficiency, with an ongoing effort to improve work processes to increase production. There is, at best, negligible concern for people. These managers consider staff to be a means of production. The task manager is unconcerned by their leadership style's potential negative impact on staff, such as conflict or stress.

The middle-of-the-road manager is located directly in the middle of the grid, at the (5,5) position. This manager appears to balance the concern for task and the concern for people to boost morale and satisfaction. On the surface, this may seem to be an efficient approach to management, but this balancing act is often challenging to sustain over time. One might consider the middle-of-the-road manager the perfect politician. These managers play both sides of the field, depending on situational factors They will tell you exactly what they think you want to hear and then tell someone else exactly what they want to hear, even if this contradicts what they told you. This is not to suggest that the middle-of-the-road manager operates exclusively on political alliances. However, it should be clear that under the best circumstances, balancing an equal concern for people and a concern for production is challenging.

The country club manager is at the upper left on the grid (1,9). This individual is most concerned with ensuring that employees' needs are met and that the work environment is comfortable and friendly. The lack of focus on production diminishes the overall capacity for employees to meet or exceed organizational goals. This style of management will probably not lead to many successful ventures based on production expectations.

The final position is in the grid's upper-right corner (9,9). Blake and McCanse (1991) labeled this position team management (formerly the ideal manager). As this label suggests, the team manager develops a sense of purpose and accomplishment in both concern for people and concern for the task. This is not a balancing act as was described for the middle-of-the-road manager; it is a theoretically perfect combination of concern for people and concern for task. Khan (2010, p. 12) relates that the ideal [team] manager "works to motivate employees to reach their highest level of accomplishment. They believe in creating a situation whereby people can satisfy their own needs by commitment to the organization's objectives."

Blake and McCanse added two more styles in 1991: the opportunistic management style and the paternalistic management style. The opportunistic management style refers to a manager who uses any combination of the five basic styles for personal reward and advancement. The purpose of the opportunistic manager's performance and effort is to realize personal gain. The paternalistic management style refers to a manager who uses both 1,9 and 9,1 styles but does not integrate the two. In other words, the person acts fatherly or motherly toward their employees but is the key decision maker, and this manager rewards loyalty but punishes noncompliance.

The grid is a useful tool for identifying leadership style, both perceived and real. Managers are often surprised at where they score on the grid. Scores may lead to self-reflection and increased understanding of their management style, which provides opportunities for increasing managerial effectiveness.

Conclusion

Trait and behavioral theories focused attention on the individual. Were differences found? Yes. Were the researchers able to produce a clear set of traits or behaviors that can be used to definitely distinguish leaders? No. Examining the findings across numerous studies, we uncover a lack of consistency and modest relationships. However, it is important not to diminish the importance of the early leadership research or of the contribution these efforts made as traits and behaviors have reemerged in contemporary leadership theories and behavioral competencies.

The theoretical evolution of leadership has led us to the next generation of research: contingency theories. Some researchers suggest the questionable reliability and disputed validity of early leadership research efforts may be attributed to the absence of a single important dimension known as the contingency factor. The term "contingency" refers to the leader's contextual situation. "Effective leaders analyze the factors of the situation, task, followers, and the organization, and then choose the appropriate style" (Osland et al., 2001, p. 290). The leadership and management traits and behaviors that work in one organizational context might not be effective in another. Factors both internal and external to the organization change, and leaders and organizations must change in response, particularly in health care. Consider a few of the impetuses that are dramatically reforming the healthcare system, such as the call for quality and performance in concert with cutting costs and the economic, social, technological, and political environments. All of these factors (and more) provide compelling reasons for contingency leadership theory in attaining organizational goals.

Discussion Questions

1. Is leadership synonymous with management, or is leading just one of the many things that a manager does? In what ways are they the same or different?
2. Explain the findings of Lewin's behavioral studies on leadership styles and behaviors.
3. Discuss the contributions and the weaknesses of trait theory.
4. Discuss the results of the Ohio State studies in terms of their significant impact on leadership research.
5. Explain the difference between the University of Michigan studies and the Ohio State studies.
6. Explain Blake and Mouton's Leadership Grid in relation to previous leadership research.

CASE STUDY AND EXERCISES

Case Study 10-1 Leadership Style

A small group of nurses at a large community hospital were unhappy about their work environment and met daily during lunch to discuss the situation. A recent change in the hospital's senior management was causing a high level of uncertainty and anxiety among the nursing staff. The nurses felt overworked as a result of the industry's current nursing shortage. Their wages and benefits had been stagnant, with no salary market adjustments for the past 2 years. The nurses saw the situation as management requiring them to do more work with fewer resources and with no appreciation or recognition of their efforts. Whenever the nurses approached management about these matters, they perceived their concerns as falling on deaf ears, since no changes were ever made.

Feeling that they had no other choice, the nurses contacted a labor union. The labor union began an organizing effort in the hospital shortly thereafter, waging an aggressive campaign over a 6-week period. There was tremendous peer pressure, as some of the well-respected members of the nursing staff became active leaders for unionization, although they had not been among the initial group of nurses who had contacted the union. The election was held, and the union was voted in by two-thirds of the nursing staff. In the weeks that followed, the original group of nurses remarked that they were surprised by the union's victory; they had only wanted to scare management into making changes to their work environment. Using Blake and Mouton's Leadership Grid, explain the leadership style displayed by management to the nursing staff.

Exercise 10-1

Write a description of an effective manager. Write words that you would use to describe an effective leader. When you review your list, consider the differences and similarities in your adjectives. How did the review of the concepts in the chapter influence your word choices? Are you comfortable distinguishing the roles? To what degree, if at all, do you believe that a manager should also be a leader or that a leader should also be a manager?

Exercise 10-2

Think of some individuals who you believe to be really exceptional leaders. What, if anything, do they have in common?

Think of some individuals who you believe to be truly poor leaders. What, if anything, do they have in common?

Do your answers identify traits or behaviors? Which do you personally view as dominant in effective leadership: traits or behaviors?

Exercise 10-3

Have you ever known people who were successful leaders in one situation and failures in another? Why do you think this happened?

Exercise 10-4

On a blank piece of paper, draw a picture of a leader. Once your picture is complete, answer the following questions:

- What does this picture say about you?
- What does this picture say about what traits you associate with leadership?
- How might implicit biases be a part of your conceptualization of a leader?

Exercise 10-5 Leadership Questionnaire

Objective: To determine the degree that a person likes working with tasks and other people.
Time: 45 minutes

Instructions

1. Complete the 18 items in the Questionnaire section.
2. Transfer your answers to the two respective columns provided in the scoring section. Total the score in each column and multiply each total by 0.2. For example, in the first column (people), if you answer 5, 3, 4, 4, 3, 2, 5, 4, 3, then your final score is $33 \times 0.2 = 6.6$.
3. The total score for the first column (people) is plotted on the vertical axis in the matrix section, and the total score for the second column (task) is plotted on the horizontal axis. Intersect the lines to see which leadership dimension you normally operate out of:
   - Task manager (authoritarian)
   - Impoverished manager
   - Ideal manager (team leader)
   - Country club manager

Questionnaire

Below is a list of statements about leadership behavior. Read each one carefully, then, using the following scale, decide the extent to which it actually applies to you. For best results, answer as truthfully as possible.

Never		Sometimes			Always
0	1	2	3	4	5

1. _____ I encourage my team to participate when decision-making time comes and I try to implement their ideas and suggestions.

2. ______ Nothing is more important than accomplishing a goal or task.
3. ______ I closely monitor the schedule to ensure a task or project will be completed in time.
4. ______ I enjoy coaching people on new tasks and procedures.
5. ______ The more challenging a task is, the more I enjoy it.
6. ______ I encourage my employees to be creative about their job.
7. ______ When seeing a complex task through to completion, I ensure that every detail is accounted for.
8. ______ I find it easy to carry out several complicated tasks at the same time.
9. ______ I enjoy reading articles, books, and journals about training, leadership, and psychology, and then putting what I have read into action.
10. ______ When correcting mistakes, I do not worry about jeopardizing relationships.
11. ______ I manage my time very efficiently.
12. ______ I enjoy explaining the intricacies and details of a complex task or project to my employees.
13. ______ Breaking large projects into small manageable tasks is second nature to me.
14. ______ Nothing is more important than building a great team.
15. ______ I enjoy analyzing problems.
16. ______ I honor other people's boundaries.
17. ______ Counseling my employees to improve their performance or behavior is second nature to me.
18. ______ I enjoy reading articles, books, and trade journals about my profession; and then implementing the new procedures I have learned.

Scoring Section

After completing the questionnaire, transfer your answers to the spaces below:

People	Task
Question	**Question**
1.	2.
4.	3.
6.	5.
9.	7.
10.	8.
12.	11.
14.	13.
16.	15.
17.	18.
Total	Total
× 0.2 =	× 0.2 =
(Multiply the total by 0.2 to get your final score)	(Multiply the total by 0.2 to get your final score)

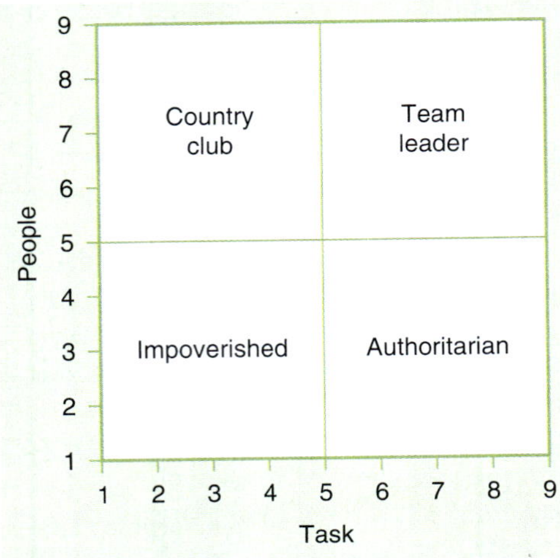

Figure 10-3

Matrix Section

Plot your final scores on the graph below (**Figure 10-3**) by drawing a horizontal line from the people score (vertical axis) to the right of the matrix, and drawing a vertical line from the task score on the horizontal axis to the top of the matrix. The area of intersection is the leadership dimension that you operate out of.

The Results

This chart will give you an idea of your leadership style.

However, like any other instrument that attempts to profile a person, you have to take in other factors, such as how your manager and employees rate you as a leader, do you get your job done, do you take care of your employees, or are you helping to "grow" your organization.

You should review the statements in the survey and reflect on the low scores by asking yourself, "If I scored higher in that area, would I be a more effective leader?" And if the answer is yes, then it should become a personal action item.

References

Bass, B. M. (1990). *Bass & Stogdill's handbook of leadership* (3rd ed.). Free Press.

Blake, R. R., & McCanse, A. A. (1991). *Leadership dilemmas-grid solutions*. Gulf Publishing.

Blake, R. R., & Mouton, J. S. (1964). *The managerial grid*. Gulf Publishing.

Dorfman, P., Javidan, M., Hanges, P., Dastmalchian, A., & House, R. (2012). GLOBE: A twenty year journey into the intriguing world of culture and leadership. *Journal of World Business, 47*(4), 504–518. Drucker, P. F. (2018). *Essential Drucker*. Routledge.

Ford, H. (1922). Ford ideals: Being a selection from "Mr. Ford's page" in The Dearborn Independent. Dearborn Publishing Company.

Geier, J. G. (1967). A trait approach to the study of leadership in small groups. *Journal of Communication, 17*(4), 316–323.
Gladding, S. T. (1995). *Group work: A counseling specialty*. Prentice Hall.
Hellriegel, D., Slocum, J. W., & Woodman, R. W. (1995). *Organizational behavior*. West Publishing.
Hernandez, S. R., O'Connor, S. J., & Meese, K. A. (2018). Global efforts to professionalize the healthcare management workforce: The role of competencies. *Journal of Health Administration Education, 35*(2), 157–174.
Khan, A. (2010). The dilemma of leadership styles and performance appraisal: Counter strategies. *Journal of Managerial Sciences, 4*(1), 1–30.
Kirkpatrick, A., & Locke, E. (1991). Leadership: Do traits matter? *Academy of Management Executive, 5*(2), 48–60.
Kotter, J. (1988). *The leadership factor*. Free Press.
Lewin, K. (1951). *Field theory in social science*. Harper & Row.
Likert, R. (1961). *New patterns of management*. McGraw-Hill.
Lussier, R., & Achua, C. (2012). *Leadership: Theory, application, and skill development*. Cengage Learning.
Luthans, F. (2002). *Organizational behavior* (9th ed.). McGraw-Hill.
Mann, R. D. (1959). A review of the relationships between personality and performance in small groups. *Psychological Bulletin, 56*(4), 241–270.
Osland, J., Kolb, D., & Rubin, I. (2001). *Organizational behavior: An experiential approach* (7th ed.). Prentice Hall.
Razik, T. A., & Swanson, A. D. (1995). *Fundamental concepts of educational leadership and management*. Prentice Hall.
Robbins, S. P. (2005). *Essentials of organizational behavior* (8th ed.). Prentice Hall.
Stogdill, R. M. (1948). Personal factors associated with leadership: A survey of the literature. *The Journal of Psychology, 25*(1), 35–71.
Stogdill, R. M. (1974). *Handbook of leadership: A survey of theory and research*. Free Press.
Winder, R. (2003). Organizational dynamics and development. *Futurics, 27*(1/2), 5.
Zaccaro, S. J., Kemp, C., & Bader, P. (2004). Leader traits and attributes. In J. Antonakis, A. T. Cianciolo, & R. J. Sternberg (Eds.), *The nature of leadership* (pp. 101–123). Sage.

CHAPTER 11

Contingency Theories and Situational Models of Leadership

LEARNING OUTCOMES

After completing this chapter, the student should be able to:

- Appreciate the contributions of contingency theories in understanding leadership.
- Distinguish between the various contingency theories.
- Apply the various contingency theories of leadership to today's work environments.

Overview

Leadership is a complex concept involving factors that extend beyond the individual to include situational factors. The simplicity of examining leadership based on individual traits and behaviors gives way to a more complex situation as we add the interrelationships of leadership style, personal and professional values, one's ability to influence, employee relationships, employee development, and the variability of other situational factors. In contingency theories, the critical component becomes the characteristics of the situation rather than the individual. Analyzing contingent factors and properly matching leadership style to the situation can allow an individual, in the proper context, to effectively move an organization toward its strategic goals by influencing other organizational members to participate in the collaborative effort to achieve corporate success and economic sustainability.

Understanding the development and application of leadership theory prepares the healthcare manager to fulfill three explicit administrative responsibilities: predict, explain, and control. Successful leaders must predict how, when, where, and why things happen. Prediction permits the leader to enhance opportunities and diminish threats which constantly arise in the workplace. The ability to explain these occurrences instills a sense of confidence in peers and employees, further augmenting the leader's legitimacy in various situations. Finally, a leader recognizes and accepts the role of control, whereby individuals are influenced to achieve strategic goals and organizational sustainability.

A contingency is an event that may occur but is not likely or intended. It is a possibility that must be prepared for, and it is dependent on chance or uncertainty. As such, contingency leadership is about possessing the knowledge, skills, and abilities to respond to a changing situation. Analyzing and responding to the contingencies that influence leader effectiveness may allow one to succeed in an ever-changing healthcare environment. Healthcare leadership is about stepping up in times of uncertainty and moving forward to minimize potential threats and capture opportunities to benefit the organization. With recent years bringing an unexpected pandemic, sociopolitical changes, and rapid advancements in artificial intelligence (AI), it is not hard to see the need to anticipate and respond to the unexpected.

This chapter discusses contingency leadership theories and their implications for the leader, the employee, and the healthcare organization. To maximize your understanding of these theories, consider how they apply to you and your work environment. Developing knowledge and applying contingency theories will enhance your ability to accomplish your managerial responsibilities to predict, explain, and control.

Fiedler's Contingency Theory

In studies of the relationship between leadership style and situation variables, Fiedler and his associates (1965, 1967, 1974) posit that individuals have dominant leadership characteristics that are well established and generally inflexible. In Fiedler's theory, leaders are either task-oriented (active, controlling, and structuring) or human relations–oriented (passive, permissive, and considerate). Fiedler believed that an individual's leadership style was grounded and somewhat inflexible; therefore, leaders would improve their effectiveness by being placed in situations that best suited their orientation. Situations that display more variability and provide contingencies are analyzed across three dimensions:

- *Leader–Member Relations*: The degree of certainty, trust, and deference between the subordinate and the leader. This factor addresses the manager's perception of their cooperative relations with subordinates. In other words, is the cooperation between the manager and subordinates good or poor? (Rating: good or poor.)
- *Task Structure*: The extent to which job assignments are clear through the implementation of formalization and policy. This factor relates to whether the work task is highly structured, subject to standard procedures, and subject to adequate measures of assessment. Specific tasks are easy to structure, standardize, and assess, such as an assembly line operation. (Rating: high or low.)
- *Leader Position Power*: The degree of control and influence the leader legitimately possesses in dealing with organizational activities. This factor, which is highly dependent on the support the leader receives from senior management, asks whether the manager's level of authority is based on punishing or rewarding behavior. For example, does the manager derive authority from providing bonuses for meeting predetermined goals or terminating employees for failure to meet the objectives? (Rating: strong or weak.)

A leader's contribution to group performance is determined by the leader's style (i.e., task or relations) in conjunction with situation variables (i.e., relationships, task structure, and power position). Effective leaders seek or are placed in situations that best match their leadership style.

Fiedler's research and the identification of leadership styles were based on a questionnaire known as the Least Preferred Coworker (LPC) Scale. Fiedler (1970) developed the LPC by asking the participants to describe their most- and least-preferred coworkers. Each participant was asked to think of all others with whom they had ever worked and then to say the person with whom they had worked best (i.e., most-preferred coworker) and then the person with whom they had worked least well (i.e., least-preferred coworker [LPC]). From the items identified, Fiedler created a scale with contrasting adjectives (pleasant/unpleasant, supportive/hostile, considerate/inconsiderate, and agreeable/disagreeable) to measure whether a person was task-oriented or relations-oriented. Fiedler believed that the ratings individuals ascribed to their least-preferred coworker reflected more about themselves than about the person they least enjoyed working with. Thus, individuals who scored the LPC in relatively favorable terms were labeled "relations-oriented," while individuals who scored the LPC in relatively unfavorable terms were labeled "task-oriented."

Assessing the three situational dimensions (leader–member relations, task structure, and position power) can determine four levels of situational favorableness. **Figure 11-1** identifies these four levels in a continuum of situational favorableness, from Very Unfavorable to Unfavorable and Favorable to Very Favorable.

Fiedler's research suggests that leadership effectiveness depends on aligning leadership style with situational favorableness. A situation is favorable when the leader is trusted (good leader–member relations), tasks are well-defined (high task structure), and the leader has authority (strong position power). Conversely, a situation is unfavorable when the leader lacks trust from members, tasks are unclear (low task structure), and authority is weak. A task-oriented leader is most effective in both highly favorable and highly unfavorable conditions. However, in moderate situations—neither favorable nor unfavorable—a relationship-oriented leader achieves better results.

In a very unfavorable situation (i.e., leader-member relations are poor, there is low task structure, and the leader has little position power), one can understand the importance of a task-oriented leadership approach. But why would a task-oriented leadership approach best suit a very favorable situation? In a favorable situation, the leader–member relationship is good, the task structure is high, and the position power is strong. This combination provides an environment where individuals are prepared to be guided and expect to be told what to do. For example, Fiedler suggests considering the captain of an airliner during its final landing. We would hardly want the captain to turn to the crew for a discussion on how to land the plane!

Fiedler's contingency theory made a tremendous contribution toward contingency theories for three reasons. It was the first theory to systematically account for situational factors (i.e., relationships, task structure, and position power). Second, the theory considers the leader's

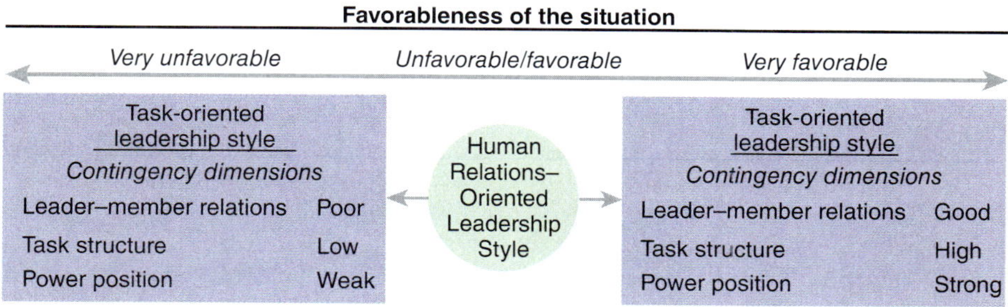

Figure 11-1 Fiedler's Contingency Theory

dominant orientation (i.e., a function of a leader's needs and personality), not the leader's behavior (Tosi & Mero, 2003). As Tosi and Mero (2003) point out, although this orientation may affect the leader's behavior, the leader's orientation toward their group determines how effective the group will be. Third, because the leader's orientation is relatively stable, it is not likely that a leader will change orientations when confronted with different situations, though the leader can change their behavior when necessary and when the leader wants to (Tosi & Mero, 2003). Fiedler believed that it would be easier to change the situation (i.e., work environment) to fit the leader's style. However, organizational and situational change may be challenging or occur very slowly. Therefore, an organization should not choose a leader who fits a situation but should change the situation to suit the style of its leader, since the leader's personality is not likely to change (Fiedler, 1970) (see **Case Study 11-1**). This concept is a major criticism of Fiedler's theory because it is difficult to enact.

In further work, Fiedler and colleagues introduced other variables into the original contingency theory (Fiedler, 1995; Fiedler & Garcia, 1987; Fiedler et al., 1979). Fiedler (1996) suggests that when leaders are under stress, their intelligence and experience tend to interfere with each other, diminishing the leader's ability to think rationally, logically, and analytically. Fiedler and Garcia (1987) refer to this reconceptualization as cognitive resource theory.

CASE STUDY 11-1 The New Chief Safety and Compliance Officer Position

Ben, CEO of a 300-bed community hospital in the Midwest, received an urgent call from Paul, the hospital's director of nursing. Paul appeared distressed as he explained, "A patient received the wrong blood type during a transfusion. The nurse noticed the reaction, but the patient died shortly after. Since the incorrect blood type may not always be fatal, we can't be certain it caused her death. She had multiple serious conditions." He also reminded Ben that the state's Medical Error Oversight Board must be notified.

Ben was shocked. Just two months earlier, the hospital had reported another error—a metal clamp left inside a patient after surgery due to a missed X-ray order. Although no harm was done, the hospital's chief operating officer, Harry Benson, had promised new procedures to prevent future mistakes.

Ben thanked Paul and instructed him to report the incident to the oversight board. He then prepared to meet the patient's family to express sympathy and assure them the hospital would investigate.

After Paul left, Ben realized immediate action was needed. Harry had been responsible for implementing safety policies, but his efforts were insufficient. Instead of relying on Harry, Ben decided to establish a Chief Safety and Compliance Officer position. This new leader would report directly to him and have full authority to enforce safety measures.

Ben quickly drafted the job description. The new officer would develop and implement compliance and safety policies, oversee system-wide training, and ensure adherence to safety protocols. They would also monitor compliance activities and enforce disciplinary actions when necessary.

The ideal candidate would hold an MHA or a related degree, have 10 years of safety and compliance experience, including 7 years in health care and 5 years in management. The role offered a competitive salary and benefits.

Ben knew this was a critical step toward building a stronger safety culture. The hospital could not afford another preventable error.

Using Fiedler's contingency theory, analyze the situational factors and determine what type of individual would be the most effective for Ben to hire. Could he change situational factors instead of hiring a new leader? If so, what changes would you recommend?

This theory describes how group performance is a construct of a complex interaction between (1) two leader traits—intelligence and experience, (2) one type of leader behavior—directive leadership, and (3) two aspects of the leadership situation—interpersonal stress and the nature of the task (Yukl, 1998). In other words, cognitive resource theory states that (1) a leader's intellectual abilities correlate positively with performance under low stress but negatively under high stress and (2) a leader's experience correlates negatively with performance under low stress but positively under high stress (Fiedler, 2008). For example, leaders under stress will fall back on their previously learned knowledge and behavior (e.g., relying on intuition and hunches); therefore, the greater the range of their experience, the better their performance will be. Under low-stress conditions, more experienced leaders are not challenged and tend to get bored and cut corners (Fiedler, 1996).

House's Path–Goal Leadership Theory

Path–Goal leadership theory was introduced by Evans (1970) and further developed by House (1971). House (1971) suggests that effective leaders provide the path, the support, and the resources to assist subordinates in attaining organizational goals. This theory combines elements of the Ohio State studies (i.e., consideration and initiating structure) with expectancy theory of motivation.

Four separate but fully integrated components make up House's Path–Goal leadership theory: Leadership Behaviors, Environmental Contingency Factors, Subordinate Contingency Factors, and Outcomes; see **Figure 11-2**. The first component, Leadership Behavior, identifies four specific leadership styles:

1. The *directive* leader provides employees with a detailed understanding of expectations, a plan to accomplish those expectations, and the resources to achieve the tasks. The directive leadership style can increase employees' motivation and satisfaction where role ambiguity exists.

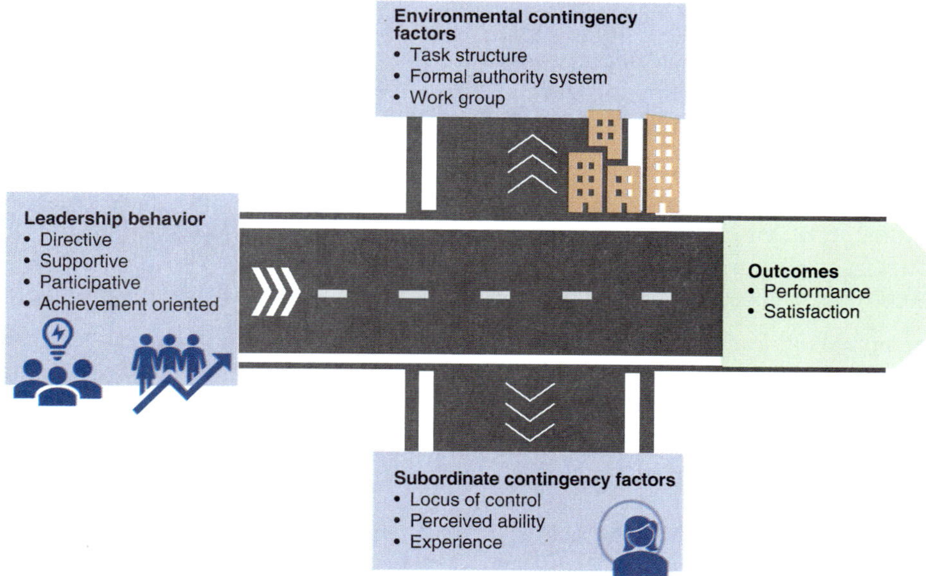

Figure 11-2 House's Path–Goal Leadership Theory

Data from Robbins, S. P. (2003). *Organizational behavior* (10th ed.). Upper Saddle River, NJ: Prentice Hall, p. 326.

2. The *supportive* leader shows concern for people, ensures that the work environment does not impede specific tasks that lead toward organizational goals, and creates a supportive atmosphere. This leadership style may increase employee motivation and satisfaction when tasks are routine or stressful.
3. The *participative* leader seeks input from multiple internal sources, including the technical core of employees, to assist in the decision-making process. The participative leader maintains responsibility for the final decision but includes the workforce in the process, ultimately enhancing buy-in from affected parties. The participative leadership style can improve motivation and satisfaction in uncertain or changing environments.
4. The *achievement-oriented* leader establishes stimulating goals and expects high levels of performance in achieving them. This style of leadership creates an environment of trust in which the leader acknowledges the workforce's abilities to accomplish organizational goals.

Whereas Fiedler proposed that leadership styles were grounded and inflexible, House proposed that leadership styles are adaptable and that managers may be called on to utilize any one of the four identified styles of leadership, depending on the situation (Razik & Swanson, 1995; Robbins, 2005).

Leadership style depends on two contingency factors: environmental and subordinate. House considered external dynamics, which are referred to as environmental contingency factors. These factors include (1) clarity of the task to be performed, (2) hierarchical authority systems, and (3) group dynamics (i.e., workgroup members' relationships). These factors are generally considered to be outside the control and influence of the worker and the manager. The second set of contingency factors, considered internal dynamics, is called subordinate contingency factors. These factors include the employee's locus of control; knowledge, skills, and abilities (real or perceived); and experience. Subordinate contingency factors are characteristics exhibited by the employees (Robbins, 2005).

The integration of leadership style, environmental contingency factors, and subordinate contingency factors leads to outcomes (performance and satisfaction). According to House and Mitchell (1974), a leader's role is influencing subordinates' perceptions and motivating them toward achieving the desired outcomes. To be effective, managers should do the following:

1. Increase personal payoffs to subordinates for work goal attainment.
2. Provide coaching and direction when needed.
3. Clarify expectations of workers.
4. Reduce frustrating barriers.
5. Increase opportunities for personal satisfaction contingent on effective performance.

The appropriate leadership style that a manager should use is the one that compensates for any quality that the employee lacks (e.g., experience, ability) or the work setting (i.e., task structure). The leadership style should not duplicate what is already available to the employee. For example, the nurse manager should not provide direction (i.e., directive leadership style) on completing a patient's history and physical to a nurse with 20 years of experience. However, the nurse manager should provide direction, training, or both, when a nurse with 20 years of clinical experience but little or no experience with technology must use an electronic medical records system for the first time to document a patient's history and physical.

Tannenbaum and Schmidt's Continuum of Leadership Behavior

Tannenbaum and Schmidt (1958, 1973) conducted one of the first studies that indicated a need to evaluate the situational factors before implementing a particular leadership style (Ott, 1996). The Continuum of Leadership Behavior model is based on the variety of behaviors noted in earlier leadership studies, particularly the distinction between task and human relations orientation. This model identifies two styles of leadership, which occur across a continuum from boss-centered (task) to subordinate-centered (relationship).

As **Figure 11-3** illustrates, the Tannenbaum and Schmidt (1958) model covers a range of leadership behaviors. The model identifies the amount of authority (boss-centered) used by the manager and the amount of freedom afforded to employees (subordinate-centered). At one end of the continuum (boss-centered), the manager takes complete control of the situation, makes a decision, and announces it to the employees. There is no effort to solicit feedback, ideas, or input. At the other end of the continuum (subordinate-centered), the manager and employees collaboratively make decisions within clearly defined organizational constraints. Within the two extremes of the continuum lie many managerial options to include or exclude employee involvement in decision-making processes. The appropriateness of the behavior depends on situational (contingent) factors.

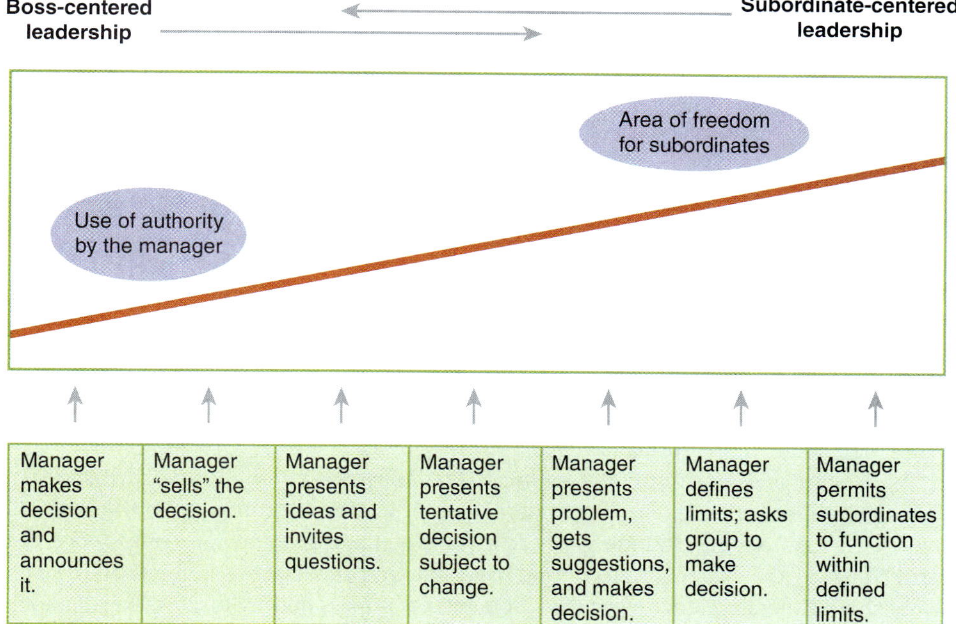

Figure 11-3 Tannenbaum and Schmidt Continuum of Leadership Behavior

Reproduced from Tannenbaum, R., & Schmidt, W. H. (1958, March–April). How to choose a leadership pattern. *Harvard Business Review, 36*(2), 96. Used with Permission.

How do managers determine where on the continuum they should position themselves? Determinants may include (1) the manager's style of leadership, (2) the culture of the organization, (3) the complexity of the task at hand, or (4) the relationship between the manager and the employee, specifically the level of confidence the manager has in the employee and the manager's level of comfort in delegating a task or seeking participation in the decision-making process. Another important situational factor is the employee's acceptance of this participation and acknowledgment of responsibility for delegated tasks. When an employee desires to participate, the subordinate-centered leadership is appropriate. When an employee avoids involvement, the boss-centered leadership style is suitable.

One approach is not universally preferred over the other. Situational factors will determine which is appropriate. Today's healthcare managers face an onslaught of ongoing critical decisions for which they are accountable and responsible. With this in mind, managers must function effectively at each place on the leadership continuum. Attempts to maintain a subordinate-centered position on the continuum will not meet the organizational needs when a manager must make a decision that requires information that employees might not possess or when the situation is so critical that there is no time to collaborate with employees.

Given appropriate time to seek involvement in a decision, the subordinate-centered approach is preferred for obvious reasons. Employees who are permitted to participate in the decision-making process tend to be less threatened by the impending change because they feel that they are part of the solution rather than being observers who have no control over what may or may not happen. Unnecessary exclusion from a participatory effort can create an environment of distrust, fear, hopelessness, and anger. A manager's decision as to where they should be positioned on Tannenbaum and Schmidt's continuum is critical to both the task and how the people affected by the positioning perceive the manager.

Four Stages of Learning Competence and Leaders' Behaviors

Contingency leadership models involve assessing the situation and context, which includes the employees' skills and competence. The Four Stages of Competence have been adapted from the early work of Broadwell and Adams in the 1960s and 1970s (Broadwell, 1969; Adams, n.d.). It explains how individuals progress from an initial lack of awareness and skill to the point where the skill can be performed automatically. It is widely applied in education, workforce development, and leadership contexts because it provides a structured framework for understanding learning progression and performance development.

In leadership and organizational settings, the Four Stages of Competence model (See **Table 11-1**) emphasizes that an employee's development requires ongoing support. Effective leaders are responsible for understanding where a team member falls on the competence continuum and adjusting their direction, feedback, oversight, and expectations accordingly. Leadership behaviors should therefore align with developmental readiness and maturity rather than relying on a single, uniform approach. When the leadership style is mismatched to the employee's competence level, adverse outcomes can occur, such as reduced confidence, preventable errors, disengagement, and slower skill advancement. There are four stages of competence (See **Figure 11-4**):

- **Unconscious Incompetence**—The learner lacks both knowledge and awareness of their knowledge gap. Individuals may underestimate the complexity of the task or associated risk

Table 11-1 Leader Behaviors for the Four Stages of Competence

Stage	Example Nurse Profile	Leadership Behaviors	Primary Leadership Approach
Unconscious Incompetence	Newly hired or new-graduate nurse unfamiliar with required tasks and risks. May not know which questions to ask.	Provide detailed instruction, clear expectations, safety protocols, and observation opportunities	Highly directive
Conscious Incompetence	Nurse aware of skill deficits and seeking improvement	Offer structured practice, feedback, mentoring, and emotional normalization	Directive with high support
Conscious Competence	Nurse able to perform skills at acceptable level with focus and effort	Provide monitored autonomy, case review, problem-solving discussion, and increasing responsibility	Coaching and collaborative
Unconscious Competence	Expert nurse demonstrating consistent, high-quality performance	Job autonomy and the teaching of others	Delegating and empowering

Data from Adams, L. (n.d.). *Learning a new skill is easier said than done.* Gordon Training International. http://www.gordontraining.com/free-workplace-articles/learning-a-new-skill-is-easier-said-than-done/.

of the task. Leaders should clearly communicate required standards, define performance expectations, and introduce foundational knowledge.

- **Conscious Incompetence**—The learner recognizes personal limitations and the need for skill development. This stage may be accompanied by doubt or frustration. Leaders can be

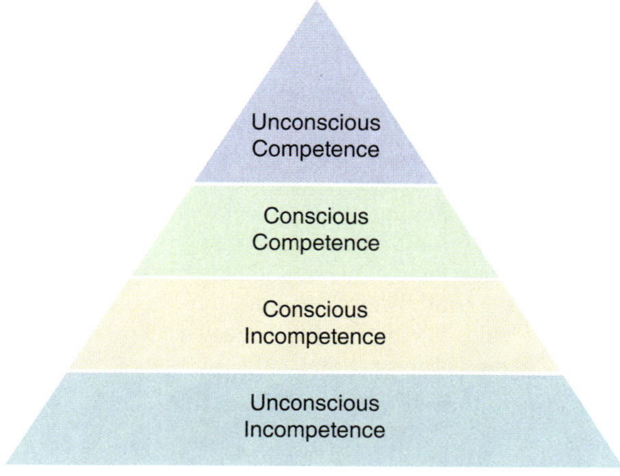

Figure 11-4 Hierarchy of Competence

Modified from Kokcharov, I. (2017). Hierarchy of competence (adapted from Noel Burch) [SVG]. Wikimedia Commons. https://commons.wikimedia.org/wiki/File:Competence_Hierarchy_adapted_from_Noel_Burch_by_Igor_Kokcharov.svg

most effective by providing structured learning opportunities, constructive feedback, guided observation, and reassurance that learning involves gradual progression.

- **Conscious Competence**—The learner demonstrates the skill reliably but must maintain deliberate concentration. Reference tools, supervision, or repeated practice often support this. Leaders can encourage independent problem-solving while still offering availability for questions and case review.
- **Unconscious Competence**—The learner demonstrates full proficiency, in which performance is effortless, efficient, and adaptable to varying circumstances. At this point, leaders may assign greater autonomy, encourage contributions to improvement activities, and involve the individual in peer teaching or precepting.

Leader–Member Exchange Theory

Whereas the contingency theories discussed thus far relate leadership style to general situational and subordinate factors across a group of employees, leader–member exchange theory (LMX) directs us to the differentiated relationships that arise between individual subordinates and their supervisors.

The foundation for LMX comes from the work of George Graen and James Cashman (1975), who coined the phrase Vertical Dyad Linkage (VDL) to describe how leaders develop dyadic (two-person) relationships with subordinates that affect the behavior of both the leader and the subordinate. Over time and through role-taking, role-making, and routinization (see **Exhibit 11-1**), the leader cognitively assigns subordinates to an in-group or an out-group. The

Exhibit 11-1 The Three Phases of LMX

This theory states that leader–subordinate relationships evolve through three stages:

- Role-Taking: Leaders assess their skills and abilities when new members join.
- Role-Making: New members begin working on tasks. Leaders subconsciously classify them into:
    - In-Group: Loyal, skilled, and motivated members who gain the leader's trust. They receive challenging tasks, training, growth opportunities, and more one-on-one time with the leader.
    - Out-Group: Members are perceived as unmotivated or untrustworthy. They receive less engagement, fewer opportunities, and routine work with minimal leader interaction.
- Routinization: Relationship patterns become established.
    - In-Group members maintain their status by showing trust, respect, and dedication. They are often seen as rising stars and receive ongoing support and opportunities.
    - Out-Group members may dislike or distrust the leader. Once labeled, moving to the In-Group is difficult, often requiring a job change.

This classification shapes leader interactions and often becomes self-fulfilling, reinforcing each group's trajectory.

Data from Mind Tools. (n.d.). Leader-member exchange. MindTools.com. http://www.mindtools.com/pages/article/leader-member-exchange.htm

leader perceives individuals assigned to the in-group as more committed to organizational goals and more likely to fulfill responsibilities with higher performance levels. The in-group is "rewarded with more of the leaders' positional resources (i.e., information, confidence, and concern) than individuals assigned to the out-group" (Luthans, 2002, p. 583). For example, a group of early careerists are enrolled in the hospital's management development program, in which they must interact with the vice president of human resources, the facilitator of the program. The young careerists who are considered to be in the in-group may have a higher number of interactions with the vice president than those who are considered to be in the out-group. For instance, if Valerie's personality is similar to the vice president's, then the vice president may spend extra time meeting with and coaching Valerie regarding her career development. This high level of interaction will increase the likelihood that Valerie will be in the vice president's in-group and that Valerie and the vice president will develop a high-quality relationship. Additionally, Valerie may be given special projects during the development program that will further enhance her career opportunities within the hospital because she is in the vice president's inner circle. Bob, another of the young professionals, may have relatively little interaction with the vice president outside of the program's scheduled training time because the vice president dislikes Bob's communication style. Therefore, Bob would be in the vice president's out-group, and Bob and the vice president would have a low-quality relationship.

Not surprisingly, in-group members report fewer problematic issues with leader–member interactions and higher levels of responsiveness with the leader than out-group members. Additionally, in-groups are more often led with less emphasis on formal authority to control and influence. In comparison, out-groups are more often supervised with a stronger emphasis on formal authority to control and influence. The mere nature of the high quality of the leader–member relationship that occurs with the in-group generates individuals who accept greater responsibility and exhibit higher levels of contribution to organizational goals (Graen & Ginsburgh, 1977; Liden & Graen, 1980).

The Leader–Member Exchange (LMX) theory takes VDL one step further. LMX examines the characteristics of individuals belonging to the in-group, noting similarities between in-group members and the leader in the dyadic relationship. Individuals with high self-efficacy will tend to form in-group relationships with the leader. In this dyadic relationship, the leader perceives the follower to be more friendly, approachable, and similar in personality to the leader themselves. The perception of similarity becomes a very important factor for inclusion in the in-group and the resultant development of relationships and contributions to task accomplishment. However, this can have the effect of leaders developing and promoting people within the organization who look and think like themselves. This may lead to reduced diversity of managers and leaders within the organization, which can lead to groupthink and discrimination. Leaders must be aware of their own internal biases when investing time and resources in developing their employees. Are only employees who look, act, and think like the leader getting fair opportunities?

According to Robbins (2005, p. 163), "Studies confirm many of the LMX predictions that leaders do differentiate among followers and those with in-group status have higher performance ratings, lower turnover intentions, and higher satisfaction with superiors than those in the out-group."

Conclusion

Contingency theories help us understand that one leadership style is not effective across all the variable situations in organizations. The leader who can respond to ever-increasing levels of environmental uncertainty by utilizing more than one leadership style will most likely increase employees' motivation, satisfaction, and productivity. Managers should not underestimate the importance of applying the appropriate leadership style based on the accurate analysis of situational factors.

Discussion Questions

1. Describe Fiedler's Contingency Model. What is the impact of his assumption that leadership style is fixed?
2. Summarize Path-Goal leadership theory. What theories of motivation can you tie to the assumptions of the model?
3. Identify healthcare situations in which Tannenbaum and Schmidt's Continuum of Leadership Behavior would suggest the autocratic leadership style as the most appropriate.
4. Discuss the role of leadership style in response to an employee's level of competence as described in the Four Stages of Competence model.
5. What impact does the assignment of employees to the in-group or out-group (LMX) have on workers' performance and satisfaction?
6. Apply the contingency theories discussed in this chapter as they relate to your work environment to assess the appropriate style of leadership and the implications for motivation, satisfaction, and productivity.

Exercise 11-1 Applying the Four Stages of Competence

Write a brief description of a personal learning experience—academic, clinical, or work-related—in which you were in each of the following stages:

- Unconscious Incompetence (you did not yet know what you did not know)
- Conscious Incompetence (you recognized your lack of skill or understanding)
- Conscious Competence (you could perform the task but had to think carefully about it)
- Unconscious Competence (the skill became automatic and familiar)

After describing your experiences, answer the following questions:

1. How did your confidence, motivation, and performance change as you moved through each stage?
2. What kinds of support or guidance from a leader, instructor, or peer were most helpful at each stage?
3. Would a different type of support or leadership approach have improved your learning at any stage?
4. Which stage do you find most challenging, and why?
5. How might understanding these stages influence the way you lead or teach others?

Form a group of three or four individuals and share your reflections. Discuss similarities and differences in how people experience the stages and the types of leadership behaviors that are most effective for supporting learners at each point in the process.

CASE STUDY 11-2 What Can Joe Do About Betty?

Just before quitting time, Joe, the hospital's health information department manager, watched his three new trainees struggle with the complex electronic medical records software. Across the room, Betty, an expert with the system, finished her work early as usual. She gathered her belongings and left without acknowledging her coworkers.

"There goes the answer to my problem," Joe thought. With her expertise, Betty would be an ideal coach for the new employees. However, she had refused training duties, saying she wasn't comfortable instructing others, didn't want responsibility for their work, and preferred working alone.

Joe was surprised by her refusal. He had been promoted to department manager over Betty despite her seniority and experience, largely because he enjoyed mentoring and helping others. He didn't want to force Betty into the role but needed a solution. The training budget was nonexistent, and no one else had her level of expertise.

As Betty walked to the parking lot, she thought, "Why would I help Joe? I should have been promoted instead of him. I trained him when he started here! Just because he has a master's degree, he got the job over me. Senior management overlooked my experience."

She resented the situation. "I don't care what happens now. I only have 5 years until retirement and my full pension. As long as I do my job well, Joe can't interfere with my plans. Not that he could anyway—he barely understands the software. It takes real technical expertise, which I have and he doesn't."

Using Fiedler's contingency theory, explain what style of leadership Joe should use with Betty, given the current situation in his department.

CASE STUDY 11-3 A New Employee Scheduling System

You are the director of human resources at Baptist Health System, overseeing over 4000 employees across hospitals, clinics, and home medical services. You plan to implement new software to automate employee scheduling, replacing the outdated system and saving the organization thousands annually. Frank, an employee in the Office of Technology (OT), has the expertise needed, but he is already overworked. His boss, Jane, has granted limited access to his time, provided it does not interfere with his duties.

Scenario One

After obtaining Jane's permission, you email Frank: "I need you to assist my staff in implementing a new software application to upgrade and automate employee scheduling. This must be completed within 2 weeks. My assistant will contact you tomorrow to discuss the details so you can start immediately."

Scenario Two

You schedule a meeting with Frank the next day: "Frank, I understand you have experience with database conversions, and Jane told me you're the best person for this project. Like many healthcare organizations, we face challenges in labor cost control and maintaining adequate staffing for high-quality patient care.

"Baptist has relied on outdated scheduling software that no longer meets our needs. We require a new system that is flexible, scalable, and integrates with our existing time and attendance system to share real-time data across facilities. The current 14-day delay is unacceptable. Additionally, The Joint Commission has strict reporting requirements that we must meet efficiently.

"This project is critical, and I'd like your input on how we can successfully implement it over the next 30 days. How can you help us reach this goal?"

Discuss how Frank would react to Scenario One and Scenario Two at each stage of the level of competence in the Four Stages of Competence model.

Exhibit 11-2 Leadership Style Survey

Directions

This questionnaire contains statements about leadership style beliefs. Next to each statement, circle the number that represents how strongly you feel about the statement by using the following scoring system:

- Almost Always True: 5
- Frequently True: 4
- Occasionally True: 3
- Seldom True: 2
- Almost Never True: 1

Be honest about your choices, as there are no right or wrong answers—this is only for self-assessment.

Leadership Style Survey

1. I always retain the final decision-making authority within my department or team.	5	4	3	2	1
2. I always try to include one or more employees in determining what to do and how to do it. However, I maintain the final decision-making authority.	5	4	3	2	1
3. I and my employees always vote whenever a major decision has to be made.	5	4	3	2	1
4. I do not consider suggestions made by my employees, as I do not have the time for them.	5	4	3	2	1
5. I ask for employee ideas and input on upcoming plans and projects.	5	4	3	2	1
6. For a major decision to pass in my department, it must have the approval of each individual or the majority.	4	3	2	1	
7. I tell my employees what has to be done and how to do it.	5	4	3	2	1
8. When things go wrong and I need to create a strategy to keep a project or process running on schedule, I call a meeting to get my employees' advice.	5	4	3	2	1
9. To get information out, I send it by email, memos, or voicemail; very rarely is a meeting called. My employees are then expected to act upon the information.	5	4	3	2	1
10. When someone makes a mistake, I make a note of it and tell them not to ever do it again.	5	4	3	2	1
11. I want to create an environment where the employees take ownership of the project. I allow them to participate in the decision-making process.	5	4	3	2	1
12. I allow my employees to determine what needs to be done and how to do it.	5	4	3	2	1
13. New hires are not allowed to make any decisions unless it is approved by me first.	5	4	3	2	1
14. I ask employees for their vision of where they see their jobs going and then use their vision where appropriate.	5	4	3	2	1
15. My workers know more about their jobs than me, so I allow them to carry out the decisions to do their job.	5	4	3	2	1
16. When something goes wrong, I tell my employees that a procedure is not working correctly and I establish a new one.	5	4	3	2	1

17. I allow my employees to set priorities with my guidance. 5 4 3 2 1
18. I delegate tasks in order to implement a new procedure or process. 5 4 3 2 1
19. I closely monitor my employees to ensure they are performing correctly. 4 3 2 1
20. When there are differences in role expectations, I work with them to resolve the differences. 5 4 3 2 1
21. Each individual is responsible for defining their job. 5 4 3 2 1
22. I like the power that my leadership position holds over subordinates. 5 4 3 2 1
23. I like to use my leadership power to help subordinates grow. 5 4 3 2 1
24. I like to share my leadership power with my subordinates. 5 4 3 2 1
25. Employees must be directed or threatened with punishment in order to get them to achieve the organizational objectives. 5 4 3 2 1
26. Employees will exercise self-direction if they are committed to the objectives. 5 4 3 2 1
27. Employees have the right to determine their own organizational objectives. 5 4 3 2 1
28. Employees seek mainly security. 5 4 3 2 1
29. Employees know how to use creativity and ingenuity to solve organizational problems. 5 4 3 2 1
30. My employees can lead themselves just as well as I can. 5 4 3 2 1

On the fill-in lines, mark the score of each item on the questionnaire. For example, if you scored Item 1 with a 3 (Occasionally), then enter a 3 next to Item 1. When you have entered all the scores for each question, total each of the three columns.

Item	Score	Item	Score	Item	Score
1	_____	2	_____	3	_____
4	_____	5	_____	6	_____
7	_____	8	_____	9	_____
10	_____	11	_____	12	_____
13	_____	14	_____	15	_____
16	_____	17	_____	18	_____
19	_____	20	_____	21	_____
22	_____	23	_____	24	_____
25	_____	26	_____	27	_____
28	_____	29	_____	30	_____
TOTAL	_____	TOTAL	_____	TOTAL	_____
Authoritarian Style (autocratic)		Participative Style (democratic)		Delegative Style (free rein)	

This questionnaire is to help you assess what leadership style you normally use. The lowest score possible for a leadership style is 10 (all answers are "Almost never"), while the highest score possible for a style is 50 (all answers are "Almost always").

The highest of the three scores indicates what style of leadership you normally use. If your highest score is 40 or more, it is a strong indicator of your normal style. The lowest of the three scores is an indicator of the style you use least. If your lowest score is 20 or less, it is a strong indicator that you normally do not use this leadership style.

If two of the scores are close to the same, you might be going through a transition phase, either personally or at work, except: if you score high in both the participative and the delegative, then you are probably a delegative leader.

If there is only a small difference between the three scores, then this indicates that you have no clear perception of the leadership style you use, or you are a new leader and are trying to feel out the correct style for you.

Available at: www.nwlink.com/~donclark/leader/survstyl.html. Created July 15, 1998; last update August 21, 2010.

References

Adams, L. (n.d.). Learning a new skill is easier said than done. Gordon Training International. http://www.gordontraining.com/free-workplace-articles/learning-a-new-skill-is-easier-said-than-done/

Broadwell, M. M. (1969, February). Teaching for learning. *The Gospel Guardian, 20*(9), 1-3.

Evans, M. G. (1970). The effects of supervisory behavior on the path-goal relationship. *Organizational Behavior and Human Performance, 5*(3), 277–298.

Fiedler, F. E. (1965). Engineer the job to fit the manager. *Harvard Business Review, 43*(5), 115–122.

Fiedler, F. E. (1967). *A theory of leadership effectiveness*. McGraw-Hill.

Fiedler, F. E. (1970). The contingency model: A theory of leadership effectiveness. In C. W. Backman & P. F. Secord (Eds.), *Problems in social psychology* (pp. 279–289). McGraw-Hill.

Fiedler, F. E. (1995). Cognitive resources and leadership performance. *Applied Psychology: An International Review, 44*(1), 5–28.

Fiedler, F. E. (1996). Research on leadership selection and training: One view of the future. *Administrative Science Quarterly, 41*(2), 241–250.

Fiedler, F. E. (2008). The curious role of cognitive resources in leadership. In R. E. Riggio, S. E. Murphy & F. J. Pirozzolo (Eds.), *Multiple intelligences and leadership*. Lawrence Erlbaum Associates.

Fiedler, F. E., & Chemers, M. M. (1974). *Leadership and effective management*. Scott, Foresman.

Fiedler, F. E., & Garcia, J. E. (1987). *New approaches to effective leadership: Cognitive resources and organizational performance*. Wiley.

Fiedler, F. E., Potter, E. H., Zais, M. M., & Knowlton, W. (1979). Organizational stress and the use and misuse of managerial intelligence and experience. *Journal of Applied Psychology, 64*(6), 635–674.

Graen, G., & Cashman, J. F. (1975). A role-making model of leadership in formal organizations: A developmental approach. *Organizational and Administrative Sciences, 6*, 143–165.

Graen, G., & Ginsburgh, S. (1977). Job resignation as a function of role orientation and leader acceptance: A longitudinal investigation of organizational assimilation. *Organizational Behavior and Human Performance, 19*(1), 1–17.

House, R. J. (1971). A path-goal theory of leader effectiveness. *Administrative Science Quarterly, 16*(3), 321–338.

House, R. J., & Mitchell, T. R. (1974). Path–goal theory of leadership. *Journal of Contemporary Business, 3*(4), 81–97.

Liden, R. C., & Graen, G. (1980). Generalizability of the vertical dyad linkage model of leadership. *Academy of Management Journal, 23*(3), 451–466.

Luthans, F. (2002). *Organizational behavior* (9th ed.). McGraw-Hill.

Ott, J. S. (1996). *Classic readings in organizational behavior* (2nd ed.). Wadsworth.

Razik, T. A., & Swanson, A. D. (1995). *Fundamental concepts of educational leadership and management*. Prentice Hall.

Robbins, S. P. (2005). *Essentials of organizational behavior* (8th ed.). Prentice Hall.

Tannenbaum, R., & Schmidt, W. (1958). How to choose a leadership pattern. *Harvard Business Review, 36*(2), 95–101.

Tannenbaum, R., & Schmidt, W. (1973). How to choose a leadership pattern. *Harvard Business Review, 51*(3), 1–10.

Tosi, H. L., & Mero, N. P. (2003). *The fundamentals of organizational behavior: What managers need to know*. Blackwell.

Yukl, G. (1998). *Leadership in organizations* (4th ed.). Prentice Hall.

CHAPTER 12

Contemporary Leadership Theories

LEARNING OUTCOMES

After completing this chapter, the student should be able to:

- Define transformational leadership.
- Identify similarities and differences between transformational and transactional leadership.
- Discuss the application of transformational leadership style in the modern health management setting.
- Identify characteristics common to charismatic, servant, and collaborative leaders.
- Describe the effect of charismatic, servant, and collaborative leadership on organizational outcomes and attaining strategic organizational goals.
- Discuss the development of behavioral competencies for healthcare leaders.

Overview

This chapter examines various contemporary leadership theories, including transformational, charismatic, servant, and collaborative leadership approaches. These theories build on both individual trait and behavior and contingency leadership theories. When examining leadership, the focus is typically on an individual who has sufficient sources of power to exert influence and control over members of the organization to achieve organizational goals. The flaw in using this approach is the narrow focus on the individual. A more appropriate assessment of leadership includes the characteristics of the leader and peers, supervisors, and the organization. This broader perspective provides a more detailed examination of the leader, the external environment, and the situation—all factors that determine appropriateness of leadership style. Contemporary theories also emphasize emotion, vision, and values.

While contemporary theories recognize the complexities of leadership and expand the multiplicity of variables that affect it, they also return us to individual characteristics and behaviors. Novick, Morrow, and Mays (2008) suggest that transformational leadership seemingly involves the reemergence of trait-based theories. Indeed, numerous studies in the past few decades have focused on personality traits of effective transformational, transactional, and charismatic leaders (DeHoogh et al., 2005). Many researchers credit this resurgence to the work of Judge, Bono, Ilies, and Gerhardt (2002), who group the numerous traits identified in leadership studies into a "Big Five" personality framework. Stronger and more consistent relationships emerged when similar traits were organized into five categories (Openness to Experience, Conscientiousness, Extroversion, Agreeableness, Neuroticism–OCEAN). This five-factor view of personality provided a new framework for linking personality and leader behavior and effectiveness in studies on charismatic, transformational, and transactional leadership (Bryman, 1992; Den Hartog & Koopman, 2001; Digman, 1990). Another individual trait that has received considerable attention is emotional intelligence (EI). Emotional intelligence involves the ability to monitor one's and others' feelings and emotions, differentiate among them, and use this information to guide one's thinking and actions (Salovey & Mayer, 1990).

While innate personality traits play a role in leadership, the variance explained by personality remains limited. A leader may have intrinsic traits that enhance or allow leadership to emerge, but must also have knowledge, skills, vision, and values to influence followers and facilitate individual and organizational performance. Therefore, we will conclude this chapter with a brief review of the development of behavioral competencies for healthcare leadership.

Transformational Versus Transactional Leadership

Defining "transactional leadership" and "transformational leadership" helps establish a foundation for how each approach is appropriate and vital to an organization's success.

In general terms, transactional leadership is directed toward task accomplishment and the maintenance of good relations between the leader and subordinates through consideration of performance and reward. The transactional leadership model has been considered the most prevalent leadership model used in health care (Schwartz & Tumblin, 2002). In contrast, transformational leadership is directed toward influencing and managing institutional change and innovation through revitalization and vision (Dessler, 1998).

Leader behaviors include characteristics identified as consideration and initiating structure. *Consideration* is the recognition that individuals have needs and require relationships; *initiating structure* denotes an emphasis on tasks and goals. Burns (1978) reported that transactional leadership style is based on both consideration and initiating structure. Transactional behaviors are "largely oriented toward accomplishing the task at hand and maintaining good relations with those working with the leader by exchanging promises of rewards for performance" (Dessler, 1998, p. 350). Transactional leaders seek to maintain the status quo and reward subordinates for doing what is expected. Expectations of performance and the resultant rewards are clearly identified and delivered on completion of the agreement. As DeHoogh et al. (2005, p. 840) put it, "[T]ransactional leaders influence followers through task-focused behaviors; they clarify expectancies, rules and procedures, emphasizing a fair deal." Trastek, Hamilton, and Niles (2014) relate that the transactional leadership model is unable to account for the complex motivations of healthcare providers, and it fails to build trust between the leader and followers. "Your reward is your paycheck" would be a statement reflective of transactional leadership.

In contrast to the transactional leadership model, the transformational style of leadership incorporates emotion, values, and vision to motivate individuals and seeks to change the status quo. Transformational leadership is all about change, innovation, improvement, and entrepreneurship through vision and inspiration. Osland, Kolb, and Rubin (2001, p. 297) state that "transformational leaders are value-driven change agents who make followers more conscious of the importance of task outcomes. They provide followers with a vision and motivate them to go beyond self-interest for the good of the organization."

Transformational leadership establishes subordinate effort and performance that extends beyond that which occurs as a result of transactional leadership. These two approaches to leadership are not mutually exclusive; most leaders exhibit both transactional and transformational behaviors in different intensities and amounts (Bass, 1990b; Luthans, 2002). According to Bass (1990b) and Luthans (2002), each leadership approach differentiates itself by identifying four specific characteristics that are unique to each style.

Transactional Leadership

- *Contingent Reward*: Contracts exchange of rewards for effort; promises rewards for good performance; recognizes accomplishments.
- *Management by Exception (an active approach)*: Watches and searches for deviations from rules and standards; takes corrective action.
- *Management by Exception (a passive approach)*: Intervenes only if standards are not met.
- *Laissez-Faire*: Abdicates responsibilities; avoids making decisions.

Transformational Leadership

- *Charisma*: Provides vision and a sense of mission; instills pride; gains respect and trust.
- *Inspiration*: Communicates high expectations; uses symbols to focus efforts; expresses important purposes in simple ways.
- *Intellectual*: Promotes intelligence, rationality, and careful problem solving.
- *Individualized Consideration*: Gives personal attention; treats each employee individually; coaches; advises.

Transformational leadership elevates the level of insight about the importance and value of outcomes through the growth of subordinates by encouraging followers to question their own way of doing things. Transactional leadership constitutes behavior that operates through consideration and covenants between the leader and the follower.

Transformational Leadership: A Contradictory View

Kotter (1995) provided a contradictory view as to the success of incorporating transformational efforts. Kotter noted that transformational change (through transformational leadership) is conducted under many banners: cultural change, reengineering, and total quality management, to name a few. The purpose of transformational leadership is to address the essential changes necessary to respond to an ever-changing, globally competitive environment.

Kotter (1995) added that transformational leadership resulting in successful change is best executed in phases and that failure to address each phase to the fullest significantly diminishes the capacity to succeed. As illustrated in **Table 12-1**, Kotter identified eight transformational phases and associated errors and provided strategies to enhance leader success by addressing the errors.

Table 12-1 Eight Specific Errors That Diminish the Transformational Effort

Phase	Transformational Errors	Processes to Enhance Transformational Success
1	Failure to create a true sense of urgency	Establish a sense of urgency by examining market and competitive realities and conducting a SWOT analysis (strengths, weaknesses, opportunities, and threats)
2	Failure to create a powerful guiding coalition	Form powerful coalitions by assembling groups of teams with the power to effect change
3	Failure to create a clearly understood vision	Create a vision with direction and focus consistent with organizational strategies
4	Failure to adequately communicate the vision	Use all available channels of communication to convey the change and lead by example
5	Failure to remove obstacles in moving toward transformational change	Remove obstacles, change systems and structures, encourage creativity and innovation through empowerment
6	Failure to systematically plan for or create short-term successes	Plan for and recognize visible, short-term improvements through established reward systems
7	Proclaiming success prematurely	Utilize credibility to change systems, structures, processes, and policies to arrive at the vision
8	Failure to anchor the transformational change	Institutionalize the change by infusing appropriate behaviors that will lead to development and succession in the organizational culture

Data from Kotter, J. P. (1995). Leading change: Why transformational efforts fail. *Harvard Business Review, 73*(2), 59–67.

Tichy and Devanna (1986), cited by Luthans (2002, pp. 591–592), found that transformational leaders shared the following seven characteristics:

1. They identified themselves as change agents.
2. They exhibited courage.
3. They trusted people.
4. They were value-driven.
5. They valued lifelong learning.
6. They had the capability to face complexity, ambiguity, and uncertainty.
7. They were imaginative, creative, innovative, and visionary.

The Implications of Transformational Leadership for the Healthcare Industry

Because of regulatory changes, financial pressures, evolving care delivery models, and AI, healthcare organizations will be transformed in many ways in the years to come. The healthcare manager must acquire the skills, abilities, and knowledge to understand effective leadership processes and anticipate environmental change. Changes facing the healthcare manager necessitate a stronger focus on results, creativity, and innovation (Gummer, 1996). The healthcare manager will experience increasing demands to demonstrate high performance and quality outcomes while reducing costs amid decreasing revenues. Leaders must increase their transformational skills while balancing the requirements of transactional management.

Despite the importance of transformational leadership, the transactional leadership model has been considered the most dominant leadership model used in health care (Schwartz & Tumblin, 2002). A 2003 study by Thyler provides interesting insight into the hold of the transactional approach to healthcare leadership and its impact on nursing care. Thyler reported that the transactional leadership style may be causing nurses to leave the profession because they struggle ideologically with the system in which they work. Numerous other studies have been conducted on the relationship between leadership style and job satisfaction (or dissatisfaction). For example, Medley and Larochelle's (1995) research reported that staff nurses view behaviors associated with transactional leadership (e.g., negative feedback) unfavorably concerning their jobs. This study indicated that head nurses with high transformational scores were likelier to have staff nurses with higher job satisfaction scores and longer association with their staff nurses than transactional leaders. These results provide strong support for the idea that a transformational leadership approach advances retention efforts and diminishes turnover rates—a conclusion that has significant fiscal implications for healthcare facilities.

Chaffee (2001) addressed the implications of transformational leadership in a military healthcare environment. The purpose of Chaffee's study was to identify the ideal characteristics of a future Navy healthcare executive. Sixty-seven respondents reported most frequently the following characteristics of an ideal, transformational leader:

- Possesses the ability to organize teamwork.
- Possesses a clear vision.
- Teaches others to succeed and mentors others.
- Takes risks and encourages others to do so.
- Develops and maintains excellent interpersonal relationship skills.
- Possesses credibility, honesty, and integrity.
- Embraces and drives change.
- Strives for excellence and continuous improvement.
- Has excellent communication skills.
- Exhibits a passion for work.
- Maintains a focus on the organizational mission.

As Chaffee (2001, p. 241) points out, "The characteristics identified by respondents describe leadership traits rather than management skills. None of the respondents identified the traditional managerial skills of planning, organizing, coordinating, directing, and controlling. Additionally, the most frequently identified characteristics fit the definition of transformational leadership."

These leadership characteristics support four managerial competencies sustained by successful leaders (Bennis, 1984; Chaffee, 2001):

1. *Management of Attention*: The ability to get the attention of a group through a compelling vision that brings others to a place they have not been before.
2. *Management of Meaning*: The ability to make a vision clear to others and the ability to communicate ideas and create meaning.
3. *Management of Trust*: The ability to inspire trust through reliability and consistency.
4. *Management of Self*: Knowing one's skills and deploying them effectively.

Transformational leadership is well suited to today's economic, social, political, and technological conditions. It thrives on change and innovation and provides the knowledge, skills, and abilities to facilitate innovation and transformation beyond those available in a traditional approach. Doing things because that is the way they were always done is being replaced by dynamic solutions to old and new problems (Sofarelli & Brown, 1998; Trofino, 2000).

Bennis and Nanus (1985), while noting the importance of both management and leadership, recognized a philosophical dissimilarity between the two approaches: "Managers are people who do things right and leaders are people who do the right things" (p. 21). Lieutenant General George J. Flynn of the U.S. Marine Corps noted, "I know of no case study in history that describes an organization that has been managed out of a crisis. Every single one of them was led" (Sinek, 2017, p. xi). These statements' implications provoke questions about how the healthcare industry will respond to an environment in which leadership focuses less on managing technical skills and more on managing knowledge processes. Technical skills are controlled through clearly stated goals and measurable performance objectives. Mental processes have replaced the mechanistic tasks that must be carefully monitored and managed, meaning that critical decisions are arrived at through cognitive processes, not controlled through clearly stated goals and measurable performance objectives. The transformational leadership approach suits this new health services environment well.

Other Contemporary Leadership Approaches

More than 70 years ago, the Office of Strategic Services published a book titled *The Assessment of Men*, in which two types of leaders were described: (1) the leader in articulation, who was forceful and inspirational in expression and who spelled out clearly what was needed and how it was to be accomplished, and (2) the leader in action, who, by setting themselves in motion, demonstrated how to accomplish a goal and whose successes encouraged others to join in the pursuit of the goal. Either way, "the leader, by words or action, inspired others to achieve something beyond the ordinary by appealing to a goal worthy of human effort" (Curtin, 1997, p. 7).

Although transformational leadership is the primary topic of this chapter, other leadership styles and their respective characteristics also focus on transformation or change. Here, we examine some other change styles and their conceptual similarities. Bolman and Deal (1997) offer the symbolic leader for consideration. Symbolic leaders interpret and reinterpret experiences, developing the capacity to impart purpose and meaning. They use symbols to seize attention. They frame experiences in an uncertain environment, providing a reasonable interpretation and understanding of events. Symbolic leaders disseminate information through persuasive communication, primarily through stories, rites, and current and past rituals. Symbolic leaders are consistent in their use of rules and customs (Bolman & Deal, 1997).

The superleadership approach shifts power from the leader to employees, fostering self-leadership. Traditional leadership models often lack the adaptability needed in today's fast-changing work environments. With increasing employee participation and evolving organizational structures, identifying a single leadership style is challenging. Like transformational leaders who encourage personal and professional growth, superleaders empower employees to take ownership of vision and direction. These leaders guide rather than control, recognizing that leadership can emerge at all levels. Superleadership is effective because it builds a positive workplace culture, promotes self-led teams, and balances rewards with constructive feedback. This approach enhances performance by fostering employee accountability and engagement (Osland et al., 2001).

Superleaders share many qualities with empowering leaders. Among various leadership approaches, those prioritizing employees' needs are linked to improved well-being (Pearce & Sims, 2002). ***Empowering leadership***, a contemporary model, encourages employee participation in decision-making, fosters confidence, enhances work meaningfulness, and grants autonomy (Audenaert et al., 2020). This approach goes beyond delegation by actively challenging employees and providing development opportunities, benefiting both individuals and the organization in the long term.

The Charismatic Leader

> Charisma is a tricky thing. Jack Kennedy oozed it—but so did Hitler and Charles Manson. Con artists, charlatans, and megalomaniacs can make it their instrument as effectively as the best CEOs, entertainers, and Presidents. If used wisely, it is a blessing; if indulged, it can be a curse. Charismatic visionaries lead people ahead and sometimes astray. (Sellers, 1996, pp. 68–72)

Charismatic leaders exhibit high levels of self-confidence and trust in subordinates, high expectations for subordinates, and an ideological vision and purpose enacted through personal example. In return, followers of charismatic leaders demonstrate loyalty to, confidence in, and trust in the charismatic leader's values, behaviors, and vision. Relationship and connectedness are critical elements between followers and charismatic leaders. The effect is profound, often producing performance results that exceed established expectations (Luthans, 2002). Followers will transcend their self-interests for the team, department, or organization (Bass, 2008).

In light of the high esteem the charismatic leader holds, one would expect the charismatic leader to exhibit high ethical standards. This presumption, in most cases, is correct. The ethical charismatic leader will generally use their power in socially constructive ways to serve others (e.g., Mother Teresa and Martin Luther King, Jr.). However, not all charismatic leaders are ethical (e.g., Adolf Hitler and Osama bin Laden). Howell and Avolio (1992) noted that charismatic leaders "deserve this label only if they create transformations in their organizations so that members are motivated to follow them and to seek organization objectives not simply because they are ordered to do so, and not merely because they calculate that such compliance is in their self-interest, but because they voluntarily identify with the organization, its standards of conduct and willingly seek to fulfill its purpose" (Luthans, 2002, p. 590).

Although transformational and charismatic leadership components differ somewhat (Yukl, 1999), these theories are often seen as equivalent. As discussed earlier, research supports the position that transformational leadership qualities can be learned as long as the individual is comfortable and confident in the controlling and influencing roles. Thus, by combining the desire to lead with learning and understanding the position and responsibility of a transformational leader, a person may develop the capacity to transform organizations. Given this supposition and the close association between transformational and charismatic leadership, the question is, "Can an individual acquire charismatic characteristics sufficient to develop a following based on trust, expectations, and purpose?"

Benton (2003) describes a six-step plan for developing executive charisma. Sometimes these elements are also referred to as executive presence. She suggests that many people, who might otherwise be change agents, accept that, given organizational constraints and the competition among organizational leaders, they will achieve only a certain level of success. She also suggests that executive charisma is the one missing component to assuming charismatic positioning beyond one's exemplary character, instincts, judgment, integrity, and positive energy. Benton (2003, p. 10) defines executive charisma as "the ability to gain effective responses from others by using aware actions and considerate civility to get useful things done." Benton's six steps to developing executive charismatic qualities are as follows:

Step 1: Be the first to initiate
Step 2: Expect and give acceptance to maintain esteem
Step 3: Ask questions and ask for favors
Step 4: Stand tall and straight, and smile
Step 5: Be human, humorous, and hands-on
Step 6: Slow down, shut up, and listen

It is important to recognize that being the first to initiate action establishes one's willingness to accept uncertainty head-on and acknowledge that a situation can be either a problem or an opportunity to initiate transformation. This first step requires a consistent willingness to act. Recognition, as both a giver and a receiver, fulfills the second step of the plan: to provide a sense of esteem to oneself and others. This provision of esteem provides a cycle of optimism that can pervade the organization, affecting the other people involved in the transformative effort.

The third step provides for an exchange of information as required to meet organizational objectives. Choosing one's words and tone carefully while being specific and concise is important to ensuring that information is timely, relevant, and accurate. Do not be too timid to ask questions or solicit favors. Be mindful to recall favors provided and extend thanks in return. Perception is important when one is exhibiting charismatic qualities. Step four demands that the executive leader not only play the role but also look the role. Standing tall with a relaxed confidence enhances one's charismatic appearance.

Interestingly, step five mandates that charismatic leaders take on responsibilities that others will not, but without overdoing it. By this, Benton means that being human is imperative to being charismatic, but do not be too human. Be humorous with a sense of appropriateness. Do not cross social, ethnic, or gender boundaries. Stepping across acceptable boundaries into indefinable territory can quickly extinguish one's effort to create charismatic leadership qualities.

The final step involves maintaining a pace that permits decision making, implementation, and focus. Not talking (shutting up) allows one the opportunity to listen. Listening allows one to hear what others have to say, develop a response to the information, and gain the trust necessary to initiate transformational efforts. "Executive charisma is not as much about you as about your effect on others, and that comes not just from what you say and do but from what you do not say and do not do" (Benton, 2003, p. 153).

In today's modern environment, have the executive presence or charisma requirements changed? Research featured in Harvard Business Review suggests that they have. From 2012 to 2022, many of the traits associated with executive presence—including respect for others—have become more important, as have authenticity and an evaluation of one's online presence and physical presence (Hewlett, 2024).

Servant Leadership

Some scholars in the leadership area, such as Peter Senge, Warren Bennis, Peter Block, and Margaret Wheatley, see servant leadership as the emerging leadership paradigm for all corporations and institutions in the 21st century. The servant leadership concept is captured in Disraeli's following quote: "I must follow the people. Am I not their leader?"

The term "servant leadership" was first used by Robert K. Greenleaf in 1969 as a way to describe a type of leadership that focuses on serving the highest needs of other people to help others achieve their goals. Servant leadership is an approach to managing people that "begins with a clear and compelling vision that excites passion in the leader and commitment in those who follow" (Blanchard & Hodges, 2003). A servant leader values others' strengths and talents and encourages the use of these strengths and talents for the betterment of the organization.

Servant leadership focuses on the leader's development through awareness and self-knowledge. Spears (2004) identified the qualities and characteristics of servant leadership: listening, empathy, healing, awareness, persuasion, conceptualization, foresight, stewardship, commitment to people's growth, and building community. These characteristics and a moral core drive servant leaders to help people meet their goals and overcome challenges (Trastek et al., 2014).

Servant leadership recognizes the importance of performance coaching while acknowledging that individual development and performance are strongly related. According to Blanchard and Hodges (2003, p. A2), instrumental to the implementation of servant leadership are three components of performance coaching:

1. *Performance Planning*: The setting of goals and objectives.
2. *Day-to-Day Coaching*: Providing the resources and an environment conducive to accomplishing established goals.
3. *Performance Evaluation*: The timely and relevant evaluation of individual performance and the identification of professional developmental needs.

Anderson (2003) believes servant leadership can build effective hospital–physician relationships. He states that servant leaders accept as their responsibility the need to invest in the lives of their followers, believing that they are "not superior to the follower and also know that on any given day or in a given circumstance the follower may become the leader. The servant leader hopes that the follower will one day become a servant leader and, therefore, will invest in the follower's career to better ensure that this indeed happens" (Anderson, 2003, p. 45).

Studies have shown that this leadership style fosters a supportive work environment, enhances employee engagement, and improves patient satisfaction. Servant leadership in health care is associated with valued outcomes such as reduced turnover rates and improved organizational performance, underscoring its relevance in addressing complex healthcare challenges (Felix, 2023). Furthermore, research indicates that servant leadership can mitigate burnout among healthcare professionals by creating environments where employees feel valued and empowered (Alharbi & Kundi, 2023). Jenkins and Stewart (2010) reported similar results. The researchers found a positive impact on individual nurse employees' job satisfaction in departments where the nursing staff perceived that their managers had a stronger servant leadership orientation.

In their studies of healthcare leadership, Pelote and Route (2007) concluded that the most successful leaders, whom they refer to as masterpiece leaders, displayed a form of servant leadership. These leaders viewed themselves as the leader-coach first and the leader-expert second. "Masterpiece leaders create, energize, and motivate the healthcare climate; exhibit a high level of passion, excitement, and drive to perpetuate their success" (p. 282).

Many people equate servant leadership with transformational leadership; however, there are differences. The primary difference between the two leadership styles is the focus of the leader. Stone et al. (2003, p. 1) explain that

> The transformational leader's focus is directed toward the organization, and his/her behavior builds follower commitment to organizational objectives. The servant leader's

focus is on the followers, and the achievement of organizational objectives is a subordinate outcome. The extent to which the leader can shift the primary focus of leadership from the organization to the follower is the distinguishing factor in classifying leaders as either transformational or servant leaders.

Collaborative Leadership

Ibarra and Hansen (2011) define collaborative leadership as the "capacity to engage people and groups outside one's formal control and inspire them to work toward common goals—despite differences in convictions, cultural values, and operating norms." Collaborative leadership is complex because it requires a leader to achieve success by motivating individuals in multiple groups and organizations and bringing together and aligning the goals of many stakeholders (Borkowski & Deppman, 2019). Al-Sawai (2013) states that collaborative healthcare leadership requires a synergistic work environment in which multiple parties are encouraged to collaborate to implement effective practices and processes. Such collaborations promote understanding of different cultures and facilitate integration and interdependency among multiple stakeholders unified by shared visions and values.

Borkowski and Deppman (2019) point out that as healthcare reform moves the industry from segment-based delivery models to integrated systems such as accountable care organizations (ACOs), collaborative leadership becomes critical to organizational success. The leader of an ACO is expected to integrate and coordinate the various parts of health care, such as primary care, specialty services, hospitals, and home health care, and to ensure that all parts function well together to deliver efficient, high-quality, and cost-effective patient-centered care. Managers of 21st-century healthcare organizations must be able to lead diverse groups of people and facilitate their professional efforts and problem-solving within an organization and across formal organizational boundaries.

According to Carter (2006), the collaborative leader should demonstrate:

1. The confidence that the goals and objectives are achievable.
2. The skills to communicate with the stakeholders about the issues that must be addressed and the potential problem-solving approaches.
3. The ability to serve as an active listener.
4. The ability to share knowledge and authority with the collaborators.
5. The ability to assess and handle varying levels of risk in decision making and implementation.

The good news is that these behaviors and the required skill set (see **Appendix 12-A**) can be learned by dedicated leaders who commit the necessary time and effort (Borkowski & Deppman, 2019). The Turning Point Leadership Development National Excellence Collaboration has identified six key practices unique to leading a collaborative process and the necessary steps for leaders to guide successful collaborations (see **Appendix 12-B**).

Another Look at Traits and Behavior

As mentioned at the beginning of the chapter, contemporary leadership theories indicate a resurgence of interest in individual traits and behaviors. Two such theoretical constructs that are receiving considerable attention are the Big Five personality factors (Judge et al., 2002) and emotional intelligence (EI) (Salovey & Mayer, 1990). Following an examination of these constructs, we return to behaviors. Bass (1990a, b) emphasized that leadership can be learned and suggested that one of the most significant applications of transformational theory is in training individuals to become transformational leaders. The success of transformational leadership training appears to be based on actual increases in leaders' use of transformational behaviors. Identification of behaviors that define competent transformational healthcare leaders has captured the attention of both scholars and practitioners.

Big Five Personality Factors

The Big Five personality framework posits that the multitude of personality characteristics identified in theory and research can be organized into five factors that underlie all others (DeHoogh et al., 2005; Robbins, 2005), with the convenient acronym OCEAN:

> ***O****penness to Experience*: Individuals open to experience are characterized by imagination, unconventionality, a range of interests, and fascination with novelty.
>
> ***C****onscientiousness*: Conscientious individuals are dependable, responsible, achievement-oriented, organized, and proficient.
>
> ***E****xtroversion*: Extroverts tend to be social, assertive, active, and gregarious.
>
> ***A****greeableness*: Agreeable individuals are warm, generous, cooperative, and trusting.
>
> ***N****euroticism*: This dimension captures an individual's ability to withstand stress. People with low neuroticism are calm, self-confident, and secure. Some researchers describe this trait as reflecting the tendency to be anxious, insecure, and defensive.

Robbins (2005) suggests that the studies of the Big Five approach resulted in consistent and strong support for traits as predictors of leadership. DeHoogh et al. (2005) draw a different conclusion. These authors suggest considerable variability in the strength and direction of the relationships between the personality factors and transformational and transactional leadership. Such variances, they conclude, result in weak support for the Big Five factors.

The inconsistency of findings led DeHoogh et al. (2005) to suggest that it is not personality itself that is important in leadership style, but the interaction of personality characteristics and the context. Their research examined the direct measure of the Big Five personality factors and interactive relationship with emphasis on perceived leader effectiveness (transformational and charismatic leader styles were considered equivalent and contrasted with transactional). The context variable—the work environment—was defined as either dynamic (i.e., characterized by a high degree of challenge and opportunities for change) or stable (i.e., more structured and orderly). Results from this study established that the relationships between personality and leadership style differed depending on the context.

Emotional Intelligence

Emotional intelligence (EI) involves assessing one's feelings, as well as the feelings of others, then using those assessments to guide personal thought and action. EI has five distinct characteristics:

1. Self-awareness
2. Self-management or regulation
3. Self-motivation
4. Empathy or social awareness
5. Social skills

Goleman (1998) describes self-awareness as involving self-understanding and knowing one's true feelings at any moment. Self-management ensures managers can control their emotions to assist with the task while focusing on the problem's solution. Self-motivation allows the manager to stay focused on the goal and desired outcome, overcome negative emotional stimuli, and accept delayed gratification. Empathy is having a sense of what others feel and want while being sensitive to their needs. Finally, social skills relate to one's ability to read and react to social situations while interacting with other people and guiding and influencing the behavior of others.

Goleman (1998), as cited by Luthans (2002, p. 306), noted that EI is not the "end all" in determining leadership characteristics and competencies, but he concludes:

- At the individual level, elements of EI can be identified, assessed, and upgraded.
- At the group level, EI means fine-tuning the interpersonal dynamics that make groups smarter.
- At the organizational level, EI means revising the value hierarchy to prioritize emotional intelligence in the concrete terms of hiring, training, development, performance evaluation, and promotions.

Goleman (1998) believes EI is more important than IQ, proposing that EI is a better predictor of success in both personal and professional endeavors. Gibbs (1995) provided the following evidence as to the importance of EI: "IQ gets you hired, but EI gets you promoted" (p. 64).

Druskat and Wolff (2001) have extended the concept of individual emotional intelligence to teams. The members of creative, productive teams demonstrate mutual trust, a sense of group identity, and a sense of group efficacy. These emotional components enable effective participation, cooperation, and collaboration. They state (p. 83):

> Group emotional intelligence ... [is] about bringing emotions deliberately to the surface and understanding how they affect a team's work. It is also about behaving in ways that build relationships inside and outside the team and strengthen the team's ability to face challenges.

Applications of EI fit well within the healthcare industry, as reflected in **Table 12-2**.

Behavioral Competencies

Behavioral competencies define the skills, knowledge, abilities, and actions that distinguish superior performance. Spencer and Spencer (1993) describe a competency as "what outstanding performers do more often, in more situations, with better results, than average performers." There has been growing interest in developing competencies since McClelland (1961, 1985) published his work on achievement and motivation.

Table 12-2 Emotional Intelligence Components Applied to Healthcare Administration

Component	Definition	Examples in Healthcare Administration
Self-awareness	Self-understanding and knowledge of one's feelings, strengths, weaknesses, and motivations at any moment.	1. Knowing that you tend to interrupt others and insist on your way 2. Understanding what types of work arrangements will interfere with your family life
Self-regulation	Self-management to ensure that one can control their emotions to assist with the task at hand while focusing on the problem's solution	1. Able to maintain composure when an angry or aggressive patient wants a resolution to a problem with their experience 2. Learning how to work well with a new boss 3. Recognizing your contribution to an argument with a colleague

Component	Definition	Examples in Healthcare Administration
Self-motivation	Staying focused on the goal and desired outcome, overcoming negative emotional stimuli, and accepting delayed gratification	1. Pursuing excellence in your work, even if you think nobody else will notice 2. Looking at challenging assignments as opportunities to grow and learn 3. Taking on new projects
Social awareness	Having a sense of what others feel and want while being sensitive to their needs	1. Considering the perspective of doctors and nurses when making a decision that will impact them 2. Understanding that a colleague's emotions and performance at work may be related to challenges in their personal lives
Social skills	Relating appropriately to social situations while interacting with others and influencing their behavior accordingly.	1. Getting department leaders on board to support a project being implemented across the hospital system 2. Helping motivate employees to work in a manner that supports the mission and vision of the organization

Competency models provide a framework for leadership development in healthcare management. While numerous models exist, we discuss a few specific to healthcare leadership. With support from the Robert Wood Johnson Foundation, the National Center for Healthcare Leadership (NCHL) developed a framework to integrate competency-based learning and assessment into healthcare management education. This model defines technical and behavioral characteristics essential for leadership success at different career stages, including early-careerists, mid-careerists, and senior executives.

Healthcare executives may also refer to the American College of Healthcare Executives (ACHE) competency model, derived from the Healthcare Leadership Alliance (HLA). The HLA framework categorizes 300 competencies into five domains: leadership, communication and relationship management, professionalism, business knowledge and skills, and knowledge of the healthcare environment. ACHE provides a self-assessment tool to help executives identify strengths and areas for improvement. Similarly, the International Hospital Foundation (IHF) created a global competency directory to standardize leadership development across different health systems (Hernandez et al., 2018).

Do competencies alone create effective leaders? Dye and Garman (2006) argue that competency represents the capacity to perform but requires motivation and opportunity to translate into success. Competencies improve gradually through deliberate practice and feedback (p. xx). Pelote and Route (2007) emphasize that leadership competencies do not exist in isolation but interact with organizational context, such as the healthcare climate, to influence performance outcomes, including patient satisfaction and financial results.

Lieutenant General George J. Flynn observed, "Professional competence is not enough to be a good leader; good leaders must truly care about those entrusted to their care" (Sinek, 2017, p. xii). Effective leaders create an organizational culture where employees feel safe, valued, and motivated to innovate. When leaders foster an environment of trust, team performance improves, innovation increases, and organizational learning is enhanced (Edmondson & Lei, 2014).

Summary

Contemporary leadership theories acknowledge the complexity of leadership while revisiting the role of traits and behaviors emphasized in traditional models. Modern leadership approaches recognize the dynamic relationship between a leader's traits, behaviors, followers, environment, and organizational objectives. Unlike traditional leadership models, contemporary theories foster more significant interaction between leaders and followers, integrating ideological, moral, and value-based applications.

Organizations benefit from a combination of transactional and transformational leadership. Neither approach alone is sufficient to meet strategic goals. A purely transactional organization would efficiently manage tasks but struggle to adapt to change. Conversely, an organization led solely by transformational leaders would generate vision and innovation but lack the structure to implement change effectively. The ideal approach balances both styles to ensure adaptability and operational efficiency.

Leadership must be flexible to respond to different situations. In times of crisis, the preferred style depends on the circumstances. If control and efficiency are paramount, transactional leadership is beneficial. However, transformational leadership is more effective when change and innovation are needed. Blending these styles based on situational demands is crucial for effective leadership.

Research suggests that transformational, charismatic, and other contemporary leadership attributes can be learned. This is encouraging for individuals seeking professional growth. Leaders at all levels can refine their skills by assessing their strengths and weaknesses, allowing them to influence better, manage, and guide their teams.

Healthcare managers, in particular, must move beyond transactional leadership to foster higher performance and workforce engagement. By incorporating visionary and servant leadership approaches, managers can create environments where employees feel valued and supported. Given the challenges of the healthcare industry, leaders must ensure their teams feel safe, not just from external pressures but also within the organization. Aligning leadership styles with situational, environmental, and personal factors enhances workplace commitment and improves organizational performance.

Discussion Questions

1. Identify the similarities and differences between transactional and transformational leadership. Discuss the appropriateness of each style depending on situational factors.
2. Discuss the type of leadership style—transactional, transformational, servant, and collaborative—that occurs in your specific professional environment. List the positive and negative outcomes that exist as a result of the leadership approach used.
3. Debate the position that transformational and charismatic leadership can (or cannot) be learned. Be specific in your support for the position you take.
4. Discuss Benton's six-step plan for executive charisma. Would the plan work for you in your current healthcare setting?
5. Deliberate the need for transformational or collaborative leadership in the next 5 years as the healthcare environment transforms as a result of industry reform.

Exercise 12-1

It has been stated that to lead people through the complex changes facing the healthcare industry, transformational leadership is required (i.e., leaders creating an environment in which staff can best apply their knowledge, skills, and efforts, engaging commitment and developing potential). Suppose you are engaged as the consultant for Beltway Healthcare System to develop a management development program that will be the vehicle that managers can use to develop the necessary skills and knowledge to drive organizational change and improve the system's performance.

What would you propose as the goals of the management development program?

What learning methods would be best suited to achieve these goals?

Exercise 12-2 Are You a Charismatic Leader?

If you were the director of a major department in a healthcare company, how important would each of the following activities be to you? Answer yes or no to indicate whether you would strive to perform each activity.

1. Help subordinates to clarify goals and how to reach them.
2. Give people a sense of mission and overall purpose.
3. Help to get jobs completed on time.
4. Look for new product or service opportunities.
5. Use policies and procedures as guides for problem solving.
6. Promote unconventional beliefs and values.
7. Give monetary rewards to subordinates in exchange for high performance.
8. Command respect from everyone in the department.
9. Work alone to accomplish important tasks.
10. Suggest new and unique ways of doing things.
11. Give credit to people who do their jobs well.
12. Inspire loyalty to yourself and to the organization.
13. Establish procedures to help the department operate smoothly.
14. Use ideas to motivate others.
15. Set reasonable limits on new approaches.
16. Demonstrate social nonconformity.

The even-numbered items represent behaviors and activities of charismatic leaders. Charismatic leaders are personally involved in shaping ideas, goals, and direction of change. They use an intuitive approach to develop fresh ideas for old problems, and they seek new directions for the department or organization. The odd-numbered items are considered more traditional management activities, or what would be called transactional leadership. Managers respond to organizational problems in an impersonal way, make rational decisions, and coordinate and facilitate the work of other people.

If you answered yes to more even-numbered than odd-numbered items, you may be a potential charismatic leader.

Data from Sellers, P. (1996, January 15). What exactly is charisma? *Fortune, 133*(1), 68–75; Bass, B. M. (1985). *Leadership and performance beyond expectations.* Free Press; Burns, L. R., & Becker, S. W. (1986). Leadership and managership. In S. M. Shortell & A. D. Kaluzny (Eds.), *Health care management.* Wiley.

Exercise 12-3 What Is Your EQ?

A number of testing instruments have been developed to measure emotional intelligence, although the content and approach of each test varies. See the About.com Psychology website at psychology.about.com/library/quiz/bl_eq_quiz.htm for a quiz that presents a mix of self-report and situational questions related to various aspects of emotional intelligence. Take the quiz to learn more about your quotient.

Do you think you are at a higher or lower level than most people when it comes to emotional intelligence?

What might you be able to do to raise your level of emotional intelligence? How effective do you think this might be, considering that some researchers suggest that emotional intelligence can be learned and strengthened, while others claim that it is an inborn characteristic?

Exercise 12-4

Access a leadership competency assessment tool of your choice (NCHL, ACHE, etc.) Review your scores to identify strengths as well as areas to develop. Given your current strengths, how would you conceptualize your leadership style?

Appendix 12-A Traits and Skills of Collaborative Leaders

Traits	Skills
Self-confidence	Communication
Decisiveness	Social
Resilience	Influence
Energy	Analytic
Need for achievement	Technical
Willingness to assume responsibility	Continual learning
Flexibility	Self-management
Service mentality	Strategic thinking
Personal integrity	Facilitation
Emotional maturity	
Collaborative mindset	
Passion towards outcomes	
Systems thinking	
Openness	
Risk-taking	
Sense of mutuality and connectedness	
Humility	

Data from Morse, R. S. (2007). *Developing public leaders in an age of collaborative governance.* University of Delaware, Institute for Public Administration. Archived June 11, 2010, at https://web.archive.org/web/20100611105119/http://www.ipa.udel.edu/3tad/papers/workshop4/Morse.pdf

Appendix 12-B Six Key Practices and Necessary Steps for Leaders to Guide Successful Collaborations

	Practices	Action
1	Assess the environment	A collaborative leader needs to be able to recognize common interests and understand others' perspectives. Collaboration seeks goal attainment around shared visions, purposes, and value. When different points of view to an issue or problem are addressed, a collaborative leader facilitates connections and encourages group thinking that identifies clear, positive change for all participants. The first priority is to set goals. The second priority is to identify the barriers and obstacles to achieving the goals.
2	Create clarity	Having and communicating the clarity of purpose (i.e., shared vision) is a quality that characterizes collaborative leaders. Clarity allows the group members to focus so their energy can be directed toward problem solving. Visioning in relation to clarity involves the commitment to a process or a way of doing things. Mobilizing refers to helping people develop the confidence to take action and sustain their energies through difficult times.
3	Build trust	The collaborative leader must have the ability to promote and sustain trust between and among the participants for sharing of innovative approaches. If a collaborative leader fails to engender trust and openness among participants, best ideas and innovative approaches for problem solving will not be developed or shared by the group.
4	Share power and influence	The collaborative leader must allow the participants to be empowered to fully contribute to the decision-making process. Rather than being concerned about losing power through collaboration, the leader needs to recognize that sharing power actually generates strength.
5	Develop people	The collaborative leader needs to bring out the best in others, maximize the use of other people's talents and resources, build power through sharing power, and cede authoritarian ownership or control. By doing so, the leader increases others' leadership capacities by encouraging experimentation, goal setting, and performance feedback.
6	Self-reflection:	Successful collaborative leaders demonstrate high levels of emotional intelligence or maturity. Through self-reflection, leaders can examine and understand their values and assess whether their behaviors are congruent with their values. In addition, successful leaders critically consider the impact their actions and words have on the group's progress toward achieving its goals and adjust their behaviors if necessary.

Reproduced from Turning Point Leadership Development National Excellence Collaborative, sponsored by The Robert Wood Johnson Foundation.

References

Alharbi, M. F., & Kundi, G. M. (2023). Servant leadership and leadership effectiveness in healthcare institutions. *Problems and Perspectives in Management, 21*(3), 361–364. doi: 10.21511/ppm.21(3).2023.29

Al-Sawai, A. (2013). Leadership of healthcare professionals: Where do we stand? *Oman Medical Journal, 28*(4), 285–287.

Anderson, R. J. (2003). Building hospital–physician relationships through servant leadership. *Frontiers of Health Services Management, 20*(2), 45–47.

Audenaert, M., George, B., Bauwens, R., Decuypere, A., Descamps, A. M., Muylaert, J., Ma, R., & Decramer, A. (2020). Empowering leadership, social support, and job crafting in public organizations: A multilevel study. *Public Personnel Management, 49*(3), 367–392.

Bass, B. M. (1990a). *Bass and Stogdill's handbook of leadership: Theory, research and managerial applications* (3rd ed.). Free Press.

Bass, B. M. (1990b). From transactional to transformational leadership: Learning to share the vision. *Organizational Dynamics, 18*(3), 19–31.

Bass, B. M. (2008). *The Bass handbook of leadership: Theory, research and managerial applications* (4th ed.). Free Press.

Bennis, W. (1984). The four competencies of leadership. *Training and Development Journal, 38*(8), 14–19.

Bennis, W., & Nanus, B. (1985). *Leaders: The strategies for taking charge*. Harper & Row.

Benton, D. A. (2003). *Executive charisma*. McGraw-Hill.

Blanchard, K., & Hodges, P. (2003, May 12). The journey to servant leadership in work, life. *San Diego Business Journal*, A2.

Bolman, L. G., & Deal, T. E. (1997). *Reframing organizations: Artistry, choice, and leadership* (2nd ed.). Jossey-Bass.

Borkowski, N., & Deppman, B. (2019). Collaborative leadership. In L. Rubino, S. Esparza & Y. R. Chassiakos (Eds.), *New leadership for today's healthcare professionals: Concepts and cases* (2nd ed.). Jones & Bartlett Learning.

Bryman, A. (1992). *Charisma and leadership in organizations*. Sage.

Burns, J. M. (1978). *Leadership*. Harper & Row.

Carter, M. (2006). The importance of collaborative leadership in achieving effective criminal justice outcomes. *Center for Effective Public Policy*. https://cepp.com/wp-content/uploads/2021/04/The-Importance-of-Collaborative-Leadership-in-Achieving-Effective-Criminal-Justice-Outcomes-2006.pdf

Chaffee, M. W. (2001). Navy medicine: A health care leadership blueprint for the future. *Military Medicine, 166*(3), 240–247. https://doi.org/10.1093/milmed/166.3.240

Curtin, L. L. (1997). How—and how not—to be a transformational leader. *Nursing Management, 28*(2), 7–8.

De Hoogh, A. H. B., den Hartog, D. N., & Koopman, P. L. (2005). Linking the Big Five factors of personality to charismatic and transactional leadership: perceived dynamic work environment as a moderator. *Journal of Organizational Behavior, 26*(7), 839–865. https://doi.org/10.1002/job.344

Den Hartog, D., & Koopman, P. (2001). Leadership in organizations. In N. Anderson, D. Ones, H. Kepir-Sinangil, & C. Viswesvaran (Eds.). *Handbook of industrial, work & organizational psychology* (Vol. 2). Sage.

Dessler, G. (1998). *Management: Leading people and organizations in the 21st century*. Prentice Hall.

Digman, J. (1990). Personality structure: Emergence of the five-factor model. *Annual Review of Psychology, 41*(1), 417–440.

Druskat, V. U., & Wolff, S. B. (2001). Building the emotional intelligence of groups. *Harvard Business Review, 79*(3), 80–90.

Dye, C. F., & Garman, A. N. (2006). *Exceptional leadership: 16 critical competencies for healthcare executives*. Health Administration Press.

Edmondson, A. C., & Lei, Z. (2014). Psychological safety: The history, renaissance, and future of an interpersonal construct. *Annual Review of Organizational Psychology and Organizational Behavior, 1*(1), 23–43.

Felix, J. (2023). Servant leadership in healthcare: A pilot study. *Journal of Business Studies Quarterly, 12*(4), 1–13.

Freshman, B., & Rubino, L. (2002). Emotional intelligence: A core competency for health care administrators. *Health Care Manager, 20*(4), 1–9.

Gibbs, N. (1995, October 2). Emotional intelligence: The EQ factor. *Time*. https://web.archive.org/web/20101008023911/www.time.com/time/magazine/article/0,9171,983503,00.html

Goleman, D. (1998). *Working with emotional intelligence*. Bantam Books.

Grossman, R. J. (2000). Emotions at work. *Healthcare Forum Journal, 43*(5), 18–22.

Gummer, B. (1996). Go team go: The growing importance of teamwork in organizational life. *Administration in Social Work, 19(4)*, 85–100.

Hernandez, S. R., O'Connor, S. J., & Meese, K. A. (2018). Global efforts to professionalize the healthcare management workforce: The role of competencies. *Journal of Health Administration Education, 35*(2), 157–174.

Hewlett, S. A. (2024). The new rules of executive presence. *Harvard Business Review, 102*(1–2), 134–139.

Howell, J. M., & Avolio, B. J. (1992). The ethics of charismatic leadership: Submission or liberation? *Academy of Management Perspectives, 6*(2), 43–54.

Ibarra, H., & Hansen, M. T. (2011). Are you a collaborative leader? *Harvard Business Review, 89*(7/8), 69–74.
Jenkins, M., & Stewart, A. C. (2010). The importance of a servant leader orientation. *Health Care Management Review, 35*(1), 46–54.
Judge, T., Bono, J., Ilies, R., & Gerhardt, M. (2002). Personality and leadership: A qualitative and quantitative review. *Journal of Applied Psychology, 87*(4), 755–768.
Kotter, J. P. (1995). Leading change: Why transformation efforts fail. *Harvard Business Review, 73*(2), 59–67.
Luthans, F. (2002). *Organizational behavior* (9th ed.). McGraw-Hill.
McClelland, D. C. (1961). *The achieving society*. Free Press.
McClelland, D. C. (1985). *Human motivation*. Scott, Foresman.
Medley, F., & Larochelle, D. R. (1995). Transformational leadership and job satisfaction. *Nursing Management, 26*(9), 64JJ–64NN.
Novick, L., Morrow, C., & Mays, C. (2008). *Public health administration: Principles for population-based management*. Jones and Bartlett Publishers.
Ornelas, J. (2003). *The effect of servant leadership on organizational outcomes*. [Conference presentation]. American College of Healthcare Executives 2003 Congress, Chicago, IL.
Osland, J., Kolb, D., & Rubin, I. (2001). *Organizational behavior: An experiential approach* (7th ed.). Prentice Hall.
Pearce, C. L., & Sims, H. P., Jr. (2002). Vertical versus shared leadership as predictors of the effectiveness of change management teams: An examination of aversive, directive, transactional, transformational, and empowering leader behaviors. *Group Dynamics: Theory, Research, and Practice, 6*(2), 172–197.
Pelote, V., & Route, L. (2007). *Masterpieces in health care leadership*. Jones & Bartlett Publishers.
Robbins, S. P. (2005). *Essentials of organizational behavior* (8th ed.). Prentice Hall.
Salovey, P., & Mayer, J. (1990). Emotional intelligence. *Imagination, Cognition, and Personality, 9*(3), 185–211.
Schwartz, R. W., & Tumblin, T. F. (2002). The power of servant leadership to transform health care organizations for the 21st-century economy. *Archives of Surgery, 137*(12), 1419–1427.
Sellers, P. (1996). What exactly is charisma? *Fortune, 133*(1), 68–72.
Sinek, S. (2017). *Leaders eat last: Why some teams pull together and others don't*. Penguin.
Sofarelli, D., & Brown, D. (1998). The need for nursing leadership in uncertain times. *Journal of Nursing Management, 6*(4), 201–207.
Spears, L. C. (2004). Practicing servant-leadership. *Leader to Leader, 34*, 7–11.
Spencer, L., & Spencer, S. (1993). *Competence at work: Models for superior performance*. John Wiley & Sons.
Stone, A. G., Russell, R. F., & Patterson, K. (2003, August). *Transformational versus servant leadership: A difference in leader focus*. Servant Leadership Research Roundtable: School of Leadership Studies, Regent University. https://www.regent.edu/acad/global/publications/sl_proceedings/2003/stone_transformation_versus.pdf
Thyler, G. (2003). Dare to be different: Transformational leadership may hold the key to reducing the nursing shortage. *Journal of Nursing Management, 11*(2), 73–79.
Tichy, N. M., & Devanna, M. A. (1986). *The transformational leader*. Wiley.
Trastek, V. F., Hamilton, N. W., & Niles, E. E. (2014). Leadership models in health care—A case for servant leadership. *Mayo Clinic Proceedings, 89*(3), 374–381.
Trofino, A. J. (1995). Transformational leadership in health care. *Nursing Management, 26*(8), 42–47.
Trofino, A. J. (2000). Transformational leadership: Moving total quality management to world-class organizations. *International Nursing Review, 47*(4), 232–242.
Yukl, G. (1999). An evaluation of conceptual weaknesses in transformational and charismatic leadership theories. *The Leadership Quarterly, 10*(2), 285–305.

Other Suggested Readings

Atchison, T. (2005). *Leadership's deeper dimensions: Building blocks to superior performance*. Health Administration Press.
Conger, J. A., & Kanungo, R. N. (1988). Behavioral dimensions of charismatic leadership. In J. A. Conger, & R. N. Kanungo (Eds.), *Charismatic leadership* (pp. 79–91). Jossey-Bass.
Dixon, D. L. (1998). The balanced CEO: A transformational leader and capable manager. *Healthcare Forum Journal, 41*(2), 26–29.
Lee, F. (2008). *If Disney ran your hospital: 9½ things you would do differently*. Health Administration Press.
Yukl, G. (1989). Managerial leadership: A review of theory and research. *Journal of Management, 15*(2), 266.

PART IV

Intrapersonal and Interpersonal Issues

In Part IV, we explore various intrapersonal and interpersonal issues. Chapters 13 and 15 focus on stress and conflict, respectively, and how the adverse effects of both can be avoided or at least minimized. Having an optimal level of stress and conflict in our lives is good. It can lead us to work efficiently and effectively with creativity. However, when we experience too much stress or conflict, productivity levels may decrease, and we may experience problems with our physical and mental health. In Chapter 14, we discuss the various ways in which individuals approach decision making. Managers face different issues (that cause stress and conflict) and therefore use different decision-making models—some more effective than others.

CHAPTER 13

Stress in the Workplace and Stress Management

LEARNING OUTCOMES

After completing this chapter, the student should be able to understand:

- The definition of stress.
- The process model of stress and coping.
- How stress can negatively affect individuals and organizations.
- The various forms of stress.
- The three stages of the General Adaptation Syndrome.
- The definition and phases of burnout.
- The four categories of stress in the workplace.
- The various coping strategies available to organizations and individuals.
- The definition of stress management and the various programs used by organizations.

Overview

Stress is a complex and highly personalized process. Because individuals' varying abilities to cope with different forms and levels of stress can cause stress levels to vary widely, even in identical situations, people are affected in different ways. These factors include their level of self-efficacy, adaptability, and the resources available to them.

Cognitive-transactional theory defines stress as "a particular relationship between the person and the environment that the person appraises as taxing or exceeding his or her resources and endangering his or her well-being" (Schwarzer, 2004, p. 343). Lazarus and his associates (Lazarus, 1991; Lazarus et al., 1985; Lazarus & Folkman, 1984) argue that individuals may perceive the same stressful situation differently based on their cognitive appraisal. Some individuals see a specific situation as a threat; others see the same situation as a challenge or an opportunity.

As **Figure 13-1** illustrates, an individual's situation assessment includes demand appraisals or resource appraisals. Demand appraisals relate to the person's perception of (1) physical demands,

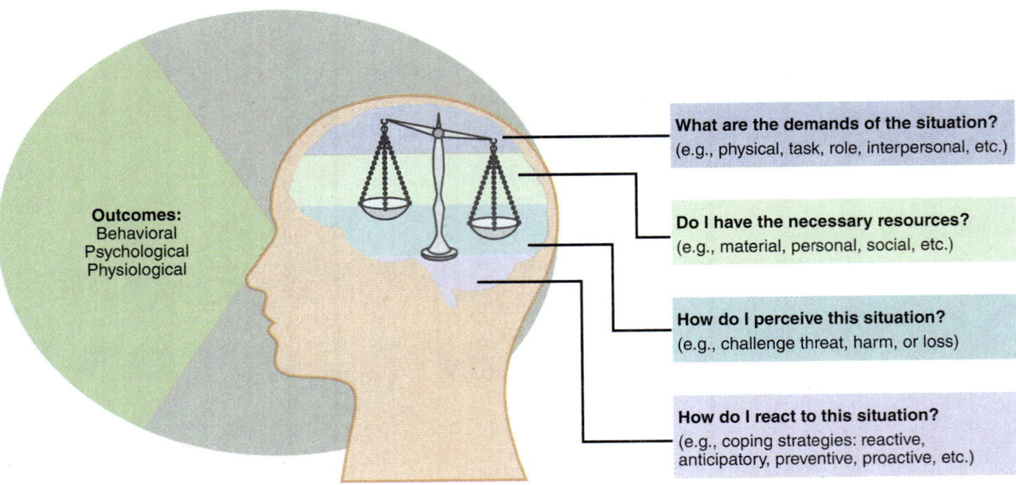

Figure 13-1 The Process Model of Stress and Coping

(2) task demands, (3) role demands, and (4) interpersonal demands (see **Table 13-1**). Resource appraisals may be material, personal, or social. Material appraisals ask, "Do I have the necessary resources to complete this task?" Personal resource appraisals refer to an individual's internal coping options. Individuals who are affluent, healthy, capable, and self-confident are generally less vulnerable to stressful events. Social resource appraisals relate to external coping options available to an individual, such as obtaining assistance from others, receiving emotional support (reassurance), and advice or additional information necessary to complete the task (Lazarus, 1991; Schwarzer, 2004).

The person's appraisal of the situation results in one of three perceptual outcomes: challenge, threat, or harm/loss. When a situation is viewed positively, the person sees the situation as a challenge and an opportunity to achieve personal growth. When the situation is viewed as a threat, the person perceives danger from physical injury or diminished self-esteem. For example, a task demand perceived to be difficult, ambiguous, unexpected, or time-consuming with an unrealistic deadline is more likely to induce a threat outcome than an easy task that can be thoroughly prepared for and solved conveniently without time constraints. If the appraisal is viewed as harm or loss, the person has determined that damage has already occurred, such as loss of self-worth, a lowering of the person's social standing, or physical injury (Lazarus, 1991; Schwarzer, 2004).

Building on Lazarus' work, Schwarzer's (2004) process model illustrates that, based on an individual's perception of the situation, the individual may engage in various coping strategies to manage the experience of stress. Combining an individual's perception of the situation (appraisals) and the coping strategies employed (reactive, anticipatory, preventive, or proactive) will determine the resulting consequences, which may be behavioral, psychological, physiological, or combinations of the three (see **Table 13-2**).

In this chapter, we first examine the factors that contribute to a person's experience of stress in the workplace. Although many extra organizational factors contribute to an individual's experience of stress, such as a pending divorce, housing conditions, and the general economy, this chapter focuses primarily on stress in the workplace. Second, we examine the various coping methods from an organizational and individual perspective.

Table 13-1 Demand Appraisals

Physical Demands

- Indoor climate and air quality
- Temperature
- Illumination and other rays
- Noise and vibrations
- Office design

Task Demands

- Occupational category
- Routine jobs
- Job future ambiguity
- Interactive organizational demands (e.g., interface with various constituencies, such as boundary spanning)
- Work overload

Role Demands

- Role conflict
- Interrole
- Intrarole
- Person/role (i.e., conflicting values or beliefs)
- Role ambiguity
- Work/home demands

Interpersonal Demands

- Status incongruity
- Social density (i.e., interpersonal need for space and distance)
- Abrasive personalities
- Leadership style
- Team pressures
- Diversity

Data from Quick, J. C., Quick, J. D., Nelson, D. L., & Hurrell, J. J., Jr. (1997). *Preventive stress management in organizations.* American Psychological Association.

Table 13-2 Individual Distress: Behavioral, Psychological, and Physiological Consequences

Behavioral Consequences

- Tobacco use
- Alcohol use
- Drug abuse
- Accident proneness
- Violence
- Eating disorders

(continues)

Table 13-2 Individual Distress: Behavioral, Psychological, and Physiological Consequences *(continued)*

Psychological Consequences
■ Burnout
■ Family problems
■ Anxiety disorders
■ Sleep disturbances
■ Sexual dysfunction
■ Depression
■ Conversion reaction and somatization
Physiological Consequences
■ Hypertension, heart disease, and stroke
■ Cancer
■ Back pain, arthritis, and other musculoskeletal conditions
■ Peptic ulcer disease and other gastrointestinal conditions
■ Headache
■ Diabetes mellitus
■ Liver cirrhosis and other alcohol-related diseases
■ Lung disease
■ Skin disease
■ Other diseases (e.g., HIV, chronic fatigue syndrome, etc.)

Data from Quick, J. C., Quick, J. D., Nelson, D. L., & Hurrell, J. J., Jr. (1997). *Preventive stress management in organizations.* American Psychological Association.

Work-Related Stress

Stress is a common phenomenon in today's workplace. Numerous surveys and studies confirm that occupation-related pressures are adults' leading source of stress. Stress, which the World Health Organization has called the "health epidemic of the 21st century," is costly as a result of accidents; absenteeism; employee turnover; loss of productivity; direct medical, legal, and insurance costs; workers' compensation awards; and tort and Federal Employers' Liability Act judgments (American Institute of Stress, 2004). Prior to the pandemic, societal costs attributable to health worker burnout in the United States were approximately $4.6 billion (NASEM, 2019). Up to 77% of workers reported experiencing work-related stress in the last month, with negative impacts, such as emotional exhaustion, lower productivity, and a desire to quit (American Psychological Association, 2023).

Workplace Violence

In addition to the effects of stress on health and financial or family problems, it may lead to verbal and physical violence. Workplace violence is not an uncommon problem in the healthcare industry. It costs U.S. hospitals and health systems $2.7 billion annually due to preparedness and prevention measures, unreimbursed medical care, and additional training and security measures (American Hospital Association, 2017). Workplace violence can occur both in interactions between coworkers and with patients and their families.

It is estimated that healthcare workers are five times more likely to be the victims of workplace violence relative to other professions (U.S. Bureau of Labor Statistics, 2020). Healthcare workers often face violent and aggressive or derogatory behaviors from patients and their family members. One nurse reports, "I've been bitten, kicked, punched, pushed, pinched, shoved, scratched, and spat upon. I have been bullied and called very ugly names. I've had my life, the life of my unborn child, and my other family members threatened, requiring a security escort to my car" (The Joint Commission, 2018).

In addition to workplace violence from patients and visitors, "horizontal violence" occurs among different members of the healthcare team. Horizontal violence is defined as "hostile, aggressive, and harmful behaviors toward coworkers via attitudes, actions, words, or other behaviors, such as bullying, incivility, or hazing" (Jones et al., 2023). For example, female physicians have highlighted the prevalence of microaggressions from a predominantly female nursing staff (Molina et al., 2020).

Stressors

Everyone encounters stress daily, but the effects on an individual depend on many factors. Stress causes, known as stressors, can take several forms, such as positive or negative, external or internal, or short-term (acute) or long-term (chronic).

Positive and Negative Stressors

A certain degree of stress is necessary for good mental and physical health; it can be viewed as constructive stress, which compels us to act optimally, helping us achieve our goals. Hans Selye (1956, 1974), a Canadian physiologist referred to as the grandfather of stress research, coined the term "eustress," incorporating the Greek root *eu* for "good," to describe good or positive stress. Selye suggested thinking of eustress as euphoria plus stress. It is only when stress is poorly managed or becomes overwhelming that the negative effects appear; this poorly managed stress is referred to as distress (see **Figure 13-2**).

Distress refers to the stressful events' unhealthy, harmful, and destructive outcomes (Quick et al., 1997). Distress may have behavioral, physiological, or psychological effects on the individual. This is referred to as an individual's fight-or-flight response. In the fight-or-flight response, certain chemicals in the brain cause a reaction to potentially harmful stressors or warnings (e.g., danger, harassment, and noise). Selye (1956) studied the physiological effects of the fight-or-flight response, resulting in his description of General Adaptation Syndrome (GAS). GAS describes the three phases an individual undergoes when encountering a stressful situation: the alarm, resistance, and exhaustion.

The first stage of GAS, the alarm phase, occurs when an individual's fight-or-flight response is elicited for mobilization and geared for either a fight or flight. In the second stage, resistance, the individual fights or escapes the stressor, and the acute fight-or-flight response ceases. The third stage, exhaustion, occurs when the individual can no longer adapt to the stressor (Jacobs, 2001). In the first two stages, alarm and resistance, bodily responses are adaptive and beneficial.

In the final stage, exhaustion, an individual's stress may be reflected in behavioral, physiological, or psychological illnesses. Physiological illnesses related to stress may include chronic headaches or fatigue, hypertension, ulcers, and heart disease. Psychological illnesses or the emotional symptoms of stress in the exhaustion stage are rooted in frustration or depression. According to

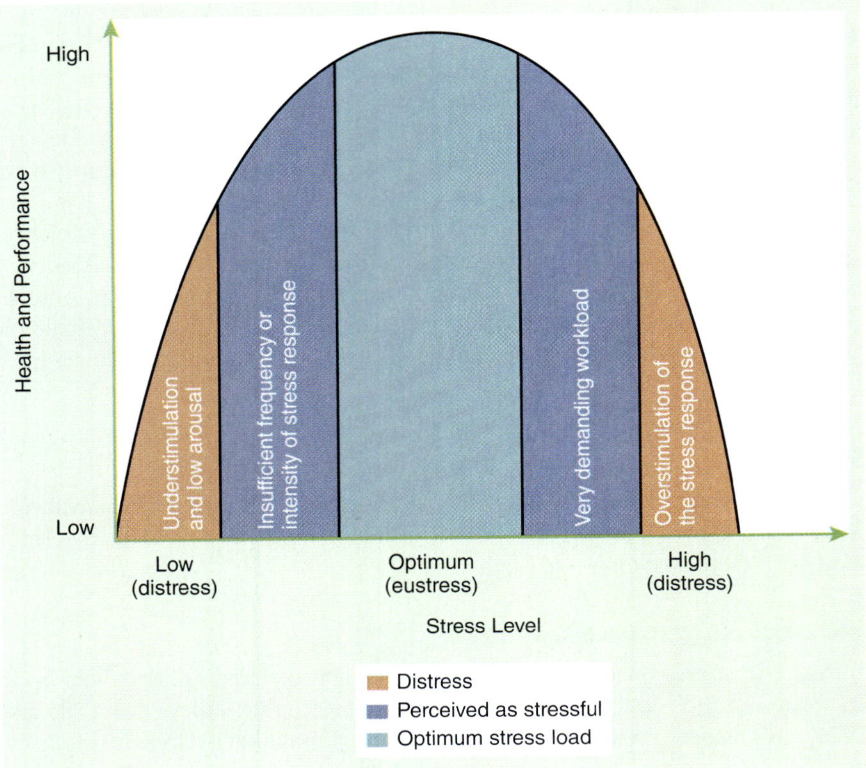

Figure 13-2 Distress–Eustress (an Expanded Yerkes–Dodson Curve)

Data from Quick, J. C., Quick, J. D., Nelson, D. L., & Hurrell, J. J., Jr. (1997). *Preventive stress management in organizations.* American Psychological Association.

von Onciul (1996), these emotional symptoms are the behavioral consequences of the exhaustion stage, which may include emotional outbursts, violent or antisocial behavior, eating disorders, and general indifference and reduced attention to personal issues, such as exercise and appearance. The individual may exhibit other mental challenges in the exhaustion stage, such as the inability to concentrate and poor memory retention. This causes impaired performance, poor judgment, and indecisiveness as well as a negative attitude toward life and work, possibly leading to the misuse of alcohol and drugs (von Onciul, 1996).

Internal or External Stressors/Acute or Chronic

Individuals can experience two categories of stressors: external or internal. External stressors can be physical conditions, such as excessive temperatures, or psychological environments, such as abusive relationships. Internal stressors can be physical illnesses or psychological tendencies, such as an individual's personality type. These stressors are either short-term (acute) or long-term (chronic). Short-term acute stress is reacting to a real or perceived immediate threat (the fight-or-flight response). Long-term chronic stressors are those that are continuous, such as work pressures, ongoing relationship problems, and financial concerns (see **Table 13-3**).

Table 13-3 External and Internal Stressors (Acute and Chronic)

External	Internal
Environment—Noise, poor lighting or bright lights, extreme temperatures of hot or cold, confined spaces, violence and other threats to personal safety, general economy, global uncertainty, technology, war	*Lifestyle*—Unhealthy lifestyles, excessive caffeine, smoking, drinking, drugs, lack of sleep, trying to do too much (e.g., supermom)
Other People—Rudeness, domineering attitudes, aggression, peer pressure, and discrimination	*Mental State*—Pessimism, self-criticism, self-helplessness, unrealistic expectations, and lack of flexibility
Work—Excessive rules and policies, poor interpersonal relationships, lack of communication, mergers, downsizing, long or irregular hours, unrealistic deadlines, retraining, discrimination, and promotion or demotion	*Personality*—Perfectionism, workahclism, perceived expectation of others and oneself, and other Type A personality characteristics
Major Life Events—Death of a loved one, poor health or disability, loss of job, new job, marriage, divorce, financial worries, relocation, new baby, aging parents, and pending retirement	
Everyday Hassles—Commuting, misplacing keys or other important items, poor customer service, standing in lines, dealing with teenagers at home	

Beliefs About Stress

Research on stress suggests that one's beliefs about stress are associated with whether or not stress leads to heart damage or increased mortality. A 2012 study asked participants whether they had experienced high or low levels of stress over the past year and then linked responses to public death records. They found that people who indicated experiencing high levels of stress were 43% more likely to die. However, the study also asked whether people believed stress harmed their health. Surprisingly, the people who experienced high stress but did not believe that stress was harmful were no more likely to die than were those who experienced low stress (Keller et al., 2012). These results suggest that an individual's beliefs about stress are significant in shaping whether or not stress will harm that person's health. Another study that examined people in a stressful environment studied an intervention that helped people see their body's stress response as positive. For example, breathing faster brings more oxygen to the brain. Subjects who were taught to believe that stress could be helpful instead of harmful to their health had a different physiological response that minimized potential heart damage compared to those who believed that stress was harmful to health (Jamieson et al., 2012). These findings suggest that stress and beliefs about stress may be important factors in how stress affects one's health.

Burnout

Stress occurs when job requirements do not match the employee's capabilities, resources, or needs. Studies show that stressful working conditions are associated with increased absenteeism, tardiness, and turnover, which affect an organization's productivity and profitability. An extreme case of job-related stress is known as burnout.

First discovered in the 1970s, burnout has been recognized as an occupational hazard in people-oriented professions, such as health care, human services, and education (Maslach &

Goldberg, 1998). Burnout symptoms include overwhelming exhaustion; feelings of frustration, anger, and cynicism; and a sense of ineffectiveness and failure. Burnout is a significant issue among healthcare workers. Healthcare professionals have reported substantially higher degrees of burnout than managers who are not employed in the healthcare industry (Golembiewski & Boudreau, 1991). Harvard School of Public Health announced burnout as a public health crisis (Jha et al., 2019). In 2018, a survey found that 78% of physicians reported experiencing symptoms of burnout (Hawkins, 2018). An earlier study reported that 33% of new nurses seek another job within one year (Lucian Leape Institute, 2013). Suicide rates are 1.4 times and 2.27 times higher among physicians than in the general population for males and females, respectively (Schernhammer & Colditz, 2004). This has resulted in estimates of more than 300 suicides per year (Frank et al., 2000), which equates to roughly two full medical school classes (Association of American Medical Colleges, 2017).

Burnout can seriously affect a healthcare organization's ability to provide good patient care and its bottom line. A more engaged workforce is associated with higher patient satisfaction and a lower incidence of medical errors (Shanafelt et al., 2010). One study found that replacing one full-time physician, including lost revenue, recruitment, and startup costs, costs approximately $1.2 million (Schutte, 2012). If multiple physicians leave or reduce clinical hours because of burnout, the result could generate millions of dollars in additional costs. Furthermore, as a society, it takes at least 12 years to create one physician (considering undergraduate and medical school and residency training). Therefore, when a physician leaves the field of medicine altogether, it takes a long time to produce a replacement. There is a physician shortage in the United States, which is expected to worsen in future years. Total shortfalls are expected to reach 30,000–100,000 physicians by 2036, and current shortfalls are estimated to be in the tens of thousands (Shanafelt et al., 2016; American Medical Association, 2023).

Maslach and Jackson (1981) identified three dimensions associated with burnout: emotional exhaustion, depersonalization, and diminished personal accomplishment.

- Emotional exhaustion results in apathy and loss of concern, a feeling that one has reached the end of one's rope. As their emotional resources are depleted, healthcare professionals feel that they cannot give of themselves emotionally or psychologically.
- Depersonalization is characterized by the development of negative and cynical attitudes toward the workplace and people with whom one interacts (patients and coworkers in the case of healthcare professionals). Depersonalized individuals distance themselves and see other people as things or objects.
- Diminished personal accomplishment is characterized by the tendency to evaluate oneself negatively, including viewing oneself as performing poorly in the job, which is viewed as having no worth or meaning (low professional efficacy).

Golembiewski and his associates (Golembiewski, 1986, 1990; Golembiewski & Boss, 1991; Golembiewski & Boudreau, 1991) studied over 13,000 managers and healthcare professionals regarding burnout. The researchers found that varying degrees of burnout existed and that healthcare workers experienced the most advanced phases (Golembiewski & Boudreau, 1991). As illustrated in **Table 13-4**, Golembiewski's phase model suggests that employees suffering from burnout first experience depersonalization, which induces feelings of inadequacy, followed by diminishing personal accomplishment, and ending with emotional exhaustion. Golembiewski and Boudreau relate that employees show growing deficits or deficiencies as they move from phase to phase:

Table 13-4 Golembiewski's Phases of Burnout

	Phase	Phase	Phase	Phase	Phase	Phase	Phase	Phase
Dimensions of Burnout	I	II	III	IV	V	VI	VII	VIII
Depersonalization	Lo	Hi	Lo	Hi	Lo	Hi	Lo	Hi
Personal Accomplishment	Lo	Lo	Hi	Hi	Lo	Lo	Hi	Hi
Emotional Exhaustion	Lo	Lo	Lo	Lo	Hi	Hi	Hi	Hi

Reproduced from Golembiewski, R. T. (1986). The epidemiology of progressive burnout: A primer. *Journal of Health and Human Resources Administration, 9*(1), 18. Reprinted with permission.

- Broad ranges of perceptions or attitudes about the worksite deteriorate; for example, satisfaction and job involvement fall, and tension at work increases.
- Performance appraisals tend to decrease.
- Physical symptoms increase.
- Turnover increases.
- Self-esteem decreases.
- Various clinical indicators of mental health show deterioration.
- The quality of social and emotional life at work declines; for example, group cohesiveness is down, and social support falls.

Causes of Burnout

Christina Maslach's research identifies six key causes of burnout, each resulting from a mismatch between the individual and their work environment. These factors reflect systemic organizational issues rather than individual shortcomings (Maslach & Leiter, 2022; Maslach et al., 2001):

- **Workload:** Excessive or sustained demands can deplete physical and emotional resources, leading to exhaustion. Burnout often arises when staff operate in constant crisis mode or are assigned responsibilities beyond their capacity.
- **Control:** A lack of autonomy or influence over work-related decisions contributes to stress. Situations where employees are held accountable without having decision-making authority undermine motivation and increase emotional strain.
- **Reward:** Inadequate compensation, insufficient recognition, or lack of intrinsic satisfaction can diminish morale. When appropriate rewards do not match effort, burnout becomes more likely.
- **Community:** Poor quality workplace relationships, including isolation, conflict, or a lack of mutual respect, can lead to cynicism and emotional withdrawal from work.
- **Fairness:** Perceptions of inequity, favoritism, or discrimination erode trust in leadership and contribute to emotional fatigue and disengagement.
- **Values:** Misalignment between an individual's values and the organization's mission or practices can create moral distress. When employees are asked to act against their ethical beliefs or engage in work perceived as meaningless, burnout risk increases.

While addressing workload is important, it is not the sole lever for reducing burnout. In healthcare environments where staffing shortages may persist, organizations must also address these other factors to mitigate burnout effectively.

Presenteeism

Symptoms of burnout may include lower job performance and satisfaction, higher job tension and turnover, and increased absenteeism. However, a low absenteeism rate does not always indicate that employees are not suffering from burnout. "Presenteeism" is when employees show up for work but are less productive because of illness. A study of 29,000 U.S. employees estimated that absenteeism and presenteeism cost U.S. industry more than $60 billion a year and that more than three-fourths of lost productivity is explained by presenteeism, not by absenteeism (Stewart et al., 2003). Dow Chemical Company estimates that presenteeism has the most significant health-related economic impact on the company, ahead of absenteeism, health insurance, and workers' compensation (Berry et al., 2004). A study of British workers found that the number of sick days workers take was halved between 1993 and 2017, likely owing to a changing workplace culture that is not supportive of taking sick time off. A survey found that only 42% of senior managers thought having the flu was a serious enough reason to miss work (Rubinstein, 2019). In health care, workers who continue to work with contagious illnesses, such as the flu, can have serious and sometimes deadly effects on immunocompromised patients. (See **Case Study 13-1**.)

CASE STUDY 13-1 Presenteeism: A Public Health Hazard

On January 19, 2005, an urban 100-bed, two-floor nursing home reported initial cases of nausea, vomiting, and diarrhea in three residents and one staff member. General infection control measures were implemented: hand hygiene reinforcement, contact isolation, and enhanced disinfection. Over the next two days, seven more residents and four additional staff developed symptoms. Two symptomatic staff were sent home following consultation with the infection control team.

The public health department was notified, and stricter controls were enacted: dining room closure, suspension of group activities and new admissions, visitor restrictions, and changes in staffing to limit personnel movement between units. Staff with symptoms were to be evaluated by Employee Health, although no systematic screening was in place.

Over 10 days, 23 residents and 18 staff developed gastrointestinal symptoms. Norovirus genotype 2 was confirmed via lab tests. Despite recommendations, many symptomatic staff continued working, often reporting symptoms only after arriving at work. Some also had ill family members. Infection Control contacted affected staff to reinforce stay-at-home guidelines and clarify return-to-work procedures, which required Employee Health clearance. Per diem and registry staff were used to address staffing needs.

No new cases were reported from days 13 to 17. However, on day 18, an ill staff member reported to work, followed by two resident cases on day 21. With voluntary compliance proving insufficient, the public health department mandated adherence to "back-to-work" rules: symptomatic employees could return only after 48 symptom-free hours and clearance by Employee Health. The outbreak's final case occurred on day 24. Infection control measures were lifted on day 34.

Data from Widera, E., Chang, A., & Chen, H. L. (2010). Presenteeism: A public health hazard. *Journal of General Internal Medicine, 25*(11), 1244–1247. https://doi.org/10.1007/s11606-010-1422-x

Causes of Workplace Stress

Workplace stress can be related to (1) individual task demands, (2) individual role demands, (3) group demands, and (4) organizational demands (Kinicki & Williams, 2003) (see **Table 13-5**).

- Individual task demands include unrealistic deadlines; fear of failure; new technology; lack of necessary resources (e.g., poor physical work environment, such as noise, heat, and crowding); work overload; lack of control; and repetitive, unchallenging work (work underload).
- Individual role demands include job ambiguity, role conflict, and difficulty balancing work and family life.
- Group demands include poor interpersonal relationships with coworkers and supervisors, inadequate support, and lack of participation in decisions.
- Organizational demands encompass politics, communication problems, excessive rules and regulations, organizational structure and culture, lack of career development activities, and change without clear strategic direction.

How these various demands can affect employees' stress levels is illustrated in **Case Study 13-2**.

Table 13-5 Job Stressors

Categories of Job Stressors	Examples
Individual Task Demands (factors unique to the job)	■ Workload (overload and underload) ■ Pace, variety, or meaningfulness of work ■ Autonomy (e.g., the ability to make your own decisions about your own job or about specific tasks) ■ Shift work or hours of work ■ Physical environment (noise, air quality, etc.) ■ Isolation at the workplace (emotional or working alone)
Individual Role Demands (role in the organization)	■ Role conflict (conflicting job demands, multiple supervisors or managers) ■ Role ambiguity (lack of clarity about responsibilities, expectations, etc.) ■ Level of responsibility ■ Difficulties balancing work and personal lives
Group Demands	■ Relationships at work with supervisors, coworkers, and subordinates ■ Threat of violence, harassment, etc. (threats to personal safety) ■ Lack of participation in decision making ■ Inappropriate leadership/management styles (autocratic versus participatory)
Organizational Demands (including organizational structure and climate)	■ Management/leadership styles ■ Communication patterns ■ Career development opportunities (under-/overpromotion) ■ Job security ■ Unplanned change ■ Overall job satisfaction

Data from Murphy, L. R. (1995). Occupational stress management: Current status and future directions. In C. L. Cooper & D. M. Rousseau (Eds.), *Trends in organizational behavior* (Vol. 2, pp. 1–14). John Wiley & Sons.

CASE STUDY 13-2 Stress in Today's Workplace

The longer he waited, the more anxious David became. For weeks, he had experienced aching muscles, poor appetite, restless sleep, and persistent fatigue. Initially, he ignored the symptoms, but his increasing irritability led his wife to insist on a medical evaluation. As he waited in his physician's office, lost in thought, he was startled when Theresa took a seat beside him. They had been close when she worked in the billing department at the drug-manufacturing company where David still worked, though she had left three years earlier for a position at a local health maintenance organization (HMO). A brief exchange soon turned into familiar conversation.

"You left at the right time," David said. "After the reorganization, job security vanished. It used to be that doing your work meant keeping your job, but not anymore. Expectations haven't changed, even though fewer staff are doing more work. I'm working 12-hour shifts, six days a week, and I still hear the machines humming in my head at night. People are calling in sick just to get a break. Morale is terrible—they're even bringing in consultants to find better workflows."

Theresa nodded. "I miss everyone, but I may not have made the best move. The phones at the HMO never stop. Calls are routed automatically, and I even have to schedule bathroom breaks. Most callers are upset, and I try to help, but I can't make promises without my supervisor's approval. I'm stuck between customer expectations and company policies. The environment is so tense that the reps don't even talk to each other—we just stay in our cubicles until quitting time."

She added, "My mother's health is failing, but I can't use sick time to care for her. Now I'm here dealing with migraine headaches and high blood pressure. Many of the other reps are seeing the employee assistance counselor and taking stress management classes. That helps a little, but real change is needed. Without changes to how the organization operates, stress will continue to wear people down."

Job Conditions That May Lead to Stress

- *The Design of Tasks*: Heavy workload, infrequent rest breaks, long work hours, and shift work; hectic and routine tasks that have little inherent meaning, do not utilize workers' skills, and provide little sense of control.
  Example: David works to the point of exhaustion. Tied to the computer, Theresa is allowed little room for flexibility, self-initiative, or rest.
- *Management Style*: Lack of participation by workers in decision making, poor communication in the organization, lack of family-friendly policies.
  Example: Theresa needs to get her supervisor's approval for everything, and her employer is insensitive to Theresa's family needs.
- *Interpersonal Relationship*: Poor social environment and lack of support or help from coworkers and supervisors.
  Example: Theresa's physical isolation and the tension within the office reduce her opportunities to interact with her coworkers or receive help from them.
- *Work Roles*: Conflicting or uncertain job expectations, too much responsibility, too many "hats" to wear.
  Example: Theresa is often caught in a difficult situation trying to satisfy both the members' needs and her employer's expectations.
- *Career Concerns*: Job insecurity and lack of opportunity for growth, advancement, or promotion; rapid changes for which workers are unprepared.
  Example: Since the reorganization at the drug-manufacturing facility, everyone, including David, is worried about their future with the company and what will happen next.
- *Environmental Conditions*: Unpleasant or dangerous physical conditions, such as crowding, noise, air pollution, or ergonomic problems.
  Example: David is exposed to constant noise at work.

Modified from National Institute for Occupational Safety and Health. (1999). *Stress at work. DHHS (NIOSH)* (Publication No. 99-101). https://www.cdc.gov/niosh/docs/99-101

Coping with Stress

Coping with stress at work can be defined as "an effort by a person or an organization to manage and overcome demands and critical events that pose a challenge, threat, harm or loss to that person and that person's functioning or to the organization as a whole" (Schwarzer, 2004, p. 342). Coping is considered one of the top skills of effective managers. With population samples from business, education, health care, and state governments, Whetten and Cameron (1993) identified 402 effective managers based on responses from peers and superiors. Responses from the participants revealed that coping with stress was second on a list of 10 skills attributed to effective managers.

Stress is inevitable, but the degree of stress experienced can be modified in two ways: by changing the environment, the individual, or both. This is referred to as stress management. Stress management can refer to a narrow set of individual-level interventions (e.g., relaxation training, biofeedback, and meditation) or a broader meaning that includes any stress intervention (Murphy, 1995). However, stress management interventions need to target characteristics of the individual worker, the job, and the organization to be successful.

Schwarzer (2004) provides managers with a model using four perspectives to assist themselves and others in coping with job-related stress, as shown in **Figure 13-3**. The differences between perspectives are based on time-related stress appraisals and the perceived certainty of critical events or demands. The four perspectives are (1) reactive coping, (2) anticipatory coping, (3) preventive coping, and (4) proactive coping.

- *Reactive* coping refers to efforts to deal with a stressful encounter that either is ongoing or has already happened, such as a job loss or demotion.
- *Anticipatory* coping pertains to efforts to deal with an inevitable event that is certain to occur soon, such as public speaking, a job interview, or downsizing.
- *Preventative* coping refers to an effort to build up resistance resources, whereby the individual's stress level is reduced (the severity of impact is minimized) if a critical event is expected to occur. For example, an individual might return to school to earn a master's degree in health administration or complete the requirements to become a board-certified healthcare executive in anticipation of a possible job loss due to a merger or buyout.
- *Proactive* coping is building up general resources that facilitate movement toward challenging goals and personal growth, such as resilience training and learned optimism (Schwarzer, 2004).

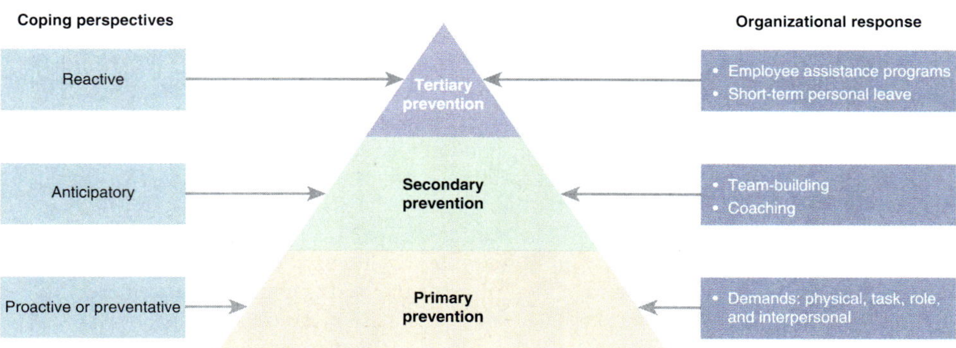

Figure 13-3 Four Coping Perspectives

As Schwarzer (2004, p. 349) points out, "The distinction between these four perspectives of coping is highly useful because it moves the individual's focus away from mere responses to negative events toward a broader range of risk and goal management that includes the active creation of opportunities and the positive experience of stress."

Individual Coping Strategies

At the individual level, one of the best techniques for reducing stress is through the relaxation response (see **Exhibit 13-1**). However, relaxation is a reactive coping strategy due to an individual's appraisal of a threat or harm/loss situation, such as failing to meet a work goal, conflict with a colleague or supervisor, or job loss. Reactive coping strategies do little, if anything, to solve the underlying problems. Therefore, employees need to learn to use preventive and proactive coping strategies so that their fight-or-flight response is not automatically engaged at the first sign of stress (Schwarzer, 2004).

Friedman (1999) recommends training employees to manage stress by enhancing their problem-solving and conflict resolution skills and developing leadership capabilities. For instance, employees anticipating increased workloads can be trained in advance to delegate tasks, practice effective time management, and strengthen their social support networks. In addition, employees should learn to balance work, family, and leisure activities—although this may be especially difficult for individuals with workaholic tendencies. Adopting a healthy lifestyle, including proper nutrition and regular physical activity, has provided a protective buffer against stress (Schwarzer, 2004). Moreover, training in learned optimism and resilience has demonstrated effectiveness in helping employees reframe perceived threats as challenges, thereby converting distress into eustress.

Learned Optimism

Based on extensive psychological research, Martin Seligman (1991) developed and applied the concept of learned optimism to workplace productivity. According to Seligman, pessimistic individuals are more likely to give up when faced with obstacles, whereas optimistic individuals tend to persist. The theory of learned optimism proposes that people can counteract pessimistic thinking by identifying and disputing their negative thoughts and beliefs.

Exhibit 13-1 Evidence-Based Stress Reduction Strategies

- *Relaxation Response*: One of the most well-documented techniques for reducing stress is through the relaxation response, a term coined by Dr. Herbert Benson of Harvard Medical School to describe a state of deep, mindful rest that offsets the physical effects of stress by lowering heart rate, blood pressure, and breathing rate. The relaxation response can be elicited at any time and place by sitting comfortably with your eyes closed, breathing slowly, letting your muscles relax, and repeating a certain word, sound, phrase, or prayer for 10 minutes while disregarding all other thoughts.
- *Daily Gratitude*: Positive psychologist Dr. Martin Seligman conducted randomized placebo-controlled trials of various interventions to improve well-being. Writing down "three blessings" or three things that went well during the day and why they went well every day for just 1 week increased happiness and decreased depressive symptoms for 6 months.

Data from Optimistic people live longer. (2003, January). *Tufts University Health and Nutrition Letter, 20*(11), 4–5; Seligman, M. E., Steen, T. A., Park, N., & Peterson, C. (2005). Positive psychology progress: Empirical validation of interventions. *American Psychologist, 60*(5), 410–421.

Importantly, optimism differs from the general notion of positive thinking. Drawing on attribution theory, Seligman (1991) emphasized that individuals interpret events through an explanatory style, which includes three key elements: stability, globality, and locus of control.

- Stability refers to whether outcomes are perceived as temporary or permanent. Optimists tend to interpret adverse outcomes as temporary and isolated, whereas pessimists view them as lasting and likely to recur. Conversely, optimists regard positive outcomes as stable and repeatable, while pessimists see them as fleeting.
- Globality concerns whether outcomes are specific to one situation or generalizable across life. Optimists view positive events as broadly applicable and adverse events as context-specific. In contrast, pessimists interpret positive outcomes as random and adverse outcomes as reflecting their entire life experience.
- Locus of control refers to whether individuals attribute outcomes to internal factors (e.g., effort) or external factors (e.g., luck). Optimists credit success to their own actions and attribute failures to external circumstances. Pessimists, by contrast, often see success as due to luck or others' efforts and failure as stemming from their deficiencies.

Pessimists typically attribute adverse events to causes that are stable, personal, and pervasive. Optimists, on the other hand, attribute failure to temporary, external, and specific causes. Optimists possess high self-efficacy and perceive setbacks as challenges to overcome, often viewing adversity as an opportunity for growth (Seligman & Csikszentmihalyi, 2000). Pessimists often lack this sense of agency. They may believe that their actions do not influence outcomes, leading to low motivation, procrastination, and depression (Seligman, 1991) see **Exhibit 13-2**. This pattern of attribution can result in learned helplessness, wherein individuals, having experienced a lack of control in the past, no longer attempt to change future outcomes—even when circumstances improve (Seligman, 1991). Persistent self-blame also undermines self-efficacy, reinforcing a cycle of helplessness (Bandura, 1997).

Exhibit 13-2 Learned Helplessness

Learned helplessness is an acquired condition that negatively impacts an individual's physical, emotional, mental, and spiritual well-being. It occurs when people who experience failure at a task, often numerous times, determine that the task cannot be accomplished, at least not by them, and so they stop trying. They internalize their failures (self-blame) and develop a helpless attitude.

A study on learned helplessness examined stress levels in two groups subjected to the same loud and unpleasant noise (Hiroto, 1974). One group was given a button to turn the noise off, while the second group was not given any way to turn it off. The subjects who were denied control over the noise experienced significant stress and called the noise "unbearable." The group that had the option of turning off the noise considered the noise only "unpleasant" but chose not to turn off the sound. Knowing they had the option of turning the noise off was enough.

Following the sound session, the researchers observed that the group that had been subjected to helplessness in the noise experiment tended to act helpless in subsequent situations, whereas the group that had been given control to turn off the noise in the experiment looked for and chose to exercise control over subsequent situations. Both helplessness and empowerment are learned conditions. Once learned, they are extended into other areas of life.

Optimism may serve as a buffer against the physiological effects of stress. Research suggests that optimists have better immune function than pessimists. It is not that optimists experience fewer stressful situations than pessimists; optimists are more adept at coping with such situations, so they can work through the problems and develop solutions rather than feeling helpless or like victims.

Organizational Coping Strategies

At the organizational level, when reactive or anticipatory coping occurs, managers' efforts focus on reducing the harm or loss to the organization. Managers using reactive or anticipatory coping are concerned with putting out fires rather than using their efforts to develop and implement preventive and proactive coping strategies, which are more beneficial for the organization and the employee. For example, preventive coping is called for when no specific event is envisioned; but rather when a more general threat in the distance comes into view, such as an economic decline, a potential merger or downsizing, an aging workforce, or new technology (Schwarzer, 2004).

The healthcare industry uses preventive coping strategies to deal with the envisioned future shortage of healthcare leaders as the workforce ages. Health systems anticipate that many of their hospitals' baby-boom generation C-suite leaders might retire in the coming decade. Many organizations have formal succession-planning programs where they identify high-potential leaders for more targeted training and development to prepare to fill future executive roles. Knowing that it takes a long time to cultivate leaders capable of operating at the C-suite level, these programs often start years in advance to ensure a new generation is ready to lead when current leaders retire.

Preventive and proactive coping are primary or organizational prevention (Quick et al., 1997). Organizational prevention is designed to enhance an employee's health and performance at work by eliminating the stressors that lead to distress. Methods to accomplish this include modifying work demands and improving relationships in the workplace (Schwarzer, 2004). Anticipatory coping is related to secondary prevention; the goal is to change individual stress responses to necessary demands. Reactive coping may be referred to as tertiary prevention, which attempts to minimize the amount of individual and organizational distress that results when organizational stressors and resulting stress responses have not been adequately controlled (Quick et al., 1997) (see **Figure 13-3**).

To illustrate these coping concepts, consider the following scenario: A physician displays inappropriate behavior* toward a nurse (a stressor), which leads to the nurse experiencing anxiety (a stress response) and, in turn, the nurse resigns (an organizational consequence of distress). Primary prevention would attempt to eliminate the stressor by having the hospital establish a zero-tolerance policy regarding inappropriate physician behavior (preventive, proactive coping, or both). Secondary prevention would address the problem by providing programs to improve interpersonal relations between physicians and nurses (anticipatory coping). These programs may include improving team building and communication skills, whereby the physician recognizes that nurses are an integral part of the patient's healthcare team, and interactions should therefore be based on mutual respect and trust. Tertiary prevention might include establishing an employee assistance program designed to help nurses cope with inappropriate behavior by physicians.

The preceding example is based on a study that linked inappropriate physician behavior with nurses leaving nursing. Rosenstein (2002) found daily interactions between nurses and physicians strongly influence nurses' morale. Survey respondents indicated that they were concerned with the significance of nurse–physician relationships, and over 90% of all respondents reported witnessing disruptive physician behavior and saw a direct link between

*Inappropriate physician behavior may be defined as "any inappropriate behavior, confrontation or conflict, including verbal abuse to physical and sexual harassment" (Rosenstein, 2002, p. 26).

this disruptive behavior and nurse satisfaction and retention. In addition, 30% of the nurse respondents reported knowing at least one colleague who had resigned because of disruptive physician behavior.

Subsequent research by Rosenstein and O'Daniel (2005, 2006, 2008) found almost equal disruptive behavior in nurses and other hospital employees. However, more disconcerting was the downstream negative impact of disruptive behavior on stress levels, loss of focus, concentration, communication, collaboration, and information transfer, resulting in medical errors, adverse events, and significant compromises in patient safety, quality, and even mortality.

Joy in Work

The Institute for Healthcare Improvement has suggested the "Joy in Work" framework to help senior leaders, managers, and individuals identify their roles in reducing stress and burnout in the workplace by seeking to increase joy in work. This results in happy, healthy, and productive employees (see **Figure 13-4**). The basic premise is that employees can better withstand the inevitable stressors in health care if they can find joy in their work.

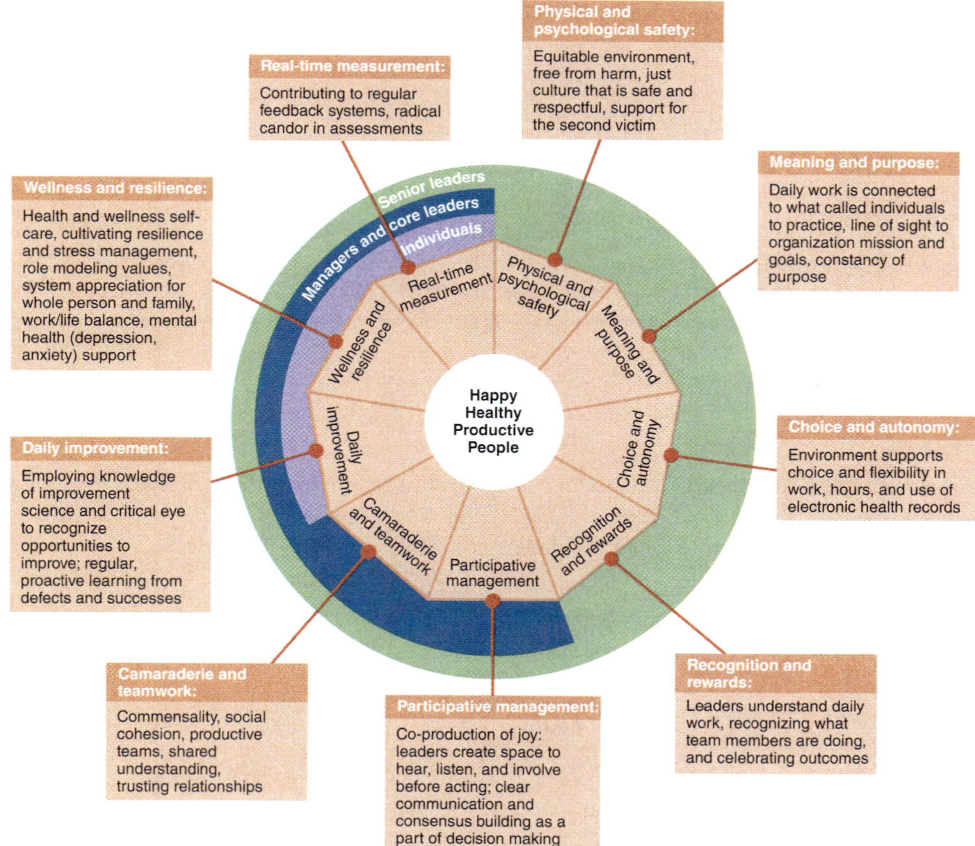

Figure 13-4 Components for Improving Joy in Work

Reproduced from Perlo, J., Balik, B., Swensen, S., Kabcenell, A., Landsman, J., & Feeley, D. (2017). *IHI framework for improving joy in work* (IHI White Paper). Institute for Healthcare Improvement. https://www.ihi.org/

Table 13-6 Description of Components for Improving Joy in Work

Physical and Psychological Safety.	*Physical*—People feel safe from physical harm at work. *Psychological*—People feel free to change, to share feedback and ideas, and to admit mistakes.
Meaning and Purpose	People feel that they are making a difference and can connect their daily work to the organization's mission and purpose.
Choice and Autonomy	People can choose how they structure and accomplish their daily work, and have a voice in changes that affect them.
Recognition and Rewards	People are recognized for their contributions and rewarded accordingly.
Participative Management	Managers encourage and engage others in their decision-making processes and regularly gather and incorporate feedback.
Camaraderie and Teamwork	People feel they are a part of a team and have mutual support and companionship at work.
Daily Improvement	A proactive approach to improvement is a part of daily practice across the organization.
Wellness and Resilience	The organization values and invests in the wellness and well-being of its employees. Self-care is seen as part of the larger organizational effort, not a stand-alone solution.
Real-time Measurement	Systems allow for regular feedback and performance monitoring to support ongoing improvement.

Data from Perlo, J., Balik, B., Swensen, S., Kabcenell, A., Landsman, J., & Feeley, D. (2017). *IHI framework for improving joy in work* (IHI White Paper). Institute for Healthcare Improvement. https://www.ihi.org/resources/Pages/IHIWhitePapers/Framework-Improving-Joy-in-Work.aspx

The IHI suggests nine components that are critical for improving joy in work (see **Table 13-6**).

Job Design

Another important component of reducing work-related stress is job design. Proper job design accommodates an employee's mental and physical abilities. According to the MFL Occupational Health Centre (2000), employers can design better jobs by doing the following:

- Clearly defining jobs and responsibilities that reduce role conflict and role ambiguity
- Giving workers a say in how they do their jobs
- Giving workers opportunities to learn new skills
- Allowing time for social interactions among workers
- Making work schedules flexible for responsibilities outside of work
- Communicating about job security
- Training managers to apply participative-management styles as part of a culture that emphasizes open communication, support, and mutual respect
- Implementing effective performance-management systems with clear expectations and procedures that are understood by managers and staff
- Ensuring that effective change management accompanies organizational change

An employee's work setting may create physical stress because of noise, lack of privacy, poor lighting, or ventilation. Therefore, organizations should redesign employees' physical settings to minimize distressful effects (i.e., primary preventive and proactive coping). For example, Williams (2003) found that the odds of feeling stress because of fear of accident or injury were 7.2 times higher for employees working in healthcare occupations than those in management, business, finance, or science. This high source of workplace stress among healthcare workers may be caused by their constant exposure to the risk of infection, long hours, and irregular shifts. Other studies have shown that creating pleasant and suitable work areas can elevate an employee's job satisfaction, safety, and mental health, which may indirectly improve job performance.

Stress Management Programs

Organizations are developing comprehensive health promotion strategies for their employees, including various individual-level stress management programs (Schwarzer, 2004). Stress management programs often involve breathing and stretching exercises, yoga, meditation, and massage. The program's goal is to lessen the adrenaline response to minor stress. For example, St. Paul Fire and Marine Insurance Company conducted several studies on the effects of stress-prevention programs in hospital settings. Program activities included (1) employee and management education on job stress, (2) changes in hospital policies and procedures to reduce organizational sources of stress, and (3) establishment of employee-assistance programs. In one study, the frequency of medication errors declined by 50% after prevention activities were implemented in a 700-bed hospital. In a second study, there was a 70% reduction in malpractice claims in 22 hospitals that implemented stress-prevention activities. In contrast, claims were not reduced in a matched group of 22 hospitals that did not implement stress-prevention activities (Jones et al., 1988).

In another example, Baptist Health South Florida (BHSF), the largest nonprofit healthcare organization in South Florida, provides a holistic approach to the well-being of its staff. The organization sponsors a healthy lifestyle program for its employees, the Wellness Advantage. On-site fitness coaches are available to employees at the system's six hospital fitness centers to provide screening and personal training. Discounts are offered to employees who choose the meals designated "healthy" in the system's cafeterias. For employees who face life-threatening illnesses, the system offers flexible, reduced scheduling to maintain some level of employment during stressful times. Senior management believes that the organization's success, as measured by patient satisfaction, physician satisfaction, employee satisfaction, clinical outcomes, and operating profits, is directly owed to its employees' "healthy" infrastructure. Baptist Health's commitment to its employees is recognized nationally. The National Business Group on Health has recognized Baptist Health's longtime commitment to its employees by naming the health system one of the Best Employers for Healthy Lifestyles (Baptist Health South Florida, 2015; May, 2004).

To meet both organizational and individual goals regarding stress management, Crampton and colleagues (1995) provide the following recommendations:

Preventive and Proactive Coping (Primary Prevention)

1. Identify the major stressors in the workplace and assess which ones are controllable. Organizations should do more than provide stress management techniques. If the causes of stress can be reduced or eliminated, they should be. Organizational-level strategies might include redesigning employees' jobs; improving the selection, placement, and orientation of new

employees; providing employees with more participation and autonomy in decision making; disseminating information; providing needed education and training; reducing workloads or the pace of work; modifying work schedules to be compatible with demands and responsibilities outside of work; conducting time management programs; clearly defining work roles; providing opportunities for career development; and providing emotional and task support.

2. Communicate with employees about the benefits of stress management. Explain what stress is and the health implications of excess stress or distress. Encourage employees to lead healthier lives by lowering their stress on the job and at home.

Anticipatory Coping (Secondary Prevention)

1. Help employees identify their stressors and stress-tolerance levels. Before learning how to deal with stress, employees must identify the stressors to which they react because not everyone responds the same way to the same stressors. To aid in this process, organizations can conduct health-risk appraisals that test their employees' stress levels.
2. Develop individualized stress management programs that meet the needs of the organization's employees. Programs should be topic-specific and should be implemented in stages. If all aspects of a program are implemented at once and parts fail, employees will lose faith in the program and management. This will be another cause of anxiety and stress for the employee. Stress management programs may include learning relaxation and meditation techniques, developing a sound support system, undertaking outside hobbies, setting realistic goals, developing time management skills, and learning when to say no rather than taking on more than one can handle.
3. Communicate with employees. Providing more information about their jobs and other factors that affect them will allow employees to feel more in control of their circumstances and can help build cohesion. Organizations must also communicate and describe the stress management strategies that are available to employees and must help employees develop personalized action plans.

Reactive Coping (Tertiary Prevention)

1. Make sure employees learn to recognize symptoms of distress. These may include gastrointestinal problems, rapid pulse, frequent illness, insomnia, persistent fatigue, irritability, lack of concentration, and increased use of alcohol, drugs, or both. Common methods used to help identify stressors and symptoms include self-report measures (e.g., interviews and surveys), behavioral measures (e.g., observation and performance measures), and physiological stress measures (e.g., heart rate and blood pressure).
2. Exercise and a nutritious diet are two of the most agreed-upon stress management techniques. Organizations can help employees by providing information and access to physical recreation facilities or equipment, establishing on-site facilities, or providing memberships to local health clubs. One type of organizational stress management program provides employees with access to an employee assistance program, a corporate psychologist, a toll-free hotline, or some other form of counseling assistance. These programs can help employees deal with a variety of problems that range from learning to cope to dealing with substance abuse.
3. Help employees keep a positive perspective on life and feel a sense of purpose. It is important for employees to feel that they are making a valuable contribution to the organization.

Summary

Stress has become a widely used but misunderstood term, and several misconceptions exist. The first misconception is that all stress is negative. A certain degree of stress is necessary for good mental and physical health; it can be viewed as positive or constructive stress, which compels us to perform optimally and achieve our goals. The second misconception is that nothing can be done to eliminate or diminish workplace distress. Organizations and individuals can use preventive or proactive (primary prevention) coping strategies to change adverse events into positive experiences and growth opportunities.

In the past, the phrase "healthy organization" almost always denoted a firm's financial health. However, "healthy organizations" studies suggest that policies that benefit workers' health also benefit the organization's bottom line. Today, the healthy organization focuses not only on financial soundness but also on its employees' physical and mental well-being. Healthy employees create stronger businesses and healthier profits.

Discussion Questions

1. Define "stress" and explain the difference between eustress and distress.
2. Discuss the various components of the stress and coping process model.
3. Discuss the adverse effects of distress from both an organizational and individual perspective.
4. Describe the various forms of stress.
5. Describe the three stages of the General Adaptation Syndrome and the positive and negative effects that occur in each stage.
6. Discuss the symptoms of burnout using Golembiewski's phase model.
7. Discuss the four categories of causes of stress in the workplace.
8. Discuss and provide examples of the various coping strategies available to organizations and individuals.
9. Discuss the concept of learned optimism and how it relates to coping with stress by individuals.
10. Discuss what the term "stress management" means and available interventions for organizations and individuals.

CASE STUDY 13-3 Why Are All the Employees Leaving?

The administrator of a large physician group practice is becoming alarmed about the growing level of turnover the organization has recently been experiencing. It has already passed the industry average, and they are concerned about the practice's capacity to staff the medical clinics for the upcoming flu season. In conducting exit interviews, they have learned that the employees who are leaving generally liked their work and felt that their salaries were fair. However, they were unhappy with the way their managers treated them, which was creating stress in their lives. They are leaving to take less-stressful positions in other healthcare organizations.

Discussion Questions

1. How should the managers behave differently so that the employees experience less stress on the job?
2. What strategies can the organization use so that the employees experience less stress on the job?
3. What could the individual employees do to help manage their own stress levels more effectively?

CASE STUDY 13-4 Scott's Dilemma

Scott, a licensed physical therapist, had worked for four years at a rehabilitation facility in an urban Southwest city. He had been satisfied with his work environment and found fulfillment in helping patients regain their independence. That changed after a system-wide reorganization brought in a new supervisor, George, from a Midwest facility.

Almost immediately, George criticized Scott's care plans and patient interactions. Despite previously receiving strong performance reviews, Scott was stunned when George gave him a poor evaluation. In response, Scott extended his hours and worked harder, hoping to meet expectations. Nevertheless, George continued to find fault. Staff meetings became stressful as George routinely belittled Scott in front of colleagues.

Over time, Scott's mental and physical health deteriorated. He felt isolated from family, friends, and coworkers, experienced sleep and appetite disturbances, and no longer enjoyed his work. He began calling in sick more often and even imagined confronting George, which only added to his distress.

George encouraged others to avoid Scott, further isolating him. As coworkers aligned with George's perspective, they began viewing Scott as the problem and distanced themselves to avoid conflict.

Seeking resolution, Scott approached George directly, expressing his concerns and desire to improve the situation. George, however, interpreted this as insubordination and intensified his hostility. Scott then turned to Human Resources, who advised him to document the mistreatment. When HR addressed the issue with George, his behavior worsened.

As a final step, Scott brought the issue to George's supervisor, Rebecca. After speaking with George, who portrayed Scott as unproductive and defiant, Rebecca placed a formal reprimand in Scott's file for insubordination.

Discuss the symptoms of stress that Scott is experiencing. What recommendations can you make to Scott for coping with his stress?

Data from Pinto, J., Vecchione, M., & Howard, L. (2004, October). Case discussion: Workplace bully. Paper presented at the 12th Annual International Conference of the Association on Employment Practices and Principles, Ft. Lauderdale, FL.

References

American Hospital Association. (2017). *Cost of community violence to hospitals and health systems*. https://www.aha.org/guidesreports/2018-01-18-cost-community-violence-hospitals-and-health-systems

American Institute of Stress. (2004). *Job stress*. https://www.stress.org

American Psychological Association. (2023). *Work in America 2023: Workplaces as engines of psychological health and well-being*. Accessed April 4, 2025, from https://www.apa.org/pubs/reports/work-in-america/2023-workplace-health-well-being

Association of American Medical Colleges. (2016). *Applicants and matriculants data. Table A-1: U.S. Medical School Applications and Matriculants by School, State of Legal Residence, and Sex, 2016–2017*. https://web.archive.org/web/20170708225910/https://www.aamc.org/download/321442/data/factstablea1.pdf

American Medical Association. (2023, October 25). *AMA president sounds alarm on national physician shortage*. https://www.ama-assn.org/press-center/press-releases/ama-president-sounds-alarm-national-physician-shortage

Bandura, A. (1997). *Self-efficacy: The exercise of control*. W. H. Freeman & Company.

Baptist Health South Florida. (2015). *Awards and recognition*. https://baptisthealth.net

Barefoot, J. C., Dahlstrom, W. G., & Williams, R. B. (1983). Hostility, CHD incidence, and total mortality: A 25-year follow-up study of 255 physicians. *Psychosomatic Medicine, 45*(1), 59–63.

Berry, L. L., Mirabito, A. M., & Berwick, D. M. (2004). A health care agenda for business. *MIT Sloan Management Review, 45*(4), 56–64.

Crampton, S. M., Hodge, J. W., Mishra, J. M., & Price, S. (1995). Stress and stress management. *SAM Advanced Management Journal, 60*(3), 10–18.

Evans, G. W., & Carrere, S. (1991). Traffic congestion, perceived control, and psychophysiological stress among urban bus drivers. *Journal of Applied Psychology, 76*(5), 658–663.

Fox, M. L., Dwyer, D. J., & Ganster, D. C. (1993). Effects of stressful job demands and control on physiological and attitudinal outcomes in a hospital setting. *Academy of Management, 36*(2), 289–318.

Frank, E., Biola, H., & Burnett, C. A. (2000). Mortality rates and causes among US physicians. *American Journal of Preventive Medicine, 19*(3), 155–159.

Friedman, I. A. (1999). Turning our schools into a healthier workplace: Bridging between professional self-efficacy and professional demands. In R. Vandenberghe & A. M. Huberman (Eds.), *Understanding and preventing teacher burnout* (pp. 166–175). Cambridge University Press.

Ganster, D. C., & Fusilier, M. R. (1989). Control in the workplace. In C. L. Cooper & I. T. Robertson (Eds.), *International review of industrial and organizational psychology*. Wiley.

Goh, J., Pfeffer, J., & Zenios, S. A. (2016). The relationship between workplace stressors and mortality and health costs in the United States. *Management Science, 62*(2), 608–628.

Golembiewski, R. T. (1986). The epidemiology of progressive burnout: A primer. *Journal of Health and Human Resources Administration, 9*(1), 16–37.

Golembiewski, R. T. (1990). Differences in burnout, by sector: Public vs. business estimates using phases. *International Journal of Public Administration, 13*(4), 545–559.

Golembiewski, R. T., & Boss, R. W. (1991). Shelving levels of burnout for individuals in organizations: A note on the stability of phases. *Journal of Health and Human Resources Administration, 13*(4), 409–420.

Golembiewski, R. T., & Boudreau, R. (1991). Healthcare professional attend thyself: The epidemiology of burnout in several settings. *International Journal of Public Administration, 14*(1), 43–57.

Hawkins, M. (2018). *2018 Survey of America's physicians: Practice patterns & perspectives*. The Physicians Foundation. https://physiciansfoundation.org/wp-content/uploads/2018/09/physicians-survey-results-final-2018.pdf

Hiroto, D. S. (1974). Locus of control and learned helplessness. *Journal of Experimental Psychology, 102*(2), 187–193.

Jacobs, G. D. (2001). The physiology of mind-body interactions: The stress response and the relation response. *The Journal of Alternative and Complementary Medicine, 7*(Suppl. 1), S83–S92.

Jamieson, J. P., Nock, M. K., & Mendes, W. B. (2012). Mind over matter: Reappraising arousal improves cardiovascular and cognitive responses to stress. *Journal of Experimental Psychology: General, 141*(3), 417.

Jha, A. K., Iliff, A. R., Chaoui, A. A., Defossez, S., Bombaugh, M. C., & Miller, Y. R. (2019). *A crisis in health care: A call to action on physician burnout*. Massachusetts Medical Society, Massachusetts Health and Hospital Association, Harvard T.H. Chan School of Public Health, and Harvard Global Health Institute. https://content.sph.harvard.edu/wwwhsph/sites/21/2019/01/PhysicianBurnoutReport2018FINAL.pdf

The Joint Commission. (2018, April 17). *Sentinel event alert: Issue 59*—Addressing workplace violence in healthcare. https://www.jointcommission.org/en/knowledge-library/newsletters/sentinel-event-alert/issue-5

Jones, J. W., Barge, B. N., Steffy, B. D., Fay, L. M., Kunz, L. K., & Wuebker, L. J. (1988). Stress and medical malpractice: Organizational risk assessment and intervention. *Journal of Applied Psychology, 73*(4), 727–735.

Jones, C. B., Sousane, Z., & Mossburg, S. (2023, October 31). *Addressing workplace violence and creating a safer workplace*. PSNet. https://psnet.ahrq.gov/perspective/addressing-workplace-violence-and-creating-safer-workplace

Karasek, R. A. (1979). Job demands, job decision latitude, and mental strain: Implications for job redesign. *Administrative Science Quarterly*, *24*(2), 285–310.

Karasek, R. A., Baker, D., Marxer, F., Ahlbom, A., & Theorell, T. (1981). Job decision latitude, job demands, and cardiovascular disease: A prospective study of Swedish men. *American Journal of Public Health, 71*(7), 694–705.

Keita, G. P., & Hurrell, J. J., Jr. (Eds.). (1994). *Job stress in a changing workforce: Investigating gender, diversity, and family issues*. American Psychological Association.

Keller, A., Litzelman, K., Wisk, L. E., Maddox, T., Cheng, E. R., Creswell, P. D., & Witt, W. P. (2012). Does the perception that stress affects health matter? The association with health and mortality. *Health Psychology, 31*(5), 677.

Kinicki, A., & Williams, B. K. (2003). *Management: A practical introduction*. McGraw-Hill.

Lazarus, R. S. (1991). Progress on a cognitive-motivational-relational theory of emotion. *American Psychologist, 46*(8), 819–834.

Lazarus, R. S., DeLongis, A., Folkman, S., & Gruen, R. (1985). Stress and adaptational outcomes: The problem of confounded measures. *American Psychologist, 40*(7), 770–779.

Lazarus, R. S., & Folkman, S. (1984). *Stress, appraisal, and coping*. Springer.

Lucian Leape Institute. (2013). *Through the eyes of the workforce: Creating joy, meaning, and safer health care*. National Patient Safety Foundation.

Maslach, C., & Goldberg, J. (1998). Prevention of burnout: New perspectives. *Applied Preventive Psychology, 7*(1), 63–74.

Maslach, C., & Jackson, S. E. (1981). The measurement of experienced burnout. *Journal of Occupational Behavior, 2*(2), 99–113.

Maslach, C., & Leiter, M. P. (2022). *The burnout challenge: Managing people's relationships with their jobs*. Harvard University Press.

Maslach, C., Schaufeli, W. B., & Leiter, M. P. (2001). Job burnout. *Annual Review of Psychology, 52*(1), 397–422. https://doi.org/10.1146/annurev.psych.52.1.397

May, E. L. (2004). Are people your priority? How to engage your workforce. *Healthcare Executive, 19*(4), 8–16.

MFL Occupational Health Centre, Inc. (2000, March). *Stress at work*. http://www.mflohc.mb.ca/

Molina, M. F., Landry, A. I., Chary, A. N., & Burnett-Bowie, S. A. M. (2020). Addressing the elephant in the room: Microaggressions in medicine. *Annals of Emergency Medicine, 76*(4), 387–391.

Murphy, L. R. (1995). Occupational stress management: Current status and future directions. In C. L. Cooper & D. M. Rousseau (Eds.), *Trends in organizational behavior* (Vol. 2). Wiley.

National Academies of Sciences, Engineering, and Medicine. (2019). Taking action against clinician burnout: A systems approach to professional well-being. The National Academies Press. https://doi.org/10.17226/25521

National Institute for Occupational Safety and Health. (1999). *Stress at work. DHHS (NIOSH)* (Publication No. 99-101). https://www.cdc.gov/niosh/docs/99-101

Perlo, J., Balik, B., Swensen, S., Kabcenell, A., Landsman, J., & Feeley, D. (2017). *IHI framework for improving joy in work*. IHI White Paper. Institute for Healthcare Improvement. https://www.ihi.org

Quick, J. C., Quick, J. D., Nelson, D. L., & Hurrell, J. J., (1997). *Preventive stress management in organizations*. American Psychological Association.

Rosenstein, A. H. (2002). Nurse–physician relationships: Impact on nurse satisfaction and retention. *American Journal of Nursing, 102*(6), 26–34.

Rosenstein, A. H., & O'Daniel, M. (2005). Disruptive behavior and clinical outcomes: Perceptions of nurses and physicians. *American Journal of Nursing, 105*(1), 54–64.

Rosenstein, A. H., & O'Daniel, M. (2006). Impact and implications of disruptive behavior in the perioperative arena. *Journal of the American College of Surgeons, 203*(1), 96–105.

Rosenstein, A. H., & O'Daniel, M. (2008). Managing disruptive physician behavior: Impact on staff relationships and patient care. *Neurology, 70*(17), 1564–1570.

Rotter, J. B. (1966). Generalized expectancies for internal versus external control of reinforcement. *Psychological Monographs: General and Applied, 80*(1), 1–28.

Rubinstein, P. (2019, February 27). Why do ill people still come into work? *BBC*. http://www.bbc.com/capital/story/20190227-how-to-tell-your-boss-youre-sick-and-why-you-should

Savery, L. K., & Hall, K. (1986). Tight rein, more stress. *Harvard Business Review, 65*, 160–164.

Schernhammer, E. S., & Colditz, G. A. (2004). Suicide rates among physicians: A quantitative and gender assessment (meta-analysis). *American Journal of Psychiatry, 161*(12), 2295–2302.

Schutte, L. (2012). What you don't know can cost you: Building a business case for recruitment and retention best practices. *Journal of Association of Staff Physician Recruiters, 19*. Summer 2012. https://web.archive.org/web/20170922021227/http://www.aspr.org/?696

Schwarzer, R. (2004). Manage stress at work through preventive and proactive coping. In E. A. Locke (Ed.), *Handbook of principles of organizational behavior*. Blackwell Publishing.

Seligman, M. E. P. (1998). *Learned optimism*. Free Press. (Original work published A. A. Knopf, 1991).

Seligman, M. E. P., & Csikszentmihalyi, M. (2000). Positive psychology: An introduction. *American Psychologist, 55*(1), 5–14.

Seligman, M. E., Steen, T. A., Park, N., & Peterson, C. (2005). Positive psychology progress: Empirical validation of interventions. *American Psychologist, 60*(5), 410–421.

Selye, H. (1956). *The stress of life*. McGraw-Hill.

Selye, H. (1974). *Stress without distress*. Hodder & Stoughton.

Shanafelt, T. D., Balch, C. M., Bechamps, G., Russell, T., Dyrbye, L., Satele, D., . . . Freischlag, J. (2010). Burnout and medical errors among American surgeons. *Annals of Surgery, 251*(6), 995–1000.

Shanafelt, T. D., Dyrbye, L. N., West, C. P., & Sinsky, C. A. (2016). Potential impact of burnout on the US physician workforce. *Mayo Clinic Proceedings, 91*(11), 1667–1668. doi:10.1016/j.mayocp.2016.08.016

Simmons, B. L., & Nelson, D. L. (2001). Eustress at work: The relationship between hope and health in hospital nurses. *Health Care Management Review, 26*(4), 7–18.

Spector, P. E. (1986). Perceived control by employees: A meta-analysis of studies concerning autonomy and participation at work. *Human Relations, 39*(11), 1005–1016.

Stewart, W. F., Ricci, J. A., Chee, E., Morganstein, D., & Lipton, R. (2003). Lost productive time and cost due to common pain conditions in the U.S. workforce. *Journal of the American Medical Association, 290*(18), 2443–2454.

U.S. Bureau of Labor Statistics. (2020). *Injuries, illnesses and fatalities*: Workplace violence in healthcare, 2018. https://www.bls.gov/iif/factsheets/workplace-violence-healthcare-2018.htm

Von Onciul, J. (1996). ABC of work related disorders: Stress at work. *British Medical Journal, 313*(7059), 745–748.

Whetten, D. A., & Cameron, K. S. (1993). *Developing managerial skills: Managing stress*. HarperCollins.

Williams, C. (2003). Sources of workplace stress. *Perspectives on Labour and Income, 4*(6), Statistics Canada Catalogue No. 75-001-XIE. https://www150.statcan.gc.ca/n1/pub/75-001-x/00603/6533-eng.html

Yerkes, R. M., & Dodson, J. D. (1908). The relation of strength of stimulus to rapidity of habit-formation. *Journal of Comparative Neurology and Psychology, 18*, 459–482.

Other Suggested Readings

Seligman, M. E. (2012). *Flourish: A visionary new understanding of happiness and well-being*. Simon and Schuster.

National Academy of Medicine. (2024). *National Plan for Health Workforce Well-Being*. The National Academies Press. https://doi.org/10.17226/26744

CHAPTER 14

Decision Making

LEARNING OUTCOMES

After completing this chapter, the student should be able to explain:

- The difference between the rational and bounded rationality approaches to decision making.
- The limitations of using intuitive decision making and the heuristics or biases approach.
- How framing heuristics affect escalation of commitment.
- The four basic styles of decision making.
- The Vroom-Yetton-Jago Decision-Making Method and the related factors.

Overview

Managers face both well-structured and poorly structured problems, requiring different decision-making models. Well-structured problems are routine, familiar, and easily defined, allowing managers to follow established policies. For example, if two employees request the same vacation time, a manager may follow company policy and grant the request based on seniority.

Middle and senior managers often deal with poorly structured problems, which are complex, new, and lack complete information. This is especially relevant in health care, where changing regulations, evolving payment models, and system consolidations create uncertainty.

Decision making can be rational or influenced by limitations. The rational approach involves a systematic process when time and resources allow. However, in the fast-paced healthcare environment, managers often face constraints, limiting their ability to evaluate every possible solution. This is known as bounded rationality. Given limited time, personal biases, and incomplete information, managers may rely on intuition or mental shortcuts, known as heuristics, to make decisions efficiently.

Rational Approach

The rational approach to decision making, also called the economic rationality model, involves a systematic analysis of the problem followed by the choice and implementation of a solution in a logical, step-by-step sequence (Daft, 2004). The rational model is considered the ideal method of decision making, as illustrated in **Figure 14-1**.

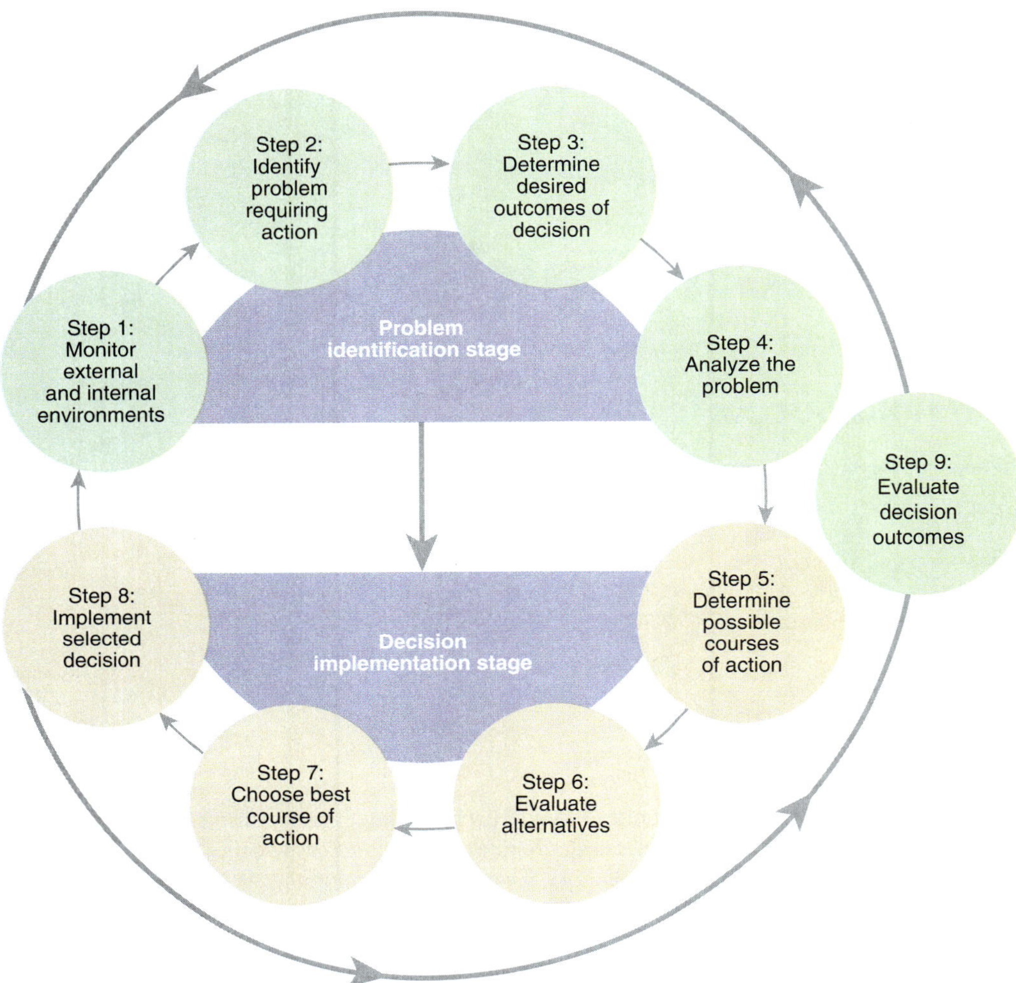

Figure 14-1 Steps in the Rational Approach to Decision Making

1. *Monitor the External and Internal Environments*: Managers need to monitor the external environment first and then the internal environment for needed changes to the status quo. These changes can arise from reviewing financial statements, performance evaluations, industry indices, competitors' activities, new regulations, and the like.
2. *Identify the Problem Requiring Action*: The manager responds to the needed change by identifying important issues, such as where, when, who are the stakeholders affected and involved, and how current activities will be influenced.
3. *Determine Desired Outcomes of the Decision*: The manager determines what performance outcomes need to be achieved by the decision.
4. *Analyze the Problem*: The manager needs to fact find the causes of and issues surrounding the problem. Additional data will be generated in this process so the appropriate alternatives can be generated.

5. *Determine Possible Courses of Action*: Before moving ahead with a decisive action plan, the manager must have a clear understanding of the various options available to achieve the desired outcomes. The manager should seek input from stakeholders and evidence-based research for varying ideas and suggestions.
6. *Evaluate Alternatives*: The manager assesses each alternative's merits and the probability that it will achieve the desired outcomes.
7. *Choose the Best Course of Action*: This step is critical to the decision process. The manager uses their analysis of the problem, outcomes, and alternatives to select the single best course of action for success.
8. *Implement the Selected Decision*: Finally, the manager allocates the necessary resources and gives directions to ensure that the selected decision is carried out.
9. *Evaluate the Decision*: Finally, the manager needs to assess if the decision met the desired outcomes and communicate the results to others. Thereafter, the monitoring activity (step 1) begins again.

The rational model may be the ideal, but under most circumstances, managers do not have complete information about a problem or all the plausible alternatives. In addition, managers are constrained by limited time and resources, personal biases, and other factors, which make rational decision making unrealistic. Therefore, managers are bounded (limited) regarding their rational decision making. The concept of bounded rationality embraces the realism that evaluation of alternatives and decision making are constrained by human actions (Forest & Mehier, 2001).

Bounded Rationality Model

The bounded rationality model of decision making, proposed by Simon (1957), recognizes that individuals have cognitive limitations that prohibit the processing of all the necessary or optimal information for decision making; therefore, an individual will limit their search for information before making a decision. Dequech (2001, p. 913) explains the concept of bounded rationality in the following manner:

1. Individuals often pursue multiple objectives, which may be conflicting. The alternatives from which to choose in order to pursue these objectives might not have been given to the decision maker, who must then adopt a process for generating alternatives.
2. The limits in the decision maker's mental capacity compared with the complexity of the decision environment usually prevent the decision maker from considering all the alternatives. Those limits are also present when the decision maker has to consider the consequences of the alternatives, so the decision maker employs some heuristic procedure for that purpose.
3. Finally, the decision maker adopts a satisfying strategy rather than an optimizing strategy, searching for solutions that are "good enough," given the realistic aspiration levels.

The expression "bounded rationality" denotes the type of rationality to which managers resort when their environment is too complex relative to their cognitive limitations. Because of these limitations, managers may employ intuitive or heuristic strategies for decision-making.

Intuition

Intuitive decision-making can be understood as a cognitive "short-circuiting," in which a decision is reached even though the reason for the decision cannot be easily described (Hall, 2002). In other words, intuitive decision making involves using one's professional judgment based on past experiences rather than sequential logic or explicit reasoning (Daft, 2004). Agor (1985, 1986a, b) suggests that intuition is most useful to managers in situations of uncertainty. Agor advocates reliance on intuition when a high level of uncertainty exists, when there is little precedent, when variables are not scientifically predictable and analytical data are of little use, when facts are limited and do not clearly point the way to go, when several alternatives seem plausible, and when time is limited and there is pressure to come up with the right answer.

There is some debate about the degree to which an individual's intuitive ability can be developed and improved (Bennett, 1998). Some researchers argue that intuitive abilities are closely related to personality types (Myers, 1980). Others claim that job characteristics or situational factors encourage managers to develop and improve their intuitive abilities (Agor, 1986a, b; Behling & Eckel, 1991; Wally & Baum, 1994). The Four Stages of Competence model is frequently applied to learning and training, but can provide some insights into the ability to develop intuition (Broadwell, 1969). This model describes the progression from unawareness to mastery of a skill. The stages are:

1. **Unconscious Incompetence**: At this stage, individuals are unaware of their lack of skill or knowledge. They do not recognize the deficit or the value of acquiring the new skill.
2. **Conscious Incompetence**: Here, individuals become aware of their lack of skill and understand the importance of acquiring it. This stage can be uncomfortable as learners recognize their deficiencies but have not yet developed the competence to overcome them.
3. **Conscious Competence**: Learners have acquired the skill but need to concentrate to perform it. They understand the steps involved and can execute them reliably, but the process is not yet automatic.
4. **Unconscious Competence**: At this final stage, the skill becomes second nature, and individuals can perform it effortlessly without conscious thought. The skill is executed fluidly and automatically.

As a leader makes more decisions over time and evaluates whether they were effective, they are likely to move along these stages until decision making becomes more intuitive.

Heuristics or Biases Approach

In addition to using intuition to deal with the problems of uncertainty and complexity, managers use judgmental heuristics strategies to simplify their decision making. Heuristics are guidelines or "rules of thumb" that help to make our world manageable by simplifying complex tasks (Kahneman et al., 1982; Tversky & Kahneman, 1974). Heuristic processing strategies enable managers to cut through overwhelming data by applying simplifying assumptions to the information. The use of heuristics may result in accurate predictions, but it can also lead to an array of errors and biases. Tversky and Kahneman (1974) describe three commonly used heuristics: (1) availability, (2) representativeness, and (3) anchoring and adjustment.

- **Availability bias** is an intuitive technique in which the perceived probability of an event is influenced by the ease of recollection. More easily recalled events are given a higher probability of recurring. More frequent events are often the most easily recalled, but the most easily recalled are not necessarily the most frequent (Hall, 2002). Ease of recall is also affected by salience (i.e., the degree to which some information is perceived as being more relevant to the decision being made) related to the emotional strength of a memory; memories associated with strong emotions are recalled more easily. For example, performance appraisals of staff are affected by the use of availability heuristics by managers while evaluating them. It is common to find the most recent and vividly etched event, positive or negative, influencing the appraisal. (See **Case Study 14-1**.)

CASE STUDY 14-1 Just Like the Others

Dr. Smith walked into the patient's room after quickly reviewing the chart. The patient was a 42-year-old woman with a long history of diabetes. The patient was complaining of needing to urinate frequently throughout the day, which is a sign of uncontrolled diabetes. When Dr. Smith entered the room, he noticed the patient was very obese and was wearing clothes that were quite worn with a few holes here and there. "Oh great. Another low-income patient who doesn't manage their diabetes. Ten bucks says this person is still eating sugary foods and can't get their insulin right. No wonder they have to urinate all the time." Dr. Smith typically counsels 4–5 patients a week about managing their diabetes, and finds that his lower-income patients do not always seem to have the health literacy to really understand his instructions. Without asking many questions, Dr. Smith started lecturing the patient on eating better foods and doing a better job of managing her insulin. When she protested that she was doing all of those things, he just reinforced the importance again.

Six months later, Dr. Smith got a call from the hospital's lawyer. The patient had a tumor in her pelvic region that was putting pressure on her bladder, increasing her urinary frequency. The cancer had progressed quickly and had metastasized to her lungs. The lawyer informed him that he was named in a lawsuit from the patient, claiming that he negligently refused to listen to her concerns and misdiagnosed her, thus resulting in her metastatic cancer.

Discussion

Dr. Smith used the availability heuristic when giving his diagnosis. Symptoms of mismanaged diabetes were very salient and accessible to Dr. Smith, because he saw several cases per week, often among low-income patients. Dr. Smith also used the representativeness heuristic by comparing the patient to former patients based on her appearance. Had Dr. Smith listened to the patient and created a robust differential diagnosis in addition to relying on his previous experience, he would have realized that the patient's symptoms could have been due to other causes, such as a tumor.

- **Representativeness bias** is an intuitive technique whereby probabilities are evaluated according to the degree to which the given sample matches, or is representative of, a class of samples or populations. (See Case Study 14-1.)
- In the workplace, representativeness heuristics can be traced as the reason behind many cases of employee discrimination. **Anchoring and adjustment bias** is an intuitive technique that is used when a series of estimates is used to obtain a proposed answer to a current problem. People create a preliminary solution on the basis of initial information (anchoring) and then modify the answer when more information becomes available (adjustment). For example, when the salary of a new employee is being set, the anchoring and adjustment heuristic is used. The employee's starting salary is invariably set close to the last paid salary without regard to what the new job description may entail. In other words, the initial value significantly influences the process of the adjustment toward the new value, irrespective of the rationality in the choice of the initial value. (See **Case Study 14-2**.)

As Case Studies 14-1 and 14-2 illustrate, there are many similarities between clinical decision making and managerial decision making. Extensive literature exists regarding the use of intuition and heuristics in medical decision making because of the high degree of uncertainty within the practice of medicine. As Sox et al. (1988, p. 17) point out, "Medicine is the art of making decisions without adequate information." As such, decisions made by clinicians through the use of intuition or heuristics can have a tremendous impact on healthcare managers. Clinicians make the decisions as to the commitment of scarce resources to patients and the associated care and

CASE STUDY 14-2 How Much Am I Worth?

Kim was really excited to start her new job. She had just graduated and was finally going to work in an entry-level position at a big hospital in town. When the hiring manager, John, was negotiating Kim's salary, he asked what her salary expectations were. Because she had only ever worked student jobs, she wasn't really sure what the salary should be for this type of position. She tried to look it up online, but it was hard to find accurate information for this particular title. She knew her college friends who were teachers were making about $45,000 a year, so she said, "around $45,000." John said that he would start her at $47,000. "Wow!" Thought Kim. "That's pretty good for my first real job, and I got even more than I asked for, plus awesome benefits! I am so excited!" John thought to himself, "Wow! That was cheap. The last person I hired for that role started at $65,000." After a few months, Kim became friends with the other employee who had the same role, Sarah. In passing, Sarah casually mentioned that she was a little disappointed with her starting salary of $65,000 because she was making $75,000 at her last job in a different industry. When Kim heard about Sarah's higher salary for doing the same job, she wasn't so happy with the $47,000 anymore. She made an appointment with John to discuss a raise. He replied, "I'm sorry, Kim, but HR will only let me go up a little bit from the starting salary without a different title."

How was the anchoring and adjustment heuristic used by Kim, John, and Sarah?

treatment plans (Hall, 2002; Thompson, 2003). However, it is the responsibility of healthcare managers to provide the resources for clinicians to perform their work, and their health systems are judged on the clinical outcomes of the patient populations they serve. Therefore, healthcare managers need to appreciate not only how intuition and heuristics play a part in their own decision making but also how they affect the decision making of clinicians because both affect the achievement of organizational goals. (See **Case Study 14-3**.)

CASE STUDY 14-3 Cognitive Errors in Clinical Decision Making

Heuristic processing helps clinicians manage complex information by applying simplifying assumptions. However, heuristics can lead to cognitive errors in medical decision making. Common heuristics include:

- **Availability error** occurs when clinicians misjudge disease probability based on recent experiences. Overestimation happens after encountering a dramatic case, such as a missed pulmonary embolism in a young, healthy patient, leading to unnecessary imaging in similar cases. Underestimation occurs when limited experience skews judgment, such as a junior resident who, after seeing only benign cases of chest pain, conducts superficial evaluations even in high-risk populations.
- **Representation error** arises when clinicians assess disease probability based on how well a case matches classic symptoms, without considering disease prevalence. For example, a healthy 60-year-old man with vague chest pain may not fit the typical myocardial infarction (MI) profile but remains at significant risk due to the condition's prevalence. Conversely, suspecting aortic dissection in a healthy 20-year-old with sharp chest pain ignores the disorder's rarity, making pneumothorax or pleuritis

more likely. Representation errors also occur when positive test results in low-prevalence populations are incorrectly assumed to indicate disease rather than a false positive.

- **Anchoring error** occurs when clinicians stick to an initial diagnosis despite contradicting evidence. For instance, diagnosing pancreatitis in a patient with a history of alcohol-related episodes is reasonable, but if pancreatic enzyme levels are normal and the patient denies recent alcohol use, dismissing these contradictions instead of reconsidering the diagnosis (e.g., acute MI) represents an anchoring error. Conflicting data should prompt further investigation rather than be disregarded.

Data from Porter, R. (Ed.). (2013). *The Merck manual of diagnosis and therapy.* Merck Sharp & Dohme Corp. https://www.merckmanuals.com/professional

Escalation of Commitment and Framing Heuristics

In addition to Tversky and Kahneman's (1974) three commonly used heuristics, escalation of commitment is another bias that can lead to poor decision making. Staw (1981) defines this as a situation where a manager continues investing resources into a failing project. One reason for this is the reluctance to admit mistakes (Staw & Ross, 1987). Research shows that managers who feel personally responsible for a failing decision are more likely to allocate additional resources than those not involved in the initial choice (Staw, 1981). This behavior is commonly described as "throwing good money after bad."

A notable example is the bankruptcy of the Allegheny Health System in Pennsylvania, where leaders failed to adjust their plans despite clear financial difficulties (Bottles, 2001). In the public sector, examples include Vancouver's Expo '86, Chicago's Deep Tunnel project, and the Washington Public Supply System (Staw & Ross, 1987). Expo '86 was intended to break even financially, but escalating costs led British Columbia to implement a lottery to cover a $300 million deficit.

Another cause of escalation is framing heuristics, where decision making is influenced by how information is presented. Despite both statements conveying the same information, Levin, Schnittjer, and Thee (1988) found that individuals viewed experimental cancer treatment more favorably when told it had a 40% success rate rather than a 60% failure rate.

To avoid escalation of commitment, Staw and Ross (1987) recommend that managers:

- Recognize their bias toward escalation.
- Identify escalation as overcommitment to a strategy, often by ambiguously defining failure or ignoring concerns from others.
- Gain an outsider's perspective to evaluate the strategy more objectively.

Decision-Style Model

Managers have different styles when it comes to making decisions and solving problems. Rowe and Boulgarides (1983, 1998) developed a decision-style model that proposes that managers differ along two dimensions in the way they approach decision making: value orientation and tolerance for ambiguity. Value orientation reflects the extent to which an individual focuses on either task and technical concerns or people and social concerns when making decisions. Tolerance for ambiguity reflects the extent to which a person has a high need for structure or control in their life.

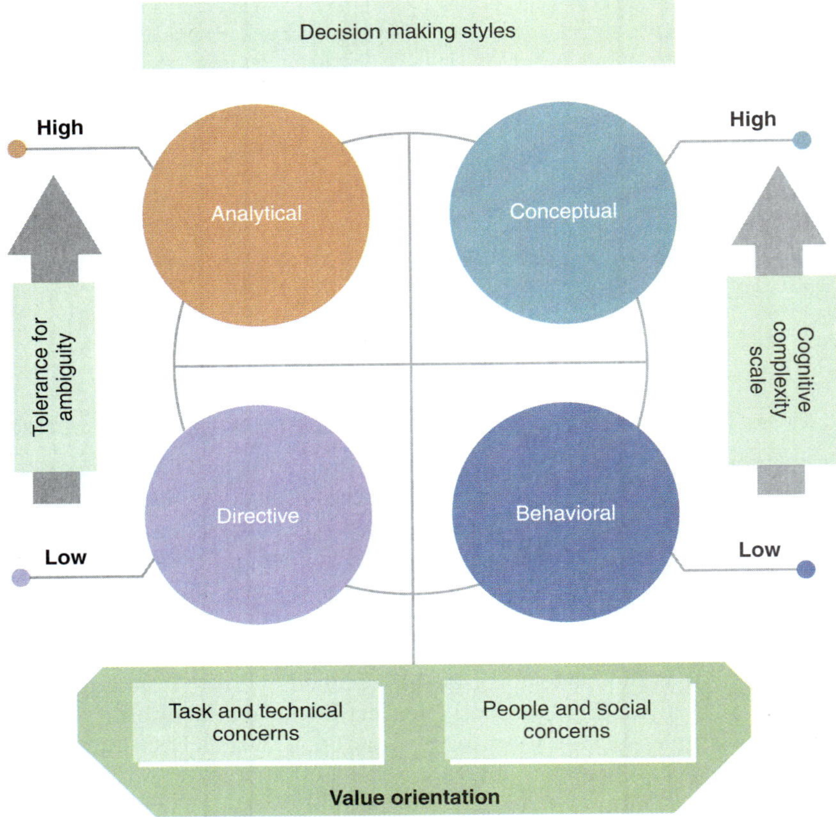

Figure 14-2 Decision-Making Styles

Modified from Rowe, A. J., & Boulgarides, J. D. (1983). Decision styles: A perspective. *Leadership & Organization Development Journal, 4*(4), 3–9.

Figure 14-2 illustrates that the decision-style model encompasses four basic styles: directive, analytic, conceptual, and behavioral. Boulgarides and Cohen (2001, pp. 59–60) describe the four basic styles as follows:

1. *Directive*: The decision maker who uses this style has a low tolerance for ambiguity and low cognitive complexity. The focus is on technical decisions, and this style is generally autocratic. The decision maker may adopt this style because of a high need for power. Because of the lack of information and the few alternatives, speed and satisfactory solutions are typical. The decision makers tend to be focused and are frequently aggressive. Generally, they prefer structure and specific information, which is given verbally. Their orientation is internal to the organization and short-range. They tend to operate with tight controls. Although they are efficient, these decision makers have a high need for security and status. They have the drive that is required to achieve results, but they also want to dominate others.
2. *Analytic*: This decision maker has a much greater tolerance for ambiguity than the directive-style manager and also has a more cognitively complex personality that leads to the

desire for more information and the consideration of many alternatives. The analytic style contains an autocratic bent because of the focus on technical decisions and the need for control. The analytic style is typified by the ability to cope with new situations (but in a structured manner) and problem solving. Position and ego are important to individuals who use an analytic decision-making style. These individuals often reach top positions in an organization or start their own companies. They are not quick in decision making, enjoy variety, and prefer written reports. They also enjoy challenges and examine every detail in a situation.

3. *Conceptual*: Including both high cognitive complexity and people orientation, managers with this decision-making style tend to use data from multiple sources and to consider many alternatives. Like individuals using the behavioral decision-making style, conceptual-style decision makers share goals with subordinates in trusting and open relationships. These individuals tend to be idealists who may emphasize ethics and values in their behavior. They are generally creative and can readily understand complex relationships. Their focus is long-range and have a high organizational commitment. They are achievement-oriented and value praise, recognition, and independence. They prefer loose control over power and will frequently encourage the participation of those they lead. They may be characterized as thinkers rather than doers.
4. *Behavioral*: Although low on the cognitive complexity scale, this leader has a deep concern for the organization and the development of people. Behavioral-style managers tend to be supportive and are concerned with subordinates' well-being. They provide counseling, are receptive to suggestions, communicate easily, show warmth, are empathetic, are persuasive, and are willing to compromise and accept a looser style of control. With low data input, this style tends toward a short-range focus and uses meetings primarily for communicating. These managers avoid conflict, seek acceptance, and tend to be more people-oriented, but sometimes are insecure.

Of the four decision-making styles, individuals tend to resort to a single, dominant style (i.e., default mode of decision making). However, with training, managers can effectively use all four styles as different situations are presented.

Vroom-Yetton-Jago Decision-Making Model

A good decision-making method under one set of circumstances might not be considered so under other conditions. A classic contingency model for decision making was first described by Vroom and Yetton (1973). Fifteen years later, Vroom and Jago (1988) replaced the decision tree system of the original model with an expert system based on mathematics; see **Figure 14-3**. The contingency model for decision making suggests that individuals should consider choosing from five types of decision processes based on a number of factors. Two of the five processes are autocratic (AI and AII), two are consultative (CI and CII), and one is group-based (GII). This decision-making model can be used to choose between individual and group decision-making strategies.

The five decision processes as described by Vroom and Yetton (1973) are as follows:

1. *Autocratic I (AI)*: Completely autocratic. You solve the problem or make the decision yourself, using the information available to you at the present time.
2. *Autocratic II (AII)*: Request specific information. You obtain any necessary information from team members or subordinates and then decide on the solution to the problem yourself. You may or may not tell subordinates the purpose of your questions or give information about the

	Five types of decision processes																		
	Autocratic AI			Autocratic AII					Consultative CI	Consultative CII						Collaborative GII			
1. Is the quality of the decision important?	Y	N	N	Y	Y	Y	Y	Y	Y	Y	Y	Y	Y	Y	Y	Y	Y	Y	N
2. Is the team commitment to the decision important?	N	N	Y	Y	Y	N	N	Y	Y	Y	Y	Y	Y	Y	N	Y	Y	Y	Y
3. Do you have the information to make the decision on your own?	Y			Y	N	N	N	N	N	Y	N	N	N	N	N	Y	N	N	
4. Is the problem well-structured?					Y	Y	Y	Y	Y		N	Y	N	Y	N		Y	N	
5. If you made the decision yourself, would the group support it?			Y	Y	Y			Y	Y	N	Y	N	N	N	N	N	N	N	N
6. Does the group share organizational goals?					N	N	Y	Y	Y	N		Y	N	N		Y	Y	Y	
7. Is conflict over the decision likely?							N	N	Y			N					Y		

Figure 14-3 Vroom-Yetton-Jago Decision-Making Model

problem or decision you are working on. The input provided by subordinates responds to your request for special information. They do not play a role in the definition of the problem or in generating or evaluating alternative solutions.

3. *Consultative I (CI)*: One-on-one discussion. You share the problem with the relevant team members or subordinates individually, getting their ideas and suggestions without bringing them together as a group. Then you make the decision. This decision may or may not reflect your subordinates' influence.
4. *Consultative II (CII)*: Group discussion. In a group meeting, you share the problem with your team members or subordinates, obtain their ideas and suggestions, and make a decision that may or may not reflect your subordinates' influence.
5. *Group (GII)*: Consensual group decision making. You share the problem with your team members or subordinates as a group. Together, you generate and evaluate alternatives and attempt to reach agreement (i.e., consensus) on a solution. Your role is much like that of a facilitator, coordinating the discussion, keeping it focused on the problem, and making sure that the critical issues are discussed. You can provide the group with information or ideas that you have, yet you do not try to pressure them to adopt your solution, and you are willing to accept and implement any solution that has the support of the entire group.

Many people find this decision-making model helpful when answering the following seven yes-or-no questions, as shown in Figure 14-3.

1. Is there a quality requirement? Is the nature of the solution critical? Are there technical or rational grounds for selecting among possible solutions?
2. Do I have enough information to make a high-quality decision?
3. Is the problem structured? Are the alternative courses of action and methods for their evaluation known?
4. Is acceptance of the decision by subordinates critical to its implementation?

5. If I decide by myself, is it reasonably sure that my subordinates would accept it?
6. Do subordinates share the organizational goals to be obtained in solving this problem?
7. Is conflict among subordinates likely in obtaining the preferred solution?

For example, in the case in which the quality requirement (question 1) is low (e.g., the nature of the solution is not critical) and team commitment (question 2) is also not critical, the method suggests that you should make the decision on your own (i.e., choose method AI). Alternatively, if team commitment is critical, you would consider question 5 about the certainty of acceptance if you made the decision on your own. If people are likely to accept your decision, the method suggests once again making the decision on your own (i.e., AI). However, if acceptance of your decision is not reasonably certain, the method suggests a consensual group method (i.e., GII) to help overcome this.

Situational factors that may influence the model include the following:

- When decision quality is important and followers have useful information, then AI and AII are not the best methods.
- When the leader sees decision quality as important but followers do not, then GII is inappropriate.
- When decision quality is important, the problem is unstructured, and the leader lacks the information or skill to make the decision alone, GII is best.
- When decision acceptance is important and followers are unlikely to accept an autocratic decision, AI and AII are inappropriate.
- When decision acceptance is important but followers are likely to disagree with one another, AI, AII, and CI are not appropriate because they do not allow differences to be resolved.
- When decision quality is not important but decision acceptance is critical, then GII is the best method.
- When decision quality is important, all agree with this, and the decision is not likely to result from an autocratic decision, then GII is best.

The Vroom-Yetton-Jago model works best when there are clear and accessible opinions about the decision quality, importance, and decision acceptance factors. However, these are not always known with any significant confidence.

Summary

In this chapter, we have discussed the various methods managers use in their decision-making processes. The rational approach is used when there is sufficient time for an orderly, thoughtful process. However, due to limited resources, such as time and information, managers may be bound in their rational decision making and rely on intuitive, heuristic, and biased approaches.

Discussion Questions

1. Explain the difference between the rational and bounded rationality approaches to decision making.
2. Explain the limitations of using the intuitive and the heuristics or biases approach to decision making.

3. Describe how framing heuristics affect a manager's escalation of commitment.
4. Discuss the four basic styles of decision making.
5. Explain the various situational factors that may influence the Vroom-Yetton-Jago decision-making model.

Exercise 14-1

There are times when you have made good decisions. You knew it was a good decision at the time, and when you looked back on it later, you recognized that it was a good decision. Even now, you still think it was a good decision. There are also times when you have made poor decisions. You might have felt uneasy about it at the time, and when you look back on it, you recognize that it was a poor decision. Analyze the factors that you think contributed to both your good decisions and your poor decisions.

Exercise 14-2

Your hospital has 2,000 doses of a vaccine against a deadly virus that is sweeping the country, with no prospect of obtaining more. The virus is airborne, highly contagious, and more likely to result in death for those who are older or have poor health status. Your hospital is brimming with patients who have the virus, many coming through the emergency department and residing within the ICU. Your hospital has over 3,700 clinical employees ranging from nurses to physicians, from outpatient to ICU. You also have 600 non-clinical employees, some of whom work in offices and some who clean patient rooms or do other functions. How do you allocate the vaccine doses and why? Describe each step in your decision-making process.

Exercise 14-3

Project Implicit at Harvard has created a series of tests to help people better understand their own implicit biases so that they can become aware of how these biases could influence decisions and behavior. Choose one of the tests on their website (https://implicit.harvard.edu/implicit/takeatest.html), and discuss what you learned about yourself from the results.

References

Agor, W. H. (1985). Intuition as a brain skill in management. *Public Personnel Management. 14*(1), 15–24.

Agor, W. H. (1986a). How top executives use their intuition to make important decisions. *Business Horizons, 29*(1), 49–53.

Agor, W. H. (1986b). The logic of intuition: How top executives make important decisions. *Organizational Dynamics, 14*(3), 5–18.

Behling, O., & Eckel, N. (1991). Making sense out of intuition. *Academy of Management Executive, 5*(1), 46–54.

Bennett, R. H. (1998). The importance of tacit knowledge in strategic deliberations and decisions. *Management Decision, 36*(9), 589–600.

Bottles, K. (2001). The good leader. *Physician Executive, 27*(2), 74–76.

Boulgarides, J. D., & Cohen, W. A. (2001). Leadership style vs. leadership tactics. *Journal of Applied Management and Entrepreneurship, 6*(1), 59–73.

Broadwell, M. M. (1969, February 20). Teaching for learning (XVI). *The Gospel Guardian, 20*(41), 1–3a.

Daft, R. L. (2004). *Organization theory and design* (8th ed.). South-Western.

Dequech, D. (2001). Bounded rationality, institutions, and uncertainty. *Journal of Economic Issues, 35*(4), 911–929.

Eisenhardt, K. M., & Bourgeois, L. J., III. (1988). Politics of strategic decision making in high velocity environments: Towards a mid-range theory. *Academy of Management Journal, 31*(4), 737–770.

Forest, J., & Mehier, C. (2001). John R. Commons and Herbert A. Simon on the concept of rationality. *Journal of Economic Issues, 35*(3), 591–605. https://doi.org/10.1007/s007120100082

Hall, K. H. (2002). Reviewing intuitive decision-making and uncertainty: The implications for medical education. *Medical Education, 36*(3), 216–224.

Hayashi, A. M. (2001). When to trust your gut. *Harvard Business Review, 79*(2), 59–65.

Kahneman, D., Slovic, P., & Tversky, A. (Eds.). (1982). *Judgment under uncertainty: Heuristics and biases*. Cambridge University Press.

Levin, I. P., Schnittjer, S. K., & Thee, S. L. (1988). Information framing effects in social and personal decisions. *Journal of Experimental Social Psychology, 24*(6), 520–529.

Maidique, M. A. (2011, August 15). Decoding intuition for more effective decision-making. *Harvard Business Review*. http://blogs.hbr.org/2011/08/decoding-intuition-for-more-ef/

Myers, I. (1980). *Introduction to type*. Consulting Psychologists Press.

Peters, T. J., & Waterman, R. H., Jr. (1984). *In search of excellence: Lessons from America's best-run companies*. Warner Books.

Rowe, A. J., & Boulgarides, J. D. (1983). Decision styles: A perspective. *Leadership & Organization Development Journal, 4*(4), 3–9.

Rowe, A. J., & Boulgarides, J. D. (1998). *Managerial decision making*. Macmillan.

Simon, H. A. (1957). *Administrative behavior* (2nd ed.). Macmillan.

Simon, H. A. (1987). Making management decisions: The role of intuition and emotion. *Academy of Management Perspectives, 1*(1), 57–64.

Sox, H. C., Blatt, M. A., Higgins, M. C., & Marton, K. I. (1988). *Medical decision making*. Butterworths.

Staw, B. M. (1981). The escalation of commitment to a course of action. *Academy of Management Review, 6*(4), 577–587.

Staw, B. M., & Ross, J. (1987). Knowing when to pull the plug. *Harvard Business Review, 65*(2), 68–74.

Thompson, C. (2003). Clinical experience as evidence in evidence-based practice. *Journal of Advanced Nursing, 43*(3), 230–237.

Tversky, A., & Kahneman, D. (1974). Judgment under uncertainty: Heuristics and biases. *Science, 185*(4157), 1124–1131. https://doi.org/10.1126/science.185.4157.1124

Vroom, V. H., & Jago, A. G. (1988). *The new leadership: Managing participation in organizations*. Prentice Hall.

Vroom, V. H., & Yetton, P. W. (1973). *Leadership and decision-making*. University of Pittsburgh Press.

Wally, S., & Baum, R. (1994). Personal and structural determinants of the pace of strategic decision making. *Academy of Management Journal, 37*(4), 932–956.

Other Suggested Readings

Agor, W. H. (1984). *Intuitive management: Integrating left and right brain management skills*. Prentice Hall.

Ashforth, B. E. (2001). *Role transitions in organizational life: An identity-based perspective*. Lawrence Erlbaum Associates.

Bates, B. (1975). Physician and nurse practitioner: Conflict and reward. *Annals of Internal Medicine, 82*(5), 702–706.

Brett, J. F., Northcraft, G. B., & Pinkley, R. L. (1999). Stairways to heaven: An interlocking self-regulation model of negotiation. *Academy of Management Review, 24*(3), 435–451.

Davis, M. H., Capobianco, S., & Kraus, L. (2004). Measuring conflict-related behaviors: Reliability and validity evidence regarding the conflict dynamics profile. *Educational and Psychological Measurement, 64*(4), 707–731.

Elangovan, A. R. (2002). Managerial intervention in disputes: The role of cognitive biases and heuristics. *Leadership & Organization Development Journal, 23*(7), 390–399.

Friedman, R. A., Tidd, S. T., Currall, S. C., & Tsai, J. C. (2000). What goes around comes around: The impact of personal conflict style on work conflict and stress. *International Journal of Conflict Management, 11*(1), 32–55.

Gigerenzer, G. (2007). *Gut feelings: The intelligence of the unconscious*. Penguin Group.

Kahneman, D. (1991). Judgment and decision making: A personal view. *Psychological Science, 2*(3), 142–145.

Kilmann, R. H., & Thomas, K. W. (1977). Developing a forced-choice measure of conflict-handling behavior: The MODE instrument. *Educational and Psychological Measurement. 37*(2), 309–325.

Kolb, D. M., & Putman, L. L. (1992). The multiple faces of conflict in organizations. *Journal of Organizational Behavior, 13*(3), 311–324.

McWilliams, C. (2003). Healthcare decision making for dementia patients: Two problem cases. *Internet Journal of Law, Healthcare and Ethics, 2*(1), 12–19.

O'Connor, K. M., DeDreu, C. K., Schroth, H., Barry, B. Lituchy, T. R., & Bazerman, M. H. (2002). What we want to do versus what we think we should do: An empirical investigation of intrapersonal conflict. *Journal of Behavioral Decision Making, 15*(5), 403–418.

Shelton, C. D., & Darling, J. R. (2004). From chaos to order: Exploring new frontiers in conflict management. *Organization Development Journal, 22*(3), 22–41.

Thomas, K. W. (1992). Conflict and conflict management: Reflections and update. *Journal of Organizational Behavior, 13*, 265–274.

CHAPTER 15

Conflict Management and Negotiation Skills

LEARNING OUTCOMES

After completing this chapter, the student should be able to understand:

- The definition of conflict.
- The four basic types of conflict.
- The five levels of conflict.
- The five conflict-handling modes.
- The three major negotiation models.

Overview

Conflict is a natural part of human relationships and is present in professional and personal settings (Thomas, 1976). It is particularly common in work environments, including health care. While definitions vary, Thomas (1992a, b) identifies three common components: perceived incompatibility of interests, interdependence between parties, and interaction. Rahim (1985) defines conflict as an "interactive state" marked by disagreement or incompatibility between individuals or groups. For this discussion, conflict occurs when one party feels negatively affected by another.

Healthcare organizations are especially prone to conflict due to high stress, strong emotions, scarce resources, competition, downsizing, mergers, excessive regulations, diversity, and competing stakeholder demands (Gardner, 1992; Johnson, 1994). Research shows that managers, both in health care and other industries, spend about 30% of their time dealing with conflict, often considering it one of the least enjoyable aspects of leadership (McElhaney, 1996; Robbins, 1990; Shelton & Darling, 2004; Thomas & Schmidt, 1976).

However, conflict is not inherently negative. Like stress, it can be either constructive or destructive. Positive conflict can drive change, encourage problem solving, boost motivation, improve work quality, and increase job satisfaction (Cosier & Dalton, 1990). Negative conflict can divert focus from goals, harm psychological well-being, and lower work quality. It can cause resentment, anxiety, and stress, contributing to poor performance and employee turnover. Studies estimate that over 65% of performance issues stem from strained relationships, and conflict accounts for up to 50% of involuntary employee departures (Dana, 2001; Watson & Hoffman, 1996). In health care, unconstructive conflict can undermine teamwork, leading to higher rates of medical errors, morbidity, and mortality (Forte, 1997).

First, we will discuss the various types and levels of conflict. Second, we examine the various methods to deal with conflict effectively, referred to as conflict resolution or conflict management. This discussion includes individual decision making and the negotiation skills that are necessary for effective conflict management.

Types of Conflict

There are four basic types of conflict: goal, cognitive, affective, and procedural (Kolb & Bartunek, 1992). Goal conflict occurs when two or more desired or expected outcomes are incompatible. It may involve inconsistencies between individual or group values and norms (e.g., standards of behavior). Cognitive conflict occurs when the ideas and thoughts within an individual or between individuals are incompatible. Affective conflict emerges when the feelings and emotions within an individual or between individuals are incompatible. Procedural conflict occurs when people differ over the process to use for resolving a particular matter. As illustrated in **Case Study 15-1**, the different types of conflict are not mutually exclusive.

CASE STUDY 15-1 Authority in Conflict

"Dr. Patel on line two for you, Evelyn."

Evelyn Harper, chair of the hospital board, knew this wouldn't be a social call. As head of surgical services, Dr. Sameer Patel rarely contacted her unless he had concerns about leadership decisions—and lately, those calls had been frequent.

"Evelyn," he began without preamble, "I oversee surgical quality and patient safety. When that's compromised, it's my responsibility to act. Agreed?"

Evelyn paused, mentally reviewing governance protocols. Dr. Patel's clinical influence was significant, but formal authority over staffing decisions did not lie with him. "Tell me what happened," she replied.

Dr. Patel launched into the situation. The dispute centered around Rachel Monroe, the nursing manager responsible for perioperative scheduling. Following hospital policy, Rachel had implemented a new rotation system to improve training and cross-coverage. But in doing so, she often assigned nurses to procedures they were less familiar with, which many surgeons viewed as a risk to efficiency and safety. Some also alleged that Rachel gave preferential assignments to a few favored physicians, escalating tensions.

That morning, after a tense exchange outside the OR, Dr. Patel informed Rachel she was no longer permitted to oversee surgical staffing. Rachel appealed immediately to the chief operations officer, Denise Rios, who reinstated her and reminded Dr. Patel that staffing decisions fell under her administrative domain—not his.

"He told me I don't understand clinical care and that he'd take it up with the board," Denise reported later to Evelyn. "I'm trying to run a safe, efficient hospital. But I can't do that if department heads bypass the process and go straight to you every time they disagree. And frankly, the next time I'm told to stay in my administrative lane, I won't be so composed."

Evelyn understood the pressure on both sides—but with staff morale and patient care at stake, she needed to find a way forward—quickly.

Discuss the different types of conflict represented in this case.

SCARF Model

David Rock's SCARF model provides a valuable framework for understanding and managing conflicts by addressing five key domains of human social experiences: Status, Certainty, Autonomy, Relatedness, and Fairness (Rock, 2008). In the context of conflict management, these domains can trigger either a reward or threat response in the brain. Conflicts escalate when one or more of these domains are perceived as threatened, leading to defensive reactions. By recognizing and addressing these underlying threats, individuals can better navigate conflicts. For example, ensuring fairness and transparency can reduce resentment, while maintaining autonomy allows individuals to feel in control. Understanding and respecting these domains can help resolve conflicts by addressing the root causes rather than just the surface-level issues.

Levels of Conflict

There are five levels of conflict: intrapersonal conflict (within a person), interpersonal conflict (between or among individuals), intragroup conflict (within a group), intergroup conflict (between or among groups), and interorganizational conflict (between or among organizations).

Intrapersonal Conflict

Intrapersonal conflict occurs within the individual and may involve some form of goal, cognitive, or affective conflict. Intrapersonal goal conflict happens when several alternative courses of action are available and when the positive or negative outcome is important to the individual (Locke et al., 1994). Brehm and Cohen (1962) identified three types of intrapersonal conflict that may develop, involving alternative courses of action:

- *Approach/Approach*: The approach/approach type occurs when an individual must choose between two or more alternatives, each expected to have a positive outcome. For example, Judy Lewis, a recent graduate of a local university's master of health services administration (MHSA) program, has been offered job positions in two healthcare organizations. The first is a managed care coordinator position with a national, publicly held laboratory company. The second is a network analyst position with a fast-growing third-party administrator. The salary levels of the two positions are comparable.
- *Avoidance/Avoidance*: The avoidance/avoidance type occurs when an individual must choose between two or more alternatives, each of which is expected to result in a negative outcome. For example, after Judy Lewis accepted the position as the managed care coordinator with the laboratory company, management announced that the company is rightsizing because of a recent merger. Judy presented two options: retain her position by relocating to the organization's headquarters, which is 1000 miles away from her hometown, or be laid off.

- *Approach/Avoidance*: The approach/avoidance type occurs when an individual must choose an alternative that is expected to have both positive and negative outcomes. Judy Lewis chooses the relocation option. Although she realizes that she will gain valuable experience working in the organization's corporate headquarters, where she will have opportunities for advancement, she is unhappy about leaving her family, friends, and familiar surroundings.

Intrapersonal conflict may also result from cognitive dissonance, which occurs when individuals recognize inconsistencies in their thoughts and behavior. Individuals seek consistency among their beliefs and opinions (i.e., cognitions); when an inconsistency arises between one's beliefs or attitudes and one's behavior (i.e., dissonance), something must change to eliminate or lessen the conflict. When there is a discrepancy between an individual's attitude and behavior, the individual's attitude is likely to change to accommodate their behavior, thereby reducing or eliminating the intrapersonal conflict (Brehm & Cohen, 1962).

In the workplace, dissonance occurs most often in role conflict. The three types of role conflict are (1) the person and the role, (2) intrarole, and (3) interrole. Person–role conflict occurs when the expectations of a work role are incompatible with the individual's needs, values, or ethics. For example, a pharmaceutical representative believes that making untested claims about a new drug is unethical, but their work role requires them to do so. Intrarole conflict occurs when an individual experiences different expectations from their role. For example, a hospital's purchasing manager who reports administratively to the vice president of operations and functionally to the medical director may face conflicting expectations, as the former may, because of decreasing reimbursements, stress cost efficiency by restricting choices of prosthesis devices in the surgery department. In contrast, the latter may emphasize having whatever prostheses the surgeons prefer to use available without regard to cost. Interrole conflict occurs when a clash between work and nonwork role demands. For example, if an individual must travel extensively or work excessive hours, it may conflict with their family's needs or desire to spend time together.

Interpersonal Conflict

Interpersonal conflict is a natural outcome of human interaction. Interpersonal conflict involves two or more individuals who believe that their attitudes, behaviors, or preferred goals are in opposition. Kottler (1996) relates that there are three major sources of interpersonal conflict: (1) personal characteristics and issues, (2) interactional difficulties, and (3) differences around perspectives and perceptions of the issues. Porter-O'Grady (2003, p. 36) summarize these components as follows:

- *Personal Characteristics and Issues*: Due to the diversity of today's workplace, an extensive range of differences exists between people and cultures. These differences are embedded with emotional content related to variations in beliefs, behaviors, roles, and relationships. Individuals function in the context of these diverse characteristics, further validating differences others see in us.
- *Interactional Difficulties*: As we mature and socialize, we learn effective communication and relational skills. A lack of communication skills, combined with our personal and cultural differences, creates powerful deficits in our ability to relate to one another. Because of this broad-based inadequacy, relational conflicts regularly emerge.
- *Perspective and Perceptive Differences*: When combined with personal differences and communication inadequacies, dissimilarity in how people view issues and interactions is a common source of interpersonal conflict. This source of conflict may include erroneous perceptions based on incomplete information, disparate interpretations of meaning, or personal bias.

Many interpersonal conflicts involve goal conflict or role ambiguity. Role ambiguity involves a lack of clarity or understanding of expectations about an individual's work performance. Misunderstandings often result from perceptual differences regarding an issue or process. Unclear performance expectations can easily intensify interpersonal conflicts and undermine healthy relationships. "I did not know that was my job" is reflective of role ambiguity. Role ambiguity may cause stress reactions, such as aggression, hostility, and withdrawal behavior (Jackson & Schuler, 1985).

Intragroup Conflict

Intragroup conflict involves clashes among some or all of a group's members, often affecting the group's processes and effectiveness. Jehn and Mannix (2001) suggest that there are three types of intragroup conflict: (1) relationship, (2) task, and (3) process.

- Relationship conflict is an awareness of interpersonal incompatibilities. It includes affective components, such as feeling tension and friction. Relationship conflict involves personal issues, such as dislike among group members, and feelings, such as annoyance, frustration, and irritation.
- Task conflict is an awareness of differences in viewpoints and opinions about a group task. Like cognitive conflict, it pertains to conflict about ideas and differences of opinion about the task. Task conflicts may coincide with animated discussions and personal excitement, but by definition, they lack the intense negative interpersonal emotions commonly associated with relationship conflict.
- Process conflict is an awareness of controversies about how task accomplishment will proceed. More specifically, process conflict pertains to duty and resource delegation issues, such as who should do what and how much responsibility should be assigned to different people. For example, when group members disagree about who is responsible for completing a specific duty, they experience process conflict.

Intergroup Conflict

Intergroup conflict involves opposition and clashes between groups. Under extreme conditions of competition and conflict, the groups develop attitudes toward one another that are characterized by a failure to communicate, distrust, and a self-interest focus (see **Case Study 15-2**). Nulty (1993) relates that there are four categories of intergroup conflict: (1) vertical conflict, (2) horizontal conflict, (3) line–staff conflict, and (4) diversity-based conflict.

- Vertical conflict occurs between employees at different levels in an organization. For example, when supervisors attempt to control subordinates, subordinates may resist because they believe that control infringes too much on their autonomy to perform their jobs. Vertical conflict may also arise because of poor communication, goal or value incompatibility, or role ambiguity (Pondy, 1967).
- Horizontal conflict occurs between groups of employees at the same hierarchical level in an organization. It occurs when each department or team strives only to achieve its own goals, disregarding the goals of other departments and teams, especially if those goals are incompatible (see **Case Study 15-3**; see also Pondy, 1967).
- Line–staff conflict occurs over authority relationships. Most managers are responsible for the processes that create the organization's services or products. Staff managers often serve an advisory or control function that requires specialized technical knowledge. Line managers

CASE STUDY 15-2 Lines in the Sand

Jason Caldwell, vice president of clinical services at Brookside Medical Center, rubbed his temples as he reviewed the email marked "Urgent – Scope of Practice Concern." The message, signed by several members of the orthopedic department, objected to an emerging initiative from the hospital's rehabilitation medicine team. Physical medicine physicians had begun advocating for expanded procedural privileges, including the use of ultrasound-guided joint injections—procedures traditionally performed by orthopedic surgeons.

The orthopedists argued that while ultrasound was useful, it could not replace the clinical judgment and technical expertise developed through years of surgical training. They asserted that the proposed change would dilute the quality of care, create confusion in treatment protocols, and threaten the hospital's liability posture. The final paragraph delivered an unmistakable warning: "If the administration proceeds with this policy change, we will need to reconsider our support for joint surgical consults across shared service lines."

Jason leaned back in his chair. This wasn't the first time interdepartmental tensions had emerged, but the tone of this message signaled a more entrenched resistance. He understood both perspectives—rehabilitation specialists had increasingly strong data supporting the safety and efficacy of minimally invasive techniques, while surgeons were understandably protective of procedural boundaries they believed safeguarded outcomes and professional identity.

He glanced at the calendar. A cross-disciplinary task force meeting was scheduled for Friday, but after this message, it was unlikely to be anything but combative. Jason knew the hospital couldn't afford fractured teamwork—especially with patient volumes climbing and regional competitors advertising their "integrated care teams."

He sighed. "Another maze of conflict," he muttered. "And no one's handing out maps."

Discuss the intergroup conflicts reflected in this case.

CASE STUDY 15-3 Competing Priorities

Lena Torres, director of inpatient nursing, closed the budget planning spreadsheet and walked briskly to the conference room. She was already bracing for the upcoming meeting with Marcus Flynn, director of clinical operations for diagnostic imaging. Over the past 6 months, their departments had clashed repeatedly over patient flow, particularly around delays in transferring patients between units and imaging services.

Lena's team had been under pressure to reduce length of stay and improve discharge times, which required efficient turnaround from ancillary departments. But radiology's bottlenecks—limited tech availability, last-minute add-on exams, and slow post-procedure reports—meant nurses were often left waiting, delaying discharges and backing up admissions from the ED.

Marcus, meanwhile, had his own metrics to hit. Facing increased demand and limited staff, he had optimized scheduling to increase throughput of outpatient imaging. He had reallocated staff accordingly, which unintentionally deprioritized inpatient requests.

"It's not that we don't care about the inpatient side," Marcus had explained at the last meeting. "But if we miss outpatient volume targets, we lose referral contracts. That affects revenue."

Lena disagreed. "And if we can't move patients efficiently through the hospital, we lose beds, staff burn out, and our HCAHPS scores take a hit. That affects revenue, too."

Both had valid points—and both were under pressure from senior leadership to show improvement in their respective areas. But neither felt supported in balancing the hospital's broader goals against their own department's needs.

As the meeting began, the tension was palpable. Each director came prepared with data, but little trust. Without a coordinated plan or shared accountability, Lena and Marcus were not just managing departments—they were managing a growing divide.

Discuss the horizontal conflict reflected in this case.

may feel that staff managers are intruding on their areas of legitimate authority. Staff personnel may specify the methods and partially control the resources used by line managers. Line managers often believe that staff managers reduce their authority over employees, although their responsibility for the outcomes remains unchanged (March & Simon, 1993).

- Diversity-based conflict relates to race, gender, gender identity or expression, age, ethnicity, and religion. These conflicts may encompass all five levels: intrapersonal, interpersonal, intragroup, intergroup, and interorganizational.

Interorganizational Conflict

Interorganizational conflict occurs between organizations as a result of interdependence on membership and divisional or system-wide success. For example, as Longest and Brooks (1998) point out, healthcare organizations participate in various forms of organizational integration. The most extensively integrated organizations are integrated delivery systems (IDSs). Senior managers become increasingly involved in interorganizational conflict as healthcare reform increases integration levels. Integration involving extensive linking of providers at different points in the patient care continuum—especially when IDSs are linked with insurers or health plans and perhaps with suppliers in highly integrated situations—brings into close interactive proximity what are often quite disparate organizations. Conflicts are unavoidable, and the knowledge and skills to manage them effectively are imperative. Interpersonal and collaborative competence is, of course, required of senior managers in all settings, but in an IDS, such competence becomes more complex overall, especially given the new dimension of managing interorganizational conflict (Longest & Brooks, 1998).

Conflict Management

As Winder (2003, p. 20) points out:

> Disagreements between people are an inherent and normal part of life. These disagreements can stem from differences in perceptions, lifestyles, values, facts, motivations or procedures. Differing goals, expectations or methods can turn disagreements into conflict, which can be damaging to both parties. Conflict may also be positive and beneficial in that it can force clarification of policy or procedures, relieve tensions, open communications and resolve problems. In its negative form, conflict can direct energy from real tasks, decrease productivity, reduce morale, prevent cooperation, produce irresponsible behavior, break down communication, and increase tension and stress, all resulting in loss of valuable human resources.

Understanding how conflict arises in the workplace helps anticipate situations that may become conflictual. However, individuals must also understand how they cope with or handle

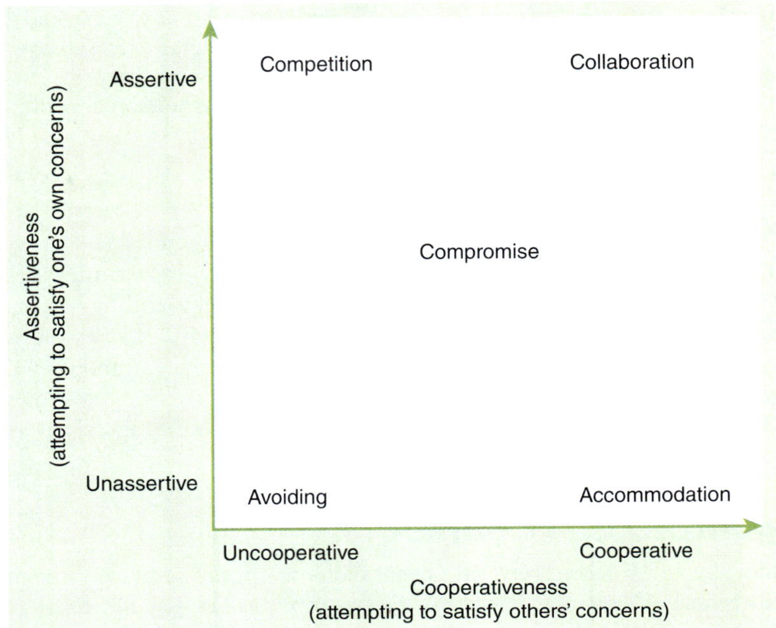

Figure 15-1 Thomas and Kilmann's Two-Dimensional Taxonomy of Conflict-Handling Modes

these conflictual situations. Thomas and Kilmann (1974), building on Blake and Mouton's (1964) work in leadership, identified five conflict-handling modes. Thomas and Kilmann describe the five conflict-handling modes in two dimensions: (1) assertiveness (i.e., attempt to satisfy one's concern) and (2) cooperativeness (i.e., attempt to satisfy others' concerns). The five conflict-handling modes are (1) competition, (2) avoidance, (3) compromise, (4) accommodation, and (5) collaboration; see **Figure 15-1**.

Competition

Competition involves assertive, uncooperative behaviors and follows a win/lose approach. A competing individual prioritizes their objective over the concerns of others (Rahim et al., 1992). Managers using this style often employ coercive power, such as demotions, dismissals, or negative performance evaluations, to gain compliance (Winder, 2003). When peer conflict occurs, competition-style managers may escalate issues to supervisors to enforce decisions in their favor (Blake & Mouton, 1984).

This approach is practical when dealing with trivial matters, making quick decisions in emergencies, or implementing necessary but unpopular policies (Dewine et al., 1991; Rahim et al., 1992). It is beneficial when enforcing cost-cutting measures or addressing employee performance issues.

Collaboration

Collaboration is a highly assertive and cooperative style that seeks a win/win outcome. Collaborating managers strive to find solutions that maximize benefits for all parties (Winder, 2003). This approach emphasizes openness, sharing information, and exploring differences to achieve a mutually acceptable resolution (Rahim et al., 1992).

Collaboration is ideal for complex issues requiring input from multiple stakeholders. It fosters creative problem solving and strategic decision making, especially when addressing long-term objectives. However, collaboration demands mutual respect, parity in power, and sufficient time and organizational support (Winder, 2003). If power imbalances exist, collaboration may not be effective.

Compromise

Compromising balances assertiveness and cooperation, involving give-and-take negotiations where each party concedes something to reach an agreement (Rahim et al., 1992). This approach is practical when parties have mutually exclusive goals or powerful groups (e.g., labor and management) reach a deadlock in negotiations.

However, overreliance on compromise can be counterproductive (Winder, 2003). First, it may address surface-level issues while ignoring deeper conflicts. Second, it encourages quick resolution rather than exploring optimal solutions. Third, it may lead to suboptimal decisions that fully satisfy neither party. While compromise is effective when a total win/win solution is unattainable, it often results in only partial satisfaction (Kabanoff, 1991).

Accommodation

Accommodation is cooperative but unassertive, prioritizing others' needs over one's own (Winder, 2003). Accommodating managers downplay differences to maintain harmony. While sometimes perceived as weak or submissive, this style can be beneficial in defusing emotionally charged conflicts, maintaining short-term stability, or when the issue is more important to the other party (Rahim et al., 1992; Winder, 2003).

Lee (1990) suggests that accommodation is ineffective as a dominant style but useful when harmony is critical. It can also be a strategic choice, yielding on minor issues to secure advantages in future negotiations.

Avoidance

Avoidance is unassertive and uncooperative, characterized by withdrawal, sidestepping issues, or passing responsibility to others (Rahim et al., 1992). Avoiding conflict may reflect an attempt to let the issue resolve itself or an aversion to confrontation. However, ignoring significant problems can frustrate others and harm organizational goals (Winder, 2003).

Consistent avoidance can escalate unresolved conflicts, creating long-term dysfunction. While avoidance may be appropriate for trivial disputes or when more information is needed before addressing an issue, overuse leads to frustration and organizational inefficiency.

Conflict Negotiation Models

Rubin and Brown (1975) define negotiation as the process of two or more parties deciding what each will give and take in an exchange. Since the 1960s, there has been extensive research in conflict resolution and conflict management. From this research, three major negotiation models have been developed: (1) distributive, (2) integrative, and (3) interactive. Each of these models is associated with different goals and indicators of success, and each may be appropriately applied in different contexts (Winder, 2003).

Distributive Model

The distributive model divides scarce resources (Lewicki et al., 1992; Stevens, 1963; Walton & McKersie, 1965). This win/lose, zero-sum approach, also called hard bargaining, views negotiators as adversaries competing for the larger "piece of the pie." Agreements are reached through concessions, often using tactics, such as withholding information, guarded communication, power positioning, threats, and distorted demands (Walton & McKersie, 1965). Brett and Shapiro (1998) compare distributive negotiation to a game of tug-of-war, where one side wins when the other weakens and is forced to concede.

Winder (2003) identifies four win/lose strategies in distributive negotiation:

1. "I want it all"—Making extreme offers and conceding minimally, pressuring the other party into significant concessions while refusing to reciprocate.
2. "Time warp"—Setting an arbitrary deadline for acceptance and warning that the offer will be withdrawn if not accepted by a specific time.
3. "Good cop, bad cop"—Alternating sympathetic and threatening behavior to manipulate the other party.
4. Ultimatum tactic—Using "take it or leave it" offers, with one side refusing to concede and expecting the other to make all concessions (Fisher et al., 1991).

This model favors one side and is often used in high-stakes, competitive negotiations where relationships are secondary to outcomes.

Integrative Model

The integrative negotiation model is currently one of the most frequently used conflict resolution models because of its collaborative versus confrontational approach (Follett, 1940, 1942; Lewicki et al., 1992; Walton & McKersie, 1965).

Integrative negotiation is a cooperative, interest-based, agreement-oriented approach to dealing with conflict viewed as a win/win or mutual-gain dispute. Integrative negotiation is a process by which parties explore options to achieve mutual gains rather than unilateral gains. Parties recognize and define a problem, search for possible solutions, evaluate the solutions, and select one that maximizes joint gains (Lewicki et al., 1992).

Filley (1975), building on the work of Walton and McKersie (1965), developed an integrative decision-making model. Filley's six-step approach is as follows:

1. Create an environment that promotes equality, cooperation, communication, and information sharing.
2. Review and adjust perceptions.
3. Review and adjust attitudes (i.e., create processes that maximize information sharing and clear the air of past hostilities and negative attitudes).
4. Define the problem.
5. Search for alternatives.
6. Achieve consensus.

Integrative negotiation is based on a value system that stresses interpersonal trust, cooperation, a willingness to share information, combined with open communication, and a search for mutually acceptable outcomes (Lewicki et al., 1992). This model looks beyond the existing resources and aims to expand the alternatives and increase the available payoffs to both parties through joint problem solving (Winder, 2003).

Fisher and Ury (1981) and Fisher et al. (1991) define integrative negotiation as "principled negotiation." They suggest that negotiations should be grounded in substantive concerns when the participants do the following:

- Separate the people from the problem. In other words, separate the conflicting issues from the personal relationships. Negotiators should be hard on the issues, but do so in a cooperative relationship with the other party.
- Focus on interest or need rather than position. In other words, do not allow individual egos to negate the negotiation process. This requires trust, respect, and open communication by both parties.
- Identify the best alternative to a negotiated agreement (BATNA) for both parties. This is essentially the next best option if an agreement cannot be reached. By identifying BATNAs, the parties' goal will be to achieve better outcomes than their BATNA through negotiations.
- Invent options or alternatives that provide mutual gain. Brainstorming, before and during meetings, can assist in developing creative alternatives.
- Insist on using only objective criteria to judge solutions. When negotiations are based on objective rather than subjective criteria, discussions focus on equitable solutions, not false assumptions.

The integrative-conflict model encourages equitable solutions to problems. Negotiators are viewed as partners who cooperate in searching for a fair agreement that meets the interests of both sides and seeks to maximize the gain for all the parties involved (Winder, 2003; see also See **Case Study 15-4**).

Interactive Model

When negotiations become locked into a win/lose situation, a third party may be invited to assist in resolving the issues (Schwarz, 1994). Interactive problem solving is a form of third-party consultation or informal mediation. Third-party facilitators can be mediators, arbitrators, or consultants. Depending on the situation, a third-party facilitator may have high or low control of the conflict-resolution process and the outcomes. For example, the third party in intraorganizational conflicts is often the person in the hierarchy to whom the contesting parties report (Lewicki et al., 1992). The mediator/supervisor would highly control the conflict-resolution process and the outcomes in this situation. Mediators usually have high control of the conflict-resolution process and low control of the outcomes (as demonstrated by the VPMA in Case Study 15-4). In contrast, arbitrators have low control of the conflict-resolution process and high control of the outcomes.

Interactive negotiation generally facilitates a deeper analysis of the problems and issues that force the conflict. According to Winder (2003), interactive negotiation usually begins with an analysis of the needs of each of the parties and a discussion of the constraints faced by each side that make it difficult to reach a mutually beneficial solution to the conflict. After the analytical dialogue, the parties engage in joint problem solving rather than a fight to be won. Interactive negotiation is less focused on directly helping parties reach binding agreements (excluding arbitration) and more devoted to improving communication, increasing perspectives and understanding, enabling the parties to reframe their substantive goals and priorities, and engaging in more creative problem solving. Other goals include improving the openness and accuracy of communication, improving intergroup expectancies and attitudes, reducing misperceptions and destructive patterns of interaction, inducing mutual positive motivations for creative problem solving, and ultimately building a sustainable working relationship between the parties (Winder, 2003).

CASE STUDY 15-4 Creating a Win-Win Situation

The anesthesiology department at a hospital faces significant financial difficulties. Department leaders request additional funding from senior administrators, warning that without it, they will lose staff and be forced to close operating rooms. Administrators refuse, arguing that funding one department would lead to similar demands from others. They also remind the anesthesiology group that their exclusive contract is a privilege and suggest that if rooms close, the hospital may consider other anesthesiology providers. To resolve the dispute, the senior vice president for medical affairs (VPMA) is called in to mediate.

Addressing the Problem and Managing Emotions

Fisher's **Principled Negotiation** emphasizes attacking the problem, not the people involved. If both sides dig into their positions—closing rooms versus denying the contract—the discussion will devolve into personal conflict rather than problem solving. The VPMA must first acknowledge that negotiation is an emotional process and encourage each side to consider the other's perspective before reacting.

Both parties should agree to ground rules requiring honesty, respect, and fairness to build trust. The goal is to focus on interests rather than entrenched positions. The anesthesiology group's interest may be increasing salaries and retaining staff without excessive workloads. The hospital's interest may be maximizing operating room usage to attract high-volume surgeons.

Exploring Interests and Avoiding Misconceptions

Both sides must recognize their multiple interests rather than reducing the issue to simple demands. Statements like "We will close an operating room" overshadow the real concerns. The VPMA should guide discussions away from preconceived notions—not all anesthesiologists seeking stipends are greedy, and not all administrators ignore clinical realities. Solutions should not be discarded before fully exploring the problem.

Finding Common Ground and Capitalizing on Differences

A shared goal exists to keep operating rooms open, benefiting both groups financially. However, if common ground is difficult to establish, differences can present opportunities for solutions.

For example, the hospital might propose expanding evening coverage in exchange for a stipend. The anesthesiology group may argue that they lack the staff for such an expansion and that additional coverage isn't necessary. Instead of a deadlock, they can explore alternative solutions. Reducing room turnover time and improving procedure scheduling could meet the hospital's need for efficiency while allowing anesthesiologists to maintain manageable workloads.

Basing Solutions on Objective Data

Once options emerge, discussions should shift to objective criteria. The VPMA should require both sides to present data before negotiating a solution. The anesthesiology group should provide benchmarks on salaries, workloads, and staffing models, while the hospital should gather information on stipends at other institutions, legal considerations, and performance metrics.

By focusing on interests, exploring creative solutions, and using objective data, the negotiation can lead to a mutually beneficial agreement rather than a divisive outcome.

Data from Tarantino, D. P. (2004). The role of the physician executive in negotiation. *Physician Executive, 30*(5), 71–73.

Benefits of Skilled Conflict Resolution and Negotiation

Managers need to understand and appreciate that negotiation is not a zero-sum game. Managers who demonstrate effective conflict-resolution skills are often seen as competent, effective leaders (Gross & Guerrero, 2000; Stamato, 2004). A study by Eckerd College's Management Development Institute (2003) found a significant link between a person's ability to resolve conflict effectively and their perceived effectiveness as a leader and suitability for promotion. The study sample consisted of 172 employees (90 male and 82 female) from five different types of organizations. Approximately one-half of the participants were middle-level managers or higher in their organization, all participating in a program focusing on workplace conflict. The study revealed a strong correlation between certain conflict-resolution behaviors and perceived effectiveness as a leader and promotion potential. Employees perceived as good at creating solutions, expressing emotions, and reaching out were considered more effective. By contrast, destructive behaviors, such as winning at all costs, displaying anger, demeaning others, and retaliating, were the worst behaviors in terms of career advancement and leadership. Avoidance behaviors were particularly problematic for would-be negotiators because individuals who are uncomfortable with negotiating or perceive themselves as unskilled or ineffective in negotiating often avoid conflict and thus fail to manage differences effectively. Of particular significance is the study's finding that negotiation skills are an important aspect of leadership.

Summary

In this chapter, we discussed conflict's positive and negative outcomes and pointed out that conflicts originate from various sources. We can predict with 100% certainty that managers will deal with conflict and negotiation during their work. Conflict-handling behavior can be learned, and managers should adapt their behavior to the situation to be resolved. Collaborative behavior is strongly desired to manage conflict and reflects positively on the individuals who use this approach.

Discussion Questions

1. Explain the definition of conflict.
2. Describe the four basic types of conflict.
3. Discuss the five levels of conflict.
4. Describe the five conflict-handling modes.
5. Describe the three major negotiation models.

CASE STUDY 15-5 Healthcare System Versus Insurance

Oakville Health System to No Longer Accept ConnectedCare Insurance After Negotiations Fail

At the end of the month, ConnectedCare Insurance will no longer be accepted at Oakville Health System, the largest health system in the state, after negotiations on reimbursement rates failed. Oakville, the only Level 1 Trauma Center in hundreds of miles, handles complex cases from a vast referral area. The change will affect an estimated 30,000 policyholders.

"ConnectedCare Insurance is asking for rates so low that it's impossible to keep our doors open," said Oakville CEO Sanjeet Mulpur. "We haven't had these issues with any other insurer. They have a history of strong-arming health systems into accepting absurdly low rates."

Last month, Oakville sent 40,000 letters to past patients with ConnectedCare insurance, warning that they may soon face out-of-pocket costs.

"We recognize Oakville provides unique, costly services, and we reimburse them accordingly," a ConnectedCare spokesperson said. "However, they charge significantly more than other health systems for common services and tests."

Oakville opposes an out-of-network designation, arguing that some patients would have no choice but to come to their facilities due to the severity of their illness.

"They demand in-network status despite their outrageously high costs," said ConnectedCare's spokesperson. "If we agreed, it would undermine employers' ability to offer insurance plans that reward cost-effective care providers."

Mulpur argued that ConnectedCare wants Oakville's rates to mirror those of smaller hospitals, ignoring the complexity of its services.

"We cannot support a program that prioritizes cost over quality," Mulpur said. "If we're the only provider of specialized treatments, why should patients pay more to access them? ConnectedCare made $8 billion in profits last year—at the expense of hospitals and patients."

Oakville believes ConnectedCare's policies harm patients, dictating what is "medically necessary" regardless of physician recommendations. The insurer has faced similar conflicts with other large health systems.

Both sides remain committed to negotiations, though tensions are high.

"We are willing to be reasonable, but what they're asking for is insane," Mulpur said. "They've given us nothing workable."

ConnectedCare responded: "Despite our attempts at compromise, Oakville has chosen to take a dramatic step that will harm patients. We hope they reconsider so we can reach a resolution that ensures affordable access to care."

Discussion Questions

1. What level of conflict is represented in this case?
2. What type of negotiation style did Oakville Health System use in this case?
3. What type of negotiation style did ConnectedCare use in this case?
4. Who are the winners and losers in this conflict?

Data from Auglair, H. (2019). *UAB to no longer accept UnitedHealth care after negotiations fail.* Al.com.

CASE STUDY 15-6 Operating Under Pressure

Dr. Carla Benson, Chief Medical Officer at Riverpoint Medical Center, stared at the flagged message in her inbox. It was from Dr. Leo Barrett, Chair of Orthopedic Surgery, and the subject line read: "OR Access – Immediate Action Needed." She had seen variations of this message before, but the urgency in Barrett's tone suggested tensions were escalating.

Riverpoint, a 600-bed academic hospital in the Mid-Atlantic, supported over 900 physicians, including faculty, fellows, and private specialists. The institution operated 22 surgical suites—none of which were permanently assigned. While this approach was intended to promote equity, it had become a breeding ground for frustration among department leaders.

Before responding, Benson scheduled individual meetings with department chairs.

Dr. Renee Park, Director of Urology

"We're being boxed out," Park explained. "Urology shares OR space with ENT and Plastics, and we're drowning in backlog. OR time is the gateway to growth. Without predictable access, we can't recruit new faculty or handle patient volume."

Park also warned that primary care providers had begun referring cases elsewhere due to excessive wait times.

Dr. Malcolm Greene, Chair of Neurosurgery

When Benson walked by the neurosurgical wing at 10 a.m. on Friday, three ORs sat unused. Greene's assistant confirmed the department's weekly teaching rounds ran until noon.

"Malcolm says they're optimizing long-term outcomes through education," she offered. "Besides, we're rarely behind on scheduled cases."

Dr. Priya Shah, Director of Ophthalmology

"I've built in some safeguards," Shah admitted during their meeting. "I pre-book slots with 'buffer' cases. If something falls through, we keep the flow moving. It reduces patient complaints and keeps my team on schedule."

She was unapologetic. "If Orthopedics wants more time, they can come talk to me. I'm open to a trade."

Dr. Leo Barrett, Chair of Orthopedic Surgery

Barrett arrived with data in hand. "Carla, you brought me in to expand surgical services. But we're stuck. I need four rooms. I get one—on a good day. I can't run a high-volume program by pleading for time or competing with phantom cases."

He was particularly frustrated with the lack of transparency. "We're losing patients to nearby hospitals with more predictable access."

Dr. Tomas El-Amin, Chief of Anesthesiology

Finally, Benson met with El-Amin, whose department was under pressure for delayed turnover times.

"I understand the concern," he said. "But we're an academic center. My attendings are working with med students, residents, and CRNAs. Teaching takes time. If leadership wants efficiency above education, we need to reconsider our mission—or invest in more staff."

The Challenge Ahead

Benson understood that the current model was unsustainable. But any changes to OR access would provoke resistance. Should scheduling be based on volume? Revenue? Teaching contribution? And how could emergency cases be prioritized without compromising fairness?

As she looked at the whiteboard in her office, she scribbled one word: *balance*. Finding it, she knew, would be the hard part.

Discussion Questions

1. What are the underlying issues driving the conflict over operating room scheduling at Riverpoint Medical Center?
2. Why have these issues escalated into interdepartmental tension rather than being resolved collaboratively?
3. Evaluate how each department leader has handled the conflict so far. What strategies have helped or hindered progress? Would you have approached the situation differently? Why or why not?
4. Imagine you are Dr. Carla Benson, the Chief Medical Officer tasked with resolving this conflict. What sources of influence or authority can you draw upon? What possible solutions could you implement, and how might each affect stakeholders? What should be your key priorities moving forward?

CASE STUDY 15-7 What Went Wrong?

Tim Hardwood, CEO of Community Health System, hung up the phone with a heavy sigh. He had just received the news from Mary Martin, vice president of human resources, that negotiations had stalled between the health system and the service employees' union. Mary had told him, "As of now, the 2,000 service employees at our three hospitals are without a contract and threatening to strike. But don't worry, Tim. I told the union negotiators that the health system is prepared to handle a strike."

"A strike!" Tim thought. "The media will have a field day with this! What went wrong?"

Jim Brentward, one of the union negotiators, sat across the table from Mary Martin. Jim told Mary that his members understood that Community Health System was having financial difficulties because of the current state of the industry with decreasing reimbursements and increasing regulations, but the union members were not pleased with the organization's proposed offer for salary increases and benefits package over the next 4 years. Jim said, "Unless the health system signs a contract by 5:00 p.m. Friday with acceptable salary and benefit increases, members of the union are threatening to strike." He continued, "The union plans to hold an informational picket on Thursday, and although the union doesn't want to strike, it's a strong possibility. After the informational picket, we will hold a strike vote and see what our members have to say about the situation."

Mary was shocked by Jim's comments. She simply could not believe that Community Health's service employees would threaten to strike! Because of her position as vice president of human resources, Mary knew that the service employees represented by Jim's union were at the bottom end of the healthcare system's pay scale. These employees included patient transporters, housekeeping, and cafeteria workers. Mary also knew that the union benefits paid to members during a strike equaled only 50% of the employee's weekly salary. Mary felt confident that because they had too much to lose financially, the employees would never vote to strike. In addition, she knew that Community Health System was considering outsourcing its dietary departments to Thomson Healthcare Food Services. If the employees did strike, although Mary considered that very unlikely, dietary services would continue without interruption. Knowing this inside information, Mary decided that she wasn't going to let Jim and the other union negotiators bully her. Mary told Jim that the healthcare system would not give in to the union's demands and was prepared for a strike.

Explain to Tim Hardwood what went wrong. If you were hired as the mediator, how would you go about resolving the situation to achieve a win/win agreement?

CASE STUDY 15-8 Healthy Conflict Resolution

"Cindy, please reschedule my afternoon clinic. I'm going to be out for the rest of the day," says Dr. Jones, a senior physician in a hospital-owned multispecialty group.

Cindy, pulling off her telephone headset, turns from the patient registration window. "But, Dr. Jones, you're double booked this afternoon because you already canceled twice this month. Some of these patients have been waiting over three months to see you!"

Jones glances at the waiting room and, already heading toward the exit, shrugs. "I'm sure you'll smooth things over. Just tell them I got called to an emergency."

Cindy suspects otherwise. Because the weather is nice, she believes Jones is taking off with a couple of colleagues to go sailing or play a round of golf. He posts on social media about these hobbies, sports a tan, arrives late, and leaves early. Enough is enough. She calls her manager and requests an urgent meeting.

The manager, sensing Cindy's frustration, arranges coverage so they can talk privately. "This happens all the time," Cindy says. "I won't work another day under these conditions." The manager calms Cindy and promises to escalate the issue to the chief of the department.

The situation quickly escalates, involving the chief medical officer, the executive director, human resources, and a union representative before Jones is even informed. When he is finally called into a meeting with the chief medical officer and HR director, he is blindsided.

"That was weeks ago! Cindy never said a word to me. We've been working together like nothing happened." Jones is even more shocked to learn that Cindy has been keeping track of how often he cancels, leaves early, or starts late.

His surprise turns to anger within minutes. The damage is done. Cindy and Jones can no longer work together.

Jones is now labeled a disruptive physician. Other doctors distance themselves from Cindy, fearing they could be next. Cindy resigns. Jones, feeling betrayed and unappreciated, resents both his staff and employer.

If you were the manager in this case, how would you have handled the situation?

Data from Pierce, K. P. (2009, January/February). Healthy conflict resolution. *Physician Executive, 35*(1), 60–61.

CASE STUDY 15-9 Conflict-Handling Styles

For each of the five scenarios that follow, determine the most appropriate conflict-handling style(s).

Scenario One

A radiologist on the staff of a large community hospital was stopped after a staff meeting by a colleague in internal medicine. On Monday of the previous week, the internist referred an elderly man with chronic, productive cough for a chest X-ray, with a clinical diagnosis of bronchitis. On Thursday morning, the internist received the radiologist's written X-ray report with a diagnosis of "probable bronchogenic carcinoma." The internist expressed his dismay that the radiologist had not called him much earlier with a verbal report. Visibly upset, the internist raised his voice, but did not use abusive language.

How should the radiologist handle this conflict with the internist?

Scenario Two

The Family and Community Medicine Division of a large-staff model HMO serves a population that is ethnically diverse. The senior management team of the HMO, spurred by repeated complaints from representatives of one racial group, has encouraged the division, all of whose physicians are White, to diversify. Several Black and Hispanic physicians with strong credentials apply for the open positions, but none are hired. Weeks later, a young female family physician learns from several colleagues that the division director has identified her as racist and the obstructionist to recruiting. The comments attributed to her are not only false, but are also typical of discriminatory statements that she has heard the division chief utter. The rumors about her "behavior" have circulated widely in the division.

How should the young female family physician handle this conflict with the division chief?

Scenario Three

A manager who reports to the vice president for clinical affairs (VPCA) of a tertiary-care hospital hired a young woman to supervise development of a large community outreach program. During the first 4 months of her employment, several behavioral problems came to the VPCA's attention: (1) complaints from community physicians that the coordinator criticizes other physicians in public; (2) concerns from two community leaders that the coordinator is not truthful; and (3) complaints about written reports about the project that label and blame others, sometimes in language that is disrespectful. The VPCA spoke several times to the manager about these problems. The manager reported other dissatisfactions with the coordinator's performance, but he showed no sign of dealing with the behavior. Two more complaints come in, one from an influential community leader.

How should the VPCA handle this conflict with the manager?

Scenario Four

The medical school in an academic health center recently implemented a problem-based curriculum, dramatically reducing the number of lectures given and substituting small-group learning that focuses on actual patient cases. Both clinical and basic science faculty are feeling stretched in their new roles. In the past, dental students took the basic course in microanatomy with medical students. The core lectures are still given, but at different times that do not match with the dental-curriculum schedule. The anatomists insist that they don't have time to teach another course specifically for dental students. The dean has informed the chair of the Department of Anatomy and Cell Biology that some educational revenues will be redirected to the dental school if the faculty do not meet this need.

How should the dean handle this conflict with the chair of the Department of Anatomy and Cell Biology?

Scenario Five

The partners in a medical group practice are informed by the clinic manager that one physician member of the group has been repeatedly upcoding procedures for a specific diagnosis. This issue first came to light 6 months ago. At that time the partners met with him, clarified the Medicare guidelines, and outlined the threat to the practice for noncompliance. He argued with their view, but ultimately agreed to code appropriately. There were no infractions for several months, but now he has submitted several erroneous codes. One member of the office staff has asked whether Medicare would consider this behavior "fraudulent."

How should the partners handle the situation with the other physician partner?

References

Baron, R. A., & Richardson, D. R. (1994). *Human aggression* (2nd ed.). Plenum Press.

Blake, R. R., & Mouton, J. S. (1964). *The managerial grid*. Gulf Publishing.

Blake, R. R., & Mouton, J. S. (1984). *Solving costly organizational conflicts*. Jossey-Bass.

Brehm, J., & Cohen, A. (1962). *Explorations in cognitive dissonance*. John Wiley & Sons.

Brett, J. M., Shapiro, D. L., & Lytle, A. L. (1998). Breaking the bonds of reciprocity in negotiations. *Academy of Management Journal, 41*(4), 410–424.

Cosier, R. A., & Dalton, D. R. (1990). Positive effects of conflict: A field assessment. *International Journal of Conflict Management, 1*(1), 81–92.

Dana, D. (2001). *Conflict resolution: Mediation tools for everyday worklife*. McGraw-Hill.

Dewine, S., Nicotera, A. M., & Parry, D. (1991). Argumentativeness and aggressiveness: The flip side of gentle persuasion. *Management Communication Quarterly, 4*(3), 386–411.

Filley, A. C. (1975). *Interpersonal conflict resolution*. Scott, Foresman.

Fisher, R., & Ury, W. (1981). *Getting to yes: Negotiating agreement without giving in*. Penguin Books.

Fisher, R., Ury, W., & Patton, B. (1991). *Getting to yes: Negotiating agreement without giving in* (2nd ed.). Penguin Books.

Follett, M. P. (1940). Constructive conflict. In H. C. Metcalf & L. Urwick (Eds.), *Dynamic administration: The collected papers of Mary Parker Follett* (pp. 30–49). Harper (Original work published in 1926).

Follett, M. P. (1924). *Creative experience*. Longmans, Green.

Forté, P. S. (1997). The high cost of conflict. *Nursing Economic$, 15*(3), 119–123.

Gardner, D. L. (1992). Conflict and retention of new graduate nurses. *Western Journal of Nursing Research, 14*(1), 76–85.

Gross, M. A., & Guerrero, L. K. (2000). Managing conflict appropriately and effectively: An application of the competence model to Rahim's organizational conflict styles. *International Journal of Conflict Management, 11*(3), 200–226.

Jackson, S. E., & Schuler, R. S. (1985). A meta-analysis and conceptual critique of research on role ambiguity and role conflict in work settings. *Organizational Behavior and Human Decision Processes, 36*(1), 16–78.

Jehn, K. A., & Mannix, E. A. (2001). The dynamic nature of conflict: A longitudinal study of intragroup conflict and group performance. *Academy of Management Journal, 44*(2), 238–251. https://doi.org/10.2307/3069453

Johnson, M. (1994). Conflict and nursing professionalization. In J. M. Dochterman & H. K. Grace (Eds.), *Current issues in nursing* (4th ed., pp. 643–649). Mosby.

Kabanoff, B. (1991). Equity, equality, power, and conflict. *Academy of Management Review, 16*(2), 416–441.
Kolb, D. M., & Bartunek, J. M. (1992). *Hidden conflict in organizations: Uncovering behind-the-scenes disputes*. Sage.
Kottler, J. (1996). *Beyond blame: A new way of resolving conflicts in relationships*. Jossey-Bass Publishers.
Lee, C. (1990). Relative status of employees and styles of handling interpersonal conflict. *International Journal of Conflict Management, 1*(4), 327–340.
Lewicki, R., Weiss, S., & Lewin, D. (1992). Models of conflict, negotiation and third party intervention: A review and synthesis. *Journal of Organizational Behavior, 13*(3), 209–252.
Locke, E. A., Smith, K. G., Erez, M., Chah, D. O., & Schaffer, A. (1994). The effects of intra-individual goal conflict on performance. *Journal of Management, 20*(1), 67–92.
Longest, B. B., & Brooks, D. H. (1998). Managerial competence at senior levels of integrated delivery systems. *Journal of Healthcare Management, 43*(2), 115–135.
Management Development Institute, Eckerd College. (2003). Leadership effectiveness study—Conflict and your career. http://www.conflictdynamics.org/
March, J., & Simon, H. (1993). *Organizations* (2nd ed.). Blackwell.
McElhaney, R. (1996). Conflict management in nursing administration. *Nursing Management, 27*(3), 49.
Nulty, P. (1993, February). Look at what unions want now. *Fortune, 127*, 128–133.
Pondy, L. R. (1967). Organizational conflict: Concepts and models. *Administrative Science Quarterly, 12*(2), 296–320. https://doi.org/10.2307/2391553
Porter-O'Grady, T. (2003). When push comes to shove: Managers as mediators. *Nursing Management, 34*(10), 34–38.
Rahim, M. A. (1985). A strategy for managing conflict in complex organizations. *Human Relations, 38*(1), 81–89.
Rahim, M. A., Garrett, J. E., & Buntzman, G. F. (1992). Ethics of managing interpersonal conflict in organizations. *Journal of Business Ethics, 11*(5/6), 423–432.
Robbins, S. (1990). *Organization theory* (3rd ed.). Prentice Hall.
Rock, D. (2008). SCARF: A brain-based model for collaborating with and influencing others. *NeuroLeadership Journal, 1*(1), 1–9.
Rubin, J. Z., & Brown, B. R. (1975). *The social psychology of bargaining and negotiation*. Academic Press.
Schwarz, R. M. (1994). *The skilled facilitator: Practical wisdom for developing effective groups*. Jossey-Bass.
Shelton, C. D., & Darling, J. R. (2004). From chaos to order: Exploring new frontiers in conflict management. *Organization Development Journal, 22*(3), 22–41.
Stamato, L. (2004, July/August). The new age of negotiation. *Ivey Business Journal Online*. https://iveybusinessjournal.com/publication/the-new-age-of-negotiation/
Stevens, C. M. (1963). *Strategy and collective bargaining negotiation*. McGraw-Hill.
Tarantino, D. P. (2004). The role of the physician executive in negotiation. *Physician Executive, 30*(5), 71–73.
Thomas, K. W. (1976). Conflict and conflict management. In M. Dunnette (Ed.), *Handbook of industrial and organizational psychology* (pp. 889–935). Rand McNally College.
Thomas, K. W. (1992a). Conflict and conflict management: Reflections and update. *Journal of Organizational Behavior, 13*(3), 265–274.
Thomas, K. W. (1992b). Conflict and negotiation processes in organizations. In M. Dunnette & L. M. Hough (Eds.), *Handbook of industrial and organizational psychology* (2nd ed., Vol. 3, pp. 651–717). Consulting Psychologists Press.
Thomas, K. W., & Kilmann, R. H. (1974). *Thomas-Kilmann conflict mode instrument*. Xicom, Inc.
Thomas, K. W., & Schmidt, W. (1976). A survey of managerial interests with respect to conflict. *Academy of Management Journal, 19*(2), 315–318.
Walton, R. E., & McKersie, R. B. (1965). *A behavioral theory of labor negotiations: An analysis of a social interaction system*. McGraw-Hill.
Watson, C., & Hoffman, L. R. (1996). Managers as negotiators. *The Leadership Quarterly, 7*(1), 63–85.
Winder, R. (2003). Organizational dynamics and development. *Futurics, 27*(1/2), 5–30.

Other Suggested Readings

Agor, W. H. (1984). *Intuitive management: Integrating left and right brain management skills*. Prentice Hall.
Ashforth, B. E. (2001). *Role transitions in organizational life: An identity-based perspective*. Lawrence Erlbaum Associates.
Bates, B. (1975). Physician and nurse practitioners: Conflict and reward. *Annals of Internal Medicine, 82*(5), 702–706.
Brett, J. F., Northcraft, G. B., & Pinkley, R. L. (1999). Stairways to heaven: An interlocking self-regulation model of negotiation. *Academy of Management Review, 24*(3), 435–451.
Davis, M. H., Capobianco, S., & Kraus, L. (2004). Measuring conflict-related behaviors: Reliability and validity evidence regarding the conflict dynamics profile. *Educational and Psychological Measurement, 64*(4), 707–731.

Elangovan, A. R. (2002). Managerial intervention in disputes: The role of cognitive biases and heuristics. *Leadership & Organization Development Journal, 23*(7), 390–399.

Friedman, R. A., Tidd, S. T., Currall, S. C., & Tsai, J. C. (2000). What goes around comes around: The impact of personal conflict style on work conflict and stress. *International Journal of Conflict Management, 11*(1), 32–55.

Gigerenzer, G. (2007). *Gut feelings: The intelligence of the unconscious*. Penguin Group.

Kahneman, D. (1991). Judgment and decision making: A personal view. *Psychological Science, 2*(3), 142–145.

Kilmann, R. H., & Thomas, K. W. (1977). Developing a forced-choice measure of conflict-handling behavior: The MODE instrument. *Educational and Psychological Measurement, 37*(2), 309–325.

Kolb, D. M., & Putman, L. L. (1992). The multiple faces of conflict in organizations. *Journal of Organizational Behavior, 13*(3), 311–324.

McWilliams, C. (2003). Healthcare decision making for dementia patients: Two problem cases. *Internet Journal of Law, Healthcare and Ethics, 2*(1), 12–19.

O'Connor, K. M., DeDreu, C. K., Schroth, H., Barry, B., Lituchy, T. R., & Bazerman, M. H. (2002). What we want to do versus what we think we should do: An empirical investigation of intrapersonal conflict. *Journal of Behavioral Decision Making, 15*(5), 403–418.

Shelton, C. D., & Darling, J. R. (2004). From chaos to order: Exploring new frontiers in conflict management. *Organization Development Journal, 22*(3), 22–41.

PART V

Groups and Teams

People are social beings and need affiliation and a sense of belonging. Groups help to satisfy these needs. In Chapter 16, we examine group dynamics. "Group dynamics" is a term created by Kurt Lewin and used to describe the subfield of organizational behavior that attempts to understand the nature of groups, how they develop, and how they interact within the group, with other groups, and with their environments. Chapter 17 discusses various types of groups and their related functions. Chapter 18 examines the use of teams in today's complex health service organizations. Healthcare delivery "takes a village." Few tasks can be performed from start to finish by one person. To complete a task requires resources from many individuals. Today, we see the widespread use of interdisciplinary teams to deliver effective and efficient health care.

CHAPTER 16

Overview of Group Dynamics

LEARNING OUTCOMES

After completing this chapter, the student should be able to describe:

- The importance of group dynamics.
- The characteristics that define a group.
- The meaning of group interaction and methods to measure it.
- What motivates individuals to join and remain in groups.
- The roles that members assume in groups and the importance of these roles.
- Group norms and how they are formed and sustained.
- The factors that contribute to or inhibit group cohesiveness.
- The impact of conformity on group performance.
- The impact of groupthink on group decision making.

Overview

Human beings are social animals. Although we are born into and singularly leave the world, we spend most of our time working, worshiping, learning, and playing in groups. Because we spend so much time in groups, there is great interest in understanding their inner workings and their members. This research is called the study of group dynamics, which attempts to understand how people interact with, influence, and are influenced by others within groups.

Understanding group dynamics is essential to the success of an organization. Due to the complex nature of healthcare delivery, accomplishing our work is nearly impossible without groups and teams. When individuals transition from a staff role to a management role, their objective moves from being an individual performer to accomplishing work through others. It is increasingly rare for managers to work independently. For example, it is estimated that, on average, managers spend 50–80% of their working day in one group or another. In the healthcare setting, this estimate is not surprising. Healthcare managers, both clinical and administrative, participate in numerous work groups and teams daily, such as operating room teams, disease management teams, patient safety committees, biomedical ethics committees, patient care teams, trauma teams, and emergency-preparedness and disaster-management teams. The movement toward value-based care will increase the importance of teams in health care (Taplin et al., 2013). Additionally, as healthcare systems expand geographically and integrate vertically, more managers may find themselves working on virtual teams with people they may have never met face to face. To manage groups effectively, managers must understand group formation and development, structure, and interrelationships with individuals, other groups, and organizations (Turner, 2001).

Our discussion of groups is divided into three sections. We define a group, discuss why individuals join groups, and then examine the interactions and behavior of members within a group. Although "groups" and "teams" are often used interchangeably, there are differences. The concept of groups is broader than the concept of teams; therefore, not every group is a team. Katzenbach and Smith (1993) highlight that teams are special groups with highly defined tasks and roles and demonstrate high group commitment. Because of these characteristics, we discuss the nature of teams separately.

What Is a Group?

Social scientists usually define a group using four characteristics: (1) two or more people in social interaction, (2) a stable structure, (3) common interests or goals, and (4) the individuals perceiving themselves as a group. For example, two patients waiting to be treated in a hospital's emergency department are not a group. This collection of two individuals is not a group because (1) there is no interaction between the two patients, nor are they attempting to influence each other; (2) patients in an emergency department constantly change, so a stable environment does not exist for future interactions; (3) although patients may have similar goals (e.g., restoring health or alleviation of pain), they are not working in a coordinated effort to achieve a common goal; and (4) these patients do not perceive themselves as a group, only as individuals occupying space in the exact location at the same time. However, a group exists when volunteer members of the local chapter of the American Heart Association meet to plan the next fundraising event or when a multidisciplinary group of clinicians convenes to develop evidence-based guidelines for patients admitted to the hospital with congestive heart failure. These groups represent collections of individuals with a common interest or goal in a stable environment (although members may join and leave the group at various times) wherein members interact with one another to influence each other. One crucial factor relating to group dynamics is understanding the interactions that occur between a group's members.

Group Interaction

Tubbs (2001) defines group interaction as the process by which members of a group exchange verbal and nonverbal messages to influence one another. Interaction includes talking, listening, nonverbal gestures, texts, emails, and any other behavior people assign meaning to. By observing these interactions, we can better understand the dynamics within a group. Bales's Interaction Process Analysis is a tool that can provide insight into the content of the members' communication (see **Figure 16-1**).

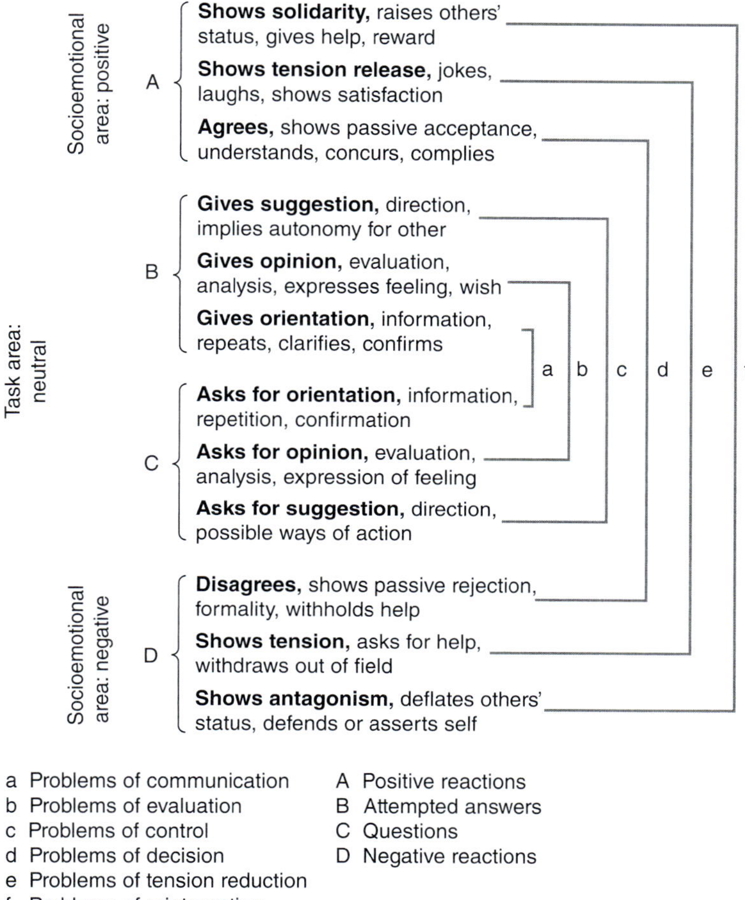

Figure 16-1 Bales's Interaction Process Analysis

Reproduced from Bales, R. F. (1950). *Interaction process analysis: A method for the study of small groups.* University of Chicago Press.

As Sprott (1958) noted, Bales's Interaction Process Analysis includes 12 interaction categories; these interactions relate to either emotion or task. The emotional responses are either positive (items 1–3) or negative (items 10–12). Task responses are giving information (items 4–6) or asking for information (items 7–9). The 12 categories are also grouped into pairs, as noted in **Table 16-1**. The interactions of these 12 categories greatly influence the roles assumed by members and group norms.

Why Do People Join Groups?

Individuals join groups for many reasons, which are explained by Maslow's Hierarchy of Needs. Individuals join groups to satisfy their need for belonging (i.e., the need to have close contact with others and to be accepted by them) in addition to social and affection needs. Groups can satisfy

Table 16-1 Bales's Interaction Process Analysis: Twelve Categories Paired

Pairs	Description	Example
f	Orientation	How well do the group members cohere? Bales gives the example of a man who makes an offensive remark directed at another member (item 12); however, another team member standing up for their offended colleague would be in category 1.
e	Emotional response only	Bales gives the example of a member sighing heavily and examining his fingernails.
d	Acceptance or rejection	This is where decisions are made. If positive, the member may show understanding, passive acceptance, and compliance with the decision. The member may show disagreement, passive rejection, and a lack of assistance if negative.
c	Control	Asking for suggestions, such as "I think we should do this," or "How do you think we ought to tackle this?" a member is getting the others to commit themselves. By committing themselves, members limit their future choices. This method brings other members under control, which may or may not lead to resentment.
b	Opinion	"Have we done that?" "We ought to make sure that we do this." Any comments that involve summarizing the issues.
a	Orientation	Setting out the problem and giving factual information.

Data from Bales, R. F. (1950). *Interaction process analysis: A method for the study of small groups.* University of Chicago Press.

an individual's need for safety by reducing the sense of powerlessness and anxiety, which may be experienced in ambiguous or threatening situations. Members may join because group affiliation can be essential to an individual's self-esteem and social identity. People need to have a favorable opinion of themselves, which they gain partly from acceptance by others in a group and evidence that other group members share their views and values. A group can also help members achieve stated goals that they could not have achieved alone.

Group membership can satisfy several needs for an individual, in addition to the member contributing to other members and the group achieving objectives. However, deciding whether to join a group or to continue membership in a group poses an approach–avoidance conflict. To resolve the conflict, an individual will perform a cost–benefit analysis of the relationship. Members will continue with their association if the rewards (satisfaction of needs) outweigh or equal the costs of being a member, such as required participation time and financial commitment. This cost–benefit analysis is analogous to Adams's equity theory of motivation.

Roles of Group Members

As introduced by Benne and Sheats (1948), functional role theory identified the functional roles that individual group members assumed in small group interactions. The three roles identified were task, maintenance, and individual (sometimes called "self-centered") roles (see **Exhibit 16-1**). Task-oriented roles focus on goal accomplishment, maintenance roles focus on

Exhibit 16-1 Benne and Sheats's Functional Roles of Group Members with Examples

Role	Function	What They Might Say
TASK ROLES: Getting the job done		
Initiator-contributor	Generates new ideas.	What if we tried a new approach to streamline this process?
Information-seeker	Asks for information about the task.	Can someone explain how this policy is supposed to work?
Opinion-seeker	Asks for input from the group about its values.	What do you all think is the best outcome here?
Information-giver	Offers facts or generalizations to the group.	According to the latest report, our readmission rates have dropped.
Opinion-giver	States their beliefs about a group issue.	I believe we should prioritize patient safety over budget constraints.
Elaborator	Explains ideas and offers examples.	To clarify, this means we would rotate staff every two weeks.
Coordinator	Shows relationships between ideas.	That aligns with what Jenna mentioned earlier about workflow.
Orienter	Shifts the direction of discussion.	Let's refocus on what our original goal was.
Evaluator-critic	Measures actions against objectives.	Does this proposal meet our quality benchmarks?
Energizer	Stimulates higher activity.	Let's pick up the pace—this could be a big win for the team!
Procedural-technician	Performs logistical tasks.	I'll set up the Zoom link and organize the documents.
Recorder	Keeps records of actions.	I've documented our decisions and shared them in the meeting notes.
MAINTENANCE ROLES: Keeping social relationships intact		
Encourager	Praises ideas of others.	That's a great point, thanks for sharing it.
Harmonizer	Mediates differences.	It sounds like you're both aiming for the same outcome.
Compromiser	Seeks middle ground.	What if we combine both suggestions into one plan?

(continues)

Exhibit 16-1 Benne and Sheats's Functional Roles of Group Members with Examples *(continued)*

Role	Function	What They Might Say
MAINTENANCE ROLES: Keeping social relationships intact		
Gatekeeper/ expediter	Keeps communication open.	Let's make sure everyone has a chance to speak.
Standard setter	Suggests criteria or standards.	We should hold ourselves to a 24-hour turnaround standard.
Group observer	Records and gives feedback.	I noticed we collaborate best when everyone contributes.
Follower	Goes along with the group.	I'm fine with whatever the group decides.
INDIVIDUAL ROLES: Looking out for one's own interests or needs		
Aggressor	Attacks or deflates others.	That's a terrible idea, and it'll never work.
Blocker	Resists group movement.	I still think we shouldn't change anything.
Recognition seeker	Seeks attention.	Just so you know, this idea is something I pioneered last year.
Self-confessor	Shares irrelevant personal info.	This reminds me of my vacation last summer!
Dominator	Manipulates or asserts control.	We're doing it my way because I've done this before.
Help seeker	Looks for sympathy.	I'm just not sure I can keep up with all of this.

relationships, and individual roles focus on individual needs (such as power or recognition), which can harm the group's overall success. Benne and Sheats's task and maintenance roles are similar to the two communication patterns—task-oriented and socioemotional—that Bales (1950, 1953, 1970, 1999) identified in his research on group members' interactions. Bales's task role relates to a member's activities that help the group accomplish its goals (e.g., concern for production), and the member's socioemotional role is described as the activities that the member performs to promote harmonious relations within the group (e.g., concern for people; see **Table 16-2**).

Members may assume different roles depending on the needs of the individual or the group. Bales found that some members engaged in more task and socioemotional activities than others and, as a result, were offered leadership status in the group. However, Bales also found that the person who engaged in the most task activities was not the same person who performed the most socioemotional activities. Therefore, two leaders emerged: the task leader, who was rated as having the best ideas, offering the most guidance, and being most influential in forming the group's opinions, and the socioemotional leader, who was the best liked. The usual explanation for the emergence of the second leader is that a task leader's sense of purpose gives rise to activities

Table 16-2 Comparison of Members' Roles

Benne and Sheats (1948)	Bales (1950)	Belbin (1981, 1993)	Description (Belbin, 1993)
Task	Task-oriented	Chairman	Also referred to as the coordinator, the mature and confident person who enables others to give their best, keeps the team oriented toward its goals, and is rarely the source of ideas
Task	Task-oriented	Shaper	The top-down leader, energetic, challenging, and pressurizing, who drives their ideas to conclusion
Task	Task-oriented	Plant	The creative and unorthodox problem solver, probably not very gooc with people
Maintenance	Socioemotional	Teamworker (positive)	An interpersonally perceptive and caring person who enables individuals to work together, but who may be indecisive under pressure
Task	Task-oriented	Completer/ finisher	The rules person who dots the i's and crosses the t's and will not give up until the job is satisfactorily completed, and who may be a worrier
Task	Task-oriented	Company worker	The person who implements, gets things done to meet goals, and may be somewhat inflexible
Task	Task-oriented	Resource investigator	The person who is out and about, seeking new ideas and exploring opportunities, and who may become bored with routine
Individual (negative)	Socioemotional	Monitor/ evaluator	The person who is judgmental, looking for faults, and seeking to prevent errors but who may not inspire others
Task	Task-oriented	Specialist	The person who is single-minded and dedicated, who has unique knowledge but whose contributions are limited to that knowledge

(e.g., unpopular orders, sharp criticism) that hurt group members' feelings. The second leader emerged to smooth things over and restore harmony to the group.

Belbin (1981, 1993, 2004) studied how team performance was directly affected by members' roles. Belbin developed the Team Role Theory, which proposes that nine (originally eight) personality-related team roles must be fulfilled for optimal operation of a management team. The roles are chairman/coordinator, shaper, plant, teamworker, completer/finisher, company worker/implementer, resource investigator, monitor/evaluator, and specialist. Belbin's nine roles can be categorized as task/task-oriented, maintenance/socioemotional positive, or individual/socioemotional negative according to Benne and Sheats's Functional Role Theory and Bales's Interaction Analysis; see Table 16-2. All groups need task leadership, attention to detail, and a concern for people to be effective. Understanding the various members' roles is important for comprehending the interactions that either push a group toward or hinder the group from meeting its goals, including member satisfaction with the interactions. The role(s) a member assumes and the resulting interactions greatly influence the group's norms.

Group Norms

Every group has a set of norms, which is an implied code of conduct about what is acceptable and unacceptable member behavior. Norms can be written or unwritten; positive, negative, or neutral; and applied to all members of the group or only to certain members. In addition, groups will apply "punishment" or sanctions to members whose behavior deviates from the group's norms. Norms can dictate the performance level of groups (e.g., high- or low-productivity work groups), the appearance of group members (e.g., bankers wear dark suits), or the social arrangement within the group (the chair of the committee sits at the head of the conference table).

Most organizations have formal rules of conduct, delineated in their policies and procedures. For example, a hospital would have written policies on clinical research protocols, infection-control procedures for handling blood and other body fluids, the proper attire to be worn in operating room suites, and processes to ensure that the correct patient (and correct body part) is operated on (see **Exhibit 16-2**).

Exhibit 16-2 Surgical Checklist

The implementation of a surgical checklist that guides the surgical team through a series of tasks and communications before, during, and after the surgery represents an example of written formal rules of conduct. Research by the World Health Organization found that implementing such a checklist reduced postoperative complications and death rates by over 30% (Haynes et al., 2009).

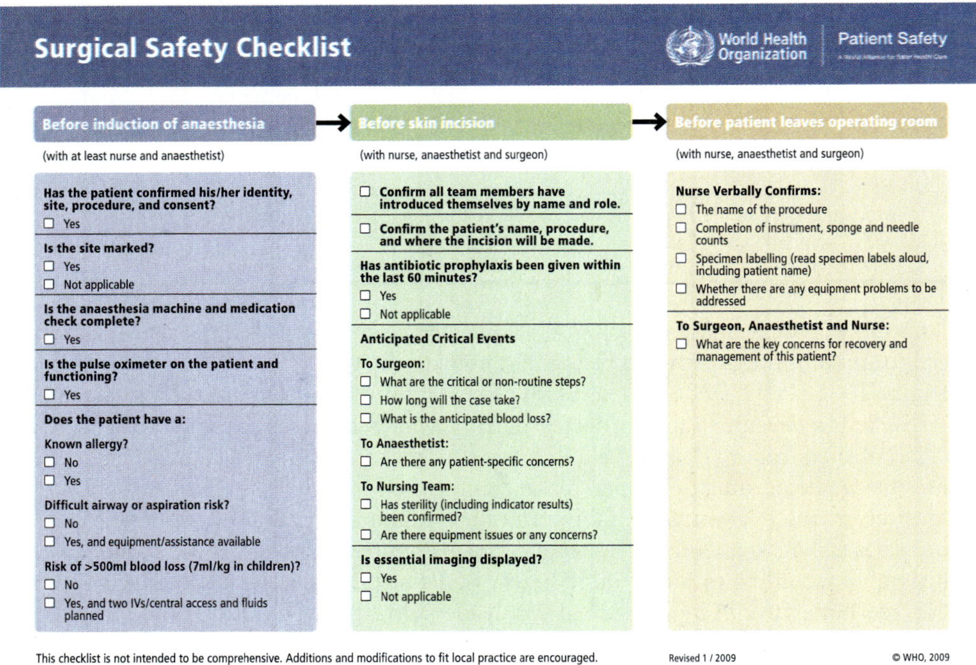

Surgical Safety Checklist

World Health Organization | Patient Safety

Before induction of anaesthesia → **Before skin incision** → **Before patient leaves operating room**

Before induction of anaesthesia

(with at least nurse and anaesthetist)

Has the patient confirmed his/her identity, site, procedure, and consent?
- ☐ Yes

Is the site marked?
- ☐ Yes
- ☐ Not applicable

Is the anaesthesia machine and medication check complete?
- ☐ Yes

Is the pulse oximeter on the patient and functioning?
- ☐ Yes

Does the patient have a:

Known allergy?
- ☐ No
- ☐ Yes

Difficult airway or aspiration risk?
- ☐ No
- ☐ Yes, and equipment/assistance available

Risk of >500ml blood loss (7ml/kg in children)?
- ☐ No
- ☐ Yes, and two IVs/central access and fluids planned

Before skin incision

(with nurse, anaesthetist and surgeon)

- ☐ **Confirm all team members have introduced themselves by name and role.**
- ☐ **Confirm the patient's name, procedure, and where the incision will be made.**

Has antibiotic prophylaxis been given within the last 60 minutes?
- ☐ Yes
- ☐ Not applicable

Anticipated Critical Events

To Surgeon:
- ☐ What are the critical or non-routine steps?
- ☐ How long will the case take?
- ☐ What is the anticipated blood loss?

To Anaesthetist:
- ☐ Are there any patient-specific concerns?

To Nursing Team:
- ☐ Has sterility (including indicator results) been confirmed?
- ☐ Are there equipment issues or any concerns?

Is essential imaging displayed?
- ☐ Yes
- ☐ Not applicable

Before patient leaves operating room

(with nurse, anaesthetist and surgeon)

Nurse Verbally Confirms:
- ☐ The name of the procedure
- ☐ Completion of instrument, sponge and needle counts
- ☐ Specimen labelling (read specimen labels aloud, including patient name)
- ☐ Whether there are any equipment problems to be addressed

To Surgeon, Anaesthetist and Nurse:
- ☐ What are the key concerns for recovery and management of this patient?

This checklist is not intended to be comprehensive. Additions and modifications to fit local practice are encouraged.

Revised 1 / 2009

Reproduced from World Health Organization. (n.d.). *WHO surgical safety checklist*. World Health Organization. https://www.who.int/patientsafety/topics/safe-surgery/checklist/en/

However, in most instances, group norms (i.e., acceptable behavior of group members) are unwritten and learned by members through their interactions with others. For example, Crandall (1988) studied groups of cheerleaders, dancers, and female sorority members with high rates of eating disorders and noted that these groups adopted the behaviors of binging and purging as normal methods of weight control. The most popular members of the group binged and purged at the rate established by the norms of the group, and those who did not binge and purge when they first joined the group were more likely to take up the practice the longer they were members of the group. This alignment of behavior within a group is part of an individual's socialization process. This process of socialization explains how unwritten norms become the "standards" for the group, as members begin to internalize the group's norms as their own behavioral standards. As such, norms do not just maintain order within the group; they also maintain the group itself (Youngreen & Moore, 2008).

Since most group norms are unwritten, they are usually not easily identified until violated. When group norms are violated, members of the group will attempt to convince the "deviant" to conform to the group's standards of behavior. If the use of persuasion is not successful, the group may punish the member by withdrawing any "special" status that the member may hold, or the group may psychologically reject (e.g., ignore) the member. The final consequence for a member who refuses to conform would be dismissal from the group. Through this process, members learn the range or boundaries of acceptable behavior within a group. For example, Feldman (1984) describes the norms about productivity that frequently develop among factory workers. A person produces 50 widgets and is praised by their coworkers; a person produces 60 widgets and is sharply teased by coworkers; a person produces 70 widgets and is ostracized by coworkers. If the group norm of producing 50 widgets allows for an acceptable pace of work, the group member who produces 70 widgets may either make the rest of the group look lazy or cause management to raise the target number of widgets to be produced, resulting in an uncomfortably fast pace of work. Not all behavior deviations will be enforced, only those violations that significantly impact the group meeting its goals (see **Table 16-3**). Norms are powerful forces not only in affecting the behavior of group members, but also in determining the degree of cohesiveness and conformity of the group.

Table 16-3 Why Norms Are Enforced

Four Conditions Under Which Group Norms Are Most Likely to Be Enforced	Example
If norms facilitate group survival	Group members do not disclose certain project details so that their work cannot be replicated by another group.
If norms simplify or make predictable what behavior is expected of group members	Employees are expected to be present at the office during the same hours each day so that clients always know where to find team members.
If norms help the group to avoid embarrassing interpersonal problems	Members do not discuss politics at work so that members with strongly held beliefs do not create conflict or ostracize other members.
If norms express the central values of the group and clarify what is distinctive about the group's identity	Long white coats are worn by physicians so that patients know which care provider is their medical doctor and to symbolize a high level of training and expertise.

Data from Feldman, D. C. (1984). The development and enforcement of group norms. *Academy of Management Review, 9*(1), 47–53.

Cohesiveness

The degree of cohesiveness (e.g., camaraderie) of a group is determined by various factors, which may include members' dependence and physical location or proximity. The more significant factors tend to be (1) the size of the group, (2) experience of success by the group, (3) group status, and (4) outside threats to the group.

Size of the Group

Researchers have determined that the size of the group directly impacts the cohesiveness of a group. When there are too many members, it becomes too difficult for members to interact. Luft (1984, p. 23) concluded that "cohesion tends to be weaker and morale tends to be lower in large groups than in comparable smaller ones." What is the acceptable group size? Kameda, Stasson, David, Parks, and Zimmerman (1992) suggest that the optimum group size appears to be five members. Five-member groups are small enough for meaningful interaction yet large enough to generate an adequate number of ideas (Tubbs, 2001). Small groups may also avoid the problem of social loafing.

Social Loafing

Diffusion of responsibility refers to the phenomenon by which an individual feels less responsible for a task when they are part of a group. For example, people are more likely to call for an ambulance when they see a car wreck if there are no other cars on the road. However, if the car wreck occurs in the middle of a busy highway with lots of other cars around, people are more likely to assume that somebody else in traffic will make the call. Perhaps you ignore the full trash can, hoping that your roommate will take care of it. A specific consequence of the diffusion of responsibility that occurs in working groups is called social loafing.

Social loafing refers to the decreased effort of individual members in a group when the size of the group increases (Tubbs, 2001). Ringelmann (1913) identified this social phenomenon when he noticed that as more and more people were added to a group pulling on a rope, the total force exerted by the group rose but the average force exerted by each group member declined. The reason is that some members' performance became mediocre because they assumed that other members would pick up the slack. Karau and Williams (1993) found that social loafing occurs across work populations and tasks. However, the researchers noted that if the participants' dominant culture emphasized collectivism versus individualism as described by Hofstede's four dimensions of national culture (Hofstede, 1984), the degree of social loafing decreased.

Subsequent studies revealed that when an individual's contribution is identified and the person is held directly accountable for and rewarded for their behavior, social loafing may be eliminated (Kerr, 1983; Kerr & Bruun, 1981; Shepperd, 1993; Szymanski & Harkins, 1987). Beyerlein, Freedman, McGee, and Moran (2002) stress that personal accountability by each group member for their role and responsibilities is required to achieve an effective collaborative team. When accountability is lacking, members will usually act in support of their own self-serving interests. For example, members will sometimes hold back if they believe that other members of their group are not expending equal efforts toward accomplishing the task.

Experience of Success

Prior success of a group in reaching its goals has a direct impact on the degree of cohesiveness. No one wants to stay on a losing team. When a group fails to attain its goals, members display a lack of unity by infighting, finger-pointing, or disassociation.

Group Status

Cohesiveness is more prominent when admission into the group is more difficult to obtain because of various barriers or high criteria, such as education levels. This perception of status, whether real or not, creates a feeling of being in the "in-group" for the individuals who were able to overcome the barriers for admission into the group—for example, a physicians' group.

Outside Threats to the Group

The cohesiveness of a group will increase if its members perceive that an external force may prevent the group from reaching its goals. Members of the group will unite to display a unified front to the opposing force. Cohesive groups will also unite against nonconforming members who threaten the esprit de corps of the group. Therefore, cohesive groups exert pressure on members of the group to conform.

Managers should encourage cohesive work groups because research has shown that cohesive units demonstrate a higher level of productivity than less cohesive groups do. However, managers need to be aware that group norms may mediate the relationship between cohesiveness and performance. On the one hand, if norms support performance-related activities, then cohesiveness is likely to improve performance. On the other hand, if norms support limited output or engagement in irrelevant tasks, cohesiveness may undermine performance (Berkowitz, 1954).

In conclusion, group cohesiveness is a product of social identification. According to Hogg and Abrams (1990), the more positive a member feels about their group, the more motivated the person is to promote in-group solidarity, cooperation, and support. In turn, the more cohesive a group is, the more likely its members will interact socially and influence one another (Turner, 1987). Because of these interactions, we find that more cohesive groups tend to eventually pressure their members toward a higher degree of conformity, and a high degree of conformity can lower the performance level of the group.

Conformity

Strong group norms and high degrees of group cohesiveness can hamper the performance of a group because of conformity pressures. Conformity involves the changing of an individual's perceptions or behaviors to match the attitudes or behaviors of others. This "normative social influence" occurs when we conform to what we believe to be the norms of the group in order to be accepted by its members.

One of the earliest studies in the conformity area was Sherif's (1936) experiment that involved the autokinetic effect. Sherif pointed a light in a dark space that, although stationary, appeared to move. Subjects were asked, both as individuals and as members of a group, to estimate the amount of movement they observed. When in groups, the subjects changed their original estimates to more closely fit the answers of the other members. This experiment demonstrated the individual's urge to conform.

Asch (1952) also conducted conformity studies. In Asch's experiments, eight people were seated around a table. Seven of them were actually the experimenters. However, the eighth person, the subject, was unaware of this situation. The group was shown two cards; each card contained different lengths of vertical lines (i.e., no two lines matched in length on either card). The participants were asked to say which of the lines matched the length of another. One after another, the participants announced their decisions. The experimenters had been told to give an incorrect response. The eighth subject sat in the next-to-last seat so that all but one of the other participants had given an obviously incorrect answer before the subject gave their answer. Even though the correct answer was obvious (i.e., no two lines matched in length on either card), Asch found that one-third of the subjects conformed to the majority, one-third never conformed, and the remaining one-third gave conforming responses at least once. This experiment was designed to create pressure on subjects to conform to others, which in fact they did.

Although Asch's experiment has been criticized for being unrealistic (i.e., in the real world, individuals would be making decisions on subjects more complex and more important than the length of a line), it did confirm that "humans have the tendency to conform to the goals and ideas of a small group and tend to be unwilling to go against the group even if they know the group is wrong" (Asch, 1960).

Not all people conform. There is evidence that those who do not conform tend to have a healthy level of self-esteem, mature social relationships, and are flexible and open-minded in their thinking. For example, Crutchfield (1955) and Tuddenham (1958) found that there is a correlation between high intelligence and other personality traits and low conformity. Another important aspect of conformity is that it may lead to "groupthink."

Groupthink

Strong conformity pressures reflect members' attempts to maintain harmony within the group. However, conformity may hamper a group's performance by decreasing innovation and increasing faulty decision making. Janis (1982) referred to this situation as "groupthink." Groupthink refers to conditions under which efforts to maintain group harmony undermine critical thought and lead to poor decisions (Janis, 1982; Janis & Mann, 1977). Janis, as cited by Tubbs (2001, p. 236), identified eight symptoms of groupthink:

Type I: Overestimation of the group—its power and morality

1. An illusion of invulnerability which creates excessive optimism and encourages taking extreme risks.
2. An unquestioned belief in the group's inherent morality, inclining the members to ignore the ethical or moral consequences of their decisions.

Type II: Closed-mindedness

1. Collective efforts to rationalize to discount warnings or other information that might lead the members to reconsider their assumptions before they recommit themselves to their past policy decisions.
2. Stereotyped views of enemy leaders as too evil to warrant genuine attempts to negotiate or as too weak and stupid to counter whatever risky attempts are made to defeat their purposes.

Type III: Pressures toward uniformity

1. Self-censorship of deviation from the apparent group consensus, reflecting each member's inclination to minimize to themselves the importance of their doubts and counterarguments.
2. A shared illusion of unanimity concerning judgments conforming to the majority view (partly resulting from self-censorship of deviations, augmented by the false assumption that silence means consent).
3. Direct pressure on any member who expresses strong arguments against any of the group's stereotypes, illusions, or commitments, making clear that this type of dissent is contrary to what is expected of all loyal members.
4. The emergence of self-appointed mindguards—members who protect the group from adverse information that might shatter its shared complacency about the effectiveness and morality of its decisions.

Was groupthink the downfall of HealthSouth? (See **Exhibit 16-3**.) Many former senior managers of HealthSouth, a nationwide provider of rehabilitative services headquartered in Birmingham, Alabama, were indicted and in some cases found guilty of fraudulently and systemically inflating the company's earnings and assets by approximately $4 billion during the 1990s.

Managers must be careful because group members sometimes desire to maintain their close team relationships—or, in the HealthSouth case, "the family relationship"—at all costs. When group members operate in a groupthink mode, it may affect their decision making. For example, consider a doctor who has proposed a new medical procedure for joint replacements. Some team members are initially resistant because of high training demands, even though the new procedure would establish best practices. To preserve harmony in the group, other staff members go along with the resisting members. In this case, the team has succumbed to group thinking instead of critical thinking.

Exhibit 16-3 Five HealthSouth Officers Charged with Conspiracy to Commit Wire and Securities Fraud

Count 1 of the Information alleges that from approximately 1994 onward, AYERS, EDWARDS, MORGAN, and VALENTINE, in conspiracy with Owens, Smith, Harris, and others, devised a scheme to fraudulently inflate HealthSouth's publicly reported earnings and asset values. The conspirators provided the Chief Executive Officer (CEO) with internal financial reports accurately reflecting HealthSouth's performance. After review, instructions were issued to ensure reported earnings met or exceeded Wall Street expectations.

Accounting staff were then directed to manipulate financial records to reach these earnings targets. These staff members met in so-called "family" meetings, where strategies were discussed to falsify books in order to bridge the gap—referred to as the "hole"—between actual and desired financial results. Fraudulent entries used to close this gap were called the "dirt."

The conspirators instructed defendants to make false entries in various financial records, including revenue, assets, and earnings. This included inflating asset values across multiple accounts, such as Property, Plant, and Equipment (PP&E), cash, inventory, and goodwill. To further the scheme, when external parties, such as auditors or buyers requested documentation, conspirators produced records that concealed fraudulent entries. In some cases, they manufactured supporting documents and altered account codes to deceive auditors.

The conspiracy was coordinated and sustained over years, with clear intent to mislead stakeholders, including investors and regulators, about HealthSouth's true financial condition.

Modified from U.S. Department of Justice. (2003, April 3). Press releases. https://www.justice.gov/archive/opa/pr/2003/April/

Many researchers studied the culture of the National Aeronautics and Space Administration (NASA) after the *Challenger* disaster and found evidence of this type of groupthink. Engineers did not voice their concerns and criticism because of the strong team spirit and camaraderie at NASA. In other words, when groups display a high degree of cohesiveness, it is especially important to guard against groupthink.

Suggested safeguards against groupthink include (1) soliciting outside expert opinions during the decision-making process, (2) appointing a devil's advocate to challenge majority views, (3) hypothesizing alternative scenarios of a rival's intention, and (4) reconsidering decisions after a waiting period. However, Bennis (1976) argues that a devil's advocate will be ignored if the group perceives the member as only role-playing.

Summary

Many factors influence our behavior. Group dynamics is a complex subject that attempts to provide us with some understanding of how individuals interact with one another and how those interactions become visible in our resulting behavior. Burton and Dimbleby (1995) developed a model, using interpersonal communication as the foundation, to help us understand the complexity of group dynamics (see **Figure 16-2**).

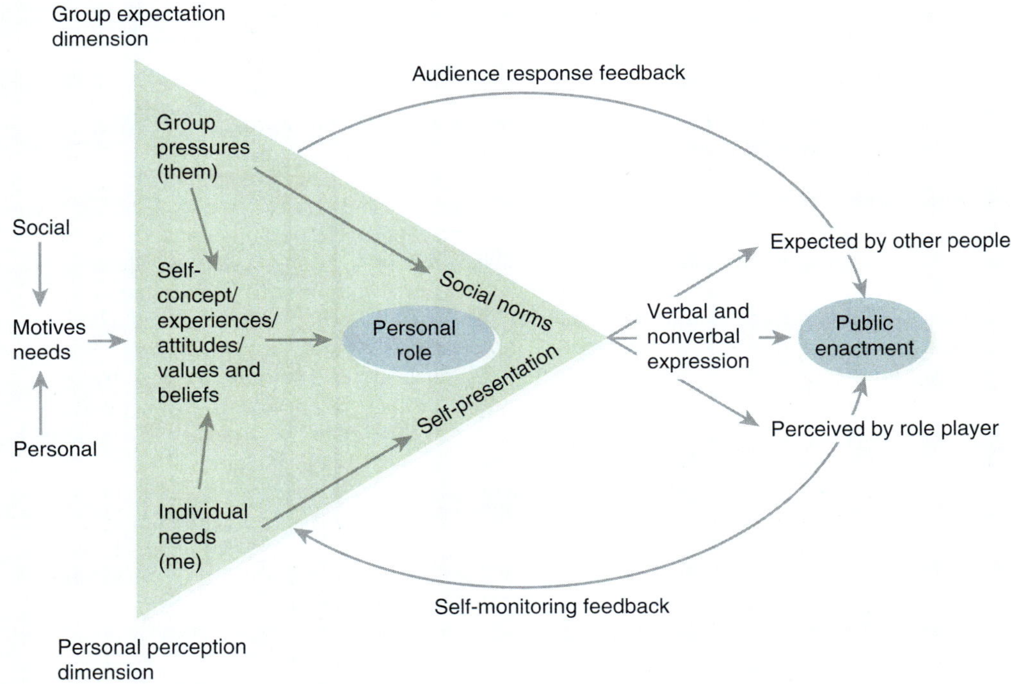

Figure 16-2 The Interface of Me and Them

The figure is titled "The Interface of Me and Them." When examining the model, you will notice that the bottom half is concerned with "me" and the top half represents "them." The process begins with an individual's needs or motivation, which triggers the "whole of self." The triangle represents various interactions with our groups that are filtered through our self-concept, which, taken together, form our personal roles. We then communicate our role and receive feedback from both ourselves (did I play the role correctly?) and others (did they confirm my behavior was correct?) to restart the process of redefining who we are as an individual (personal role).

Discussion Questions

1. Define the study of group dynamics and discuss why it is important to today's managers.
2. Describe the four characteristics that define a group and provide examples of nongroups and groups.
3. Explain what is meant by "group interaction."
4. Discuss how group interactions can be measured.
5. Discuss why people join groups and what sustains their membership.
6. Explain the importance of the various roles that members assume in groups.
7. Discuss how group norms are formed and sustained within groups.
8. Explain how group cohesiveness is developed and sustained.
9. Discuss why conformity can inhibit a group's performance.
10. Explain what behavior is displayed by a group engaging in groupthink.

Exercise 16-1

Form small groups of four to five individuals and discuss the following statement:

> Often employees do not act or react as individuals but as members of groups.

When discussing this statement, the group members should share experiences of working in groups. Can you recall an instance in which you gave in because of the pressure to conform? Have you experienced a nonconformist in one of your groups? How did you or other members of your group react to "deviant" behavior in your group?

Exercise 16-2

Form small groups of four to five individuals. Using the worksheet "Be the Best We Can Be Team Norms," discuss how the answers to the questions can assist the group with developing team norms so that each member understands their expected behaviors.

Be the Best We Can Be Team Norms

1. When I am upset with someone I will:
2. One way I can avoid making premature assumptions is:
3. When a member of the group is not contributing, we will:
4. One thing I think we could do to resolve differences among us as a team could be:
5. One thing important to me about how we communicate (email, text, F2F, how quickly should people respond, etc.) is:

6. When someone comes to complain to me about another person on our team I or we will:
7. One way I'd like to be recognized or appreciated is:
8. One thing our group could do when we forget our Team Commitments and want to get back on track could be:

Reprinted with permission from Guilmartin, N. (2009). *The power of pause: How to be more effective in a demanding, 24/7 world.* John Wiley & Sons.

Exercise 16-3

Analyze the level of group cohesiveness in one of the groups to which you belong.

References

Asch, S. (1952). Effects of group pressure on the modification and distortion of judgments. Reprinted in G. E. Swanson, T. M. Newcomb, & E. L. Hartley (Eds.), (1965). *Readings in social psychology* (2nd ed.). Holt, Rinehart & Winston.

Asch, S. (1960). *Social psychology*. Prentice Hall.

Bales, R. F. (1950). *Interaction process analysis: A method for the study of small groups*. University of Chicago Press.

Bales, R. F. (1953). The equilibrium problem in small groups. In T. Parsons, R. F. Bales & E. A. Shils (Eds.), *Working papers in the theory of action* (pp. 111–167). Free Press.

Bales, R. F. (1970). *Personality and interpersonal behavior*. Holt, Rinehart & Winston.

Bales, R. F. (1999). *Social interaction systems: Theory and measurement*. Transaction.

Belbin, R. M. (1981). *Management teams: Why they succeed or fail*. Elsevier/Butterworth-Heinemann.

Belbin, R. M. (1993). *Team roles at work*. Elsevier/Butterworth-Heinemann.

Belbin, R. M. (2004). *Management teams: Why they succeed or fail* (2nd ed.). Elsevier/Butterworth-Heinemann.

Benne, K., & Sheats, P. (1948). Functional roles of group members. *Journal of Social Issues, 4*(2), 41–49.

Bennis, W. (1976). *The unconscious conspiracy: Why leaders can't lead*. AMACOM.

Berkowitz, L. (1954). Group standards, cohesiveness, and productivity. *Human Relations, 7*(4), 509–519.

Beyerlein, M. M., Freedman, S., McGee, C., & Moran, L. (2002). *Beyond teams: Building the collaborative organization*. Jossey-Bass/Pfeiffer.

Burton, G., & Dimbleby, R. (1996). *Between ourselves: An introduction to interpersonal communication*, Bloomsbury Academic, an imprint of Bloomsbury Publishing Plc.

Crandall, C. S. (1988). Social contagion of binge eating. *Journal of Personality and Social Psychology, 55*(4), 588–598.

Crutchfield, R. (1955). Conformity and character. *American Psychologist, 10*(5), 191–198.

Feldman, D. C. (1984). The development and enforcement of group norms. *Academy of Management Review, 9*(1), 47–53.

Haynes, A. B., Weiser, T. G., Berry, W. R., Lipsitz, S. R., Breizat, A. H. S., Dellinger, E. P., … Merry, A. F. (2009). A surgical safety checklist to reduce morbidity and mortality in a global population. *New England Journal of Medicine, 360*(5), 491–499.

Hofstede, G. (1984). *Culture's consequences: International differences in work-related values* (Vol. 5). Sage.

Hogg, M., & Abrams, D. (1990). Social motivation, self-esteem and social identity. In D. Abrams & M. Hogg (Eds.), *Social identity theory: Constructive and critical advances* (pp. 28–47). Harvester Wheatsheaf.

Janis, I. L. (1982). *Groupthink: Psychological studies of foreign policy decisions and fiascoes* (2nd ed.). Houghton Mifflin.

Janis, I. L., & Mann, L. (1977). *Decision making: A psychological analysis of conflict, choice, and commitment*. Free Press.

Kameda, T., Stasson, M. F., David, J. H., Parks, C., & Zimmerman, S. (1992). Social dilemmas, subgroups, and motivational loss in task-oriented groups: In search of an "optimal" team size in division of work. *Social Psychology Quarterly, 55*(1), 47–56.

Karau, S. J., & Williams, K. D. (1993). Social loafing: A meta-analytic review and theoretical integration. *Journal of Personality and Social Psychology, 65*(4), 681–706.

Katzenbach, J. R., & Smith, D. K. (1993). *The wisdom of teams: Creating the high-performance organization*. Harvard Business School Press.

Kerr, N. L. (1983). Motivation losses in small groups: A social dilemma analysis. *Journal of Personality and Social Psychology, 45*(4), 819–828.

Kerr, N. L., & Bruun, S. E. (1981). Ringelmann revisited: Alternative explanations for the social loafing effect. *Personality and Social Psychology Bulletin, 7*(2), 224–231.

Luft, J. (1984). *Group processes: An introduction to group dynamics* (3rd ed.). National Press.

Ringelmann, M. (1913). Recherches sur les moteurs animés: Travail de l'homme [Research on animate sources of power: The work of man]. *Annales de l'Institut National Agronomique*, 2e série, tome XII, 1–40.

Shepperd, J. A. (1993). Productivity loss in performance groups: A motivation analysis. *Psychological Bulletin, 113*(1), 67–81.

Sherif, M. (1936). *The psychology of social norms*. Octagon Books.

Sprott, W. J. H. (1958). *Human groups*. Penguin Books.

Szymanski, K., & Harkins, S. G. (1987). Social loafing and self-evaluation with a social standard. *Journal of Personality and Social Psychology, 53*(5), 891–987.

Taplin, S. H., Foster, M. K., & Shortell, S. M. (2013). Organizational leadership for building effective health care teams. *Annals of Family Medicine, 11*(3), 279–281.

Tubbs, S. L. (2001). *A systems approach to small group interaction*. McGraw-Hill.

Tuddenham, R. (1958). The influence of a distorted norm upon individual judgment. *Journal of Psychology, 46*(2), 227–241.

Turner, J. (1987). *Rediscovering the social group*. Basil Blackwell.

Turner, M. E. (2001). *Groups at work: Theory and research*. Lawrence Erlbaum Associates.

U.S. Department of Justice, Northern District of Alabama. (2003, April 3). Five HealthSouth officers charged with conspiracy to commit wire & securities fraud [Press Release]. https://www.justice.gov/archive/opa/pr/2003/April/03_crm_205.htm

Youngreen, R., & Moore, C. D. (2008). The effects of status violations on hierarchy and influence in groups. *Small Group Research, 39*(5), 569–587.

CHAPTER 17

Groups

LEARNING OUTCOMES

After completing this chapter, the student should be able to describe:

- Importance of a group's size.
- Three broad categories of groups.
- Difference between informal and formal groups.
- Different types of task groups.
- Five stages of group development.
- Seven stages of group decision making.
- Different methods for group decision making.

Overview

This chapter discusses the composition, structure, formation, and decision-making processes of groups. The optimum size for a group is five members. However, we will find groups with fewer than five members and groups with more. When a group has fewer than five members, problems may arise relating to an inability to make decisions and lower levels of creativity (Tubbs, 2001). If the group becomes too large, subgroups may form, distracting from the group's primary purpose, and a majority of the group's time may end up being used for functioning purposes (e.g., organizing members and assigning roles) rather than the required task (Tubbs, 2001). All these situations can cause frustration among the members and stifle the group's ability to reach its goal.

Types of Groups

Groups can be categorized into three broad groups: primary, secondary, and reference. In the workplace, groups operate under an informal or formal structure.

Primary Groups

Primary groups include one's family, close friends, and peers. Social psychologists tend to see primary groups as those that (1) involve regular contact between members of the group, whether through direct face-to-face interaction, technology, or other means, and (2) are relatively small (20 or fewer members) (Blackler & Shimmin, 1984). In addition, primary groups (1) involve cooperation, (2) share common goals, (3) are familiar with all members, and (4) have an understanding of the roles of each member.

Primary groups powerfully influence a member's self-concept and the development of the individual's perceptions and attitudes. During an individual's childhood and adolescence, the family unit strongly impacts the development of the individual's personality and future behaviors, both socially and in the workplace.

Secondary Groups

Secondary groups comprise the larger circle of people we associate with. During the adult years, associations with work and professional groups will influence an individual's attitudes and perceptions through various interactions with these different groups. For example, Jane Kerry, RN, is a member of a family group, a group of close-knit friends that meet monthly for dinner, the president of her local bridge club, a member of the hospital's neonatal unit nursing staff, and a member of the hospital's quality improvement committee. Jane is also a member of larger groups: She is a member of the hospital's pediatric department, the hospital's nursing staff, and a member of the community in which the hospital is situated. In addition, she is a member of the American Nurses Association. Whether she is a short-term or long-term member of these groups, each group will influence Jane's behavior.

Reference Groups

"Reference group" is a term coined by Herbert Hyman (1942, 1968) to designate a group that an individual uses as a point of reference in determining their judgments, preferences, and behaviors. A person uses a reference group as an anchor point for evaluating their own beliefs and attitudes. Even though an individual may or may not be a member and may or may not aspire to be a reference group member, the group can significantly influence the person's values, opinions, attitudes, and behavior patterns. For example, one might say, "I'm not like *those* people" or "I am like those people." A reference group's influence on an individual may be positive or negative. An individual may pattern their beliefs and behavior to be congruent with or opposite to the group. Churches, labor unions, and political parties are examples of reference groups that can be positive or negative for specific individuals. The size of a reference group can range from a single individual (e.g., a movie star, athlete, or supermodel) to a large aggregate of persons, such as a political party or a religious institution.

Informal or Formal Group Structure

In the workplace, two types of groups can be found: informal groups and formal groups.

Informal Groups

The informal group (or clique) is organized based on the members' common interests or goals. Membership is voluntary and not part of the organization's official structure. Although informal groups usually have a short life cycle, they can significantly affect the organization's current and future operations. They can influence attitudes, perceptions, group norms, and communication networks.

For example, a small group of nurses at a large community hospital were unhappy about their work environment and met daily during lunch to discuss the situation. A recent change in the hospital's senior management caused high uncertainty among the clinical staff. The nurses also felt overworked because of the shortage of well-recognized nurses. Their wages and benefits had been stagnant, with no salary market adjustments for the past 3 years. No changes were ever made whenever the nurses approached management about these matters. This informal group of nurses decided to contact a labor union. The union began an organizing effort in the hospital shortly thereafter, holding an aggressive recruitment campaign. There was tremendous peer pressure, as some of the well-respected members of the nursing staff became active leaders for unionization, although they had not been among the initial organizing group. The election was held, and two-thirds of the nursing staff voted in the union. In the weeks that followed, the clinical nursing staff remarked that they were surprised by the union's victory; they had only wanted to scare management into making changes to their work environment.

Many cliques in the workplace can exist harmlessly, but managers need to be aware that some informal groups can be a powerful force within their organization. With an understanding of their influence, managers can use informal groups to initiate positive changes. Researchers have found that groups with informal leadership were sometimes more productive than groups without informal leaders. This occurs because information often spreads more easily through informal leaders than through formal channels (Marion et al., 2016). For example, a free standing outpatient surgical center administrator wanted to begin a cross-training program for the clinical staff to improve the organization's performance. The administrator knew that staff would resist this "new" concept because of their past failures to implement change. They enlisted the support of a group of nurses who had developed into a close-knit group. This was also the nursing group to which other clinical staff members looked for guidance on patient care issues. The administrator secured the support of the informal group by showing how the change would improve the quality of care for the patients (e.g., a more knowledgeable workforce), patient satisfaction (e.g., shorter wait time for procedures to be performed), and job security (e.g., an increase in the organization's financial stability). Because of the support of this group of nurses, the change was successfully implemented with minimal resistance from staff. Furthermore, the good outcomes that the administrator predicted would occur did happen. These outcomes positively reinforced the relationship between the informal nursing group and management.

Informal groups meet the needs of individuals and therefore have a strong influence on the members' behaviors. If managers are aware of these groups, they can be enlisted to assist the organization in achieving its goals (see **Case Study 17-1**). There are several ways that managers can incorporate informal leaders into the change process (Krueger, 2013):

- Keep informal leaders informed and encourage them to ask questions and challenge assumptions.
- Give frequent feedback and share results.

CASE STUDY 17-1 Using Informal Groups to Promote Organizational Goals

The clinic's chief executive officer (CEO) was known for consistently seeking, listening to, and incorporating the views of others. While she worked effectively through the formal hierarchy, she also regularly sought the views of physicians and employee influence leaders. These influential leaders were part of a group that met to provide input, shape ideas, and provide accurate information to those who looked to them for the inside scoop. Their role in helping to sell others on new directions was clearly recognized.

For example, when it came time to consider affiliating the clinic with another healthcare organization, influential leaders visited and came back to share their feelings with a broad cross-section of the organization. Many who listened to them would have been more skeptical if the information presented had come from the CEO's lips.

Modified from Peters, L. H., & O'Connor, E. J. (2001). Informal leadership support: An often overlooked competitive advantage. *Physician Executives, 27*(3), 35–39. Reprinted with permission.

- Get buy-in from employees on which informal leaders should be involved in helping to lead the change.
- Incorporate the feedback provided by the informal leader and ask for suggestions.
- Distribute various elements of the change or project to different formal leaders to avoid one person dominating the process.

Formal Groups

Formal groups are created by an organization and are part of its formal structure. They can be a long-term team (e.g., a functional or command group) or a short-term team (e.g., an ad hoc committee).

An entity's organizational chart specifies and outlines a functional or command group. For functional groups, members are grouped by similar tasks, such as financial and administrative services, ancillary services, human resources and organizational development, and nursing services (see **Figure 17-1**). For command groups, members are formed into subgroups under the leader's legitimate power position in the organization. For example, all laboratory technicians report to the manager of laboratory services. The manager forms a group of laboratory technicians to discuss the implementation issues of providing clinical support for the hospital's new outpatient clinic.

Task groups consist of two or more individuals focused on a specific objective, project, or issue. These groups may be short-term or long-term and are evaluated based on their goals. Unlike functional or command groups, task group members may come from different departments and organizational levels, selected for their relevant knowledge, experience, or authority. For example, a hospital CEO might form a multidisciplinary task force on disaster preparedness, including representatives from administration, patient care, information technology, and physical plant.

Task groups, such as those responsible for policymaking or coordination, may be permanent and can operate for a year or longer, even indefinitely. In contrast, ad hoc task groups are temporary and formed to address a specific problem or issue. Their duration typically ranges from one month to one year, depending on the complexity of the task. For instance, hospitals often create short-term ad hoc groups in response to natural disasters. These groups often disband once the immediate concern is resolved.

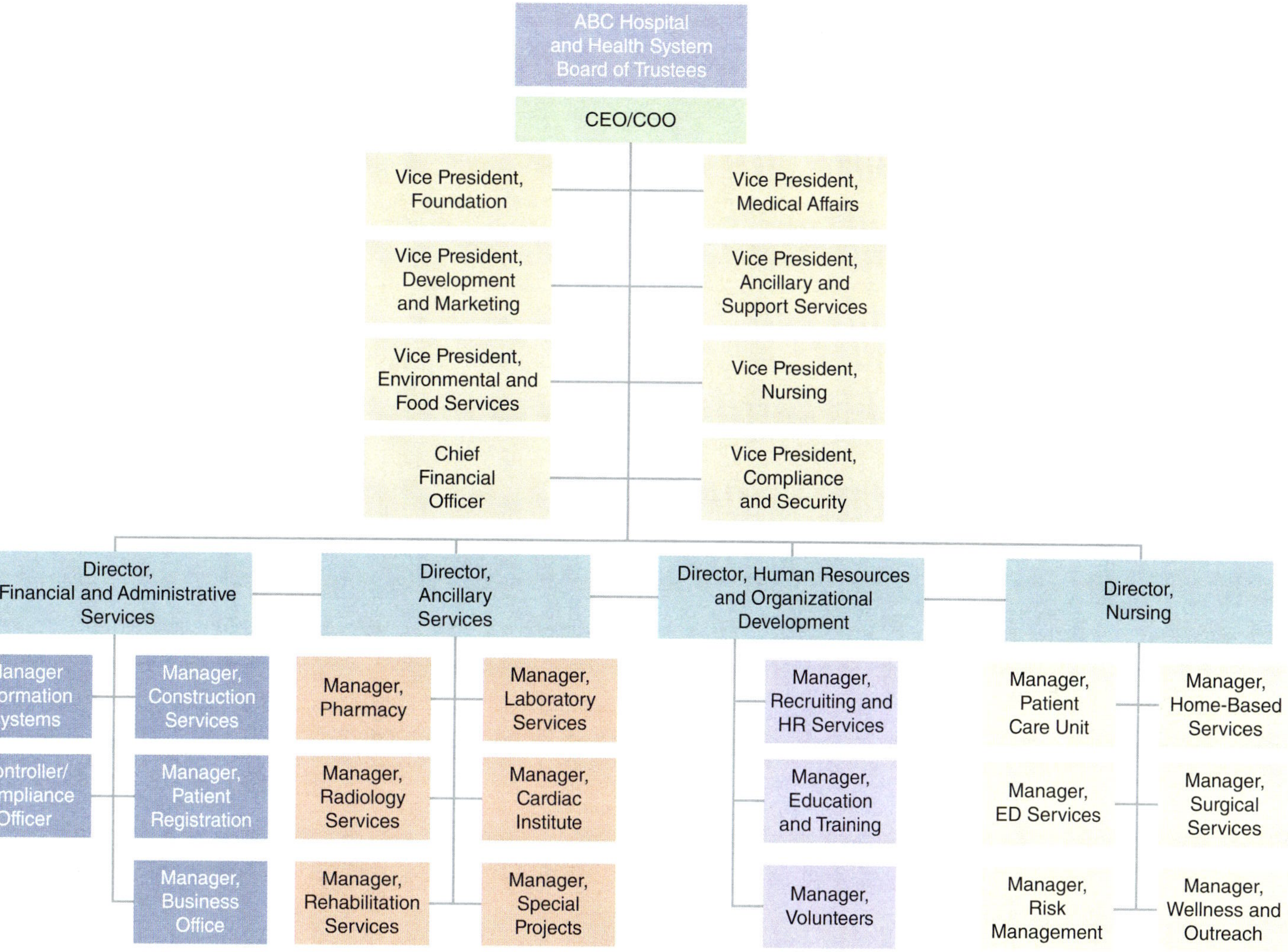

Figure 17-1 Organizational Chart for ABC Hospital and Health System

Group Development

Groups go through five sequential stages of development. Based on their leadership or members' prior experiences, some groups can move through these stages more quickly than others. Because of the same factors, some groups may never experience all five stages. The five stages of development are as follows:

1. *Forming*: During the forming stage, members try to determine the group's appropriate behaviors and core values. They focus on exchanging functional information, task definition, and boundary development. They begin to establish tasks and determine how they might meet objectives. During this initial stage, members must understand the reason or purpose for joining the group and find a social niche in the group.
2. *Storming*: The second stage of group development is characterized by high levels of emotion because members try to find their group identity and assert their individuality. At this stage, members are claiming their social power within the group, and a hierarchy is established as people question authority, react to what is supposed to be accomplished, and jockey for power within the group. Intermember criticism, scapegoating, and judgments may accompany this struggle for control.
3. *Norming*: In the third stage, the development of cohesion and structure occurs when the group's standards, key values, and roles are accepted. The gradual development of cohesion occurs after the conflict in the second stage. In this third stage, the rules for behavior are explicitly and implicitly defined. There is a greater degree of order and a strong sense of group membership.
4. *Performing*: In the fourth stage, members have found their roles within the group, and their energy is focused on the task. The group works through the problems it confronts, and when the task is near completion, it moves to the final phase.
5. *Adjourning*: Adjourning is the final stage of group development, representing the dissolution or termination of membership in the group.

Group Decision Making

Group decision making is the process of arriving at a judgment based on the feedback of multiple individuals. Such decision making is a key component of an organization's functioning because organizational performance involves more than just individual action. Therefore, managers need to understand how the group process affects group decision making.

Group decision making usually takes longer than an individual decision (Nour & Yen, 1992). However, research confirms that groups produce more and better solutions to problems than do average individuals working alone, and the choices that groups make will be more accurate and creative (Robbins, 2003). This is due to the higher levels of communication, coordination, and collaboration that occur within groups during the decision-making process (Nour & Yen, 1992). When groups are willing to challenge assumptions (which can involve more conflict), they will likely arrive at a better decision.

Four factors play an important part in a group's decision quality. First, the group should be diverse; members should have differences in experiences, individual knowledge, talents, skills, culture, and age (Butterfield & Bailey, 1996). Second, the members need to feel that they are in a safe environment to express their ideas freely; this will help the group avoid conformity and groupthink. This concept is often called psychological safety. Third, the degree of task interdependence must be high; if the task is too simple, members can solve the problem individually with no assistance from other members. Fourth, the group must have the potency for success; the members believe that the group can be effective (Shea & Guzzo, 1987).

Rational Decision-Making Processes

Peterson (1997) and Burn (2004) provide a seven-stage model that illustrates the process by which groups make decisions; see **Figure 17-2**:

- *Stage 1—Problem Definition*: The better informed the group members are, the better they are at formulating the problem or issue at hand. Clarity about the problem is necessary for a high-quality decision.
- *Stage 2—Identify Alternatives*: Groups sometimes limit and restrict options based on the ideas and perceptions of only a few members. Inclusivity and careful review of all available options expand problem-solving alternatives. Members sometimes believe that they must choose the first alternative for the sake of time or that they do not have all the relevant information.
- *Stage 3—Gather Information*: Information needs to be gathered about all possible consequences based on the identified alternatives. Groups often neglect to take the time to gather all relevant information and do not develop a process by which all members can contribute to gathering information.

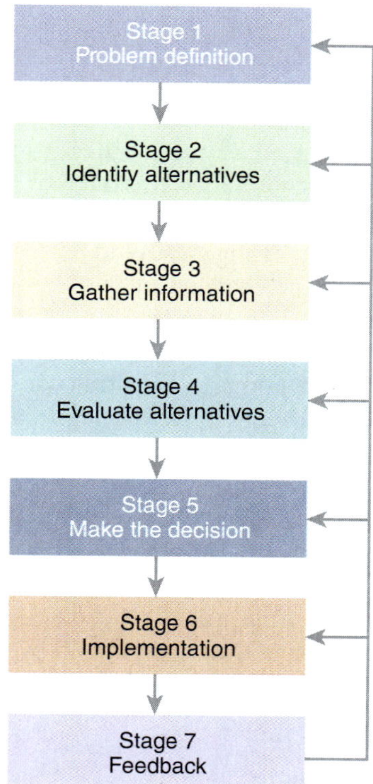

Figure 17-2 Group Decision Process Model

- *Stage 4—Evaluate Alternatives*: The group must objectively analyze all of the available alternatives and potential consequences. The challenges that emerge during this stage include developing processes to ensure that all information is reviewed, that higher-status members do not dominate, and that decisions are not made for any member's personal gain. Group members could choose the first available alternative that meets minimal standards and convince themselves and others that it is the most appropriate. Therefore, rational and objective criteria are needed to prevent flawed decisions.
- *Stage 5—Make the Decision*: The method by which the group chooses to make the decision is extremely important. Some members may try to control and bolster their own ideas without supportive evidence. Lower-status members might vote with higher-status members when the vote is by a show of hands; the vote might change drastically if there is a secret ballot.
- *Stage 6—Implementation*: The challenges at this stage involve resolving all of the tasks necessary to fully implement the decision, including identifying all of the needed resources.
- *Stage 7—Evaluate the Outcome:* After implementation, a step that is often disregarded is evaluating the outcome. Have processes been developed so that the decision group can measure the success or relevance of the outcome? Did the decision meet the goals and objectives? This critical inquiry is essential to learning from the experience.

A group's collective information processing takes time to develop. This may be due to members not being aware of the group's information resources or members being hesitant to provide information to the group. Some groups provide structured techniques so that every member participates equally, and positive interaction is encouraged. These strategies include brainstorming, the nominal group technique, and the Delphi technique.

Brainstorming

Brainstorming involves taking a designated amount of time (usually 5–7 minutes) to generate as many ideas as possible with no discussion of their feasibility or practicality. The originator of this technique (Osborn, 1957) believed that members' tendencies to judge and criticize other people's offerings deter members from freely expressing creative ideas. Osborn hypothesized that the more ideas a group developed, the greater the chance that the ideas would be of high quality. However, research does not support Osborn's hypothesis. Brainstorming groups do not produce more or higher-quality ideas than those that are generated individually (Mullen et al., 1991). Some factors that may reduce the performance of brainstorming groups include social loafing, apprehension about being judged by others, and the tendency for introverted people to withdraw when in the company of extroverted members, who may compete and try to dominate the brainstorming process. People also have a difficult time thinking and listening to others at the same time. Dennis (1996) contends that computer-based brainstorming, a technique in which group members interact electronically, often anonymously and simultaneously, eradicates interpersonal pressure. The advantages are that they are less likely to forget what they are sharing as they type; the written record of all contributions can be made available for all and at any time; and because of the anonymity, lower-status members do not feel the pressure of the evaluation of their contribution by other members.

Nominal Group Technique

The nominal group technique is a brainstorming technique that is implemented on an individual and nonverbal basis. The information obtained is then pooled. This technique allows the group to communicate without the risks involved in verbal communication. A typical five-step process begins with a period of silence, during which group members write down their ideas independently. A round-robin recording of ideas follows this. Third, the leader calls on each member to share one idea at a time and writes each idea down in view of the total group. Fourth, there is a group discussion of each idea on the list, and all ideas are clarified and evaluated. Fifth, the participants identify and privately rank their ideas in order of preference, then vote; the vote is recorded, the voting pattern is discussed, and the highest-ranked idea is discussed. The nominal group technique has been used extensively in business and government because of its efficiency and its capacity to limit emotional arguments.

The Delphi Technique

The Delphi technique is intended to help with the challenge faced by group members who may lack the experience to understand that the information they hold is needed to generate and evaluate options or alternatives. This technique uses a series of written communications to collect and synthesize the opinions of a group of experts into a decision. A carefully devised letter is sent to several experts to define the problem and ask them for possible solutions. The leader collects and collates the responses for each of the experts and sends them back to the experts for commentary and additional solutions. The leader collects the letters and analyzes them for consensus. If a clear consensus emerges, a decision can be made. If not, the process is repeated until consensus is achieved. This process can be time-consuming, and the same result may be achieved through a face-to-face meeting of experts.

Irrational Decision-Making Processes

The "Garbage Can" Decision-Making Process

Unlike the rational decision-making model described earlier, in which groups follow a step-by-step process to arrive at the best solution to a problem, the "garbage can" model of decision making is a process that does not begin with a problem and end with a solution. In this process, many types of independently generated problems and solutions are placed in a "garbage can" (see **Figure 17-3**). Managers and other participants then search through the "garbage can" looking for interesting, suitable, or important "problems" and "solutions" (Cohen et al., 1972; Lovata, 1987; Schmid et al., 1987). Although the "garbage can" decision-making approach is not very efficient, the process is appropriate for group decision making in organizations in which the technologies are not clear, the involvement of participants fluctuates in terms of the amount of time and effort given, and choices are inconsistent and not well defined (Cohen et al., 1972; Lovata, 1987; Schmid et al., 1987).

The "garbage can" model is often referred to as political or antirational because it disconnects problems, solutions, and decision makers from one another. Cohen et al. (1972) relate that specific decisions (i.e., choices) do not follow an orderly process from problem to solution but are outcomes of several relatively independent streams of events within the organization:

1. Problems identified in organizations usually require attention because there are performance gaps.
2. Solutions are ideas that have been identified to solve one or more problems, which are independent and distinct from the problems that they might be used to solve (e.g., in some cases, solutions are answers looking for a problem).

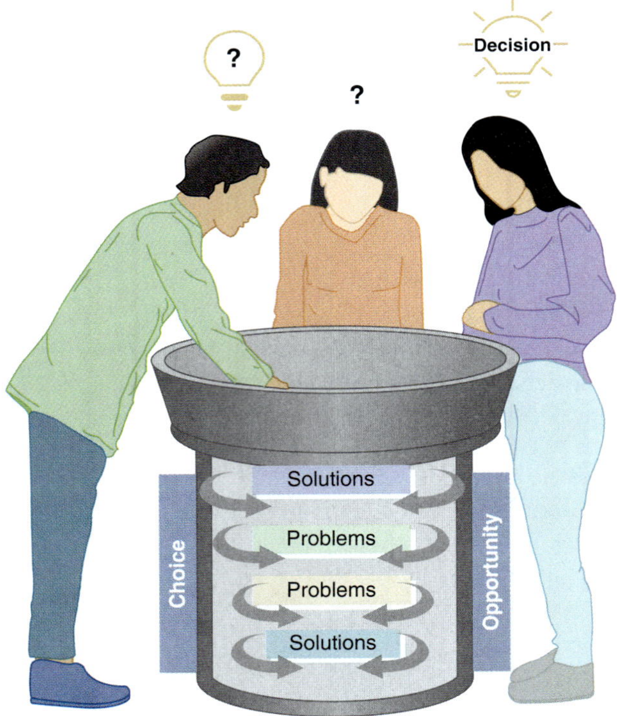

Figure 17-3 Illustration of Independent Streams of Events in the "Garbage Can" Model of Decision Making

Reproduced from Daft, R. L. (2004). Organization theory and design (8th ed.). Mason, OH: Thomson South-Western.

3. Participants come and go, and levels of participation vary for each problem and each solution, depending on the demands on participants' time or on other situational factors.
4. Choices are made only when the combination of problems, solutions, and participants allows the decision to happen (i.e., when they are in alignment).

Consequently, the alignment of the problems, solutions, and individuals often occurs after the opportunity to make a decision about a problem has passed, or it may occur even before the problem has been discovered (Cohen et al., 1972). The "garbage can" model provides a real-world representation of the nonrational manner in which decisions are often made in an organization. In a broad sense, the model provides some clue to understanding "how organizations survive when they do not know what they are doing" (Cohen et al., 1972).

Summary

Groups remain the context for most of our social and work activities. The powerful impact that groups have on people and the powerful influence that people have on groups merit our ongoing attention.

Discussion Questions

1. Discuss why the size of a group is important to performance.
2. Explain the different broad categories of groups.
3. Describe the difference between informal groups and formal groups.
4. Discuss the various task groups within an organization and their purposes.
5. Explain the five stages of group development.
6. Discuss the factors that may hinder the effectiveness of a group decision-making process.
7. Explain the seven stages of group decision making.
8. Describe the various methods for group decision making.

Exercise 17-1

Analyze the last poor decision made by a group of which you were a member. What do you think contributed to the group's poor decision? Did the group think of alternative possibilities? Did the group move too quickly through any of the development stages? If so, did this cause a lack of cooperation or poor communication?

Exercise 17-2

Form small groups of four or five individuals and, within 10 minutes, brainstorm as many solutions as possible that address the following situation:

> A small nonprofit organization for which you serve on the board of directors needs to raise $500,000 to support its programming needs.

After the exercise has been completed, personally reflect on the group interactions. Did you notice any factors that might have reduced the performance of the group (e.g., social loafing, apprehension of being criticized by others, dominant behavior by one or more members, etc.)?

References

Blackler, F., & Shimmin, S. (1984). *Applying psychology in organizations*. Methuen.

Burn, S. B. (2004). *Groups: Theory and practice*. Thompson Wadsworth.

Butterfield, J., & Bailey, J. J. (1996). Socially engineered groups in business curricula: An investigation of the effects of team composition on group output. *Journal of Business Education, 72*(2), 103–106.

Cohen, M. D., March, J. G., & Olsen, J. P. (1972). A garbage can model of organizational choice. *Administrative Science Quarterly, 17*(1), 1–25.

Daft, R. L. (2004). *Organizational theory and design* (8th ed.). Thomson South-Western.

Dennis, A. R. (1996). Information exchange and use in small group decision making. *Small Group Research, 27*(4), 532–551.

Hyman, H. H. (1942). The psychology of status. *Archives of Psychology, 269*, 5–91.

Hyman, H. H. (1968). Reference groups. In D. Sills (Ed.). *International encyclopedia of the social sciences* (Vol. 13, pp. 353–359). Macmillan and Free Press.

Krueger, D. L. (2013). Informal leaders and cultural change. American Nurse Today, 8(8). https://www.myamericannurse.com/informal-leaders-and-cultural-change/

Lovata, L. M. (1987). Behavioral theories relating to the design of information systems. *MIS Quarterly, 11*(2), 147–149.

Marion, R., Christiansen, J., Klar, H. W., Schreiber, C., & Erdener, M. A. (2016). Informal leadership, interaction, cliques, and productive capacity in organizations: A collectivist analysis. *The Leadership Quarterly, 27*(2), 242–260.

Mullen, B., Johnson, C., & Salas, E. (1991). Productivity loss in brainstorming groups: A meta-analytic integration. *Basic and Applied Social Psychology, 12*(1), 3–23.

Nour, M. A., & Yen, D. C. (1992). Group decision support systems: Towards a conceptual foundation. *Information & Management, 23*(2), 55–64.

Osborn, A. F. (1957). *Applied imagination*. Scribner.

Peterson, R. S. (1997). A directive leadership style in group decision making can be both virtue and vice: Evidence from elite and experimental groups. *Journal of Personality and Social Psychology, 72*(5), 1107–1121. https://doi.org/10.1037/0022-3514.72.5.1107

Robbins, S. P. (2003). *Organizational behavior* (10th ed.). Prentice Hall.

Schmid, H., Dodd, P., & Tropman, J. E. (1987). Board decision making in human service organizations. *Human Systems Management, 7*(2), 155–161.

Shea, G. P., & Guzzo, R. A. (1987). Group effectiveness: What really matters? *Sloan Management Review, 28*(3), 25–31.

Tubbs, S. L. (2001). *A systems approach to small group interaction*. McGraw-Hill.

CHAPTER 18

Work Teams and Team Building

LEARNING OUTCOMES

After completing this chapter, the student should be able to define the following:

- Difference between stable teams and teaming.
- Various types of teams.
- Differences between a virtual or hybrid team and conventional types of teams.
- Various approaches for building team performance.
- Various organizational barriers to effective team building.
- Common characteristics of successful teams.

Overview

What is the difference between groups and teams? Does a group of people who happen to be thrown together in a surgical suite or primary care office constitute a team? No, not all groups meet the definition of a team (see **Case Study 18-1**).

In general, groups are much broader than teams. Teams are special groups with highly defined tasks and roles that demonstrate high group commitment (Katzenbach & Smith, 1993). We begin this chapter by discussing teams. We then examine the various types of teams, their characteristics, and the factors that either promote or hinder their effectiveness.

Almost every organization uses some form of problem-solving team, the most common being the self-managing work teams found in most Fortune 1000 companies. Managers need to understand the complexity of teams in terms of their work design, the composition of the members, and the factors that enable teams to achieve high levels of performance and effectiveness.

CASE STUDY 18-1 Halloween in the Trauma Unit

Dr. Andrea Martinelli, a trauma surgeon, loathed working in the trauma surgery unit on Halloween, any holiday involving fireworks, or after a big win for the local college football team. Drunk drivers, burn victims, and shooting victims seemed to roll in at an unstoppable pace. Although she usually worked the day shift, she was required to take some night shifts. She checked in for her Halloween night shift at 6 p.m., and immediately the action started. "Dr. Martinelli, you've got a patient prepped and ready in Room 6. Major car accident, and he's bleeding out." As she walked into the room, Dr. Martinelli thought, "Who will I be working with this time?" She entered a room bustling with nurses, residents, a surgery fellow, two nursing students, a scrub tech, an anesthesiologist, and a nurse anesthetist, and she realized that she didn't know any of them. This was a large hospital, and because of different shift schedules and turnover, she rarely worked with the same configuration of people. She could tell that the patient was crashing fast. "Okay, everyone, I'm Dr. Martinelli. Let's get started."

Teams and Teaming

A team is a small group of people who are committed to a common purpose, possess complementary skills, and have agreed on specific performance goals for which the team members hold themselves mutually accountable (Katzenbach & Smith, 1993) (see **Case Study 18-2**). On the basis of this definition, a team (1) should be composed of a small number of members (preferably an odd number, such as five or seven) to encourage consensus without discord, (2) must have specific goals, and (3) must contain members with mutual accountability, requiring interdependence and collaboration of efforts (Gordon, 2002).

Many of the groups in health care do not fit neatly into the given definitions of either a group or a team. Recall that one of the defining elements of a group is a stable structure. According to this formal definition, a variety of strangers who are quickly assembled in an operating room, as in Case Study 18-1, does not qualify as a group. Health care is filled with examples of people coming together quickly for a specific purpose and then disbanding to form new configurations. These changes can occur daily, even hourly. For example, an anesthesiologist overseeing four surgical rooms will work with four different combinations of nurses, surgeons, technicians, residents, and students at any point during the day. Depending on the number of operating rooms in a hospital and staff turnover, it may be weeks or months before a particular configuration is repeated. Similarly, an oncologist, a doctor of internal medicine, a radiation oncologist, and a surgeon from another hospital may convene to determine the best path forward for a cancer patient. For the next patient, that oncologist may be working with a completely different set of specialists. What shall we call such a collection of people? A group? A team?

Amy Edmondson (2012) of Harvard Business School calls this phenomenon "teaming," which she defines as "teamwork on the fly." She argues that stable teams of people who work together over time can be highly effective, such as a basketball team that practices thousands of hours together and wins a national championship. However, the current reality is that healthcare teams are often more like players in a game of pickup basketball in the park. Edmondson suggests that stable teams are insufficient when companies face complex and uncertain tasks that need rapid resolution. Teaming can be highly effective because it allows the right experts from different

CASE STUDY 18-2 Kaiser Permanente Facilities Use TeamSTEPPS to Improve Obstetrics and Other Patient Care

A Well-Functioning Care Team

Implementing AHRQ's TeamSTEPPS® to improve teamwork and communication, Kaiser Permanente in Northern California reduced the dosage of labor-inducing drugs by approximately 15%, without increasing C-section rates, from 2015 to 2017. Kaiser trained its staff at 16 medical centers and a skilled nursing facility across the state. As a result, perinatal teams have successfully used TeamSTEPPS strategies to standardize and reduce variation in dosing of labor-inducing drugs.

TeamSTEPPS is an evidence-based, customizable program aimed at optimizing performance among teams of healthcare professionals, enabling them to respond quickly and effectively to whatever situations arise. AHRQ developed it in collaboration with the Department of Defense and launched it in 2006.

Initially, Kaiser's main focus was to train teams for three new hospitals prior to their opening and to "build TeamSTEPPS expertise at the regional risk management and patient safety department in Oakland to support the new teams," explained Celia Ryan, MSHA, RN, executive director of risk and patient safety. Officials were so pleased with the results that they expanded TeamSTEPPS implementation to training teams in emergency departments, operating rooms, and inpatient units in all of Kaiser's Northern California hospitals.

In total, 45 Kaiser teams have completed TeamSTEPPS "train the trainer" programs since 2014. Staff have been trained across a wide variety of units, including emergency departments, intensive care, coronary care, cardiac catheterization laboratories, neonatal intensive care, medical, surgery, telemetry, interventional radiology, environmental services, perioperative (including preoperative, operating room, and postanesthesia care), perinatal (labor and delivery, nursery, and the mother and baby), and skilled nursing units.

The perinatal teams at Kaiser commonly use the following TeamSTEPPS strategies:

- Huddle—An ad hoc meeting and planning session used to reinforce plans that are already in place. This allows for on-the-spot assessment and reassessment. Huddles are held daily with multidisciplinary teams comprised of obstetricians, certified nurse midwives, residents, registered nurses, anesthesiologists, and pediatric specialists who review the patient's status, any concerns about her condition or treatment, and fetal monitoring.
- Debrief—An after-action review or information-sharing session intended to improve team performance and effectiveness. Debriefs help identify and resolve concerns and address the timely acquisition of additional staff assistance when needed.
- SBAR—An acronym that stands for Situation, Background, Assessment, and Recommendation. This technique facilitates prompt and effective communication among staff. A "baby SBAR" is used to ensure situational awareness between the obstetrician and neonatal teams to establish the delivery approach and anticipate potential resuscitation needs.

"During times of high volume, huddles have improved workflows and situational awareness," said Paul Preston, M.D., staff anesthesiologist and safety educator for The Permanente Medical Group. "Debriefs have also been critically useful—specifically post-delivery and for real-time learning—and have contributed to improvements in the obstetrics hemorrhage team response and C-section decision-to-incision time," he noted.

Reproduced from Agency for Healthcare Research and Quality. (2018, April). *Kaiser Permanente facilities use TeamSTEPPS to improve obstetrics and other patient care.* https://www.ahrq.gov/news/newsroom/case-studies/201716.html

fields and disciplines to be assembled to accomplish a complex task. With industry changes and reforms, evolving diseases and treatments, and the explosion of new scientific knowledge, it is no surprise that health care is filled with examples of teaming.

Types of Teams

Cohen and Bailey (1997) determined that teams can be organized into the following four categories: (1) work teams, (2) parallel teams, (3) project teams, and (4) management teams.

- *Work teams* are continuing work units that are responsible for producing goods or providing services. Traditional work teams are directed by managers who make most of the decisions about what is done, how it is done, and who does it. However, an alternative form of work team with a variety of labels—self-managing, autonomous, semiautonomous, self-directing, empowered—is gaining favor. Self-managing work teams involve employees, not managers, deciding how to carry out tasks, allocating the work within the team, and making decisions. Examples include primary care, surgical, and emergency department teams (Taplin et al., 2013).
- *Parallel teams* draw members from different work units or jobs to perform functions that the regular organization is not equipped to perform well. They exist in parallel with the formal organizational structure. They generally have limited authority and can make recommendations only to individuals higher up in the organizational hierarchy. Parallel teams are used for problem-solving and improvement-oriented activities. Examples include quality improvement teams, employee resource groups, quality circles, and patient satisfaction task forces.
- *Project teams* are time-limited and produce one-time outputs. Examples include a new electronic health record implementation team or a new facility design and construction team. Project team tasks are typically nonrepetitive and involve considerable application of knowledge, judgment, and expertise. A project team's work may represent either an incremental improvement over an existing concept or a radically different new idea. Project teams often draw their members from different disciplines and functional units to apply specialized expertise to the project. For example, a new drug-development team of a pharmaceutical company would draw its members from research and development, marketing, finance, and manufacturing. When a project is completed, the members either return to their functional units or move on to the next project. Cross-functional project teams enhance project success as a result of their capacity to handle multiple activities simultaneously rather than sequentially. This saves time for organizations concerned with the rapid development of new services and products owing to competition.
- *Management teams* coordinate and provide direction to the subunits they are responsible for, laterally integrating interdependent subunits across key business processes. The management team is responsible for the overall performance of a business unit. Its authority stems from the hierarchical rank of its members. It includes the managers responsible for each subunit, such as vice presidents of nursing, compliance and security, finance, and medical affairs. At the top of the organization, the top management team establishes and manages the organization's strategic direction and performance. Management teams can help organizations achieve a competitive advantage by applying collective expertise, integrating disparate efforts, and sharing responsibility for organizational success.

Virtual and Hybrid Teams

The virtual team has emerged along with technological advances and was rapidly accelerated during the COVID-19 pandemic when nonclinical teams were forced to work remotely, and some clinical teams expanded their use of telemedicine in a remote setting. Unlike conventional teams, a virtual team works across space, time, and organizational boundaries using technology to facilitate communication and coordination. Virtual teams are also referred to as remote teams, due to their existence away from the organization's physical location. A hybrid team is one that includes both a virtual and in-person component. Outside of a purely clinical setting, it is rare today to find a team that does not do at least some of its work in a virtual setting. Virtual and hybrid teams are less common in health care than in some other industries because much of the work in health care requires being in the same location as the patient. However, there has been a growing trend toward virtual and hybrid work during and following the COVID-19 pandemic (Efimov et al., 2024; Kumar, 2024). In the healthcare and social assistance industry, it is reported that 59% of employees are fully on-site, 23% are hybrid, and 18% are fully remote (Barrero et al., 2025). As virtual and hybrid teams become more common, managers must be able to understand how to facilitate their performance and cohesion.

Organizations can benefit from virtual and hybrid teams through access to previously unavailable expertise and enhanced cross-functional interaction. By using virtual teams, organizations can assign the right person to the job, regardless of where the person lives. However, the dimension of physical distance between members does affect the way in which team members interact. Roebuck and Britt (2002) advise that for a virtual team to be successful, members must be firmly committed to the team's purpose and to each team member. They must want their collaborative work to be successful and be willing to go the extra mile. For example, Rush University Medical Center in Chicago implemented a pilot program known as Virtual Integrated Practice, in which primary care physicians recruit and organize their own off-site interdisciplinary teams consisting of social workers, dietitians, pharmacists, and other healthcare providers to manage and coordinate care for geriatric patients with chronic disease. These teams collaborate virtually, using email, phone, and fax to plan and deliver coordinated patient care. A comparison of four practices using the virtual integrated practice model to four similar practices that provided the usual care found that the virtual integrated practice program reduced emergency department visits, enhanced patient satisfaction and understanding of their medical condition(s) and medications, increased physician knowledge, and boosted referrals to interdisciplinary team members (Rothschild & Lapidos, 2009).

One issue that managers must consider when creating virtual teams is the possibility of social isolation. Gen Z reports the highest loneliness at 71%, followed by 65% of Millennials (Cigna, 2023). Social interaction with one's team at work can be a positive experience for employees. The workplace is often a place where people make friends, with 76% of Americans reporting that they have met at least one friend through work (Ballard, 2019). Therefore, managers must consider the well-being of virtual team members who may not benefit from social interaction in a traditional work setting.

Building Team Performance

Teamwork does not always come naturally to healthcare professionals; healthcare cultures too often emphasize autonomy and working within professional boundaries (Bartunek, 2011). Yet a lack of effective teamwork and communication among and between teams of caregivers can have serious consequences for patients' safety. To deliver safe and effective care, staff members in high-risk areas, such as emergency departments, intensive care units, labor and delivery units, and operating rooms must work as cohesive, high-functioning teams. A highly cohesive team will be more cooperative and effective in achieving the goals that they set for themselves (Oxford Centre, 2011). Daft and Marcic (2009) relate that members of a highly cohesive team focus on the process, not the person; respect one another; are fully committed to team decisions; and hold each member accountable to the team.

Katzenbach and Smith (1993) developed the team performance curve to illustrate how small groups may develop into high-performing teams (see **Figure 18-1**). Katzenbach and Smith (1993, p. 85) found that, "unlike teams, working groups rely on the sum of 'individual bests' for their performance. They pursue no collective work products requiring joint efforts. By choosing the team path instead of the working group, people commit to taking the risks of conflict, joint work products, and collective action necessary to build a common purpose, set goals, approach, and mutual accountability. People who call themselves teams but take no such risks are at best pseudoteams."

Although there is no guaranteed "how-to" recipe, Katzenbach and Smith (1993, pp. 119–127) list eight approaches to building team performance. These steps are most appropriately applied to stable or semi-stable teams:

1. *Establish Urgency and Direction*: All team members need to believe that the team has urgent and worthwhile purposes and want to know the expectations. The best team charters are clear enough to indicate performance expectations but flexible enough to allow teams to shape their own purpose, goals, and approach.
2. *Select Members on the Basis of Skills and Skill Potential, Not Personality*: Teams must have the complementary skills needed to do their jobs. Three categories of skills are relevant: (1) technical

Figure 18-1 The Team Performance Curve

Reproduced from Katzenbach, J. R., & Smith, D. K. (1993). *The Wisdom of Teams: Creating the High-Performance Organization.* Harvard Business School Press.

and functional, (2) problem-solving, and (3) interpersonal. The key issue for potential teams is striking the right balance between members who already possess the needed skill levels and those whose skill levels will develop after the team starts. Margerison and McCann (1989) have performed extensive research on the "people" side of successful team building. On the basis of studies incorporating over 5000 managers, they developed the Team Management Wheel, which assists managers in selecting the right balance for their teams regarding roles (advisers, explorers, organizers, and controllers) and linking skills (e.g., the main role of the team leader) (see **Exhibit 18-1** and **Figure 18-2**).

Exhibit 18-1 The Team Management Wheel

The Margerison–McCann Team Management Wheel defines members' roles and is based on the following eight characteristics:

1. *Reporter–Advisor*: Those who prefer work involving gathering and sharing of information. Supporters, helpers, collectors of information, knowledgeable, flexible.
2. *Creator-Innovator*: Those who prefer work that generates and encourages experiments with new ideas. Imaginative, creative, enjoy complexity, future-oriented.
3. *Explorer–Promoter*: Those who prefer work that involves investigation and presentation of new opportunities. Persuaders, influential and outgoing, easily bored.
4. *Assessor–Developer*: Those who prefer work that involves planning to ensure that ideas and opportunities are feasible in practice. Analytical and objective, idea developers, experimenters.
5. *Thruster–Organizer*: Those who prefer work that allows them to arrange and organize the way work is done. Results-oriented, analytical, organizers, and implementers.
6. *Concluder–Producer*: Those who prefer work that can be implemented systematically to produce regular outputs. Practical, production-oriented, like schedules and plans, value effective efficiency.
7. *Controller–Inspector*: Those who prefer work involving controlling and auditing procedures and systems. Controller, detail-oriented, inspectors of standards and procedures, low need for personal interaction.
8. *Upholder–Maintainer*: Those who prefer work that involves upholding and conserving processes and procedures. Conservative, loyal, supportive, strong sense of right and wrong, motivation based on purpose.

The hub of the Team Management Wheel is the Linker, and that is often the main role of the team leader, although it is important for all team members to contribute to this activity. The Linker circle can be expanded into a full-range team leadership model that describes three levels of Linking that should be practiced, to varying degrees, by everyone in an organization.

At the first level of Linking are the skills arranged around the outside of the model. These skills are the People Linking Skills. They create the atmosphere in which the team works, by promoting harmony and trust. Thus, everyone in a team has a responsibility to implement this level of leadership.

- Active Listening
- Communication
- Team Relationships
- Problem Solving and Counseling
- Participative Decision Making
- Interface Management

(continues)

Exhibit 18-1 The Team Management Wheel *(continued)*

Inside the People Linking Skills are the Task Linking Skills. These skills create a solid core or foundation on which the work of the team relies. They promote confidence and stability.

- Work Allocation
- Team Development
- Delegation
- Objectives Setting
- Quality Standards

These skills tend to apply more to people on the second rung of the leadership ladder—those in more senior positions in a team, responsible for guiding others. This guiding may be done in either a supportive or a directive way but should not violate the first level of People Linking Skills. The challenge is to find the balance at which the six People Linking Skills and five Task Linking Skills can coexist.

At the core of the Linking Skills Wheel are the two Leadership Linking Skills of Motivation and Strategy. Leadership Linking is the third step on the leadership ladder and applies to leaders who have organizational responsibility for strategy. They need to implement these two skills along with the People and Task Linking Skills to achieve the status of the Linker Leader, a term that is used to describe someone who is effective at implementing all three levels described in the Linking Skills Wheel.

Figure 18-2 Margerison–McCann Team Management Wheel

Reproduced from Margerison, C., & McCann, D. (n.d.). Margerison–McCann Team Management Wheel. Team Management Systems. https://www.teammanagementsystems.com. Reprinted with permission.

3. *Pay Attention to First Meetings and Actions*: Initial impressions always mean a great deal. When potential teams first gather, everyone alertly monitors the signals given by others to confirm, suspend, or dispel assumptions and concerns they have going in. They pay attention to the people in authority: the team leader and any executive who set up, oversee, or otherwise influence the team. What leaders do is more important than what they say.
4. *Set Some Clear Rules of Behavior*: All real teams develop rules of conduct to help them achieve their purpose and performance goals. The most critical early rules pertain to attendance ("no interruptions to take phone calls"), discussion ("nothing is off-limits"), confidentiality ("the only things to leave this room are what we agree will leave this room"), analytic approach ("facts are friendly"), end-product orientation ("everyone gets assignments and does them"), constructive confrontation ("no finger pointing"), and often the most important: contributions ("everyone does real work").
5. *Set and Seize upon a Few Immediate Performance-Oriented Tasks and Goals*: Most teams trace their advancement to key performance-oriented events that forge them into a cohesive group. Potential teams can set such events in motion by immediately establishing a few challenging yet achievable goals that can be reached early on.
6. *Challenge the Group Regularly with Fresh Facts and Information*: New information causes a potential team to redefine and enrich its understanding of the performance challenge, thereby helping the team to shape a common purpose, set clear goals, and improve on its common approach.
7. *Spend Lots of Time Together*: Common sense tells us that teams must spend a lot of time together, especially at the beginning. The time spent together must include both scheduled and unscheduled time. Creative insights and personal bonding require impromptu and casual interactions, which are just as important as time spent analyzing spreadsheets, interviewing customers, and so on. These meetings or interactions need not always be face-to-face. Use of technology is encouraged.
8. *Exploit the Power of Positive Feedback, Recognition, and Reward*: Positive reinforcement works well in a team context. There are many ways to recognize and reward team performance, of which direct compensation is only one. Ultimately, satisfaction in the team's performance becomes the most cherished reward. Until the goal is reached, however, team leaders must find other ways to recognize and reinforce individual and team contributions and commitment.

Recall that teaming usually involves a group of people who come together (often quickly) to solve a complex problem and then disband. Therefore, some of the steps listed by Katzenbach and Smith might not be possible when teaming takes place, such as spending lots of time together. Edmondson (2012) suggests behaviors necessary for successful teaming in **Table 18-1**.

Common Characteristics of Successful Teams

Hackman (2011) has studied teams for many years, and he has identified six enabling conditions for effectiveness. The team must (1) be real, (2) have a compelling purpose, (3) consist of the right members, (4) establish and follow clear norms of conduct, (5) work in a highly supportive context, and (6) receive well-timed team coaching. Elaine Biech, as cited by Gordon (2002, p. 184), outlines the 10 most commonly mentioned characteristics for successful teams:

- *Clear Goals*: Clear goals allow everyone to understand the function and purpose of the team.
- *Defined Roles*: Defined roles allow team members to understand why they are on the team and enable clear individual- and team-based goal setting.

Table 18-1 Behaviors of Successful Teaming

Behaviors of Successful Teaming	Description	Healthcare Examples
Emphasizing purpose	Define the purpose of the project or task and how it aligns with shared values.	Clinicians can unite under their shared value of doing what is best for the patient.
Building psychological safety	Create an environment in which it is expected that people can speak up and disagree without being punished. Exhibit curiosity, ask thoughtful questions, and demonstrate "situational humility," which is acknowledging that the project is complex, and we don't know all the answers.	The concept of shared governance in health care means that each member of the care team has shared responsibility in decision making for the patient (versus the outdated "Just do what the doctor says" mentality).
Embracing failure	Create an environment in which members know that failures are expected to occur, and it is okay to admit failure and ask for additional help.	A nonjudgmental mortality and morbidity (M&M) conference can be held to openly discuss clinical errors and develop solutions.
Putting conflict to work	Encouraging members to develop curiosity and inquire about different viewpoints instead of focusing on winning other people over to a certain point of view.	Doctors and nurses can listen to each other with a spirit of curiosity to avoid professional clashes.

Data from Edmondson, A. C. (2012). Teamwork on the fly. *Harvard Business Review, 90*(4), 72–80.

- *Open and Clear Communication*: Effective communication is considered the most important aspect of team building. It hinges on effective listening.
- *Effective Decision Making*: Effective decision making is critical, and for a decision to be effective, the team must be in agreement with the decision and must have reached agreement through a consensus-finding process.
- *Balanced Participation*: Balanced participation ensures that all members are fully engaged in the efforts of the team. Participation is also directly linked to leader behaviors. Effective team leaders should not see their role as authoritarian and should strive to be seen as the team's mentor or coach.
- *Valuing Diversity*: The team must recognize each member's expertise and value variety of knowledge, skills, perspectives, and abilities. In the world of teams, diversity consists of all elements of one's lived experience, background, and skills.
- *Managed Conflict*: Managed conflict requires that all team members feel safe to freely state their points of view without fear of reprisal. For teams, managed conflict is almost akin to brainstorming, in that conflict allows the team to openly discuss ideas and decide on common goals.
- *Positive Atmosphere*: A positive atmosphere requires a climate of trust. One way of developing trust is to allow team members to come together in a positive atmosphere. Allowing team members to become comfortable with one another will generate a positive atmosphere, leading to enhanced creativity and problem-solving.

- *Cooperative Relationships*: Cooperative relationships are a must, and team members should recognize that they need one another's knowledge and skill to complete the given task(s).
- *Participative Leadership*: Participative leadership includes having good leadership role models as well as leaders who are willing to share responsibility and recognition with the team.

Reflection and *appreciative inquiry* can be added to Biech's list of successful team characteristics. Teams should be encouraged to allocate time for reflection and debriefing on the results of their actions and decisions. Appreciative inquiry can help with this process by encouraging honest communication and analysis by the group (Drew & Coulson-Thomas, 1996). Appreciative inquiry encourages members to identify and reflect on periods of excellence and achievement. By looking at the past, members can develop a vision of what they want to accomplish in the future. They build on what worked best to reach their goal.

Barriers to Effective Teamwork

The barriers to effective teamwork fall into four categories: (1) lack of management support, (2) lack of resources, (3) lack of leadership, and (4) lack of training (see **Table 18-2**). If these barriers exist in an organization, the likelihood that groups would be given the opportunity to develop into high-performing teams is limited. Teams need management support, proper leadership, adequate resources, and training to reach their full potential.

Dunphy's (1996) research supports the idea that teams contribute significantly to the productivity and efficiency of organizations. In today's environment, hospitals and other healthcare

Table 18-2 Barriers to Effective Teamwork

Category	Description
Management	Lack of sufficient support and commitment from senior management
Management	Pressure for short-term results
Management and leadership	Political meddling and power politics
Management and leadership	Lack of trust among team members and with leadership (i.e., communication is closed and risk taking is not encouraged or rewarded)
Leadership	Lack of clear vision, goals, and objectives
Leadership	Unwillingness to allow teams the necessary autonomy and decision-making powers
Leadership	Poor communication and interpersonal skills
Leadership and resources	Failure to recognize and reward group efforts
Resources	Insufficient release time from other duties for team members
Training	Inadequate training and skills development
Training	Lack of project management skills

Data from Drew, S., & Coulson-Thomas, C. (1996). Transformation through teamwork: The path to the new organization? *Management Decision, 34*(1): 7–17.

providers are seeking innovative ways to reduce medical errors and costs while increasing quality of care and customer and employee satisfaction. Effective, high-performing teams can help accomplish these goals. However, team building is a process that takes time and resources. Management needs to invest today to reach tomorrow's goals.

Summary

In conclusion, Messmer (2004, pp. 13–14) provides an excellent guide to assist managers in the coordination of activities for building an effective team (see **Exhibit 18-2**).

Exhibit 18-2 Questions to Ask for Team Effectiveness

1. Planning and Purpose
   - Have I clearly defined the team's mission and primary objectives?
   - Have I identified the expertise and skill sets needed to achieve these goals?
   - Do I understand how long the team will be active and what the key deadlines are?
   - Have I clarified whether the team will generate ideas, implement solutions, or both?
   - Will the team operate independently or in coordination with other departments?
2. Project Readiness
   - Have I fully researched the impact this project will have on the organization's financial, operational, and human performance?
   - Am I prepared to explain the project's importance clearly at the first meeting?
   - Have I created a timeline, resource guide, or supporting materials to distribute?
3. Team Member Selection
   - Am I evaluating candidates based on both technical expertise and communication skills?
   - Have I consulted others for recommendations and reviewed each candidate's availability with their direct manager?
   - Have I selected a team coordinator to organize and share updates consistently?
4. Team Engagement and Structure
   - Have I planned an initial meeting to review goals, gather input, and confirm expectations?
   - Have I established protocols for conflict resolution, budget approvals, and decision-making processes?
   - Did I revise and share the final action plan based on team feedback?
5. Leadership and Support
   - Am I encouraging team members to solve problems independently rather than micromanaging?
   - Am I recognizing and supporting reasonable risks that lead to innovation?
   - Do I regularly check in on workload balance and make adjustments as needed?
6. Team Participation and Inclusion
   - Am I monitoring team dynamics to ensure inclusive participation during meetings?
   - Do quieter members feel encouraged to contribute alongside more vocal participants?
7. Motivation and Morale
   - Do I begin meetings by recognizing recent wins or progress?
   - Am I maintaining a positive tone, even during challenging periods?
   - Have I acknowledged project milestones and celebrated team successes?
8. Reflection and Strategy
   - Am I continually evaluating team performance and making improvements?
   - Have I aligned the team's work with broader organizational goals?
   - Is my leadership style helping the team stay focused, motivated, and collaborative?

Discussion Questions

1. Explain why teams and groups are not the same.
2. Describe the various types of teams that are used in today's organizations.
3. Explain the difference between a traditional work team and a self-managing work team.
4. Discuss the positive and negative issues of using a virtual or hybrid team rather than a conventional-type team.
5. Explain the difference between a working group and a high-performing team.
6. Explain the various approaches managers can use to build team performance.
7. Discuss the various organizational barriers to team effectiveness.
8. Are there other characteristics of a successful team that can be added to Biech's list?

Exercise 18-1

List and describe the types of teams that are most commonly found in your organization. What are the purposes of the teams?

Exercise 18-2

List the teams of which you are a member. Select one of these teams to analyze. Is it a high-performing team? If so, why is it? If not, why isn't it? What changes need to be made to increase the probability that it could become a high-performing team?

Exercise 18-3

Using recent news headlines, describe an example of teaming in which a group of people came together briefly to solve a complex problem.

References

Ballard, J. 2019. "Millennials Are the Loneliest Generation." YouGov. July 30, 2019. https://today.yougov.com/society/articles/24577-loneliness-friendship-new-friends-poll-survey

Barrero, J. M., Bloom, N., Buckman, S., & Davis, S. J. (2025). *Survey of Working Arrangements and Attitudes March 2025 updates*. https://wfhresearch.com/wp-content/uploads/2025/03/WFHResearch_updates_March2025.pdf

Bartunek, J. M. (2011). Intergroup relationships and quality improvement in healthcare. *BMJ Quality and Safety, 20*(Suppl. 1), i62–i66.

Browne, R. (2018, May 30). 70% of people globally work remotely at least once a week, study says. *CNBC*. https://www.cnbc.com/2018/05/30/70-percent-of-people-globally-work-remotely-at-least-once-a-week-iwg-study.html

Cigna Group. (2023). Vitality in America 2023 Report. https://filecache.mediaroom.com/mr5mr_thecignagroup/182356/FINAL_Vitality_Report.pdf

Cohen, S. G., & Bailey, D. E. (1997). What makes teams work: Group effectiveness research from the shop floor to the executive suite. *Journal of Management, 23*(3), 239–290.

Daft, R., & Marcic, D. (2009). *Understanding management* (6th ed.). Cengage Learning.

Drew, S., & Coulson-Thomas, C. (1996). Transformation through teamwork: The path to the new organization? *Management Decision, 34*(1): 7–17.

Dunphy, D. (1996). Organizational change in corporate settings. *Human Relations, 49*(5), 541–552.

Edmondson, A. C. (2012). Teamwork on the fly. *Harvard Business Review, 90*(4), 72–80.

Efimov, I., Harth, V., & Mache, S. (2024) "That was one of my most difficult and biggest challenges": Experiences, preconditions and preventive measures of health-oriented leadership in virtual teams—A qualitative study with virtual leaders. *BMC Public Health, 24*(1), 1338.

Gordon, J. (2002). A perspective on team building. *Journal of the American Academy of Business, Cambridge, 2*(1), 185–188.
Hackman, J. R. (2011). *Collaborative intelligence: Using teams to solve hard problems*. Berrett-Koehler Publishers.
Katzenbach, J. R., & Smith, D. K. (1993). *The wisdom of teams: Creating the high-performance organization*. Harvard Business School Press.
Kumar, R. (2024) Navigating remote work in medical: Strategies for enhancing virtual team collaboration and performance. *Indian Journal of Basic and Applied Medical Research, 13*(3), 31–40.
Lawler, E. E., III (1999). Employee involvement makes a difference. *Journal for Quality and Participation, 22*(5), 18–20.
Margerison, C., & McCann, D. (1989). Managing high-performance teams. *Training & Development Journal, 43*(11), 52–60.
Messmer, M. (2004). Project teams that get results. *Strategic Finance, 85*(8), 13–14.
Oxford Centre for Staff and Learning Development. (2011). *Characteristics of a group—Cohesiveness*. https://web.archive.org/web/20120603010018/https://www.brookes.ac.uk/services/ocsld/resources/small-group/sgt107.html
Roebuck, D. B., & Britt, A. C. (2002). Virtual teaming has come to stay—Guidelines and strategies for success. *Southern Business Review, 28*(1), 29–39.
Rothschild, S. K., & Lapidos, S. (2009, November 25). Virtual teams that coordinate care for chronically ill geriatric patients reduce emergency department visits and improve medication compliance, referral patterns, and patient outcomes. AHRQ Health Care Innovations Exchange. https://innovations.ahrq.gov/profiles/virtual-teams-coordinate-care-chronically-ill-geriatric-patients-reduce-emergency
Taplin, S. H., Foster, M. K., & Shortell, S. M. (2013). Organizational leadership for building effective health care teams. *Annals of Family Medicine, 11*(3), 279–281.

Other Suggested Readings

Biech, E. (Ed.). (2001). *The Pfeiffer book of successful team-building tools: Best of the annuals*. Jossey-Bass/Pfeiffer.
Wise, H., Beckhard, R., Rubin, I., & Kyte, A. L. (1974). *Making health teams work*. Ballinger Publishing Co.

PART VI

Managing Organizational Change

In Part VI, we explore planned organizational change and how it is managed at the micro-level. To lead organizational change effectively, a leader must apply all the theories and concepts discussed throughout this textbook. Success depends on the leader, or change agent, leveraging their knowledge of motivation, leadership, group dynamics, team building, and conflict management, along with strong communication and negotiation skills. In Chapter 19, we explain the concepts and theories related to change management and analyze how healthcare organizations can implement successful change initiatives.

In Section Two, Part VII, we shift our focus to the macro-level and discuss how organizations should be designed and structured to enhance their effectiveness and performance. These are key ideas for managers to consider when implementing change within their organizations.

CHAPTER 19

Managing Resistance to Change

This chapter discusses planned organizational change and how to manage it. To manage organizational change, a leader must apply all the theories and concepts discussed in this textbook so far. To succeed, the leader, or change agent, must use their knowledge of motivation, leadership, group dynamics, team building, conflict management, and communication and negotiation sk lls. This chapter describes the concepts and theories of change management and explores how healthcare organizations successfully implement their change initiatives.

LEARNING OUTCOMES

After completing this chapter, the student should be able to:

- Identify the drivers of change.
- Understand the various change models.
- Identify the various barriers to change.
- Understand the step-by-step change process.

Overview

Planned change arises from a single change or series of changes in organizational goals and objectives (e.g., increased patient satisfaction). These changes may originate from an organization revising its mission, creating a new vision, or responding to other internal or external forces. Unplanned change arises from the unexpected and impinges on the organization's well-be:ng. Unplanned changes occur because of sudden shifts in the industry, reduced demand for a product or service, the emergence of new therapies and treatments, cybersecurity breaches, changes in technology, depressed economic conditions, natural disasters, sudden policy and reimbursement changes, or pandemics.

Whether planned or unplanned, many changes within an organization will meet with resistance because, as Lippitt (1973, p. 3) noted, "change is a very complex phenomenon involving the multiplicity of man's motivations in both micro and macro systems and that a man gets satisfied with his equilibrium and is resistant to changing his status quo." Resistance to change is not limited to clinical or entry-level administrative staff. Resistance may also be expressed by middle managers, senior executives, and even board members. Therefore, it is a top priority for managers to understand the factors involved in change management. If managers understand these factors, they can increase employees' readiness for change, reducing resistance to organizational change.

Drivers of Change

Organizations function within three identifiable environments: external and social, industry and task, and internal (see **Figure 19-1**). The primary forces creating the need for change originate in an organization's external and industry environments. Change occurs as the organization attempts to respond to and adapt to these environments' new demands.

Today's organizations face many challenges. In the external and social environment, political polarization, global crises, pandemics, and changing regulations are affecting healthcare organizations in unprecedented ways. Economic forces include other countries' economic threats of inflation, deflation, recession, trade wars, and sanctions. Advances in technology and the rapid evolution of artificial intelligence are major forces affecting today's businesses.

Health care has always been a dynamic industry, but more so in the past two decades. New reimbursement models, escalating costs, funding uncertainty, an aging population, a pandemic, and changing regulations have resulted in an environment fraught with survival struggles. Rapid technological changes, persistent clinician burnout, and consolidation among healthcare systems and insurers have added to the challenges. In addition, the availability of accurate and inaccurate information online has changed how patients interact with the healthcare system and its providers. These external forces affect all organizations, directly impacting the healthcare industry/task

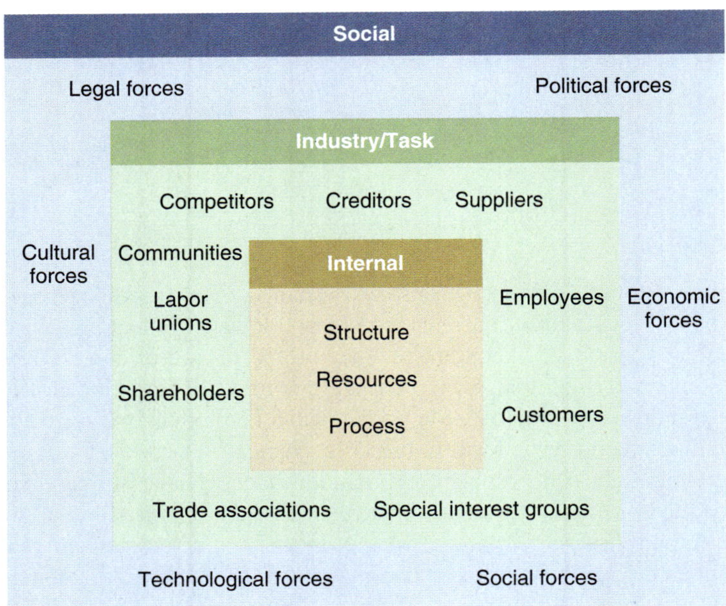

Figure 19-1 Environments

Data from Wheelen, T. L., Hunger, D., & Hunger, J. D. (1998). *Strategic management and business policy* (6th ed., p. 10). Addison-Wesley.

environment. For example, patients have become informed consumers of healthcare services' value and costs; cloning and gene modification capabilities have challenged an organization's ethical practices; special interest groups, such as insurance companies and pharmaceutical companies, have directly affected the way health services organizations do business; and technological advances in artificial intelligence, new drugs and treatments, telemedicine, and security breaches, have had far-reaching effects on the healthcare industry. With their ever-changing health policies and regulations, federal, state, and local governments have had a direct and significant impact on the industry, and the politicization of health care means that major swings can be felt industry-wide.

In addition to external forces, internal forces influence change within health services organizations. Internal forces are related to an organization's structure, processes, and resources. Because of the many external factors cited above, healthcare organizations are experiencing decreasing reimbursements and increasing costs, resulting in smaller profit margins. In addition, the organizations are being challenged to deliver patient-centered care with value-based outcomes. As a result, healthcare systems are considering and engaging in redesign to include more alignment and inclusion across systems (Fischer et al., 2009), such as vertically integrated models along the continuum of care, accountable care organizations, and joint ventures with insurers and employers. Whatever the reasons that create a need for change, management must develop and implement a planned response to ensure the organization's future effectiveness.

Resistance to Change

Although resistance to change is often deeply embedded in organizations, there are situations in which individuals will embrace change. This generally occurs when they perceive that the change will benefit them somehow. Kirkpatrick (2001) identified change outcomes that would cause individuals to react positively to change:

- *Security*—The change may increase demand for an individual's skill set.
- *Money*—The change may involve salary increases.
- *Authority*—The change may involve promotion.
- *Status/prestige*—There may be changes in titles, work assignments, and additional decision-making responsibilities.
- *Better working conditions*—The physical environment, including new equipment and updated technology, may change.
- *Self-satisfaction*—Individuals may feel a greater sense of achievement and challenge.

However, managers need to be aware that most organizational change efforts will be met with resistance. Resistance to change may arise from two sources: organizational barriers and individual barriers. Organizational barriers may include (1) lack of a change agent, (2) inadequate finances or capacity, (3) poor leadership, (4) resistance to change by senior management, (5) lack of necessary technology, (6) time restraints, or (7) poor market conditions. Overcoming organizational barriers to change may be beyond the manager's control and is usually a topic in a strategic management course. Because our concern is understanding the behavior-oriented change process, we will focus on understanding the individual's barriers or resistance to change.

Individuals' Barriers to Change

For individuals, resistance to change may involve affective, behavioral, and cognitive components (Palmer et al., 2009). The affective component relates to how an employee feels about the change, the cognitive component relates to how the employee thinks about the change, and the behavioral

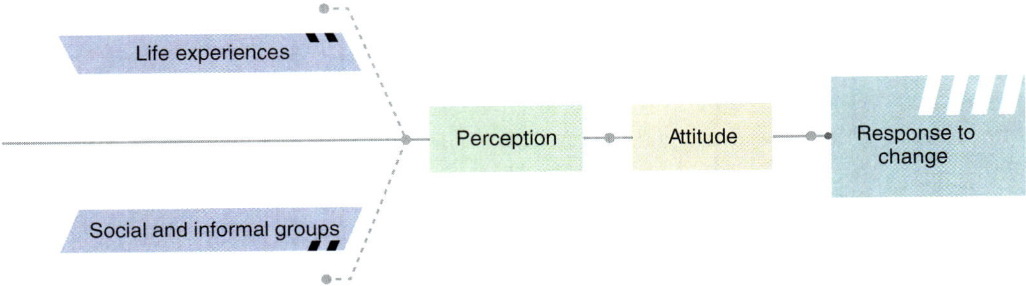

Figure 19-2 Model for Change

Data from MANAGEMENT AND MORALE by F. J. Roethlisberger, Cambridge, Mass.: Harvard University Press, Copyright © 1941 by the President and Fellows of Harvard College. Copyright © renewed 1969 by Fritz Jules Roethlisberger. Used by permission. All rights reserved.

component relates to what the employee does when confronted with the need to change (Palmer et al., 2009). For most individuals, contextual factors determine how they react (Bareil et al., 2007).

The results of the famous Hawthorne Studies showed that employees behave differently simply because they are being observed. Roethlisberger (1941) proposed that an individual's attitudes affect their response to change. In other words, how a person feels about a change determines their response. Feelings are not random. Feelings and/or attitudes toward an object are based on the collective experience of one's life; thus, different employees may be affected differently when faced with the exact change in the workplace.

As illustrated in **Figure 19-2**, Roethlisberger suggested that two primary forces influence an individual's perception, attitude, and response toward change. The first force consists of the worker's cumulative life experiences. The second, which functions within the formal organizational setting, is the influence of the social forces or informal groups. The identification of these social forces subsequently led to considerable research efforts in the area of group dynamics. These studies revealed the great potential for social forces to directly influence an individual's behavior and beliefs, which serve as the foundations for establishing or changing an attitude.

Employees may resist change as a result of many issues. Palmer et al. (2009, pp. 163–168) provide us with some of the commonly cited barriers:

- Discomfort with uncertainty
- Perceived adverse effects on interests
- Perceived breach of psychological contract
- Lack of clarity as to what is expected
- Excessive change

Discomfort with Uncertainty

Employees require a stable psychological condition in the workplace. When changes occur, professional and personal insecurity issues are kindled, primarily by a lack of knowledge and understanding of the changes and the official causes. Management's failure to provide realistic information promptly adds to employees' uncertainty. This uncertainty often results in lower morale, increased absenteeism, and reduced quality and quantity of output.

Perceived Negative Effects on Interests

Employees may lack an understanding of the likely effect of the change on their interests, which can relate to numerous factors, such as their level of authority, status, salary, autonomy, and job security. Employees find it easier to support changes that they perceive as nonthreatening to their interests and will resist those that are seen as damaging to these interests.

Perceived Breach of Psychological Contract

Employees form beliefs about the nature of the reciprocal relationships between them and their employers—that is, a "psychological contract." Change often disrupts employees' expectations. The employee–employer psychological contract becomes unbalanced as historical feelings of trust and perceptions of honest relationships become questionable.

Lack of Clarity as to What Is Expected

Resistance to change may result from management's failure to provide a clear message at the organizational level about the behavior expected of employees. As Gadiesh and Gilbert (2001, p. 74) noted, "A brilliant business strategy … is of little use unless people understand it well enough to apply it."

Excessive Change

Resistance to change can be characterized in two ways. The first form occurs when an organization is pursuing several change initiatives simultaneously, and employees perceive them as unrelated or in conflict. The second form occurs when the organization introduces numerous change projects before other changes have been completed, and employees feel that their resources (including their time) are being spread too thin, not allowing the initiatives to be effectively implemented. Such "waves of change" may cause employee initiative fatigue and burnout.

Creating and influencing readiness for change within an organization helps managers prevent or minimize the likelihood of resistance to change (Armenakis et al., 1993). Readiness for change refers to organization members' shared determination to implement a change (change commitment) and shared belief in their collective capability to do so (change efficacy) (Weiner, 2009). Armenakis et al. (1993) identified five elements for developing organizational readiness for change: (1) create a clear and compelling message for the need for change (discrepancy); (2) demonstrate that it is the right change (appropriateness); (3) ensure that employees demonstrate self-efficacy (i.e., confidence in skills and ability) supported by the required organizational infrastructure (i.e., technology, policies, procedures, managerial talent) for successful change implementation and continued sustainability (efficacy); (4) ensure that key leaders, both formal and informal, visibly support the change (principal support); and (5) help employees understand how the change benefits them (personal valence).

Lewin's Change Model

To fully understand the influence of group dynamics on an individual's attitude toward change, consider the work of Kurt Lewin (1947) and his model of Force Field Analysis. Lewin's model lets us view change as a series of forces working in different directions. In effect, forces and interests

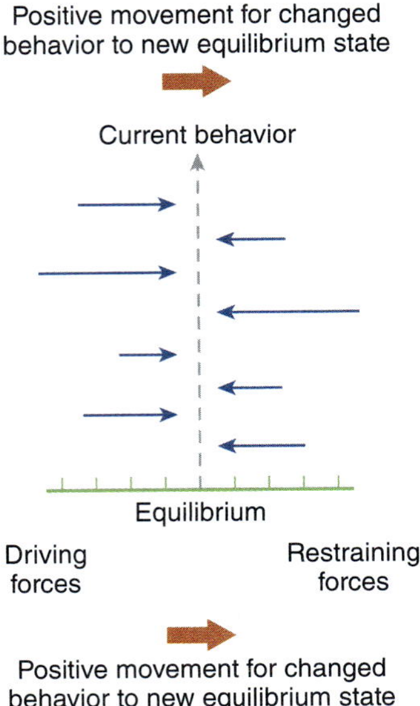

Figure 19-3 Lewin's Force Field Analysis

within an organization that push for change may be offset by forces and interests that strive to maintain the status quo (see **Figure 19-3**).

For change to be implemented, the strength of the forces for change (i.e., driving forces) must increase, and the strength and position of opposing forces (i.e., restraining forces) must be reduced or removed. Employing this model requires an improved managerial understanding of the external and internal environments. Identifying each force makes it possible to distinguish between forces and issues that may be changed and those that cannot.

According to Lewin (1947), change can be enacted in one of two ways: by increasing the force for change in the desired direction or reducing the strength of opposing forces. Borkowski and Allen's (2002) research on physicians' nonacceptance of clinical practice guidelines in their medical practice illustrates the application of Lewin's Force Field Analysis in the change process. Clinical practice guidelines are essential tools to reduce variances of medical services received by patients and improve the quality of care by establishing "best practices." As such, there is great concern about why these guidelines have been unsuccessful in significantly influencing physician practice patterns. Borkowski and Allen suggested that the driving forces for accepting and implementing clinical practice guidelines represented knowledge and attitudinal change and were viewed positively by physicians. In contrast, the restraining forces represented changes imposed by some external force that physicians resented viewed negatively; see **Table 19-1**.

When these forces or variances are understood, a realistic approach to planning change can be undertaken. As reflected in **Figure 19-4**, Lewin provides us with a three-step process for implementing planned change:

1. *Unfreeze*: Workers who actively resist change or a new initiative understand variances between current practices and behavior and desired activities and behavior. Using the clinical guidelines example, unfreezing may occur when managers effectively communicate the need for

Table 19-1 Suggested Driving and Restraining Forces Regarding Physicians' Acceptance of Clinical Practice Guidelines

Driving Forces	Restraining Forces
High-quality patient care (e.g., professional competence)	Administrative edicts (e.g., cost control)
Best practices (e.g., evidence-based findings)	Legislative mandates (e.g., laws and regulations)
Effective use of limited resources	Financial penalties and incentives
Good educational tools	Licensing and accreditation mechanisms
Convenient sources of advice	Utilization review

Data from Borkowski, N., & Allen, W. (2002). Using organizational behavior theories to manage clinical practice guideline implementation. *Journal of American Academy of Business, 1*(2), 365–370.

change (driving forces), such as mortality and morbidity rates, hospital readmission data, and best practices benchmarks.

2. *Change*: Based on new objectives, a series of revised policies, procedures, and operating practices is implemented. Members of the affected workforce must understand the reasons for change and participate in designing new approaches. Participating in the change design,

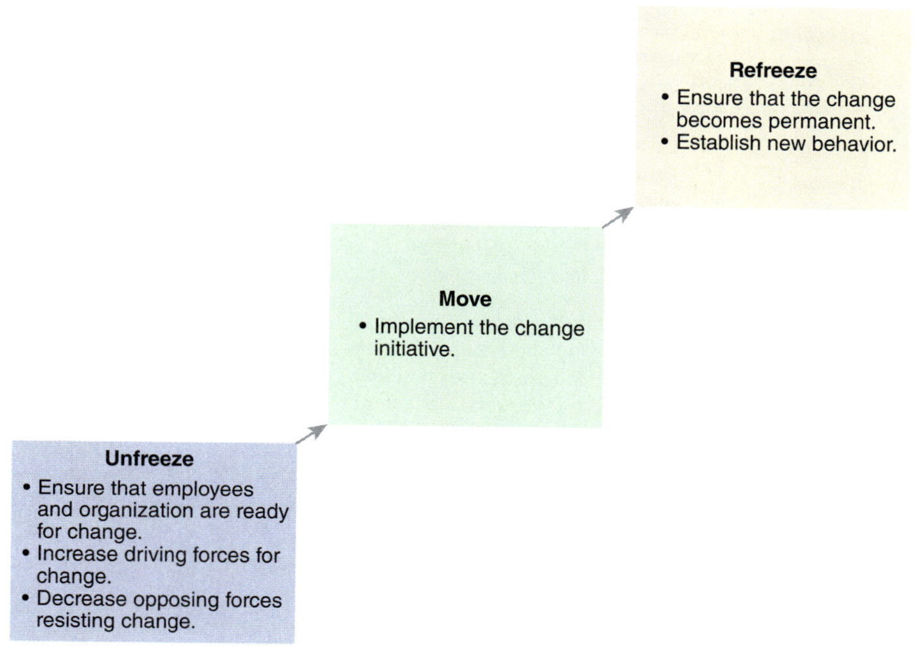

Figure 19-4 Lewin's Three-Step Change Process

followed by appropriate training and reorientation, allows workers to buy into the latest approaches. Physician participation (directly or indirectly) in developing a clinical practice guideline increases its acceptance, as measured by hospitals' reduced length of stay and inpatient costs (Borkowski & Allen, 2002).

3. *Refreezing*: Changes are implemented, monitored, and adjusted where necessary. Subsequent changes in daily activities reinforce new organizational goals. Continuous monitoring ensures successful operating practices. For example, an audit of and feedback on physicians' practice patterns is a familiar reinforcement managers use.

Based on Lewin's change model, Kotter (1995, 1996) identified eight steps for managers to follow for successful organizational change. The first four steps change the status quo (i.e., unfreezing), steps 5 through 7 introduce new policies (i.e., change), and step 8 institutionalizes the changes (i.e., refreezing). The eight steps, as described by Kotter and Cohen (2002), are listed in **Table 19-2**.

Table 19-2 Steps for Organizational Change

Lewin's Change Model—Kotter's 8 Steps for Successful Organizational Change	
Unfreeze	1. *Establish a Sense of Urgency*: The first step must be to unfreeze the organization's current state and establish a sense of urgency about the need for change (i.e., the desired new state). Managers need to increase the feeling of urgency (e.g., by discussing crises, potential crises, or significant opportunities) so that employees start telling each other that something must be done about the problems and opportunities. 2. *Create a Powerful Guiding Coalition*: Management needs to create a powerful guiding coalition. This group spans the organization's functions and levels (i.e., includes members not part of senior management). This requires pulling together the right people with the right characteristics and sufficient power to drive the change effort. 3. *Develop a Vision*: Management must create the right compelling vision to direct the change effort and assist the guiding team in developing a bold strategy for making the vision a reality. 4. *Communicate the Vision*: Management must use every vehicle possible to communicate the new vision and strategies, including teaching new behaviors by the example of the guiding team. Managers need to send transparent and credible messages about the direction of the change, using words, actions, and technology to open communication channels and overcome confusion and distrust.
Change	5. *Empower Others to Act on the Vision*: Management must eliminate barriers to change and encourage risk-taking and creative problem-solving. It must also change systems, structures, processes, and procedures that hinder employees from achieving the vision. 6. *Plan for and Create Short-Term Wins*: Management must plan for visible short-term performance improvements to diffuse cynicism, pessimism, and skepticism. In addition, employees who are involved in the upgrades must be recognized and rewarded. These strategies build momentum by "speaking" to what employees deeply care about. 7. *Consolidate Improvements and Produce More Change*: Management should use the credibility achieved by short-term wins to create more change. This may include hiring, promoting, and developing employees who can reinvigorate the change process with new projects and themes and assume change agent roles.

Lewin's Change Model—Steps for Successful Organizational Change	
Refreeze	8. *Institutionalize New Approaches*: Management must reinforce changes by highlighting connections between new behaviors and organizational success. Managers should use the employee orientation and promotions processes and the power of emotion to enhance new group norms and shared values.

Data from Kotter, J. P., & Cohen, D. S. (2002). *The heart of change*. Harvard Business Review Press.

Transformation of Health Care Organizations

Many healthcare entities implement change management to transform their organizations to deliver high-quality patient care. For example, Lukas, C. V. et al. (2007) examined 12 healthcare systems that either participated in the Robert Wood Johnson Foundation's Pursuing Perfection program or had reputations for long-standing commitments to improvement and high-quality care. The researchers identified five interactive elements as being critical for the successful transformation of a healthcare organization; see **Figure 19-5**.

1. *Strong impetus to change*: The impetus to change can be external or internal to the organization. In most cases, external pressure for change is the strongest impetus (e.g., regulatory, changes in reimbursement schemes).
2. *Leadership commitment to quality*: Leadership is critical for organizational transformation. Leaders must demonstrate authentic passion for and commitment to quality and steer the change through the organization's structures and processes to maintain urgency, set a consistent direction, reinforce expectations, and provide resources and accountability to support the change.
3. *Improvement initiatives that actively engage staff in meaningful problem solving*: Improvement initiatives must actively engage staff across disciplines and hierarchical levels in problem solving focused on objective, meaningful, urgent issues (e.g., eliminating never events and reducing unnecessary readmissions). These initiatives, such as clinical redesign and improved operations, must be built into routine new work practices that are visible, easier to perform, more reliable, and more efficient than old practices.
4. *Alignment to achieve consistency of organizational goals with resource allocation and actions at all levels of the organization*: Changes must be aligned with the organizational mission and strategic direction. Therefore, changes must be consistent with the organization's plans, processes, information technology, resource decisions, actions, results, and analysis to support key organization-wide goals.
5. *Integration to bridge traditional intraorganizational boundaries among individual components*: To succeed, change initiatives must be integrated across intraorganizational boundaries to improve coordination and continuity of care (e.g., patient flow, case management, electronic medical records). Extensive integration is needed to break down barriers between departmental silos so that the system operates as an entirely interconnected unit to support organization-wide goals.

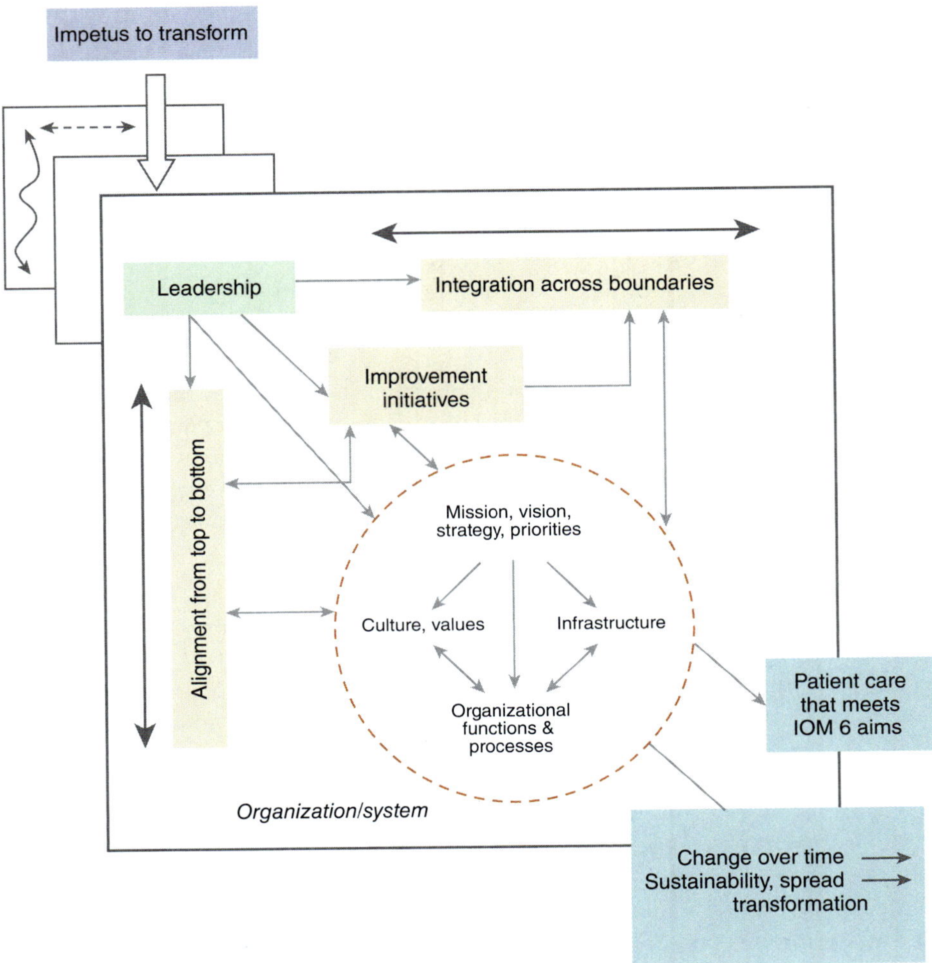

Figure 19-5 Key Elements of Organizational Transformation to Deliver High-Quality Patient Care

Reproduced from Lukas, C. V. D., Holmes, S. K., Cohen, A. B., Restuccia, J. D., Cramer, I. E., Shwartz, M., & Charns, M. P. (2007). Transformational change in health care systems: An organizational model. Health Care Management Review, 32(4), 309–320. Figure 1, p. 314. https://doi.org/10.1097/01.HMR.0000296785.29718.5d

Summary

The primary objective of change is to ensure the future competitive sustainability of an organization. The rationale and need for change arise from both external and internal forces. For successful implementation, managers need to recognize and appreciate employees' attitudes, considering the various organizational and individual barriers likely to create resistance to the required change. In addition, management should use a documented, step-by-step process that includes specific opportunities for feedback, evaluation, and adjustments. As Peter Senge (1990) advocates, organizations must develop the capacity to adapt and change continuously. Senge (1990) relates that organizations must learn to create attributes and implement practices that (1) dismiss old ways of thinking, (2) share ideas freely, (3) create an organizational vision, and (4) establish a collective effort to design a plan to achieve the vision. Becoming a continuously learning organization requires management to commit to change and develop an open organizational culture.

Discussion Questions

1. Identify and describe the drivers of change.
2. Explain the components of Roethlisberger's change model.
3. Explain the concept of Lewin's change model.
4. Identify and explain the various barriers to change.
5. Describe the steps used by managers in the change process.

Case Study

Case Study 19-1 Smyrna University Hospital Department of Internal Diseases: Finally Walking Side by Side

Smyrna University

Smyrna University (now referred to as Aegean University and Ege University Hospital) was founded as the fourth university of Turkey and the first university of the Aegean region, in accordance with the decision of the "Turkish Ministry of Education" under the law 6595 in May 1955. The rapidly growing university not only supported the well-educated workforce of the Aegean region, but also was the *only* research and education institution that contributed to the commercial, health, social, and cultural development of the Aegean region. Soon after the establishment of the Turkish Higher Education Council in 1981,[1] the university separated into two universities. While Smyrna University continued its academic activities under the same name, a new government university named September University[2] was founded in 1982. This new university was the second state university of the Aegean region and founded with faculties that transferred from Smyrna University.

Smyrna University has played a vital role in the establishment and development of new universities since 1982. The university played a fundamental role in education for the Aegean region and in 2001 it became the guarantor for the foundation of the first private university in Izmir. Today, Smyrna University represents Turkish universities in the "500 Leading Universities of

1 The Council of Higher Education was established in 1981. It is a fully autonomous supreme corporate public body responsible for the planning, coordination, governance, and supervision of higher education within the provisions set forth in the Constitution (Articles 130 and 131) and the Higher Education Law (Law No. 2547). It has no political or governmental affiliation. In 2024, there were 204 universities in Turkey, 79 of which have private foundation status.

2 September University (now referred to as Dokuz Eylül University) was founded on July 20, 1982. Seventeen previously established institutions of Smyrna University and various other higher education institutes were affiliated to the university in the same year. It reached 41 academic units by 1992 and has since expanded further.

World" and according to the evaluation of "University Ranking by Academic Performance," the university is the fifth leading educational institution in Turkey (http://www.hurriyetegitim.com/kurum/1004015144/izmir/onlisans-lisans/ege-universitesi.aspx).

Soon after its founding, Smyrna University started its first academic year (1955–1956) with 90 students. Today, more than 50,000 students are educated in 11 faculties, 8 institutes, 13 vocational schools, 1 state conservatory, and 26 research centers. There are more than 3,200 academicians and 4,000 administrative staff employed by the university.

Smyrna University Faculty of Medicine and Hospital

Smyrna University Faculty of Medicine[3] was one of the first two faculties of Smyrna University, and was founded in 1955. During its early years, education for fundamental sciences was conducted in several buildings, prefabs, and temporary structures around Bornova,[4] where other subunits of faculty, including internal diseases, child care, and chest diseases, conducted classes in buildings belonging to various hospitals around the city. In 1971, the university was moved to its permanent campus, which was located in Bornova, and since then Smyrna University Faculty of Medicine has maintained its academic, research, and healthcare activities on this campus. In 1981, the university restructured its academic activities as a result of Higher Education Law No. 2547.[5] With this new regulation, all departments of Smyrna University Faculty of Medicine were grouped under three major scientific divisions. Each division included major medical departments.

In addition to its academic activities as a medical school, the faculty has sustained healthcare services under the name of Smyrna University Faculty of Medicine Hospital. All of the academic staff in the university also work as physicians in the Smyrna University Faculty of Medicine Hospital. Therefore "Smyrna University Hospital" is often referred to as a "university hospital," with duties in excess of simply patient care, such as the following:

1. **Medical Education**: Training current and future doctors and resident physicians, and providing clinical education.
2. **Research Center**: Creating new knowledge through conducting basic science and clinical investigation.
3. **Patient Care**: Delivering comprehensive healthcare services to patients through one or more hospitals.

As a result of all these duties, Smyrna University Faculty of Medicine Hospital always keeps in step with recent developments in patient care and treatments. Today, the healthcare services operate in three different hospitals located throughout the campus:

1. Smyrna University Faculty of Medicine Children's Hospital
2. Smyrna University Faculty of Medicine Adult's Hospital
3. Smyrna University Faculty of Medicine Oncology (Cancer Care) Hospital

The future physicians who complete their theoretical "clinical education" are then tasked to work as interns in the university hospital. Those interns who choose to continue their careers in internal diseases will be the future members of Department of Internal Diseases (DID)[6] of the "Adult Hospital" of the university. The DID has been developing patient care services since 1958 and today operates in 4 different buildings located throughout the campus with 52 academic staff, 100 medical staff, 65 nurses, and 370 employees. The DID is the largest clinic of the hospital and, moreover, in terms of academic members, it would not be an exaggeration to compare the department with the other faculties of the university.

---

3 Symrna University Faculty of Medicine will be abbreviated as "faculty" for the rest of this case.

4 Bornova is one of the counties of Izmir, which is located very close to the city center.

5 Date of enactment: November 4, 1981. Published in the Turkish Official Gazette No: 17506; Date: November 6, 1981. For the full body of the act, see the official site of Turkish Official Gazette http://www.resmigazete.gov.tr/default.aspx and please refer to http://www.cepes.ro/services/pdf/Turkey3.pdf for the English translation.

6 The "Department of Internal Diseases" will be abbreviated as DID for the rest of this case.

Internal Diseases Department Needed a New Head, Early Elections, and an Unexpected Candidate: Prof. Dr. Selim

Since the establishment of the DID as a separate department in the Medical Sciences Division,[7] nine individuals were elected in succession for the head position. Prof. Dr. Selim acted as a vice head for the DID during the illness of the ninth head, Prof. Dr. Gurhun. Unfortunately, the illness was so serious that Selim's temporary agency position lasted for nearly a year. In that trial period, he found that he was ready to serve as permanent head and that there was much to be done in the DID. Acquiring the head position would enable him to impose his ethical codes on the DID team, including patients, nurses, residents, and medical staff. After the mourning period for Prof. Dr. Gurhun, Prof. Dr. Selim decided to stand as a candidate for the head of DID. However, he discovered that people were ready to protest and were not very pleased with his candidacy. There was one other candidate, but Selim won the race by a one-vote margin.

This large department had been managed by Prof. Dr. Selim since 2002. He felt at home there, having spent time in the DID as a physician, as an academician, as a manager, and all at once for most of the time. He had been working in the faculty since his graduation from the Smyrna University Faculty of Medicine in 1981. His admirable commitment to the faculty was not only because he had been a member of the faculty for 30 years but also because his father—as mayor of Izmir in 1955—had signed the foundation protocol and worked hard to establish the university in its early years.

Both the local and national press had started to talk about the changes in the DID of Smyrna University Hospital. What was happening there? In order to evaluate the antecedents and consequences of this change under the supervision of the new head, a meeting was arranged with Prof. Dr. Selim.

When the meeting started, it was nearly 7 p.m. Although a tired man was expected, who would not be able to interview for more than 30 minutes, Prof. Dr. Selim instead stood ready with an inspiring smile and full of vim and vigor. He greeted the interviewers with a warm handshake and made sure that everybody was comfortable in this hospitable room. The room was elegant and cozy, with one of the walls decorated with photos of previous department heads. He offered tea and cookies and gave permission to record the whole interview, which took nearly 2 hours.

As of 2011, Prof. Dr. Selim was in his third continuous term as DID's head. From the beginning he spent hours walking around the patient rooms, talking to them and listening as they poured out their grievances. He spent almost all his time at the hospital. He said, "We are more than physicians. The white coat we wear means treating all patients equally, regardless of their status, race, gender, and any other features." Patients were not his only concern; he also stayed in touch with students, academics, and medical and administrative staff of DID. It sometimes took him nearly an hour to reach his office from the other end of the "20 meters" corridor that leads to his own consulting room because on the way he answered any question directed to him, shook each hand offered, and listened to any problems without refusal. He stated that it was very important for him to be in touch with everybody around him, believing that he could learn important details about the department that might have been missed through formal communication. For example, in one of his long walks, Prof. Dr. Selim felt completely helpless about what he heard about a promising young lady: She had abandoned her medical education in her second year due to some financial problems. This event triggered Prof. Dr. Selim to establish a charitable fund in the faculty that supported the education of the poor students. With the voluntary contribution of the doctors, nearly 230 students had received scholarships from this fund in the last 10 years. However, each scholarship student must have worked for faculty where needed according to their academic programs and competencies. Some worked in the library, and some helped the administrative staff with new technology,

7 As mentioned in the text, the faculty was restructured under law number 2547 and all academic activities are grouped under three major divisions.

such as computers; thus, these students were aware that they received this scholarship in return for their efforts.

The Main Problems of the Department of Internal Diseases When Prof. Dr. Selim Acquired the Head Position

In the very early days of Prof. Dr. Selim's promotion as head, there were several problems to be addressed at the DID. The staff, even the doctors, avoided Prof. Dr. Selim, choosing to walk in the opposite direction when they saw him. By doing this, they rejected Prof. Dr. Selim's preferred communication channel, face to face. In addition, no one took accountability for what they did. The problems were all around, but nobody had attempted to fix them. Therefore, DID was unable to find solutions and fell into a vicious circle where the same problems emerged repeatedly.

On the other hand, everybody complained to one another about a variety of problems at DID. Whether from habit or not, nurses, employees, and doctors—thus, nearly all members of DID—were complaining about one another. Some were for trivial reasons, but some were destructive to their relationship, such that personnel were criticizing and comparing the working hours, attendance periods, reward systems, promotions, etc. Academic promotion of some physicians had been delayed for years for personal reasons in the department. Although the procedures and requirements for promotions must follow faculty laws and regulations, these rules are ignored in most of the cases. However, according to Prof. Dr. Selim, any kind of academic appellation could not be under the control of one person; rather, it depended on the merit of that person who decisively worked hard for it. Thus, the academic promotion of doctors could not be directed by personal closeness to the head, or value attributed to their "surnames" by the society.

Another challenge faced by Prof. Dr. Selim was financing the department. The Turkish government allocated a determined amount of funding for hospitals. Each hospital then allocated those funds among departments. However, the financial funds that had been designated to DID had never been sufficient to maintain Prof. Dr. Selim's ideal department. The overall physical structure of the DID was not sufficient to satisfy contemporary health services. The patient rooms were inadequate to meet the moderate hospitalization services, and the equipment supplied to the administrative and academic staff was so limited that it even slowed down the daily routine of the department. The assistant doctors, doctors, and nurses were not allowed to use the printers in the department to print their educational materials, such as academic papers, due to the limited amount of paper supplied to DID. They could only use this paper for routine administrative activities and for patient reports.

The Consequences of Management Alteration and Leadership Style: Things Started to Change at DID

This section summarizes significant phrases from the interview with Prof. Dr. Selim that highlights the work he did at the Department of Internal Diseases.

The professor's one-year agency appointment was a great opportunity for him to draw up his road map. During this period, he saw the deficiencies of the department. Prof. Dr. Selim's main concern was to make radical changes in the department when he decided to be a candidate for the head position as the overall management principles were not overlapping with his working and ethical principles. As soon as the professor became the head of DID, his main concern was highlighting the deficiencies of the current state. Organizational members were no longer seen as negative factors; rather they were the solution centers. Prof. Dr. Selim, as the new role model, was fair, hardworking, devoted, and openminded, and he started to inspire the whole department. The winds of change started to be felt at all levels of the department. At the end of his first year as head, the number of complaint petitions started to decrease, and in the last 9 years no petitions were forwarded to the head of DID. As mentioned previously, for some of the academic promotions, the faculty laws and regulations were ruled out; however, during those 9 years no one lost any academic promotion due to a conflict of interest or personal reasons.

Members started to feel free to visit the head office whenever something went wrong within the DID, knowing that the door was always open to them with a genuine listener behind it. Prof. Dr. Selim allowed the organizational members to take active roles in decision-making processes and kept communication channels open all the time. He aimed to raise the awareness of organizational members about improper applications. Therefore, members of DID were ready to take responsibility for their mistakes, believing that problems needed a solution for the well-being and success of DID. At last they were walking side by side in the corridors. The best example of the positive effects in the DID could easily have been interpreted from the latest newspaper account, entitled "Halil Ibrahim Library Lends Books to Patients in DID at Smyrna University Hospital." An employee named Halil Ibrahim was distributing books to patients in DID at the end of working hours from his "mobile library." He had worked as a janitor in DID for 15 years when Prof. Dr. Selim became head of the department. He had tried to distribute books and newspapers to patients in the past, but he could not continue due to his limited income. Soon after he shared his idea with Prof. Dr. Selim, he was given a book cart where he could place books and walk around the corridors easily. Prof. Dr. Selim also started a second-hand book campaign for the Halil Ibrahim Mobile Library. With this campaign, nurses, doctors, academicians, and even patient relatives brought books to him. There was no such service in any other department of the faculty or in any other private or public hospital around Izmir. All these examples were major indicators of the multidimensional effects of all staff, from the head to janitor, on the development of organizations with effective projects and valuable staff contributions.

Soon after he started to work as the head, Prof. Dr. Selim began to look for new financial resources for the department, although it was not his area of responsibility. The initial funds raised were used to meet the daily administrative needs of the department. Thus, for example, scarcity of paper for both assistants and administrative staff was no longer a problem for the department.

As mentioned before, in DID, the patient rooms had not been meeting the requirements of modern physical health conditions, with 6–8 beds in less than 20 square meters and a communal toilet on each floor. In fact, this is the leading problem of the Turkish healthcare sector. As of 2007, in Turkey, the total number of doctors per 100,000 people is only 123; this number is 567 in Italy, 330 in France, and 287 in Armenia. On the other hand, the total number of patient beds per 10,000 people is 28 (https://www.ceicdata.com/en/turkey/health-statistics/tr-hospital-beds-per-1000-people) (http://www.biyoetik.org.tr/files/hekim%20sayisi%20yetersiz%20mi.pdf:19.09.2011), which means that in Turkey the attainability and fair distribution of healthcare services were very limited. The need for beds for patients was a larger problem for university hospitals, where nearly 60–70% of all teaching hospital patients entered because of serious illnesses that required long-term treatment (Yiğit & Ağirbaş, 2004). Therefore, in order to increase the number of patients treated, the hospital administration preferred to increase the number of patient beds per room. However, on the other hand, this increase decreased the quality of healthcare services supplied to patients. As mentioned previously, Smyrna Hospital was one of those university hospitals that experienced a similar patient bed problem because of the huge gap between supply and demand of healthcare services in Turkey. The solution found for rooms has been the leading contribution of Prof. Dr. Selim to both DID and the Faculty of Medicine. Prof. Dr. Selim's offer for two-bed patient rooms with air conditioning and a private toilet had initially increased the tension in the academic committee in those days when the general belief was to hospitalize as many patients as possible regardless of the number of nurses and health conditions. In Turkey, the majority of the hospitals tried to increase the number of patients treated and, therefore, regardless of the insufficient healthcare services due to the inadequate number of doctors and nurses they employed, they chronically invested in increasing the number of beds. However, Prof. Dr. Selim interpreted that, "I always believe the number of nurses is the main determinant of the number of patients as each person deserves the best condition for hospitalizing."

With the help of donations and different sources of financial aid, DID started to make modifications in patient rooms. At each stage of the construction, the professor had asked for the assistance of end users of these modifications. During the construction of new patient rooms, he always collaborated with the organizational members, knowing that they were the ones who would work under renewed conditions.

For example, for the location, ergonomics, and decoration of nursing centers, he held long discussions with the nurses and modified the existing centers according to the feedback he received from them. Soon after they had started to renovate the patient rooms, the microbiology department complained to the dean about the modification, accusing the DID of causing infection in hospitalized patients. The unavoidable fallout of such modifications, like the smell and dust, and chemicals, such as paints and polishes, were impacting the hygiene of the entire building where DID operated. Prof. Dr. Selim stated, "I am sure that they were all right about their complaints. Although we have taken all the necessary precautions, the dust and the noise spread around had bothered the other departments. Especially the microbiology department was very sensitive to it, as they were operating on the ground floor of our building." The dean, who considered Prof. Dr. Selim's arguments to be reasonable, had not taken any legal action about the complaints of the microbiology department, and the renovation continued. This was the very best proof of the administrative support given to Prof. Dr. Selim for his longstanding efforts to transform DID into an enhanced place for both patients and healthcare staff.

The hospital administration assigned additional rooms for DID in the existing building. However, all these rooms needed similar modifications. As mentioned before, due to insufficient financial resources, DID had to raise its own funds for the modification of these rooms. This time the required funding was more than the hospital could support individually; therefore, Prof. Dr. Selim spoke to the rector about his ideas and got the permission to take this subject to the Izmir representative of the governing political party. By chance, the Izmir representative was trying to contact Prof. Dr. Selim for a health problem at that time, and he promised to help him, although due to his heavy schedule he was not able to head the fundraising drive himself. Prof. Dr. Selim continued to search for other sources of donations and contracted two of Izmir's philanthropic families. Both agreed to help Prof. Dr. Selim and did more than they promised to do at the very beginning of the project. One of these families committed to helping him just because Dr. Ali Selim, Prof. Dr. Selim's father, was a person whom the family admired. Prof. Dr. Selim added, "There again I felt the admirable inheritance I took over from my father. Thank god I had those wonderful traces and the powerful shadow of my father in my life." So the modification of patient rooms was completed, and ever since DID has operated on two floors with facilities that best suit proper health conditions and the demands of patients.

> . . . then the rooms were ready to meet the proper health conditions. Thus, there was no doubt that we made a successful change! But it was just the beginning and unfortunately the easiest part of an organizational change. I am very sure that all those changes might turn out to be a waste of time, energy, and money if the staff would not appreciate the things done in the department. That was the newest and the most difficult problem of our department that I had experienced. When I acquired the head position I also acquired the team that I have been working with. They were sharing the vision and principles of the previous head and they were far away from adopting my principles and sharing my desire for change.

As stated previously, in Turkey, in governmental bodies, when you acquire a position you also acquire the staff. Thus, the managers were not involved in the decision process of hiring and selecting the people they were going to work with. Rather, they had to work with selected employees before they had been promoted to that position, and furthermore they had to choose among candidates that were sent to them whenever a position must be filled. However, Prof. Dr. Selim believed that sustainable development could only be achieved if and only if the new structure of the DID was internalized by all members of the department. So he kept in touch with the organizational members all the time, listened to them, and tried to be a solution partner for problems in DID.

Despite the insufficient HR policies discussed, the head nurse, Alaz, was his instant counselor and best supporter during those hard days. He vaguely recalled their first meeting and how he tested her personality and compatibility with his ethical codes.

> There was no doubt that Alaz was a very young "head nurse"; however, she was the

one whom I was looking for. The smile on her face and the light in her eyes gave me an instant impression of an honest personality. Her wide sense of perspective under different circumstances and sense of justice soon justified my first thoughts about her.

The harmony between them had triggered Prof. Dr. Selim to think of transferring daily routine business to the control of the head nurse. From then on, only strategic projects and complex problems related to DID were discussed with the DID's head. DID was no longer a place where "the head orders and the rest obeys." Prof. Dr. Selim said:

> Her existence in the head nurse position made me feel comfortable because from the "director's chair" things might have been blurred or you saw them only from the point that they were shown to you. Soon after I delegated the leading of a reasonable amount of daily routines to Alaz, I realized that by doing this I was both indirectly kept in touch with the nurses and their problems, and caught any detail that may have been missed if I had worked alone. Finally, I have created an organizational climate of my dreams that was very supportive and open to new ideas for better conditions.

Prof. Dr. Selim was not only executing the administrative duties; rather he was a full-time physician and an academician. He carefully considered university education and its major objectives. Education could be achieved through transferring knowledge, encouraging the students by developing their competencies, and enlightening the exact nature of attitudes and behaviors. The first two could easily be done by words, but the latter could only be achieved by example.

The following quotation from the interview proved that Prof. Dr. Selim supported the opinion mentioned above:

> Today we are living in the age of technology, where everybody could easily access knowledge. So, successful educators or managers helped their followers to use the knowledge and transfer it into competencies that distinguished them from others. I have been working very hard to make DID a better place for all stakeholders. We renovated the rooms, redesigned the job descriptions, reorganized the working conditions, and reapplied the rules and principles of the hospital. The best thing about all those changes is that, this team is ready to survive in this new system. Thus if I leave the position today, without any question, they will allow the sustainability of "new DID." This is not because I established a perfect system; rather it is all about the cooperation and coordination. My major role during this great transition was distributing justice and sustaining the fair progress of the change. Today, I am very pleased with the atmosphere we finally achieved. However, I now started to think that there is a life outside the walls of this clinic, which is very precious. I have been devoted myself to DID but doing this caused me to miss the life out there.

Discussion Questions

1. Using Lewin's Force Field Analysis, illustrate the change process in DID.
2. Analyze the change process of DID according to the most appropriate model(s) of a Planned Organizational Change, giving examples from the case.
3. According to John Kotter, there are eight pitfalls to be avoided for the success of a change program. Discuss whether Prof. Dr. Selim made any of these mistakes, supporting your answer with examples from the case.
4. Discuss the leadership practices of Prof. Dr. Selim during the change process of DID. Which leadership theory (theories) do you think best describe(s) his leadership style?
5. According to the major concerns and definitions of an organizational change process, what may happen to DID if Prof. Dr. Selim is not a candidate in the coming election?

Data from Borkowski, N., & Deckard, G. (2014). Case studies in organizational behavior and theory for health care. Jones & Bartlett Learning.

References

Armenakis, A. A., Harris, S. G., & Mossholder, K. W. (1993). Creating readiness for organizational change. *Human Relations, 46*(6), 681–704.

Bareil, C., Savoie, A., & Meunier, C. (2007). Patterns of discomfort with organizational change. *Journal of Change Management, 7*(1), 13–20.

Borkowski, N., & Allen, W. (2002). Using organizational behavior theories to manage clinical practice guideline implementation. *Journal of the American Academy of Business, 1*(2), 365–370.

Fischer, E., Berwick, D., & Davis, K. (2009). Achieving health care reform: How physicians can help. *New England Journal of Medicine, 360*(24), 2495–2497.

Gadiesh, O., & Gilbert, J. L. (2001). Transforming corner-office strategy into frontline action. *Harvard Business Review, 79*(5), 73–79.

Kirkpatrick, D. L. (2001). *Managing change effectively: Approaches, methods, and case examples*. Routledge.

Kotter, J. P. (1995). Leading change: Why transformation efforts fail. *Harvard Business Review, 73*(2), 59–67.

Kotter, J. P. (1996). *Leading change*. Harvard Business School Press.

Kotter, J. P., & Cohen, D. S. (2002). *The heart of change*. Harvard Business Review Press.

Lewin, K. (1947). Frontiers in group dynamics. *Human Relations, 1*(1), 5–41.

Lippitt, G. L. (1973). *Visualizing change: Model building and the change process*. University Associates.

Lukas, C. V., Holmes, S. K., Cohen, A. B., Restuccia, J., Cramer, I. E., Shwartz, M., & Charns, M. P. (2007). Transformational change in health care systems: An organizational model. *Health Care Management Review, 32*(4), 309–320.

Palmer, I., Dunford, R., & Akin, G. (2009). *Managing organizational change: A multiple perspective approach*. McGraw-Hill Irwin.

Roethlisberger, F. J. (1941). *Management and morale*. Harvard University Press.

Senge, P. M. (1990). *The fifth discipline*. Doubleday.

Weiner, B. J. (2009). A theory of organizational readiness for change. *Implementation Science, 4*, 67. doi:10.1186/1748-5908-4-67

Wheelen, T. L., Hunger, D., & Hunger, J. D. (1998). *Strategic management and business policy* (6th ed.). Addison-Wesley.

Other Suggested Readings

Bardwick, J. M. (1991). *Danger in the comfort zone*. AMACOM.

Burke, W. W. (1987). *Organization development: A normative view*. Addison-Wesley.

Lewin, K. (1951). *Field theory in social science*. Harper & Row.

Mone, M. A., McKinley, W., & Barker III. V. L. (1998). Organizational decline and innovation: A contingency framework. *Academy of Management Review, 23*(1), 115–132.

Riggio, R. E. (2003). *Introduction to industrial/organizational psychology* (4th ed.). Prentice Hall.

Sheehy, G. (1995). *New passages: Mapping your life across time*. Random House.

Tomasko, R. M. (1987). *Downsizing*. AMACOM.

Zand, D. E. (1995). Force field analysis. In N. Nicholson (Ed.), *Blackwell encyclopedic dictionary of organizational behavior*. Blackwell.

SECTION TWO

Macro Level—"The Organization"

PART VII

Organization Theory and Design

Part VII includes four related topics. In Chapter 20, the history of organization theory is discussed, as is the importance of developing a learning organization. Chapter 21 describes an organization's choices that define how it relates to the external environment. The chapter examines the numerous issues associated with organizational strategy and how it relates to an entity's structure. Chapter 22 describes the contextual factors a manager must consider regarding how the organization is structured to ensure it can successfully interact with the environment. Chapter 23 discusses the internal characteristics of the organization that make up the structural dimension. The structural dimension's various elements determine how an organization's multiple parts will be organized to coordinate and control the entity's activities. What we learn from these four chapters is that organizational structures are a result of the influence of multiple factors, and that they have an important impact on an organization's effectiveness and performance.

CHAPTER 20

Overview and History of Organization Theory

LEARNING OUTCOMES

After completing this chapter, the student should be able to understand:

- The definition of organization theory.
- The definition of an organization.
- The components of an organization's formal structure.
- The factors that determine the stability and uncertainty of an organization's environment.
- The importance of the classic management theorists regarding the development of organization theory.
- The difference between closed and open systems.
- What is meant by the term *learning organization*.

Overview

Organization theory (OT) is commonly referred to as the study of the behavior and nature of organizations in their environments. Although OT emerged from sociology, economics, political science, and psychology, similar to organizational behavior (OB), its focus is the organization as a whole. In other words, OT relates to the macro-level study of organizations versus the micro-level focus of OB, the study of individual and group behaviors in the workplace.

An organization may be defined as a collection of people working together (i.e., social entity) under a defined structure to achieve predetermined outcomes through coordinated activities (i.e., processes). Organization theory addresses the many issues associated with an organization's design and structure. Organization design may be viewed as the formal arrangement of departments, divisions, functions, and people interacting and linked together within an entity. As such, the concept of organization design is creating the structure and developing the relationships to achieve an organization's goals (Kast & Rosenzweig, 1985). Structure is the result of the design process, which is reflected by the clustering of these various departments and divisions, to coordinate and control activities (and people) to obtain the organization's goals. Kast and Rosenzweig (1985, p. 234) define an organization's formal structure as follows:

- The pattern of formal relationships and duties—the organizational chart plus job descriptions.
- How the various activities or tasks are assigned to different departments or people in the organization (differentiation).
- How these separate activities or tasks are coordinated (integration).
- The organization's power, status, and hierarchical relationships (authority system).
- The planned and formalized policies, procedures, and controls that guide the activities and relationships of people in the organization (administrative system).

The formal structure of a company is reflected by its organizational chart, which reveals its complexity. The complexity of an organization's structure is related to many factors. For example, the more differentiated and diverse the organization's activities are, the more integration is required, resulting in a more complex structure. Factors affecting an organization's structure are its size, technology, strategies, and external environment.

All organizations function within different environments. For example, the external and social environment affects all organizations to varying degrees. This includes sociocultural, political and legal, economic, and technological forces. The industry and task environment is more specific. It consists of those forces that an organization must continuously interact with that directly affect the company's ability to achieve its predetermined outcomes (i.e., goals). These forces include suppliers, customers, regulators, and competitors. The number of forces an organization needs to deal with regularly, how diverse these forces are, and how rapidly these forces are changing affect the stability or uncertainty of the organization's environment, which, in turn, impacts its structure. Burns and Stalker (1961, pp. 119–120) related that:

> Different types of organizational structures are suitable for particular environmental conditions. An organization with well-defined tasks and a rigidly hierarchical system of decision-making [*mechanistic* structure] is argued to be appropriate for stable environmental conditions. Where the environment changes, an *organic* form of organizational structure is deemed more appropriate, in which tasks are flexibly defined and participants cooperate based on expertise and not hierarchical positions.

Later in this chapter, we will discuss how various factors affect an organization's structure, but first, we will provide a brief overview of the history of OT so managers can better understand why organizations select specific structures to achieve their goals.

History of Organization Theory

Max Weber

The historical roots of OT can be found in the concepts developed during the Industrial Revolution in the late nineteenth and early twentieth centuries. During this period, Max Weber (1864–1920), a German sociologist considered the founding father of OT, developed a framework of administrative characteristics that allowed large organizations to play a positive role in the larger society by being "rational" and efficient.

Weber (1947) viewed an organization as a closed system (i.e., autonomous and isolated from environmental forces) with rules and procedures enforced by an individual with rational and legal authority. Weber believed that manager–subordinate relationships should be impersonal, with no reference to personal preferences, thereby ensuring that the manager did not permit emotional attachments or personalities to interfere with rational organizational decisions (Longest et al., 2000).

The six key administrative characteristics of Weber's rational and efficient organization, which is referred to as a bureaucratic organizational structure, are as follows:

1. *Hierarchy of Authority*: To ensure clear communication of supervision and subordination positions (i.e., designations).
2. *Hiring (and Promoting) of Technically Qualified Workers*: To ensure that hiring and promotions are based on merit rather than favoritism, and that those hired view their positions as full-time, primary careers.
3. *Consistent System of Rules*: To ensure consistent and effective pursuit of organizational goals.
4. *Extensive Use of Written Documents*: To ensure that decisions are made and communicated through written rules and records.
5. *Functional Specialization and Division of Duties*: To ensure efficient operations, each worker will carry out specific tasks and duties based on his or her skill and training.
6. *Separation of Position from Worker*: To ensure that an individual worker does not have "rights" to any aspect of their position, thereby eliminating the ability to pass the position on to friends or family once their contract ends.

Weber's rational bureaucracy model dominated social science thinking about organizations until World War II. At this time, others began criticizing Weber's ideas because his model ignored much of what happens in organizations—conflicts, workarounds, and informal leadership. According to Selznick (1948, 1957), the central issue was that "bureaucracies" were not and should not act like machines because they consisted of human beings, and people will not imitate machines. Bureaucratic organizations are generally viewed as inefficient because of their functional design and slow decision-making capabilities. However, Burns and Stalker (1961) noted that bureaucratic-type structures are suited for organizations in stable environments with routine tasks, but not those operating in industries with unstable environments and nonroutine tasks—for example, companies operating in the healthcare industry!

Henri Fayol

Another individual who impacted OT was Henri Fayol (1841–1925), a French industrialist. Fayol (1949) developed a set of rules for managers to follow to be successful. His set of rules consisted of three parts: (1) activities of management, (2) principles of management, and (3) elements of management.

Based on his management/administrative experiences, Fayol argued that all activities within organizations could be divided into six main groups:

1. Technical (production, manufacturing, and adaptation)
2. Commercial (buying, selling, and exchange)
3. Financial (search for and optimum use of capital)
4. Security (protection of property and persons)
5. Accounting (stocktaking, balance sheet, statistics, and costs)
6. Managerial (planning, organization, command, coordination, and control)

According to Fayol, the six groups of activities are interdependent, and management's role is to ensure that all six activities work smoothly to achieve the organization's goals.

The second part of Fayol's set of rules is the 14 management principles. Although Fayol described these principles as flexible and adaptable rather than rigid and absolute, he stressed that managers' adherence to the principles will contribute to a more effective organization (Miner, 2002). Fayol's management principles are listed and applied to health care in **Table 20-1**, with division of work (specialization), unity of command, and scalar chain being the most important.

Table 20-1 Fayol's 14 Principles of Management in Health Care

Principle	Description	Healthcare Application
Division of work (specialization)	Specialization limits the number of tasks and activities an individual does so that they can become more efficient at performing them with greater quality and similar effort.	An orthopedic surgeon who specializes in hip replacements can perform this type of surgery faster and with better outcomes than a general surgeon who performs numerous types of surgeries.
Authority and responsibility	Managers should exercise authority because of their formal position, expertise, and experience. Responsibility must be commensurate with authority.	Because of his official role and advanced skills, the nurse manager should exercise authority over staff nurses and take greater responsibility for nursing services provided.
Discipline	Discipline is adherence to a formal or informal contract between employees and employers. It requires good managers, equitable agreements, and warning and disciplinary actions when needed.	Hospitals have an employee code of conduct that outlines expected behaviors and grounds for suspension or termination for not adhering to required policies, such as patient confidentiality.
Unity of command	An individual should receive orders from one supervisor only. Dual command is to be avoided.	An ICU nurse reports directly to her nurse supervisor rather than to a nurse supervisor and a physician supervisor. However, dual command is frequent in health care, creating role conflict.
Unity of direction	A group of activities with the same objective should be placed under a single manager with a single plan.	An outpatient clinic has one administrator who ensures consistent direction for the organization.
Subordination of individual interests to the general interest	The organization's interests must take precedence over those of individuals or groups.	Adherence to a hospital's operating room safety protocols must take precedence over the preferences of an individual surgeon.
Remuneration of personnel	Payments should be fair and equitable, reward well-directed effort, and not exceed reasonable limits.	Clinicians should be compensated according to their training, experience, expertise, and performance.
Centralization	The amount of centralization and decentralization may vary depending on the situation, firm size, personal characteristics of the manager, reliability of subordinates, and business conditions.	The vice president of quality and safety has a small, high-performing, experienced team. Therefore, he delegates decision making for establishing safety protocols to his team.

Principle	Description	Healthcare Application
Scalar chain	The scalar chain is the line of authority from top management to the lowest ranks. Communication should occur up and down the scalar chain of authority. If following the chain creates delays, cross-communications can be allowed.	During normal operations, an employee must follow the established chain of command to request changes in procedures. However, during an emergency situation, such as a pandemic, organizations created "employee idea forums" to quickly implement procedural changes and respond to new problems as they arise.
Order	There should be a specific place for everything and everyone. This principle means good organization and selection and implies the existence of an organizational chart.	Medical supplies are strategically located throughout the hospital close to where the work is performed, and frontline workers are assigned to specific units.
Equity	Employees should be treated with kindness and justice, eliciting devotion and loyalty. A sense of equity should permeate the whole scalar chain.	Healthcare workers have formed and joined labor unions due to actual or perceived inequities in wage standards and lack of or insufficiencies of workplace protections.
Stability of tenure of personnel	Employees and managers need time to settle into their jobs before achieving maximum performance. (Turnover is inefficient.) Stability of tenure promotes loyalty to the organization, its purposes, and values.	Replacing one physician due to turnover is estimated to cost over $1 million, including recruitment costs and lost revenues.
Initiative	Creating and executing a plan and having the freedom to do so are particularly valuable to an organization in difficult times. Managers who facilitate subordinates' initiatives (versus top-down initiatives) are superior because they lead to employee satisfaction and motivation.	The concept of shared governance is a pillar for nursing magnet-designated hospitals. This model incorporates a decision-making model focused on empowering the people who care for the patients. This approach allows for better nurse satisfaction and patient outcomes.
Esprit de corps	Unity and harmony should be fostered, and conflict minimized. Verbal communication should be used whenever possible because it permits rapid conflict resolution.	A nursing unit celebrates its team successes (e.g., zero patient infection rate) to develop a sense of camaraderie among peers.

Abbreviation: ICU, intensive care unit.

Data from Miner, J. B. (2002). *Organizational behavior: Foundations, theories, and analyses* (pp. 65–68).

The third part of Fayol's set of rules is the elements of management, which are composed of five activities:

1. Planning
2. Organizing

3. Commanding
4. Coordinating
5. Controlling

As described in **Table 20-2**, these activities are more task-oriented than people-oriented. Although developed almost a century ago, Fayol's management elements provide a helpful framework for understanding the nature of managerial work and continue to be widely used in management training (Miner, 2002).

Table 20-2 Fayol's Five Elements of Management

Element	Description	Application to Health Care
Planning	Planning involves assessing the future, making provisions for it, and developing a plan of action based on contributions from throughout the business.	Developing a strategic plan with specific tactics to achieve the hospital's goals
Organizing	Organizing involves developing an organizational structure, allocating human resources to ensure the accomplishment of objectives, and evaluating managerial personnel.	Forecasting patient volumes to ensure sufficient nursing staff are hired and trained to meet proper nurse-to-patient ratios
Commanding	Commanding activates the organizational structure. It involves thoroughly knowing the personnel, being knowledgeable about employer–employee agreements, setting a good example, conducting periodic organization audits, establishing unity of direction, avoiding excess detail, and generally fostering unity, energy, initiative, and loyalty.	Efforts by managers and leaders to motivate employees with regular assessment of employee engagement, as well as annual performance reviews for improvement feedback
Coordinating	Coordinating harmonizes an organization's various activities and ensures multiple departments work harmoniously rather than operating in isolation as ends in themselves. Units know their role in the total effort and the interdependencies between them. The need to facilitate horizontal communication is evident.	Reorganizing individual units and departments into service lines, such as oncology or transplant services
Controlling	Controlling is checking the realities of operations against plans and taking steps to correct deviations. It assumes the existence of up-to-date plans and the use of sanctions to achieve compatibility with them promptly. Inspections should be impartial and objective.	Use of external accreditation agencies, such as The Joint Commission (JCAHO) or Det Norske Veritas (DNV) to conduct site visits to ensure the hospital is operating according to specific standards

Data from Miner, J. B. (2002). *Organizational behavior: Foundations, theories, and analyses.* M.E. Sharpe.

Frederick Taylor

The third classic management theorist we will discuss is Frederick Taylor (1856–1915). Taylor (1911) developed the well-known framework of scientific management. Based on his work experiences, Taylor was primarily concerned with managing production workers to achieve maximum efficiency. Taylor's four basic principles of management were the following:

1. Develop a science for each person's work. This involves determining how the work can best be performed by experimenting with it, conducting time-and-motion studies, and, often, applying mathematical formulas.
2. Scientifically select the best individual for the job, train that person to perform the job better, and pay higher wages to reward the increased productivity.
3. Cooperate with the workers to ensure that the work is done in the prescribed manner; combine knowledge of the job (principle 1) and the worker selected (principle 2). This should include, but not be limited to, providing for increased earnings for those who follow the prescribed methods most closely.
4. Divide the work so that activities, such as planning, organizing, and controlling are the responsibility of management; the worker, in contrast, has the responsibility for doing. This division is predicated on the assumption that most workers cannot create the science of their work.

Taylor believed that organizational efficiency was achieved by creating jobs that economized time, human energy, and other productive resources. As such, Taylor placed a strong emphasis on the exception principle. By establishing output standards, managers would only need to give their attention to those workers whose established standards were not met (or exceeded). Although Taylor preferred that managers deal with one worker at a time, he was aware that group influences might produce changes in output (Miner, 2002).

Open-Systems Theory

Classical theories were well suited to the Industrial Age to create large, efficient organizations, but the "people" and "environment" components were missing. Although the human relations/behavioral management movement started to emerge in the 1920s due to the famous Hawthorne Studies (Homans, 1950; Roethlisberger & Dickson, 1939), the bureaucratic approaches remained the primary focus for OT until the late 1970s and early 1980s. At this time, new directions for OT appeared in the literature. These theories emphasized that organizations were open systems interacting with and dependent upon unstable environments. Over the past 40 years, much research has been disseminated regarding the need for organizations to be flexible and adaptable to acquire the necessary resources to meet the needs of their changing environments. This is referred to as open-systems theory.

Katz and Kahn (1978) developed a framework for open-systems theory that encompasses four phases: (1) inputs into the organization, (2) the transformation of those inputs within the system, (3) outputs, and (4) recycling. See **Figure 20-1**. As previously noted, an organization is a group working under a defined structure to achieve stated goals through coordinated activities. These activities require the use of human, material, and financial resources. An organization must obtain the necessary input resources (e.g., employees, materials/supplies, capital) from its environment and efficiently transform them into outputs (i.e., goals). These outputs provide

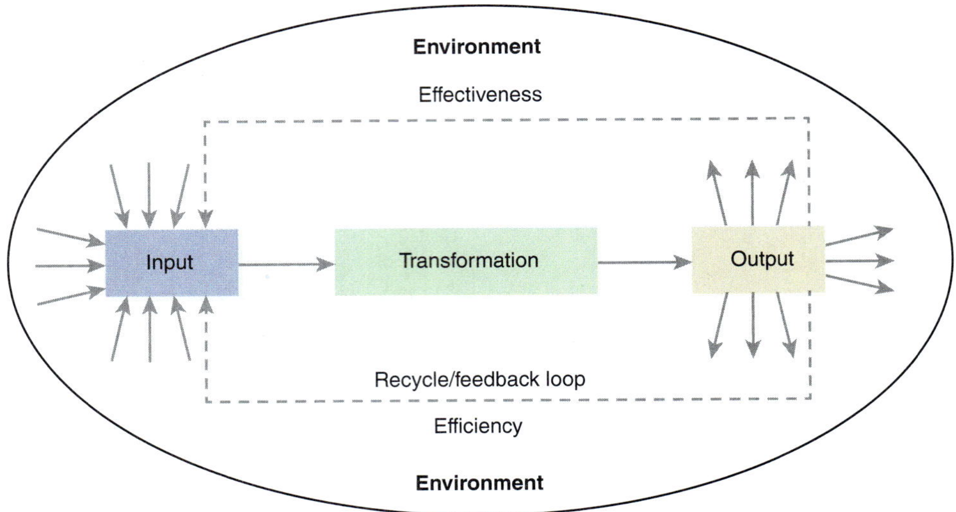

Figure 20-1 Four Phases of an Open System

another external resource (e.g., dollars) so that the organization can acquire the required input resources again.

Organizations need to create more outputs than they consume. In addition, the organization must produce outputs required and valued by purchasers (i.e., external environment). In other words, an organization must be efficient and effective to survive. An organization must interact effectively with its environments to achieve these results, as shown in **Figure 20-2**. An open-systems organization is not passive: It needs to reach out and attempt to influence its environment, but at the same time, the organization will be influenced by its environment. If the company's environment is stable, the organization can emphasize efficiency (bureaucratic approach) more. When the environment is unstable, the company must emphasize efficiency and effectiveness.

Today's healthcare environment is anything but stable. As reflected in Figure 20-2, a healthcare organization must interact with the general and industry environments and numerous stakeholders with conflicting demands. For example, hospitals must accommodate demands for uncompensated care while balancing criticism of cost shifting, for high-quality care while experiencing nursing and other clinician shortages, and for providing jobs and decent wages with declining profit margins due to lower reimbursements and changing payment schemes from payors (Arndt et al., 1999).

On an annual basis, the American College of Healthcare Executives (ACHE) surveys hospital CEOs regarding the 10 most pressing issues affecting their community hospitals (nonfederal, short-term, nonspecialty hospitals) to identify specific areas of concern. As reflected in **Exhibit 20-1**, financial problems remain one of the uppermost concerns for hospital CEOs in 2023, only topped by workforce challenges (e.g., continuing personnel shortages after COVID-19).

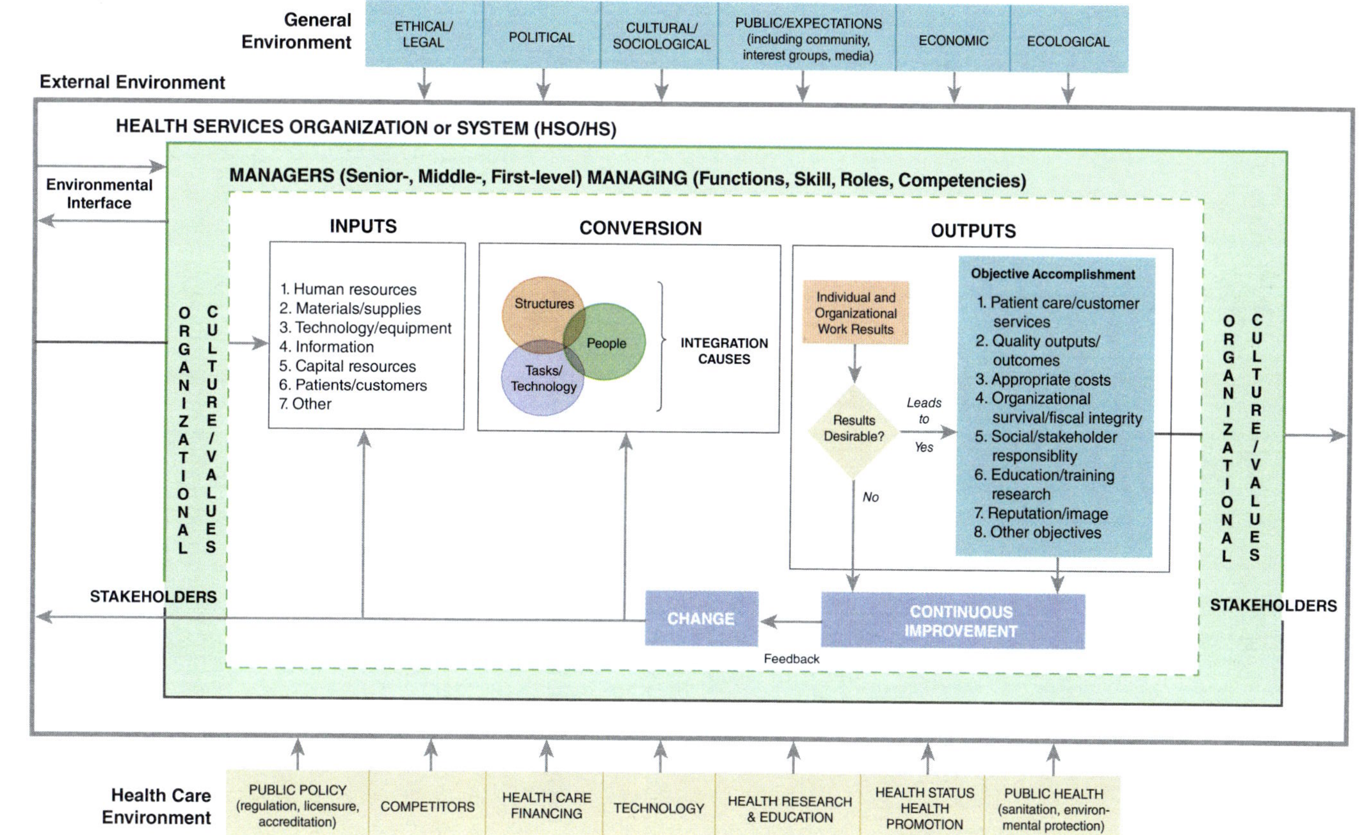

Figure 20-2 Open-System Theory

Reproduced from Longest, B. B. & Darr, K. (2014). *Managing Health Services Organizations and Systems*, Sixth Edition; reprinted by permission of Health Professions Press, Inc. (www.healthpropress.com).

Exhibit 20-1 **Top Issues Confronting Hospitals**

The following table ranks each issue in order of importance according to 241 U.S. hospitals' CEOs.

Issue	2023 Rank
Workforce challenges	1
Financial challenges	2
Behavioral health and addiction issues	3
Access to care	4
Governmental mandates	5
Patient safety and quality	6
Patient satisfaction	7
Technology	8
Physician-hospital relations	9
Population health management	10
Reorganization	11

Data from American College of Healthcare Executives. (2023). *Top issues confronting hospitals, 2023*. Author.

The Learning Organization

ACHE's annual survey results included concerns only recently expressed by hospital CEOs—transition from volume to value and price transparency—reflecting the fact that healthcare organizations are complex and always changing because of their need to adapt to their external environment and to develop and maintain relationships with various stakeholders and constituents of the system. Healthcare managers must be flexible and willing to learn new things by consistently questioning the status quo. But this goal has been difficult to achieve in the past! As noted by Donald Berwick (2002), the former administrator for the Centers for Medicare and Medicaid Services, CEO of the Institute for Healthcare Improvement, and one of the architects of the Institute of Medicine's *Crossing the Quality Chasm* report, "The quality chasm in health care reflects one crucial deficit: deeply embedded incapacities—a learning disability—at the heart of the healthcare industry. This disability is historical, cultural, and structural" (Institute of Medicine, 2001, p. 301).

Managers in today's unstable and complex healthcare environment must understand that what worked in the past will not work in the future. Therefore, organizations need to "learn." In a learning organization, problem solving is key, unlike the traditional organization designed for efficient performance (see **Figure 20-3**). Learning organizations "promote communication and collaboration so that everyone is engaged in identifying and solving problems, enabling the organization to experiment, improve and increase its capability continuously" (Daft, 2007, p. 29).

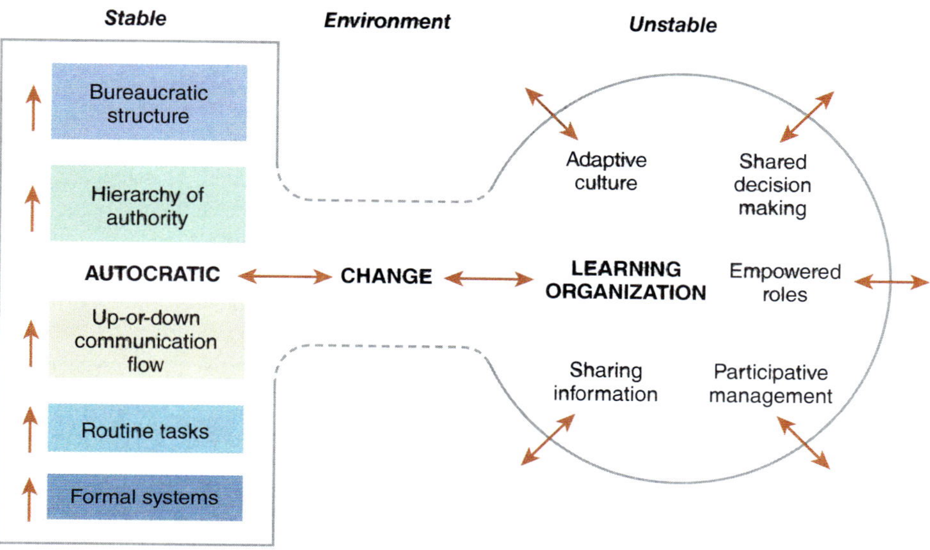

Figure 20-3 Learning Organization

The idea of the learning organization became popular largely through Peter Senge's book, *The Fifth Discipline*, first published in 1990. Senge outlined five characteristics of a learning organization: personal mastery, mental models, shared vision, team learning, and systems thinking. The five characteristics are described as follows (Hartzell, n.d.):

1. *Personal mastery* refers to the need for an individual worker to have personal professional development goals on which to focus energy; the organization must recognize and nurture these goals.
2. *Mental models* refer to how we make sense of the world and react to it. In the context of the learning organization, mental models can be considered part of the organization's culture, which is mindful and respectful of the intricacies and theories that provide the framework for how effective organizations function.
3. Building a *shared vision* implies that the organization and its members have a shared vision; the organization consciously blends individual aspirations with company goals.
4. *Team learning* stresses the importance of collaboration, shared dialogue and decision making, and mutual accountability in work groups.
5. *Systems thinking*, also known as the "fifth discipline" in that it integrates the previous four, acknowledges that organizations are complex systems of interrelationships. That is, marketing depends on finance, finance depends on information technology (IT), IT depends on research and development, and so on.

Senge believed that these interrelationships must be carefully examined and understood to uncover opportunities, problems, and possibilities within them.

As noted, organizations are open systems that must interact with and adapt to the environment to survive. Over the past three decades, rapid changes in the healthcare industry have forced managers to reorient toward an open-systems mindset and recognize that their organizations are part of a complex, interconnected whole (Daft, 2007). Open-systems theory assumes that all large organizations are made up of subsystems, each of which receives inputs from other subsystems and turns them into outputs for use by other subsystems (see **Table 20-3**). The subsystems are interdependent and interrelated. As described by Senge's fifth discipline—systems thinking—organizations must achieve balance between their subsystems to be successful.

For example, the sales and marketing department of a national retail-based clinic company might grow very quickly as patients and insurers need and want efficient, cost-effective care for minor emergencies (versus going to hospital emergency departments). However, if the organization's human resources department cannot keep pace with hiring qualified nurse practitioners to staff the mini-clinics, the entire organization could break down. Thus, subsystems within an organization must maintain a state of balance as the organization adapts to environmental influences.

Table 20-3 Subsystems of an Open System

Subsystem	Description	Healthcare Example
Production subsystems	Components that transform inputs into outputs. Other subsystems are typically built around the production subsystem.	This subsystem would include the nursing, medical staff, pharmacy, and radiology departments in a hospital.
Maintenance subsystems	Maintain the social involvement of employees in an organization. Activities in this group include providing benefits and compensation, creating favorable work conditions, empowering employees, and fulfilling other employee needs.	In health care, these functions typically reside within the human resources or the organizational development department.
Adaptive subsystems	Serve to gather information about threats and opportunities in the environment and then respond with innovations that allow the organization to adapt to these conditions.	This would be an integral part of the hospital's strategic management culture, with oversight by the executive management team and coordination within the organization's planning department.
Supportive subsystems	Perform acquisition and distribution functions within an organization. Acquisition activities include securing resources, such as employees and supplies, from the external environment (i.e., human resources and purchasing departments). Supportive subsystems would also include those activities and efforts to transfer the product or service outside the organization.	A hospital's supportive subsystems include medical records and patient billing departments.
Managerial subsystems	Direct the activities of other subsystems in the organization. These managerial functions set goals and policies, allocate resources, resolve conflicts, and generally work to facilitate the organization's efficiency.	These subsystems would include clinical and administrative leaders at all levels of a healthcare organization.

Data from Katz, D., & Kahn, R. L. (1978). *The social psychology of organizations.* John Wiley & Sons.

Katz and Kahn (1978) identified five subsystems that are important to the success of all organizations. Each of these subsystems may also be made up of subsystems.

High-Reliability Organizations

The high-reliability organization is an example of a learning organization applicable to the healthcare industry. High-reliability organizations operate in complex domains and must sustain safe operations because failure can result in catastrophic consequences, such as air traffic control centers, aircraft carriers, or nuclear plants. This concept has been applied to health care as lapses in hospital safety can have catastrophic consequences and harm or even death for patients. High-reliability organizations are unique because there are countless opportunities for failure, and conditions constantly change, resulting in an endless array of possible problems. Each patient is unique in health care, and the methods for maintaining patient safety can change frequently. The Agency for Healthcare Research and Quality suggests that high-reliability organizations have five core characteristics, outlined in **Table 20-4**.

Table 20-4 Characteristics of a High-Reliability Organization

Characteristic	Description
Preoccupation with Failure	Everyone is aware of and thinking about the potential for failure. People understand that new threats emerge regularly from situations that no one imagined could occur, so all personnel actively think about what could go wrong and are alert to minor signs of potential problems. The absence of errors or accidents leads not to complacency, but to a heightened sense of vigilance for the subsequent possible failure. Near misses are viewed as opportunities to learn about systems issues and potential improvements, rather than as evidence of safety.
Reluctance to Simplify	People resist simplifying their understanding of work processes and how and why things succeed or fail in their environment. People in HROs understand that the work is complex and dynamic. They seek underlying rather than surface explanations. While HROs recognize the value of standardization of workflows to reduce variation, they also appreciate the complexity inherent in the number of teams, processes, and relationships involved in daily operations.
Sensitivity to Operations	Based on their understanding of operational complexity, people in HROs strive to maintain a high awareness of operational conditions. This sensitivity is often referred to as "big picture understanding" or "situation awareness." It means that people cultivate an understanding of the context of the current state of their work about the unit or organizational state—i.e., what is going on around them—and how the current state might support or threaten safety.
Deference to Expertise	People in HROs appreciate that the people closest to the work are the most knowledgeable. Thus, people in HROs know that in a crisis or emergency, the person with the greatest knowledge of the situation might not be the person with the highest status and seniority. Deference to local and situation expertise results in a spirit of inquiry and de-emphasis on hierarchy in favor of learning as much as possible about potential safety threats. In an HRO, everyone is expected to share concerns with others, and the organizational climate is such that all staff members are comfortable speaking up about potential safety problems.

(continues)

Table 20-4 Characteristics of a High-Reliability Organization *(continued)*

Characteristic	Description
Commitment to Resilience	Commitment to resilience is rooted in the fundamental understanding of the frequently unpredictable nature of system failures. People in HROs assume the system is at risk for failure, and they practice performing rapid assessments of and responses to challenging situations. Teams cultivate situation assessment and cross-monitoring to identify potential safety threats quickly and either respond before safety problems cause harm or mitigate the seriousness of the safety event.

Abbreviation: HRO, high-reliability organization.

Reproduced from Agency for Healthcare Research and Quality. (2019). Patient Safety Network. *Patient Safety Primer: High Reliability*. Available from https://psnet.ahrq.gov/primer/high-reliability

Summary

This chapter provided an overview of organization theory and its historical roots based on the works of Max Weber, Henri Fayol, and Frederick Taylor. Since the Industrial Revolution, a wealth of information has emerged with the study of OT. We have abandoned Weber's original concept that organizations are closed systems and developed an understanding that organizations are part of a complex, interconnected whole. Organizations are open systems that must interact with and adapt to the environment to survive. The learning organization attempts to interact with its environment effectively by promoting communication and collaboration throughout the entity's subsystems. Communication and cooperation are achieved through the organization's design and structure. Additional conditions for high-reliability organizations must be present to achieve continuous learning and avoid harm. Organization design may be viewed as the formal arrangement of departments, divisions, functions, and people interacting and linked together within an entity. Structure is the result of the design process. The organization's structure is reflected by the clustering of various departments, divisions, and so forth to coordinate and control activities (and people) to achieve the organization's goals.

Discussion Questions

1. Define OT.
2. Define an organization.
3. Describe the components of an organization's formal structure.
4. Describe the factors that determine the stability and uncertainty of an organization's environment.
5. Explain the importance of the classic management theorists in developing OT.

6. Describe the difference between closed and open systems.
7. Describe what is meant by the term "learning organization."
8. Describe the five components of a high-reliability organization.

Case Exercise

Visit the Institute for Healthcare Improvement's website, www.ihi.org a nonprofit organization dedicated to improving the quality of healthcare systems through education, research, and demonstration projects (https://www.ihi.org/library/blog). Break into small groups, choose a story on the blog and discuss the achievements of selected health service organizations (HSOs) working to improve patient care.

1. How are these HSOs demonstrating that they are "learning" organizations?
2. How are they similar or dissimilar to your organization?

CASE STUDY 20-1 Same Pandemic, Different Response

During the COVID-19 pandemic, two hospitals in the same large metropolitan city had very different experiences.

To save money, United Oak Hospital typically kept about 1 month of supplies on hand, including personal protective equipment (PPE), such as surgical masks and gowns and N95 masks used to filter airborne pathogens. United Oak's senior leadership team was very focused on financial performance and often pushed to pay lower salaries than other hospitals in the city. They also kept staffing levels as low as possible to ensure they could meet their financial goals. As a result, nurses and physicians often felt overworked and burned out, and they would leave to work at different hospitals in the city with better pay, better hours, and better patient loads.

When the pandemic hit, United Oak Hospital was unprepared to handle the influx of patients. Within a week, its PPE was out of stock, and national shortages made it difficult to procure more. The administration resorted to asking their doctors and nurses to use garbage bags and bandanas to protect themselves from the virus while caring for their sick patients. Employees began to post pictures of the working conditions on social media, which generated national outrage over the working conditions. The hospital was inundated with patients, most of whom had tested positive for COVID-19. Their intensive care unit beds were filled, and all ventilators were in use for unstable patients in critical condition as a result of the virus. Morale was completely eroded among the staff, and frequent medical errors were being made amid the high stress. On a particularly tumultuous day, a group of nurses refused to leave the break room unless the administration brought in more nurses to help with the overwhelming number of patients.

Just across town, Belton Hospital was flooded with COVID-19–positive patients in critical condition, but their experience was completely different. Belton Hospital had developed a culture that valued courage, teamwork, and learning for decades. When various diseases, from smallpox to Ebola, threatened the community, Belton Hospital was always the first to volunteer to treat these patients. As a result, Belton had developed significant expertise in infectious disease management. With a heightened awareness that contagious diseases could spread quickly within its city, Belton built negative-pressure rooms to contain the spread of disease, kept a 6-month supply of PPE on hand, and maintained vigilance about adhering to safety protocols. In the past, Belton had made mistakes in handling specific cases involving infectious diseases and had conducted careful analysis to ensure that systems and protocols were changed to prevent future errors. The leadership team at Belton Hospital believed its people were its most valuable assets and worked hard to create a positive and motivating working environment and retain top talent in the city. When the COVID-19 pandemic hit, Belton Hospital was ready. Its CEO rounded through each unit, encouraging the frontline staff, "This is what we've been preparing for decades! We are in this together!" When the SARS epidemic in Asia occurred several years before, Belton Hospital proactively created contingency plans to develop makeshift PPE and ventilators if need ever arose. They quickly put these plans into place, starting with an N95 mask resterilization process. Local news media interviewed physicians and nurses at Belton Hospital, who shared that although they were scared, they were ready and prepared. The clinical teams pulled together to provide high-quality care despite the stress of the pandemic.

Discussion Questions

1. Which of Fayol's 14 Principles of Management were demonstrated at Belton Hospital? Which ones were missing from United Oak Hospital?
2. Describe how management from each hospital considered their external environment, and how this led them to different decisions regarding PPE and staffing.
3. Which components of a high-reliability organization did Belton Hospital demonstrate?

References

American College of Healthcare Executives. (2023). *Top issues confronting hospitals: 2023*. https://healthcareexecutive.org/archives/march-april-2024/top-issues-confronting-hospitals-2023

Arndt, M., & Bigelow, B., (1999). In their own words: How hospitals present corporate restructuring in their annual reports. *Journal of Healthcare Management*, *44*(2), 117–132.

Berwick, D. (2002). Quality chasm factors. *Health Affairs (Millwood)*, *21*(5), 301–302.

Burns, T., & Stalker, G. M. (1961). *The management of innovation*. Tavistock.

Daft, R. L. (2007). *Organization theory and design* (9th ed.). Thomson South-Western.

Dyrbye, L. N., Shanafelt, T. D., Sinsky, C. A., Cipriano, P. F., Bhatt, J., Ommaya, A., West, C. P., & Meyers, D. (2017, July 5). *Burnout among health care professionals: A call to explore and address this underrecognized threat to safe, high-quality care*. National Academy of Medicine. https://nam.edu/burnout-among-health-care-professionals-a-call-to-explore-and-address-this-underrecognized-threat-to-safe-high-quality-care/

Fayol, H. (1949). *General and industrial management*. Pitman.

Hartzell, S. (n.d.). How companies become learning organizations. Study.com. https://study.com/academy/lesson/how-companies-become-learning-organizations.html

Homans, G. C. (1950). *The human group*. Harcourt, Brace.

Institute of Medicine (2001). *Crossing the quality chasm: A new health system for the 21st century*. National Academy Press. https://www.nap.edu/catalog/10027/crossing-the-quality-chasm-a-new-health-system-for-the-21st-century

Kast, F. E., & Rosenzweig, J. E. (1985). *Organization and management: A systems and contingency approach*. McGraw-Hill.

Katz, D., & Kahn, R. L. (1978). *The social psychology of organizations*. John Wiley & Sons.

Longest, B. B., Rakich, J. S., & Darr, K. (2000). *Managing health services organizations and systems* (4th ed.). Health Professions Press.

Miner, J. B. (2002). *Organizational behavior: Foundations, theories, and analysis*. Oxford University Press.

Roethlisberger, F. J., & Dickson, W. J. (1939). *Management and the worker*. Harvard University Press.

Senge, P. M. (1990). *The fifth discipline: The art and practice of the learning organization*. Doubleday.

Selznick, P. (1948). Foundations of the theory of organization. *American Sociological Review*, *13*(1), 25–35.

Selznick, P. (1957). *Leadership in administration: A sociological interpretation*. Row, Peterson.

Taylor, F. W. (1911). *The principles of scientific management*. Harper & Brothers..

Weber, M. (1947). *The theory of social and economic organizations* (A. M. Henderson & T. Parsons, Trans.). Free Press.

Other Suggested Readings

Chuang, Y., Ginsberg, L., & Berta, W. B. (2007). Learning from preventable adverse events in health care organizations: Development of a multilevel model of learning and propositions. *Health Care Management Review, 32*(4), 330–340.

Cunningham Wood, J., & Wood, M. C. (Eds.). (2002). *Henri Fayol: Critical evaluations in business and management*. Routledge.

Fells, M. J. (2000). Fayol stands the test of time. *Journal of Management History*, 6(8), 345–360.

Lawler III, E. E., & Worley, C. (2006). *Built to change: How to achieve sustained organizational effectiveness*. Wiley.

March, J. G., & Simon, H. A. (1958). *Organizations*. Wiley.

Society for Healthcare Strategy and Market Development of the American Hospital Association (2005). *Futurescan: Healthcare trends and implications, 2005–2010*. Health Administration Press.

CHAPTER 21

Strategy and Structure

LEARNING OUTCOMES

After completing this chapter, the student should be able to understand:

- The definition of organizational strategy.
- The roles of the different levels of management in the strategic process.
- The three levels of strategy.
- The overall process of strategic planning, and the content and purposes of each step.
- The relationship of culture and structure to the strategic planning process.
- The Miles and Snow organizational types and their environment–strategy–structure-process relationships.

Overview

Organizational strategy deals with the choices that define how it relates to the external environment. Because the organization's external environment is constantly changing, strategy is an ongoing and continual process. An effective strategy is not reactive to change but proactive in anticipating the need for change, planning appropriate change, and consistently implementing that change. Like structure, strategic choices are long-term and too complex to adjust quickly and effectively in the short term.

Understanding strategy is critical to an organization's achieving superior long-term results. Selection and effective implementation of appropriate strategies are of even greater importance for health services organizations, as they operate in an industry subject to greater change pressures and external threats than organizations in more stable industries.

Strategy

Organizational strategy is a process and a mindset or way of viewing the environment. From a process standpoint, strategy is an integrated approach, including assessing the organization and its environment, developing and selecting long-term organizational direction, and implementing strategies to accomplish the organization's vision and objectives. The strategic process, however, also requires an executive mindset that allows the organization to choose its direction and successfully achieve its vision. The ideal strategic environment combines an appropriate strategic mindset with an effective strategic process.

By definition, strategy provides the means to accomplish the entire organization's mission, vision, and objectives. A defining element of a plan is the focus on the organization as a whole rather than individual units or parts of the organization. The other defining element of strategy is an external focus—a view that the organization does not stand alone but is part of and dependent on a wider external environment. Understanding and planning appropriate responses to environmental changes is key to the strategic planning process.

Strategy is a series of sequential steps in the description of the process discussed later in this chapter. In some organizations, it may be nothing more than that. However, to be effective, strategy needs to be an ongoing process, a continual cycle formulated and implemented at all levels within the organization. A strategy that is ingrained and integrated into day-to-day management is successful. A strategy that is simply a set of documents on the CEO's desk, no matter how well written, is a failed strategy.

An organization's structure and culture are among the most critical long-term factors impacting an organization's ability to accomplish its mission and vision. An appropriate match between the overall organization's direction and its chosen competitive strategies, structure, and culture greatly increases its chances of long-term success.

Governance

Strategy is an essential part of the organizational governance process. Healthcare organizations may be for-profit, not-for-profit, or governmental entities. In all cases, an effective governance process is key to ensuring that the aims of those providing long-term capital resources to the entity (e.g., stockholders, funding organizations, and legislative bodies) are accomplished. An oversight body (such as a board of directors) is established for the organization with primary responsibility to the stockholders (for-profit), communities (not-for-profit), or other providers of long-term capital.

In exercising their responsibility for oversight, the board must consider the organization's long-term and short-term directions. The strategic planning process provides three key documents to the board, through which the board exercises control over the organization's direction. These are the strategic plan, the medium-term plan (sometimes called a 5-year plan), and the budget. By reviewing and approving these documents, the board indicates its agreement with management's proposals for the organization's future direction.

Organizational success in the era of health reform is dependent upon good governance. As hospitals, health systems, and other health services organizations embark on transformational change, their boards must lead it (Jarousse, 2014). Exceptional boards ensure that there is a strong link between the organization's priorities and the needs and concerns of stakeholders (e.g., community, employees, physicians, employers, patients, and other constituent groups) and that the organization has the necessary infrastructure in place to help the board govern effectively (Health Research and Educational Trust, 2007). The board can focus on identifying the dimensions of organizational performance that must be monitored and evaluated to meet stakeholder needs. The Balanced Governance Scorecard model (see **Figure 21-1**) suggests that boards need to focus simultaneously on four dimensions of performance to ensure that the organization meets

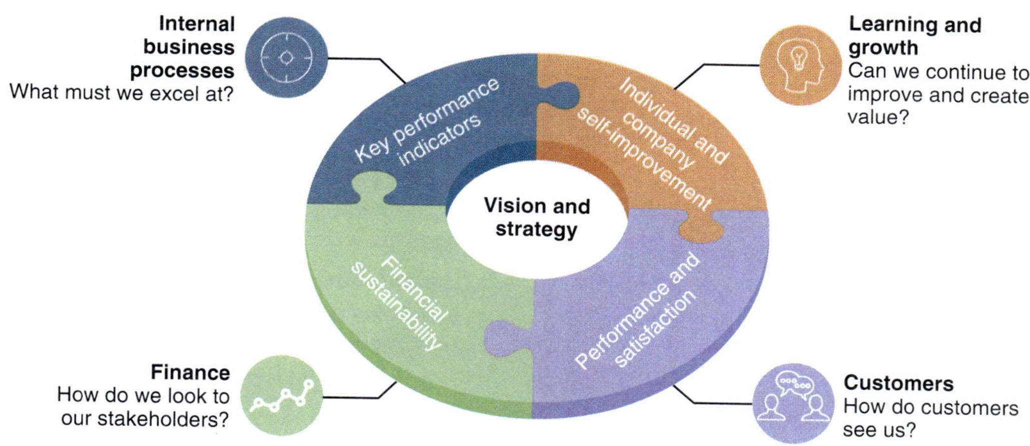

Figure 21-1 The Balanced Governance Scorecard Model

its obligations to stakeholders: organizational goals, executive performance, quality of care, and financial health (Pointer et al., 2005). According to Pointer, Totten, and Orlikoff (2005), to meet organizational performance objectives, key board activities include the following:

- Formulating a vision of what the organization should become to maximize stakeholder benefit
- Developing the key goals the organization must accomplish
- Ensuring that management's strategies are aligned with and will lead to achieving the goals

Management

Although executive management and the board are ultimately responsible for determining strategy and are accountable for the organization's accomplishments, that does not mean that strategy should be a "C-suite show." Developing and implementing an effective strategy requires the input and cooperation of all managers at all organizational levels. A plan's communication and coordination components are just as important as the content developed during the process. For this reason, operational and functional level managers, along with administrative and clinical personnel, should be integral parts of the development process of the organization's plans and strategies.

During the assessment stage, management should seek broad participation to perform a thorough assessment. Similar to the internal analysis, it is equally essential that management actively seek input to assess the external and competitive environments. The best strategic ideas, environmental perceptions, and competitive insights often come from middle- and lower-level managers, as well as administrative and clinical staff, who have closer contact with the organization's patients, customers, vendors, and other stakeholders.

Input and feedback may be present at all stages, but during the strategy development phase, senior management is responsible for the earlier stages (values, mission, and vision). Responsibility gradually expands to include more divisional management during the objectives and strategy-setting stages. During the implementation phase, participation expands further, from the divisional and higher functional levels in the medium-term plan to all levels of management for the annual objectives and budget stages. Finally, strategic evaluation is the responsibility of senior management.

Three Levels of Strategy

According to Hofer and Schendel (1978), strategy has three interrelated levels. The strategy-setting process addresses these sequentially. Understanding the various levels of strategy can help one understand the strategic process and an individual manager's role within that process.

- *Level 1: Corporate Strategy*: Corporate-level strategy answers the questions of what businesses the organization is in and what the emphasis is between those different businesses. For example, a large healthcare enterprise may compete in Alabama's acute care hospital and primary care clinic market segments. Senior management decides on these businesses and their scope, and then allocates how much of the organization's limited resources to each.
- *Level 2: Business Strategy*: Once the corporate strategy has defined the business and level of resource availability, the business strategy is developed to define how the organization will compete within the defined business, given the resources the organization has been allocated. In our example, if the primary care clinic division of the organization has been assigned high growth objectives and relatively modest resource allocations, management may develop a business strategy of partnering with other businesses (such as a grocery or drugstore chain) rather than adopting a stand-alone facility strategy. For example, Sharp Healthcare and Carolinas HealthCare System partnered with CVS's retail-based MinuteClinics. This collaboration allowed the health systems to leverage MinuteClinic's widespread, convenient, and accessible locations to reach more patients, particularly those lacking regular access to primary care.
- *Level 3: Functional Strategy*: After determining the corporate and business strategies, attention is directed toward creating compelling and consistent functional strategies. Almost all strategy implementation is accomplished at the functional level through operational planning. Operational plans include standing plans (policies, standard operating procedures, rules, and regulations), single-use plans (specific programs and projects), and budgets. As such, senior management needs to review all functional strategies to ensure that they support the organization's business strategies and are consistent with the strategy of other functional units (e.g., finance, operations, marketing).

Within individual functions (e.g., operations or finance), there are numerous choices regarding which functional strategy to implement (or whether the existing functional strategy requires change). For example, the choice of accounting functional strategy may be whether the health system will do billing and collections from individual hospitals or the corporate location.

These functional strategy choices repeat themselves throughout the organization. Consistent functional strategies that fully support the organization's chosen business strategy and build on the organization's strengths are key to successfully implementing the organization's corporate and business strategy.

The Strategy Process

The strategic planning process contains four parts: strategic assessment, developing strategy, implementing strategy, and evaluating strategy. These four parts are highly interrelated and include several steps (see **Figure 21-2**). Because the typical cycle for the process is annual, all steps should be documented in writing for clarity, future evaluation, and efficiency in repeating the process the following year.

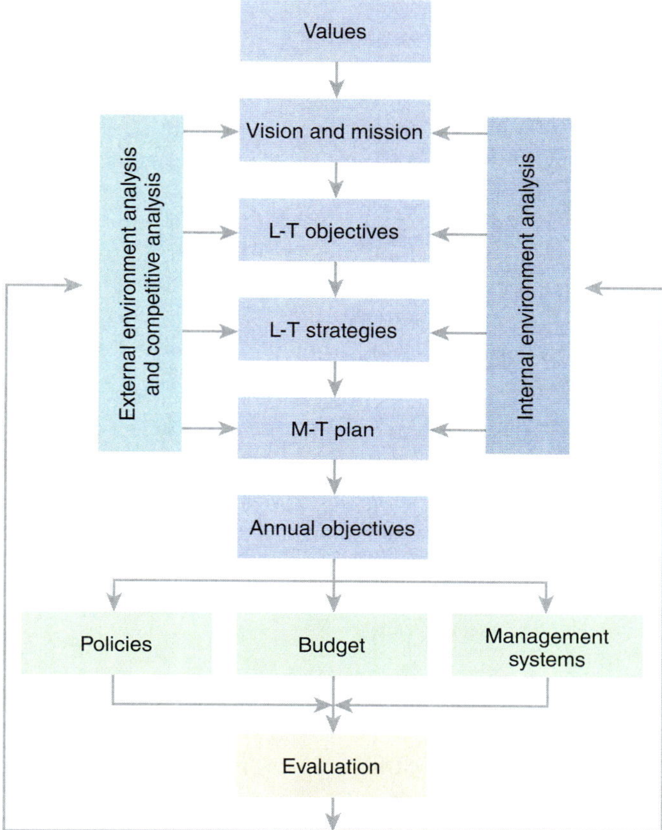

Figure 21-2 The Strategic Planning Process

Assessment

Values

The process begins with an assessment of the organization's values, which is accomplished through organizational governance. In large for-profit or not-for-profit organizations, there are several steps. First, the "owners" select a board of directors (or trustees) representing their values. The board, in turn, appoints a senior management team that reflects the owners' values.

Values can be a commitment to serve the community (not-for-profits) or a desire to deliver high financial returns to owners (for-profits). Many studies show that successful companies place a great deal of emphasis on their values. A clear statement of these values is an essential first step in strategic planning. As Lencioni (2002) noted, "Core values are the deeply ingrained principles that guide all of a company's actions." Decisions and trade-offs at all other steps of determining and implementing strategy require consistency with the organization's stated values.

Internal Environmental Analysis

Next, management thoroughly analyzes the organization's current internal environment. A frequently used approach is to explore the organization's strengths and weaknesses. Strengths are those aspects of the organization that are better than the industry's average, and weaknesses are those that are below the industry's average. Examples of internal areas addressed in the analysis would be the various functions (e.g., finance, operations, and marketing) and organizational and managerial factors that cut across functions. This would include organizational structure, culture, historical context, management stability, nonfinancial control systems currently in place (e.g., Six Sigma, Balanced Scorecard, etc.), and formal and informal planning systems.

As Figure 21-2 shows, this analysis (as well as the external and competitive analyses) is completed over several steps in the strategic planning process. It begins by analyzing the largest, most significant factors. As the process moves from the highest level (vision and mission) to more specific and detailed analysis stages, it continues to a more detailed and thorough analysis.

External Environmental Analysis

The external analysis is focused on two levels: the industry and the macroenvironment. Several tools exist to analyze the industry. For example, Michael Porter's Five Forces model (1980) gives managers a better understanding of the industry context in which the organization operates. According to Porter (1980), industry structure is shaped by five forces:

1. Bargaining power of suppliers
2. Bargaining power of buyers and customers
3. Threat of new entrants
4. Threat from substitutes
5. Competition among existing players

Trend analysis is also a standard tool for industry analysis. In any case, it is important to understand the industry's current structure and major trends.

Reviewing the major external threats and opportunities is a common approach to macroenvironmental analysis. PESTEL Analysis is used to evaluate environmental trends that could impact the organization, specifically political, economic, social, technological, environmental, and legal forces (see **Figure 21-3**).

Competitive Analysis

Before deciding on the organization's strategic direction, it is also essential to understand its major competitors. This analysis would compare each competitor's market position, strengths, and weaknesses, as well as the competitors' current strategies and objectives. Also, it would be essential to understand each competitor's potential response to the plan the organization might be considering. For example, suppose a children's hospital opens a labor and delivery service line. In that case, it must anticipate how the other general acute care hospitals within the community with a labor and delivery service line will respond, and how this might create tension in existing interorganizational relationships. As a goal, organizations should seek to know as much about each major competitor as they know about themselves. All competitor intelligence should always be gathered in legal and ethical ways.

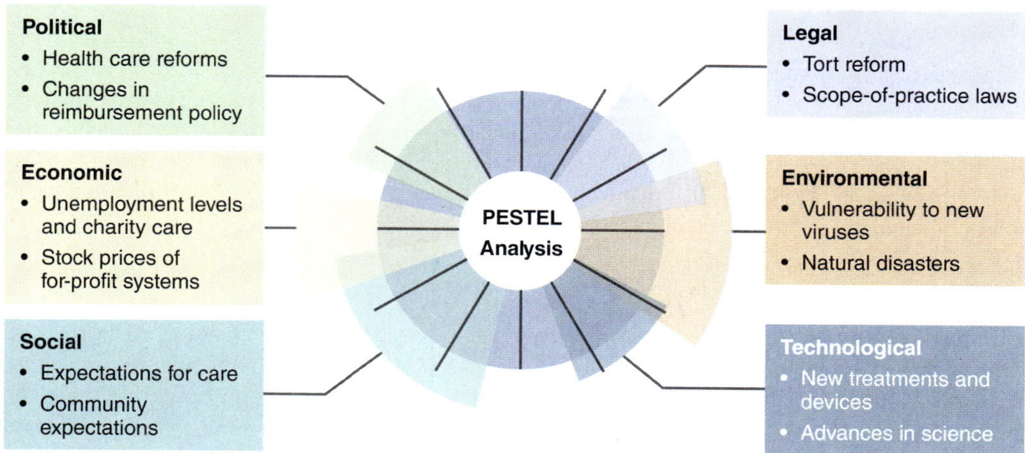

Figure 21-3 PESTEL Analysis

Developing Strategy

Vision and Mission

After thoroughly assessing the environment, management must determine the most appropriate long-term direction for the organization. The vision reflects the organization's aspirations—what it wants to become. For example, Hartford Hospital in Connecticut's vision is "to be nationally respected for excellence in patient care and most trusted for personalized coordinated care." The vision sets the tone and overarching direction for the rest of the strategy development phase and provides the organization with an easily understood and unifying common purpose.

The mission has four purposes:

1. Defining the organization
2. Providing direction (making the vision more specific)
3. Serving as a basis for resource allocation
4. Differentiating this organization from others competing in the same industry

It is usually a one- or two-sentence statement describing why an organization exists and is used to help guide decisions about priorities, strategies, and responsibilities. It accomplishes these purposes by defining four aspects of the organization: products or services, customers, markets, and philosophy (consistent with the vision). For example, the mission statement of Jackson Health System, located in southern Florida, is "To build the health of the community by providing a single, high standard of quality care for the residents of Miami-Dade County."

Of these aspects, the most critical to effective strategy is a clear definition of the organization's markets: where and with whom they compete, directly and indirectly, and a defined understanding of who the customers are. Customers can include direct customers (e.g., patients) and indirect customers (e.g., those paying for the products and services, such as third-party payers).

Long-Term Objectives

Objectives and goals reflect the desired end state. These are usually stated in 3- to 5-year terms. They can be of many types, but often reflect long-term objectives in the areas of growth, financial return, or customer perceptions (such as quality of care). An example of an objective for a hospital could be to "increase outpatient revenues from 20% of net revenues to 45% within 5 years." Strategic long-term objectives reflect organization-wide objectives and not those of individual units or functional areas.

Long-Term Strategies

Long-term strategies reflect how the objectives will be accomplished. They are corporate- or business-level strategies. For example, a plan to carry out the outpatient revenue objective could be "establishing three new community clinics that would provide outpatient services within the current market area." Typical organizations should have no more than three to five long-term strategies.

Effective long-term strategies and objectives need to be critically evaluated on several criteria before acceptance. These criteria include fit with the defined values, vision, and mission; consistency with external trends; feasibility of financial and managerial resources; organizational competencies to implement the strategies successfully; and potential impact on the competitive environment, including likely competitor counter-strategies.

Implementing Strategy

The key to a successful implementation of strategy is its integration with the organization's daily operations. An analytical and thorough process of reflecting strategy in the daily decisions of middle and lower management substantially increases the likelihood of strategic ideas becoming strategic realities.

Medium-Term Plan

Management looks mainly to annual plans and budgets as a guide in their daily decision process, so a "bridge" is necessary. The medium-term plan breaks down the 3- to 5-year long-term strategies and objectives into shorter, more actionable stages.

In addition to breaking down long-term strategies and objectives into 1-year periods, significant functional actions are mapped and sequenced, and financial implications are considered. Most large strategic programs require a series of essential actions within the various functional areas of the organization. The medium-term plan places these in their proper sequence. In our community clinics expansion example, locations must be determined before equipment is purchased or employees are hired and trained.

The final element of the medium-term plan includes a financial forecast for the 5 years, including the costs and expenses of the planned strategic actions. Of particular importance would be cash-flow forecasts showing how the new strategies would be financed and repaid.

Annual Objectives

All functional and financial objectives from the medium-term plan are listed. This is the beginning point for expanding on these objectives. A hierarchy of objectives is then created from the top down, eventually establishing annual objectives for each budget unit within the organization.

These objectives, if collectively carried out, would lead to accomplishing all strategic, financial, and functional objectives listed in the medium-term plan for the year.

Although this process must be top-down to ensure strategic consistency throughout the organization, that does not mean lower levels of the organization are not involved. Once a departmental manager or director has their objectives for the year, dividing them among individual units and developing the specific methods of accomplishment should reflect a team effort within the department.

Budget

Much has been written about the budget process, and a wide variety of budgeting methods exist. However, the only way to accomplish the strategic objectives is to build the budget around the annual unit objectives determined in the prior step. If, on the other hand, the budget is based on last year plus a percentage, it is decoupled from the strategic plan, and the likelihood of strategic accomplishment is low (unless the strategy for this year is to copy last year).

In building a budget around the unit's annual objectives, staffing and spending levels necessary to accomplish the goals are determined, and then these amounts are budgeted. This would apply to both operating and capital budgets. If the strategy for the year requires substantial changes from "business as usual," this could mean that some units may lose 50% of their budgets, while other units' budgets may double or triple. If management is unwilling to reflect strategic priorities in the budgets, then resources are not being allocated based on strategy and key objectives will not be met.

Policies

In practice, the strategic process often neglects policies and procedures. This oversight can severely threaten strategic change. In making the daily decisions that cumulatively either accomplish or fail to accomplish the organization's total strategy, middle- and lower-level managers rely on two primary guides: their budget and the organization's policies and procedures.

Policies accumulate over time, with older organizations having many more than younger organizations. These policies are often not well integrated, and may even conflict with one another, because they are often issued in response to a negative event. For example, one day several patients' checks bounce, so a new policy prohibiting the acceptance of checks as a method of payment is established. Because there is seldom any strategic input into policies, strategic change can contain many landmines. Consequently, it is best practice to review all policies annually in terms of how they support the new strategic direction. If policies are found that hinder strategic accomplishment, they need to be either changed or abolished.

Management Systems

In addition to the budget and policies, some organizations may have other management systems in place, such as a Six Sigma quality-improvement initiative. If other systems exist within the organization, it is critical that they be integrated with the strategic planning system so that they reinforce the strategic effort rather than hinder strategic accomplishment. Of particular note is the Balanced Scorecard (Kaplan & Norton, 1996) (Figure 21-1). This approach can be very helpful in the operational implementation of strategy if it is well integrated with the overall strategic planning process.

Evaluating Strategy

After year-end, and as the first step in the new strategy cycle, management evaluates the effectiveness of the prior year's strategies, including accomplishment of the year's strategic objectives. This begins with a review of the major strategic assumptions in the year's plan and a determination of whether those assumptions were, overall, accurate. If there was a major change to one of the critical strategic assumptions, a meaningful evaluation is not possible, and management may decide to shorten this step or skip it entirely. In our primary care clinic expansion example, suppose the organization had planned to open a clinic in October. However, the bank that was to finance the clinic build-out and equipment was being acquired by another financial institution due to its inability to meet federal capital requirements. As a result, the bank canceled the healthcare organization's credit line in January. Because of the changed lending environment, it took until August for the organization to obtain a new credit line with another bank. This delay in the clinic opening the following year, due to a major problem beyond the organization's control, does not reflect on the strategy's validity and may cause management to delay the evaluation until the following year. It is important to caution that this is not a place for management excuses, and such major events should be extremely rare.

If the assumptions did not change in any significant manner, then management must evaluate the strategic effectiveness. This evaluation can be of either a quantitative or qualitative nature (or both). Quantitative methods would look at the specific, measurable objectives that were supposed to occur during the year and compare the plan to what actually happened. If, in our clinic example, an objective was to increase outpatient revenue from 20% to 25% during the first year (on the way to the 45% long-term goal), then management would objectively determine whether the 25% goal was met. On the qualitative side, if a goal was to improve skills of middle management to handle the expansion through intensive training efforts, management would subjectively assess whether that goal had been met.

If the annual strategy objectives were met overall and no major changes in the environment were forecasted, usually the organization will continue with the current strategies and objectives for the next year. However, if the strategic analysis pointed to a shortfall, management would need to find the cause of the shortfall. There are two possibilities: poor or excessively ambitious strategies, or poor implementation of the strategies. The bias at the executive level is to blame execution, while the bias at the operational levels is to blame the strategy. For an effective evaluation, biases need to be set aside, and the analysis needs to be factual. Incorrect identification of the root causes of any shortfall inevitably leads to delays in fixing the problems and potentially severe financial consequences for the organization. After completion of the strategic evaluation, the process begins anew in the next year's planning cycle with a review of the prior assessments and revisions.

The Role of Structure

Structure plays a dual role in the strategic planning process. It is an important consideration in the internal evaluation phase and a critical element in implementation. During internal evaluation, the effect of structure on the organization's strategic focus, level of efficiency, integration of functions, and capacity to implement change is assessed. The structure chosen may also create or eliminate strategic competencies within functions. For example, centralized research and development departments are more likely to focus on new product breakthroughs and other long-term research at a strategic level. Decentralized research and development units, on the other hand, are more likely to focus on shorter-term process and product improvements at an operational level.

Once the assessment and strategy development phases have been completed, and the process moves into implementation, the organization's current structure must be assessed in terms of its appropriateness to implement the chosen strategic objectives. A critical issue in a decentralized organization, for example, would be whether the decentralization is on the same basis as the strategy. In our example, if the strategic direction is to customize services and delivery models at different primary care clinics, then the structure should be decentralized on the basis of geographic locations. If, on the other hand, the strategic direction is to serve as efficient "feeders" to the hospitals, then the structure would be much more centralized with few duplicated functions. These different strategic directions could well result in different structural alignments for various units, such as billing and collections, and diagnostic services.

If structural changes are needed in the organization as a result of changes in strategic direction or ineffective prior implementation efforts, this change needs to be built into the medium-term plan. A change of structure is a major organizational change, requiring careful and thorough planning.

Culture and Strategy

Like structure, organizational culture is also considered at the internal assessment and implementation stages of the strategic planning process because it is regarded as the most powerful influence on how people behave in organizations. Although the concept of organizational or corporate culture is of more recent origin, culture has long been the purview of anthropologists (O'Toole, 2014). For example, in 1871, British anthropologist E. B. Tylor (p. 1) defined culture as the "complex whole which includes knowledge, belief, art, morals, law, custom, and any other capabilities and habits acquired ... as a member of [a] society."

Because an organization's existing culture can be a significant strength or weakness, it should be evaluated during the internal evaluation phase. At this stage, it may also be helpful to assess subcultures within units that may become critical to potential strategies. For example, suppose there is a culture of constant conflict between physicians and other professionals within the surgical units of the hospital. That conflict may not be an issue for our primary care clinic expansion strategy if the culture is cooperative and collaborative in the hospital's outpatient units. However, these cultural issues need to be known in advance so that, during the implementation phase, managers and clinicians for the new primary care clinics are drawn from the hospital's outpatient units and not from surgical units. If a strategic change is being considered, a thorough cultural analysis during assessment can prove helpful later in the process.

Culture will be a primary strategic consideration during the implementation phase. If the existing culture supports the new strategy, the odds of success are much higher than if the culture is neutral to the change. A neutral culture will require more management, change support, and organizational development efforts during implementation.

Finally, a culture that opposes the planned strategic change usually presents a significant roadblock. Management guru Peter Drucker has often stated that an organization's culture would trump any attempt to create a strategy that was incompatible with its culture. A significant cultural change at the strategic level within an existing organization may be unrealistic, leaving managers with few other strategic implementation options, none perfect. If the new strategy is deemed essential to the organization, implementation must proceed. The best choice in these circumstances is usually to try to tweak the strategy's implementation approach (without changing the long-term objectives) to make it more palatable to the culture. Other choices are to use a high level of outsourcing (to companies with more appropriate cultures) or to use coercive power to impose the change (usually a disastrous choice). If culture is going to be a problem, it may be worthwhile for the organization to revisit the strategic choice to ensure that this is the direction they want to go.

Matching Strategy and Structure

Based on research in 84 organizations (including 19 hospitals), Miles and Snow (1978) proposed four organizational types, in terms of their general characteristics, strategy sets, and internal characteristics and behavior; see **Figure 21-4**. They suggested a close relationship exists between a successful organization's internal factors, chosen competitive environments, and practical strategies. Later research (Brown & Iverson, 2004; Zahra & Pearce, 1990) supported the major concepts of these typologies, although some specific functional matches had mixed research results.

Miles and Snow identify four organizational types: defenders, prospectors, analyzers, and reactors. They point out that these types of organizations may need some adjustment in particular industries.

Defenders

These organizations have narrow product and market domains, industry-specific experienced executives, and do not search outside their defined markets for new opportunities. Their strategies are to penetrate deeper into current markets, maintain prominence within their chosen markets, and grow cautiously and incrementally.

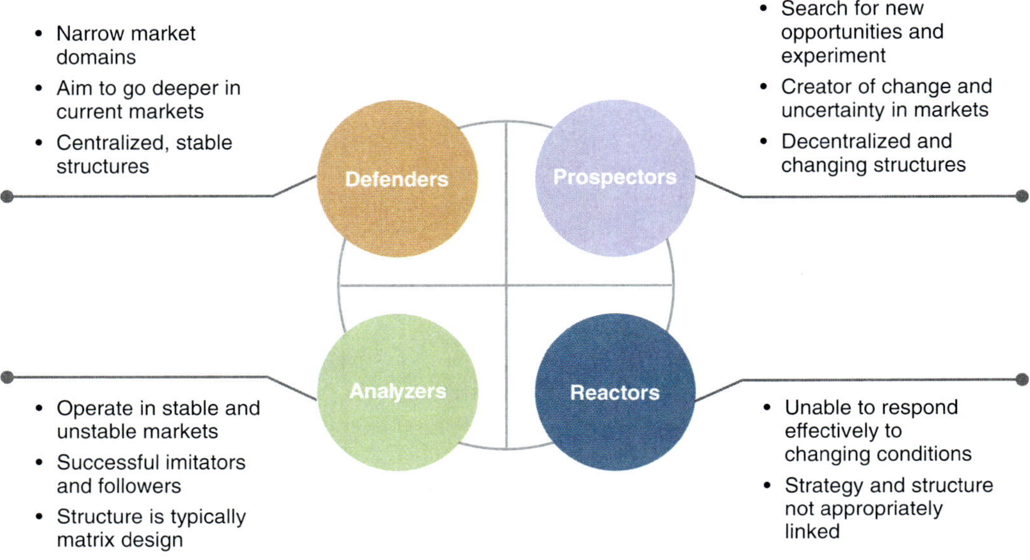

Figure 21-4 Miles and Snow's Four Organizational Types

Their structures are functional and stable with centralized controls and vertical information flows. They promote from within, focus on continual efficiency improvements, have formal job definitions, and use intensive (deep, detailed) planning systems. The politically dominant functions are finance and operations. Lincare Holdings, part of the Linde Group, is an example of an efficiency-focused organization with a narrow product/market domain. A high percentage of its revenues is from Medicare and Medicaid reimbursements, and its product line primarily provides oxygen and respiratory therapy services to patients in the home.

With a primarily internal focus, defenders perform best in the stable environments they seek and maintain. Significant strategic risks for defenders are the continued viability of their narrow domains and their relative inflexibility to change if needed.

Prospectors

These organizations continually search for market opportunities and experiment with potential responses to emerging environmental trends. Miles and Snow view this type of organization as creating change and uncertainty within markets. Their strategies look to a carefully monitored, broad product/market domain that undergoes frequent change. Their growth is uneven and in spurts from new products and new markets.

Structures often change and tend to be product-based. Information flows to decentralized decision makers with results-oriented controls. There is low formalization in job descriptions; the organization views its technology as people rather than machines; and conflict resolutions are usually handled through integrators, such as project managers. Efficiency is sacrificed for flexibility, with broad-based planning systems. The politically dominant functions are marketing, research, and development. UnitedHealth Group is an example of an organization with a frequently changing product/market domain, including consulting and processing services, plan administration, a full range of risk-based health insurance plans, pharmacy benefit management, and dental and disability solutions. Frequent structural changes are reported as changes in their product and market domains.

Prospectors with a primarily external focus perform best in the unstable and changing environments they seek. Should their product domains become more stable and cost-sensitive, prospectors face significant strategic risks, including inefficiency and a higher cost structure.

Analyzers

Analyzers operate in both stable and changing environments. In a stable environment, these organizations adopt efficient formal structures and processes, while in unstable areas, they monitor competitors for successful ideas and adopt the most promising ones. Their strategies are successful imitation and avid followers of change, using extensive market surveillance. Growth is usually through market penetration, but may also occur from product or market development.

The structure is usually a matrix, with a functional organization in the stable areas and a product organization in the unstable regions. Planning is intensive and broad, with complex control systems that can make trade-offs between efficiency and effectiveness. Because of its dual nature and need for different structures and processes in the two areas, maintaining an analyzer organization is difficult in practice. The politically dominant functions are marketing, applied research, and operations. A community hospital may pursue this strategy to maintain efficiency (and low costs) in ongoing operations. Still, it must also react to changes and instability in the technical, competitive, and reimbursement environments.

Analyzers, with their dual focus, perform best in mixed environments. The significant strategic risks for analysts are their need to straddle the middle and preserve power balances, which prevent them from aggressively pursuing either an efficiency or effectiveness strategy if the environment should shift firmly to one side or the other.

Reactors

These organizations have top managers who perceive change in their environments, but cannot respond effectively. With an inconsistent strategy-structure relationship, they seldom adjust until forced to do so by external pressures. According to Miles and Snow (1978), this final organizational type is unable to succeed because of one of three strategic issues: (1) management cannot create a viable strategy; (2) management develops a strategy, but structure and processes are not appropriately linked; or (3) management continues with a strategy no longer suitable to the changed external environment.

During the 2000s, Pfizer was an example of a reactive organization due to its inability to adapt to a changed regulatory and technological environment. Pfizer had to deal with a lengthier (and more challenging) new drug approval regulatory environment, patents expiring on major blockbuster drugs, generics obtaining increasing market share, inefficient and high-cost-fragmented structures, and an organizational culture resistant to change. Other examples include many community hospitals that have been unable to adapt to a shift toward outpatient-based care models, more rigorous reimbursement policies, or demographic changes in their service areas.

The Miles and Snow (1978) typology demonstrates the close relationship and critical need to link strategy to the external environment, internal structure, and processes. Although there are other successful models in the healthcare sector beyond the four Miles and Snow present, the idea that the external environment, the strategy, and an organization's internal structure and processes must be carefully coordinated remains a central tenet of a winning strategy.

Summary

Strategy plays a critical role in organizational success. Through a few major decisions, an effective strategy guides the organization through changing environments, conflicting stakeholder demands, and uncertain economic and regulatory times. The strategic planning provides an integrated approach to environmental assessment, strategy development, implementation, and evaluation. This top-to-bottom integrated strategic process can significantly improve an organization's chances of realizing its long-term vision.

The ideal situation is an organization that understands and selects a suitable competitive environment, develops strategies that match the chosen external environment, and designs organizational structures and processes best suited to implement those strategies.

Discussion Questions

1. Discuss how the healthcare external environment differs from that the average U.S. company faces. Explain this at both the industry and macroenvironment levels.

2. Explain the differences in how personal values are reflected in an organization's values between an entrepreneurial healthcare firm and a large governmental health agency. Do you think these differences change the typical values that each type of organization has?
3. Discuss at least three different types of healthcare organizations and how their differences could affect their strategic planning process.
4. Using as an example a healthcare organization you are familiar with (or have researched), explain the competitive domain they have chosen, their strategies to compete, and their structure and processes. Are there mismatches? If so, what changes would you recommend?

CASE STUDY 21-1 Strategy, Stability, and Strength

Bronson's Journey to Excellence

Excellence has always been a focus of Bronson Methodist Hospital, a not-for-profit tertiary hospital based in Kalamazoo, Michigan. But it was not until 1999 that the organization adopted the Baldrige criteria and put into place a systematic approach to organizational excellence.

In the mid-1990s, as Bronson designed and prepared to move into a new, all-private-room facility, Bronson's leadership seized the opportunity to raise the bar on the quality of their internal processes so they could match the quality of the hospital's new state-of-the-art patient-care environment. The building project became a catalyst for moving the organization's culture from "good" to "great."

When the Baldrige criteria for health care became available in 1999, Bronson was poised and ready to begin using the model—a systems perspective for understanding performance management provided by the Baldrige Performance Excellence Program (www.nist.gov/baldrige). They were attracted to this model because the Baldrige criteria are not prescriptive; they do not tell an organization what to do. Instead, the criteria challenge an organization to review and understand how it is doing things. This was precisely the formula for self-evaluation that Bronson was looking for to become a "great" hospital and sustain long-term success. Since implementing the Baldrige criteria, Bronson has achieved strong performance improvement and results in every key area measured, including low Medicare patient mortality; high overall patient, employee, and physician satisfaction; and national recognition for workplace excellence. They have seen significant improvement in use of prophylaxis, registered nurse turnover rate, and the integration and use of technology; Bronson also has pioneered efforts to reduce waste and pollution. As a result of these and many other accomplishments, Bronson Methodist Hospital was named one of six recipients—from across American industries—of the Malcolm Baldrige National Quality Award in November 2005.

A critical component of the organization's success can be attributed to Bronson's Leadership System. In the past, they had been unable to clearly articulate exactly how we led the organization. Working with the Baldrige criteria compelled us to specifically delineate and document how the organization "fits" together in terms of strategy, performance standards, action, results, and accountability. As a result of this work, we created the Strategic Management Model to provide Bronson with a systematic approach that aligns all of our planning, including strategic, workforce, financial, capital, and information technology. Because strategy is the foundation for success, we have found that the consistent use of this tool has contributed greatly to our organization's evolution.

Focus: Bronson's strategy revolves around our Plan for Excellence, which captures the

Table 21-1

<table>
<tr><td colspan="3">VISION
Bronson will be a national leader in healthcare quality</td></tr>
<tr><td colspan="3">Clinical Excellence
Achieve excellent patient outcomes</td></tr>
<tr><td colspan="2">Customer and Service Excellence
Enhance service excellence, staff competency, and leadership</td><td>Corporate Effectiveness
Achieve efficiency, growth, financial, and community benefit targets</td></tr>
<tr><td>Philosophy of Nursing Excellence
Respect
Compassion
Expertise
Impact
Pride</td><td>Values
We believe in, and our actions will reflect:
Care and respect for all people
Teamwork
Stewardship of resources
Commitment to our community
The pursuit of excellence</td><td>Commitment to Patient Care Excellence
Healing with our knowledge
Caring with our hearts
Working together for Bronson patients and families</td></tr>
<tr><td colspan="3">MISSION
Provide excellent healthcare services</td></tr>
</table>

Reproduced from Sardone, F. J., & Reinoehl, S. (2006). Strategy, stability and strength: Bronson's journey to excellence. *Healthcare Executive, 21*(3), 16–20. Reprinted with permission.

vision, mission, values, and service expectations of all staff and leaders (see **Table 21-1**). It includes our strategies, the "three Cs": clinical excellence, customer service excellence, and corporate effectiveness. They use the plan extensively during employee, physician, volunteer, and other stakeholder interactions to effectively communicate the hospital's vision and actively engage them in achieving it.

In the early years of using the Baldrige criteria to focus our planning, they realized that the hospital's mission and vision also needed to be refined and focused. The mission at the time was: *We are committed to improving the health of those we serve by providing services that are of value, that are comprehensive, and that are accessible through an integrated network of cooperating providers.*

As Bronson talked with stakeholders, they realized that this mission seemed too "corporate" in its language and was difficult to understand. Furthermore, it only vaguely addressed community health and partnerships with other organizations, which was difficult to measure. They decided our mission should be succinct, direct, and measurable and address the needs of anyone seeking our services whether they are members of the community or not. Thus, the mission today is simply:

> *Provide excellent health care services:* This mission is easy to communicate, deploy, and measure. In a similar vein, they rewrote our vision, which was: *Bronson and its partners will be the system of choice in our region.*

The old vision focused on being the best in our area. But to truly raise the bar on organizational performance, it was critical that they benchmark against the best in the nation. As a result, the current vision is: *Bronson will be a national leader in healthcare quality.*

This vision has driven the organization and helped fuel performance improvement processes. The simplification of the mission and vision now keeps the entire organization focused and moving in a clear direction.

Re-evaluation: An important component of our Strategic Management Model is the Strategic

Input Document (SID), which informs the planning process. The SID is a formal compilation of assumptions about the environment and how those assumptions will affect Bronson during the year. Leaders look at developments in the community; changes occurring in competing organizations; governmental issues on the local, state, and national levels; and the needs and wants of our stakeholders. While Bronson always had considered these issues during the annual planning process, they had never formally documented them so that they could refer to them easily; prioritized challenges; and most importantly, continuously re-evaluated them throughout the year. The SID is a simple, yet critical, process improvement. It helps Bronson to react quickly to environmental changes yet stay on task with our plan.

Accountability: Before they adopted the Baldrige criteria and developed the Strategic Management Model, Bronson did not use scorecards to set targets and track our progress formally. As they implemented the Strategic Management Model, they designed detailed tactics based on metrics to achieve goals aligned with the three Cs. For example, the clinical excellence goal of reducing Medicare mortality—which is reported to our board in an overall scorecard—cascades down to specific measurable activities on leader- and staff-level scorecards. These detailed tactics are like strings that are attached from Bronson's overall goals to every person in the organization. Thus the entire workforce, employees and physician partners, know exactly how their efforts contribute to the organization's success. Not only do scorecards reinforce the responsibility that staff have in achieving the hospital's overall goals, but also—because of the metrics, which include "meet," "exceed," and "far exceed" scoring criteria—staff know exactly where they stand at any given time. Bronson monitors the impact of our efforts to improve accountability through our scorecards and employee and physician opinion surveys which asks whether they understand our strategic direction and their role in reaching organizational goals.

Heightening the sense of accountability among staff also was made easier when they modified the vision and made a conscious decision to bring Bronson's strategic plan to light at all levels of the organization. Today, even their specific tactics are widely publicized throughout the hospital. Such disclosure has made a huge difference with the leadership team, employees, medical staff, and volunteers, who feel more connected to the vision.

Ownership: In the past, Bronson's strategic planning was primarily orchestrated by the vice president of Planning. In an effort to improve results, they created Strategic Oversight Teams for each of the three Cs, led by members of the executive team. The teams establish short- and long-term plans for their "C," develop the accompanying scorecards, and monitor results. With this approach to planning, there is more ownership of the plan at the executive level and with leaders and key physicians who now feel as though they own the plan.

Integration: When Bronson first began using the Baldrige criteria, we treated it as a separate process and convened a separate committee. This changed when they realized the true value of the Baldrige model is in integrating it into what you do every day to run your organization.

Once Bronson did this, they understood how it was going to make them a better business. By aligning the six categories of the Baldrige criteria, Bronson learned the importance of examining the interrelationships among all facets of the organization. For example, through the process, they realized that they were approving capital purchases separately from our strategic planning cycle. Now, their capital and technology planning are wrapped into one process. Bronson holds a day-long retreat focused on reviewing and prioritizing clinical technology as part of developing the next year's strategic plan and budget. Prior to using the Baldrige criteria, many processes were people-dependent. Fortunately, they employed excellent people who did a great job of carrying out the work assigned to them; however, they realized that this was risky in both the short and long terms. If those people left the organization, how would the processes be sustained? Tools like the Plan for Excellence, the SID, the Strategic Oversight Teams, and scorecards are now hardwired into the work; they are documented and repeatable. This helps ensure that organizational stability and the high-quality service and excellent outcomes will be sustained in the future, regardless of any personnel changes.

Using the Baldrige criteria has dramatically changed how Bronson serves our patients. Community preference for Bronson as the area's "best hospital" was at a record high during this timeframe. Independent study data show there is a 32-point gap between Bronson and its closest competitor. This preference has translated into market growth as well: inpatient volume at Bronson grew 34% between 2000 and 2005.

Since being named a Baldrige recipient last November, Bronson has received numerous phone calls and emails from organizations across the United States asking how to win the award. There is no formula for winning; it is all about the journey to excellence and what each organization learns about itself along the way.

Using the Baldrige criteria has dramatically changed how Bronson runs the business, and they are very proud to now be considered a role model organization that others can learn from. The tools it provides allow for continuous improvement that can strengthen and sustain any organization for years to come.

Discussion Questions

1. Using the strategic planning model as a guide, discuss how Bronson currently carries out each step in the model.
2. Explain how Bronson links the various steps together. Are the steps in the same sequence as the model?
3. Discuss several changes you would recommend to Bronson to improve their strategic planning process.
4. Do you think Bronson is trying to become one of the three successful Miles organizational types? If so, which one? If not, why not?

References

Brown, W. A., & Iverson, J. O. (2004). Exploring strategy and board structure in nonprofit organizations. *Nonprofit and Voluntary Sector Quarterly, 33*(3), 377–400.

Drucker, P. F. (1974). *Management: Tasks, responsibilities, practices*. Harper & Row.

Hartford Hospital. (n.d.). Mission, vision, & values. https://hartfordhospital.org/about-hh/mission-vision-values

Health Research and Educational Trust (2007). *Building an exceptional board: Effective practices for health care governance*. Report of the Blue Ribbon Panel on Health Care Governance. https://hscrc.maryland.gov/documents/public-interest/hospitalgovernance/ctrhlthcaregovernance_2007.pdf

Hofer, C. W., & Schendel, D. (1978). *Strategy formulation: Analytical concepts*. West Publishing.

Jackson Health System. (n.d.). Mission. Retrieved October 18, 2025, from https://jacksonhealth.org/about-us/

Jarousse, L. A. (2014). Transforming governance: Leading in an era of reform. *Hospitals & Health Networks, 88*(3), 41–46. https://web.archive.org/web/20150909040943/http://www.hhnmag.com/Magazine/2014/Mar/gatefold-transforming-governance

Kaplan, R. S., & Norton, D. P. (1996). Linking the balanced scorecard to strategy. *California Management Review, 39*(1), 53–79.

Lencioni, P. (2002). Make your values mean something. *Harvard Business Review, 80*(7), 113–117.

Miles, R. E., & Snow, C. C. (1978). *Organizational strategy, structure, and process*. McGraw-Hill.

O'Toole, J. (2014). Organizational culture. *Strategy+Business, 77*, 78–81.

Pointer, D. D., Totten, M. K., & Orlikoff, J. E. (2005). Trustee workbook 2: The balanced scorecard: A tool for maximizing board performance. *Trustee: The journal for hospital governing boards, 58*(4), 17–20.

Porter, M. E. (1980). *Competitive strategy: Techniques for analyzing industries and competitors*. Free Press.

Tylor, E. B. (1871). *Primitive culture: Researches into the development of mythology, philosophy, religion, art, and custom*, (Vol. 1). J. Murray. https://quod.lib.umich.edu/m/moa/ABC123

Zahra, S. A., & Pearce, J. A., II. (1990). Research evidence on the Miles-Snow typology. *Journal of Management, 16*(4), 751–768.

Other Suggested Readings

Begun, J. W., & Kaissi, A. A. (2005). An exploratory study of healthcare strategic planning in two metropolitan areas. *Journal of Healthcare Management, 50*(4), 264–275.

Chan, S. (2002). The importance of strategy for the evolving field of radiology. *Radiology, 224*(3), 639–648.

Covaleski, M. A., & Dirsmith, M. W. (1981). MBO and goal directedness in a hospital context. *Academy of Management Review, 6*(3), 409–418.

Crotts, J. C., Dickson, D. R., & Ford, R. C. (2005). Aligning organizational processes with mission: The case of service excellence. *Academy of Management Executive, 19*(3), 54–68.

Ford, R. C., Sivo, S. A., Fottler, M. D., Dickson, D., Bradley, K., & Johnson, L. (2006). Aligning internal organizational factors with a service excellence mission: An exploratory investigation in health care. *Health Care Management Review, 31*(4), 259–269.

Kershaw, R., & Kershaw, S. (2001). Developing a balanced scorecard to implement strategy at St. Elsewhere Hospital. *Management Accounting Quarterly, 2*(2), 28–35.

Rivers, P. A., Fottler, M. D., & Parker, M. (2005). Environmental assessment of the Indian Health Service. *Health Care Management Review, 30*(4), 293–303.

Steiner, G. A., Miner, J. B., & Gray, E. R. (1982). *Management policy and strategy* (2nd ed.). Macmillan.

Williams, J., Smythe, W., Hadjistavropoulos, T., Malloy, D. C., & Martin, R. (2005). A study of thematic content in hospital mission statements: A question of values. *Health Care Management Review, 30*(4), 304–314.

CHAPTER 22

Organization Structures: Contextual Dimension

LEARNING OUTCOMES

After completing this chapter, the student should be able to understand:

- How each element of the contextual dimension relates to an organization's structure.
- The differences between mechanistic and organic systems.
- The advantages and disadvantages of the four basic organizational structures.
- The importance of the various horizontal linkage mechanisms.
- What is meant by population ecology.
- What institutional theory means, and the three mechanisms associated with institutional isomorphism.
- The various strategies organizations use to develop and sustain interorganizational relationships.

Overview

To be an effective leader, an individual must consider a given situation's internal and external constraints. The same concept holds true for designing an organization's structure. For managers to effectively structure their organizations for high performance, they must consider various internal and external constraints. Some constraints may be the organization's culture or size, how the organization adapts to its environment, and differences among resources, operating activities, and strategies. Daft (2007) refers to these constraints as the contextual dimension of organizational design (see **Table 22-1**).

Contextual Factors

Contextual factors are important and interrelated in explaining what goes on inside organizations. For example, what measurement is used when describing the organization's size? Does the organization use the number of employees, physical capacity (e.g., number of hospital beds), organizational inputs or outputs (e.g., 50,000 annual emergency room visits), or the organization's yearly

Table 22-1 Organizational Contextual Dimensions

Dimension	Description	Healthcare Organizations
Size	Size typically reflects the number of people in the organization, division, or unit.	Typically measured by number of employees (i.e., full-time equivalents [FTEs]). Other size measures, such as total patient net revenue, total inpatient discharges, total outpatient visits, number of beds, or total assets, also reflect magnitude. Still, they do not indicate the size of the "people" part of the system.
Technology	Technology refers to the tools, machinery, physical equipment, and accumulated knowledge and techniques used to produce its services and/or products.	This includes medical devices, information systems, diagnostic knowledge and processes, and treatment modalities.
Environment	The environment includes all elements outside the organization's boundary. Key elements include the industry, government, customers, and competitors in the same industry.	This includes, among others, insurance companies and other payors, competing hospitals, patients, the Centers for Medicare and Medicaid Services (CMS), and pharmaceutical companies.
Goals and strategies	Goals are the organization's intent, and strategies are the plans of action that describe resource allocation and activities for dealing with the environment to accomplish the organization's goals.	Goals and strategies define the scope of the organization's current and future operations and the relationships with employees, patients, payors, and competitors.
Culture	An organization's culture is the underlying set of key values, beliefs, understandings, and norms employees share. Although unwritten, an organization's culture can be observed in its stories, slogans, ceremonies, uniforms, and design.	Healthcare organizations typically have a formal written statement of values regarding ethical behavior, commitment to employees, clinical excellence, or patient service. These statements provide a framework for decision making and hold organizational members together and accountable.

Data from Daft, R. L. (2007). *Organization theory and design* (9th ed., p. 20). Thomson South-Western.

revenues or net assets? Although Kimberly (1976) suggests that these various size measurements may be highly intercorrelated in some instances, managers must be clear about the measurement used. Most research relating size to organizational structure has been based on the number of people employed by the organization. Blau (1968) found that increasing organizational size (number of employees) was related to increasing differentiation (number of levels, departments, etc., within an organization). Increasing differentiation is related to an increased need for control and coordination. The widely cited Aston studies, which were a series of comparative investigations into the sources of organizational structure carried out over the 1960s and 1970s (Pugh et al., 1963; Pugh et al., 1968), found that increasing size is related to increasing structuring of organizational activities and decreasing concentrations of authority. As the organization gets larger, it becomes more complex to manage, therefore needing more structures to coordinate among its various parts.

Technology is another important factor relating to an organization's structure. The contextual factor of technology has three components: (1) machine technology (i.e., facilities and equipment), (2) application of knowledge for effective performance of certain tasks and activities, and (3) organizational technology—the techniques used in the transformation of inputs into outputs (Kast & Rosenzweig, 1985). Three questions need to be answered when assessing an organization's technical system:

1. Are the organization's tasks and problem-solving needs standardized?
2. Is the organization's technical system stable or dynamic?
3. Is the organization's technical system complex or straightforward?

To answer the first question, Perrow (1967) provides us with the following guidelines: (A) if problem solving is standardized, with few exceptions, it can be described as routine technology; (B) if problem solving is difficult, with many exceptions, the technology is described as nonroutine. To assist in answering questions 2 and 3, Kast and Rosenzweig (1985) relate that when considering organizational technologies, managers need to determine (1) the degree of complexity of the technology and (2) whether the technology is stable or dynamic. Organizational technologies can range from simple and stable (i.e., person-tool) to dynamic and complex (i.e., continuous process or advanced technology). For example, a nurse practitioner diagnosing a patient for strep throat by obtaining a culture is stable and straightforward. In contrast, a team of surgeons performing a multiple-organ transplant operation would be considered dynamic and complex technology.

Woodward (1965) and her associates noted a close relationship between the type of technology, the average span of control, the number of levels of management, and the organization's success. Miles and Snow (1978) demonstrated the critical need to link the other contextual factors of environment, goals, strategies, and culture to an organization's internal structure and processes.

The contextual dimension describes the organizational setting that influences and shapes the structure and design of the entity (Daft, 2007). In other words, given the situation, the organizational structure of an organization must "fit" with its environment and between its subsystems to achieve the company's goals. Because no two organizations are identical (different goals, cultures, size, etc.), managers need to appreciate that there is no one best way to structure an organization (Lawrence & Lorsch, 1967). For example, an organization making a standard product or offering a standardized service using the same processes and procedures will use routine technologies and a bureaucratic structure to achieve maximum efficiency (e.g., Shouldice "Hernia" Hospital in Canada). In contrast, organizations with nonroutine activities dealing with unpredictable environments will use flexible technologies and a nonbureaucratic structure. Burns and Stalker (1961, 1994) termed these bureaucratic and nonbureaucratic structures mechanistic and organic systems, respectively.

Mechanistic and Organic Systems

Burns and Stalker (1961, 1994) developed the mechanistic and organic systems theory when their research found that technology and market forces exerted pressures on organizations that made particular organizational forms desirable. The researchers found that mechanistic systems are suitable for stable conditions and are characterized by repetitive tasks, a clear hierarchy of control, vertical communication, and standardized technologies. Organic systems have the opposite characteristics and are therefore appropriate to changing conditions that introduce new problems and requirements for action (i.e., innovation). The organic system requires a dynamic, changing structure that is not feasible for all organizations. As such, Burns and Stalker noted that there are stages on the continuum between the two polar points (mechanistic and organic), and organizations may operate within both systems simultaneously; see **Figure 22-1**. For example, a pharmaceutical company's research and development division may operate as an organic system, whereas the manufacturing division may work as a mechanistic system.

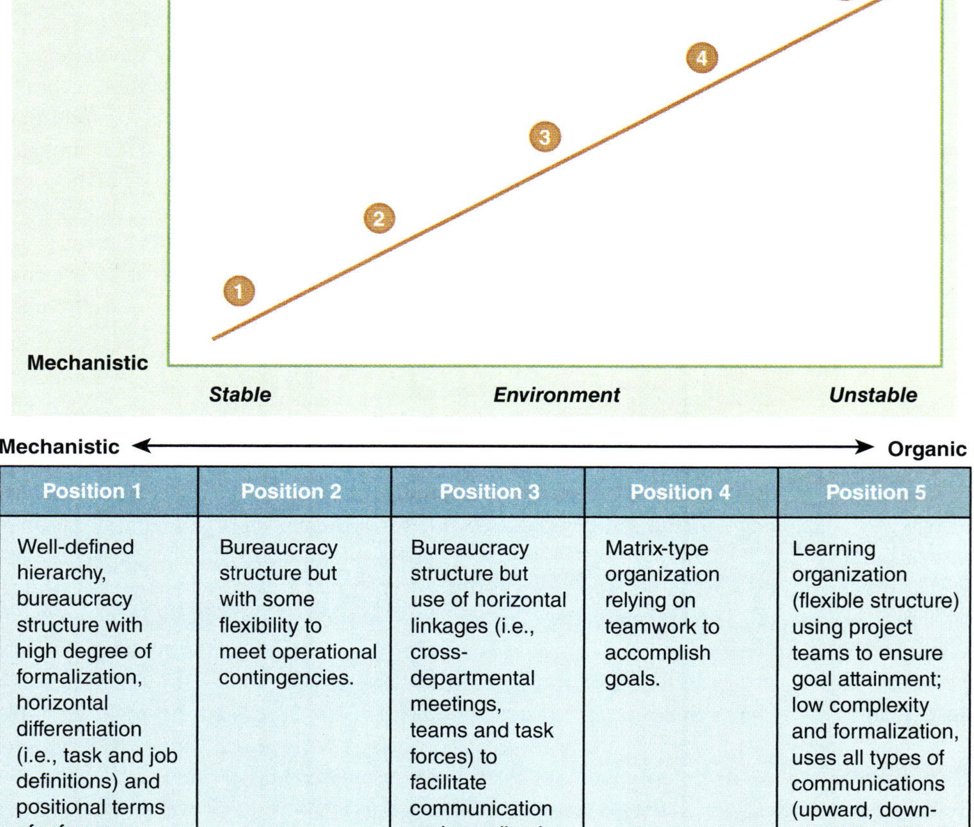

Mechanistic ⟵⟶ Organic

Position 1	Position 2	Position 3	Position 4	Position 5
Well-defined hierarchy, bureaucracy structure with high degree of formalization, horizontal differentiation (i.e., task and job definitions) and positional terms of reference, downward communications with little participation in decision making.	Bureaucracy structure but with some flexibility to meet operational contingencies.	Bureaucracy structure but use of horizontal linkages (i.e., cross-departmental meetings, teams and task forces) to facilitate communication and coordination of operational activities.	Matrix-type organization relying on teamwork to accomplish goals.	Learning organization (flexible structure) using project teams to ensure goal attainment; low complexity and formalization, uses all types of communications (upward, downward, lateral) to coordinate activities with high degree of participation in decision making based on expertise rather than position.

Note: Burns and Stalker noted that there are stages on the continuum between the two extreme points (mechanistic and organic) and that organizations may operate within both systems simultaneously.

Figure 22-1 Positions on the Mechanistic and Organic Continuum

Understanding mechanistic and organic systems allows us to explore an organization's structure, taking into consideration its complexity (e.g., size, goals, environment). As Burton, DeSanctis, and Obel note (2006, p. 57), "a poor choice of structure leads to opportunity losses that can be a threat to the organization's short-term efficiency and effectiveness as well as its long-term viability."

An organization's structure can be defined as the clustering of its various departments, divisions, and so forth to coordinate and control activities (and people) to achieve the company's goals. Structure involves two issues: (1) how to organize the firm into smaller subunits and (2) how to coordinate the subunits so the firm's goals will be achieved (Mintzberg, 1979). The company's organization chart can determine how an entity has structured itself. The organization chart depicts the degree or level of vertical differentiation of the company (i.e., the depth of the hierarchy—top to bottom), vertical operational responsibilities (i.e., communication and coordination activities connecting the top and bottom of an organization), and sometimes, but not always, the horizontal linkages (i.e., communication and coordination activities across organizational departments). In this chapter, four basic structure configurations will be presented. We will discuss how these structures emerged and how and why they changed.

Organization Structures

A multiplicity of models exists regarding organizational configurations. Most of these models use variations of one or more of the four basic organizational structures. The four basic organizational structures are simple, functional, divisional, and matrix (Miles & Snow, 1978). As noted, these four basic structures can be combined in different organizational patterns and/or forms. Variations can be found across the organization's work units, departments, and divisions, and up and down the hierarchy. For example, if an organization is designed with a divisional structure, within the division's subunits may be a functional, matrix, another divisional, or hybrid form of these basic structures (Burton et al., 2006).

Simple Structure

The simple organizational structure is prevalent because, in many industries, including health care, most organizations are small and therefore do not need a complex structure. Simple structures have the following characteristics: (1) centralized decision making, (2) low specialization (i.e., division of labor), and (3) high degree of informality (i.e., limited written rules, policies, and procedures). Although this simple structure may provide job enlargement because employees are not bound by formality or division of labor, it also may lead to inefficiencies and conflicts if employees do not understand their roles and responsibilities. An example of a simple structure is a sole practitioner's (e.g., a physician's) office. The physician is "senior management," responsible for making the practice's clinical and administrative decisions. Although there is a clear distinction between the roles of clinical and nonclinical professionals working in the office, administrative personnel usually multitask between front desk duties, obtaining needed referrals, coding, billing, and so on. Within small physicians' offices, policies and procedures are generally communicated verbally, with little to no documentation except when required by local, state, or federal regulations.

Functional Structure

As the physician's practice grows, it may evolve into a functional structure with employees working in departments based on their roles and responsibilities (see **Figure 22-2**). This structure enhances the functioning of each subunit. For example, if all billing and coding employees work

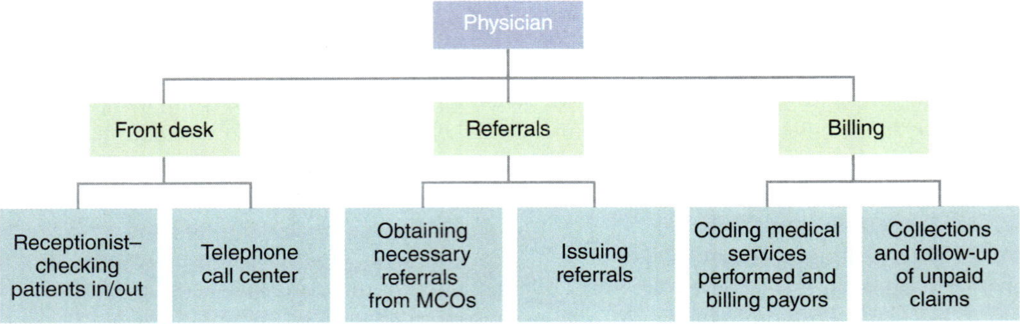

Figure 22-2 Functional Structure—Physician's Office

in the same department, they will increase their expertise by sharing knowledge and supporting one another. This structure allows the physician's practice to achieve efficiency because of the economies of scale. However, this structure makes communication and coordination among different departments more difficult and limits flexibility because of the centralization.

Divisional Structure

A divisional structure divides the organization's operations into product/service or customer segments or geographical locations. For example, a managed care organization may be divisionally structured by its customer segments—Medicare, Medicaid, and commercial members. Each division is responsible for product and service lines, customer bases, or geographic locations with supporting functional units, such as finance, marketing, and human resources. A divisional structure is decentralized, which allows for flexibility and quick responses to environmental changes. However, this structure results in duplication of resources because each division has the same administrative operations. In addition, it does not support the exchange of knowledge between people working in the same profession (i.e., human resources, marketing, finance) because employees work in different divisions (see **Figure 22-3**).

Many national and multi-state organizations have a divisional structure. They may have a central corporate office, then organize their hospitals and clinics into regional structures that have their own leadership. This allows for some standardization across sites, while also recognizing that each location has a unique patient population and culture, and allowing for some flexibility

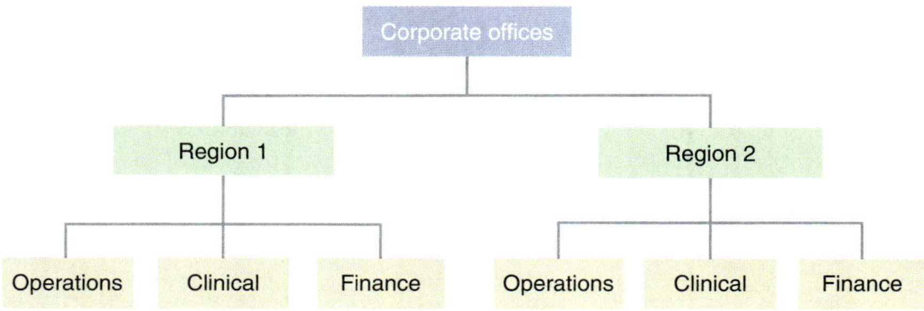

Figure 22-3 Divisional Structure

in how the local hospital cares for its unique community. By creating a divisional structure, the organization can balance economies of scale by having a central office that doesn't duplicate services (e.g., information technology, billing, and group purchasing are "corporate" services to the divisions) and through each division's ability to focus on patients and customers at the local level.

Matrix Structure

The matrix structure combines the functional and divisional structures. The matrix organization was developed to improve management's control over a product or project within a multifunctional firm (Scott & Davis, 2006). The matrix structure is reflected in an organization chart with the various products and projects (each with a nonfunctional orientation) on the horizontal axis, and the functional contributors to those products and projects on the vertical axis. Because of the "cross-representation" (i.e., product/service and function), an employee will be accountable to both a product/project manager as well as a functional manager. For example, a hospital may organize under clinical service lines while maintaining permanent functional units (see **Figure 22-4**). The cardiovascular services line is assigned a clinical service line (CSL) manager responsible for directing the operations of all medical and surgical cardiac care, including the hospital's cardiac catheterization laboratory. As such, some nurse employees would have two managers: a functional manager (director of nursing) and a CSL manager.

This type of structure is not easy to implement because of the dual authority. However, the matrix structure eliminates the duplication of skills and responsibilities by identifying functions or common components shared by multiple divisions, services, or products within an organization. Matrix organizations provide clear accountability within a specific business function and allow more efficient allocation of specialized skills. By taking advantage of the shared services and abilities and not having to develop and manage those skills, the service product line manager can better focus on their goals (see **Case Study 22-1**).

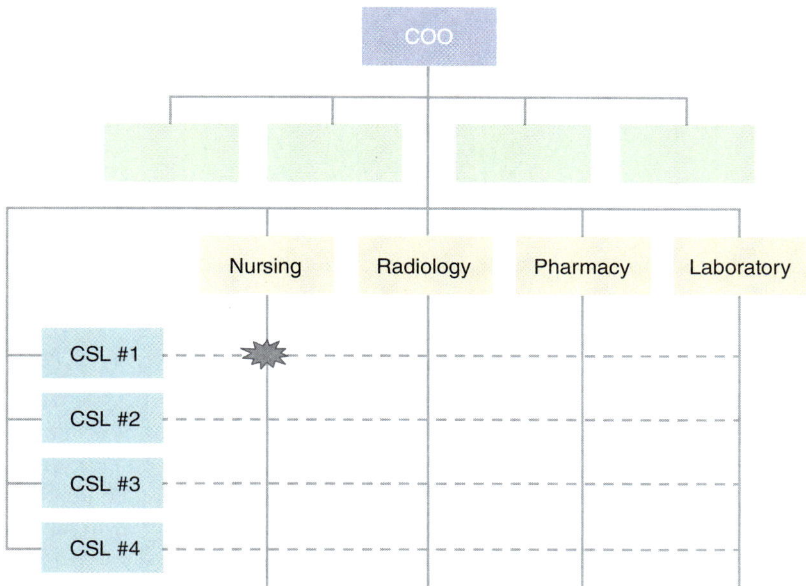

Figure 22-4 Matrix Structure

CASE STUDY 22-1 SSM St. Joseph Hospital[1]

In 1996, the financial situation at SSM St. Joseph Hospital of Kirkwood, Missouri, was in crisis mode. However, SSM Health Care had no intention of closing the facility. It was determined to make the hospital stronger and more efficient by initiating radical structural changes. St. Joseph reorganized into a decentralized structure around clinical service lines (CSLs) with one core objective: to provide the best patient care possible.

Due to this situation, St. Joseph implemented the CSL model for surgical, cardiovascular, women's and children's, and senior services. For each CSL, a clinical director with a nursing background was assigned. Each CSL director reported to the chief operating officer and was responsible for overseeing their CSL, developing a business plan with growth strategies, and improving operational efficiencies, customer satisfaction, and clinical outcomes.

The hospital also formed a nursing leadership team that included all clinical directors with nursing units and departments from emergency department services, nursing service operations, and home health care. The team's challenge was to guide everyone through this cultural transition while performing at the same high level. The CSL structure helped limit territorial issues and foster positive growth by enabling departments to work together. For example, rooms needed to be emptied and cleaned quickly for new admissions because of rapid patient turnover. The housekeeping department could not meet the new demand. When the problem surfaced, the CSL director met with the housekeeping director and other staff members and developed a housekeeper float role to solve it.

In comparing a functionally structured organization with St. Joseph's new matrix organizational structure, one senior manager commented that the patient turnover problem's quick response and change in a centralized organization with clear departmental lines would have been challenging. Territorial issues would have taken center stage in more traditional structures, obstructing problem-solving. However, "when people come together around patient care, they don't have to deal with maintaining departments. Their priority becomes determining what the patient needs and then providing care to the patient. When we focus on patient care, employees agree that the solution to every issue and the reason behind every dollar spent centers on adding value and enhancing patient or physician satisfaction. And that agreement empowers employees to achieve the organization's success."

Epilogue: Less than 10 years after implementing its matrix structure, SSM St. Joseph received the 2005 Missouri Quality Award, became the first winner of the Missouri PRO Quality Award, and was a 2007 recipient of the Premier Award for Quality in the area of acute myocardial infarction, or heart attack.

[1]On March 30, 2009, after 54 years of operations, SSM St. Joseph Hospital of Kirkwood moved to SSM St. Clare, the community's replacement hospital.

Data from Green, G. (2000). Beyond the barriers of centralized learning, everyone works for a common goal: Clinical service lines bring patients into focus. *Nursing Management, 31*(3), 40–43.

The value of the matrix structure is its flexibility in responding to environmental pressures (Miner, 2002). Because the matrix structure increases interdependencies, increased communication and collaboration are required. New behavior patterns must be learned if managers and employees are to function effectively in a matrix structure. As Miner (2002) suggests, this can be facilitated through a team-building process to identify expectations, objectives, leadership, roles and responsibilities, decision modes, communication, and conflict-resolution modes. In addition to team building, employee development will be needed to provide knowledge and skills relevant to the matrix structure. Because of the complexity of the matrix structure, Miner (2002, p. 496) states that three conditions must be present for an organization to consider this form:

1. Two or more critical sectors, such as functions, products, services, markets, or geographical areas, must simultaneously be highly salient for goal accomplishment.
2. The need to perform uncertain, complex, and interdependent tasks must exist, so a sizable information-processing capacity is required.
3. There must be a need to realize economies of scale by using limited human resources effectively.

Because of the matrix structure's complexity and the major role that power conflicts can play, some organizations use horizontal linkages to achieve coordination and communication across departmental units.

Horizontal Linkages

Horizontal linkages are methods employed by an organization to overcome the barriers found in the functional structure, such as a lack of coordination and poor information flow. Although horizontal linkage mechanisms are usually not reflected in the firm's organization chart, they are nevertheless part of its structure (Daft, 2007). Organizations can use any one or many of the following structural alternatives to improve horizontal coordination and information flow (Daft, 2007, pp. 95–99):

- *Information Systems*: Technology, such as information systems and electronic health records, can enable staff, administrators, and clinicians to routinely exchange information about problems, opportunities, activities, and patient treatment decisions.
- *Liaison Role*: An individual is located in one department but is responsible for communicating and coordinating with another department.
- *Task Forces*: A temporary committee can be composed of representatives from each department affected by a problem.
- *Full-Time Integrator*: The integrator coordinates several departments but does not report to or is assigned to one of the functional units. Integrators need excellent interpersonal skills because, in most cases, they have little authority but all the responsibility! For example, a clinical nurse leader is a lateral care integrator who may coordinate with everyone who provides care for the patient, such as physicians, respiratory therapists, and social workers, to ensure care is effectively coordinated. Some hospitals use patient liaisons or advocates to help coordinate the patient's experience, navigate them through the health system, and ensure their care is well coordinated across units.
- *Teams*: Teams are used when activities among departments require coordination over a long period.

As previously mentioned, there is no best way to structure an organization; however, most firms use one or more (i.e., hybrid) basic structures to achieve their goals. This is evident within the healthcare industry, where most organizations share remarkable structural similarities. Why is this so? The answer may be found within the population ecology and institutional theories.

Population Ecology

Population ecology is a theory about the "survival of the fittest" in populations of organizations (Carroll & Hannan, 2000). A population is defined as a set of organizations engaged in similar activities with similar forms (e.g., technology, structure, products/services, goals, and personnel). Hannan and Freeman (1977, 1989) related that long-term change in the diversity of organizational forms within a population occurs through the selection process rather than adaptation because most organizations have structural inertia (i.e., a tendency to maintain their internal structure regardless of other factors or concerns) that hinders adaptation when the environment changes. Hannan and Freeman argue that there are many limitations on the ability of organizations to change. The limitations come from substantial investment in facilities, equipment, and specialized personnel; limited information; established viewpoints of decision makers; the organization's successful history that justifies current procedures; and the difficulty of changing corporate culture (Daft, 2007, p. 183). Because of these barriers, true transformation tends to be a rare and unlikely event for organizations (Hannan & Freeman, 1989).

Organizations that are unable to adapt and, therefore, become incompatible with the environment are eventually replaced through competition with organizations that do meet the environment's demands (see **Figure 22-5**).

Stinchcombe (1965) noted that if two populations of organizations occupy the same market niche while differing in some organizational characteristic, the population with the less-fit environmental characteristic will be eliminated. As a result of the selection and retention process, organizational forms within a population become consistent over time. Consistency of form relates to the legitimacy of an organization. Suchman (1995, p. 574) describes legitimacy as "a generalized perception or assumption that the actions of an entity are desirable, proper or appropriate within some socially constructed system of norms, values, beliefs and definitions." The legitimacy of an organization is the focus of institutional theory. Although institutional theory differs from population ecology in that institutional theory explores how organizations adapt to their environment and how population ecology theory examines organizations' relationships to their environment from the selection perspective, both theories help explain why healthcare organizations share structural-form similarities.

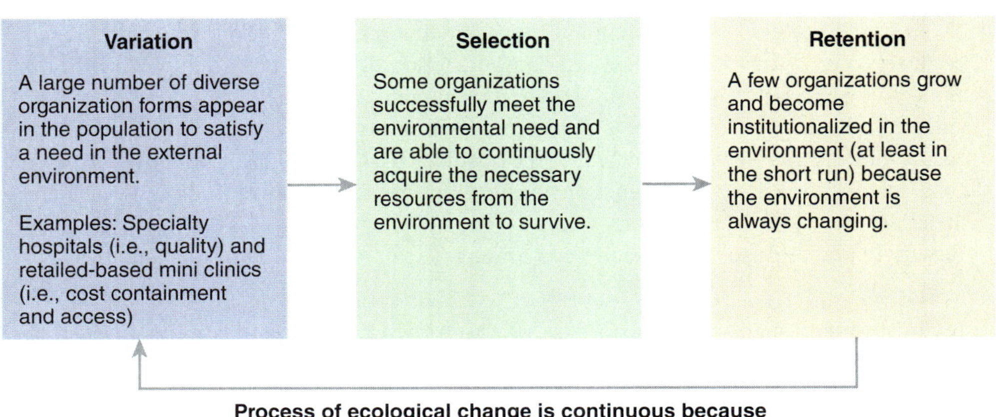

Figure 22-5 Process of Ecological Change

Institutional Theory

DiMaggio and Powell (1983, p. 147) observed that "structural changes in organizations are less and less driven by competition and that bureaucratization and other forms of organizational change occur as the result of processes that make organizations more similar without necessarily making them more efficient." This process of "homogenization," referred to as institutional isomorphism, is described as the constraining process that forces one unit in a population to resemble other units that face the same set of environmental conditions. DiMaggio and Powell proposed three mechanisms through which institutional isomorphism change occurs: coercive, mimetic, and normative.

1. *Coercive isomorphism* may result from pressure from other organizations on which a focal organization is dependent, or it may be caused by the cultural expectations within the society where the organization functions. Perhaps more than in any other type of business, external environmental forces bring change to the healthcare industry. For example, the Leapfrog Group, a consortium of large employers, uses its collective purchasing power to require hospitals to implement some standards regarding patient safety and quality-of-care issues; the largest purchasers of hospital services, federal and state governments, use their funding status to determine what medical services are provided to which patient groups in what settings (i.e., inpatient or outpatient); and regulators, such as The Joint Commission determine what organizational and medical standards will be followed within the industry. DiMaggio and Powell (1983, p. 154) hypothesized that "the greater the dependence of an organization on another organization, the more similar it will become to that organization in structure, climate, and behavioral focus." As such, healthcare entities adapt their organizations to fit the needs of their funding agencies and regulators, with little time or resources available for innovation. Delbecq (1995) pointed out that preoccupation with reimbursement rules and regulations (e.g., reactiveness) may cause healthcare organizations to lose sight of the pervasiveness of the need for continuous change (e.g., proactiveness).
2. *Mimetic isomorphism* is a response to uncertainty. In situations in which a clear course of action is unavailable, organizations tend to model themselves after similar organizations in their field that they perceive to be more successful: "We are hiring a Chief Wellness Officer to address physician burnout because Stanford has one!" or "That's the way Cleveland Clinic does it." Arndt and Bigelow (2000) state that in the case of hospitals, there is considerable uncertainty about technology (i.e., actual impact on patients' health) and performance measures due to continuously changing laws and regulations that require providers not only to meet strict medical standards, but also to provide proper care at all times to avoid liability actions. The more uncertain the relationship between means and ends, DiMaggio and Powell (1983, p. 154) hypothesized, "the greater the extent to which an organization will model itself after organizations it perceives to be successful." However, this modeling effect may cause a decrease in variation and diversity within the industry. DiMaggio and Powell explain that "new entrants which could serve as sources of innovation and variation, will seek to overcome the liability of newness by imitating established practices within the field" (p. 156).
3. *Normative isomorphism* results from professionalization, which includes two areas. First, members of professions receive similar training that socializes them into similar worldviews. Second, members of professions interact through professional and trade associations, which further diffuse ideas among them. The robustness of graduate health services administration programs is essential for developing organizational norms. Accreditation by the Commission

on Accreditation of Healthcare Management Education (CAHME) ensures that a program meets the standards developed by the profession and the health services industry. These standards are determined, in part, by CAHME's sponsoring organizations, which represent the healthcare industry's major professional trade associations and educational institutions. This reflects norms ingrained in these professionals as a part of their education and training. As such, the same standards influence the professional throughout their career (completing an educational program followed by membership in professional associations). However, according to Hamel (1998) and Morrison (1999), this may lead to a lack of diversity in leadership and management. Hamel states, "All too often … conversations become hard-wired over time, with the same people talking to the same people about the same issues year after year. After a while, individuals have little left to learn from each other" (p. 13).

Seizing opportunities involves change within an organization. Change can be problematic for mechanistic, bureaucratic, or functionally structured organizations because it requires new forms of coordination, information exchange, transfer of goods and services, and measurement (Stevenson & Jarillo-Mossi, 1986). But change is essential for survival. As Delbecq (1995, p. 1) points out,

> Healthcare organizations that emerge as leaders within the industry will have incorporated radical changes to deal with new patterns of reimbursement and simultaneous changes in core medical services—changes that incorporate new technology and push down costs. They will also have to cope with radical changes in information and quality systems.

In 2001, the Institute of Medicine (IOM) made the following recommendations for revamping the nation's healthcare system to improve patient care:

- Healthcare providers, payers, policy makers, purchasers, and patients should commit to a national effort to raise healthcare quality to "unprecedented levels."
- Providers, patients, and payers should agree to a "redesign" of the processes by which care is delivered.
- The federal government should identify "priority conditions" that need to be addressed first and provide resources to "stimulate innovation" and "initiate the change process."
- Healthcare organizations should fully support the changes needed to improve care.
- Participants in the healthcare industry should foster an environment for change in healthcare delivery by creating an "infrastructure to support evidence-based practice," facilitating the use of information technology, and aligning "payment incentives" to encourage quality.

How can healthcare organizations drive this change process versus reacting to changes imposed by others? Hamel (1998) suggested that there are five areas an organization can develop to achieve strategy innovation, a term used to describe the capacity to reconstruct the existing industry model in ways that create new value for customers and produce new wealth for all stakeholders. The five areas identified are (1) new voices, (2) new conversations, (3) new passions, (4) new perspectives, and (5) new experiments.

Hamel (1998) noted that new voices provide previously underrepresented constituencies (e.g., young people, newcomers to the organization) a larger share of voice in the strategy creation process, making it a pluralistic process. Hamel explained that new conversations create dialogue across all organizational and industry boundaries. "Opportunities for new insights are created when one juxtaposes previously isolated knowledge in new ways" (Hamel, 1998, p. 13). New passions release individuals' deep sense of discovery to search for new wealth-creating strategies. Hamel suggested that individuals will eagerly embrace change when allowed to participate in creating their organization's future. New perspectives enable individuals to reinvent their industry and their organization's capabilities by searching for new opportunities to fulfill environmental needs. By experimenting with new forms, organizations will learn which ones satisfy the environment's needs.

Interorganizational Relationships

One method organizations use to adapt to their environment is to create interorganizational relationships. Interorganizational relationships allow an entity to keep its core form but provide the organization with necessary resources and flexibility for adaptation. Interorganizational relationships are resource transactions, flows, and linkages between two or more organizations (Daft, 2007, p. 172). These relationships are strategies used by organizations to reduce their dependence on the environment or to share resources. Interorganizational relationships may be between or among organizations that provide similar services (i.e., horizontal integration) or between or among dissimilar but related organizations to provide a continuum of services (i.e., vertical integration). We will examine these relationships through resource dependency theory and the use of collaborative networks.

Resource Dependency Theory

Resource dependency theory states that all organizations exchange resources with the environment, which are essential for survival, and that organizations will attempt to acquire them without creating dependencies (Pfeffer & Salancik, 1978). In other words, organizations seek to establish relationships with other organizations to obtain scarce resources by attempting to (1) minimize their dependence on other organizations or (2) increase control over resources that maximize the dependence of other organizations on themselves (Ulrich & Barney, 1984). By achieving either or both of these outcomes, the organization increases its power with other organizations. Resource dependency theory aims for the organization to have sufficient power to influence the environment so that scarce resources are available to it (Pfeffer, 1981).

According to Pugh and Hickson (1996), the amount of dependence on a resource is based on two factors: (1) the importance of the resource to the organization and (2) how much discretion or monopoly power those who control a resource have over its allocation and use. For example, hospitals need nurses for patient care, and colleges and universities provide the education for Bachelor of Science in Nursing (BSN) degrees. As such, hospitals are dependent on higher education institutions for their current and future nursing workforce. Physicians control which hospital their patients will be admitted to for services. Hospitals need high occupancy rates to remain financially viable, so they depend on physicians to admit their patients to their facilities. Surgeons decide at which facility they will perform their surgical cases. Hospitals, as well as outpatient surgery centers, are dependent on surgeons for their essential resource, patients for surgery. Based on resource dependency, healthcare organizations will develop short-term and long-term strategies to address their dependency issues. For example, a hospital may use an outside agency to provide skilled nurses to cover its short-term shortages. This strategy would be cost-prohibitive in the long run. As such, hospitals may offer scholarships to nursing students pursuing a BSN degree in exchange for a work commitment after graduation. Some hospitals have funded nursing faculty positions so more students could be admitted into the various nursing programs. Others, such as Baptist Health South Florida (Baptist), have partnered with a local college to establish an on-site nursing educational program. Baptist capitalized on an opportunity to partner with a local college by helping the college manage the long waiting list for candidates to enter their nursing programs. The college faced the same challenges as many nationwide educational facilities—limited classroom space, too few faculty, and inadequate funding to meet these needs through campus resources. This initial partnership became the model for future partnerships within the community for advanced nursing education (BSN and MSN). It demonstrated the presence of a strong outreach program between the community and Baptist. The on-site program provided classroom space on the hospital's campus and funding for adjunct faculty who were Baptist nurse employees, allowing an additional 90 students annually to enter the program. These students received full scholarships and stipends while attending the Baptist Hospital campus nursing program, completed their clinical rotations at a Baptist facility, and received faculty support from incumbent employees. Once they completed the program, these nurses were given preferential employment opportunities. In less than 3 years, the number of newly graduated nurses hired per year by Baptist increased from approximately 80 to 136. Due to the success of this innovative nursing educational program, Baptist has expanded to partner with two additional universities.

As previously noted, resource dependency theory aims for the organization to have sufficient power to influence the environment so that scarce resources are available. This is precisely what Baptist achieved. The on-site nursing program has influenced its environment and now has a direct source of future nurse employees. In addition, by providing classroom space, adjunct faculty, and funding for other full-time faculty positions, the local college has increased its dependence on Baptist. Resource dependency can create win–win opportunities for all parties, as reflected in Baptist and its local college partnerships.

Collaborative Networks

Collaboration is another interorganizational relationship that can create win–win opportunities. Collaborative networks are organizations that join to become more competitive and share scarce resources. For example, a group of community health centers (CHCs) discovered that by linking together and creating a network, they could receive the advantages and expertise of an extensive health system while remaining independent. This unique and powerful alliance, Health Choice Network (HCN), is a national model of a successful collaboration among 37 CHCs and one of several Health Resources and Services Administration–sponsored health center–controlled networks. HCN's mission is to provide high-quality service, support, and expertise to its member organizations and to act as a vehicle for strategic efforts that strengthen its community member partners (Health Choice Network, 2008). The shared functions integrated through the network are finance, information technology, electronic health records, clinical support, disease management programs, and managed care contracting. In today's healthcare environment of cost containment, reduced reimbursement, and advancing technologies, collaborative networks are becoming more common as organizations attempt to remain competitive in their environments.

Co-opetition

A relatively new concept in the healthcare industry is co-opetition, which refers to alliances formed between competitors. "Co-opetition" describes the relationship when organizations compete against and cooperate simultaneously. Although relatively new to health care, co-opetition has been common in other industries. For example, U.S. milk producers and distributors competing with one another over various milk and dairy products brands launched a joint advertising campaign, "Got Milk?" Their goal was to reestablish milk as a primary source of nutrition and breakfast food to fight the pressure of substitution from other nondairy and breakfast foods. As such, these "co-opeting" alliances are used not only to extend or complement each organization's capabilities but also to eliminate potential threats to the "partners" (Chalhoub, 2007).

According to Ernst & Young (2004), co-opetition is one of the more powerful trends driving change in the industry. The following scenario illustrates this:

> Hospital A and Hospital B are competitors in the area. Each has 50 percent of the inpatient cardiology market, and each has a group of dedicated cardiologists who compete against the others to provide outpatient cardiology imaging services. Hospital A and its cardiology group joint venture with an outpatient center with new cardiac CT/MRI (computed tomography/magnetic resonance imaging) equipment to ease this competition. This equipment streamlines the work of cardiologists by allowing on-the-spot reading of the imaging so that more tests can be ordered if needed. As such, the center provides convenience for patients and their families. This patient-centered approach shifts business from Hospital B and other service providers in the area. Although Hospital A and its cardiologists still compete on providing echocardiograms, they are generally ahead of others because of the inpatient and outpatient business they pull in from their co-opetition (LeTourneau, 2004, p. 82).

Co-opetition is multifaceted in terms of what it means to hospitals and other healthcare organizations today (see **Case Study 22-2**). The key to effective co-opetition is mutual trust among the partners. If approached with open communication and awareness of a larger context, it can represent win–win opportunities for all involved parties.

CASE STUDY 22-2 Crossing Competitive Lines in Crisis

When a novel respiratory virus swept across the country in early spring, the impact was immediate and overwhelming. Within two weeks, hospital beds were full, ventilators were in short supply, and frontline staff began reporting critical shortages of protective gear. To make matters worse, international supply chains had collapsed, delaying shipments of essential medical supplies and test kits.

In Riverbend County, three hospitals that had long viewed each other as fierce rivals found themselves facing the same enemy—a deadly threat to their community. County General, Westside Regional, and Valley Health System had historically competed for patients, funding, and staff. But as the number of infections surged beyond projections and each hospital reached capacity, it became clear that old rivalries had to give way to new realities.

Leaders from all three systems began meeting via daily video calls. One of the first collaborative breakthroughs came when Valley Health engineers shared a method for safely re-sterilizing N95 masks using hydrogen peroxide vapor. Rather than keeping the process internal, they offered to reprocess masks for all hospitals in the region, preserving thousands of units of PPE.

Meanwhile, Westside Regional, which had an underused lab facility, redirected its staff and equipment to focus on increasing the area's testing capacity. By working with local biotech firms and public health officials, Westside was able to convert its lab into a high-throughput testing site. County General, the largest of the three, offered its parking structure as a drive-through testing and later immunization hub.

As cases surged, the three hospitals collaborated with the local emergency management agency to construct tented field hospitals on county fairgrounds. Staffing, equipment, and patient triage protocols were coordinated to ensure the best use of resources and reduce duplication.

By the time the vaccine rollout began, the partnership had evolved into a regional response coalition, including health departments, emergency services, and academic institutions. Despite historical competition, the crisis created a lasting model for cross-institutional collaboration.

Discussion Questions

1. Did the hospitals in Riverbend County work collaboratively with former competitors? What factors might have made this possible during a crisis?
2. Using Resource Dependence Theory, identify the external entities each hospital became reliant upon during the crisis. How did these dependencies influence their decision making?
3. What role did trust, transparency, and shared purpose play in forming the coalition? How might these factors be fostered outside of a crisis?
4. What lessons from this partnership could be applied to other complex or "wicked" problems in health care?
5. How can competitive health systems balance autonomy with collective action when faced with system-wide challenges?

Summary

This chapter presents four basic organizational structure configurations as a conceptual framework that managers can use to understand how structures emerge and how and why they change over time.

Discussion Questions

1. Describe how each element of the contextual dimension relates to an organization's structure.
2. Discuss the differences between mechanistic and organic systems.
3. Discuss the advantages and disadvantages of the four basic organizational structures.
4. Describe the importance of the horizontal linkage mechanisms and discuss when each would be used within an organization's structure.
5. Describe population ecology and how it differs from institutional theory.
6. Describe the three mechanisms associated with institutional isomorphism and how each affects organizations' homogeneity.
7. Discuss organizations' various strategies to develop and sustain interorganizational relationships.

CASE STUDY 22-3 Bayer AG of Germany

Bayer AG of Germany—the company best known in the United States for its Bayer aspirin products—is one of the largest and oldest chemical and healthcare products companies in the world. Because of massive sales gains and increased activity overseas in the early 1980s, Bayer announced a reorganization in 1984.

Bayer had been successful with a conventional organizational structure that was departmentalized by function. However, in response to new conditions, the company wanted to create a structure that would allow it to achieve three primary goals: (1) shift management control from the then–West German parent company to its foreign divisions and subsidiaries; (2) restructure its business divisions to more clearly define their duties; and (3) flatten the organization, or empower lower-level managers to assume more responsibility, so that top executives would have more time to plan strategy.

Bayer selected a relatively diverse matrix management format to pursue its goals. It delineated all of its business activities into six groups under an umbrella company called Bayer World. Within each of the six groups were several subgroups made up of product categories, such as dyestuffs, fibers, or chemicals. Likewise, each of its administrative and service functions were regrouped under Bayer World into one of several functions, such as human resources, marketing, plant administration, or finance. Furthermore, top managers who had formerly headed functional groups were given authority over separate geographic regions, which, like the product groups, were supported by and entwined with the functional groups. The net effect of the reorganization was that the original nine functional departments were broken down into 19 multidisciplinary, interconnected business groups.

After only 1 year of operation, Bayer management lauded the new matrix structure as a resounding success. Not only did matrix management allow the company to move toward its primary goals, but it also had the added benefits of increasing its responsiveness to change and emerging opportunities, and of helping Bayer to streamline plant administration and service division activities.

Discussion Questions

1. Bayer AG of Germany's reorganization occurred in the early 1980s. Research the company and determine whether the organization continues to operate under a matrix structure. If yes, what, if any, structural changes have occurred in the past 25 years? If no, what organizational structure does the company currently use and why?

CASE STUDY 22-4 Organizational Structure: A Driver of Performance

Would you build a house without laying a foundation? The result would be four walls lacking any grounding and with little stability. Similarly, it is impossible to build a high-performing organization without first constructing a strategy. Nonetheless, across all industries, less than 10 percent of strategic plans are executed and realized. How can this happen if the primary responsibility of management is to develop and execute strategies that will help the enterprise realize its vision and mission?

Hospitals that *do* successfully execute strategies share a key common element: an organizational structure that insists upon clear role focus, fosters accountability, and requires manageable spans of control. Moreover, high-performing hospitals and healthcare systems design their management structures to execute strategies. They consider organizational structure as they would any other resource (e.g., capital, workforce, physicians) and deploy it according to the strategic needs of the company. In short, hospital strategies should not just inform organizational structure, but determine it.

One of the most performance-driven healthcare companies in America today utilizes this approach to organizational design. Several years ago, executives at this large healthcare system realized that their ambulatory strategies were not keeping pace with market demands. Accordingly, a single corporate position was created with responsibility for outpatient services at all of the system's hospitals. This new job, and the new structure, was born out of strategic need and focused accountability. The result was an enhanced focus on outpatient development, streamlined outpatient decision-making processes, and, ultimately, improved hospital ambulatory services performance.

Considerations in Restructuring Your Organization

Look at your current organizational structure. Assess your strategic initiatives and how you will execute your plans on the basis of the current decision-making structures and accountabilities. Such an assessment will encompass an analysis of management requirements and should include a review of the following focal points:

- Strategic plan.
- Organizational control structure.
- Management responsibilities.
- Physician leadership.

An example of an organization that has employed this form-follows-function approach is St. Joseph's Hospital.

Strategic Plan

St. Joseph's strategic plan includes three major initiatives:

Develop cancer, cardiac services, and neurosciences as distinctive, market-leading service lines.

Expand the outpatient strategy to include new facilities in two markets within St. Joseph's primary service area.

Significantly upgrade quality and patient safety throughout St. Joseph's facilities.

These initiatives are fairly typical for metropolitan tertiary hospitals; what distinguishes high-performing organizations, however, is successful execution—and the structure that enables it.

Control Structure

Control structures need to encompass patient care functions, patient care support functions, and administrative support functions. The way these functions are aligned varies dramatically between organizations and defines both culture and accountabilities within the hospital. At St. Joseph's Hospital, leadership responded to a change in the hospital's strategic plans by also revising the control structure. The new, revised strategy shifted the hospital's major spheres of organizational responsibility, prompting a leadership structure that was reflective of the institution's goals:

An outpatient executive dedicated to the growth of outpatient centers, with line accountability for staff in the outpatient areas.

A service line dyad for each major program that links a clinical director with a physician leader. The dyad is accountable for service line development and profitability.

A clinical quality structure headed by the Chief Medical Officer with direct oversight and reporting from clinical quality and patient safety personnel.

In the traditional environment, the control structure is organized in a purely functional way that does not respond to the business of health care: the provision of high-quality care within a service line. Patients do not seek nursing services, radiology, or physical therapy or the other traditional departments within a hospital. Instead, they want care to treat their heart condition, cancer, or other illness or injury. In the traditional departmental control structure, it is difficult to implement service line strategies that bridge multiple departments because there is not a direct line of accountability between the service line director and the department managers. The department managers are held accountable for the performance of their department, rather than the performance and growth of the service line, leading to competing priorities.

This structure creates a "silo" mentality that optimizes performance within narrowly focused units but in which a patient and physician perspective is disconnected, inconvenient, and confusing. These service lines (e.g., cancer, heart, and so forth) should represent the new control structure of your hospital, since they ultimately drive hospital performance. High-performing organizations look to service line or discrete clinical program areas to help define the control structure (organizational reporting and hierarchy structure) of their hospital.

In **Figure 22-6**, a traditional hospital organizational structure is compared to that same organization that adapted its structure to implement its key strategies.

Managerial roles within hospitals rarely change following development of a new strategy, such as a shift to a service line focus. This stagnancy is counterproductive: As you implement key strategies around growth, clinical services, quality, and safety, the control structure of your organization must change to reflect your strategies. One of the biggest complaints that physicians, staff, and managers make about hospital leadership is the slow pace of decision making. This is probably a symptom of larger control structure issues. If your control structure does not reflect your strategy, you are probably suffering from an inefficient decision-making process involving too many sign-offs.

A leadership structure for an oncology service line is presented in **Figure 22-7** as an example of a service line leadership group. This group makes the key decisions for the service line, and their reporting relationships are depicted in the multidisciplinary executive-level organizational chart.

Management Responsibilities

Management responsibilities include those functions that must be regularly executed; these responsibilities vary according to the control structure. There are administrative management (staff) functions required by all control centers and additional responsibilities related to the management of patient care (line management) functions. Building on our example of St. Joseph's, a management structure might include site administrators for each ambulatory site and functional managers within each service line (for example, cath lab manager reporting to the cardiac dyad, radiation therapy reporting to the cancer dyad, and so forth).

Management responsibilities should be determined on the basis of your strategy and plan for execution through the modified control structure.

Physician Leadership

Just as the administrative organizational structure must reflect strategic objectives, so must the physician leadership structure. In many academic organizations, there are formal physician leadership structures (e.g., department chairs, service or section chiefs) that include employed physicians rather than traditional elected members of the medical staff. If you are contemplating a service line initiative, you must adapt your physician leadership structure to accommodate different responsibilities and objectives.

Strong physician leaders from a range of clinical areas within the service line are critical to driving change and engendering support from the medical staff. If you are committed to effective, service line–based management, hiring a medical director for each major line may be a logical step to ensuring credibility with affected physicians and accelerating service line development. You should also consider a management or advisory role for non-employed physicians.

Engineering a Structure Built for Success

Good leaders do not put their employees in a position where they are destined to fail. Success requires clear lines of authority and accountability, and those in authority need the right tools to meet performance expectations. Some organizations have created a "matrix" service line management structure, appointing a vice president of a clinical service without formal line authority or control over the deployment of resources. Others have created mixed models, where the head of a service line may have direct control over functions that directly relate to the service (e.g., radiation oncology reports to cancer and the cath lab to cardiology) but indirect influence over shared services (such as radiology or inpatient care). This influence often comes in the form of operational councils or committees where multiple users of these services have an opportunity to explain their needs and priorities. Although either structure can work, keep in mind that the leader is more likely to succeed if there is greater control—and thus, accountability—for the resources and the performance of those resources within that service line.

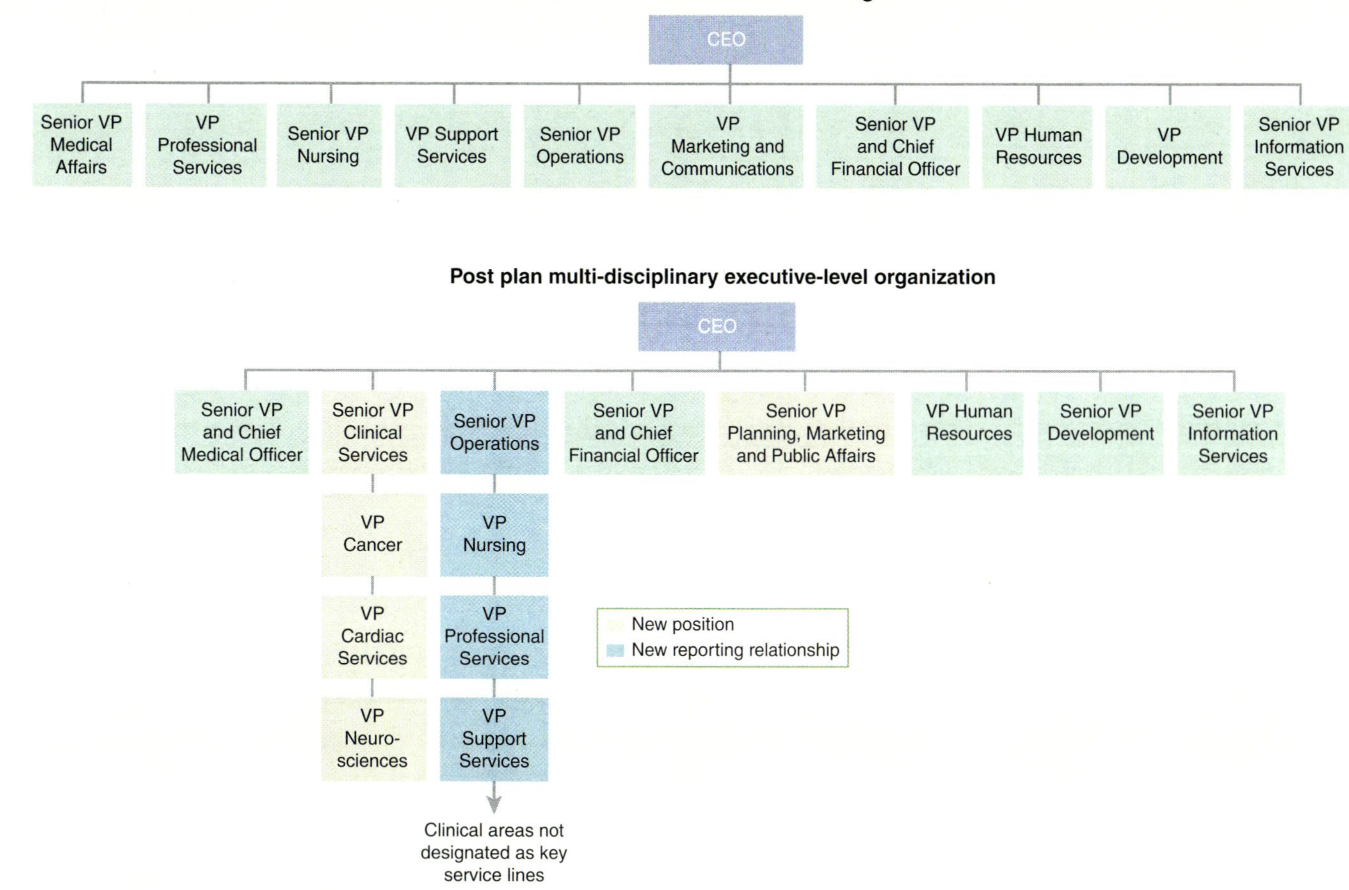

Figure 22-6 Traditional vs. Post Plan Multi-Disciplinary Executive Organization

Reprinted with permission, ECG Management Consultants, Inc.

Role

- Maintain authority over leadership group activities.
- Provide guidance and leadership.
- Set strategic direction and context.
- Oversee progress/accountability.

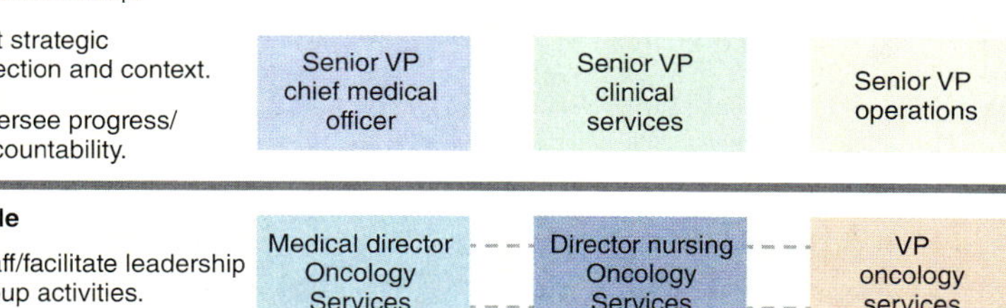

Leadership group functions

- Participate in and drive business planning activities.
- Facilitate capital budgeting.
- Drive business development activities.
- Perform activities related to technology assessments and product standardization.
- Assist in physician planning and recruiting.
- Develop and oversee quality programs.

Role

- Staff/facilitate leadership group activities.
- Maintain accountability for service line development/performance.
- Complete business planning activities.

Figure 22-7 Oncology Services Leadership Group

Reprinted with permission, ECG Management Consultants, Inc.

Lessons Learned

Strategic planning does not end when the report is finalized; it must also include a revised organizational structure. If you aren't willing to take the time to reconsider and assess your management structure as you explore your strategic direction, then don't waste your resources on strategy development.

Implementation of changes in organizational structure, reporting relationships, span of control, and role focus requires a thoughtful, measured, and sensitive approach. And you must be prepared for the effect of changing individuals' jobs and responsibilities. As your organizational structure changes, some of your managers will feel disenfranchised and perhaps move on to other opportunities.

This raises a tough question. Do you design the structure and jobs around your valued people, or design the structure and positions with a focus on performance and then assign the right people to those roles? The right answer is a combination of both. Performance-driven organizations employ talented and effective managers in roles that foster accountability and decision making to achieve the organization's strategic goals. They leverage the talent they currently have, but do not design important roles around the strengths, weaknesses, or desires of managers. You also need to recognize instances in which your current resources lack the appropriate seasoning or skill set to fill the positions and when it is necessary to make a strategic hire.

Having the right people in the right roles is a critical step, but you must cement changes in your organizational structure by tasking your management team with developing business and operating plans under the new rubric. For example, when migrating to a service line structure, require that the service line management team develop a business plan to hardwire the new strategy and structure and provide a canvas upon which the new team can paint the future. The process of drafting and revising a business plan will help the management group not only refine its focus, but also begin working as a team.

Reprinted with permission, ECG Management Consultants, Inc.

Discussion Questions

1. How does organizational structure impact performance of new strategies?
2. What key considerations are needed when redesigning your management structure?
3. Discuss effective service line management and leadership structures.
4. How does a manager "hardwire" new reporting relationships?

References

Arndt, M., & Bigelow, B. (2000). The transfer of business practices into hospitals: History and implications. In J. D. Blair, M. D. Fottler, & G. T. Savage (Eds.), *Advances in health care management: Vol. 1*, pp. 339–368. JAI/Elsevier Science.

Begun, J. W., Tornabeni, J., & White, K. R. (2006). Opportunities for improving patient care through lateral integration: The clinical nurse leader. *Journal of Healthcare Management*, *51*(1), 19–25.

Blau, P. M. (1968). The hierarchy of authority in organizations. *American Journal of Sociology*, *73*(4), 453–467.

Briggs, J. (2007, August). Partnerships: Rx for hospitals. *Oakland Business Review*.

Burns, T., & Stalker, G. M. (1961). *The management of innovation*. Tavistock.

Burns, T., & Stalker, G. M. (1994). *The management of innovation* (Rev. ed.). Oxford University Press.

Burton, R. M., DeSanctis, G., & Obel, B. (2006). *Organizational design: A step-by-step approach*. Cambridge University Press.

Carroll, G. R., & Hannan, M. T. (2000). *The demography of corporations and industries*. Princeton University Press.

Chalhoub, M. S. (2007). A framework in strategy and competition using alliances: Application to the automotive industry. *International Journal of Organization Theory and Behavior*, *10*(2), 151–183.

Daft, R. L. (2007). *Organization theory and design* (9th ed.). Thomson South-Western.

Delbecq, A. L. (1995). The hidden competitive weapon supporting innovation in health care. *Physician Executive*, *21*(5), 18–23.

DiMaggio, P. J., & Powell, W. W. (1983). The iron cage revisited: Institutional isomorphism and collective rationality in organizational fields. *American Sociological Review*, *48*(2), 147–160. https://doi.org/10.2307/2095101

ECG Management Consultants, Inc. (2007). The strategic imperative of adapting the hospital's management structure [White paper]. https://www.ecgmc.com

Ernst & Young, LLP. (2004). Practical governance: Co-opetition—The new governance challenge.

Green, G. (2000). Beyond the barriers of centralized nursing, everyone works for a common goal: Clinical service lines bring patients into focus. *Nursing Management*, *31*(3), 40–43.

Hamel, G. (1998). Strategy innovation and the quest for value. *Sloan Management Review*, *39*(2), 7–14.

Hammer, D., & Franklin, D. (2008). Beyond bolt-ons: Breakthroughs in revenue cycle information systems. *Healthcare Financial Management*, *62*(2), 52–60.

Hannan, M. T., & Freeman, J. (1977). The population ecology of organizations. *American Journal of Sociology*, *82*(5), 929–964.

Hannan, M. T., & Freeman, J. (1989). *Organizational ecology* (pp. 3–27). Harvard University Press.

Health Choice Network (2008). http://www.hcnetwork.org/

Institute of Medicine (2001). *Crossing the quality chasm: A new health system for the 21st century*. National Academy Press.

Kast, F. E., & Rosenzweig, J. E. (1985). *Organization and management: A systems and contingency approach*. McGraw-Hill.

Kimberly, J. (1976). Organizational size and the structuralist perspective: A review, critique and proposal. *Administrative Science Quarterly*, *21*(4), 571–597.

Lawrence, P., & Lorsch, J. (1967). *Organization and environment*. Irwin.

LeTourneau, B. (2004). Co-opetition: An alternative to competition. *Journal of Healthcare Management*, *49*(2), 81–83.

Malonis, J. A. (2000). Bayer AG of Germany. Encyclopedia of Business (2nd ed). Thomas Gale.

Miles, R. E., & Snow, C. C. (1978). *Organizational strategy, structure, and process*. McGraw-Hill.

Miner, J. B. (2002). *Organizational behavior: Foundations, theories and analyses*. Oxford University Press.

Mintzberg, H. (1979). *The structuring of organizations*. Prentice Hall.

Morrison, I. (1999). Leadership and white space: The struggle for strategy innovation in health care. *Health Forum Journal*, *42*(3), 18–25.

O'Quinn, M., & Mulqueen, K. C. (2007). "Recreate Jackson:" A turn-around tale. *hfm*, 82–87.

Perrow, C. (1967). A framework for the comparative analysis of organizations. *American Sociological Review*, *32*(2), 194–208.

Pfeffer, J. (1981). *Power in organizations*. Pitman.

Pfeffer, J., & Salancik, G. (1978). *The external control of organizations: A resource dependence perspective*. Harper & Row.

Pugh, D. S., & Hickson, D. J. (1996). *Writers on organizations*. Sage.

Pugh, D. S., Hickson, D. J., Hinings, C. R., Lupton, T., McDonald, K. M., & Turner, C. (1963). A conceptual scheme for organizational analysis. *Administrative Science Quarterly*, *8*(3), 289–315.

Pugh, D. S., Hickson, D. J., Hinings, C. R., & Turner, C. (1968). Dimensions of organizational structure. *Administrative Science Quarterly*, *13*(1), 65–105.

Scott, W. R., & Davis, G. F. (2006). *Organizations and organizing: Rational, natural, and open systems perspectives*. Prentice Hall.

Stevenson, H. H., & Jarillo-Mossi, J. C. (1986). Preserving entrepreneurship as companies grow. *Journal of Business Strategy*, *7*(1), 10–23.

Stinchcombe, A. L. (1965). Social structure and organizations. In J. P. March (Ed.), *Handbook of organizations* (pp. 142–193). Rand McNally.

Suchman, M. C. (1995). Managing legitimacy: Strategic and institutional approaches. *Academy of Management Review*, *20*(3), 571–610.

Ulrich, D., & Barney, J. B. (1984). Perspectives in organizations: Resource dependence, efficiency, and population. *Academy of Management Review*, *9*(3), 471–481.

Woodward, J. (1965). *Industrial organization: Theory and practice*. Oxford University Press.

Other Suggested Readings

Boblitz, M. C., & Thompson, J. M. (2005). Assessing the feasibility of developing centers of excellence: Six initial steps. *hfm*, *59*(10), 72–84.

Borkowski, N., & Gordon, J. (2006). Entrepreneurial organizations: The driving force for improving quality in the healthcare industry. *Journal of Health and Human Services Administration*, *28*(4), 531–549.

Burns, L. R. (1989). Matrix management in hospitals: Testing theories of matrix structure and development. *Administrative Science Quarterly*, *34*(3), 349–368.

Hall, R. H. (1996). *Organizations: Structures, processes, and outcomes* (6th ed.). Prentice Hall.

Kaplan, R. S., & Norton, D. P. (2006). How to implement a new strategy without disrupting your organization. *Harvard Business Review*, *84*(3), 100.

Miller, D., & Friesen, P. H. (1980). Momentum and revolution in organizational adaptation. *Academy of Management Journal*, *23*(4), 591–614.

Perrow, C. (1986). *Complex organizations: A critical essay* (3rd ed.). Random House.

Ruef, M., & Scott, R. W. (1998). A multidimensional model of organizational legitimacy: Hospital survival in changing institutional environments. *Administrative Science Quarterly*, *43*(4), 877–904.

Scott, R. W., Ruef, M., Mendel, P. J., & Caronna, C. A. (2000). *Institutional change and healthcare organizations: From professional dominance to managed care*. University of Chicago Press.

CHAPTER 23

Organization Design Parameters: Internal Characteristics

LEARNING OUTCOMES

After completing this chapter, the student should be able to understand:

- The five organizational parts of an organization, as described by Mintzberg.
- The importance of communication to the coordination and control of organizational activities.
- How each element of the structural dimension relates to organization design.

Overview

The core issue [of the quality chasm in health care] is fragmentation, and the solution lies in forms of assembly and cooperation that the prevailing structures in health care cannot achieve. Disciplines divide from disciplines, organizations from organizations, events from events. Patients cross over these boundaries time and again, and their needs get lost in the disorder.

—Donald Berwick (2002)

Burton, DeSanctis, and Obel (2006) describe an organization's complexity as the property or characteristic of its structure based on the breakdown of subunits by two dimensions: vertical differentiation and horizontal differentiation. "It is the height and width of the organization's hierarchy. The vertical differentiation reflects the depth of the hierarchy—top to bottom—and the horizontal differentiation refers to the degree of task specialization across the hierarchy" (p. 69). In this chapter, we will focus on the formal division of the organization into subunits (i.e., horizontal differentiation) based on various parameters. These parameters are shaped by the following questions (Mintzberg, 1979, p. 66):

1. How many tasks should a given position in the organization contain, and how specialized should each task be?
2. To what extent should the work content of each position be standardized?
3. What skills and knowledge should be required for each position?
4. On what basis should positions be grouped into units and units into larger units?
5. How large should each unit be, and how many individuals should report to a manager?
6. To what extent should the output of each position or unit be standardized?
7. What mechanisms should be established to facilitate mutual adjustment among positions and units?
8. How much decision-making power should be delegated to the managers of line units down the chain of command?
9. How much decision-making power should pass from the line managers to the staff specialists and operators?

The preceding questions relate to the fundamental issues of structure and design. Daft (2007) organizes these questions into the organizational design's structural dimension (see **Table 23-1**). These design parameters, or "internal characteristics," create the basis for an organization's structure.

The design parameters determine how the various parts of an organization will be organized to coordinate and control the entity's activities. In his seminal work on organizational

Table 23-1 Structural Dimension of Organization Design

Dimension or Parameter	Description	Healthcare Examples
Formalization	The degree to which the organization controls how work will be completed. This includes written procedures, job descriptions, regulations, policy manuals, and unwritten rules and requirements.	An organization that requires all surgeons to document a set checklist would be more formalized than one that allows each surgeon to choose how they manage the case.
Specialization	The degree to which organizational tasks are subdivided into separate jobs (also called the division of labor). If specialization is high, each employee performs a narrow range of tasks. If specialization is low, each employee performs a broader range of functions in their job (i.e., job enlargement).	Examples: orthopedic surgeon versus a general surgeon; a medical or surgery nurse versus an ICU nurse; an organization development consultant versus a human resource generalist.
Hierarchy of Authority	This is also called span of control and describes (1) who reports to whom and (2) the number of employees reporting to a supervisor. When spans of control are narrow, the hierarchy will be tall, and when spans of control are vast, the hierarchy will be shorter.	Tall span of control: A bedside nurse reports to a nurse supervisor, who reports to a nurse manager, who reports to a nurse director, who reports to a nurse vice president, who reports to the chief nursing officer.

Dimension or Parameter	Description	Healthcare Examples
Centralization	The decision-making position or level in the hierarchy. If decision making is at the top of the hierarchy, the organization reflects centralized decision making; when decision making is delegated to lower hierarchy levels, it is referred to as decentralized decision making.	A large health system with multiple hospitals centralizes its support functions, such as human resources, information technology, and legal, at the system level.
Professionalism	The level (or average number of years) of formal education and training of employees.	Most healthcare organizations have a high level of professionalism, with some clinicians needing up to 15 years of formal school and training before treating patients independently.

Data from Daft, R. L. (2007). *Organization theory and design* (9th ed.). Thomson South-Western.

structures, Mintzberg (1979), one of the leading scholars in organization theory, breaks down organizations into five basic but interrelated parts: (1) strategic apex (senior management), (2) middle line (middle management), (3) operating core, (4) technostructure, and (5) support staff (see **Figure 23-1** and **Exhibit 23-1**).

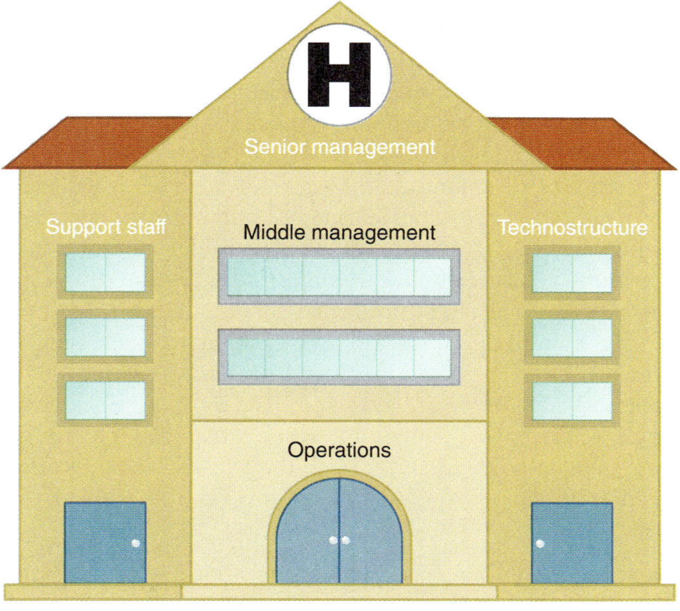

Figure 23-1 The Five Basic Parts of an Organization

Exhibit 23-1 Five Basic Parts of Organizations

Senior management is what Mintzberg called the *strategic apex*. It is responsible for ensuring that the organization effectively serves its mission, serves the needs of the organization's various stakeholders, and manages the organization's relationships with its environment.

Middle management (middle line) links senior management to the operating core. This chain runs from the senior managers just below the strategic apex to the first-line supervisors (e.g., the nurse supervisor) who have direct authority or supervision over the operating-core members. In general, this chain of authority is scalar; that is, it runs in a single line from top to bottom.

The *operating core* is the heart of every organization, the part that produces the essential outputs that keep it alive. The operating core of the organization encompasses those members who perform the basic work related directly to the production of services and products. The members perform four prime functions: (1) securing the inputs for production; (2) transforming the inputs into outputs; (3) distributing the outputs that result from the transformation process; and (4) providing direct support to the input, transformation, and output functions.

The *technostructure* includes the staff who serve the organization by affecting the work of others. These employees design systems that standardize the organization's work processes and outputs. Technostructure employees are removed from the operating workflow—they may design it, plan it, change it, or train the people who do it, but they do not do it themselves. As such, technostructure employees spend much of their time in informal communication.

An organization's *support staff* comprises employees who perform support services to the organization outside of its operating workflow, such as public relations and legal counsel. Although an organization can outsource many of these functions, the existence of support staff reflects the organization's attempt to encompass more boundary activities to reduce uncertainty and control its own affairs.

Modified from Mintzberg, H. (1979). *The structuring of organizations*. Prentice Hall.

The five organizational parts allow managers to better understand the complexity of and the interrelationships among the subsystems within an organization, and how the five organizational parts form is based on the company's environment, mission, size, and requirements to coordinate and control its activities to accomplish its goals.

Managers' proper use of communication forms and methods is essential for coordinating and controlling an organization's activities. Communication activity and frequency increase as activity and task variety increase. The form, technique, and direction of communication change depending on whether the manager deals with routine activities and tasks (vertical communication) or nonroutine activities and tasks (horizontal communication). To better understand the importance of proper communication, we will now examine the increasing need and direction for communication when interdependence between or among departments regarding an organization's workflow exists.

Interdependence refers to the extent to which organizational units depend on one another for resources or materials to accomplish their tasks. There are three types of interdependence: pooled (minimal), sequential (medium), and reciprocal (high) (Thompson, 1967) (see **Figure 23-2**).

- Pooled interdependence means that each organizational unit is relatively independent because work does not flow between or among units. With pooled interdependence, there is a low need for coordination, most of which is accomplished by standardizing activities.

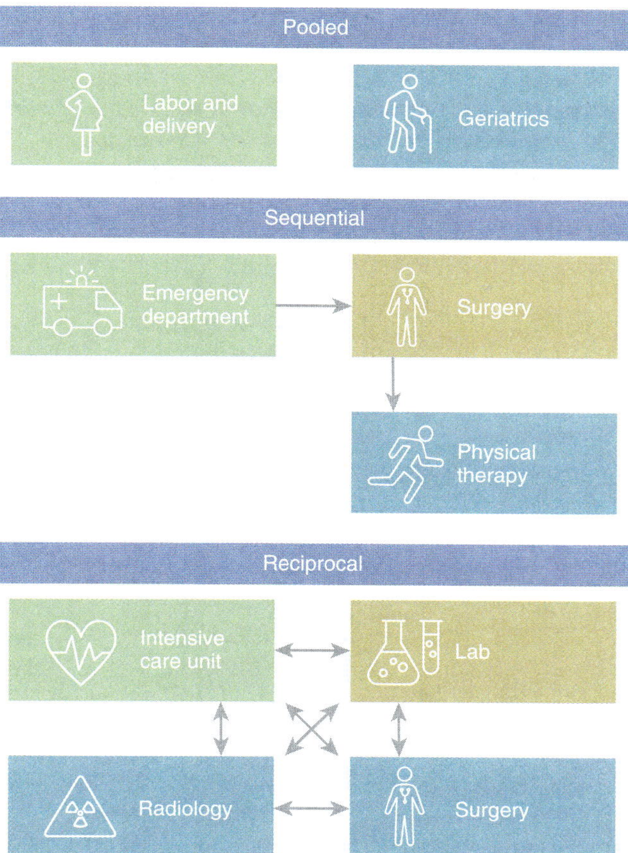

Figure 23-2 Types of Interdependence

Because there is a low need for coordination, communication between units is minimal, with formalized rules and procedures.

- Sequential interdependence relates to a one-way flow of resources, where the output of one unit becomes the input of another unit (e.g., assembly line). With sequential interdependence, there is increased dependence and sharing of resources; therefore, there is an increased need for coordination between organizational units. Because this is a one-way flow of resources, managers can use task forces to coordinate horizontal linkage, with frequent communications relating to planning, schedules, and feedback.
- Reciprocal interdependence means that the output of unit one becomes the input for unit two, which transforms the input and sends it back to unit one as its input. Hospitals are an excellent example of reciprocal interdependence because they provide coordinated services to patients (Daft, 2007). Consider a patient admitted to a hospital for a knee replacement operation. The patient will move back and forth from radiology, surgery, the intensive care unit (ICU), the medical/surgical floor, physical therapy, etc.

To achieve this high level of coordination, a horizontal organizational structure would be recommended, as well as permanent teams to ensure open and frequent communication between and among organizational units to deal with any problems or issues. However, managers should be aware that the culture of health care can directly and strongly oppose this shared communication even at the most local levels. Healthcare workers often have a strong preference for creating and using their own solutions. They are not always willing or eager to learn—or share learnings—with other departments, units or divisions. George Halvorson, former chairman and CEO of Kaiser Foundation Health Plan and Hospitals, used the change of nurse shift information transfer process, a universal basic task, as an example to illustrate his point:

> Hospitals are open 24 hours daily, so multiple shifts are needed for each work site and unit. At the end of each shift, the nurses from the prior shift take some time to brief the new set of nurses about each patient in the relevant work unit. This is essential for the continuity of patient care. It is a job that has to be done three times a day—hopefully very well, because the quality of the information sharing affects the quality of care for each patient.
>
> Unfortunately, that process is not always done well or efficiently. It can take much time. The communication process itself can too easily create factual errors. It is a typical type of care linkage deficiency that we may more readily expect from outpatient clinical care. However, it is a bit more surprising when it happens in an institution as formal and highly organized as a hospital. In the real world, each floor in a hospital is likely to have its separate information transfer process, "invented here, by us." Hospital staff do not typically seek the best method for transitioning that information. Process improvement as a desirable cultural value does not appear on many healthcare radar screens.
>
> For the nurse shift transfer process, simply implementing an easy-to-use, standardized, well-thought-out, carefully designed information checklist for each patient can cut the transfer time from nurse to nurse from more than half an hour per shift change to less than 15 minutes while hugely reducing communication errors about individual patients. Patient care improves. Nurse efficiency improves. Care linkages improve. The nurses who are tired and worn out at the end of their shifts get to go home a bit earlier. Everyone wins!

Now that we have a greater understanding of the five interrelating parts of an organization and the need for proper communication to coordinate and control an organization's activities, we will continue our discussion of each design parameter that makes up the structural dimension of organizational design.

Elements of the Structural Dimension

The design parameters that comprise the structural dimension of organizational design are: formalization, specialization, hierarchy of authority, centralization, and professionalism.

Formalization

Formalization is the degree to which the organization communicates how the work will be performed, who will do the job, and under what circumstances or constraints the work will be done. This is usually measured by the amount of written documentation in the organization. Documentation includes procedures, job descriptions, regulations, and policy manuals. Monitoring and feedback systems (e.g., budgets, production measurement systems, performance reviews) reinforce the degree of formalization. However, as Burton, DeSanctis, and Obel (2006) point out, an organization can have high formalization even though rules, policies, procedures, and so on are not "written down." Rules can be communicated through training procedures, behavior modeling, or verbalized working codes that people are expected to learn over time. In highly formal organizations, there are penalties for "breaking the rules." Formalization is considered low when an organization lacks powerfully written or unwritten accepted rules of conduct. When formalization is low, there is high variance in the methods and procedures used to govern the organization's work (Burton et al., 2006). In this situation, employees must use their judgment in deciding how the work will be performed. This flexibility is appropriate when employees deal with situations without "preprogrammed" answers. Organizations with low formalization usually deal constantly with new conditions for which precedents do not exist, such as scientific research (Hall, 1996).

All organizations, except the smallest ones, need formalization to avoid chaos. However, too much formalization may cause an organization to become bureaucratic, prohibiting creativity and innovation. Most organizations operate between relatively high formalization and relatively low formalization (Burton et al., 2006).

Specialization

Specialization refers to the degree to which organizational tasks are subdivided into separate jobs (i.e., division of labor). If specialization is high, each employee performs a narrow range of functions in their job. If their specialization is low, each employee performs various tasks.

Dividing work into specialized tasks and organizing them into distinct departments was one of the basic foundations of Max Weber's rational bureaucracy model. Weber's (1947) idea of functional specialization applied to persons within an organization and relations between larger units or divisions of the organization. Weber argued that such specialization is essential to a rational bureaucracy and that the specific boundaries separating one functional division from another must be fixed by explicit rules, regulations, and procedures (Miner, 2002). In addition, the principles of Taylor's (1911) scientific management included subdividing work into measurable and manageable units to achieve "maximum efficiency" of an entity's operations. This required managers to (1) divide the work into separate tasks, (2) develop a science for each person's work, (3) initiate controls to ensure the work is done in the prescribed manner, and (4) train the person to be able to perform his or her job better.

The growth and current status of medical specializations provide an excellent example of division of labor. Today, more than 60 medical specialties and subspecialties are formally recognized by training and certification. In his book *Divide and Conquer: A Comparative History of Medical Specialization*, George Weisz (2006) provides the historical context of the creation of specialists from generalists, giving attention to this process's cultural and institutional dimensions. For example, Weisz relates that hospitals played an essential role in influencing the legitimization and value of medical specialization by providing the venues for treating illnesses and pursuing clinical research and opportunities for clinical training. Support of specialization continues today with hospitals creating centers of excellence around selected service lines, such as cardiology, oncology, and orthopedics. In addition, a wide variety of specialized organizational forms support medical specialization, such as specialty hospitals, free-standing renal disease units, retail-based urgent-care centers, neighborhood health centers, and home health agencies. As Scott, Ruef, Mendel, and Caronna (2000) point out, these specialized organizational forms reflect service "unbundling," whereby a cluster of services once performed in a generalized community-based hospital is disaggregated and re-formed as separate units. This unbundling reinforces the specialization of medical practice. In addition to medical specialties, nurses can and do specialize, although this is more closely related to locus of practice than to differences in training. For example, nurses can specialize (and receive certification) in the areas of child-care nursing, gerontological nursing, maternity nursing, medical–surgical nursing, nurse anesthesia, nurse midwifery, nurse practitioner studies, nursing administration, nursing education, oncology nursing, psychiatric nursing, public health nursing, and rehabilitation nursing.

Kast and Rosenzweig (1985) noted that the more specialization within an organization, the greater the requirement for sophisticated methods of coordination and integration of activities. This leads to increasing levels of organizational complexity, making the role of managers more difficult! The following vignettes in **Exhibit 23-2** describe quality-of-care issues that may arise due to the lack of coordination and integration of specialized services of a hospital's subsystems. The vignettes illustrate the fragmentation of today's U.S. healthcare system due to specialization. Managers need to develop the proper coordination and control mechanisms to achieve the system "redesign" goals stated in the Institute of Medicine's 2001 report, *Crossing the Quality Chasm: A New Health System for the 21st Century*.

Exhibit 23-2 Vignettes

Vignette One

Howard came into Hospital A's outpatient renal dialysis center for hemodialysis on Tuesday, Thursday, and Saturday afternoons. One day, the renal dialysis nurse noticed during a routine foot check that Howard had an ulcer on his left foot that would require daily wound dressings for at least 3 weeks. The renal dialysis nurse called the hospital's home health division to schedule a home care nurse to change the dressing on Howard's nondialysis days. The home care nurse asked the renal dialysis nurse, "Where are you calling from again?" The renal dialysis nurse repeated that she was calling from the hospital's outpatient renal dialysis center. There was a pause, and then the home care nurse responded, "Well, that explains why Peter is never home on Tuesday and Thursday afternoons for us to check his blood sugar. I didn't know he was on dialysis! You know, we've been seeing him for 6 months at the request of the hospital's diabetes clinic—does the diabetes nurse manager know?"

Vignette Two

Mary was admitted for surgery to Hospital B on Monday after her weekly treatment at the hospital's community-based hemodialysis center. During her hospitalization, she received dialysis in the hospital's inpatient hemodialysis unit. On Friday afternoon, after her treatment, the surgeon discharged her from the hospital. On Monday morning, when Mary was late for her hemodialysis appointment, a nurse from the hospital's community hemodialysis unit called the hospital's inpatient unit. The unit secretary said, "Mary was discharged on Friday, didn't you know?" "No, we didn't, we're part of the hospital's outpatient division and therefore do not receive discharge notifications." The nurse called Mary's home, but there was no reply. The nurse became concerned and called 911. The paramedics found Mary unconscious at home and immediately brought her to the hospital's emergency room. Shortly after readmission, Mary had a cardiac arrest and required resuscitation. Mary later told the hemodialysis nurse, "After I was discharged, I went home by taxi and managed to crawl up the stairs to my apartment—there's no elevator, you know, and dialysis always makes me feel tired, so I went straight to bed. When I woke up, I was too weak to get to the phone in the living room to call for help." Mary remained in the hospital as an inpatient for 3 weeks and required intradialytic parenteral nutrition for 3 months.

Data from Ravenscroft, E. F. (2005, June). Access within a fragmented healthcare system: A nurse's perspective on Romanow. Nursing Leadership—Online Exclusive.

Hierarchy of Authority

Hierarchy of authority refers to a manager's span of control. Span of control describes (1) who reports to whom and (2) the number of employees reporting to a supervisor. If an organization is structured so that, on average, each manager has few people reporting to them, the resulting shape will be tall and narrow (see **Figure 23-3**). If each manager's average span of control is increased, the resulting shape is flatter, and the number of levels in the hierarchy will be less (Miner, 1973).

As companies grow, they tend to increase the number of hierarchical levels, with a pronounced positive relationship between size (as measured by the number of employees) and levels (Hickson et al., 1969). An interesting side note is the effect of flat and tall structures on employees' job satisfaction. A comprehensive survey of more than 1500 managers in both tall and flat organizations revealed that for the group as a whole, those in flat structures were no more satisfied than those in tall structures (Porter & Lawler, 1964). However, in smaller companies (under 5000 employees), there was a tendency for the flat structure to be associated with greater job satisfaction; in the larger companies, this relationship was reversed—that is, job satisfaction was greater in the tall structure (Miner, 1973).

Early theorists believed that organizations should have narrow spans of control. For example, Fayol (1949) believed that when the work was nonroutine, the span of control for each manager should be fewer than six employees. When the job was routine, he recommended 20 or 30 employees for each manager. Over the years, considerable research has been done regarding

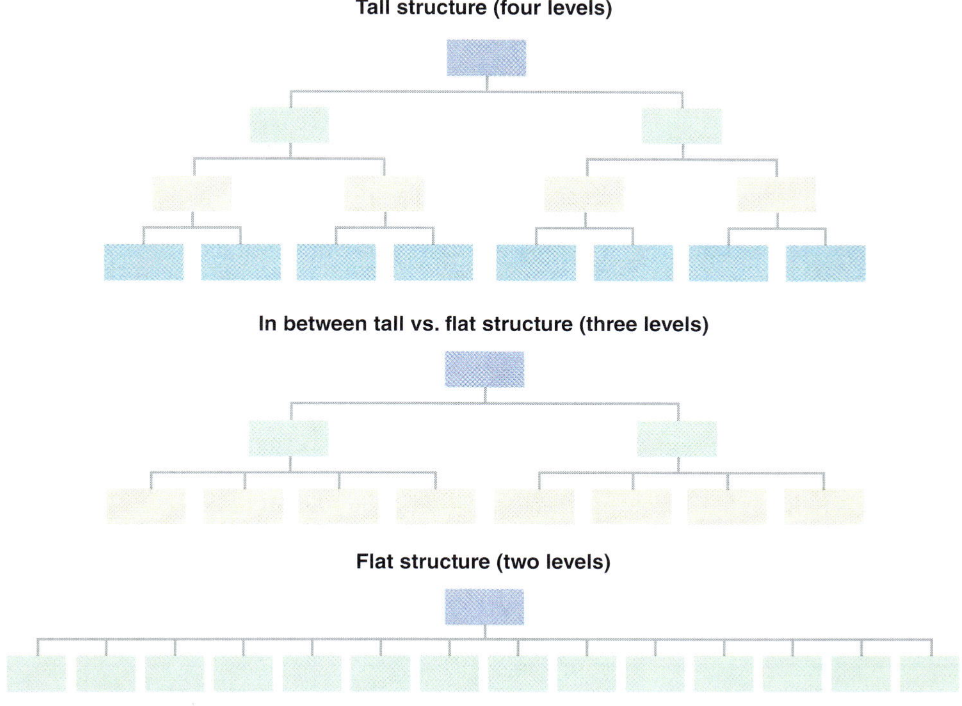

Figure 23-3 Tall Versus Flat Organization Structures

spans in various organizations, and certain factors are consistently associated with the size of the spans of control. Woodward's (1965) work with multiple manufacturing companies in the United Kingdom is the most widely cited research in this area. Woodward found a close relationship between the type of technology, the average span of control, the number of levels of management, and the organization's success.

Small-batch and unit-production firms (such as medical device manufacturers) usually had three levels of management: frontline, middle, and senior management. When these organizations had three levels, they were more likely to succeed than others with more or fewer levels. In large-batch and mass-production firms, such as pharmaceutical companies, the typical and desirable number of levels rose to four. In the continuous-process firms, such as hospitals, the average levels of management were six. For example, in nursing, you may have a frontline manager, such as a charge nurse, a unit manager, a division director, a senior director, a vice president, and a chief nursing officer. Organizations in the continuous-process category with fewer or more levels in the hierarchy were usually less successful. As previously noted, Woodward's work was related to industrial companies' use of technology. However, as discussed earlier in this chapter, service organizations' technologies also influence organizational structure due to interdependence.

All things being equal, a wide span of control is more efficient because it requires fewer managers. However, it is essential to recognize that, at some point, effectiveness will decline. Therefore, Miner (1973) provides us with certain generalizations regarding span of control:

- The optimal span for most situations ranges from 5 to 10 employees per manager. Larger spans (e.g., 8–10 employees) are most appropriate at higher organizational levels where greater resources for diverse decision making are needed.
- The size of the core operations span is influenced by the type of technology and the costs associated with smaller spans. Spans below 10 employees may not be economically feasible because of the number of managers required despite other potential advantages.
- In establishing a span of control for a specific situation, factors, such as the desirability of group solidarity, the need for job satisfaction, the amount of power required, the nature of the work, the stability of the environment, and the extent of operational support for the manager (i.e., assistants) must be taken into account.

Centralization

Centralization is the degree to which decision making is concentrated with the senior management team at the top of the organization's hierarchy. Decentralization is the extent to which decision-making authority is moved down the organizational structure and shared with many employees, as seen in **Figure 23-4**. Generally, when the organization's operating activities are relatively routine with a high degree of uniformity, there is likely to be considerable centralization of decision making. When the work is less routine and many individuals with professional specialization and training are involved, decision making is delegated to lower levels and professionals (Hage & Aiken, 1969; Hall, 1962). For example, a decentralized form would be required for day-to-day operating decisions in organizations employing professionals. As Miner (1973) noted, professionals, such as physicians, attorneys, accountants, and consultants, must make their own decisions regarding their patients and clients with reference to the particular circumstances existing at a time. Attempts to centralize such decisions often result in a considerable loss of professional staff to the organization. Furthermore, the requisite knowledge and information is typically available at the level of the practicing professional.

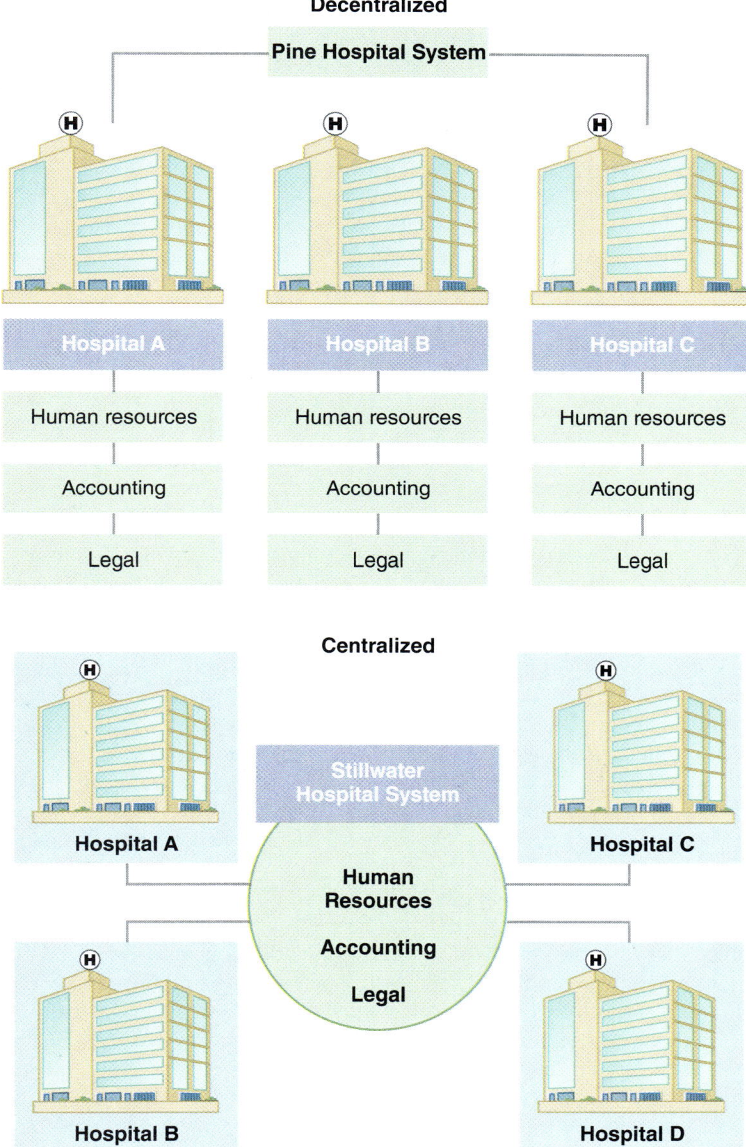

Figure 23-4 Centralized Versus Decentralized Health Systems

A high degree of decentralization is appropriate (1) when an organization is operating in an unpredictable environment, which is constantly changing and characterized by high risk, or (2) when an organization becomes large and complex in terms of product and service lines and markets. In these situations, the organization needs to respond quickly to new cues in the environment whenever they arise. A very centralized decision structure could easily result in outdated responses or in no response at all! However, even under those conditions that make decentralization most desirable, the practice should not be carried to the point where senior management becomes relatively powerless (Miner, 1973). When this occurs, organizations become much less effective (Tannenbaum, 1968). Therefore, even when an organization may be considered decentralized, a number of decision-making activities should remain centralized at the top level. Some of these activities, in addition to strategic planning, would be setting company-wide policies, finance, accounting systems, some research, activities relating to mergers and acquisitions, approval of capital expenditures above certain dollar amounts, senior management selection and compensation, negotiating with unions for collective bargaining settlements, and public relations. For example, ProMedica Health System, one of the country's most integrated health systems, operates as a decentralized system with the corporate office providing the organization's overall strategic direction. In **Exhibit 23-3** are excerpts of an interview with Alan Brass, former CEO and president of ProMedica Health System, as he explains how a decentralized organization with consistency in implementing strategic goals resulted in ProMedica being recognized in 2007 as the nation's best-performing healthcare system (see Evans, 2008).

Exhibit 23-3 ProMedica

ProMedica is composed of over 70 corporations and joint ventures, serving 27 counties throughout Ohio and Michigan. It is made up of 12 acute-care hospitals and more than 300 sites and centers. It employs over 14,000 individuals, and more than 4.4 million patient encounters are generated system wide annually (see http://www.promedica.org/).

Under the leadership of Alan Brass, ProMedica's former CEO and president, ProMedica served its communities through five divisions—ProMedica Ambulatory and Acute Care; ProMedica Physician Group; ProMedica Health, Education, and Research Corporation; ProMedica Continuing Care Services Corporation; and ProMedica Insurance Corporation. According to Alan Brass, "All the business units except continuing care are decentralized. The air and land transport network, durable medical supplies, visiting nurses, and other components of the continuing care can be managed more efficiently if they cut across the counties that ProMedica serves."

Brass states, "ProMedica's corporate office does certain things, and the operating units do other things. We want the boards of our regional hospitals and businesses to be responsible and accountable. That can happen only if we believe in and follow a decentralized model." For example, the corporate office produces "a robust five-year strategic plan, one that includes input from the community and is fully communicated, reviewed, and assessed constantly, so that the executive officers and their decentralized boards know the plan as well as the CEO." The local officers and boards then take responsibility and accountability in their communities for the system's facilities and services, continuum of care, and quality standards.

ProMedica's corporations, sites, managers, and employees operate under the strategic plan. "You have to know who you are and where you are. Unless an integrated delivery system (IDS) consistently applies its strategic plan throughout the organization, it cannot maintain and sustain itself today. In putting together an IDS the size of ProMedica, which is getting larger and larger, you need to be very consistent in application," Brass asserts.

"The consistency of application starts at the CEO level, but it goes up and down. It goes up to the board and to all of the executive officers, managers, and supervisors." Brass says, "We formulate strategies for the company and its business units in March and April. I'm the first one out of the gate saying to the 14 presidents, 'Here is what I have; here's what I want to see done next year; here's what I want to work toward; here's what I want to see you building into your plan.' They take those strategies, move them into their local business units, and add the appropriate strategic thrusts for their areas. Whether in the case of board nominating, planning, or financial decision processes, we rely on the decentralized model extensively." For example, in figuring out revenues, the regional presidents need to work with their financial officers and the parent company's chief financial officer to figure out what their reimbursements will be and whether there will be policy changes that will affect their bottom lines.

For Brass and ProMedica, "It is essential in 'growing' a company to ensure that its various components' culture fits together. It is crucial to be explicit and forthright in communicating what the parent company is looking for, what is important, and what is not." That philosophy relates to decentralization, consistency, teamwork, and concentration on quality and delivery, which Brass says drives ProMedica.

Reproduced from Deloitte Health Care Review. (2004, July/August). *CEO says decentralization, consistency, and concentration on delivery and quality account for ProMedica's rapid rise to the fourth most integrated U.S. health system*. Washington, DC: Author.

To determine whether an organization's decision making is more centralized or decentralized, one needs to consider who is making operational decisions. If strategic decisions are made at the top level of the organization, but the subunits make operational decisions, the organization would be considered decentralized (Burton et al., 2006). In addition, centralized organizations have more levels of management with narrow spans of control, whereas decentralized organizations have fewer levels of management with wider spans of control.

Healthcare organizations decentralize by delegating decision-making authority to those employees closest to the organization's patients, clients, or customers. Delegating gives employees more freedom to implement positive changes that directly impact their and the organization's performance. However, as Miner (2002) points out, managers must proceed cautiously when delegating decision-making authority. Several studies have been conducted to determine the effectiveness of delegating decision-making authority. Miner (1973) reported that, in simulation studies, it was found that although some employees will go well beyond the freedom delegated to them, others will not use the freedom given. Thus, delegating decision-making authority may be less critical to the outcome than the individual tendencies of employees to make their own decisions or defer to their managers. Some employees are unwilling to risk making decisions and being held accountable. They may claim that their freedom of action is restricted when, in fact, it is merely that they do not want to accept responsibility for their own decisions. As such, if delegation is to improve organizational effectiveness, employees must be recruited or developed who are willing to accept delegation and make decisions (Miner, 1973).

Professionalism

Professionalism refers to the level or average number of years of formal education and training of employees. The higher the level of professionalism and the more professionals employed within an organization, the greater the need for a decentralized structure. There is a large body of literature on professional organizations and the sociology of the professions (Friedson, 1984; Larson, 1977; Parsons, 1968; Scott, 1982). Much of the sociological theory on professionals has pertained to the mechanisms of control over professionals, including socialization in the profession, a desire to serve others, control by professional peers within and outside the employing firm, reputation in the community, bureaucratic controls from the hierarchical supervision within firms, and client control (Hodgson, 2002; Sharma, 1997; Tolbert & Stern, 1991).

Management of highly motivated and largely autonomous professionals is always challenging. Therefore, managers need to understand the professionals' culture (i.e., why they act the way they do) to reduce conflicts and resistance to change within the organization. For example, when an organization's interests, standards, or procedures conflict with the opinions of peers in the profession, professionals will usually side with their profession, because most professionals identify more closely with the profession than with the organization (Alvesson & Willmott, 2002; Bolton, 2004). This has been called the "clash of cultures" between corporate and professional cultures. Corporate culture reinforces the conflict between professionals and managers by formalizing roles, relationships, and procedures that are inimical to professionals' predispositions. For example, managers must coordinate and control the diverse activities and individuals contributing to organizational goals. However, professionals expect to maintain self-control over applying their field of knowledge, establish their agenda, and be controlled by no less than their peers (Clegg, 1981; Hodgson, 2002). This professional culture of self-control and autonomy results from professionals' prolonged training and socialization into their profession. This lengthy and rigorous process causes professionals to govern themselves by internalized social–regulative rules and norms (Philip et al., 1986; Raelin, 1986). For example, physicians emphasize preserving independent medical decision making to uphold their ethical obligations to provide the best care possible, regardless of cost. In contrast, healthcare managers are interested in standardizing healthcare delivery because of concerns over rising healthcare costs, medical errors, and wide variations in physicians' practice patterns. These attempts at standardization have resulted in confusion, frustration, and conflict between physicians and managers because professionals will resist attempts to exert control over them or in any way limit their freedom to make crucial decisions independently (Freidson, 2001; Kleinke, 1997; O'Connor & Lanning, 1992; Raelin, 1986). As such, managers need to establish an environment that effectively reduces the tension between the needs of physicians (i.e., clinical autonomy and independence) and the needs of the organization (i.e., control of resources and variations in patients' outcomes) (Marcus, 1985; Meyer & Tucker, 1992).

Summary

Mintzberg (1979, p. 2) states that:

> Every organized human activity—from the making of pots to placing a man on the moon—gives rise to two fundamental and opposing requirements: the division of labor into various tasks to be performed and the coordination of these tasks to accomplish the activity. An organization's structure can be defined simply as the sum total of the ways in which it divides its labor into distinct tasks and then achieves coordination among them.

It is a manager's responsibility first to determine the necessary activities to achieve the organization's goals, followed by dividing the activities on a logical basis into departments that perform the specialized functions, and finally to implement the systems necessary to coordinate and control the activities and individuals who perform the tasks. Considering all the variables that must be considered and evaluated, this is a challenge—the environment, technology, strategies, processes, etc. As Hall (1996) noted, organizational structures are a consequence of the simultaneous impact of multiple factors. Structure should reflect the organization's situation, age, size, type of technology needed for its services or products, and the extent to which its environment is complex and dynamic. However, based on decades of research, managers can use a few rules of thumb. Larger organizations need more formalized structures—more rules, more planning, more detailed job descriptions—as do those in stable environments and mass production. Organizations in more complex environments need higher degrees of decentralization; those diversified in many markets need divisional instead of functional structures (Miller & Friesen, 1984). The higher the routineness of job functions, the more mechanistic the structure, and the greater the interdependence of activities or processes, the more organic the structure. How does this all come together? The ideal state occurs when the company's strategy, ideally suited to the current external environment, is matched by the organization's design and structure, which allows for the optimal implementation of the entity's strategy. However, managers must always consider one crucial factor: culture. There's an old saying in business that "culture trumps strategy every time." The most carefully thought-out design will not accomplish the company's goals unless its culture supports it. This would include the formal rules and procedures that govern employees, the practices and communication they follow, and the congruence of the values the organization espouses and practices (Monteiro, 2002).

Discussion Questions

1. Describe the five organizational parts of an organization and their significance to organizational design.
2. Discuss why the proper communication form and method are necessary to coordinate and control organizational activities.
3. Describe each element of the structural dimension and how it relates to organization design.

CASE STUDY 23-1 Mitigating Hazards Through Continuing Design: The Birth and Evolution of a Pediatric Intensive Care Unit

Introduction

A recent report published by the Institute of Medicine (IOM, 2001) found that medical errors kill as many as 100,000 people each year in American hospitals. The report argues that many medical errors stem from structural problems in healthcare organizations and the U.S. healthcare system, suggesting that increasing patient safety is (at least in part) an organizational design problem. To the surprise of interested healthcare managers and professionals, the literature on organizational safety and design offered little guidance on designing a safe hospital and organizations for hazardous environments more generally.

William Howard Taft Children's Hospital Pediatric Intensive Care Unit

Pediatric intensive care is a complex and unpredictable domain. The potential for treatment-induced complications abounds. Children often react differently from adults. Even minor procedures, such as injections or intravenous line insertions, can cause patients to become agitated and move in unpredictable ways.

William Howard Taft Children's Hospital (WHTCH) established a new pediatric intensive care unit (PICU) in 1988 to meet the challenges associated with treating children in critical condition. WHTCH is a tertiary children's hospital in a geographic area more than three times the size of Vermont. The population is 2.5 million, with 500,000 under the age of 15. In 1988, WHTCH brought in a pediatric intensivist as the director of the new PICU. A second intensivist joined the unit a year later, and these two physicians headed the unit until 2000, when they both left the hospital. During their tenure, the PICU grew from an initial size of 8 beds to 25 beds with an average daily census of 21 children, including an average of 9 on ventilators. By 1999, the PICU had more than 1300 admissions per year, making it one of the largest PICUs in the United States in terms of both number of beds and admission rate.

The Evolution of Organizational Design in the Pediatric Intensive Care Unit

The Setting

Many medical organizations follow a model of treatment that delineates the attending physician as the primary decision maker, more or less solely responsible for the care of their patients and the management of their medical outcomes. Therefore, if one physician establishes a care plan but is unavailable when another sees the patient, the second physician may change the care plan without interacting with the first. Because traditional physician roles in this model are highly individualistic, the teamwork aspect of care is often missing. In this model, physicians may be unaware that each one works differently, and doctors are not incentivized to forge agreed-upon plans. The physician answers to the patient, not to another physician, and medical doctors rarely accept advice from peers on how to practice medicine.

Furthermore, while a physician's relationship with other doctors is one of independence and individual responsibility, their relationship with nurses and other healthcare personnel is usually one of hierarchy and authority. This model dictates unidirectional planning and communication, with the physician as director in a vertical hierarchy. The physician remains the "final common pathway" for patient care decision making. In the PICU director's experience, many physicians underscored their authority through belligerence and criticism, leading nurses and other support staff to live in fear of physicians. He had seen that the culture of fear encouraged nurses to think independently as little as possible and focus instead on avoiding the physician's notice. In this environment, nurses, therapists, and residents quickly learned that the path of least resistance was to follow physician instructions to the letter. The PICU director observed how interactions among physicians and staff unnecessarily complicated patient care.

The Birth of a Pediatric Intensive Care Unit

With these experiences in mind, the first pediatric intensivist came to WHTCH as PICU director in 1988. The PICU did not exist as a distinct unit within the broader 627-bed medical center. Before this, critically ill children were either treated in the adult ICU or transferred to other hospitals with pediatric facilities. With the intensivist's arrival, the adult ICU donated eight beds and the PICU began to function independently.

From the beginning, the new PICU director saw founding a new unit as an opportunity to diverge from the traditional design of critical-care units as he had seen it. He was a Navy combat veteran from the Vietnam War. As a pilot, he had witnessed firsthand how a rigid hierarchy with authority enforced through verbal abuse caused accidents in hazardous situations. When he left the Navy and entered medical school, he found a similar design.

During his training, the first intensivist noticed a sharp distinction between the bedside caregiver, typically a resident nurse who spends long hours monitoring individual patients or small groups of patients, and the physician, whose responsibilities include attending to a larger number of patients, with less time spent monitoring each patient. Because of their experience with individual patients over long periods, bedside caregiver, such as nurses, are often the first organizational members to detect slight changes in patient conditions that signal latent health problems. Therefore, while the information necessary to care for a child may come from advanced knowledge of disease processes or discussions with other experts, it may also come from intimate knowledge gained by bedside nurses. The intensivist noted that physicians with whom he was familiar relied on information from laboratory values, radiographic findings, and physician colleagues as resources to make effective decisions. However, he often overlooked information from the bedside staff.

The intensivist wanted to design a unit that avoided the mistakes of the U.S. Navy and departed from the worst aspects of organizational design in traditional medical units as he saw them. To this end, he believed the unit's design should involve nurses and other support staff more equally in patient care decisions. When the PICU began admitting patients, the intensivist asked nurses for their opinions on patient treatment options and invited them to perform some tasks traditionally reserved for doctors. This approach was not well-received at first. Accustomed to traditional roles, some nurses became resentful, suggesting that the intensivist was asking them to work too hard or to do his job as well as their own. Other nurses saw the intensivist's behavior as a sign of incompetence or lack of confidence and became concerned about his abilities as a physician. This initial reaction surprised the new PICU director and convinced him that instituting his desired participative organizational design in the unit would require a long-term commitment and evolving effort. He saw that many nurses did not feel adequately trained to take on the added responsibilities he offered them.

During the PICU's first months, non-dedicated nurses and respiratory care practitioners worked some shifts in the PICU and elsewhere in the hospital. Based on the resistance to delegating some decision-making responsibilities to nurses, the intensivist decided that his design interventions could work only with dedicated support personnel. This was true for two reasons. First, because people resisted roles other than those they had become accustomed to through training and experience, only dedicated staff members could accumulate enough experience with a new design to begin to trust it. Second, even if nurses could be convinced to participate in patient treatment decisions, they needed additional training to do so successfully. This type of training would be possible only with a relatively small number of dedicated nurses. Early in his tenure, the PICU director approached hospital administration to request a dedicated nursing staff. Administrators granted the request. Later, the director also asked for dedicated respiratory care practitioners. While initially resistant, administrators also eventually granted this request.

As the intensivist continued encouraging nurses to assist in making patient care decisions, many dedicated nurses (and later the dedicated respiratory care practitioners) began warming to his approach. At this point, participative decision making in the unit was informal and primarily involved queries about staff members' observations about patients and requests for their opinions about appropriate treatment options. Several nurses and respiratory care practitioners working in the unit at the time report that the intensivist's approach made them feel valued, but they did not feel qualified to offer suggestions on patient treatment options. The intensivist started teaching staff members about medical decision making in response to this concern. He introduced lessons through conversations with care staff and increasingly invited staff members to attend his physician's rounds.

Growth

The PICU director's inclination to involve the support staff in patient care decisions was reinforced by necessity. He made an early policy decision not to turn away children referred to the PICU. This policy contrasted sharply with prior practices in the original adult ICU, which resulted in the admission of only 40% of referred children (the ICU turned away children that they could not treat with available equipment, and also deemed some children to be in insufficiently critical condition for admission). The new PICU policy quickly raised the admission rate to more than 90% (and eventually as high as 99%) of referred children.

WHTCH's PICU admitted more than 500 children during its first year, while the PICU director was its only physician. This is a heavy workload for a pediatric intensivist. For reference, an average PICU has one physician for every 4–5 beds and roughly 200–300 admissions per year. The focal PICU, with eight beds and more than 500 admissions, had roughly double this ratio in its first year. Thus, besides involving staff members to improve patient care, the intensivist realized he needed their help.

Eleven months after the PICU was established, a second intensivist came to the unit as assistant director of critical care. The PICU director recruited him specifically because of his fire department emergency medical services background. The second intensivist independently concluded that organizational structures in fire departments could handle emergencies more effectively than those in the medical centers with which he had experience.

Despite adding a second intensivist, the patient-physician ratio at the PICU remained high. The PICU admitted roughly 900 children in its second year, nearly 1200 in its third, and 1400 in its fourth. The unit's growth quickly outstripped its allotted 8-bed space in the adult ICU. During its second year, the PICU moved into a new building with 25 beds. A study published shortly thereafter found that 40% of PICUs in the United States have 4–6 beds, while those with more than 18 beds make up less than 6% of the national total. The latter averaged 1277 ± 63 patient admissions per year. According to these numbers, WHTCH's PICU was one of the largest PICUs in the country by its third year. This growth resulted from a pediatric critical-care transport system established by the second PICU intensivist in 1989, allowing the unit to transport and accept highly critical children from other less-equipped hospitals. WHTCH's pediatric critical-care transport system quickly grew into one of the largest of such systems in the country.

At the end of 1994, an intermediate ICU was established as a separate unit at WHTCH. The intermediate ICU served three purposes related to the functions of the PICU: It admitted children who required a high level of nursing attention, but not the same level of critical care as patients in the PICU; it took recovering PICU patients who no longer required intensive care; and it housed the WHTCH cardiothoracic ICU, where children with heart conditions were treated. Establishing the intermediate ICU increased the severity of conditions treated in the PICU because the less critical patients were referred directly to the intermediate ICU.

Staff Training as Continuing Design

Because of his background, the second intensivist enthusiastically supported the PICU director's push to delegate care decisions and functions to nurses, respiratory care practitioners, and residents. The first intensivist's efforts had secured the unit a dedicated nursing staff, many of whom learned to enjoy taking an active role in treatment decisions. Yet nurses and other staff members complained that they lacked the expertise to make critical medical decisions. The PICU's emerging design required a high level of distributed knowledge, expertise, and authority. As both intensivists wanted to increase bedside caregiver participation in the PICU further, they made attaining this level of staff medical knowledge one of the major drivers behind their design efforts.

While the first intensivist previously conducted informal lessons, training became increasingly formalized after the second intensivist's arrival. The intensivists began teaching staff members how to identify medical problems that brought children to the PICU. They taught caregivers how to identify and treat disease-related complications or inappropriate medical care. The intensivists also gave staff members formalized decision-making aids to help them know when to treat a patient and when to ask for help. They taught staff members to break down a patient's symptoms into categories, assess the severity of each category, and begin treating the most acute symptoms while calling for additional help if needed.

To further facilitate decentralized decision making, the intensivists said they would respond immediately to staff questions. They gave out their personal phone numbers and encouraged staff to feel comfortable calling them if they were absent and the attending physician could not assist.

Both intensivists continued to teach informally when opportunities arose and initiated formal in-service training sessions for all staff members on duty. As part of the training, the intensivists encouraged staff members to read medical journals and textbooks to educate themselves further. Several former nurses and respiratory care practitioners report that they became so interested in what they learned in these training sessions that they returned to school for advanced degrees.

Furthermore, all staff members, regardless of position and disciplinary background, were encouraged to attend the physicians' rounds on the PICU floor. These rounds included an educational component to ensure that staff possessed the abilities necessary to function across roles. During rounds, the intensivists practiced wheeling a blackboard around the PICU to write notes and draw diagrams to facilitate staff training.

While residents and fellows commonly participate in physicians' rounds at hospitals, the level of participation instituted at the focal PICU was extraordinary. Morning rounds routinely include all residents, the fellow (if on service), lead respiratory therapist, charge nurse, pharmacist, social worker, and the patient's bedside nurse and respiratory therapist. As PICU staff members became accustomed to participating in physicians' rounds, they undertook larger roles. Nurses began presenting patients and discussing treatment options with the physicians.

One intensivist notes that it took several years before staff members were trained well enough to implement his vision of an optimally decentralized PICU design. Before this time, staff members did not have the knowledge to participate in medical decisions and treatments to the extent he desired. Thus, establishing the PICU's decentralized design was a process rather than an event.

Supporting Staff Decisions

As staff members received more training, they began to feel comfortable accepting more responsibility, and the two intensivists increasingly delegated authority to them. However, specialists from other hospital departments were unaccustomed to such a degree of knowledge distribution and occasionally resisted decisions made by staff when treating PICU patients. The PICU directors developed a policy always to support their staff members' decisions in these situations. While staff members' decisions were not always right, the two PICU intensivists believed that their decentralized design improved response times and decision quality on average because staff with direct information about critical situations made essential care decisions. Distributed decision-making authority reduced the need for information to flow through the chain of command and back to the bedside caregiver.

The PICU directors also assigned bedside caregivers to ensure standard and consistent patient treatment plans. As situations developed and additional people and resources responded to critical events at the PICU, arriving members were trained to inquire about and use information from bedside caregivers to assess the situation and develop a common treatment strategy. This was one of the PICU's central design elements, and also perhaps the source of its most significant difference from other units in the hospital.

When the second intensivist arrived in the PICU, he brought the notion of post-event debriefings from his experience in emergency services, and frequent debriefings were quickly institutionalized in the unit. He routinely conducted open debriefings for all involved staff following major events. While most large healthcare organizations utilize some form of post-crisis debriefing, the intensivists believed that these meetings tended to be rare and typically restricted to physicians, residents, and hospital administrators. Debriefings at the PICU became unusual in their frequency and inclusiveness. The purpose of these debriefings was twofold: First, to encourage staff to learn from an experience while it was still fresh, and second, to act as a form of therapy for staff members. These sessions allowed staff members to talk through their emotions and prepare themselves to return to work.

Resistance and Buffering

The decentralization and elevated educational focus designed into the unit encountered opposition from some staff members. As a result of their academic focus, some of the physicians' rounds lasted longer than usual. This was, and still is, one of the busiest PICUs in the country, and some staff members considered the rounds a waste of time. Some resistance to the goal of increasing staff autonomy also arose. While most of the staff embraced or at least cooperated with the intensivists' push to delegate decision making, the approach required a significant commitment by staff members to learn how to perform new duties.

However, internal resistance to the decentralized design in the focal PICU was not nearly as strong as resistance from other departments in the hospital. Colleagues from different departments increasingly discussed the PICU's design and processes with the intensivists, at times to advise the intensivists of resistance from administration, and at other times to argue that staff members made poor care decisions. Hospital administrators and some physicians from different departments also saw the practice of staff members attending in-service training and physicians' rounds as a waste of time and resources.

To preserve their desired organizational design in light of these concerns, the PICU directors developed formalized protocols to constrain bedside caregiver discretion within certain boundaries. For instance, they created new rules requiring bedside caregivers to open the airways of new patients before beginning to design a treatment plan. This rule ensured that patients were stable before staff members began to think about appropriate treatments and gave staff members time to consult with physicians as needed. In addition, the new protocols required PICU staff to ask for assistance under specified conditions. When a patient exhibited one or more of a particular set of symptoms, they were required to get a second opinion from another staff member before proceeding with treatment; when a patient exhibited one or more of a second set of symptoms, they were required to ask a PICU physician for assistance; and when a patient had one or more of a third set of symptoms, they were required to call a specialist from another department in the hospital for a consultation.

By following these guidelines for decision making, bedside caregivers maintained their ability to make decisions regarding routine patient care without consulting physicians while avoiding further conflicts with outside specialists. The metarules placated administrators and physicians outside the PICU by giving them indirect but formalized control over caregiver activities, because physicians could modify rules governing the breadth and scope of allowable discretion. While the PICU's initial design called for broad staff decision-making authority, the two intensivists realized that the new formalization created a superior organizational design. Not only did the institution of formal metarules placate hospital administration, but it also helped some staff members feel more confident in their patient care decisions.

Despite this change, some physicians in the hospital remained uncomfortable. To minimize resistance from these physicians, the two intensivists moved to buffer the PICU from the remainder of the hospital as much as possible. Early efforts in this direction led to the assignment of dedicated nurses and respiratory care practitioners to the unit. Later efforts were aimed at increasing the unit's autonomy. Before the PICU's establishment, physicians from other hospital departments (pediatricians, surgeons, cardiologists, and others) came from their home departments. They managed critically ill children in the original adult ICU as needed. This practice continued to an extent after the PICU's founding because critically ill children often required the care of medical specialists. The two intensivists came to see the porosity of the PICU's boundaries as a potential hazard to patient safety.

As their vision of an effective organizational design evolved, the two intensivists decided to minimize the unit's porosity by assuming primary responsibility over all ventilator patients. They became the main contact points for specialists outside the PICU to discuss patient matters and solicit advice regarding patient care within the unit. This simplified work for staff members but complicated the intensivists' responsibilities, because they now handled conflicts with outside physicians. Discussions about appropriate care occasionally arose between them and external specialists, diverting some of their time and attention from responding to their staff. The intensivists viewed the change positively, believing staff members could operate more effectively when buffered from external conflict.

In addition to serving as gatekeepers between the PICU and the hospital, the two founding intensivists took steps to reduce the PICU's dependence on outside expertise. They each received additional training to personally perform many of the functions that previously had required the services of a specialist. For example, at the beginning of the PICU's history, external ear, nose, and throat (ENT) specialists performed difficult intubations in the unit. When some ENTs voiced disagreement with practices in the PICU, the two lead intensivists began performing difficult intubations and training their fellows to do them. They also requested that an anesthesiology fellow be assigned to the unit to reduce their dependence on outside anesthesiologists.

The intensivists argued that the changes improved patient care in the PICU because children's conditions often deteriorated while waiting for specialists to arrive. However, these moves also further buffered the PICU and its unique design from the rest of the hospital. The second intensivist took additional steps to make PICU admission through the pediatric critical-care transport system independent of the outside hospital by training transport paramedics and PICU staff to perform functions assigned initially to hospital triage staff. In addition, the intensivists gradually discontinued offering care outside of the PICU. While the high workload within the PICU itself often precluded the intensivists from responding to pediatric emergencies in other departments, the intensivists also felt they could not maintain a consistent quality of care when working with resources and staff outside the PICU.

Reliability and Outcomes

Compared to the other PICUs, the focal PICU had normal mortality rates for a PICU of its size during its first two years. After this period, however, its mortality rate began to decline, even while the unit grew rapidly. By 1993, the focal PICU's mortality rate was 4.6%, compared to the average rate of 7.8 ± 0.8% for PICUs with more than 18 beds. Except for a brief increase in 1994, associated with establishing the intermediate ICU (which increased the average severity of the conditions of PICU patients), the mortality rate at WHTCH's PICU remained low. In 1999, the last full year that the original intensivists remained at the unit, its mortality rate was 3.5%.

Mortality rate is a poor indicator of healthcare performance, because numbers are complicated to obtain and notoriously difficult to control for the severity of a unit's caseload. We mention it here simply as an indicator that the PICU's design appears to have helped it perform well. Aside from mortality, several other indicators of patient medical outcomes also seemed to improve as the PICU's distinctive decentralized design was implemented. For instance, the unit's staff introduced several innovations that improved patient care. These innovations would not have been possible without the additional medical training and patient care discretion given to staff members in the PICU. In one case, respiratory care practitioners changed the blend of helium and oxygen when administering gas to patients with severe asthma. The innovation gave children on ventilators increased energy, allowing them to play longer. In another case, resident nurses began placing the children on their stomachs during a period when the unit experienced a higher incidence of acute lung disease. They discovered that children had better lung function in this position, with oxygen entering the blood more easily. In a third case, some respiratory care practitioners began setting ventilators to higher breath rates, sometimes reaching levels higher than those generally considered safe. Further study of the practice found that higher ventilator rates made some patients more comfortable and alert and did not cause adverse health outcomes.

The design instituted by the two managing intensivists also led to higher satisfaction and lower turnover among unit staff members. The PICU's founding director saw one of his primary responsibilities as creating a supportive environment. As a consequence of this effort, the PICU had an extremely low turnover rate for nurses and therapists, much lower than is common in intensive care generally. Several former residents reported the PICU residency as the most difficult but enjoyable of their residencies.

Culture Clash

In 1993, the PICU brought in an additional pediatric intensivist fellow to assist the original two intensivists. As the unit grew, others were hired, and the number of doctors (including fellows) soon stabilized at five. Until 1997, the only physicians assigned to the PICU were the original two intensivists, their fellows, and intensivists who had received their fellowship training in the unit. As a result, the unit's physicians strongly agreed that its decentralized design, although unorthodox, was effective.

Beginning in 1997, intensivists trained elsewhere were hired into the unit. The PICU's continuing expansion and the departure of intensivists trained in the unit for leadership positions elsewhere created vacancies. The PICU's high utilization demanded that vacancies and new positions be filled quickly, and the founding intensivists eventually turned to externally trained intensivists to expedite staffing needs.

A few externally trained intensivists did not see the value of the PICU's approach. They believed instead that the unit's design might constitute malpractice because physicians did not always control patient treatments. The new intensivists introduced notions of strict physician authority and one-way, downward communication. Although the protocols allowing staff to exercise discretion remained in place, staff members learned that the new doctors interpreted them differently than the original two intensivists did. In fact, during this period, staff members began to refer to cultural differences between "PICU north" and "PICU south" because the founding intensivists' offices were located on the south side of the unit. Concerns of malpractice liability from physicians inside the PICU resonated with negative feelings about the unit held by some physicians elsewhere in the hospital. Physicians from other departments saw the growing rift within the PICU. They became more outspoken about their disagreement, often refusing to let the two founding intensivists treat their patients even within the PICU. Some hospital administrators, never entirely comfortable with the level of autonomy at the PICU, used these concerns to argue against providing dedicated resources or supporting the unit's continued expansion. In this environment, both original intensivists chose to leave WHTCH and accept positions elsewhere in 2000.

According to staff members who remained at the PICU, the unit's design features changed following the departures of the two original intensivists. Physicians began to assert their authority over patient care decisions and ignore suggestions from bedside staff members. Staff turnover in the unit increased, and staff members who remained learned to follow the physician's instructions and keep their opinions to themselves. Although the PICU retained some procedures allowing staff discretion and might still have been considered "participative," its staff no longer enjoyed broad decision-making autonomy. Furthermore, procedures put in place to support staff autonomy were gradually discontinued. The new physicians did not encourage staff members to participate in rounds and no longer used rounds as a training opportunity. Similarly, the practice of holding post-event debriefings was discontinued, and staff members were not encouraged to participate when debriefings were held.

Although current staff members believe that the new PICU intensivists are skilled doctors and that the PICU remains a relatively safe unit, they suggest that its health outcomes are not as good as they once were. The annual mortality rate at the unit has increased since its low in 1999. Finally, as noted previously, staff turnover has increased during the same period. WHTCH's PICU remains a good unit but has lost its distinct design and may be less reliable than its previous form.

Discussion

The design of WHTCH's PICU evolved over time in response to environmental and technological demands. This resulted in an extremely decentralized decision-making structure for an industry where strictly enforced hierarchical relationships are more often the norm. The PICU also became unusually self-sufficient in an area where organizational boundaries are typically porous or unidentifiable.

The PICU's experience provides several implications for organizational design theory and practice. The case draws a connection between organizational design and leadership. The coincidence of the founders' departures and design changes at the PICU suggests the alternative explanation that good leadership, rather than organizational design, led to the PICU's performance. It may have been that the charisma and personal leadership qualities of the two head intensivists motivated staff members to achieve high performance, independent of any design interventions that were introduced. According to the PICU members with whom we spoke (including the two intensivists), this was not the case. Neither the intensivists nor other staff members claim extraordinary leadership qualities; other staff members do not attribute such to them. While most of the PICU staff accepted and came to agree with the intensivists' approach, others did not—some harboring personal dislike for the intensivists themselves. Furthermore, current staff members quickly point out that the intensivists who headed the PICU after 2000 are neither poor leaders nor poor physicians. Instead, several of them emphasized that the reason for the PICU's success stems from its design differing from those of other ICUs.

Despite these assertions that the PICU case is a design story and not a leadership story, the case suggests a closer connection between the two explanations than previously acknowledged. Organizational design is often seen in terms of impersonal structural characteristics: span of control, levels of hierarchy, formalization of rules, and so on. The PICU case instead suggests that organizational design exists at least as much in designers' visions as in organizations and formal structures. For example, the PICU director's vision for the unit was continuity of high-quality care through a highly knowledgeable, motivated, and involved support staff. While this vision did not change during the PICU's growth and evolution, many of its structural characteristics did change as the unit met new challenges. For example, when the first intensivist arrived at the unit, he did not fully appreciate the amount and formality of staff education necessary to fulfill his goals for the unit. Similarly, the two intensivists initially sought to minimize formal boundaries on staff decision-making authority. Still, they later decided that encasing staff authority in formalized metarules created a more effective design aligned with their original vision.

The PICU's design was an ongoing effort, and its most stable components centered on a vision of distributed knowledge and decentralized intensive care. To the extent that this vision existed mainly in the minds of the two PICU directors, the unit's design cannot easily be separated from its leaders. Many (perhaps most) of the design features that eventually came to characterize the PICU were not planned from the foundation of the unit. Instead, they were instituted in response to new challenges or unanticipated consequences of the unit's evolution. For example, neither intensivists anticipated the lengths they would eventually go to isolate and buffer their unit from the broader hospital. Their buffering efforts were necessitated by unexpected hostility from other hospital units to the PICU's design. The case highlights the cyclic nature of organizational design. Organizational leaders put a design in place, observe its effects on the organization, adjust the design, again observe the effects, and so on.

In another vein, the PICU experience shows that a design's origin may be as important as its content. While much work examines the adoption of legitimized forms and increasing conformity among organizational designs in a field, few perspectives address the motivation to search for alternative designs when commonly accepted forms exist. The PICU story highlights that organizational leaders with diverse prior experiences can introduce this form of divergent change. Many of the unit's design features were based on organizational designs employed by fire department emergency medical service organizations. However appropriate these designs may have been to pediatric intensive care, they were unfamiliar to nurses, therapists, and physicians. Unfamiliarity led many members of WHTCH and the PICU itself to distrust the new design. Much of the ongoing design effort undertaken by the two PICU intensivists was devoted to combating this distrust.

Similarly, the PICU case illustrates some of the unique challenges of designing an organizational subunit to operate much differently than its parent organization. Any organizational design that differs from an accepted, institutionalized model in its industry is necessarily fragile. However, the PICU's design was even more tenuous because it was at odds with accepted designs in its parent organization. While the PICU directors succeeded in implementing such a design, the unit's design required constant and effortful maintenance. The PICU's director quickly discovered that his unique design was complex for many physicians and staff members to accept. He responded by removing his unit from its parent organization and associated designs. He obtained dedicated nurses and respiratory care practitioners, unified the unit's contact with other departments through himself and his associate, and limited the need for outside specialists to enter the unit.

The PICU case suggests that buffering subunits with unique designs from their environments is essential to their operation, but also raises specific challenges. Much prior work focuses on organizations naturally buffered from outside pressures and lacking exposure to market or competitive forces. Indeed, many such organizations may be conceived of as "total institutions," as they achieve strong cultures by removing their members from outside society. The present examination reveals that such isolation takes considerable effort in multiunit organizations. While such a subunit may need to distance itself as much as possible from its parent organization, the case illustrates that resistance may develop from members of other organizational subunits and organizational leaders who perceive such buffering as a threat to their power. Without continuous buffering efforts, the unit may easily be overrun by the culture of its parent organization or its industry at large.

The case also suggests several characteristics of the PICU's design evolved in direct response to challenges posed by the unit's technology and environment. There are many examples of organizations facing similar hazards that have attempted but were unable to reach safety and operational reliability goals. Several differences exist between the PICU and the designs at these other organizations. Specifically, the PICU was highly decentralized, as its founders delegated authority throughout the organization. Organizations desiring consistent performance under hazardous conditions must be designed to give frontline employees tremendous decision-making authority and flexibility. The relationship between complex organizational environments and decentralized decision-making authority has long been acknowledged by contingency literature on organizational design. While many organizations distribute knowledge and delegate decision-making authority during abnormal operations or crises, they usually display high levels of centralization and formalization during more routine periods. However, the decentralization of decision making at WHTCH's PICU was broad-based and not confined to emergencies, suggesting that decentralized decision making need not be coupled with periods of strict hierarchy.

The PICU experience also reinforces the assertion that decentralization requires distributed knowledge. The founding intensivists devoted much time and attention to training staff members to make treatment decisions. Their experience shows that frontline employees cannot be expected to shoulder decision-making responsibilities effectively without sufficient knowledge and training. Some prior studies suggest that the high levels of training required to create such knowledge distribution may be too costly for organizations in most environments. However, despite the training requirements, the focal PICU functioned quite efficiently with such a structure. Indeed, the unit's low doctor-patient ratio was one of the conditions that necessitated decentralization.

The PICU experience also supports a growing recognition that even generally successful organizations make mistakes and must learn from them to maintain consistency. Behavioral perspectives argue that organizations and the people in them often learn through performance shortfalls, interpreting successes as a sign that change is not needed, and learning only in response to failure. Crises inevitably arise in any complex healthcare setting. Postcrisis debriefings provided opportunities and time for the staff and founders to learn from failures, and because PICU leaders did not search for "responsible" parties to blame for poor outcomes, unit members could learn from their experiences without fear of retaliation.

A recurring question for the founders, however, was whether an organization can be designed to operate reliably in some more benign way than waiting for lessons learned in blood, as failures are costly and often difficult to learn from. The leaders of the PICU did not wait for a serious accident before delegating authority, developing structures to distribute knowledge, and creating other conditions that they believed would lead to enhanced learning and performance. Instead, in designing the unit, they drew on the failures and successes of different organizations with which they had been associated. As a result, their design interventions sought to avoid strict hierarchy, absolute physician control over patient treatment, and strict individual accountability (or blame) for adverse patient outcomes.

Discussion Questions

1. How did the PICU directors continually readjust their design to meet internal and external challenges?
2. Do you believe that the PICU's design resided perhaps more in its leaders' vision than in its structures and processes?
3. What difficulties did the PICU directors encounter while attempting to institute unique designs within their subsystem of a large organization?

Reproduced from Madsen, P., Desai, V., Roberts, K., & Wong, D. (2006). Mitigating hazards through continuing design: The birth and evolution of a pediatric intensive care unit. *Organization Science, 17*(2), 239–248. Reprinted with permission.

References

Alvesson, M., & Willmott, H. (2002). Identity regulation as organizational control: Producing the appropriate individual. *Journal of Management Studies*, *39*(5), 619–644.

Berwick, D. (2002). Quality chasm factors. *Health Affairs*, *21*(5), 301–302.

Bolton, S. C. (2004). A simple matter of control? NHS hospital nurses and new management. *Journal of Management Studies*, *41*(2), 317–333.

Burton, R. M., DeSanctis, G., & Obel, B. (2006). *Organizational design: A step-by-step approach*. Cambridge University Press.

Clegg, S. (1981). Organization and control. *Administrative Science Quarterly*, *26*(4), 545–562.

Daft, R. L. (2007). *Organization theory and design* (9th ed.). Thomson South-Western.

Deloitte Health Care Review (2004, July/August). *Decentralization, consistency, and concentration on delivery and quality account for ProMedica's rapid rise to the fourth most integrated U.S. health system, CEO says*. Author.

Evans, M. (2008). Integrating efficiency: Verispan's annual ranking of the top integrated health networks shows improved operating margins along with expanded services. *Modern Healthcare*, *38*(5), 26–29.

Fayol, H. (1949). *General and industrial management*. Pitman.

Freidson, E. (1984). The changing nature of professional control. *Annual Review of Sociology, 10*(1), 1–20.

Freidson, E. (2001). *Professionalism, the third logic: On the practice of knowledge*. University of Chicago Press.

Hage, J., & Aiken, M. (1969). Routine technology, social structure, and organization goals. *Administrative Science Quarterly*, *14*(3), 366–376.

Hall, R. H. (1962). Intraorganizational structural variation: Application of the bureaucratic model. *Administrative Science Quarterly*, *7*(3), 295–308.

Hall, R. H. (1996). *Organizations: Structures, processes, and outcomes* (6th ed.). Prentice Hall.

Halvorson, G. C. (2007). *Health care reform now!: A prescription for change*. Jossey-Bass/John Wiley & Sons.

Hickson, D. J., Pugh, D. S., & Pheysey, D. C. (1969). Operations, technology and organization structure: An empirical reappraisal. *Administrative Science Quarterly*, *14*(3), 378–397.

Hodgson, D. (2002). Disciplining the professional: The case of project management. *Journal of Management Studies*, *39*(6), 804–821.

Institute of Medicine (2001). *Crossing the quality chasm: A new health system for the 21st century*. National Academy Press. https://www.nap.edu/books/0309072808/html/

Kast, F. E., & Rosenzweig, J. E. (1985). *Organization and management: A systems and contingency approach*. McGraw-Hill.

Katz, D., & Kahn, R. L. (1966). *The social psychology of organizations*. Wiley.

Kleinke, J. D. (1997). The industrialization of health care. *Journal of the American Medical Association*, *278*(17), 1456–1457.

Larson, M. S. (1977). *The rise of professionalism: A sociological analysis*. University of California Press.

Madsen, P., Desai, V., Roberts, K., & Wong, D. (2006). Mitigating hazards through continuing design: The birth and evolution of a pediatric intensive care unit. *Organization Science*, *17*(2), 239–248.

Marcus, A. A. (1985). Professional autonomy as a basis of conflict in an organization. *Human Resource Management*, *24*(3), 311–328.

Meyer, P. G., & Tucker, S. L. (1992). Incorporating an understanding of independent practice physician culture into hospital structure and operations. *Hospital & Health Services Administration*, *37*(4), 465–476.

Miller, D., Friesen, P., & Mintzberg, H. (1984). *Organizations: A quantum view*. Prentice Hall.

Miner, J. B. (1973). *The management process: Theory, research, and practice*. Macmillan.

Miner, J. B. (2002). *Organizational behavior: Foundations, theories, and analyses*. Oxford University Press.

Mintzberg, H. (1979). *The structuring of organizations*. Prentice Hall.

Monteiro, M. (2002, June 15). *Outline of organizational designs and structures and linkage to innovation.* Businessgyan. https://web.archive.org/web/20080306092215/http://www.businessgyan.com/content/view/180/434/

O'Connor, S. J., & Lanning, J. A. (1992). The end of autonomy? Reflections on the postprofessional physician. *Health Care Management Review*, *17*(1), 63–72.

Parsons, T. (1968). Professions. In D. L. Sills, & R. K. Merton (Eds.), *International encyclopedia of the social sciences, Vol. 12* (pp. 536–547). Macmillan.

Podsakoff, P. M., Williams, L. J., & Todor, W. D. (1986). Effects of organizational formalization on alienation among professionals and nonprofessionals. *Academy of Management Journal*, *29*(4), 820–831.

Porter, L. W., & Lawler, E. E. (1964). The effects of "tall" versus "flat" organization structures on managerial job satisfaction. *Personnel Psychology*, *17*(2), 135–148.

Raelin, J. A. (1986). *The clash of cultures: Managers and professionals*. Harvard Business School Press.

Ravenscroft, E. F. (2005). Access within a fragmented healthcare system: A nurse's perspective on Romanow. *Nursing Leadership—Online Exclusive*, *18*(2). http://www.longwoods.com/product.php?productid=19031&cat=252

Scott, W. R. (1982). Managing professional work: Three models of control for health organizations. *Health Services Research*, *17*(3), 213–240.

Scott, W. R., Ruef, M., Mendel, P. J., & Caronna, C. A. (2000). *Institutional change and healthcare organizations: From professional dominance to managed care*. University of Chicago Press.

Sharma, A. (1997). Professional as agent: Knowledge asymmetry in agency exchange. *Academy of Management Review*, *22*(3), 758–798.

Tannenbaum, A. S. (1968). *Control in organizations*. McGraw-Hill.

Taylor, F. W. (1911). *The principles of scientific management*. Harper and Brothers.

Thompson, J. (1967). *Organizations in action*. McGraw Hill.

Tolbert, P. S., & Stern, R. N. (1991). Organizations of professions: Governance structures in large law firms. *Research in the Sociology of Organizations*, *8*, 97–117.

Weber, M. (1947). *The theory of social and economic organization* (A. M. Henderson & T. Parsons, Trans.). Free Press.

Weisz, G. (2006). *Divide and conquer: A comparative history of medical specialization*. Oxford University Press.

Woodward, J. (1965). *Industrial organization: Theory and practice*. Oxford University Press.

Other Suggested Readings

Best, R. G., Hysong, S. J., Pugh, J. A., Ghosh, S., & Moore, F. I. (2006). Task overlap among primary care team members: An opportunity for system redesign. *Journal of Healthcare Management*, *51*(5), 295–307.

Bohmer, R. M. J. (2005). Medicine's service challenge: Blending customer and standard care. *Health Care Management Review*, *30*(4), 322–330.

Gerardi, D. (2005). The culture of health care: How professional and organizational cultures impact conflict management. *Georgia State University Law Review*, *21*(4), 857–890.

Hearld, L. R., Alexander, J. A., Fraser, I., & Jiang, H. J. (2008). How do hospital organizational structure and processes affect quality of care? A critical review of research methods. *Medical Care Research and Review*, *65*(3), 259–299.

Vera, A., & Kuntz, L. (2007). Process-based organization design and hospital efficiency. *Health Care Management Review*, *32*(1), 55–65.

Index

Note: Page numbers followed by *e*, *f*, and *t*, indicate materials in exhibits, figures, and tables, respectively.

B

C

D

K

L

M

N

Q

R

S

T

U

V

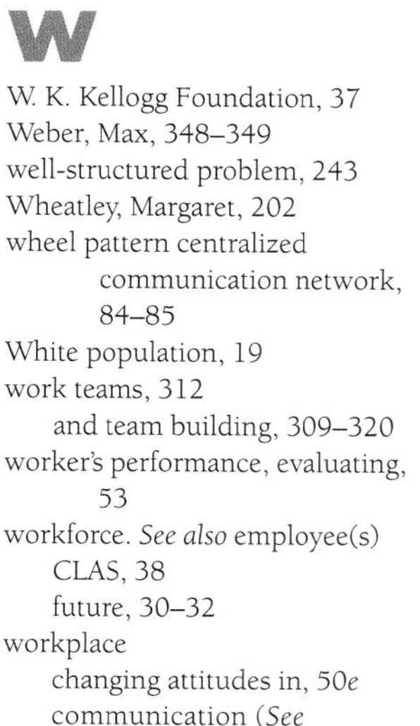

W

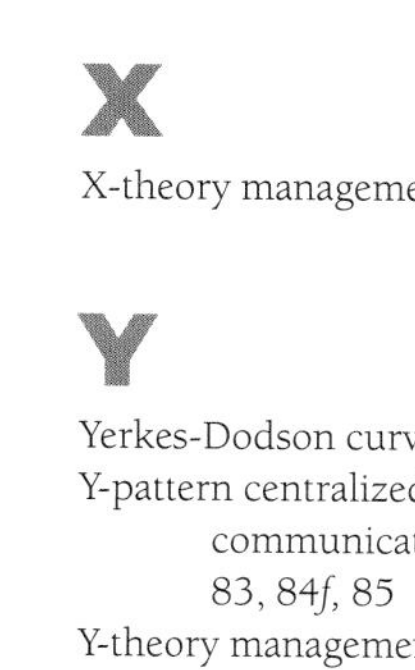

X

Y

Z